Our Selves/Our Past

Our Selves/Our Past

Psychological Approaches to American History

EDITED BY
ROBERT J. BRUGGER

THE JOHNS HOPKINS UNIVERSITY PRESS
Baltimore and London

The Johns Hopkins University Press, Baltimore, Maryland 21218
The Johns Hopkins Press Ltd., London

Library of Congress Cataloging in Publication Data

Main entry under title:

Our selves/our past.

  Bibliography: pp. 405–14
  1. United States—Civilization—Psychological
aspects—Addresses, essays, lectures.   2. Psychohistory—
Addresses, essays, lectures.   I. Brugger, Robert J.
E169.1.09   973'.01'9   80-26343
ISBN 0-8018-2312-9
ISBN 0-8018-2382-X (pbk.)

For Laura and Rebecca

Love always

CONTENTS

PREFACE

History is fun for most of us who read or write it because it calls for detective work—following clues, reconstructing logic, testing hypotheses. If indeed the historian is a kind of detective and if, as Cushing Strout tells us,*—Sigmund Freud was the Sherlock Holmes of the mind, one would expect "psychohistory" to be doubly exciting. I hope with this book to show that it can be. Collected here are representative samples of the work historians have done applying psychological theory to American history. While making clear the problems historians face in using such theory, this volume argues the need to acquaint ourselves with it in more cases than may earlier have seemed necessary. It seeks to inform and stimulate, to register achievements while suggesting how we may best proceed.

Editors are under obligation to say something of their choices and assumptions. First of all I have planned the book and written my own contributions so as to reach as wide an audience as possible. Discussing the relationship between two disciplines, the introduction and headnotes raise important conceptual issues and therefore ought to provide plenty of grist for the mills of advanced and specialized students of history. As a reader in applied psychology (by no means all of it Freudian), it should prove interesting and profitable to analysts, clinicians, and other mental health care professionals. I hope to have introduced both history and theory unforbiddingly enough to engage college students and indeed anyone who finds American history fascinating.

Secondly, I have tried to strike a balance on several scales. Besides covering the span of American history as evenly as possible, the volume includes a classic or two along with more recent work that breaks new ground or reexamines timeworn topics from a fresh perspective. Thus one finds here Stanley Elkins's study of the "slave personality," published over twenty years ago, together with Carroll Smith-Rosenberg's innovative essay on women hysterics and the pathbreaking witchcraft analysis of Boyer and Nissenbaum. To demonstrate that psychological studies need not be confined to biography, the anthology is made up of both individual and group studies—selections running from a portrait of Eleanor Roosevelt to an essay exploring subliminal themes in the abolitionists' critique of the slave South. I have

*For a reference to "The Uses and Abuses of Psychology in American History," see the Select Bibliography, Part I.

endeavored also to present as many theoretical perspectives as possible, so that one may read here Richard Bushman's Eriksonian article on Jonathan Edwards but also a character-trait study of Revolutionary Loyalists and Patriots, an Adlerian approach to Populism, and Robert Jay Lifton's "survivor guilt" interpretation of the My Lai atrocity.

Eclecticism leads directly to the problem of definition: When does an interpretation or subject become "psychological" enough to be called psychohistory? My premise has been that the work falls under that rubric when the author (in text, notes, or appendix) discusses the pertinence of formal psychological theory, uses it knowledgeably, and demonstrates a willingness to follow it wherever it leads—meaning to use it consistently or to acknowledge snags in the attempt to interweave the theory and history. Psychohistory means the deliberate use of psychology. Of course it can be used implicitly, and at some point being coy can give rise to the objection that the theory isn't really there at all. Boyer and Nissenbaum's selection, for example, illustrates principles of ego-defense mechanisms but nowhere mentions Sigmund or Anna Freud. Rather than press a point, I have included it and a few others like it for their heuristic value. They illustrate a sensibility that this book urges us to sharpen.

It may be self-evident that limitations of space have forced me to shorten many of these selections. For the sake of continuity and simplicity I have gone a step further and omitted ellipsis points—trappings of excision that in this case would be more distracting than purposeful. Especially with the Burrows and Wallace, Hull et al., Jordan, Elkins, Youngdale, and Mazlish pieces, one should refer to the original article or book for more elaborate argument and fuller documentation.

Finally I should admit that the quality of these selections is uneven and that, because psychohistorians have plenty left to do, the volume seems to overlook some inviting topics. All the same, these essays more often reflect the strengths than the weaknesses of psychology in history and, taken together, write a compelling brief for more such work. Though my headnotes occasionally raise questions, which hardly exhaust the possibilities, they are meant to be provocative, not unfriendly.

My personal thanks go to Michael Aronson, now of the Harvard University Press, who first encouraged me to undertake this anthology, and to Mary Lou Kenney, the editor and friend who made numberless suggestions and patiently saw the book through the early publishing process. Henry Y. K. Tom, social sciences editor, and Judith Stivelband, copy editor, both have been exceptionally helpful in the final stages of publication. I am indebted to the Andrew W. Mellon Foundation for the faculty fellowship that gave me a year at Harvard and time to combine this project with research and teaching there; to the students of my applied psychology seminar in Eliot House for their considerable help, much of it scholarly; and to Alan Heimert, Master of that friendly establishment, for his support and kindnesses. Many colleagues, historians and clinicians, have taken time to read portions of the manuscript and to help me with the fine points that are critical in interdisciplinary study; I owe special thanks to Vamik D. Volkan and C. Knight Aldrich, professors of psychiatry at the University of Virginia, and to members of the Psychology/Humanities study group there. Ella M. Wood, Lottie M. McCauley, Kathleen Casey, Elizabeth C. Stovall, and Vicki Kader are simply the most cheerful secretaries in academic life.

Our Selves/Our Past

INTRODUCTION

THE HOUSE OF MANY GABLES

ROBERT J. BRUGGER

The human heart might be compared to a cavern, Nathaniel Hawthorne wrote in one of his journals. Sunshine and flowers around the entrance yield, only a few steps within, to "a terrible gloom, and monsters of diverse kinds; it seems," he continued, "like hell itself."[1] One need not share Hawthorne's sense of sin and shame to agree that all of us are creatures of darkness as well as brightness, that everyone is made up of ideals, appetites, thoughts, and fears alike. Students of the past generally pay attention to what lies outside Hawthorne's cavern—not all of it sweetness and light: to political power, economic forces, and social structure. This anthology offers readers a taste of the work historians of the American experience have done while trying to probe the depths Hawthorne imagined.

I

Psychohistory may be an idea whose time has come, but its entrance has not been perfectly graceful. So outrageous are some recent books going by that description that one hesitates to use the term in polite company; while it raises the pitch of discourse where booklovers gather, the loudest sounds are often boos and catcalls. A New Yorker cartoon of a few years ago pictured a large, institutional door labeled "Psychohistory Ward." "Some people mark up walls with ugly words," Newsweek quotes the psychiatrist Robert Coles as saying, "other people do psychohistory."[2]

Americans may be particularly hostile to the genre. Writing history with a psychological approach can mean taking into account the irrational and unchanging features of human nature. Yet we prefer to see in our history the record of reason and optimism fulfilled, evidence of progress, a chronicle of challenges successfully met. Besides, while many Americans enjoy reading about the habits of film stars and the escapades of politicians, that curiosity

1

dwells side by side with a more commendable respect for privacy. Psychohistory can focus attention on sexual and other private matters which, though occasionally titillating, reach beyond traditional historical topics. While Fawn Brodie's *Thomas Jefferson; An Intimate History* (1974) sold very well, it also invited salvoes of criticism for dwelling at length on that founding father's real and possible sexual adventures. "By Sex Possessed" read the title of an essay on Brodie's book in *Commentary* magazine, wherein David Herbert Donald drily observed that Brodie seemed to be a disciple of the sexologist A. C. Kinsey. Believing that a man ought to be judged by the fullness and frequency of his sex life, Brodie, Donald concluded, had made a "heroic attempt to restore Jefferson his full humanity."[3]

Causing scholars special distress are the claims that psychohistory comprises an entirely new science, and that it reveals world-shaking truths. Lloyd deMause, a New York dabbler in history and psychoanalysis who far and away is the most conspicuous spokesman for merging those two callings, has brought down upon himself the full wrath of established historians. One of them, Jacques Barzun, emeritus professor at Columbia, argues forcefully that Clio, muse of history, needs no such new-fangled "doctoring." As if to drive home Barzun's point for him, deMause makes startling revelation the mainstay of his marketing campaign. In 1975, writing in the magazine he founded, he described psychohistory as "a science with a terrible sense of urgency . . . uncertain whether it has even one decade to learn what it must in order to make a difference in the race . . . against man's spiraling ability to destroy himself." At a meeting of the American Association for the Advancement of Science the following year deMause reported that the American Revolution was "a group psychotic episode involving the shared fantasy of regression in the mother's womb." (Put off by his slighting of the Boston Tea Party, the *Globe* of that city suggested that, had there been any psychohistorians in 1773, "they might have been pitched in right after the tea and it would have served them right.") Then, too, deMause hypes his *Journal of Psychohistory* by making regular mailings to academic membership lists. Scholars usually find his snippets on masturbation and infanticide half-baked and juvenile. Kenneth S. Lynn, who himself is no stranger to psychological theory, refers to deMause's journal as an adult comic book. Also citing the work of more serious historians, Lynn argues that "reckless psychologizing" is a "cancer" eating its way "through the whole body of the historical profession."[4]

II

Psychohistory is nothing if not controversial. But before examining more fully its own history and the reasons why it causes such controversy, one should note that in some sense every good historian is a "psycho" historian.

History concerns itself with those things worth knowing about the past, at bottom involving people, and certainly their motives, how they grow into society, why conflict divides them. One need not look long or far to find examples of American biography and history that are sensitive to the issues of character or the emotional undercurrents of political behavior. An oft-cited example of vividness in portraiture without the apparatus of psychological theory is Henry Adams's treatment of that erratic congressman of Jeffersonian Virginia, John Randolph of Roanoke. "Of all his eccentricities the most pitiful yet the most absurd were not those which sprang from his lower but from his higher instincts," Adams wrote in a biography published in 1882:

Half his rudeness and savagery was due to the pride which would allow no one to see the full extent of his weakness. At times he turned violently on himself. So in the spring of 1815 he snatched at religion and for an instant felt a serious hope that through the church he might purify his nature; yet even in his most tender moments there was something almost humorous in his childlike incapacity to practice for two consecutive instants the habit of self-control or the simplest instincts of Christianity.... If in his moments of utmost Christian exaltation he could only think he had forgiven his enemies and would hurt no human being if he had the power, what must have been his passion for inflicting pain when the devil within his breast held unchecked dominion!

Adams's psychological insights were informal, phrased in ordinary English; they strike his readers as convincing and "true" to our own experience. So do the observations of William E. B. Du Bois, the early-twentieth-century black historian, on the rage of white mobs in the post-Civil War South. "Before the wide eyes of the mob is ever the Shape of Fear," said Du Bois in his *Black Reconstruction in America* (1935):

Back of the writhing, yelling, cruel-eyed demons who break, destroy, maim and lynch and burn at the stake, is the knot, large or small, of normal human beings, and these human beings at heart are desperately afraid of something. Of what? Of many things, but usually of losing their jobs, being declassed, degraded, or actually disgraced of losing their hopes, their savings, their plans for their children; of the actual pangs of hunger, of dirt, of crime.

Like the novelist or short story writer, the most sensitive historians and biographers demonstrate a highly developed awareness of the force and flow of human feelings.[5]

But psychohistory holds out the promise that the psychology it employs is formal or theoretical rather than commonsensical, perhaps even discussed in the text, and that the union enables the historian to do what otherwise he could not. Interest in such formal linkage began as early as 1896, according to John Garraty, when the English scientist and writer Havelock Ellis described biography as "applied psychology." Among the first attempts to make the application in this country were the psychoanalytic biographies that followed Freud's visit to the United States in 1909 and the American publication of his *Introductory Lectures on Psychoanalysis* in 1920. Except for a volume on Martin

Luther, which Preserved Smith, the Cornell historian, published in 1913, most of the new psychoanalytic studies were of American subjects. Katherine Anthony offered a book on Margaret Fuller, the transcendentalist writer, in 1920; three years later Ralph V. Harlow finished a biography of Samuel Adams. Two books appeared in the 1920s on that eminent psychological subject, Edgar Allan Poe, one by Joseph Wood Krutch and another by a French emigré and disciple of Freud, Marie Bonaparte. In 1929 Gerald W. Johnson, a newspaperman and writer, had his own try with John Randolph, whom in a subtitle he described as "a political fantastic." In the early thirties Leon Pierce Clark, a practicing psychiatrist, published a psychobiography of Lincoln, and the literary critic Lewis Mumford issued a memorable book on Herman Melville.[6]

Several of the volumes on this incomplete list did contain useful insights. Every failure wants to forget his failures, wrote Harlow of Sam Adams, whose prerevolutionary career was not happy: "He may ignore them, or he may seek to deceive himself and others into a conviction that they represent, not weakness, but a peculiar virtue." "Of Poe," Krutch observed in an important passage, "it has often been said with entire truth that whatever objections might be made to the tone of his stories it could not be denied that they are without single exception 'pure,' and that though they may deal with every other horror and corruption known to man they are free from any taint of sexual indelicacy."[7] But on the whole these new psychoanalytical studies— filled with jargon, highly judgmental—deserved the cool reception they met.

By the late 1950s several trends in historical writing reopened the case for psychology in history. One was the effort to reconsider and rewrite conventional "Progressive" accounts of the American past. "Revisionist" historians wondered, for example, whether there might not be more to sectional conflict in the antebellum period than economic differences, more to the Populist and Progressive movements than the perennial quarrel between agrarian and commercial interests. This revisionist trend invited scholars to look beneath the surface or between the lines of public debate for the worries that gave such arguments their force. Reflecting the movement was the work of Richard Hofstadter, a Columbia University historian, who wrote on the fears Populist farmers had of distant, mysterious banks and railroad offices, on the status anxieties of Progressive reformers, and on what Hofstadter called "the paranoid style" in American politics.[8] Akin to Hofstadter's approach was the research of David Donald, then also teaching at Columbia. In 1956 Donald published an essay suggesting that leading abolitionists suffered their own uneasiness over changes in nineteenth-century American society and their diminishing esteem within it; four years later he registered an important advance with *Charles Sumner and the Coming of the Civil War*—the first professional historian's attempt, and a successful one, to make sustained use of Freudian theory. Yet another product of Columbia in these years was Stanley Elkins's doctoral dissertation, a study of slavery that based its case for a "Sambo" personality type on several schools of psychological thought.[9]

From an altogether different direction, from clinical experience in ego psychology, Erik H. Erikson in 1958 made his own mark on this genre by publishing *Young Man Luther*. Erikson's book attracted attention neither by making necessary sweeping changes in Reformation history nor because it was a complete biography but because it represented a dramatic attempt to make biographical and historical use of ideas Erikson had discussed earlier in *Childhood and Society* (1950). Most notable among them was the concept of an identity crisis, which American psychologists, sociologists, and other scholars had found especially interesting. Erikson's evidence was embarrassingly thin—virtually nothing is available on Luther's childhood and little on his youth—and critics cited weaknesses in Erikson's understanding of Protestant theology.[10] His achievement was in combining patterns of personality growth derived from long clinical experience with the few historical materials he had; the argument he wove in writing this experiment in what he termed "psycho-history" was plausible in large part because of the quality of mind, the humane sensibility that was so obvious on each page. Here was a convincing study of a "great man" whose own psychological peculiarities, whose own deep-felt needs intermeshed with historical forces. It was a book historians could read with craftsmanly admiration even while questioning its evidentiary soundness.

A broader, harder-to-measure surge of interest in psychological approaches to history might trace its origins to William Langer's presidential address to the American Historical Association in December 1957. Langer, a Harvard professor of European history, whose brother had written a psychoanalytic profile of Hitler for the government during World War II, chided his colleagues for their conservatism, their rationalism; the "newest history," he said, would answer the urgent need to deepen historical understanding "through exploitation of the findings of modern depth psychology." Persons who attended the meeting agree that Langer's presentation, entitled "The Next Assignment," created little stir at the time. Nonetheless in the 1960s it served as a mandate for graduate students and younger faculty members who found themselves drawn to problems that required grounding in psychological theory—or who decided simply to pursue "psychohistory" as a new and promising subfield. A young student of European intellectual history, Bruce Mazlish, made Langer's address a point of departure in collecting a book of essays on psychoanalysis and history. Psychohistory emerged as a lively topic for papers and discussion at historians' professional meetings. Psychiatrists and historians in several cities organized circles for "applied psychoanalysis." By 1972 a small number of mostly younger historians within the American Historical Association formed a Group for the Use of Psychology in History and began publishing a newsletter, now a regular quarterly, *The Psychohistory Review*.[11]

In the sixties and seventies these merging currents produced a tide of publications in "psychohistory." Many of the new books were biographies bearing resemblances to the Freudian volumes of thirty or forty years before.

One of them was partly the work of Freud himself. *Thomas Woodrow Wilson*, published in 1967, after the death of the second Mrs. Wilson, derived from a collaboration during the 1930s between the aged analyst, who detested Wilson, and William C. Bullitt, a diplomat who for political and personal reasons shared that dislike. The Freud-Bullitt book, clumsy, its Wilson grotesque, brought forward a legion of reviewers who bemoaned its literary blunders and logical errors.[12] By offering an example of how not to do psychohistory, and by demonstrating how out of place such crudity was by the late sixties, the Freud-Bullitt biography had the effect of promoting better work. Most of the psychobiographies of these years avoided the *Wilson* mistakes and relied more heavily on the Eriksonian model, which, after 1969, included besides *Young Man Luther* a prizewinning study of Gandhi. Especially well received, and reflecting the careful thought historians were now willing to give psychological theory, were Emery Battis's study of Anne Hutchinson, Richard Bushman's work on Benjamin Franklin, and Kenneth Lynn's study of the late-nineteenth- and early-twentieth-century novelist, William Dean Howells. James T. Patterson acknowledged the help of psychological theory in writing his biography of Robert Taft, published in 1972; Dorothy Ross's biography of G. Stanley Hall (1972) and Peter Shaw's *The Character of John Adams* (1976) skillfully intertwined thought with personality. The historian's growing concern with psychological theory has perhaps transformed the biographical art as it has literary criticism. It is increasingly difficult to justify biography that fails to consider the psychological element in a subject's life. "More than anything else," writes Richard Ellman in the *New York Review of Books*, "we want in modern biography to see the character forming."[13]

Yet psychologically influenced history of the sixties and seventies went beyond biography. Following the lead of Hofstadter and Donald, David Brion Davis reexamined timeworn larger topics like the antebellum "reform" movements aimed at exposing and rooting out Masons, Catholics, and Mormons; since then Davis's work has involved the complex political, cultural, intellectual—and psychological—origins of abolitionism. Winthrop D. Jordan and others have written extensively on the origins and functions of white racism in American life. More remarkably, the historian's familiarity with psychology has considerably enhanced, if not opened up, whole new areas of historical inquiry. John Demos's Eriksonian study of childhood and family patterns in seventeenth-century Plymouth colony, *A Little Commonwealth* (1970), coincided with the major publications of Philip Greven and Kenneth Lockridge on New England communities and contributed measurably to the growing historical concern with child-rearing, adolescence, sexual roles, and family relationships. Interest in psychological theory among historians has also generated studies in attitudes toward the body and sexuality; studies of the position of women in society and male beliefs about them, marriage and divorce patterns, conflict between generations, discontent among the young, aging, and dying, all involve psychological issues and call for an acquaintance with the theories and findings of clinicians. One must conclude that these days the historian who disdains formal psychology does so at his peril.[14]

III

Students of history rightly ask where one begins with psychological theory, which does after all cover topics ranging from religious cravings to conditioned response. Academic psychology departments offer courses as diverse as experimental psychology, child development, memory, clinical psychology, personality theory, perception, social psychology, cognitive development, psycholinguistics, abnormal psychology, animal psychophysics, behaviorism—and the list could go on. From our vantage point much that academic psychologists do seems harmless drudgery: What does one make of statistics measuring the reflexes of startled rats or the anxiety level of lovers? In medical schools psychiatrists-in-training examine mental illness as a condition with origins in somatic (genetic, neurological, and chemical) causes as well as personal or social disorders, and pathological states like schizophrenia and severe depression may indeed respond best to advanced drugs or carefully managed shock therapy. Such findings are of little professional interest to historians, who do not try to cure patients and who take for granted the structure of brain cells and function of nerve endings.

On the conceptual plane and a practical level these glib generalizations break down. As a rule psychologists' taxonomic or categorial issues—what fits under what heading—may not concern outsiders. But definitions of "madness" or pathology do, especially since they have changed through the centuries and because the norms for sanity a society establishes tell a great deal about it. Then too historians in their research occasionally come upon problems that simply demand expert opinion. Donald consulted with specialists on Charles Sumner's traumatic head injury. There is reason to believe that Woodrow Wilson suffered a stroke in 1906 and that it influenced his presidential leadership; future students of Wilson and the politics of his period may need technical help on this point—which in fact a medical doctor first raised. Before attempting another study of John Randolph of Roanoke one would want to research the causes and symptoms of Klinefelter's syndrome, a chromosomal imbalance.[15] Students of social history do well to consult psychological works on the relationship between nutrition and emotional well-being. Wondering about the effect of early parental deaths in the southern colonies, to move away from medical examples, one might examine clinical findings on separation and loss among present-day children. Psychologists have in fact explored the topic long enough to have compiled impressive evidence that adults who as children lost one or both parents are especially prone to nostalgia and depression. Biographers and historians of the family have read with profit psychological data on sibling rivalry—the personality characteristics typically found according to birth order.[16]

Several theories of personality[17] have come into play when historians have tried new approaches to longstanding problems or answered the attacks of colleagues on favorite historical figures. One of the references Stanley Elkins used in *Slavery* was Harry Stack Sullivan's "interpersonal theory," in which one's character derives extensively from the persons with whom one interacts, especially in formative years and especially with those people in places of authority; we are, in that sense the sum of our relationships. Elkins also relied on role psychology, the view that a person tries to control the impressions he or she leaves with others—and thereby the responses evoked—by wearing "masks," or "playing roles," in the course of everyday dealings. David Brion Davis, in a 1969 series of lectures, made use of role theory in a study of mutual suspicions between North and South in the pre–Civil War period: so fluid was antebellum society, he wrote, extending the message of Herman Melville's *Confidence Man* (1857), that one could never be certain which "masks" were authentic and which were misleading—who was reliable and truthful and who was not.[18] A clinician, Sylvan Tompkins, has defended Northern abolitionists against charges of being deranged fanatics by invoking Gordon Allport's theory of "propriate striving"; hoping to demonstrate their emotional stability and lofty intentions, Tomkins has noted that according to Allport's humanistic psychology the healthy person chooses goals to realize his potential and serve needs beyond himself.[19]

Psychology commands the attention of historians wherever it deals with the way people act and believe, and even some forms of measuring or scaling thereby find their way into historical writing. Historians in this respect trail behind sociologists and political scientists, who, perhaps because like psychologists they study the here and now, have longer-established links with psychologists than have most historians. The search for "determinants" has led a few younger historians to experiment with trait and cognitive psychology. Trait psychology systematically establishes the characteristics that mark members of a group under examination. Though the "key traits" psychologists have listed differ considerably, this method has proven of some use, for example in uncovering correlations between the background or temperament of judges and tendencies in the opinions they hand down.[20] N. E. H. Hull and colleagues, in an essay reprinted in this anthology, apply trait psychology to the study of opposing factions in Revolutionary New York, culling manuscript sources for "answers" to a kind of "questionnaire" they devised and comparing the results to traditional accounts of Loyalism and patriotism.

Cognitive psychology, concerning the development of powers of mind and patterns or styles of belief, probably will prove of more lasting value to historians. Social scientists already have used cognitive theory in working on past topics. Ole Holsti distilled from John Foster Dulles's writings and public speeches ten cardinal beliefs which made up what Holsti calls an "operational code" and by which Dulles's mind, rather like a computer, organized the "input" of information it received from the military-diplomatic world outside himself. Leon Festinger's 1957 textbook on cognitive dissonance used the Millerite movement of the 1840s to illustrate the theory that we tend to hold beliefs in a cohesive, stable structure. When outside reality or introduced beliefs conflict with the existing structure, something has to give. In the case of the Millerites, whose leader predicted the end of the world in August 1843 only to see the day pass peacefully, reality was readjusted to "fit" their cognitive pattern: either they had simply miscalculated the time or their faith was being tested by a deity who had only postponed the day of judgment. In like manner, Robert M. Cover has used cognitive dissonance theory to help explain the rulings of Virginia judges in the early republic who found themselves caught between the demands of slave law and the call of conscience.[21] The most innovative work in cognitive psychohistory may finally draw on Jean Piaget's empirical studies of intellectual growth or sophistication in reasoning among children. Different societies—because of the way each brings young people to adulthood—produce persons with different cognitive capacities. Perhaps the thinking done in a society, as evidenced in its legal theory or views of history, develops over time just as do the cognitive skills of maturing children.[22]

Concepts of cognitive psychology may introduce new questions to intellectual historians and novel ways of approaching old ones. The work of Hull et al., Holsti, and others illustrates, they argue, the adaptability of experimental psychology to historical explanation. Historians make occasional use of theory to stir or throw oil on interpretive waters and sometimes face problems that specialists can help to solve by dint of professional experience and accumulated data. But at bottom the question is whether historians should otherwise or of necessity bother with psychological literature, whether there is compelling reason for historians to be psychologically minded in the sense of studying formal theory, or for there to be something called psychohistory. According to Lloyd deMause, that reason lies in the formative power of early life; "no childhood," he is quoted within this volume as saying, "no psychohistory." A better reason lies with the theory of the unconscious: if one can agree that within us are urges or suggestions we are not always aware of and also that we "defend" ourselves in often nondeliberate ways, then all the fuss about psychology in history will appear justified. This leap of faith actually is not so frightening. Even if the unconscious cannot itself be placed under a microscope or on a dissecting table (indeed it is not a thing, and referring to it as "the unconscious" is a shorthand device), few students of human nature deny that something answering its description acts within us.[23] Everyone has his or her own example of "evidence" that it does; usually our reflections conclude less with questions about the existence of the unconscious than with puzzlement about how this feature of the mind "works" or influences us.

Though Sigmund Freud hardly discovered the unconscious, he examined it with revolutionary rigor and completeness.[24] Training as a physician in late-nineteenth-century Vienna, Freud grew interested in patients with "hysterical symptoms," or ailments and oddities with no apparent physical source. His knowledge of hypnotic practice, then the subject of much medical curiosity, and of the writings of the French student of mental disorders Jean Charcot led him to experiments by which he decided that hysterical symptoms resulted from experiences or fears that patients could not talk about when fully conscious. Freud's method soon changed from the rather unproductive one of hypnosis to "free associating" with patients while they, relaxed on a couch in his office, spoke with as little reserve as possible of their dreams, of the images and associations that came to mind as Freud tried to re-create their emotional past. The fruit of this work, the point of Freud's early essays, was the hypothesis that the mind is a study in tension between conscious and unconscious. As his clinical practice grew larger and his writings bolder, Freud modified this view of the mind's "topography" so that it was divided into the familiar tripartite order superego, ego, and id. The ego in his theory resembled a lid on a cauldron boiling with id, or unconscious impulses that called for containment, or "repression," and that in the end were two contrary drives. One was the sexual instinct (eros or libido), the other aggression (thanatos or destrudo). To love and to destroy were the deep-seated wishes which, Freud wrote in 1920,[25] made up contending yet complementary urges inside all men and women.

These primary impulses play themselves out in the developmental, or family, drama, for which Freud is probably best known. Based on his work with patients whose disturbances seemed to have origins in early life, Freud constructed a theory of psychological growth that he argued was empirically grounded in infantile animal needs and the child's early attachments to and jealousy of parents. The oral stage he described as that of an infant's total dependence on his mother, of breastfeeding, and of blissful unity with the source of all gratification; in the anal stage the child, as he masters control of the excretory functions, finds them an object of intense curiosity; in the phallic and the latency stages—roughly between the ages of five and twelve—Freud believed that children discover but hold in abeyance knowledge of sexual differences. In the genital stage young people learn about and want to act on their sexual urge. Having established these psychobiological steps, Freud argued for the formative importance of the first few years of life. Disruption of or unusual experiences in the oral or anal stages leads to "fixations"—peculiar dependencies or characterological marks that bear the imprint of the troubled phase. Abrupt or early weaning, for example, would produce adult obsession with things in or of the mouth; harsh toilet training might lead to an unusually severe sense of order, time, and spending. Freud also thought that emotional strain in adults could and did bring about temporary "regression" to one of these early stages, with any or all its signs.

The key to Freud's developmental theory was his view that the first sexual attraction in anyone's life, the first "love affair," involves the opposite-sex parent, and it invariably brings with it anxiety and often causes damage. The oedipal crisis, named for the Greek tragedy in which King Oedipus unknowingly falls in love with and weds his mother, occurs between the anal and latency periods, Freud wrote. He described a frightening situation in which each young boy finds himself: loving and "wanting" (in a primitive or presexual sense) his mother, the boy faces the swift and sure retribution of the father, who as her mate jealously guards the mother. Young girls, in an "Electra" variation, somehow have to work themselves out of a similar predicament. In the oedipal dilemma, according to Freudian theory, lie the origins of parent-child rivalry and its perplexing mixture of love and "hate"—its "ambivalent" affection. Therein Freud also placed the psychosexual roots of the superego, the consciencelike arbiter of one's thoughts and acts. Stated as simply as possible, Freud wrote that boys, unconsciously fearful that their father will literally or figuratively castrate them for their designs on the mother, make amends by adapting themselves to fatherly and, more broadly, to social dictates.

From these hypotheses pour insights and methods that fascinate any humanist. Among Freud's signal contributions was his view that there is a wholeness or coherence to mental experience, deliberate acts having roots in the unconscious and unconscious wishes in the instincts or principles he believed he had discovered; by Freud's rule of "psychic determinism" every "motion" of the mind—every fantasy, every slip, mannerism, or "fetish"—has a traceable psychic cause. While these reasons may be successfully repressed, they act on us regardless whether we are aware of them. The result is that things are not as they seem, that there is meaning beneath the surface of thought and action. The ego, as a sentry against unacceptable wishes, deflects, reverses, or denies them, mixes them with their opposites and—typically in what Freud called "dream work"—"condenses," or collapses the complex into the vividly simple. Thus in Freud's scheme an affianced person does not, for example, simply "lose" an engagement ring; he or she unconsciously makes a statement of doubt or ambivalence, otherwise unspeakable. To recognize the persuasiveness of Freud's schema one need only consider the saliency of something "forgotten" or blurted out in an emotionally charged or unguarded moment, or the suggestive richness of one's dreams. Finally, besides showing the protean or fluid quality of mental operations, the psychoanalytic system offers a method of analysis that ties together presumably distinct problems. Interpreting dreams requires the same attention to the mind's "scrambling" of urges as did Freud's work with hysterical patients; there are functional similarities among dreams, which Freud called the "royal road to the unconscious," neuroses, by which we play tricks on ourselves in failing to face squarely the sources of our distress, and art, which relies heavily on the expression of untutored wishes bubbling up from the unconscious.

Not until Freud's later years, after World War I, did he spend much time reflecting on the large implications or historical dimensions of his theory. Several later works tried to make connections between psychoanalysis and anthropology. *Totem and Taboo* (1919) argued from questionable evidence that the oedipal conflict had its prototype in actual prehistoric rivalries; at a critical point in the life of a human horde the young males, or "sons," rose up against the aging dominant male, or "father," killed him, and then, guilt-stricken, consumed his flesh. Distant human memories of this practice survived, Freud thought, in religious ceremony and in the potentially explosive veneration of charismatic leaders. He explored such leadership briefly in *Group Psychology and the Analysis of the Ego* (1920), where he discussed the libidinous bonding, the submergence of ego in group love for a single figure, which seems necessary in church, army, and mob. In *Civilization and Its Discontents* (1930) Freud wrote an overview of human history based on the need of men and women in society to repress and rechannel into constructive courses (or "sublimate") their antisocial instincts. Unable because of social convention to enjoy sexual freedom, men and women raised cities, built empires, and wrote music instead. Thus in Freud's view the human race is a necessarily unhappy lot. Instinctively licentious, men are circumscribed by taboos. Secretly yearning for the domination of a primitive father, they fear the authority "castrating" fathers impose. Beset with unattainable wishes, in their neuroses they resist true self-understanding. Freud's answer to the unhappiness of mankind was to bring to the level of consciousness as much as possible of the id, to come to terms with or unmask the superego for what it is, but finally to give in to neither oppression nor libertinism: to achieve self-mastery.[26]

These views were harsh, and not all of them won converts. As "father" of the psychoanalytic movement, Freud in theory expected and indeed received challenges from the students he trained in the method. Alfred Adler, one of Freud's Vienna circle of young disciples, broke with the master in 1911 for personal reasons but also over theoretical and therapeutic differences: Adler's "Individual Psychology" stressed the assertive tendencies—the "striving for power"—of the ego, the dangers of the "inferiority complex"; he examined patients as parts of families and placed emphasis on brief and supportive therapeutic encounters. Freud derided Adler and his followers as "buffoons" who thought they were preachers. Carl Gustav Jung, a Swiss Protestant whom Freud at first thought to be his most promising pupil, went on to become his most famous defector. Jung's concept of the unconscious went beyond Freud to embrace, at bottom, archaic images, or "archetypes," derived from man's evolutionary past. Blackness as a symbol might therefore draw on primordial fears of darkness; dreams of washing ashore or coming out of water might issue from the organism's shared memories of progressing from fish to amphibian. Jung wrote that each person has a social mask, an ideal self (or "persona"), and an evil self (or "shadow"). He introduced concepts of extrovert and introvert. Jung's orientation, metaphysical where Freud's was biological and clinical, led him to think about the meaning of life and the way one arrives at a satisfying old age. Geza Roheim, another student of Freud, made his point of departure the psychoanalytic interpretation of character and social change.[27]

These variations might deserve less space except that they prefigured and paralleled developments that made psychoanalysis far more valuable to historians than was Freud's theory by itself. Adler and Jung, studying the ego and reaching beyond infancy for influences on character, complemented the studies of Freud's daughter Anna, who, after his death, in 1939, continued his work and introduced important shifts in orthodox theory. Her subjects, instead of the well-educated, middle-class adults whom her father had treated, were primarily children, whose growth and resiliency centered Anna's attention on the ego and its adaptive strengths. In a 1923 essay Freud himself had spoken of "internalization" and "identification" as ego capacities worthy of notice;[28] Anna Freud's *The Ego and the Mechanisms of Defense* (1936) continued this line of inquiry so that the ego, instead of being squeezed between id and superego, took on functions of its own and assumed a dynamic relationship with the world outside it: the ego, for example, takes in, introjects, or internalizes surrounding values in the course of growth or as a defense against possible threats, and identifies with persons or things outside it as a means of enhancement or protection. By means of "projection" one unconsciously sees in others, while denying in oneself, qualities that are unattractive or dangerous, and by "displacement" one vents feelings—especially of anger—against something less dangerous than the thing that aroused the anger. In the same vein the ego "splits," or separates to make palatable, the hateful or redeeming qualities of someone with great power or attraction. Clinicians like Heinz Hartmann and David Rapaport joined Anna Freud in studying the coping or adaptive devices of the self.

A student of Anna Freud and Hartmann, Erik Erikson has made the subject of self in society—the point where "depth" psychology and history cross paths—one of considerable intellectual vitality.[29] Born in Denmark in 1902, Erikson's early ambitions were artistic; it was as an art student vagabonding about Europe in 1927 that quite by accident he happened to spend a summer tutoring some of Anna Freud's patients in Vienna. The young Dane found her work fascinating. He underwent the analytic process that Freud had made a requirement of all practitioners of his method, and then in 1933, feeling cramped in Freud's Vienna and having recently married an American, Erikson embarked on his own career in Boston. Affiliated with the Harvard clinic directed by Henry A. Murray, Erikson there enjoyed productive years researching and writing on children's habits of play. At the same time he developed ties with social scientists, Margaret Mead among them, and learned much from Murray, himself a leading student of personality in culture. Erikson's concern with the problem of childhood adjustments in different social settings led to fieldwork among American Indian tribes and produced additional essays in scholarly journals. In 1950 this artist-observer, who had never bothered to earn a diploma, captured the attention of scholars in more than a few disciplines with the publication of *Childhood and Society*, a book that drew together many of his previous writings but represented more than the sum of its parts.

While in it Erikson acknowledged debts to Hartmann, Murray, and others, his success was in making a theoretical statement of original value. For one thing he spoke of stages of growth that covered the entire span of a normal life. These "ages of man," each of them involving a crisis one must meet before moving along safely to the next, Erikson said, begin with the same psychobiological periods that Freud had discussed. Erikson altered the concepts and introduced new terms for them because he invested them and his other stages with social significance. Freud's oral stage Erikson called "trust versus mistrust," a time when a mother's manner of answering infantile needs—and her method varied according to social custom, Erikson found—helps to shape a person's fundamental attitudes of love and aggression toward others and the world itself. In Erikson's account, for example, Sioux mothers by their weaning practices were able to foster their infant sons' aggressive instincts and to aim them outward over the landscape to the hunting enterprise and tribal enemies. The anal stage Erikson treated as a matter of a child's learning to take and let go, or of "autonomy" when mastered properly and "shame and doubt" when the muscular-anal issues of toilet training leave psychological scars; on this point his illustration was the "saving" and "timing" culture of the salmon-fishing Yurok tribe. A child's explorations after discovering genital differences and beginning to walk— coinciding with Freud's oedipal period—Erikson analyzed as the stage of "initiative versus guilt," an age with social meaning in that it partakes of "making" and of "being on the make." Freud's latency period in Erikson's research made more sense as a stage of "industry" wherein one enters life outside the family and acquires basic skills of tools and interaction, the failure of industry leading to "inferiority."

Erikson's ideas, based he said on Freudian theory, faced issues in ego psychology that the master would probably have looked upon askance. Like Jung, for instance, Erikson with his eighth and last stage of life contemplated the psychological settlement that men and women try to reach in the winter of their lives; he described the crisis as one of "ego integrity," of either feeling fulfilled after leaving a legacy for succeeding generations or of having despaired of life's meaningfulness. Preceding such final stock-taking was the crisis of "generativity"—the mid-life assessment of one's productivity and its worth, and before that seventh stage came success or failure at finding what

Erikson called "intimacy." Men and women, he wrote, seek a mature and lasting closeness that grows out of conjugal love and the nurturance of their children. Each of Erikson's resolutions built on what had gone before: without realizing who one was and what one "stood" for in life, no intimacy was possible in Erikson's scheme. That pivotal issue of "identity or role confusion"—the problem of finding oneself in youth—Erikson defined as the quest for harmony with oneself, for "a new sense of continuity and sameness," confidence in one's character and purpose, and a sense of where one fits in society and the future.[30] Identity meant direction that included embracing an ideology or a framework that helped to organize one's perception of the world. Making Erikson generally relevant beyond the clinic was his argument in *Childhood and Society*—developed more fully since then—that society, rather than an enemy of the self as Freud wrote, is necessary to it.

Open though historians may be to the helpfulness of any psychological theory, more often than not they turn to psychoanalysis. The pieces in this anthology illustrate the pervasive influence of psychoanalytic principles; indeed Freudian insights have become part of the very language we commonly use to describe ourselves and one another. Historians find psychoanalysis useful because it speaks to the conflict and development which, in one form or another, are central to historical study. Rather than simply describing specific behavior, psychoanalysis embraces a theory of human nature, reaching beneath the conscious, dealing with the push and pull of different impulses, and involving itself with causes—or at least with the roots of the individual psyche in time. Within this tradition Eriksonian ego theory now offers historians the richest return on their reading. It promotes inquiries that tie together unconscious impulses and processes, the conscious self, beliefs, and the social reality beyond the individual.

Another value of psychoanalysis is that it remains an inherently clinical theory—a working and evolving body of theory that changes in emphasis as patients and therapists interact. The view of women in Freud's classical theory, for one thing, has undergone criticism and revision. Judith M. Bardwick, Janine Chassequet, and others now speak of a psychology of women and emphasize, as does Carroll Smith-Rosenberg in her essay in this collection, the peculiar life experiences of women.[31] Robert Jay Lifton, a pioneer in psychohistory who works within the psychoanalytic framework, has spent much of his career studying the impact of disasters and extreme stress;[32] in a selection appearing here, Lifton draws on the theory that victims of these experiences carry with them a frequently dangerous emotional residue. A number of British analysts—W. R. D. Fairbairn, Otto Kernberg, Harry J. S. Guntrip, D. W. Winnicott, and John Bowlby prominent among them—have developed an "object-relations" strain of theory that lays stress on the ways in which "libidinal and antilibidinal factors" (as Fairbairn prefers to call Freud's erotic and aggressive drives) relate to objects outside the self. The British school studies the function of such objects when internalized;

John Bowlby has studied how people adapt when these attachments change or are lost.[33] Heinz Kohut, an Austrian-born analyst now teaching at the Chicago Institute for Psychoanalysis, also has extended Freud's theory. Kohut has published extensively on the viability of "the self" as an entity partaking of superego, ego, and id and adapting to changing social situations.[34] Instrumental in establishing the Center for Psychosocial Studies in Chicago, Kohut shares with Kernberg an interest in narcissism, a topic Christopher Lasch discusses in this collection. Focused study of "the self" can be of theoretical value to biographers; the inclusion of persons and symbols as "objects" in object-relations theory should prove of interest to historians examining, say, the reasons why certain leaders or political rhetorics appeal to certain groups in particular circumstances. In any event, these growing points in psychoanalytic theory reflect an awareness that psyche and self develop within a sociocultural setting.

IV

Even a passing acquaintance with these theories should make clear that they present problems for the historian. First of all there is no single psychology, no unchanging theory, on which he or she can depend. Behaviorism, cognitive studies, child development, and the rest are subject to the refinements and reevaluation that go with continuing research. From Freud to his wayward disciples to his daughter Anna and ego psychologists like Erikson to the British students of object-relations, psychoanalysis—better maintained than many orthodoxies—has continued to evolve, split off, change in emphasis. One can argue that closeness to the clinic is a weakness instead of a strength: if psychohistory means nothing more than applying the "tools" of psychology, the historian can scarcely rely on them, and a poor craftsman it is who cannot. As Jacques Barzun and others have pointed out, when historians decide to apply a psychological theory, they have no assurance that it will remain valid long enough to get the book through its printing.[35]

Nor, if psychohistory means simply joining two disciplines, wedding two methodologies, is it likely that the marriage was made in heaven. Though history and psychology have common concerns with motives, socialization, and patterns of human behavior, differences finally outweigh similarities. Psychoanalytic therapy, for example, involves the study of a life or case history, searching a person's past. Yet the resemblance to biography is superficial. The patient's recollections and associations never stand the usual tests of historical criticism. The analyst's interpretation finally needs to make sense only to the patient in that it translates his overlaid past into the present and transfers his feelings for the therapist (as stand-in for past figures) into the open, where their oppressive power can be dealt with. The analyst's "history" tries to help a patient by reconstructing the psychic origins of pathology; the historian's analysis aims to answer questions about the past by reconstructing what men thought and did. The analyst can give and take with a patient, allowing a process to take its course; even in those rare cases when a historian is able to sit down and talk with a subject, as did Doris Kearns with Lyndon Johnson, intimate disclosures are either out of bounds or likely to be counterfeited. The more common problem is that one "cannot psychoanalyze the dead," as critics of psychohistory put it, and there is no denying the partial truth of that observation.[36]

True, too, that the scholarly purposes of psychology and history are different. Strictly speaking, studies of human nature are ahistorical, conducted without interest in time or place. We cannot be sure that the stages of life number exactly eight or that everyone has faced these crises quite as Erikson describes them regardless whether he or she lived on a Sioux reservation during the Depression, in a German village in late medieval Europe, or in British-controlled India. Erikson's stages of man, Frederick Crews wrote in 1975, are "highly moralized struggles" by which Erikson presumes "to set forth a complete life plan for his species, irrespective of cultural differences."[37] Historians disdainful of the value of psychoanalysis are quick to note that Freud's theory holds the dynamics of the unconscious, the drives of sexuality and aggression, to be constants in all men and women throughout history and thereby renders history unimportant.

It is safe to grant that at some deep level there are universals in human nature. But given the questions historians ask, they can make little use of insights on the likeness of people. Psychohistorians invite stern comment when they settle for similarity. In an article exploring the power of nineteenth-century American beliefs about the West, for example, Alan Beckman argues that the frontier myth gave expression to "the symbolic re-enactment of a universal wish drama of childhood, the Oedipus conflict, a wish drama whose enactment is necessary for the psychological development of a boy into a man." The West, in this interpretation, symbolizes the mother of early infancy, the mother who grants basic wishes and becomes the first love object of the child. The East, of course, represents civilization, order, authority— and the father, after whom the frontiersman finally patterns himself.[38] This symbolic-mythical view of the frontier may suggest deep-seated reasons for the popularity of frontier imagery in Jacksonian oratory or of James Fenimore Cooper's Leatherstocking tales among urban, middle-class readers at the time. Nonetheless it in no way helps to account for important historical differences: Americans—including those who settled the West—divided on issues like Indian and land policy, internal improvements, banks, and the schedules of protective tariffs. Psychohistory often raises the legitimate question "So what?"

While it may be the case that oedipal wishes are part of "every man's early childhood," as Beckman reminds us, the point by itself has limited relevance because historians devote so much of their time to the uniqueness of persons and historical settings. This distinction between the general and the particular, the timeless and the unique, reflects the split in principle between scientific inquiry and humanistic undertakings. Scientists seek and use covering or general laws that explain why, given certain preconditions, specific results become observable. To "explain" something in this sense means to show that the results of an experiment covered by the law could only have occurred as they did, and that at any time in the future—so long as the preconditions obtain—the same occurrence is predictable. Humanists on the other hand try to uncover meaning in the record of human experiences and expression. Their enterprise is artistic in the sense that it involves fashioning a whole from the materials at hand. Their thought and writing transcends the particular; but the effort is to appreciate or understand rather than to predict. Academic psychologists consider themselves scientists. Psychoanalysts still debate whether they practice an art or devote themselves to a science. Most historians would agree that their work falls somewhere between science and art.[39] Historians as humanists concern themselves with the meaning of ideas and symbols in the past; when as scientists they speak of explanation, they refer to their answers to questions of how and why: how and why a particular event took place or a personality developed as it did, when it did—that is, in its own historical setting.

Partaking of both art and science, history represents a disciplined imagination at work on historical sources. Historians therefore judge their writing against standards of logical tightness and soundness of evidence. Yet psychohistory often lies vulnerable on these counts. Psychoanalysis, as the discussion in the preceding section of this essay makes clear, trains attention on the "intrapsychic" tensions that lie well beneath the level of consciousness and have their roots in early childhood. Psychoanalytical studies of historical personalities thus easily fall victim to what Erikson calls "originology," a preoccupation with the earliest appearance of symptoms, or what in logic is known as the genetic fallacy. A similar trap is the reductive fallacy, the attempt to make the complicated misleadingly simple or unitary. No biographer who ascribes the work of a writer or the decisions of a politician to such simple "causation" can hope for a respectful hearing. Collapsing the answers to why questions to a childhood fixation or a single ego defense slights the array of influences that always is involved. It also makes the character under study a cartoon, a caricature.[40]

For an illustration of logical lapses one can read Freud and Bullitt's discussion of Woodrow Wilson during the *Lusitania* crisis. Politically and personally committed to peace, Wilson in the summer of 1915 was growing angry at German disregard for civilian lives and was aware that a swelling number of Americans shared his anger. In Freud and Bullitt's awkward collaboration they account for the tone of Wilson's two diplomatic messages that summer—one strongly worded, the other holding out for a change in German war policy—as symptomatic of Wilson's earlier troubled relationship with his father. "The *Lusitania* note gave release to his hostility to his father," reads the Freud and Bullitt commentary, "the supplementary instruction to his passivity to his father." By this mode of interpretation the real game is played deep within the psyche, and whether Wilson is firm with the Germans or conciliatory he "loses" in that his oedipal struggle explains his every move. A conventional historian or biographer would point to diplomatic and political considerations—to the most apparent reasons—in accounting for Wilson's conduct. Freud and Bullitt instead begin and end with the unconscious and with childhood issues—the least obvious explanations. Their neglect of the forces acting at the time on Wilson as president illustrates tunnel vision in psychohistory at its worst. Writing of unconscious drives as if they are fluids with so many pounds pressure per square inch is neither historically convincing nor, for that matter, the stuff of great literature. "Those [unconscious] desires were still in conflict," Freud and Bullitt continue. "On the one hand he wanted to express his unconscious hatred of Germany and his unconscious desire to be Jehovah. On the other hand he wanted to express his wish to be the Prince of Peace. His problem was to find some course of action which would satisfy both these charges of libido and at the same time would be acceptable to his Super-Ego. . . . If, by defeating Germany, he could dictate a permanent peace to the whole world, he would be a Prince of Peace indeed!"[41]

The question "How do you know?" is usually the most difficult for the psychohistorian to answer. Like lawyers marshaling arguments based on available evidence, historians pride themselves on their use of sources, their quick recognition of thin, faulty, or missing data. Though the strongest case one can make for psychohistory is that it tries to take into account the unconscious, the evidence suited for this approach is at best indirect, just as evidence of the childhood experiences that are so important to a psychoanalytic interpretation is almost always hard to come by. While for example Fawn Brodie's early biography of the Reconstruction congressman Thad Stevens drew upon the facts of Stevens's lameness and his highly plausible efforts to make up for his deformity, Brodie found Thomas Jefferson's "intimate history" far more elusive. Reviewers had a field day with her scavenged evidence that Jefferson was a guilt-ridden womanizer. Using Freud's dictum that we accidentally reveal what bothers us in slips of the tongue and pen (as well as in jokes and dreams), Brodie noted how words like "corruption" and "infidelity" crept into Jefferson's writings on religion and his letters about the unreliability of American and French post offices. By Freud's principle, simply adhered to, the frequent choice of such words may have masked self-indictment.

But diminishing their significance in this case are historical points that Brodie missed. The belief that the medieval church had "corrupted" Christianity was explicit in eighteenth-century religious studies; Joseph Priestly used that word in the title of his famous book on the subject. As for "infidelity," Jefferson joined both the pure and profligate in applying this term to describe fears that curious postmen and even political enemies were prying open letters (as often happened) before they were delivered. If "infidelity" denotes illicit sex, Garry Wills observed with glee in the *New York Review of Books*, perhaps Jefferson was a homosexual—since the word also cropped up in one of his letters to the South Carolinian, Ralph Izard. Brodie's evidence was not much firmer when she reached Jefferson's possible love affair with Sally Hemings, the light-skinned slave girl, while he served as minister to France. "The first evidence that Sally Hemings had become for Jefferson a special preoccupation," Brodie declared, came in his use of the term "mulatto" eight times in a log he kept while traveling in northern Europe. Being the farmer and amateur scientist he was, Jefferson carefully described the soil qualities of the countryside he visited; an earlier trip through southern France—before Sally's arrival in Paris—had yielded only one "mulatto" reference. The trouble here is that "mulatto" was a standard geological category in Jefferson's day, and the soil colors of southern France and northern Germany differed exactly as he described them.[42]

V

While the essays comprising this collection will not escape every logical or evidentiary objection, they do offer examples of psychology-in-history aware of itself, to paraphrase Emerson, or self-critical in its execution. They illustrate humanistic concern for the richness of human subjects; for problems of will or intention versus the unintentional or our vulnerability to unconscious drives; for the possible roots of intellectual, religious, and artistic creativity. They demonstrate the humanist's sensitivity to anguish and its resolution in the historical record. These essays explore the human costs of ambition, competition, technological advance, isolated achievement, and rootlessness— issues that are of particular importance in the American experience and that therefore argue specifically for American psychohistory. These essays also argue the seemingly unobjectionable point, which some students of history still do not accept, that the historian as scientist cannot solve every problem by attending to the most readily accessible reasons, the most "rational" causes, alone. The pieces in this anthology make no effort to "prove" universal laws of human behavior; they do suggest that common psychological impulses and mechanisms invite attention to altogether new problems, to the multiple levels of perceived reality, and to the psychological strategies of contented and discontented alike.

Gnawing questions of sufficient evidence probably go with the historian's territory. Critics of psychohistory rightly cite the limitations of circumstantial evidence and the outright gaffs that appear in the literature. Yet clinical evidence and psychological data—fruits of the therapeutic encounter and psychological research—can be of immense help to the historian. They provide missing pieces to the puzzle he wants to put together and point to new puzzles. Christopher Lasch's essay demonstrates how not only developments in the theory of narcissism but also clinical data on the narcissistic personality structure can shape the questions a historian asks of recent and contemporary American life. Robert Jay Lifton's therapy sessions with Vietnam veterans prompted him to use his clinical findings in writing an account of the milieu in which these ex-soldiers had grown up and of a curious massacre that Americans visited on Vietnamese civilians. In such cases a psychohistorian tries to establish a useful parallel relationship between what we know from the clinic and what we would like to know about the past. The classic example of this tactic, building by suggestive analogy, is Stanley Elkins's slave personality study, in which the experience of nazi concentration camp victims provides a framework for a discussion of plantation slavery.[43] Clinical findings in this way resemble the dotted line (for the missing years) on the historian's graph showing the rate of Southern economic growth before and after the Civil War or perhaps more accurately the durable mesh backing archivists use to hold together old manuscripts with tattered pages and missing lines.

In biography clinical-historical paralleling entails deductions about a subject's early life based on adult personality—an admittedly risky undertaking. Consider for example Jefferson's regard for his mother, a topic on which there is so little hard evidence that one of Jefferson's biographers describes Jane Randolph Jefferson, whom her son mentioned only once in all his writings, as apparently "a zero quantity" in his life. A retired New York analyst, extending Brodie's discussion, has compared Jefferson's well-documented awkwardness with women and preference for friendships with married women to clinical experience and found a very close correspondence between him and male patients whose mothers had exercised long and unsalutary dominion over their sons.[44] Trying to gain access to Jefferson through clinical profiles proves nothing, but it does provide possible answers to enduring questions about dark corners in the life of that founding father and helps us to understand him as social commentator and even political subject. In this collection Bruce Mazlish's article on Nixon enables the reader to watch as a psychobiographer cautiously tries to reconstruct the psychologically important features of a subject's early life, based on thin childhood but thick adult evidence, using theory or clinical evidence circumspectly to shape questions and supply educated guesses where the historical sources are sketchy or lacking.

All the same, psychobiographers need not depend on such adult-to-childhood reconstruction. Much recent work avoids the problem of childhood evidence by focusing on young adult and mature psychological issues, which Eriksonian ego psychology calls to our attention and for which evidence is usually more abundant. Mazlish thus makes the most of the evidence on Nixon's identity formation, choice of marriage partner, and manifest efforts to "make it," to prove himself in a world he perceived to be hostile. In like manner Joan Erikson looks closely at Eleanor Roosevelt as a woman seeking her own selfhood while endeavoring to live with and serve her strong-willed husband. In addition psychobiographers of late have made end runs on a subject's character by studying and laying stress on those historical elements that reveal by reflection. Here is a variation of Erikson's "great man" theorem, by which famous and powerful figures and their peculiar needs intersect with historical forces and change their direction. Richard Bushman's discussion of Jonathan Edwards's religious appeal helps to illuminate his audience and his society, but also delineates Edwards himself, the psychological and religious experience that produced him uniquely. By the same token Kathleen Dalton's essay on Teddy Roosevelt's popularity outlines issues that troubled Americans of his day while raising the imprint of Victorian values on Roosevelt. By and large psychobiographers have taken seriously the warning of Beatrice Cowper Green; the historian, she chided, "just as much as the psychologist, should . . . have more in his or her repertoire of possible explanations than an overworked Oedipal complex."[45]

It is instructive, and promising given the traditional artistic goals of biographers, that psychobiography at its best aims at persuasive coherence.[46] With that end in view biographers find psychoanalysis, for all its scientific shortcomings, nonetheless valuable because it presses us to ask how thoughts, fears, acts, refusals to act—how opposites—may form a unified historical picture. "There are no accidents" was Freud's admonition in the principle of psychic determinism; "everything fits" is the biographer's lesson: adulthood and childhood, conscious and unconscious, public and private all, in some fashion that the psychobiographer sets out to trace, make up a coherent whole. Psychohistorians and biographers therefore join in dissenting from psychoanalytic orthodoxy without, as Frederick Crews puts it, forsaking its most promising insights—"its attentiveness to signs of conflict, its hospitality to multiple significance, its ideas of ambivalence, identification, repression, and projection."[47] With his ear thus "tuned," the psychobiographer is ready to hear what Cushing Strout calls the "resonance" that occurs when pieces of evidence at different levels of experience—like strings on a guitar—produce a "harmony" of relatedness. In the case of William James, argues Strout, this technique means studying the correspondences and suggestive connections, if not simple causality, running through James's relationship with his father, his formal philosophy, and his conflicted experience in Civil War and postwar society.[48] Erik Erikson refers to this ordering of multilayered evidence as "triple bookkeeping," and successful psychobiography adheres to the spirit of his principle.[49] Psychological theory leads, not to simplification, but to a meaningful complexity that integrates distinct elements in any biographical problem: the subject's unconscious impulses and processes, his conscious self, and his setting in society and culture.

The nonbiographical essays in this anthology illustrate a corollary to the meaningful complexity rule: "the multiplication of causes," in Frank Manuel's phrase, "is a mark of sagacity."[50] These pieces often draw back from startling conclusions for the very reason that historical logic carries the warning that explanations are seldom simple. Avoiding fallacies of reduction, Boyer and Nissenbaum, for example, set out to uncover the meaning that tied together real developments and real fears; they prepare the reader for an analysis of psychological strains by discussing the political, material, and social divisions that gave rise to them. Ronald Walters, Carroll Smith-Rosenberg, and Howard Feinstein demonstrate a healthy mix of conventional and psychological reasoning; they shun the approach that would force a psychological interpretation on the reader before he is persuaded of the need to try one. The John Demos and James Youngdale essays offer examples of the process by which a psychohistorian, eye sharpened for evidence and patterns that others may have overlooked or dismissed, points out the shortcomings of earlier treatments of a topic. After explaining the possible helpfulness of a psychological perspective, each goes on to discuss the new questions that spring to mind, to search for new kinds of evidence, and to try on all the evidence for a "fit" with the theory. The psychohistorian is by nature a revisionist. Dissatisfied with historical accounts that partake only of conscious or surface reality, he or she does not so much substitute explanations based on the unconscious elements in life, however, as explore the complex interplay between rational and less readily apparent reasons for behavior.[51]

The readings that follow also provide answers to the question where psychohistory goes after biography. Psychology, eminently the study of the individual, might seem to have no bearing on groups and historical events beyond an individual life; one therefore hears that there is a "coming crisis" in psychohistory, that psychobiography leads to a dead end.[52] Besides the empirical approach of Hull, Hoffer, and Allen—correlating personality traits to political affiliation—these essays demonstrate several ways in which the psychology of the unconscious illuminates group problems in history. All of them receive further treatment in the headnotes. One method entails the study of shared unconscious devices or processes—of ego defenses but perhaps also of "offense mechanisms"—in an episode or movement. The Boyer and Nissenbaum, Dalton, and Youngdale essays illustrate this approach, as does Jordan's selection on Jefferson insofar as it reaches for broader than biographical significance. As persons we are different; but all of us have in common the means of ego defense, and sometimes our employment of them lays out a pattern revealing cultural assumptions, particular social tensions, racial myths, ideal self-images, or political expectations. Studying patterns of ego defense involves attention to symbols, surrogates, and scapegoats, and their meaning in a specific historical setting.

Two additional approaches attempt to show ties between social circumstances and character structure. The first moves from historical setting to "group personality"—a contradiction of terms that can be a useful fiction. The essays by Elkins, Smith-Rosenberg, and Feinstein suggest that life experiences peculiar to a specific group may in fact produce shared personality characteristics. The most impressive of such studies next use those findings to ask further questions about the social arrangements that were psychologically confining or shaping. Since personality themes include ego defenses, this scheme and the preceding one overlap. Here, however, one treats the defenses of a woman hysteric or the "Sambo" role of a slave not as episodic, as in patterns of witchcraft accusations, but as part and parcel of life in a particular social stratum or within a sex or race group. The reverse of examining "group personality" based on a definable social experience is studying social norms as revealed in personal pathology, a third application of psychohistory at the group level, which Lasch's selection illustrates. This strategy moves from patterns of patienthood to themes of society at large.

Other modes of nonbiographical psychohistory grow out of developmental theory, the psychology of generations, and the dynamics of group trauma. The study of childhood, for example, opens a wide avenue for psychological questions and insights. The Burrows and Wallace piece on the American Revolution suggests how—in carefully spelled out circumstances—changes in parenting practices can help to account for adult attitudes toward political authority. Another approach building on the importance of psychological development makes the process of identity formation a stepping-off point: because in Erikson's definition identity depends so heavily on the social possibilities open to one, how certain groups of people managed this critical passage in life speaks incisively of their historical experience. Cushing Strout's article illustrates the use of an unusual source, late-nineteenth-century American fiction, to probe this issue in the cases of middle-class women and Jewish immigrants. George Forgie's essay, drawing on Freud's theory of the oedipal drama, argues that we can better understand the political behavior of certain generations by treating them as psychological subjects, an approach that awaits further exploitation in examining, say, the impact of the Great Depression. Finally, psychohistorians have made attempts to explain sudden group decisions like revolutions or severe group experiences like disasters in terms of psychological process. The least successful such studies describe a group as being like a person and then proceed as if it were true—though nations or classes are hardly persons who work out oedipal complexes or suffer psychotic episodes. In this collection Youngdale's piece on the Populists offers an example, less objectionable, of social psychology applied to group disappointment, while Lifton's essay draws on the survivor syndrome concept to explain a specific violent outburst. The theoretical formulations underlying this mode of psychohistory, about which the headnote to Lifton's discussion says more, call for further thought and experimental application.

Altogether the pieces of this anthology argue a thesis that even the archcritic of psychohistory, Jacques Barzun, might find acceptable. Barzun has insisted that history, to remain the blend of art and science that it is, must maintain a chronological dimension, be concrete in its subject matter, and qualify as memorable—by which he means both worth remembering and capable of being remembered after reading.[53] Driven into bunkers by attacks on psychohistory during the past two decades, its practitioners dug deeper when Barzun's *Clio and the Doctors* (1974) appeared. Yet his classic prescriptions deserve a close reading: they allow plenty of room for innovation in approach and subject matter and will quite likely mark the interdisciplinary work that proves of widest lasting importance. They do not slam the door on psychological analysis as completely as Barzun seemingly intended. Trying to answer questions about the past, the historian is clearly free to search other disciplines for anything that bears helpfully on a historical problem. Barzun's test for "true" history only reminds us that to be most persuasive to a readership the result of the problem-solving will have to handle the issues through time, appear in common English rather than clinical or theoretical jargon, and apply the customary (though slightly amended) rules of logic.

The point is that we ought to think of psychohistory, not as a new field or science with its own method, but as psychologically informed history, and of the psychohistorian, rather than as a sort of mutant, as a student of history with a sharpened sensibility. As Paul Monaco said in the *History of Childhood Quarterly*, disagreeing with its editor, Lloyd deMause, "What is needed is fewer new disciplines and more thinking about the old ones." Though history and psychology have different methods and objectives, the fact diminishes in importance when the historian who reads psychology remains a historian whose "proofs" and "explanations" need not stand the test of repeatable laboratory experiments and whose concerns are not truly with predictive models or therapeutic measures. The historian may well seek the help of academic psychologists or trained analysts in organizing his or her readings in theory and, while immersed in the historical evidence, consult with them on clinical findings. All the same, the interpretation finally emerges from the mind of the historian alone and partakes of all elements which, in his or her judgment, help to answer questions of how and why.[54]

The simplicity of this view is its strength. Because historians who read in psychological theory remain students of past problems, they may benefit from psychological insights without applying the method that clinicians use while treating patients. The historian may find psychologists' questions and answers interesting and suggestive, and compare them to his work. He does so without binding himself to a body of theory that may undergo change; he ties himself only to his own evidence and logic. The historian does not "apply" tools after reading in other theories and then writing psychologically. The worst psychohistory, in fact, results when theory is "applied" to—or pressed down on—a historical subject and its accompanying body of evidence. Tools are for hammering, prying, cutting. Psychological, especially psychoanalytic, theory invites another metaphor—one of adrenalin, perhaps, a substance that heightens consciousness without distorting it. Readings in psychological theory help to lend coherence and multiply causal factors; and while it may not be true that theory is only a "grab bag"[55]—one as good as another— it is always the coherence and persuasiveness of the historian's case, the winning of the reader's confidence given all the evidence, that decides the success or failure of the psychohistorians's work.

There is much to commend Hawthorne as a guest at these proceedings. While we have left his world behind, we have by no means escaped the responsibilities he portrayed so vividly in his romances. One of them is to try to understand the past, which he said weighs down on us despite ourselves. In doing so we might remember that the house of history, like Hawthorne's old New England mansion of seven gables, is a many-sided structure with enough room for guests from other disciplines and a great many windows to sit beside and look out of. History and biography, this collection seeks to demonstrate, clearly are richer when psychological theory and clinical findings are among the visitors. Such history may not yield explanation in the purely scientific sense, but if carefully and sensitively executed, it measurably improves on the commonsensical musings that brilliant scholars like Henry Adams could produce with a dash of the pen and that Jacques Barzun apparently believes everyone capable of writing.

Another of Hawthorne's responsibilities is self-knowledge, and it is important that psychologically informed history urges thinking about ourselves as well as the circumstances of our lives. It asks us to consider the relationship between self and society, and by dint of examples from the past both warns us of our frailties and enables us, if we wish, to suppose what we might make of the future. By recommending a search for the unconscious elements in a historical problem, psychohistory raises questions of how and why that extend our analytical range and lead to the self-scrutiny and the awareness of human complexity that are so important to intellectual growth and fundamental to historical understanding. In Freud's theory the process of self-discovery is at the heart of therapy: "Where the id is, there the ego shall be." In the words of Richard Ellman, who speaks of biography but whose sentiments apply to historical inquiry as a humane discipline, "to know another person who has lived as well as we know a character in fiction, and better than we know ourselves, is not frivolous. It may even be, for reader as well as for writer," he concludes, "an essential part of experience."[56]

NOTES

1. Nathaniel Hawthorne, *The American Notebooks*, ed. Randall Stewart (New Haven: Yale University Press, 1932), p. 98.

2. *Newsweek*, April 18, 1977, p. 97.

3. Fawn M. Brodie, *Thomas Jefferson: An Intimate History* (New York: W. W. Norton & Co., 1974); David Herbert Donald, "By Sex Possessed," *Commentary* 58 (July 1974):96.

4. Jacques Barzun, *Clio and the Doctors: Psycho-History, Quanto-History, and History* (Chicago: University of Chicago Press, 1974). (A briefer and more incisive version of Barzun's critique

appeared as "History: The Muse and Her Doctors," *American Historical Review* 77 [February 1972]:36–64.) *History of Childhood Quarterly* 3 (Fall 1975):200. *The Boston Globe* and deMause quoted in *New York Post*, March 12, 1976. Kenneth S. Lynn, "History's Reckless Psychologizing," *Chronicle of Higher Education*, January 16, 1978. For a biting review of the first three volumes of deMause's *History of Childhood Quarterly*, see Clifford S. Griffin, "Oedipus Hex," *Reviews in American History* 4 (September 1976):305–17. John Demos lamented the work of Glenn Davis, a deMause disciple, in a review of Davis's *Childhood and History in America* (New York: Psychohistory Press, 1977), *New York Times Book Review*, April 24, 1977. The most recent (and longwinded) dismissal of this genre is David E. Stannard, *Shrinking History: On Freud and the Failure of Psychohistory* (New York: Oxford University Press, 1980).

5. Henry Adams, *John Randolph of Roanoke*, American Statesmen, ed. John T. Morse, Jr. (Boston: Houghton, Mifflin and Co., 1882), pp. 266–67; W. E. B. DuBois, *Black Reconstruction in America: An Essay toward a History of the Part Which Black Folk Played in the Attempt to Reconstruct Democracy in America, 1860–1880* (New York: Harcourt, Brace and Co., 1935), p. 678.

6. Ellis quoted in John A. Garraty, "The Interrelations of Psychology and Biography," *Psychological Bulletin* 51 (November 1954):569. Prominent among early discussions of applied psychology in history were the writings of Harry Elmer Barnes: "Psychology and History: Some Reasons for Predicting Their More Active Cooperation in the Future," *American Journal of Psychology* 30 (October 1919):337–76; "Some Reflections on the Possible Service of Analytical Psychology to History," *Psychological Review* 8 (January 1921):22–37; and *Psychology and History* (New York: Century Co., 1925). Exploring James Harvey Robinson's use of contemporary behavioral psychology is Dorothy Ross, "The 'New History' and the 'New Psychology': An Early Attempt at Psychohistory," in *The Hofstadter Aegis: A Memorial*, ed. Stanley Elkins and Eric McKitrick (New York: Alfred A. Knopf, 1974). Katherine Anthony, *Margaret Fuller: A Psychological Biography* (New York: Harcourt, Brace; 1920); Ralph V. Harlow, *Samuel Adams, Promoter of the American Revolution: A Study in Psychology and Politics* (New York: Henry Holt and Co., 1923); Joseph Wood Krutch, *Edgar Allan Poe: A Study in Genius* (New York: Alfred A. Knopf, 1926); Marie Bonaparte, *The Life and Works of Edgar Allan Poe: A Psychoanalytic Interpretation* (London: Imago Publishing Co., 1933); Gerald W. Johnson, *Randolph of Roanoke: A Political Fantastic* (New York: Minton, Balch, 1929); Leon Pierce Clark, *Lincoln: A Psychobiography* (New York: Charles Scribner's Sons, 1933); Lewis Mumford, *Herman Melville* (New York: Harcourt, Brace, 1929). For Freud's early impact in this country, see Nathan G. Hale, Jr., *Freud and the Americans: The Beginnings of Psychoanalysis in the United States, 1876–1917* (New York: Oxford University Press, 1971).

7. Harlow, *Samuel Adams*, p. 37; Krutch, *Edgar Allan Poe*, p. 82.

8. Richard Hofstadter, *The Age of Reform: From Bryan to F. D. R.* New York: Alfred A. Knopf, 1955) and *The Paranoid Style in American Politics and Other Essays* (New York: Alfred A. Knopf, 1965). On Hofstadter's influence, see also Lester K. Little, "Psychology in Recent American Historical Thought," *Journal of the History of the Behavioral Sciences* 5 (April 1969):163–64. As evidence that interest in psychoanalytic concepts was growing in the 1950s, see Raymond DeSaussure, "Psychoanalysis and History," *Psychoanalysis and the Social Sciences* 2 (1950):7–64; Garraty, "Interrelations of Psychology and Biography"; Edward N. Saveth, "The Historian and the Freudian Approach to History," *New York Times Book Review*, January 1, 1956; Richard L. Schoenwald, "Historians and the Challenge of Freud," *Western Humanities Review* 10 (Spring 1956):99–108; Leon Edel, "Psycho-Analysis," in *Literary Biography: The Alexander Lectures, 1955–56* (Toronto: University of Toronto Press, 1957); and Frederick Wyatt and William B. Willcox, "Sir Henry Clinton: A Psychological Exploration in History," *William and Mary Quarterly*, 3d ser. 16 (January 1959):3–26. On the "paradox," "ambivalence," or "cultural tensions" influence of American Studies in these years, see the headnote to the Cushing Strout essay in this collection, chap. 11, and Little, "Psychology in Recent American Historical Thought," pp. 164–65.

9. David Herbert Donald, *Charles Sumner and the Coming of the Civil War* (New York: Alfred A. Knopf, 1960); Stanley Elkins, *Slavery: A Problem in American Institutional and Intellectual Life*

(Chicago: University of Chicago Press, 1959). Work on American topics outside the Columbia circle—books that doubtless had their own impact—included Leon Edel, *The Life of Henry James: The Untried Years, 1843-1870* (Philadelphia: J. B. Lippincott, 1953); Alexander L. George and Juliette L. George, *Woodrow Wilson and Colonel House: A Personality Study* (New York: John Day, 1956); and Fawn M. Brodie, *Thaddeus Stevens: Scourge of the South* (New York: W. W. Norton & Co., 1959).

10. Erik H. Erikson, *Young Man Luther: A Study in Psychoanalysis and History* (New York: W. W. Norton & Co., 1958). Donald B. Meyer, "A Review of *Young Man Luther,*" *History and Theory* 1, no. 3 (1961):291-97; Roland H. Bainton, "Psychiatry and History: An Examination of Erikson's *Young Man Luther,*" *Religion in Life* 40 (Winter 1971):450-78. For more on Erikson and the identity crisis, see note 30 below and the paragraph to which it refers.

11. William Langer, "The Next Assignment," *American Historical Review* 63 (January 1958):283-304; Bruce Mazlish, ed., *Psychoanalysis and History* (New York: Grosset and Dunlap, 1971). One suspects that another "pulling" influence on historians in the 1950s was the work of psychoanalytic literary critics and biographers. Besides Edel's book on James, Phyllis Greenacre's *Swift and Carroll: A Psychoanalytic Study of Two Lives* (New York: International Universities Press, 1955) drew attention from historians. See Frederick Wyatt, "Psychoanalytic Biography," *Contemporary Psychology* 1 (April 1956):105-7. On early psychohistory sessions and collaborative circles, I rely on Richard L. Schoenwald, February 25, 1980, personal communication; Richard L. Schoenwald, "Setting Up Sitting Up With Psychiatrists," *Group for the Use of Psychology in History Newsletter* 2 (May 1973):5-6; Bruce Mazlish, February 26, 1980, personal communication; Peter Loewenberg, March 11, 1980, personal communication. See also "News and Notes: An Interdisciplinary Psychoanalytic Study Group on Political Leadership in Los Angeles," *Journal of the History of the Behavioral Sciences* 5 (July 1969):271-72.

12. William C. Bullitt and Sigmund Freud, *Thomas Woodrow Wilson: A Psychological Study* (Boston: Houghton Mifflin, 1966). Among the telling attacks on this work were Erik H. Erikson, "The Strange Case of Freud, Bullitt and Woodrow Wilson I: A Dubious Collaboration" and Richard Hofstadter, "The Strange Case II: A Disservice to History," *New York Review of Books*, February 9, 1967; and Robert Coles, "Shrinking History—Part One," ibid., February 22, 1973.

13. Erik H. Erikson, *Ghandi's Truth: On the Origins of Militant Nonviolence* (New York: W. W. Norton & Co., 1969); Emery Battis, *Saints and Sectaries: Anne Hutchinson and the Antinomian Controversy in the Massachusetts Bay Colony* (Chapel Hill: University of North Carolina Press, 1962); Richard L. Bushman, "On the Uses of Psychology: Conflict and Conciliation in Benjamin Franklin," *History and Theory* 5, no. 3 (1966):225-40; Kenneth S. Lynn, *William Dean Howells; An American Life* (New York: Harcourt Brace Jovanovich, 1970); James T. Patterson, *Mr. Republican: A Biography of Robert A. Taft* (Boston: Houghton Mifflin, 1972); Dorothy Ross, *G. Stanley Hall: The Psychologist as Prophet* (Chicago: University of Chicago Press, 1974); Peter G. Shaw, *The Character of John Adams* (Chapel Hill: University of North Carolina Press, 1976). For a survey then current, see Little, "Psychology in Recent American Historical Thought," pp. 152-72. Richard Ellman, "That's Life," *New York Review of Books*, June 17, 1971, p. 3.

14. David Brion Davis, "Some Themes of Counter-Subversion: An Analysis of Anti-Masonic, Anti-Catholic, and Anti-Mormon Literature," *Mississippi Valley Historical Review* 47 (September 1960):205-24; "Some Ideological Functions of Prejudice in Ante-Bellum America," *American Quarterly* 15 (Summer 1963):115-25; *The Problem of Slavery in the Age of Revolution, 1770-1823* (Ithaca: Cornell University Press, 1975). Winthrop D. Jordan, *White Over Black; American Attitudes toward the Negro, 1550-1812* (Chapel Hill: University of North Carolina Press, 1968); Joel Kovel, *White Racism; A Psychohistory* (New York: Vintage Books, 1970); Earl E. Thorpe, *Eros and Freedom in Southern Life and Thought* (Westport, Conn.: Greenwood Press, 1978). John Demos, *A Little Commonwealth: Family Life in Plymouth Colony* (New York: Oxford University Press, 1970). For a longer list of historical work drawing (sometimes implicitly) on psychological concepts or theory, or dealing with a necessarily psychological topic, see William J. Gilmore's bibliographies, *Psychohistory Review* 7 (Fall 1978) and 8 (Winter 1979).

15. See Donald, *Charles Sumner and the Coming of the Civil War*, pp. 312–47. Edwin A. Weinstein, "Woodrow Wilson's Neurological Illness," *Journal of American History* 57 (September 1970):324–52; Edwin A. Weinstein, James William Anderson, and Arthur S. Link, "Woodrow Wilson's Political Personality: A Reappraisal," *Political Science Quarterly* 93 (Winter 1978):585–98. Randolph's probable genetic defect is outlined in a letter from Dr. Thomas B. Hall III to the editor, January 30, 1978.

16. Suggesting studies of diet and group personality are findings that diet affects pubertal development and that early maturers (especially boys, at least in the United State) are more likely as adults to be stable, sociable, and successful. Paul Henry Mussen and Mary Cover Jones, "Self-Concepting Motivations and Interpersonal Attitudes of Late- and Early-Maturing Boys," *Child Development* 28 (June 1957):243–56; J. M. Tanner, "Sequence, Tempo, and Individual Variation in Growth and Development of Boys and Girls Aged Twelve to Sixteen," in Jerome Kagan and Robert Coles, eds., *Twelve to Sixteen: Early Adolescence* (New York: W. W. Norton & Co., 1972). For a discussion of a related topic, psycho-epidemiology, see Philip Pomper, "Problems of a Naturalistic Psychohistory," *History and Theory* 12, no. 4 (1973):367–88. On death and bereavement in early Maryland and Virginia, see Daniel Blake Smith, "Mortality and Family in the Colonial Chesapeake," *Journal of Interdisciplinary History* 8 (Winter 1978):403–37 and "Family Experience and Kinship in Eighteenth Century Chesapeake Society" (Ph.D. diss., University of Virginia, 1978). On sibling rivalry and parental loss literature, see "Note on Psychological References," in Robert J. Brugger, *Beverley Tucker; Heart over Head in the Old South* (Baltimore: The Johns Hopkins University Press, 1978).

17. Recommended introductions to personality theory: James C. Coleman and William E. Broen, Jr., *Abnormal Psychology and Modern Life*, 5th ed. (Glenview, Ill.: Scott, Foresman and Co., 1976); Calvin Springer Hall and Gardner Lindzey, *Theories of Personality*, 3d ed. (New York: John Wiley, 1978); Robert T. Hogan, *Personality Theory: The Personological Tradition*, Prentice-Hall Series in Personality, ed. Richard S. Lazarus (Englewood Cliffs, N.J.: Prentice-Hall, 1976); Theodore Millon, ed., *Theories of Psychopathology and Personality: Essays and Critiques* (Philadelphia: W. B. Saunders Co., 1967); Leon Rappoport, *Personality Development: The Chronology of Experience* (Glenview, Ill.: Scott, Foresman and Co., 1972); Hendrik M. Ruitenbeek, ed., *Varieties of Personality Theory* (New York: E. P. Dutton & Co., 1964). See also chapter 4, note 21.

18. David Brion Davis, *The Slave Power Conspiracy and the Paranoid Style* (Baton Rouge: Louisiana State University Press, 1969). Elementary textbooks on role theory include Erving Goffman, *Presentation of the Self in Everyday Life* (Garden City, N.Y.: Doubleday Anchor, 1959), and *Interaction Ritual* (Garden City, N.Y.: Doubleday Anchor, 1967). For a sympathetic introduction, see Hogan, *Personality Theory*, pp. 187–205.

19. Silvan S. Tompkins, "The Psychology of Commitment: The Constructive Role of Violence and Suffering for the Individual and for His Society," in *Antislavery Vanguard: New Essays on the Abolitionists*, ed. Martin Duberman (Princeton, N.J.: Princeton University Press, 1965). Cf. Lewis Perry, "Psychology and the Abolitionists: Reflections on Martin Duberman and the Neoabolitionism of the 1960's," *Reviews in American History* 2 (September 1974):309–22. On humanistic psychology, see Gordon W. Allport, *Becoming: Basic Considerations for a Psychology of Personality* (New Haven: Yale University Press, 1955), and *the Person in Psychology* (Boston: Beacon Press, 1968); Abraham Harold Maslow, *Motivation and Personality*, 2d ed. (New York: Harper & Row, 1970), and *Dominance, Self-Esteem, Self-Actualization: Germinal Papers of A. H. Maslow*, ed. Richard J. Lowry (Monterey, Calif: Brooks/Cole, 1973); and Carl R. Rogers et al., *Person to Person: The Problem of Being Human; A New Trend in Psychology* (Walnut Creek, Calif.: Real People Press, 1967). A further listing of theoretical works and their application appears in *Psychohistory Review* 7 (Spring 1979):26–27.

20. John R. Schmidhauser, "Judicial Behavior and the Sectional Crisis of 1837–1860," *Journal of Politics* 23 (November 1961):615–80; Glendon Schubert, *The Judicial Mind Revisited: Psychometric Analysis of Supreme Court Ideology* (New York: Oxford University Press, 1974). Sociologists like Glen Elder, Kenneth Keniston, David C. McClelland, and David Riesman have given full

weight to affective, or emotional, elements in their studies of American attitudes. In a famous post-World War II examination of the "authoritarian personality," T. W. Adorno et al., tabulated the answers to a battery of selected questions designed to show what attitudes denoted incipient facism. Following the lead of Harold Lasswell and R. E. Money-Kyrle, who wrote in the 1930s, recent students of politics—James D. Barber, Fred I. Greenstein, Jeanne N. Knutson, Stanley Allen Renshon, Paul Roazen, and Robert C. Tucker chief among them—have applied psychological concepts to presidential character, mass political movements, and the relationship between leaders and followers. See the Dalton essay and the headnote to the Lifton piece, in this collection.

21. Ole Holsti, "The 'Operational Code' Approach to the Study of Political Leaders: John Foster Dulles' Philosophical and Instrumental Beliefs," *Canadian Journal of Political Science* 3 (March 1970):123–57. Leon Festinger, Henry W. Ricken, and Stanley Schacter, *When Prophecy Fails: A Social and Psychological Study of a Modern Group That Predicted the End of the World* (Minneapolis: University of Minnesota Press, 1956). Robert M. Cover, *Justice Accused: Antislavery and the Judicial Process* (New Haven: Yale University Press, 1975). But see also Henri Tajfel, "Cognitive Aspects of Prejudice," *Journal of Social Issues* 25 (Autumn 1969): 79–97; Gail Stokes, "Cognition and the Function of Nationalism," *Journal of Interdisciplinary History* 4 (Spring 1974):525–42; Robert Lewis, *Perception and Misperception in International Politics* (Princeton, N.J.: Princeton University Press, 1976). For a basic text on dissonance, see Leon Festinger, *A Theory of Cognitive Dissonance* (Evanston, Ill.: Row, Peterson, 1957).

22. Introductions to Piaget include John Flavell, *The Developmental Psychology of Jean Piaget* (New York: Van Nostrand, 1963); Jean Piaget, *Behavior and Evolution*, trans. Donald Nicholson-Smith (New York: Pantheon Books, 1978); and Howard E. Gruber and J. Jacques Vonèche, eds., *The Essential Piaget* (New York: Basic Books, 1977). See also Robert L. Soslo, ed., *Theories of Cognitive Psychology* (New York: John Wiley, 1974). On the connections between cognitive, interpersonal, and affective growth and social or political advances, see Kenneth Keniston, "Psychological Development and Historical Change," *Journal of Interdisciplinary History* 2 (Autumn 1971):329–45. A recent example of applied cognitive theory is Charles M. Radding, "The Evolution of Medieval Mentalities," *American Historical Review* 83 (June 1978):577–97.

23. For the deMause quote, see N. E. H. Hull, Peter C. Hoffer, and Steven L. Allen, "Politics and Personality," chapter 4 below. Hogan, *Personality Theory*, pp. 11–12, 23–34, makes a clever case for the unconscious mind. Positive proof that our minds have an unconscious dimension is, one must admit, difficult to obtain. How do we measure or test for tendencies that are rarely if ever articulated and heavily overlaid with personal protections and social conventions? In a philosophical vein one can go on to say that, by definition, no knower (ego or self) can be unaware of itself (that is, of repressed memories and impulses). But the most determined work of behavioral and experimental psychologists to "disprove" a dynamic unconscious falls short. Even David Stannard concludes that the concept of the unconscious, "however logically problematic, does easily appear to satisfy, in a common sense way, questions raised by phenomena ranging from dreams to forgetfulness to slips of the tongue. Thus, whether or not there actually is such a thing (or place) as the unconscious, logical argument appears at present to be capable only of raising serious doubts about it" (*Shrinking History*, p. 66).

24. On early research into the subconscious mind, see Henri F. Ellenberger, *The Discovery of the Unconscious; the History and Evolution of Dynamic Psychiatry* (New York: Basic Books, 1970). Besides Freud's Clark University Lectures, "The Origin and Development of Psychoanalysis," *American Journal of Psychology* 21 (April 1909):181–218, or the "Introductory Lectures on Psycho-Analysis" (1915–17), in *The Complete Works of Sigmund Freud*, 24 vols. (London: The Hogarth Press, 1953–74), vols. 16 and 17, the best overview of psychoanalysis is probably Philip Rieff, *Freud: The Mind of the Moralist* (New York: The Viking Press, 1959). Also valuable are A. A. Brill, ed. and trans., *The Basic Writings of Sigmund Freud* (New York: The Modern Library, 1938); Franz Alexander, *Fundamentals of Psychoanalysis* (New York: W. W. Norton & Co., 1963); Raymond Fancher, *Psychoanalytic Psychology: The Development of Freud's Thought* (New York: W.

W. Norton & Co., 1973); and Richard Wollheim, ed., *Freud; A Collection of Critical Essays*, Modern Studies of Philosophy, gen. ed. Amelie Oksunberg Rorty (Garden City, N.Y.: Anchor Press/Doubleday, 1974).

25. For Freud's later systematic writings, see *Beyond the Pleasure Principle* (1920), *Complete Works* 18:7–64, and *The Ego and the Id* (1923), ibid., 19:12–66.

26. These proto-existentialist themes in Freud are highlighted in Rieff, *Freud*, especially chapters 9–10. See also Avery D. Weisman, *The Existentialist Core of Psychoanalysis: Reality, Sense, and Responsibility* (Boston: Little, Brown, 1965).

27. Freud quoted in Paul Roazen, *Freud and His Followers* (New York: Alfred A. Knopf, 1975), p. 204. Adler's works of prominence are *The Practice and Theory of Individual Psychology*, trans. P. Radin (London: Routledge and Kegan Paul; New York: Humanities Press, 1921 [1929]) and *Understanding Human Nature*, trans. Walter Béran Wolfe (1927; rpt. Greenwich, Conn.: Fawcett Publications, 1954; see also Heinz L. Ansbacher and Rowena R. Ansbacher, eds., *The Individual Psychology of Alfred Adler: A Systematic Presentation in Selections from His Writings* (New York: Basic Books, 1956). For the development of Jungian theory, see Jung, *Psychological Types; or the Psychology of Individuation;* trans. H. Godwin Baynes (London: K. Paul, Trench, Trubner & Co.; New York: Harcourt, Brace & Co., 1923); *Analytical Psychology; Its Theory and Practice*, the Tavistock Lectures, with a Foreword by E. A. Bennet (1928; rpt. New York: Pantheon Books, 1968); and *Modern Man in Search of a Soul*, trans. W. S. Dell and Cary F. Baynes (1933; rpt. New York: Harcourt, Brace, 1962). Also helpful is Frieda Fordham, *An Introduction to Jung's Psychology* (Baltimore: Penguin Books, 1953). Representative of Geza Roheim's work are his *Social Anthropology; A Psycho-Analytic Study in Anthropology and a History of Australian Totemism*, with an Introduction by M. D. Eder (New York: Boni and Liveright, 1926), *The Origins and Functions of Culture* (1943; rpt. New York: Johnson Reprint Corp., 1968), and *Psychoanalysis and Anthropology; Culture, Personality, and the Unconscious* (New York: International Universities Press, [1950]).

28. On Freud's late-developing interest in the ego as a repressing element and in objects outside the self, see Freud, *The Ego and the Id,* and Fred Weinstein and Gerald M. Platt, *Psychoanalytic Sociology: An Essay on the Interpretation of Historical Data and the Phenomena of Collective Behavior* (Baltimore: The Johns Hopkins University Press, 1973), especially pp. 5–10.

29. Among the writings Erikson's approach has inspired or affected see Bert Kaplan, ed., *Studying Personality Cross-Culturally* (New York: Harper & Row, 1961); Cushing Strout, "Ego Psychology and the Historian," *History and Theory* 7, no. 3 (1968):281–97; Alan Roland, "Psychoanalysis and History: A Quest for Integration," *Psychoanalytic Review* 58, no. 4 (1971):631–39; a special issue on Erikson, *Psychohistory Review* 5 (December 1976); and a special issue, touching on "Erikson and Psychohistories," of the *Psychoanalytic Review* 63 (Summer 1976). The currently authoritative study of Erikson's life and research is Robert Coles, *Erik H. Erikson: The Growth of His Work* (Boston: Little, Brown and Co., 1970). But see also Frederick Crews, "American Prophet," *New York Review of Books*, October 16, 1975, together with the exchange of letters in the February 5, 1976, issue; David Gutmann, "Erik Erikson's America," *Commentary*, September 1974; and John J. Fitzpatrick, "Erik H. Erikson and Psychohistory," *Bulletin of the Menninger Clinic* 40 (July 1976):295–314.

30. Erik H. Erikson, *Childhood and Society*, rev. ed. (New York: W. W. Norton & Co., 1964), p. 261; Erik H. Erikson, "The Problem of Ego Identity," and David Rapaport, "Historical Survey of Psychoanalytic Ego Psychology," in "Identity and the Life Cycle: Selected Papers," *Psychological Issues* 4 (1959); Erik H. Erikson, *Identity: Youth and Crisis* (New York: W. W. Norton & Co., 1968).

31. For a sampling of the extensive discussion of Freud on women, see Judith M. Bardwick, *Psychology of Women: A Study of Bio-Cultural Conflicts* (New York: Harper & Row, 1971); Janine Chassequet, ed., *Female Sexuality: New Psychoanalytic Views* (Ann Arbor: University of Michigan Press, 1970); *Journal of the American Psychoanalytic Association* 24, no. 5 (1977), Special Supplement—Female Psychology; Christopher Lasch, "Freud and Women," *New York Review of Books*, October 3, 1974 and exchange of letters, ibid., December 12, 1974; and Jean Baker Miller,

32   ROBERT J. BRUGGER

ed., *Psychoanalysis and Women* (Baltimore: Penguin Books, 1974). But see also Naomi Rosenthal, "The Psychology of Women," *Psychohistory Review* 8 (Spring 1980):52-56; Carroll Smith-Rosenberg, "The New Woman and the Psycho-Historian: A Modest Proposal," *Group for the Use of Psychology in History Newsletter* 4 (December 1975):4-11; Judith M. Wellman, "Some Thoughts on the Psychohistorical Study of Women," *Psychohistory Review* 7 (Fall 1978):20-24; and note 43 below.

32. An excellent introduction to Robert Jay Lifton is his "The Sense of Immortality: On Death and the Continuity of Life," *American Journal of Psychoanalysis* 33, no. 1 (1973):3-15. His major books are *Death in Life: Survivors of Hiroshima* (New York: Random House, 1968); *History and Human Survival: Essays on the Young and the Old, Survivors and the Dead, Peace and War, and on Contemporary Psychohistory* (New York: Random House, 1970); and *The Life of the Self: Toward a New Psychology* (New York: Simon and Schuster, 1976). For a critical view of Lifton's work, see Joel Kovel, "On the New History," *Psychotherapy and Social Science Review* 4; no. 9 (1970):2-8. William G. Niederland, who apparently first used the "survivor" concept, explained it in "The Problem of the Survivor," *Journal of the Hillside Hospital* 10 (July–October 1961):233-47 and in "Clinical Observations of the 'Survivor Syndrome,'" *International Journal of Psycho-Analysis* 49, parts 2-3 (1968):313-15.

33. Fairbairn's effort to resolve problems in Freud's theory (does repression derive from the ego, superego, or both?) leads him to a far more sophisticated "endopsychic structure," in which id, ego, and superego each has its own dynamic structure; Fairbairn's ego, for example, consists of a central core cathecting with, or connecting emotionally to, an ideal object; a libidinal ego cathecting with an exciting object; an antilibidinal ego cathecting negatively or aggressively to a rejecting object. W. R. D. Fairbairn, "A Critical Evaluation of Certain Basic Psycho-Analytical Conceptions," *British Journal for the Philosophy of Science* 7, no. 25 (1956):49-60, especially pp. 57-59, and *Psychoanalytic Studies of the Personality*. Preface by Ernest Jones (London: Tavistock Publishers, 1952). Other worthwhile readings in object-relations theory include John Bowlby, *Attachment and Loss*, vol. 1, *Attachment*; vol. 2 *Separation Anxiety and Anger*, The International Psycho-Analytical Library, No. 95, ed. M. Masud R. Khan (London: The Hogarth Press, 1973); Harry J. S. Guntrip, *Psychoanalytic Theory, Therapy, and the Self* (New York: International Universities Press, 1969); Otto F. Kernberg, *Borderline Conditions and Pathological Narcissism* (New York: J. Aronson, [1975]); and Donald W. Winnicott, *The Child, the Family and the Outside World* (Baltimore: Penguin Books, 1969). See also the special issue on object relations theory, *Journal of the American Psychoanalytic Association* 27, no. 2 (1979).

34. Heinz Kohut's principal theoretical statements are *The Analysis of the Self: A Systematic Approach to the Psychoanalytic Treatment of Narcissistic Personality Disorders* (New York: International Universities Press, 1971) and *The Restoration of the Self* (New York: International Universities Press, 1977). See also a transcribed colloquium with Kohut speaking on psychohistorical problems, *Group for the Use of Psychology in History Newsletter* 3 (March 1975):3-10.

35. For an elaboration on this point, see Barzun, "History: The Muse and Her Doctors," pp. 48-49 and Bruce Mazlish, "Inside the Whales," *London Times Literary Supplement*, July 28, 1966, p. 667.

36. For a comment on the differences between historical and therapeutic purposes, see American Psychiatric Association, Task Force on Psychohistory, *The Psychiatrist as Psychohistorian*, Task Force Report 11 (Washington, D.C.: American Psychiatric Association, 1976). For earlier variations, see Wyatt, "Psychoanalytic Biography," p. 105; Hans Meyeroff, "On Psychoanalysis as History," *Psychoanalysis and the Psychoanalytic Review* 49 (Summer 1962):3-20; Robert Jay Lifton, "Psychoanalysis and History," in *History and Human Survival*, pp. 290-98; John Klauber, "On the Dual Use of Historical and Scientific Method in Psychoanalysis" *International Journal of Psychoanalysis* 49, part 1 (1968):80-88; Bruce Mazlish, "Clio on the Couch: Prolegomena to Psycho-History" *Encounter* 31 (September 1968):51; and Barzun, "History: The Muse and Her Doctors," pp. 54-57.

38. Alan C. Beckman, "Hidden Themes in the Frontier Thesis: An Application of Psychoanalysis to History," *Comparative Studies in Society and History* 8 (April 1966):361-82.

Related to Beckman's essay is Michael Paul Rogin's *Fathers and Children: Andrew Jackson and the Subjugation of the American Indian* (New York: Alfred A. Knopf, 1975). Rogin argues that the Indian was childlike, or "oral," in his simplicity, and that whites (symbolized by Andrew Jackson), as "anal" capitalists, were compelled to destroy him because the Indian was a fragment of the primitive self that was dangerously lazy and aggressive. The Indian thus had to be annihilated out of psychological self-defense. For sharp criticism of this thesis from Rogin's graduate school mentor, see William Appleman Williams, "Yankee Doodle Andy," *New York Review of Books*, August 7, 1975. Martin Quitt's interesting critique appears in *History of Childhood Quarterly* 3 (Spring 1976):543-51. See also William J. Gilmore, "The Individual and the Group in Psychohistory: Rogin's *Father's and Children* and the Problem of Jackson's Health," *Psychohistory Review* 6 (Fall-Winter 1977-78):114.

39. Beckman, "Hidden Themes in the Frontier Thesis," p. 373. Thoughtful discussions of psychohistory and historical explanation include Quin McLoughlin, "History, Science, and Psychohistory," *Psychohistory Review* 8 (Spring 1980):22-31; Faye Crosby, "Evaluating Psychohistorical Explanations," *Psychohistory Review* 7 (Spring 1979):6-16; Frank Manuel, "The Use and Abuse of Psychology in History," *Daedalus* 100 (Winter 1971):187-213; Bruce Mazlish, "Group Psychology and Problems of Contemporary History," *Journal of Contemporary History* 3 (April 1968):168-77; and John R. Seeley, "Psychoanalysis: Model for Social Science," *Psychoanalysis and the Psychoanalytic Review* 47 (Winter 1960):80-86. Also pertinent are David Herbert Donald, "Between Science and Art," *American Historical Review* 77 (April 1972):445-52; Gene Wise, *American Historical Explanations; A Strategy for Grounded Inquiry* (Homewood, Ill.: Dorsey Press, 1973); David S. Landes and Charles Tilly, eds., *History as Social Science* (Englewood Cliffs, N.J.: Prentice-Hall, [1971]); and Robert F. Berkhofer, Jr., *A Behavioral Approach to Historical Analysis* (New York: Free Press, 1969). Among basic texts on the nature and limits of historical analysis are H. Stuart Hughes, *History as Art and Science; Twin Vistas on the Past* (New York: Harper & Row, 1964) and Karl R. Popper, *The Poverty of Historicism* (Boston: Beacon Press, 1957). Also interesting are Daniel M. Taylor, *Explaining and Meaning; An Introduction to Philosophy* (Cambridge: Cambridge University Press, 1970) and George Henri von Wright, *Explanation and Understanding* (Ithaca, N.Y.: Cornell University Press, 1971).

40. Erikson uses the term "originology" in various writings, but see especially *Young Man Luther*, p. 18. On fallacies of motivation, genesis, and reduction, see David Hackett Fischer, *Historians' Fallacies: Toward a Logic of Historical Thought* (New York: Harper & Row, 1970), especially pp. 155-57 and 172-75. Also discussing logical problems in psychohistory are Cushing Strout, "The Uses and Abuses of Psychology in American History," *American Quarterly* 28, no. 3 (1976):324-42; Mazlish, "Clio on the Couch," p. 51; Lawrence Stone, "The Massacre of the Innocents," *New York Review of Books*, November 14, 1974; and Gertrude Himmelfarb, "The 'New' History," *Commentary* 59 (January 1975):75-76.

41. Bullitt and Freud, *Thomas Woodrow Wilson*, p. 169.

42. Garry Wills, "Uncle Thomas's Cabin," *New York Review of Books*, April 18, 1974; Brodie, *Thomas Jefferson*, p. 229.

43. For an interesting example of psychological theory and clinical experience helping to pose historical questions, even to supply suggestive evidence, see Nancy Chodorow, "Family Structure and Feminine Personality," in *Woman, Culture, and Society*, ed. Michelle Zimbalist Rosaldo and Louise Lamphere (Stanford, Calif.: Stanford University Press, 1974). On the issue of clinical patterns as stand-ins for historical evidence—referring to Elkins's work on slavery—see Bruce Mazlish, "Psychoanalytic Theory and History: Groups and Events," *Annual of Psychoanalysis* 6 (1978):41-57 and Keniston, "Psychological Development and Historical Change," p. 346.

44. Merrill D. Peterson, *Thomas Jefferson and the New Nation: A Biography* (New York: Oxford University Press, 1970), p. 9. Gisela Tauber, "The Role of Reconstruction in Psychoanalytic Biography: Contributions to the Understanding of the Man Thomas Jefferson," unpublished paper, submitted to *Journal of Psychohistory*, Spring 1980.

45. Beatrice Cowper Green, *AHA Newsletter* 14 (October 1976):6. For similar advice, see Alan Ryan, "The Family Mill," *New York Review of Books*, May 28, 1975, and Robert E. McGlone, "The New Orthodoxy in Psychohistory," *Psychohistory Review* 4 (September 1975):4-9.

46. Reconstructions of psychobiographical thinking, especially valuable to the beginning student, are numerous. See Brugger, "Note on Psychological References," in *Beverley Tucker*; Bushman, "On the Uses of Psychology"; Leon Edel, "The Biographer and Psycho-Analysis," in *Biography as an Art*, ed. James L. Clifford (New York: Oxford University Press, 1962), pp. 226-39; George and George, "Research Note," in *Woodrow Wilson and Colonel House*; Mazlish, "Clio on the Couch," pp. 51-54; and of course Erik H. Erikson, "On the Nature of Psycho-Historical Evidence: In Search of Gandhi," *Daedalus* 97 (Summer 1968):695-730.

47. Crews, "American Prophet," p. 9.

48. Strout, "Ego Psychology and the Historian," p. 285.

49. Erikson, *Childhood and Society*, pp. 37-38, quoted in Mazlish, "Group Psychology," p. 173.

50. Frank Manuel, "On History," *The New Republic*, November 20, 1976, p. 31.

51. Nonbiographical topics and psychological concepts or methods receive critical treatment in Nancy F. Cott, "Notes toward an Interpretation of Antebellum Childrearing," *Psychohistory Review* 6 (Spring 1978):4-20; Raimond E. Goerler, "Family, Psychology, and History," *Group for the Use of Psychology in History Newsletter* 4 (December 1975):31-38; Peter C. Hoffer, "Psychohistory and Empirical Group Affiliation: Extraction of Personality Traits from Historical Manuscripts," *Journal of Interdisciplinary History* 9 (Summer 1978):131-45; Lifton, "Psychoanalysis and History" and "Comments on Method," in *History and Human Survival*; David C. McClelland, "The Use of Measures of Human Motivation in the Study of Society," in *Motives in Fantasy, Action, and Society*, ed. J. W. Atkinson (Princeton, N.J.: Van Nostrand, 1958); Gerald M. Platt, "The Sociological Endeavor and Psychoanalytic Thought," *American Quarterly* 28, no. 3 (1976):343-59; Melvin Small, "Some Suggestions from the Behavioral Sciences for Historians Interested in the Study of Attitudes," *Societas: A Review of Social History* 3 (Winter 1973):1-19; and Judith Wellman, "Culture and Character: Some Perspectives from Psychological Anthropology for Psychohistorians," *Group for the Use of Psychology in History Newsletter* 4 (December 1975):12-30.

52. Fred Weinstein and Gerald M. Platt, "The Coming Crisis in Psychohistory," *Journal of Modern History* 47 (June 1975):202-228.

53. Barzun, "History: The Muse and Her Doctors," pp. 55-57. For the replies of John J. Fitzpatrick, William L. Langer, and Peter Loewenberg, see the *American Historical Review* 77 (December 1972):1194-97.

54. Credit for first use of the term "psychologically informed" goes to Bushman, "On the Uses of Psychology," p. 234. Paul Monaco, "Psychohistory: Independence or Integration?" *History of Childhood Quarterly* 3 (Summer 1975):127. "To define history by means of four qualities does not mean that it cannot accommodate every sort of data," comments Barzun in "History: The Muse and Her Doctors," p. 57; "The answer to the misguided use of psycho-analysis," Leon Edel pointed out many years ago—and he might have said it of psychological theory more generally—"is not to close our ears but to ask ourselves: how are we to handle this diffifult material while remaining true to our own disciplines—and avoid making complete fools of ourselves?" Edel, *Literary Biography*, p. 60. See, more recently, the thoughts of Peter Gay in the introduction to his *Art and Act: On Causes in History—Manet, Gropius, Mondrian* (New York: Harper & Row, 1976). For an example of successful collaboration between historian and analyst, see Wyatt and Willcox, "Sir Henry Clinton."

55. For the "grab bag" reference, see Gilmore, "The Individual and the Group in Psychohistory," p. 114.

56. Ellman, "That's Life," p. 7. See also Peter Loewenberg's remarks on "making syntonic what was previously distonic" in "Communications," *American Historical Review*, 77 (February 1972):242.

1

JOSEPH AND HIS BROTHERS
A Story of the Putnam Family

PAUL BOYER AND STEPHEN NISSENBAUM

A ready argument for psychologically informed history is the smudged line between rationality and irrationality in the human record. The Salem witchcraft scare of 1692, during which 142 persons were accused of witchcraft and 19 were hanged as the devil's agents, offers an especially pointed example: the roots of motivation lie tangled within us. It was by far the most serious such outbreak in early American history, and when we in this century have referred to the episode it often has been to cite the danger of hysteria and superstition. Marion Starkey's *The Devil in Massachusetts* (1949) described in colorful detail the emotional fury of adolescent girls whose anger against "witches" paralleled the Nazi persecution of Jews; in *The Crucible* (1953) Arthur Miller made witch-hunting in Salem a commentary on the ruthless hunt for communists that Joe McCarthy was then conducting with the approval of many bystanders.

Later students of Salem witchcraft have searched for its physiological and psychological sources. A graduate student in psychology, Linnda R. Caporael, argued in *Science* magazine (April 1976) that a fungus common to the rye that Salem Villagers probably grew may have caused hallucinations that the accusers believed were a witch's spell; once baked, the substance changed chemically to a form of LSD. John Demos, having earlier published a study of living conditions in Plymouth, *A Little Commonwealth*, maintained in a 1970 article that the severely cramped, maternally oppressive world of young women in colonial New England likely brought on the discontent that they, during the witchcraft craze, directed against older women of their mothers' generation.

Pursuing this second line of inquiry, Paul Boyer and Stephen Nissenbaum have discovered what they believe was a more complicated pattern. Their book, *Salem Possessed: The Social Origins of Witchcraft* (1974), builds on extensive local church, property-holding, and political records and tries to demonstrate overlapping tensions

36   PAUL BOYER AND STEPHEN NISSENBAUM

in the area of the witchcraft scare. One axis of friction lay between Salem Town—the original settlement, a prosperous seaport that was the political center of the locality—and Salem Village, where the bewitched and many of their supposed tormentors lived—a subsistence-farming area, socially less cohesive, politically an adjunct to the Town. In the perception of the Villagers, Boyer and Nissenbaum find, Salem Town represented worldliness and sin—wealth, status, the secularism of world trading, commercial values instead of the piety and simplicity of the old Puritan faith. Too, there were divisions among the Villagers themselves, who differed, for example, over the pastorate of Samuel Parris—who as minister of the Village church had the support of only a bare majority of his congregation and who spoke out strongly against encroaching materialism. There were also antagonisms based on property differences among the Villagers, a few of whom farmed superior soil or, living along the Ipswich Road that led from the Village to the Town, took advantage of their location to ship excess produce to the markets of the seaport. Boyer and Nissenbaum discover that accusers tended to be Villagers who sided with Parris and were less well off, while those accused of witchcraft—after the first few, who were widows with strange habits or otherwise socially marginal persons—tended to belong to the anti-Parris faction in the Village, to be relatively better off, or to have indirect ties to Salem Town and the "bewitching" ways of the world beyond Puritan New England.

The following piece is from chapter 6 of Boyer and Nissembaum's book and explores another dimension of the witchcraft phenomenon, family rivalry and infighting. It suits this collection first of all because it describes a setting of anger and of frustration that was especially painful for some members of the the Putnam family and that the historian can present to his readers only with empathy and an ear for psychological "truth." Indeed the malaise Boyer and Nissenbaum re-create in the book as a whole partakes of a wide variety of political uncertainties and baneful omens. This sense of impending disaster grew out of issues that were critical in early colonial New England—generational crowding on family lands, backcountry versus urban economic needs and social styles, conflict between parent towns and satellite villages, and between minister and congregation. The feeling of doom or catastrophic change is itself evidence of psychological unrest of a kind that spawns movements and that social psychologists prey upon; it is noteworthy that the feeling recurs throughout American history. Second, this chapter suggests how received traditions and symbols—here those dramatized in the Hansel and Gretel story—can help afflicted persons "see" solutions to their grievances. The omnipresence of certain themes in folklore, one might go on to say, lends credence to the Jungian view of a collective unconscious. Finally, one sees in "Joseph and His Brothers" a pattern of accuser-accused that makes sense only in terms of the ego-defense principles of displacement, projection, and denial. To accuse someone of witchcraft was indeed to use "language as symbolic action" (as the student of literature, Kenneth Burke, put it). Understanding the psychological meaning of the act enables us to decipher what at first may appear to be a random sampling of Salem residents.

To be sure the chapter raises the familiar question of sufficient proof: however skillful the essay, does one finish it convinced that the people the Putnams accused were in fact stand-ins for their real enemies?

Few SEVENTEENTH-CENTURY Salem Villagers bore the name Joseph. It seems generally to have been reserved for certain special cases: for a son born to an older couple after a lapse of several years, or for the first son born to a marriage. Thus in 1690 Thomas Wilkins gave the name to his third son, born twelve years after his next older child. And Joseph Porter, the brother of Israel and Benjamin, was the eldest son of his father's second marriage. This interesting pattern was almost certainly linked to the fact that the biblical Joseph, from whom the name derives, was the child of Jacob's old age and his first by Rachel, the favorite among his four wives and concubines.

Thomas Putnam [whose 1681 Village tax of over £10 placed him not only first among the Putnams, but well ahead of any other Salem Villager[1]] married Ann Holyoke in 1643, when he was twenty-eight, and he sired eight children by her between 1645 and 1662. Only two of these, as it happened, were male: Thomas, Jr. (born in 1653) and Edward (1654).[2] As Thomas, Jr., came of age early in the 1670's, and assumed his role as eldest son of the richest man in the Village, he could look forward eventually to occupying a similarly exalted position himself. This is not to say that his prospects were altogether untroubled. He knew that a part of his father's estate would probably have to go to provide dowries for his four living sisters, and he knew, too, that he would have to divide the bulk of his father's acreage with his younger brother, Edward. And he must have recognized, like all the Putnams in these years, that the family's holdings were relatively isolated from the commercial center of Salem Town.

For young Thomas Putnam, Jr., then, the future may have been bright, but not quite so bright as the life he already knew. To live up to his father's station, and his own expectations, it would be necessary for him to take positive action. Accordingly, at about the time his uncles John and Nathaniel were beginning their ill-starred venture in the iron business, Thomas Putnam, Jr., too, attempted to diversify. He chose, however, another form of investment: matrimony. In 1678, at the age of twenty-five, young Thomas married Ann Carr, daughter of George Carr, one of the richest inhabitants of nearby Salisbury. Thomas had reason to expect that his marriage would bring him as a matter of course the economic diversification which his uncles had attempted so clumsily to achieve on their own. Not only was his father-in-law an extremely wealthy man, but his fortune was broadly based in a variety of economic activities: George Carr controlled some 400 acres of farm land in Salisbury, he owned a shipworks there, and he operated the ferry at a principal crossing point on the Merrimack River. At his death, Carr left an estate appraised (perhaps under-appraised) at more than £1,000.[3] Thomas Putnam must have had every hope, as he married into the Carr family, of making his way, in time, into that family's varied commercial activities.

But this was not to be. For when George Carr died in 1682 (four years after Thomas Putnam's marriage into the family), his widow and two of his sons

moved decisively to hold the family enterprises under their own control. In a
bitter protest filed with the courts in June 1682, several other members of the
family (including Thomas Putnam, Jr.) charged that in settling the estate the
widow Carr and her two sons, who had been appointed executors, were
blatantly cheating the three Carr daughters, and their husbands, of their
rightful portions.[4]

But this protest had little effect: about 60 percent of the Carr estate—
including the shipyard and the ferry business—went, directly or indirectly,
to the two Carr sons, with the remaining six children receiving comparatively
modest cash bequests.[5] So vanished whatever hopes Thomas Putnam, Jr.,
may have entertained of using marriage as a vehicle to break out of his total
economic dependence on the Salem Village lands he could expect to inherit
from his father.

Still, those expectations were far from paltry. At the very least, Thomas
might have anticipated receiving from his father perhaps 300 acres, in addition to the family homestead, and—if his father followed the pattern of
modified primogeniture by which he himself (as eldest son) had come into a
double portion—perhaps considerably more.

But if Thomas Putnam, Jr., did entertain such prospects, he did not take
into account the longevity and continued sexual vigor of his father. For in
1666, the year after his first wife died, the elder Thomas had taken for his
second a widow by the name of Mary Veren. Second marriages were, of
course, the rule for widowed persons in colonial New England, but this
particular one had unexpected and far-reaching overtones. For Mary Veren
was a woman of Salen Town, the widow of a Salem ship captain named
Nathaniel Veren whose two brothers were among the more successful of the
Town's emergent merchant class. Mary Veren herself was the owner of a
house and lot in the Town, which she had purchased in her own name from one
of her brothers-in-law. A daughter by her first marriage was to wed another
Salem merchant and oft-time selectman, Timothy Lindall.[6]

The implications of his father's second marriage for Thomas Putnam, Jr.,
had deepened immeasurably in 1669 (although the sixteen-year-old youth
may not have realized it at the time) with the arrival of Joseph Putnam.
Perhaps Mary Veren had acquired some of the business acumen of the Salem
circles in which she had moved, or perhaps her new husband had decided on
his own to shift his deepest loyalties from the connections of his first marriage
to those of his second. In any case, one or both of them began to promote the
interests of their son Joseph at the expense of Thomas Putnam's other children, including Thomas, Jr., now on the threshold of manhood. When the
elder Thomas Putnam died in 1686, he left a will which bequeathed to Mary
and to Joseph—then sixteen years old—the best part of his estate, including the
ample family homestead, the household furnishings, all the barns and out-
buildings, and agricultural equipment (the "plow gear and cart and tackling
of all sorts, with all my tools [and] implements of all sorts") and many of the

most fertile acres that had been granted to old John Putnam forty years before.[7]

Thomas Putnam, Jr., and his siblings were not left out altogether. Indeed, the old man may have died half-believing he had been scrupulously fair to all his children. He had already settled Thomas and Edward on farms of their own carved from his lands, and he confirmed those grants in his will. To his daughters he gave cash bequests.

But Thomas and Edward were convinced that they had been discriminated against, and their suspicions were deepened by certain rather unusual terms in their father's will. For example, the document specified that Joseph should come into his inheritance at the age of eighteen, rather than at the usual twenty-one. (This provision betrayed real concern that Joseph by some mischance or legal maneuver—set off, perhaps, by his mother's death—might be denied his full inheritance.) Even more important, Thomas named Mary and the lad Joseph as joint executors of his will and, in a surprising clause whose full significance would emerge only gradually, he appointed none other than Israel Porter (who also served as witness) [and who was a notorious rival of the Putnams] as one of the overseers of the estate.

The depth of the grievance felt by the older children of Thomas Putnam, Sr., is revealed by the determination with which they tried to break the will. When the document was presented for probate, it was countered by a petition bearing the signatures of Thomas Putnam, Jr., his younger brother Edward, and their brothers-in-law Jonathan Walcott and William Trask. The four declared that they would be "extremely wronged" if their father's will were allowed to stand, and they pointed the finger at what they saw as the source of the wrong: the will, they said, "was occasioned to be made as it is by our mother-in-law" ("stepmother," by modern parlance). They asked the court to name Thomas Putnam, Jr., as executor, in place of Mary Veren Putnam and her son, in order for a "true inventory" to be taken "so that each of us may have that proportion of our deceased father's estate which by the law of God and man rightly belongs to us." But Mary hired a lawyer of Salem Town, and the challenge got nowhere.[8]

Thus it was that on September 14, 1687—his eighteenth birthday—Joseph Putnam became, overnight, one of the richest men in Salem Village. His 1690 tax was 40 percent higher than that of his older half-brothers; indeed, it was well above that of any of the third-generation Putnams, eight of whom had reached taxable status by that year. All the other members of the numerous family—but especially Thomas Putnam, Jr.—watched impotently while Joseph, who could only have been seen as an interloper though he bore the family name, moved quickly and effortlessly into a privileged position in the Village.

But this was not to be all. In 1690, at the unusually youthful age of twenty, Joseph Putnam took a wife: she was none other than Elizabeth Porter, the sixteen-year-old daughter of Israel Porter.[9] The young man had managed to forge a formal alliance with the one family in the Village which rivaled and even surpassed the Putnams in wealth and prestige. This marriage confirmed for the other Putnams what was already only too clear: by joining the Porter clan Joseph.Putnam had managed to break free of the narrow agrarian constraints which held the rest of the Putnams down, and to strengthen his links (already strong through his mother) to the social, commercial, and political life of Salem Town. And he had achieved all this—and here was the most galling part of the business—through no real effort of his own.

This is not to suggest that Thomas Putnam, Jr., or the other Putnams had meanwhile sunk into desperate poverty or been driven completely into the political wilderness. Thomas, like his brother, his brothers-in-law, and his Putnam cousins, still remained a fairly prosperous farmer and, in the local village sphere, an influential figure. But, in relative terms, these years of Joseph's dramatic rise saw the situation of the rest of the family remain more or less static. In the years from 1690 to 1695, while the total of Putnam taxes (excluding those paid by Joseph) rose by about 6 percent, Joseph's shot upward by about 50 percent. The tax rates of 1690 and 1695 indicate that, still in his twenties, he was the wealthiest Putnam and the second richest man in the Village. (The richest was his wife's uncle Joseph Porter, while the fourth richest was her uncle-by-marriage Daniel Andrew.) In that same five-year interval, the tax paid by Thomas Putnam, Jr., declined by about 10 percent, from £1 to eighteen shillings.[10] By 1695, this eldest son of the man who had been, by a wide margin, the wealthiest taxpayer in Salem Village ranked only sixteenth among the 105 householders on the tax rolls.

Joseph Putnam's economic rise was paralleled by an increase in his political power. From the early years onward, Thomas Putnam, Sr., and his brothers and, later, their sons had dominated Village affairs. Joseph's rise did not demolish this entrenched power, but it severely challenged it. The entirely new Village Committee elected by the dissident faction in October 1691 was made up of Joseph Putnam (still only twenty-two years old) and his newly acquired kinsmen Joseph Porter and Daniel Andrew, together with two other men of similar anti-Parris views. It was this Committee which so dramatically set itself against Samuel Parris and otherwise repudiated the policies of the group which had hitherto run the Village. The crucial meetings of late 1691, at which the Villagers voted to investigate the "fraudulent" conveyance of the parsonage to Samuel Parris in 1689, were called by Joseph Putnam. The political turbulence of this period is visually conveyed in the Village Book of Record, as the neat, methodical handwriting of Thomas Putnam, Jr. (who had served as Village clerk for years until 1691) gives way to someone else's hasty scrawl, probably that of Joseph Putnam himself.[11]

By 1692 the children of the first Thomas Putnam—and especially his eldest son's family—were prepared to believe that witchcraft lay at the root of their troubles. They were hardly the first, under similar circumstances, to reach such a conclusion. Indeed, this episode in the history of the Putnam family is echoed in what might at first seem the least likely of sources: the folk-literature of medieval Europe, in which the evil stepmother and avaricious half-sibling frequently play central roles. The father of Cinderella, for example, takes as his second wife a widow associated with high society who, with the two daughters of her previous marriage, quickly comes to "govern him entirely" (as Mary Veren was accused of doing with her husband Putnam) and to relegate Cinderella, the child of his first marriage, to the role of a menial.[12]

The parallels are even closer in *Hansel and Gretel*, even though in this most famous witch story of all, the central family (unlike the Putnams) is poor and the stepmother brings no children of her own into the household. But like Cinderella—and the older children of Thomas Putnam, Sr.—Hansel and Gretel find themselves victimized and exploited by their father's selfish second wife, who ultimately persuades her somewhat reluctant husband to abandon them to certain death in the forest. But a magical bird leads them to a cottage made of bread, cake, and sugar—an impoverished child's image of prosperity. The old witch who lives in the place captures them and treats them precisely as their stepmother had done, exploiting their labor and even plotting their murder. ("Get up, you lazybones," she orders Gretel, "fetch water and cook something for your brother. When he's fat I'll eat him up.") But instead, it is the children who kill the witch, using the method often employed in European witch trials: fire. They return home—no trouble finding their way this time—laden with the "pearls and precious stones" they have discovered hidden in the witch's house. These they show to their over-joyed father, who "had not passed a single happy hour since he left them in the wood" and who informs them that their stepmother has died in their absence. Only the original family is left to share the witch's wealth.[13]

Both structurally and psychologically, the "witch" in *Hansel and Gretel* is a symbolic projection of the stepmother herself. Each of these women exploits the brother and sister and actually tries to kill them, and after the children execute the witch, the stepmother turns out, in a most improbable coincidence, to have died at about the same time. It is tempting to speculate about what actual event may have given rise to the tale of *Hansel and Gretel*. Perhaps there existed a real stepmother who was killed by her husband's children—children who then excused their deed by calling the selfish woman a witch. Or perhaps the historical prototypes of "Hansel" and "Gretel" merely made the initial accusation of witchcraft, leaving it to the authorities to burn the hated stepmother at the stake.

If, like the real Hansel and Gretel, the Putnams had expressed their frustration and rage in one terrible act of violence directed against a solitary individual, they would probably be remembered, if at all, not as historical villains but as folk figures—again like Hansel and Gretel, or (to take a more recent example) Lizzie Borden. But as even a summary of their role in 1692 makes clear, the Putnam response, if no less deadly, was far more diffuse and indirect. In that year Thomas Putnam, Jr., testified against twelve persons and signed complaints against twenty-four. His wife, Ann; his twelve-year-old daughter, Ann, Jr.; and a servant girl in his house named Mercy Lewis were all counted among those persons afflicted by "witchcraft." Indeed, the younger Ann Putnam, who testified against at least twenty-one persons, has remained the most infamous of the band of "afflicted girls." Thomas's brother Edward participated in thirteen cases; his brother-in-law Jonathan Walcott in seven; and Walcott's daughter Mary (who lived in Thomas Putnam's house) was not far behind her cousin Ann in attracting spectral torturers, sixteen of whom assaulted her in 1692.[14]

Strangely enough, the younger Thomas Putnam and his siblings never directly attacked the two persons most obviously responsible for their difficulties: their stepmother and their half-brother. Neither Mary Veren Putnam nor Joseph Putnam was named as a witch in 1692—though family tradition long held that Joseph kept a horse saddled day and night during that summer, and never ventured forth without a gun.[15] But, in the end, his precautions proved unnecessary. Was this because Mary and her son (unlike wealthy persons living outside the Village) were simply too powerful and too immediate a presence to be challenged directly? Or would accusations against them—since they were, in spite of everything, still part of the family—have involved psychic strains too intense to be borne? Whatever the reason, it seems clear that the Putnams in 1692 (like Hansel and Gretel in the folk tale) projected* their bitterness onto persons who were, politically or psychologically, less threatening targets: notably older women of Mary Veren Putnam's generation. Against such persons they vented the rage and bitterness which they were forced to deny (or to channel through such stylized outlets as legal petitions) in their relations with Mary and Joseph.

The original "afflictions," though evidently beginning in the Parris household, quickly spread from there to the three girls who lived in the household of Thomas Putnam, Jr.: Ann, Mary, and Mercy. But the imprisonment of the first three accused witches on March 1, Sarah Good, Sarah Osborne, and Tituba, did not cause the symptoms to abate. Indeed, they now spread to Thomas's wife, Ann Putnam, Sr. By the second week in March, both mother and daughter were complaining that they were being tortured by another woman, Martha Cory. The sufferings of the elder Ann Putnam became especially acute on the afternoon of the eighteenth: already "wearied out in helping to tend my poor afflicted child and maid," Mrs. Putnam was just lying down in bed "to take a little rest" when Goody Cory's apparition appeared and "torture[d] me so as I cannot express, ready to tear me all to pieces."[16]

Like the three women already in prison, there was a taint about Martha Cory: she had given birth, years earlier, to an illegitimate mulatto son, and the young man was still living in the Cory household, just over the Village line in Salem Town, with Martha and her second husband, Giles Cory. (Martha's first husband had been a Salem Townsman named Rich—like Mary Veren she had come as a mature woman to Salem Village after having been long identified with Salem Town.) But Goody Cory was not simply another Village outcast like Sarah Good or Tituba, for her husband was a prospering though somewhat obstreperous farmer and landowner, and—a fact of considerable importance—Martha herself was a covenanting member of the Salem Village church.[17]

The accusation of such a person as Martha Cory was a key point along the psychological progression which the Thomas Putnam family, and the entire witchcraft episode, followed in 1692. For in turning on her they betrayed the fact that witchcraft accusations against the powerless, the outcast, or the already victimized were not sufficiently cathartic for them. They were driven to lash out at persons of real respectability—persons, in short, who reminded them of the individuals actually responsible (so they believed) for their own reduced fortunes and prospects. Martha Cory was the ideal transition figure: she combined respectability with a touch of deviance. If the Putnams could bring her down, they would be free, not only politically, but psychologically as well, to play out their compulsions on a still larger scale.

And they brought her down in less than two weeks. On March 19, on the strength of Edward Putnam's complaint that she had afflicted Thomas Putnam's wife and daughter, Martha Cory was arrested.[18] Others would subsequently testify against her, but initially—unlike the first three accused women—she was a Putnam family witch pure and simple.

For their next play in this deadly game of psychological projection,* the Putnams moved farther up the social and economic ladder—and thus, in a sense, that much closer to Mary Veren Putnam. It was as early as March 13 that the younger Ann Putnam first saw the new and strange female apparition. "I did not know what her name was then," she later testified, "though I knew where she used to sit in our meetinghouse." On the fifteenth, Samuel Parris's niece saw the same specter, and four days later, it appeared to Ann Putnam, Sr. By this time its identity had somehow been ascertained: it was Rebecca Nurse, a respected older woman of Salem Village, and the wife of Francis Nurse, a once-obscure artisan who in 1678 had established himself as a substantial figure in the Village by purchasing, on credit, a rich, 300-acre farm near the Ipswich Road.[19]

Rebecca was convicted largely on the basis of spectral afflictions which befell the elder Ann Putnam between March 19 and 24, 1692. At first, until Martha Cory was imprisoned, Rebecca was distinctly a secondary figure in Ann Putnam's roster of spectral visitors. But after the twenty-first, with Cory safely in prison, Goody Nurse became the dominant presence in Ann's life. On Tuesday March 22, as Mrs. Putnam would later testify, her apparition "set upon me in a most dreadful manner, very early in the morning, as soon as it was well light." The struggle which ensued, and which was to continue almost without respite for three days, was at once physical and

---

*[Here and on p. 42 the authors use "projected" and "projection" when they mean "displaced" and "displacement" (i.e., from object a to safer object b).]—Ed.

spiritual. Dressed at first "only in her shift," Nurse carried in her hand the morning of her first visitation to the Putnam household a "little red book" which she "vehemently" urged Mistress Ann to sign (to sign away what? her soul? her estate?). When Ann refused, the specter (as she put it) "threatened to tear my soul out of my body," and denied that God had any power to save her.[20] The ordeal lasted almost two hours, and it recurred intermittently for the rest of the day.

It was on the next day, Wednesday the twenty-third, that the Reverend Deodat Lawson, Parris's predecessor in the Village pulpit, visited the besieged household. When he arrived, Ann had just recovered from a "sore fit." At the Putnams' request, Lawson began to pray, but by the time he had finished, Mrs. Putnam "was so stiff she could not be bended." A little afterwards, she "began to strive violently with her arms and legs" and to shout at her tormenter: "Goodwife Nurse, be gone! be gone! be gone! Are you not ashamed, a woman of your profession, to afflict a poor creature so! What hurt did I ever do to you in my life? . . . [B]e gone, do not torment me!"[21]

The scene thereupon turned into an argument about what the future held in store for the two women. Mrs. Putnam, for her part, insisted that her spectral visitor had "but two years to live" and that then the Devil would carry her off to hell: "For this your name is blotted out of God's Book, and it shall never be put in God's Book again." But the specter of Rebecca Nurse, for its part, seems to have had the same plans in store for Ann Putnam herself: "I know what you would have . . . ," Ann told her, "but it is out of your reach; it is clothed with the white robes of Christ's righteousness."

The encounter between Ann Putnam, Sr., and "Rebecca Nurse" is the most vivid and intimate record we have of the actual process by which a "witch" was singled out for accusation, and of the degree to which the accusers felt palpably threatened by the specters which haunted them. In retrospect, perhaps, Rebecca Nurse appears the inevitable victim, since she was an ideal "substitute" for Mary Veren Putnam: both were women of advanced years, both were prosperous and respected, both were in failing health, and both were members of the Salem Town church (though Rebecca occasionally worshiped in the Village).

To be sure, there were also a number of reasons, on the conscious and "rational" level, why Ann Putnam may have resented and even feared Rebecca Nurse. Rebecca was from Topsfield, whose town authorities had for years been harassing the Putnam family by claiming that parts of their lands actually lay in Topsfield rather than in Salem Village. And her husband Francis had been involved during the 1670's in a protracted dispute with Nathaniel Putnam over some mutually bounded acreage.[22] Furthermore, Francis Nurse, though not a real leader in Village politics, was clearly identified with the faction which the Putnams opposed. Along with Joseph Putnam, Daniel Andrew, and Joseph Porter, he had been elected to the anti-Parris Village Committee which took power at the end of 1691. And it was around the Rebecca Nurse case that Israel Porter was soon to try to rally opposition to the trials. Finally, even more than Martha Cory, and through no doing of her own, Rebecca was particularly vulnerable in 1692: years earlier, her mother had been accused of witchcraft (though never arrested or brought to trial) and local gossip had it that the taint had been passed on to her daughters. (Indeed, probably because the accusations against Rebecca jogged memories about the earlier episode, her two sisters were later accused as well.)[23]

But while such circumstances made Rebecca Nurse an acceptable and even plausible "witch" once she had been accused, they did not themselves provide the emotional impetus which led to her being singled out in the first place. The source of that drive lay in the fact that Ann Putnam was unable or unwilling publicly to vent her terrible rage on its living source: her mother-in-law Mary Veren Putnam, and perhaps her own mother Elizabeth Carr— the two old women who had somehow managed over the years to deprive Ann and her family of the high station which, by birth, was rightfully theirs. Of this redirected rage, Rebecca Nurse, like Martha Cory before her, was the innocent victim.

Once Rebecca *had* been singled out, and Ann Putnam's spectral struggle with her had begun, Ann's frantic monologues reveal a great deal about the nature of her obsession: "I know what you would have... , but it is out of your reach," she insists. "[W]e judged she meant her soul," interpolated Deodat Lawson (a little defensively?) at this point in his published report of the interview; but Ann's own words remain laden with unconscious ambiguity. Indeed, it is surprising how little energy Ann devoted during these hours of her travail to accusing Rebecca of witchcraft: it is "Rebecca's" death (or, more specifically, the obliteration of her psychological presence) which obsessed her. "Be gone! Be gone! Be gone!" she cries; "Be gone, do not torment me." She insists that Rebecca's name has been "blotted out" of God's mind forever. She even ventures a prediction: her spectral visitor has "about two years to live."[24] (In fact the guess was only a little optimistic: Mary Veren Putnam survived for almost exactly three years.)

But there is guilt as well as rage in all of this [projected "sin" as well as displaced anger]: for when the family of Thomas Putnam was deprived of its birthright, first by Elizabeth Carr and then by Mary Veren Putnam, it was forced openly and perhaps even consciously to confront the fact that it cared, and cared profoundly, about money and status. The apparition which for six days urged Ann Putnam to "yield to her hellish temptations," and which denied, as Ann put it, "the power of the Lord Jesus to save my soul," was, after all, in the mind of Mrs. Putnam herself. Did she fear that, covenanting church member or no, she had indeed lost her soul?—that it was she and her husband, with their open and drawn-out pursuit of money through the county courts, who were the real witches?

Might any of the other Putnams—or Lawson himself—have sensed danger here? In any case, by this time, the family had seen (and heard) enough. Later that same day, March 23, Edward and Jonathan Putnam went to the officials to swear out a complaint against Goody Nurse, and a warrant for her arrest was issued on the spot.[25] Rebecca's public examination was held the next day. But although the scene had shifted from Ann Putnam's bedroom to the Village meetinghouse, Ann still dominated it. She called out to Rebecca (in what must have been their first non-spectral encounter in some time): "Did you not bring the Black Man with you? Did you not bid me tempt God and die? How often have you eat and drunk your own damnation?"

At this, the exhausted Mrs. Putnam fell into still another fit; with the permission of the presiding magistrates her husband Thomas carried her home.[26] Almost as soon as Rebecca was imprisoned, the elder Ann Putnam's afflictions ceased—and they would not return for over two months. For a while, at least, the obsessive presence of Mary Veren, and all she represented in the life of Thomas Putnam, Jr., and his family, had been exorcised.

To understand Thomas Putnam, Jr., and his family is to begin to understand Salem Village. For in Puritan New England, the line between public and private concerns was a thin one. Since individual behavior was scrutinized by the full community just as closely as it was by a person's own family, it is hardly surprising that public issues should so often have been approached from the perspective of family relationships. It was, for example, altogether natural (and not in mere rhetorical hyperbole) that a Connecticut legislator of the 1690's, while denouncing an outlying section of his town for seeking autonomy, lamented to his fellow lawmakers that "one of your first born, a lovely, beautiful child, should be disinherited, and lose its birthright to an inferior brat."[27]

Similarly, the family of Thomas Putnam, Jr., readily wove its personal grievances into a comprehensive vision of conspiracy against Salem Village as a whole. In this way, the "pro-Parris" Villagers (who might otherwise have remained a disorganized collection of farmers ultimately to vanish from the hisorical record without a trace) attracted a powerful and determined leadership. Most Salem Village farmers must have found the forces which threatened them amorphous and difficult to pin down; for the Putnams, however, that task was all too easy: it was Mary Veren and her son Joseph who were the serpents in Eden, and if they, or their psychological equivalents, could only be eliminated, all might again be well.

NOTES

1. Tax list, Village Records, Dec. 27, 1681.

2. Putnam genealogy: Sidney Perley, *The History of Salem*, 3 vols. (Salem, 1924–28).

3. *Records and Files of the Quarterly Courts of Essex County, Massachusetts, 1636–1683*, 8 vols. (Salem, 1911–21), 8, 348–350 (George Carr's will and estate inventory); hereafter cited as *EQC*.

4. 8 *EQC*, 354–355.

5. *Ibid.*, 348–349.

6. Perley, *History of Salem*, I, 303–304 (Veren genealogy); II, 109 (Putnam genealogy). See also 3 *EQC*, 264, for reference to Captain Nathaniel Veren.

7. Will in Eben Putnam, *History of the Putnam Family* (Salem, 1891), pp. 11–19. For a photograph of the Putnam homestead: Perley, *History of Salem*, III, 167.

8. Petition reprinted in Putnam, *History of the Putnam Family*, pp. 20–21.

9. Perley, *History of Salem*, II, 109 (Putnam genealogy) and 162 (Porter genealogy).

10. Tax lists, Village Records, Dec. 30, 1690; Jan. 18, 1695. The comparative economic standing of the two men is also vividly revealed in the Salem Town tax rolls. In the Town tax of 1697, for example, the £1/9 paid by Joseph Putnam was more than double the fourteen shillings paid by his older half-brother. *Tax and Valuation Lists of Massachusetts Towns Before 1776*, microfilm edition compiled by Ruth Crandall (Harvard University Library), reel 8: "Salem, 1689–1773."

11. Perley, *History of Salem*, III, 252 (list of selectmen); Church Records, March 27, 1693.

12. Andrew Lang, ed., *The Blue Fairy Book* (Looking Glass Library, distributed by Random House, New York, 1959), pp. 96–97.

13. *Ibid.*, pp. 331–341; quoted passages on pp. 338, 340, and 341.

14. W. Elliot Woodward, *Records of Salem Witchcraft, Copied From the Original Documents*, 2 vols. (Roxbury, Mass., Privately printed, 1864; reissued in one volume, New York, Da Capo Press, 1969), index.

15. Charles W. Upham, *Salem Witchcraft*, 2 vols. (Boston, 1867), II, 457.

16. Deposition of Ann Putnam, Sr., quoted *ibid.*, II, 278.

17. On Martha Cory, see Perley, *History of Salem*, I, 193; III, 292; on Giles Cory: 1 *EQC*, 152, 172; 4 *EQC*, 275; 6 *EQC*, 191; 7 *EQC*, 89–91, 123–124, 147–149; 10 *New England Historical and Genealogical Register* (1856), 32 (will); Sidney Perley, "The Woods: Part of Salem in 1700," *Essex Institute Historical Collections* (Salem), 51, 195.

18. Woodward, *Records of Salem Witchcraft*, I, 50.

19. *Ibid.*, I, 88–89.

20. Deposition of Ann Putnam, Sr., quoted in Upham, *Salem Witchcraft*, II, 279.

21. Deodat Lawson, *A Brief and True Narrative of Some Remarkable Passages Relating to Sundry Persons Afflicted by Witchcraft, at Salem Village Which Happened from the Nineteenth of March to the Fifth of April, 1692* (Boston, 1692), in George Lincoln Burr, ed., *Narratives of the Witchcraft Cases, 1648–1706* (New York, Charles Scribner's Sons, 1914; reissued New York, Barnes and Noble, 1968), p. 157.

22. 7 *EQC*, 10–21; 8 *EQC*, 116–121, 319–323 (Topsfield dispute). For a timber dispute which pitted the Putnams against Rebecca's family in the 1680's, see manuscript volumes of unpublished county court records, Essex County Courthouse, Salem, Mass., 47, 42–43.

23. The earlier charge against Rebecca Nurse's mother is mentioned in the testimony of Ann Putnam, Sr.—Woodward, *Records of Salem Witchcraft*, I, 95.

24. Lawson, *Brief and True Narrative*, in Burr, *Narratives*, p. 157.

25. Woodward, *Records of Salem Witchcraft*, I, 76–77.

26. Lawson, *Brief and True Narrative*, in Burr, *Narratives*, p. 159; Woodward, *Records of Salem Witchcraft*, I, 82–87, quoted passage on pp. 83–84. If Rebecca Nurse was a substitute for Mary Veren Putnam, then John Willard, against whom Ann Putnam also testified, may have been a substitute for Joseph Putnam.

27. Richard L. Bushman, *From Puritan to Yankee: Character and the Social Order in Connecticut, 1690–1765* (Cambridge, Mass., Harvard University Press, 1967), p. 66.

2

JONATHAN EDWARDS AS GREAT MAN
Identity, Conversion, and Leadership in the Great Awakening

RICHARD L. BUSHMAN

Conceivably "one of the few original intellects of modern Christianity," in the words of Perry Miller, Jonathan Edwards was a Congregationalist minister and student of religious psychology in early-eighteenth-century Massachusetts. Edwards labored to reconcile the doctrines of Puritan Calvinism with the then-new Lockean or "sensationalist" theory of the mind. The senses, he argued, were the primary means of appreciating the grandeur and glory of God and our own helplessness; no wonder, then, that the emotional faculties were the primary means of expressing joy at the conversion experience. During the Great Awakening, the series of stirring revivals that swept the colonies in the 1730s and 1740s, Edwards's theory served to underpin an approach to religious justification by which—instead of waiting passively for God to give a sign of one's election to grace—it was possible actively to prepare for the indwelling of the Holy Spirit. This preparation and the feelings that accompanied conversion were ultimately of significance beyond the strictly religious because sharing them were rich and poor, men and women, powerful and weak, old and young alike. Evangelical faith carried the theme of equality and therefore sowed seeds that flourished after the Revolution. The ideas Edwards professed on the workings of the mind no longer carry scholarly weight. He remains worth knowing, however, because a major problem he grappled with has proved to be a lasting tension in the American experience—the pull between material striving and disdain for purely material success.

A major lesson of the essay that follows is that psychobiography, rather than being merely the narrative account of a single person's character and foibles, can provide a means of examining broad historical topics: "great men" or women—particularly innovative thinkers, charismatic politicians, and religious leaders—are successful because they come to terms with personal issues that enable them to speak to the wishes or needs of their audiences. The effort to explore the place where private history and the forces of public history meet, Richard Bushman observes, owes much to the

Reprinted with permission from *Soundings: An Interdisciplinary Journal* 52 (Spring 1969):15–46.

example of Erik Erikson, whose sequel to *Young Man Luther*, *Ghandi*, was unpublished when this article first appeared. In Edwards's inner life the "sins" of pride and ambition, his relationship with authority, his inability to indulge sensuality or express emotions, all represented—directly or metaphorically—the fault lines of a restless and growing society. Thus, as Bushman notes in this selection, personality finds its way back into historical studies.

Bushman's method, which he discussed more fully in an earlier essay on Benjamin Franklin, is to read all available evidence with an eye for recurring psychological patterns. Though these themes emerge mostly from the writings the subject left as an adult, the themes can alert one to possible similar patterns and their psychological roots in early life—without, he adds, either leading one to see in the past more than is there or making adult personality nothing more than repetition of what has gone before. Bushman's patterns point the way to adjustable hypotheses about the likely initiatives and responses of a diplomat—in Franklin's case—or, as here, about the meaning a religious reformer consciously and unconsciously gave the messages that were most prominent in his writings and sermons.

Introducing the subject of psychological biography in this anthology, Edwards fits well here because the study of his career continues themes sounded in the Boyer and Nissenbaum chapter. In emotionalism, the central role of young people loosed from their usual restrictions, and in expressing anxiety over the evils of worldliness, the Great Awakening that Edwards led bears striking resemblance to the Salem witchcraft scare some forty years before.

ERIK ERIKSON'S *Young Man Luther* has raised again the question of the great man's part in history.[1] The early nineteenth-century fascination with heroes who bent the course of events through sheer determination and personal force later faded as new conceptual tools enabled historians to calculate more precisely the impact of social forces. The times, it was then believed, thrust forward the great men, and rather than shaping events to their wills, heroes were as much determined by their environments as the mass. Erikson's biography of Luther does not restore the hero to his former eminence nor discount the weight of social conditions, but it does assert that the relationship of a man and his times is an exchange that goes both ways. A single individual can bring to his age powers that enable him to mobilize forces latent in the mass of men. Not just any power, however imposing, will do. The great man's capacities must be congruent with the needs of his age; when he speaks the age must respond. But his presence does make a difference. The force of one man's will, as Erikson shows in the case of Luther, can shape history.

Through Luther, Erikson examines the nature of the great man's power and shows that his compelling qualities may grow out of his anxieties as much as his strengths. His virtue lies in his unrelenting determination to settle psychological controversies which others experience but face less decisively. While most men conceal their anxieties and compromise rather than reconcile internal conflicts, an unusual integrity in the great man compels him to harmonize the warring elements. From his anguished quest for peace comes a new personal identity and with it a magnificent release of energy and determination. The combination of a compelling new identity and individual magnetism galvanizes others, and the great man, often without calculation, finds himself at the head of a movement.

All this is extrapolation from the one biography Erikson has published, but the notions are so intriguing and *Young Man Luther* so rewarding that similar works on other men seem in order. Only when applied to a number of figures can the merit of Erikson's implicit hypotheses be measured. While of lesser magnitude than Luther and Protestantism, Jonathan Edwards and the Great Awakening of 1740 in New England were similarly related. The revivals of 1735 which foreshadowed the greater outburst in 1740 began in Edwards' parish, and for many years he was called to preach wherever ministers wished their congregations to join the movement. No one compelled sinners to face their doom more relentlessly, and no one told better the sweet raptures of grace or explained more precisely where to place one's trust. He was by common consent the most powerful spokesman for the reborn men of his generation.

To understand the sources of this influence, Erikson's model of leadership calls for a reconstruction of the leader's identity and of the emotional needs of his age, for the great man has access to the hearts of other men at the point where the spiritual needs of leader and people converge. In Erikson's scheme, identity is the shape that an individual gives to his life to satisfy himself and his society. It is constituted both by his personal likes, dislikes, habits, attitudes, fears, hopes, and capacities, and by the way he manages all these internal resources within the limitations of his social environment. As Erikson puts it, identity in the maturing person is "the accrued experience of the ego's ability to integrate all identifications with the vicissitudes of the libido, with the aptitudes developed out of endowment, and with the opportunities offered in social roles."[2] To work with this model in Edwards' case we must delineate the emerging patterns of his thought and feeling and the roles he assumed in his father's parsonage as he grew up. We must also look for strains among these components, for it was the resolution of tensions in conversion which both shaped his personal identity and prepared him for leadership in the Great Awakening.

Erikson draws heavily on psychoanalysis for his insights into Luther, and among psychological systems psychoanalysis is unusually helpful in enlarging the historian's understanding of human character. But more important than the system employed is the ability to enter into the consciousness of another person and to respond to his feelings. Psychoanalysis is particularly useful in the interpretation of early childhood, where an adult imagination is most likely to fail; but so little information on that period remains in most cases, and virtually none for Edwards, that the beginnings perforce must be neglected. Psychoanalytic insights can also help to discover patterns in the materials on later life, and in the analysis that follows I have relied more than once on Erikson's reformulation of Freud to interpret the data.[3] But sensitivity of the sort exhibited by novelists or the best literary critics is the skill most evident in Erikson's work and the one required of historians who would follow him. Effective application of his model of leadership depends mostly upon the exercise of historical imagination in translating the raw facts of a biography into a coherent and believable human experience.

I

Jonathan Edwards was born in 1703 in East Windsor, Connecticut, in the household of the Reverend Timothy Edwards.[4] East Windsor had separated from Windsor in 1694, and in the first year of its independence the parish settled Timothy Edwards as its minister. Fresh from Harvard, he soon married and moved into the house which his father, a prosperous Hartford merchant, built for him in the center of the village. Jonathan was his fifth child and first son, the only son, as it turned out, among eleven children.

The most evident import of Jonathan's genealogy is that he would be expected to attain to eminence. Differing circumstances on the ancestral lines of both mother and father pointed in the same direction: Jonathan would have to be powerful and successful, especially intellectually, to fulfill his family's hopes. Jonathan's mother, Esther, was the daughter of Solomon Stoddard and Esther Warham Mather Stoddard, a very imposing pair of parents. Solomon Stoddard was the dominant ecclesiastical figure in the Connecticut Valley and a powerful man throughout New England. His voice could disturb the Mathers in their Boston stronghold and was regarded respectfully everywhere. Most noted for successfully challenging the "New England Way" of admitting only visible saints to communion, Stoddard believed that true saints could not be discovered and that upright and orthodox people should be accepted into the Church in the hope that communion would help convert them, a view that many churches in the Connecticut Valley adopted. Solomon was also renowned for the fervency of his preaching and for the recurrent revivals in his Northampton congregation, a tradition Jonathan was to inherit and culminate.

When Solomon accepted the pulpit at Northampton, he met and soon married his predecessor's widow. The daughter of a famed Connecticut minister, and a powerful person in her own right, Esther Stoddard was widely known for her vigorous mind, strength of will, and considerable learning, traits which, along with her name, she gave to Jonathan's mother.

Esther Edwards was remembered by her friends as "tall, dignified and commanding in her appearance," yet "affable and gentle in her manners." Solomon sent her to Boston for her education, and she became especially well acquainted with the Scriptures and with theological writers. After Timothy's death she would ask in the neighborhood ladies to listen to her comments on theology. Some of the listeners thought Esther Edwards surpassed her husband in "Native vigor of understanding."[5]

Knowing this much, it seems safe to say that Esther wanted Jonathan to embody the qualities notable in her father, her mother, herself, and the man she chose to marry. To please his mother fully Jonathan would have to be a man of unusual force and intellect. Values so thoroughly inbred and virtually unchallenged through at least two generations could exert an intense pressure, all the greater because Jonathan was the only son among eleven children. The hopes which only a man child could fulfill necessarily focused on a boy who arrived after four daughters, and the hopes grew more intense as six daughters followed.

A rivalry with the other Stoddard daughters may have heightened Esther's ambition for her son. A hint of this competition infuses all the family relationships. Perhaps the goal was to produce a worthy successor to Solomon; if so, Esther triumphed, for Jonathan was chosen to take the Northampton pulpit. But he paid dearly for his success. His cousins harried him whenever he was in trouble. During the dismissal proceedings at Northampton, one cousin, Joseph Hawley, was the leading spokesman for the opposition. Another, Solomon Williams, wrote the refutation of Edwards' plea for a church of visible saints, pointedly rebuking him for attacking his honored grandfather. Still another cousin, Israel Williams, a powerful figure in civil and commercial affairs in Northampton, had a long record of opposing Edwards' ministry on various counts. As early as the college years, Elisha Mix, a roommate and a cousin on Esther's side, fell out with Jonathan and wanted to move. Jonathan's father complained to Elisha's mother of his bad conduct and reproved her for speaking ill of Jonathan before strangers.[6] This collective animus may measure the determination of the Stoddard daughters to have their sons achieve the stature of Solomon and the disappointment of Esther's sisters at seeing one who was not their own excel.

Timothy Edwards's own hopes reinforced Esther's high expectations for Jonathan. Timothy was the first in his family to attend college in three generations. His great-grandfather, Richard Edwards, was an ordained minister, a university graduate, and the teacher in the Cooper's Company school in London. He died young, and his widow married a cooper. With him and William, her only son by Richard, she migrated to Connecticut. William would have gone to college had his own father lived, but in America he took up his stepfather's trade. Whatever educational values may have been transmitted across the generations were twice focused on only sons, for William's wife bore him a single son who was named Richard in memory of a father and perhaps of a way of life not wholly forgotten. Timothy remembered of this Richard that, beside the Bible, "Other Good books were in the Season thereof Much Read in his house," providing some evidence of values surviving.[7]

William could not afford college for his son, but in the cooper's shop Richard prospered. He also built up a mercantile business that eventually outgrew one warehouse and required another. Meanwhile he rose through town offices into colonial politics, holding positions as selectman, as deputy to the General Court, and in his later years as Queen's Attorney. When it came time to choose a career for his eldest son, Richard sent Timothy to Harvard to study for the ministry, and perhaps to recover the honor and refinement of the first Richard's station. Timothy's aspirations for Jonathan were at least tinged with the frustrated desires of two generations finally promised fulfillment in a brilliant scion.

After settling in East Windsor, Timothy became well known for his great skill in preparing boys for Harvard and Yale. He simply assumed that Jonathan would be a scholar too and assimilate his father's learning in Latin, Greek, and Hebrew. All of the Edwards children studied the classical languages under Timothy, and even the girls went on for more schooling. The desks lining the parlor were constant reminders of family expectations. Jonathan quite naturally began Latin at age six when his precocity was fast becoming evident. In the family of Esther and Timothy, the early discovery of Jonathan's great abilities only heightened the parents' hopes and intensified the pressure for achievement.

More remains than the meager information about Esther and Jonathan to tell us about the probable effects of Timothy's character on his son. Timothy was a compulsively exact and exacting man. He schooled his students so well because he tolerated no errors in their recitations, just as he allowed none to himself. He memorized every word of his sermons and delivered them letter-perfect. Measuring corn for barter or in lieu of money payment on his salary, he "made the negro sweep it up very clean" and then measured the sweepings.[8] He delighted in classifying thoughts, arranging them in numbered lists. His tribute to his father "ends with a list of seventeen mercies attending the manner of his death, separates his dying words into thirty-five items, works out six ways in which he glorified God at his death, and proceeds to supply numbered particulars under each."[9]

Timothy displayed all the classic compulsive traits, order, thrift, and obstinacy. When inflation depreciated the value of his salary, he prepared lengthy comparisons of purchasing power at the time he was settled and afterwards to prove he was being cheated. He was never one to yield in disputes with his congregation, either. In the 1730's a young man in town married a local girl without her parents' permission. Timothy wished to censor the boy, but the congregation refused to concur. Considering the case a matter of conscience, Timothy denied communion to the entire town for over three years while the controversy dragged on.

Jonathan's mind, though far more sweeping, poetic, and profound than his father's, bore the marks of its training under Timothy. Jonathan too refused to give an inch when challenged. In the dismissal controversy at Northampton he would not compromise with his parishioners, nor would he yield a point in the debate with Solomon Williams on admission to communion. In all intellectual disputes Edwards stubbornly beat down his opponents, demolishing even the slightest contradictions. He had to prove himself right in every detail. Even in non-combative writings, his arguments were exhaustive. What often appears as repetition was part of a massive effort to block every conceivable loophole. The careful definitions, the close reasoning, the piling up of proofs and illustrations were the natural ways of his thorough and fastidious mind. The truth had to be expressed immaculately and in perfect order, leaving no gaps for error to invade.

His father's parsimony shaped not only Jonathan's attitude toward money—he too argued with his parish over salary—but toward ideas. Ideas were poetry and power for Edwards; with them he negotiated his peace with the universe. But they were also things to be possessed. His delight in discovering Locke was greater "than the most greedy miser finds, when gathering up handsful of silver and gold, from some newly discovered treasure."[10] He pinned papers to his coat while riding as reminders of his thoughts so that none would be lost. All of his ideas, along with many he read, were written down and carefully preserved in notebooks that came to contain many thousands of pages. The productions of mind were hoarded and treasured as valued possessions in a vast miser's store of thoughts.

Timothy's exactions were moral as well as intellectual. He required perfect obedience as well as perfect accuracy. The detailed instructions contained in letters to his family were presumably no less thorough when he was at home. Jonathan's behavior for the most part appears to have satisfied his parents. In one letter, when Jonathan was eight, Timothy said, "I hope thou wilt take Special care of Jonathan that he dont Learn to be rude and naught etc., of which thee and I have Lately Discoursed."[11] But the tenor of the comment was that naughtiness was exceptional. Not until late adolescence did the strains which Timothy's high standards imposed come out. Jonathan gratefully acknowledged that his parents' "counsel and education" had been his "making," but confessed that "in the time of it, it seemed to do me so little good."[12] The entire diary testified of the "good" of that sort of upbringing. Timothy's education implanted a conscience as meticulous and demanding as his standards of scholarship. The comment "it seemed to do me so little good" speaks of long struggles in which part of the self was hopelessly resistant to the pressures of conscience. By the time of the diary, Jonathan had conquered all obvious forms of sin and was struggling with the fine points, like wanting to stop to eat when mealtime came and an occasional listlessness in his studies. But his conscience kept asking for perfection, and he obediently renewed the daily examinations of his soul. He thought once that he must live as if he were to be the only true Christian on the earth in his generation. Timothy's education placed that much of a burden on his boy. Throughout his life, Jonathan continued to abhor himself as a "miserable wretch," "base and vile," and unworthy of God.[13]

There is some evidence that a peculiar combination of fear and love enforced Timothy's exactions. He displayed an extraordinary anxiety for his children's physical safety. An excerpt from a letter to Esther illustrates the point.

I hope God will help thee to be very careful that no harm happen to the little Children by Scalding wort, whey, water, or by Standing too nigh to Tim when he is cutting wood; and prithee take what care thou canst about Mary's neck, which was too much neglected when I was at home. . . . And Let Esther and Betty Take their powders as Soon as the Dog Days are Over, and if they dont help Esther, talk further with the Doctor about her for I wouldnt have her be neglected. . . . If any of the children should at any time Go over the River to meeting I would have them be exceeding carefull, how they Sit or Stand in the boat Least they should fall into the River.[14]

That passage may be read as the loving concern of an oversolicitous father, but, as Ola Winslow commented, "instead of quieting childish fears he raised them, as though parental guidance consisted in advance notice of potential disaster."[15] If the attitude was typical, Timothy's anxieties would have reinforced in the Edwards children the ordinary apprehensions of violent destruction. Perhaps on an unconscious level they sensed that under Timothy's apparent strength was a lively sense of the precariousness of existence. At the very least they imbibed a sense of their vulnerability. Small wonder that thunder terrified Jonathan and raised apprehensions of divine wrath.

Timothy's own vulnerability made resistance still more hazardous. Fears for his own destruction arose with anxieties about the children. The myth of his boyhood, based perhaps on fact, perhaps on his own febrile imagination, had him narrowly escaping calamities ranging from drownings and freezings to swallowing peach stones. His letters home from the military expedition which he accompanied as chaplain admonish Esther not to be "discouraged or over anxious concerning me," and follow with such quavering reassurances as, "I have still strong hopes of seeing thee and our dear children once again." His life, like the letters, was suffused with the conditional, "if I Live to come home." Or again: "Tell the children, that I would have them, if they desire to see their father again, to pray daily for me in secret."[16] The conventional sentiment may have had deeper significance in the Edwards household where the children were made to feel some of the responsibility for preserving his rather frail being, making resistance fraught with danger.

Timothy's fragility and perfectionism were slight defects, and the burdens he imposed on his children surprisingly light, considering the emotional hardships of his own childhood. Richard Edwards as one of the few men in seventeenth-century New England to seek and obtain a divorce. After three appeals and a special investigation, his complaints finally moved the magistracy. Timothy's mother, Elizabeth Tuttle, confessed pregnancy by another man three months after her marriage and was unfaithful periodically throughout the twenty-four years of her life with Richard. He never forgave her infidelity and besides bore other perversities "too grievous to forgitt and too mutch here to Relate."[17] Elizabeth's trouble was not mere weakness but a violent malice, bordering on or perhaps symptomatic of insanity. Her brother Benjamin killed their sister with an axe. Another sister killed her own son. Elizabeth threatened Richard with physical violence. Timothy grew up in the presence of distrust and hatred, dependent almost wholly on his father for steady affection and exposed to visible and explosive hostility in his mother. The insistence on rigid control and the precautions Timothy urged on the patient Esther out of fear for his own and his children's safety were modest demands from such a man.

The fear of destruction was always wrapped and muffled in love. Timothy Edwards was indeed an oversolicitous parent, moved by genuine affection and concern. Another letter asks Esther to "remember my love to each of the children, to Esther, Elizabeth, Anne, Mary, Jonathan, Eunice and Abigail," in his usual thorough way naming each individually in order of birth, and then adding, "the Lord have mercy on and eternally save them all, with our dear little Jerusha," the most recent. The next sentence tells much about the warmth of his household: "The Lord bind up their souls with thine and mine in the bundle of life."[18]

Any contemplated disobedience faced this love as well as the implicit danger of destruction. Overt rebellion struck at the loving and loved parent. Jonathan's doctrine that sin was all the more heinous for offending a God who loved the sinner with infinite compassion expressed the anguish felt by rebels in the Edwards household. Unjustifiable resistance wholly deserved its punishment, even if it were complete destruction. All of the Edwards children remained loyal to their parents and their parents' values. The resentments arising from discipline were necessarily turned inward or diverted to other objects.

A chance event in the family history may have accentuated the apprehensions which Timothy aroused. When Jonathan was seven he passed through a rare naughty spell, resisting for a moment his father's strict control. Immediately afterwards Timothy left with the military expedition for Canada and soon wrote home his quavering hopes for a safe return and the admonitions to pray for his safety. Jonathan's wish to overthrow his father's government seemed to enjoy remarkable success. Suddenly his father was gone and Jonathan was the only male in the house, a situation perfectly designed to revive the furtive romance with the mother characteristic of boyhood a few years earlier. With his conscious mind, Jonathan knew well enough where his father was and that he intended to return, but the direct fulfillment of secret wishes heightened fantasies with immense appeal to the unconscious. When word came back that Timothy had fallen ill and nearly died, the rational faculty would have to struggle desperately to convince itself that those deep wishes had not come precariously close to fulfillment. The brief release of passionate hopes compelled the internal restraining forces to grow all the stronger. All this was stored away in the expanding armory of Jonathan's exceedingly aggressive conscience.

Recreating what we can, then, from the meager facts of Jonathan's childhood, a few themes begin to emerge:

1) Both father and mother had unusually high hopes for Jonathan's intellectual prowess and for the possibility of his becoming eminent.

2) Timothy exacted extraordinarily precise moral and intellectual behavior from his son.

3) Timothy's feelings for his children were an ambivalent mixture of high demands, intense love, and fear of destruction, both theirs and his own.

II

Three essays written by Jonathan, probably between his eleventh and thirteenth years, open a window on his character as it took shape amid the high expectations of the Edwards household. One was an unfinished set of observations on the rainbow, foreshadowing the later notes on natural science. The second was the famous essay on spiders, and the third a facetious rebuttal to the notion of a material soul. The hand of Timothy encouraging and guiding Jonathan's development is seen behind the spider essay, "Of Insects." Like many other New England ministers, Timothy cultivated English correspondents, offering them, in return for their interest, notes on natural phenomena in the New World. More ambitious for his son than himself, Timothy urged Jonathan to write up his observations and send them to England where conceivably they might impress "the Learned world."[19]

"Of Insects" demonstrates how precocious Jonathan was both intellectually and socially. In the letter accompanying the essay, he self-consciously presented himself in a stylized guise suitable for his tender age and also in accord with the conventional proprieties of authorship.

Forgive me, sir, that I Do not Conceal my name, and Communicate this to you by a mediator. If you think the Observations Childish, and besides the Rules of Decorum,—with Greatness and Goodness overlook it in a Child and Conceal Sir, Although these things appear very Certain to me, yet Sir, I submit it all to your better Judgment and Deeper insight....[20]

Particularly the sentence, "Forgive me, sir, that I Do not Conceal my name, and Communicate this to you by a mediator," was an affectation entirely appropriate for his century, but one that had to be learned. Somehow from the books or the guests in the East Windsor parsonage Jonathan had picked up the mannerism and made it his own.

Obviously as Jonathan wrote this essay he did not think of himself as a young future pastor, as might be expected from his upbringing and later life. He accepted that role too; a contemporaneous letter to his sister triumphantly recounted the conversions during a revival time in East Windsor.[21] But in the essay on spiders he appeared as a natural philosopher, and the essay on the soul was weighted heavily with the gestures of an eighteenth-century man of letters.

I am informed that you have advanced an Notion that the soul is materiall and attends the body till the resurection as I am a profest Lover of novelty you must immagin I am very much entertained by this discovery (which however [old] in some parts of the world is new to us) but suffer my Curiosity a Littel further I would know the manner of the kingdom before I swear alegance.[22]

The casual, satirical tone, so redolent of fashionable prose postures, stands in marked contrast to the earnest, straightforward style of Edwards' maturity and comes as something of a relief in an anthology of his writing. The two pages on "The Soul" suggest that he toyed with more sprightly life-styles and was for a moment light-hearted before settling down to the life and death issues.

The parenthetical comment, "which however [old] in some parts of the world is new to us," indicates that imitating English manners was more than an amusing posture. Jonathan was a provincial, painfully aware that there were brilliant centers of culture and learning where ideas had grown old before the provinces even heard them. He wanted access to those centers and recognition from them. The roles of man of letters or natural philosopher were acceptable in the capitals of the English community, and, with Timothy's help, Jonathan cultivated the parts. If Timothy's expertise was limited to ancient languages, he knew of larger fields for the mind and aspired to see his son enter them.

Jonathan's strategy is reminiscent of Benjamin Franklin's, to name but one of Edwards' contemporaries with a similar youthful outlook. Franklin too was industriously perfecting his style, using Addison and Steele as his masters, with the intent of winning the attention of great ones. Success in the *New England Courant* fostered high hopes which led first to Philadelphia and then to London, where he introduced himself to polite society with a philosophical essay and a natural curiosity, a piece of asbestos. Defeated for the most part in this first assault, Franklin returned to Philadelphia and built a solid provincial base before trying again and succeeding magnificently as a natural philosopher. His scientific experiments won the recognition of the learned world and helped to establish him as the most cosmopolitan of provincials. In social terms, scientific speculation and experimentation can be interpreted as providing entry to the intellectual life beyond the provinces. Far from being unique, Edwards and Franklin simply took more seriously activities in which many educated Americans dabbled. Science and letters were avenues which talented young men could follow into the great world.

In Edwards' case, the social opportunity must also be related to his personal situation. Ascent into the great world was the fulfillment of his parents' high expectations, or, more accurately, a natural sequel to the rewards his intelligence had won at home. As his parents' ambitions for him became his own ambitions for himself, success in meeting their expectations encouraged him to aspire to success in broader spheres.

The spheres he hoped to conquer grew even larger after he entered Yale at age thirteen and learned about the marvels of Locke and Newton. Sometime during his college years he began the notes on mind and on natural science which reveal how seriously Edwards took the work of these two intellects. The natural science notes show Edwards exploring every physical phenomenon he observed and in his usual thorough and rational way explaining the facts of physics, biology, and astronomy. "The Mind" contained observations on psychology and metaphysics after the manner of Locke's *An Essay Concerning Human Understanding*. In it Jonathan laid the groundwork of his philosophical idealism.

Both sets of notes were meant to be more than a record of observations. Edwards planned two massive treatises for publication. At the head of the notes on "The Mind" is a formal title: "The Natural History of the Mental World, or of the Internal World: being a Particular Enquiry into the Nature of the Human Mind." The relationship of this work to the notes on natural science was to be explained in the introduction: "Concerning the two worlds—the External and the Internal: the External, the subject of Natural Philosophy; the Internal, our own Minds."[23] With his two volumes Edwards planned to encompass the whole of existence, the internal and external worlds. He aimed to enlarge upon and perhaps advance beyond Locke and Newton, grounding all in theological metaphysics. Edwards was well aware that his undertaking was presumptuous and cautioned himself "not to insert any disputable thing, or that will be likely to be disputed by learned men; for I may depend upon it, they will receive nothing, but what is undeniable, from me."[24] And yet confidence in his own powers and mastery of every intellectual task Connecticut had presented encouraged him to go ahead with his *Summa*. This young provincial aimed high.

The picture of Edwards thus far is relatively conflict-free. Past performance promised future fulfillment of his parents' hopes. His natural gifts and temperament suited perfectly the life they foresaw for him. Even the legacy of compulsive thoroughness and logic were put to the service of his identity as scholar and philosopher. In the family, at Yale, and hopefully in the greater English community, society confirmed his belief that the works of his mind were worthy and important and would assure him a place of high respect.

But the promise was not fulfilled exactly as forecast. The two treatises were never published. Although Edwards steadily added to his scientific and philosophical notes, they remained notes. He never publicly assumed the role of natural philosopher, and he dropped the fashionable style of a man of letters in favor of a more somber voice as preacher. His career as pastor and divine absorbed his entire life. The early work was put aside except when it served religion.

The main turning came during the conversion years, but the earliest writings reflect the tensions conversion had to resolve. More was at stake, of course, than boyish dreams of fame. The essay on spiders particularly points to the pitfalls which the high-strung Edwards conscience created even for a boy as obedient as Jonathan and which compelled him to change his life. "Of Insects" is most useful to a biographer if it is read as an unconscious allegory of human existence. Such an interpretation is not far-fetched considering that later Edwards consciously made a spider the emblem of man's plight. Aside from purely scientific curiosity, something held Edwards' attention on spiders hour after hour. During his observations he continually drew parallels with people, and at the end he discussed the ways of God with small creatures in the universal moral order.

The quality which first intrigued him was the "truly very Pretty and Pleasing" ability of spiders to swim through the air from tree to tree and float high in the sky toward the sun. By careful experimentation, he discovered that spiders emitted a fine web which the air bore upwards and which, when it grew long enough, carried away the spider. He hypothesized that it spun the web from "a certain liquor with which that Great bottle tail of theirs is filled," and which dried and rarefied when exposed. He saw the spiders on these webs "mount away into the air" and thought it afforded them "a Great Deal of their sort of Pleasure." Their delight disclosed "the exuberant Goodness of the Creator" who provided for the necessities and also "the Pleasure and Recreation of all sorts of Creatures."[25]

The pleasures of ascent, however, were short-lived, for as the spiders mounted toward the sun in the fair summer weather, they were caught in the prevailing westerly winds and carried to the sea with a great stream of other insects to be "buried in the Ocean, and Leave Nothing behind them but their Eggs." "The End of Nature in Giving Spiders this way Of flying Which though we have found in the Corollary to be their Pleasure and Recreation, yet we think a Greater end is at last their Destruction."[26] The "Greater end" of the pleasing rise was eventual destruction.

The spider's nature made him worthy of this fate. At first appearance "no one is more wonderful than the Spider especially with Respect to their sagacity and admirable way of working." Its maneuvers were "truly very Pretty." But the inner nature of the spider warranted a violent burial at sea, for in essence it was "the Corrupting Nauseousness of our Air." Were spiders in any number to die inland in winter, the spring sun would revive "those nauseous vapours of which they are made up."[27] To prevent them from smelling up the country they were taught to rise and then destroyed.

Edwards here dwelt somewhat pathetically on two themes which sound again more stridently through the "Diary": a pleasurable ascent ends in destruction, and nauseousness lies beneath the pretty appearances. In the "Diary" Jonathan firmly renounced the pleasures of rising as he saw that pride led to destruction. His schemes to achieve eminence in the world had to be abandoned in favor of a life devoted wholly to religion. A loathing of his own vileness also came to obsess him. Later he spoke of sensuality as pollution. "How sensual you have been!" he told one audience. "Are there not some here that have debased themselves below the dignity of human nature by wallowing in sensual filthiness, as swine in the mire, or as filthy vermin feeding with delight on rotten carrion?"[28] "Of Insects" suggests that Jonathan's conscience was already disturbing his complacency in prideful achievement and that the underside of the compulsive perfectionism Timothy implanted was a fear of concealed filth.

Another portentous theme appeared in the early writings. Comparing spiders to humans, Edwards said, "the soul in the brain immediately Percieves when any of those little nervous strings that Proceed from it are in the Least Jarrd by External things." In the essay on the material soul, he asked facetiously if the soul is "a number of Long fine strings reaching from the head to the foot." The image of strings suggests how delicately responsive was his nervous system and how easily jarred. When the spiders were jarred in the course of the experiments, they spun a web and drifted off. The material soul was less mobile, and the main point of the essay concerned the discomforts it suffered "when the Coffin Gives way" and "the earth will fall in and Crush it." Or more excruciating, when other souls were buried in the same grave, they "Quarril for the highest place." "I would know whether I must Quit my dear head if a Superior Soul Comes in the way." When twenty or thirty souls occupied the spot, "the undergoing so much hard Ship and being deprived of the body at Last will make them ill temper'd."[29]

The satirical portrayal of a discontented, nervous soul, growing ill-tempered as it struggled for a place in the narrow confines of the grave, suggests some of the contrasting pleasures of Edwards' famous booth in the woods. The large family of girls, the guests, the students, and the watchful, demanding eyes of Timothy left little room in the house for peaceful worship. With his boyhood friends, Jonathan built a "booth in a swamp, in a very retired spot, for a place of prayer. And besides, I had particular secret places of my own in the woods, where I used to retire myself."[30] Personal relations all too easily jarred "the little nervous strings" proceeding from his brain, and Edwards struggled hard for mastery of his responses. His diary discloses that he suffered particularly from a "disposition to chide and fret." His own overweening conscience inclined him to snap at others' weaknesses and "to manifest my own dislike and scorn."[31] He eventually decided he could permit himself no evil speaking, not even that which he once thought to be righteous reproof. The dangers of slander or undue vehemence were all too apparent. Even public worship tried him, until by concerted effort he learned to overcome his impatience.[32] Throughout his life he often walked in the fields or rode in the woods, where alone under the sky he more easily composed his soul and made peace with God.

In sum, these early writings confirm to some extent and elaborate the previous speculations on the emotional import of Edwards' early life:

1) For a time anyway, Jonathan aspired to fulfill family expectations through his philosophic writings.

2) The pleasure and excitement of rising was counter-balanced by a fear of destruction because of unworthiness or inward filthiness.

3) The tendency to chide and fret made close personal relations uncomfortable.

III

Edwards' conversion, which drew on all of these themes, occurred over a period of years in his early manhood. Near the end of his college days, a case of pleurisy brought him "nigh to the grave" and shook him "over the pit of hell." After that he grew steadily more uneasy about religion, going through "great and violent inward struggles" until he finally broke off "all ways of known outward sin." The "inward struggles and conflicts, and selfreflections" continued, and he made "seeking my salvation the main business of my life" but still did not consider himself converted.[33] Meanwhile he was studying theology in New Haven and preparing to take a temporary pulpit in New York City.

Sometime in his eighteenth or nineteenth year began a series of experiences which he later believed to be gracious. Two slightly differing accounts survive. Edwards wrote the *Personal Narrative* nearly twenty years later, after the first revivals in Northampton. What remains of the "Diary" begins in December of 1722 when he was in New York City and when he had reason to believe grace had already touched him. It records his struggles with sin and his further experiences with grace.

In the "Diary" Edwards charted his cycles of spiritual decay and recovery, the movement from spiritual dullness to the exhilarating moments of rededication. On Saturday, January 12, 1723, in the morning, he enjoyed one of the seasons of grace, and the comment he wrote directly afterwards indicates the nature of the experience. The paramount issue was renunciation of self and complete surrender to God.

I have this day, solemnly renewed by baptismal covenant and self-dedication, which I renewed, when I was taken into the communion of the church. I have been before God, and have given myself, all that I am, and have, to God; so that I am not, in any respect, my own. I can challenge no right in this understanding, this will, these affections, which are in me. Neither have I any right to this body, or any of its members—no right to this tongue, these hands, these feet; no right to these senses, these eyes, these ears, this smell, or this taste. I have given myself clear away, and have not retained any thing, as my own. I gave them to God, in my baptism, and I have been this morning to him, and told him, that I gave myself *wholly* to him. I have given every power to him; so that for the future, I'll challenge no right in myself, in no respect whatever.[34]

Edwards felt compelled to offer more than perfect obedience to God. He searched his soul to be sure nothing was left for himself; everything was given to God, his body and all its senses, all his powers, all enjoyments, the credit for all his efforts, the right to complain or rest, the right to seek anything for himself. He could not permit himself to be "in any way proud." At issue in conversion was the willingness to obliterate selfishness and give up all to God. During the controversy over admission to communion in North-ampton, he summarized in a public profession what was expected of saints and put this surrender and the accompanying obedience at the heart. The profession read in the whole:

I hope, I truly find in my heart a willingness to comply with all the commandments of God, which require me to give up myself wholly to Him, and to serve Him with my body and my spirit; and do accordingly now promise to walk in a way of obedience to all the commandments of God, as long as I live.[35]

The *Personal Narrative* shifted the stress somewhat to emphasize Edwards' reconciliation with the doctrine of "God's sovereignty, in choosing whom he would to eternal life, and rejecting whom he pleased, leaving them eternally to perish, and be everlasting tormented in Hell." Edwards did not con-sciously experience the intense fear of divine wrath which usually preceded conversion. He thought his "great and violent inward struggles" were not properly called terror, but as these comments reveal, the fear of punishment was there, probably buried too deep to be felt. The doctrine of election "used to appear like a horrible doctrine," and filled his mind with objections from his childhood up.[36]

For no discernible reason, Edwards suddenly became convinced of God's justice in election. Objections ceased and he rested easy in assurance of divine justice. In connection with this alteration, he tells of his first experience with "that sort of inward, sweet delight in God and divine things" that he later called grace. It came as he read the passage in Scripture saying, "Now unto the King eternal, immortal, and invisible, the only wise God, be honor and glory for ever and ever, Amen." As he read these words, there diffused through his soul "a sense of the glory of the Divine Being; a new sense quite different from any thing I ever experienced before."[37] As far as Edwards could tell that was the moment of his conversion, and reconciliation with divine power was the critical issue. After that, the thunder that had once terrified aroused sweet contemplations of God's glory.

The two accounts of the experience with grace are easily reconciled, for they have in common a submission to God. The "Diary" stresses the surrender of self and renunciation of pride. The *Personal Narrative* emphasizes the discovery of beauty in God's sovereign right to punish. Both forms of submission can be seen as aspects of a single experience, especially if one remembers how some common vicissitudes of childhood could prepare the way for this very combination. While engaged in passionate rivalry with his father for the love of his mother, a boy imagines himself rising in pride and power to displace his father, thereby evoking paternal wrath. Peace negotiations require both the renunciation of pride and acceptance of the father's superior power, a double surrender morally symmetrical with the two issues in Edwards' conversion.[38]

Edwards' pride could easily have awakened these old memories and their attached apprehensions because his ambition was tied so closely to intellectual achievement, which was also his father's source of pride and a form of accomplishment his mother prized. In seeking to excel as a scholar he inevitably outdid his father and won the favor of his mother. The audacity of the act, though wholly symbolic and unconscious, released the fears which Timothy's compulsive demands and the implicit threats of destruction had formed in Jonathan's conscience. The "torments of hell" included the terror the Edwards children felt toward the imminent possibility of hurting and being hurt by their loving, profoundly fragile, and threatening father. In yielding all to God, Jonathan disclaimed the old rivalry, again symbolically and unconsciously, and placated his archaic fears. The danger of rising to destruction was averted.

Edwards wanted God to sanctify every level of his being, down to the deepest, and the glory of conversion was the comprehensive transformation it wrought. Its power lay in the affinity between theological notions and intimate personal tensions. In conversion Jonathan reconciled himself to God and universal being but the religious symbols also formed bonds with long forgotten memories and with buried conflicts too explosive for consciousness to touch. Conversion resolved tensions along the full range of experience. Until that moment God was the sovereign who judged and punished, shaking men over the pit until they obeyed. The relationship was one of king to subject. As the new "sense of the glory of the Divine Being" came over Edwards upon reading the first epistle to Timothy, he felt a happy yearning to enjoy God, to "be rapt up to him in heaven" and to be "swallowed up in him forever." He prayed "In a manner quite different" from before and "with a new sort of affection." The beauty and loveliness of Christ instead of the fierce power of God impressed his mind. All of Canticles occupied him and especially the verse, "I am the Rose of Sharon, and the Lily of the valleys."

These symbols and the whole perception of the divine was softer, warmer, more sensuous.[39] The new relationship was one of lovers. At times the tone was frankly sexual. Some passages in the *Personal Narrative* overflow with a lover's passion.

The inward ardor of my soul, seemed to be hindered and pent up, and could not freely flame out as it would. I used often to think, how in heaven this principle should freely and fully vent and express itself. Heaven appeared exceedingly delightful, as a world of love; and that all happiness consisted in living in pure, humble, heavenly, divine love.[40]

Or in a different mode: "My heart panted after this, to lie low before God, as in the dust; that I might be nothing, and that God might be ALL, that I might become as a little child."[41] One of the rewards of conversion was that feelings otherwise tightly suppressed flowed freely toward God.

The venting of emotion was possible because vileness was changed to sweetness. The nauseousness of the spider was banished. Whereas sensuality had been and under that name was still described as filth and defilement, the new "delights" were of a "pure, soul-animating and refreshing nature." The happiness of heaven where the inward ardor could "freely flame out" consisted "in pure, humble, heavenly, divine love." The "ravishingly lovely" beauty of holiness was "far purer than any thing here upon earth"; everything else was "mire and defilement" in comparison.[42] In grace emotions were sweet and calm and flowed freely without polluting. Sensuality was purely joyous.

One final issue came to resolution during conversion. Edwards overcame, partially at least, his uneasiness among people. His disposition to chide and fret had disturbed his personal relations, and he had found peace most easily in solitude. In conversion he still envisioned himself "alone in the mountains, or some solitary wilderness, far from all mankind, sweetly conversing with Christ, and wrapt and swallowed up in God." But loving and even ardent relations with other Christians were possible. Another of his poetic visions pictured the soul of a true Christian as "a little white flower" standing "peacefully and lovingly, in the midst of other flowers round about." In New York he drew very close to the two saintly people with whom he lived and delighted in long intimate discussions about heaven and holiness.[43]

Edwards' social discomforts did not disappear, for his "heart was knit in affection" only "to those, in whom were appearances of true piety." Indeed he "could bear the thoughts of no other companions, but such as were holy, and the disciples of the blessed Jesus." He disliked visiting among his parishioners where small talk of the world was a necessity. Instead he invited them to his study where he could keep the discussion on religion. The woman he married, Sarah Pierrepont, had been widely reputed for her piety, and even before he met her Edwards wrote a tribute to her "wonderful sweetness" and "singular purity."[44] He could enjoy the intimacies of marriage and friendship only with those whom grace had sanctified, but at least conversion afforded that measure of untroubled intercourse.

IV

The happy visitations of grace continued during his stay in New York and into the following summer spent at his father's house. By the fall of 1723 he had agreed to settle in Bolton, a new town not far from East Windsor, but before his installation, a tutorship opened at Yale, and Edwards persuaded Bolton to release him. From June of 1724, after a winter of private study, until September of 1726, he was the senior tutor and acting Rector, with responsibility to discipline the students as well as to instruct them. After one week on the job, "despondencies, fears, perplexities, multitudes of cares, and distractions of mind" weighed him down and convinced him "of the troublesomeness and vexation of the world." For the three years of his tutorship he was in a "low, sunk estate and condition, miserably senseless" about "spiritual things."[45] The only respite came in the fall of 1725 when he fell ill at North Haven on his way home and his mother came to nurse him.

For many reasons Edwards welcomed the offer which came in 1725 to assist aging Grandfather Stoddard in Northampton. The new position took him away from Yale, and it made him heir-apparent to Solomon Stoddard's immense power. Nothing could have thrilled his mother more. The summer following his ordination, Edwards married Sarah Pierrepont, whose piety he had admired from afar and whose life in the Northampton parsonage bore out the promise of her early godliness and aristocratic upbringing. She was deeply devoted to her husband—one of her deepest sorrows was to displease "Mr. Edwards"—and her saintliness fully matched his own.[46] A daughter, the first of eleven children, was born in 1728.

Solomon Stoddard died in 1729 and Edwards became chief pastor. He seems never to have regretted the subordination of his youthful ambitions to be a natural philosopher. A ministerial career was perfectly suited to the religious identity formed in conversion. In the pulpit the lonely quest for salvation entered onto a broad stage. His office permitted him to talk freely of God's wrath, of human defilement, and of the exquisite joys of grace. Speaking objectively as pastor, Edwards exposed his soul publicly as he could never do privately. The secret yearnings and dread so long stored in the recesses of his heart became the bread and wine of an open communion with the world. Even the disposition to chide and rebuke was dignified to a duty. When he admonished, he spoke for God, expressing the righteous wrath of a Holy Father, commanding rather than being commanded, pure instead of vile, terrifying rather than being terrified. And the whole was sanctified and purged of pride because done for God and not for self.

The congregation responded to his quiet, intense preaching. From time to time under Stoddard, revivals had brought unusually large numbers into the Church. Five years after Edwards became pastor, the town experienced a livelier concern with religion than any known before. Two sudden deaths contributed to "the solemnizing of the spirits" of the young, and a controversy over Arminianism set many to asking the true way of salvation. Before long "among old and young, and from highest to the Lowest; all seemed to be siezed with a deep concern about their Eternal salvation."[47] The concern spread from town to town until churches all up and down the Connecticut Valley were reporting revivals. The suicide of Edwards' Uncle Hawley in a fit of melancholy over his state slowed the work, but five years later in 1740, when Whitefield visited New England, Northampton and other towns were ripe. The concern spread more widely than ever, engaging thousands of souls this time, and Edwards was in great demand as a preacher and counselor.

Edwards identified these conversions as being of the same species as his own. People felt the same "utter helplessness, and Insufficiency for themselves, and their Exceeding wickedness and Guiltiness in the sight of God," each one considering himself worse than all others just as he had. They were eventually brought to "a Lively sense of the Excellency of Jesus Christ" and "to have their Hearts filled with Love to God and Christ, and a disposition to Lie in the dust before him." In the process of conversion people were also "brought off from their Inordinate Engagedness after the world," though obviously in different ways from Edwards' renunciation of achievement as a philosopher. The same love for others and concern for their souls, the same heightened sense of personal wickedness, the same variations in intensity of devotion all linked the common experience to Edwards' conversion.[48]

His personal influence, of course, does not begin to explain the prevalence of the revivals. All over New England people underwent rebirth in the period of a few years. They followed Edwards, or others like him, because they were ready, not because he personally overpowered them. Something common to all, some prevailing strain on their institutions, some pressure in the culture prepared people for the new life he urged upon them. They listened because the truth of his experience was also the truth of theirs.

I have treated the consciousness of this period at length elsewhere, but even in outline the parallels with Edwards can be seen.[49] In Edwards' psyche the most serious conflict leading to conversion was the tension between prideful ambition and the fear of suffering God's wrath for indulging in pride. Conditions in New England in the early eighteenth century put large segments of the population in a similar predicament. The paramount fact of the common life after 1700 was rapid expansion—in population, in the number of new settlements, in commercial opportunities and involvements, and in the economic horizons of the ordinary man. In Connecticut, for example, population grew nearly five times as fast in the thirty years after

1700 as in the thirty years before; the number of new towns settled doubled; the number of debt cases per capita—a measure of increasing prosperity and commercial growth—increased five times.

The most important and obvious effect on most lives was to broaden economic opportunities. The new towns offered a host of tantalizing possibilities for incipient merchants. The growing markets outside New England, in Newfoundland and Halifax, in the West Indies, and in Europe, along with the expanding needs of the prospering fishing fleet provided growing outlets for farmers, and the rapid growth of population made speculation in new land very enticing. These developments permitted young men to dream dreams utterly unfeasible earlier. New England had visited a few men with prosperity from the beginning, but very few ordinary men could hope for more than a decent living. William Edwards, for example, had carried on his trade without making great advances. Richard had fared better, building on his father's business, but in the seventeenth century he was exceptionally fortunate. Not everyone could elevate himself in the eighteenth century either, but new opportunities increased the incidence of success. Examples multiplied of small storekeepers who became wealthy merchants and of thrifty farmers who doubled their estates through speculation. By later standards the stakes were small, but the prospects dazzled the first generation of the new century.

Expansion stimulated the desire to rise in the world and yet implicitly threatened destruction, the very ambivalence prominent in Edwards' life. Commercial and agricultural expansion depended heavily on risk-laden speculations: natural disasters, debt foreclosures, and unforeseen calamities of various kinds could wipe out farmers and traders. The psychic hazards were as great as the economic ones. Puritan preachers urged men to follow their callings industriously and to rise through their enterprise. But they condemned men for setting their hearts on wealth and making it their god. The increasing luxury of the eighteenth century and its "Cursed Hunger of Riches" evoked the most bitter indictments. A man never knew exactly where he stood. At one moment he rested in the assurance of his virtuous diligence and of the prosperity heaven had bestowed. At the next a warning from the pulpit started fears that the lust for gold had hopelessly corrupted his soul. Men found themselves in a dilemma comparable to the plight of Robert Keayne, a Boston merchant of the seventeenth century. Keayne prospered in Boston and maintained a respectable reputation until he was accused of unfair dealing and reprimanded in the courts. The confrontation with his guilt put him in fear for his salvation. In hopes of recovering his peace of mind, Keayne wrote an interminable testament justifying his conduct.[50] In the seventeenth century distress like his hung over the few who prospered; in the eighteenth century economic expansion exposed the entire population to these unsettling apprehensions.

Conflicts with authority magnified the guilt and fears of the ambitious.

Aspiring men fought with established authority at every level of government, in the town, in the church, and in the colonial government. With innumerable variations, involving large and small enterprises, the pattern repeated itself: ambitious men in pursuit of wealth broke through conventional restrictions and clashed with authorities bent on preserving order. The conflicts were psychically debilitating because the magistracy and ministry were thought to rule by virtue of divine investiture. Authority had a counterpart in individual consciences, and when men resisted they fought against themselves. Opposition, however well justified, partook of sinful rebellion.

Another theme in Edwards' life, his prickly relations with associates, appears in the social record also. New Englanders were notoriously litigious, quick to criticize, to sue, or to ask the church to censure. Economic expansion increased the occasions for misunderstandings and ill feeling. The competition for land and trade and for every conceivable economic advantage made enemies of former friends. Every debt case, for example, represented a dispute. A creditor always preferred to settle privately to avoid court costs. Only when prolonged appeals failed did he sue. The storekeeper or wealthy farmer grew exasperated at the delays in payment; the debtor for his part felt the terms unjust, the request for payment over-hasty, or the creditor unsympathetic. The fivefold increase in debt cases per capita in Connecticut between 1700 and 1730 represented at least as large an increase in personal quarrels arising for economic reasons.

The whole society suffered from a painful confusion of identity. People were taught to work at their earthly callings and to seek wealth; but one's business had to remain subservient to religion and to function within the bounds of seventeenth-century institutions. The opportunities constantly tempted people to overstep both boundaries, thereby evoking the wrath of the powerful men who ruled society. Even relations with neighbors deteriorated as expansion multiplied the occasions for hard feelings. At some indeterminate point social values and institutions stopped supporting the man who placed his confidence in worldly success and instead obstructed and condemned his actions. The pleasurable rise which prosperity afforded carried one at last to destruction.

A widespread uneasiness put people "upon Enquiring, with concern and Engagedness of mind, what was the way of salvation, and what were the Terms of our acceptance with God."[51] The revival preachers confronted their audience with the darkest possible view of their sins and hopeless future. They had fought against God, were filled with pride and vileness, and were worthy of unending torment in the pit of hell. This frank exposure of their dark inward side gave people the courage to bring their sins and insecurity to the surface. The man in the pulpit assuring them that he understood their guilt and the presence of others publicly manifesting their anguish provided communal support for the agonizing confrontation.

The preachers required total humiliation and submission before promising peace. The only hope for reconciliation with God was to confess to utter helplessness and to depend wholly on his grace. For those who heard, moral rectitude and a measure of prosperity suddenly furnished neither peace in this world nor a promise of God's favor in the world to come. Men stood naked under the heavens, helplessly exposed to divine wrath. Edwards noticed people passing from despair to passivity as they recognized the impossibility of earning salvation and gave themselves up to be damned or saved at God's pleasure. Then almost surprisingly hope revived. The good news of the Gospel was heard as if for the first time. The gift of grace seemed sufficient to redeem, and the convert rejoiced in new confidence, founded now on God's loving mercy. They were brought to a "Lively sense of the Excellency of Jesus Christ" and "of the Truth of the Gospel." The sense of sin continued and increased, but now contrition was combined with love and joy.[52] Men felt that they were saved.

With a new identity founded in God's gracious love, converted men renounced their former sources of confidence. The world's wealth no longer appeared so enticing. Edwards noted that in Northampton "People are brought off from Inordinate Engagedness after the World, and have been Ready to Run into the other Extreme of Too much neglecting their worldly Business and to mind nothing but Religion." People seemed to "dread their former Extravagances" and wanted to strip themselves of worldly luxury.[53] After the frenetic itinerant James Davenport urged a New London audience to discard their wigs, fine clothing, and worldly books, the people piled their possessions in a public place and burned them.

Conversion also relieved tensions with neighbors and with authority. The infusion of God's love sweetened all personal relations. "Persons are soon brought to have done with their old Quarrels: Contention and Intermeddling with other mens matters seems to be dead amongst us," Edwards wrote. He cited a number of parishes where old contentions vanished and the congregation was "universally united in hearty affection to their minister." In 1735 his own people "Generally seem to be united in dear Love, and affection one to another," and he "never saw the Christian spirit in Love to Enemies so Exemplified, in all my life." Indeed Northampton "never was so full of love, nor so full of distress as it has Lately been."[54] He composed a covenant to which his congregation subscribed in 1742, pledging themselves not to "overreach or defraud" their neighbors, or "wilfully or negligently" to default on their honest debts. They promised not to "feed a spirit of bitterness, ill will, or secret grudge," and in the management of public affairs not to let private interest and worldly gain lead them into "unchristian inveighings, reproachings, bitter reflectings, judging and ridiculing," but do everything with "christian humility, gentleness, quietness and love.[55]

The results of the revival deeply gratified Edwards. A barely suppressed elation runs throughout *A Faithful Narrative of the Surprising Work of God*, the essay in which he described the love of God and men which came over

Northampton in 1735. The Spirit of God appeared to be creating an entire society of saintly men, submissive to God and exquisitely sensitive to religion, a society which confirmed and supported the identity Edwards had assumed in his own conversion. The resonance between Edwards and his people did not continue as perfect harmony. Eventually he demanded more saintliness than they could muster, and his congregation voted 200 to 23 to dismiss him. But for more than a decade, while his words shaped the innermost lives of the reborn, his heart and theirs were as one.

V

Edwards' influence arose from the emotional congruities of his life and his people's; both felt a tension between the yearning to rise in the world and the fear of being destroyed for their pride. In a time of newly opened possibilities for success, heightened aspirations ineluctably entangled men in conflicts with established institutions and values. Widespread contention filled people with guilt, just as the stresses in Edwards' life brought him to an obsession with his unworthiness. The conflict might have been resolved by rationalizing self-interest or by justifying the right to resist authority, and many Americans followed that very course. Edwards, however, admitted his utter sinfulness, submitted all to God, and was rewarded with love, joy, and peace. The conversion of thousands during the Awakening signified the general applicability of Edwards' personal solution to the common problem and the implicit acceptance of his leadership.

The sources of pride and guilt doubtlessly varied. Edwards' intellectual ambitions and the peculiar combination of enveloping love, moral precision, and fear in his father were unique. Strictly personal circumstances could have generated pride and guilt in other lives as well. But the susceptibility to revival preaching in a large proportion of the population, more than chance can account for, is a puzzling fact. Apart from Providence, which can never be ruled out, general social conditions offer the most plausible explanation. The widening economic opportunities of the early eighteenth century, pressing men against rulers, against established institutions like town and church, and against the moral restrictions on covetousness, seem to be the most likely sources of the prevailing distress. Circumstances converged to generate tensions whose psychological structure happened to coincide with that which life in the Edwards' household formed in Jonathan.

Insofar as this analysis is convincing, it confirms Erikson's conception of leadership as the application of the leader's personal identity resolution to the needs of his age. Anyone approaching the problem of leadership, of course, must proceed with humility. Because the influence of one person on another works along subterranean psychological channels, the difficulties in arriving at uncontestable conclusions are immense. The explanation for the power of

Joseph McCarthy in the fifties remains conjectural, even when responses from actual participants are still available. But if we are not to abandon all efforts in despair, Erikson's model merits attention. Without claiming scientific certainty for its conclusions, it provides a frame within which to draw together the remaining evidence and to reconstruct lives as imaginatively and as completely as possible.

One virtue of Erikson's work is the incorporation of the personal emotional struggles of which our lives are composed into a coherent system of historical analysis. Attempts to make history "human," to "breathe life" into it, so often lead only to anecdotes or colorful quotations. Erikson's vigorous and well-articulated treatment of human feeling in the framework of his model of leadership makes the moral vicissitudes of life a central component of fundamental historical processes. He helps the historian to describe the bearing of emotions and will as coherently as the impact of the impersonal economic and social forces which once threatened to eliminate personality from historical writing altogether. This entrenchment in an analytical structure is the best assurance possible that personality will be given its due.

It should be apparent that Erikson's model does not apply to every kind of leadership. Most authorities operate within conventions which assure a measure of obedience apart from any personal qualities, and for the most part social forms contain people's anxieties without any extraordinary direction from a gifted man. But at those critical junctures where old values fail and a new order is coming, the way is open for a leader of greater charisma. Then the man of unusual courage and integrity, who successfully contends with the sufferings, self-doubts, and hopes of his time, may, more than we have imagined, exert an influence on the course of events.

NOTES

1. Erik H. Erikson, *Young Man Luther: A Study in Psychoanalysis and History*, Austen Riggs Monograph No. 4 (New York, 1958).

2. Erik H. Erikson, *Childhood and Society*, 2nd ed. (New York, 1963), p. 261. Erikson also discusses identity in "Identity and the Life Cycle: Selected Papers by Erik H. Erikson," *Psychological Issues*, I (1959), and in Richard I. Evans, *Dialogue with Erik Erikson* (New York, 1967).

3. I give an example of how psychoanalysis can illuminate incidents from adult life in "On the Uses of Psychology: Conflict and Conciliation in Benjamin Franklin," *History and Theory*, V (1966), 225–240.

4. Three biographies of Edwards' life are useful for different purposes. Ola Elizabeth Winslow, *Jonathan Edwards, 1703–1758: A Biography* (New York, 1940), places Edwards in his social setting. Perry Miller, *Jonathan Edwards* (New York, 1949), is a brilliant interpretation of Edwards' thought with suggestive comments on the social structure in the Connecticut Valley. S. E. Dwight, *The Life of President Edwards* (New York, 1830), reprints much of the source material.

5. Dwight, *Edwards*, pp. 16, 18.

6. Jonathan Edwards to Timothy Edwards, Nov. 1, 1720; fragment of a letter from Timothy Edwards to Mrs. Mix. Both are in the Andover collection now on deposit at the Edwin J. Beinecke Library at Yale. I am grateful to Andover-Newton Theological Seminary for permission to refer to this letter and also to Miss Marjorie Wynne of the Beinecke Library for giving me access to it.

7. Quoted in Winslow, *Edwards*, p. 16.

8. Quoted in Ibid., p. 21.

9. Quoted in Ibid., p. 22.

10. Quoted in Miller, *Edwards*, p. 52.

11. Winslow, *Edwards*, p. 41.

12. From the "Diary," in Dwight, *Edwards*, p. 86.

13. Ibid., pp. 81–83.

14. Winslow, *Edwards*, pp. 41, 42.

15. Ibid., p. 43.

16. Dwight, *Edwards*, p. 14; Winslow, *Edwards*, p. 41.

17. Quoted in Winslow, *Edwards*, p. 18.

18. Dwight, *Edwards*, p. 14.

19. Winslow, *Edwards*, p. 36...

20. Ibid.

21. Dwight, *Edwards*, p. 21.

22. *Jonathan Edwards: Representative Selections, with Introduction, Bibliography, and Notes*, ed. Clarence H. Faust and Thomas H. Johnson, rev. ed. (New York, 1962), p. 11.

23. The intended title page is reprinted in Dwight, *Edwards*, p. 664.

24. From the "Notes on Natural Science," reprinted in Dwight, *Edwards*, p. 702.

25. *Representative Selections*, pp. 3, 6, 7.

26. Ibid., pp. 10, 8.

27. Ibid., pp. 3, 10.

28. *The Works of President Edwards, in Four Volumes* (New York, n.d.), IV, 234.

29. *Representative Selections*, pp. 5, 11, 12.

30. Ibid., p. 57.

31. Dwight, *Edwards*, pp. 84–85.

32. Ibid., pp. 85, 88, 89, 90, 94.

33. *Representative Selections*, pp. 57, 58.

34. Dwight, *Edwards*, pp. 78–79.

35. *Works*, I, 202.

36. *Representative Selections*, p. 58.

37. Ibid., p. 59.

38. A more elaborate explication of Edwards' conversion and the psychoanalytic elements involved may be found in Richard L. Bushman, "Jonathan Edwards and Puritan Consciousness," *Journal for the Scientific Study of Religion*, V (1966), 383–396.

39. *Representative Selections*, pp. 59, 60.

40. Ibid., p. 63.

41. Ibid., pp. 63–64.

42. Ibid., pp. 62, 63.

43. Ibid., pp. 60, 63, 64, 65.

44. Ibid., pp. 64, 65.

45. Dwight, *Edwards*, pp. 106, 103.

46. Ibid., pp. 171–172.

47. *Representative Selections*, pp. 74, 75.

48. Ibid., pp. 77, 78.

49. Richard L. Bushman, *From Puritan to Yankee: Character and the Social Order in Connecticut, 1690–1765* (Cambridge, Mass.: 1967).

50. Bernard Bailyn, "The Apologia of Robert Keayne," *William and Mary Quarterly*, 3d ser., VII (1950), 568–587.

51. *Representative Selections*, p. 74.

52. Ibid., pp. 77, 78.

53. Ibid., pp. 76, 77.

54. Ibid., pp. 76–78.

55. Dwight, *Edwards*, pp. 165–167.

3

THE AMERICAN REVOLUTION
The Ideology and Psychology of National Liberation

EDWIN G. BURROWS AND MICHAEL WALLACE

Revolution means fundamental change, and historians and political scientists alike find intriguing the question why people resort to such change when they do. The American Revolution, though carrying its measure of social upheaval, was preeminently a political struggle—what we in more recent times would call a war of national liberation. Because it was, as Edwin G. Burrows and Michael Wallace point out, we must see it as an ideological and psychological matter combined, "a two fold event—on the one hand a conscious, calculated rejection of constraining ideology in favor of one that permits and compels national autonomy, and on the other an inner, emotional revulsion against colonial subjection and inferiority." Both these elements, they contend, found expression in the rhetoric of the pre-Revolutionary debate between British and American spokesmen and among Americans—particularly in the use of the "family" or the parent-child metaphor. King and Parliament according to this conceptual scheme were parents to the empire, the colonies submitting to that authority like children in the dependence they in truth exhibited for several generations.

In the sections that set the stage for the excerpt below, Burrows and Wallace make clear that early modern English political theory—as evidenced in the influential writings of Sir Robert Filmer—had indeed justified the fatherly role of monarchy in terms of the childlike capacities of subjects. In the late seventeenth century, however, this apology for the stern rule of the Stuarts gave way to the "contractualist" theory of John Locke in his *Second Treatise on Government* (1690): the basis for governmental authority was not parental prerogative but a contract with the governed. The king might remain a "father," but his rule was justified only so long as he met the needs and fulfilled the expectations of his subjects.

One does not draw the connection between political theory and practical affairs easily, but Burrows and Wallace make a highly interesting case that Locke's contract theory of political rights and obligations carried appeal because of actual changes in child-rearing patterns. Another of Locke's treatises, this one containing *Thoughts*

Reprinted with permission from *Perspectives in American History* 6 (1972):266–303. This section of the essay originally appeared as "The Psychology of Revolution and Repression."

Concerning Education (1693), had called for parenting practices that would bring young people to a sense of disciplined self-reliance; his ideas enjoyed wide currency in the 1720s and 1730s, especially among Americans during a time when they—witness the experience of Jonathan Edwards—faced expanding opportunities and an increasingly diverse socioeconomic order. Sensing these changes and determined to prepare their children for them, American parents therefore raised children who were independent enough to be equal to the challenge. Supporting this view is the work of Philip Greven, who in *Four Generations* (1970) found considerable differences in feelings of autonomy between the Revolutionary generation and its immediate forebears. In the 1770s, therefore, two lines crossed. Colonial Americans had developed the psychological basis for personal independence; British policies seemed the wrongful exactions of a political "parent."

Burrows and Wallace offer a skillful psychological analysis that weaves together political ideology, its language or symbols, and the social or everyday reasons why that language—in the context of constitutional crisis—could call for a new departure. "The assumption that children have a natural right to protest parental misconduct squared both with contractualist doctrine and with practical expectations," they conclude in a passage preceding the selection below. Or as Thomas Paine asked in his famous pamphlet *Common Sense*, "Is it in the interest of a man to be a boy all his life?"

IN TRACING the career of the parent-child analogy from a patriarchalist to a contractualist device we have as yet made no mention of the obvious transformation that occurred along the way in its affective content. Where the advocates of divine right and nonresistance had woven the analogy into their polemics with analytical deliberation, the contractualists of the Revolutionary era, Englishmen and Americans alike, seemed to take it as a kind of dramatic script that somehow required the colonists to speak the lines of rebellious children while the mother country spoke the lines of an aggrieved parent. And where the former had spun out the analogy with academic detachment, the latter turned it into a vehicle for the expression of vivid emotion. There remained the same intense concern to achieve ideological justification by reference to the abstract rights and duties of parents and children, but now, in the decade after 1765, the old language was also being used to convey strong feelings and sentiments—love, hate, anxiety, fear, anger. When Americans decried "a parent red with the blood of her children" and Englishmen denounced the colonists as "parricides" they were adding an entirely new dimension to the analogical tradition.[1]

This dimension irresistibly invites further exploration, for it appears to contain important clues to the psychological as well as ideological processes of the Revolution. Emotion, after all, is raw material for psychological inquiry, and if we could use the new, affective content of analogical thought for such an inquiry we might gain fresh insight into a wide range of problems that continue to vex students of the Revolution—why, for example, Americans accepted colonial dependency for so long then threw it off so suddenly, what distinguished rebels from Tories, why England fought to maintain imperial supremacy when at least some Englishmen recognized that the economic advantages of empire could be preserved without direct political control.

At the same time, however, there are treacherous difficulties that lie in the path of the historian who would pursue the psychological implications of the parent-child analogy. Psychology, it need hardly be said, is preeminently a science attuned to individuals; the indiscriminate application of its concepts and methodologies to collectivities (groups, nations, institutions, movements) can lead and has led to all manner of foolishness. Psychology, too is a science oriented to the living; by any reasonable clinical standards we are unlikely to recover sufficient data for the rigorous analysis of more than a handful of individuals in the past, to say nothing of the complexities that arise when ideas about the human mind and personality derived in one socio-historical context are brought to bear in another. To attempt, therefore, to offer any useful observations on the psychology of historical collectivities seems a difficult, perhaps impossible, task.

Yet this is precisely what we shall attempt to do in the remainder of this essay. We have no illusions about the perils of such an undertaking, but neither do we doubt that without a first, tentative exploration of the subject many fundamental questions about the nature and causes of the American Revolution will remain forever beyond the reach of historical understanding. If nothing else, the several hypotheses we will proceed to develop here can serve as the points of departure for further, and long overdue, discussion and investigation.

Let us begin by returning to the proposition that the analogy between parental and imperial authority had emotive as well as ideological significance in the Revolution. The first thing we are obliged to recognize is that the emotions it conveyed were those of collectivities rather than individuals—England was an injured and outraged "parent," the colonies were abused and angry "children." But England, after all, was not a parent, nor even composed entirely of parents, and the colonies were not children, nor composed entirely of children. Merely because large numbers of Englishmen and Americans indulged in this anthropopathic rhetoric—ascribing human feelings and sentiments to nonhuman entities—in no way entitles us to do likewise. It would be futile and foolhardy to contend, for example, that their analogical language makes the Revolution a gigantic oedipal struggle or perhaps a massive adolescent uprising; we want to find out what was going on in the minds of real people, and that is simply impossible to achieve by fanciful interpretations of what transpires in the fictitious "minds" of groups.

Suppose, on the other hand, we stipulate from the outset that the terms "mother country" and "child colony" must be read as purely symbolic formulations, representing the common wisdom among a substantial body of individuals about the nature and character of the groups to which they belong. We are then in a much better position to say something of value about the psychologies of those individuals, for we can draw, not on metaphysical notions of the "collective unconscious," but rather on the impressive work done in recent years on the way in which symbolic forms precede and shape conscious thought. Michael Walzer, for one, has observed that symbolization is essential to the sense of group distinctiveness because the union of men "has no palpable shape or substance; it must be personified before it can be seen, symbolized before it can be loved, imagined before it can be conceived."[2] Shared symbolic images bind otherwise discrete individuals together; they serve, as Kenneth Boulding puts it, as "the basic bond of any society, culture, subculture, or organization."[3] They may be created by solitary geniuses whose wordcraft works a "set of disconnected, unrealized private emotions" into "a public possession, a social fact."[4] Or symbols may be "a collective product, worked out by numberless men at many different levels of artistic and intellectual excellence over a long period of time."[5] But whatever their origin they become what Clifford Geertz calls "matrices for the creation of a collective conscience," and as such they provide an important insight into the way individuals think and feel about the groups of which they are part.[6]

Among the wide variety of symbolic devices that give coherence to a class or a party or a nation none is more familiar than personification, the metaphorical representation of the many as one. Uncle Sam, John Bull, Columbia, Britannia—each provides "a kind of rough summation or index of a vast complexity of images of roles and structures," and the characteristics routinely imparted to each contain major clues to what the members of the group believe to be their salient common characteristics.[7] Indeed, as Leonard Doob writes, "It would be foolhardy to assume that the personification of the nation is only a figure of speech. . . . Personification on the national level is usually so complete that it probably affords as good a basis for predicting national policy as personality traits on the level of the specific individual."[8] Similarly, the way one group personifies another—as rapacious Hun, avaricious Jew, or wild-eyed anarchist—provides an equally reliable guide to its behavior toward that group. And when Englishmen and Americans referred to England as the "parent" of colonial "children" they were cooperating in the preservation of a symbolic construct that can tell us much about their innermost conceptions of themselves and their relationship to one another.[9]

We can go still further: once a symbol has come into existence it becomes a social datum with a life and coercive authority of its own. On one level the symbol dictates behavior by shaping inarticulate assumptions and expectations, by enabling individuals "to grasp, formulate, and communicate social realities that elude the tempered language of science."[10] If Turkey was "the sick man of Europe," it did not matter that most Turks were perfectly healthy and "sickness" a concept that applies to organisms rather than states:

the metaphor stuck because it effectively encompassed and communicated a host of otherwise isolated and refractory impressions about the condition of a particular political system, and in so doing it exercised an imponderably great influence on the way foreign governments would deal with that system. And if the American colonies were England's "children," no matter that they contained a perfectly normal adult population and that "childhood" was an idea applicable only to humans: that symbol, too, commanded continuing attention because it caught the essence of a real but otherwise intangible relationship, and in so doing it would substantially influence the way Englishmen and Americans alike conceived of and responded to the possibility of separation.

On a deeper and more complex level, symbols govern behavior because they often become the objects of individual identification. The desecration of a flag, the assassination of a president, and even defeat in an international soccer match—each can provoke extraordinary exhibitions of rage, grief, and despair precisely because flags, presidents, and soccer teams, standing for things larger and more elusive than themselves, imperceptibly and unconsciously attract emotional attachments as much a part of the individual psyche as attachments to personal friends and possessions.[11] In the case of national symbols this process of identification can play so decisive a role in the formation of individual personality that Wilhelm Reich has described the "inclination to identify" as "the psychological basis of national narcissism, i.e., of the self-confidence that individual man derives from 'the greatness of the nation.' "[12] Attack the symbol of national unity and identity and you attack the identity of each and every member of the nation who accepts it: "The question of national unity," Erik Erikson emphasizes, "may become a matter of the preservation of identity, and thus a matter of (human) life and death, far surpassing the question of political systems."[13] By the same token, when the form or chief attributes of the symbol change—when it becomes male rather than female, older rather than younger, stronger rather than weaker—then there is persuasive, albeit second-hand, evidence that the self-perception of the individuals who create and sustain it is changing too. That Uncle Sam replaced Columbia, or that the American colonies grew from helpless "infants" to "sturdy youths almost out of their time," bespeaks a concomitant transformation in the personal identity of significant masses of people which is practically impossible to grasp from any other angle.[14]

Now the analysis of symbolic forms is not at all the equivalent of direct psychological investigation. Even so—and this brings us back to the almost overwhelming dilemmas that confront the psychohistorian—it may well be the only way to recapture interior attitudes, emotions, and states of mind of large numbers of people in the past without trafficking in the concepts of "group mind" and "collective unconscious." The essential thing is to appreciate the intricate interrelationship of individuality and symbolic collective identity, the way symbolic representations of the group arise out of and express the sense of common traits and destinies, mold perceptions and behavior, and influence even the innermost contours of personality and self-awareness. We have already alluded briefly to the advantages of reading the Revolutionary analogy between imperial and parental authority in this light; let us move ahead and consider, in hypothetical form, how we might thereby provide psychological solutions to four crucial historical problems: why colonial Americans accepted dependency on England for 150 years, how and why they came to reject it, why Tories balked at Independence, and why England considered it necessary to maintain colonial subordination.

The Roots of Dependency

HYPOTHESIS ONE: Americans accepted British control and authority because the objective disparity between British power and colonial power created in them a deep personal sense of comparative weakness and inferiority.

We observed in previous chapters how the parent-child analogy provided a natural law justification for colonial obedience to imperial authority. Here we should take note of the way the concept of colonial "childhood" not only legitimated British superiority, but also encapsulated a multitude of facts, impressions, and assumptions about the true relationship between England and America. It provided, in short, a symbol of American identity within the empire, and, from what we have suggested about the coercive influence of such symbols, the readiness of the Americans to accept it as an accurate statement of the colonies' standing vis-à-vis England meant that their own individual attitudes toward England would often show a childlike quality of powerlessness, inconsequence, and dependency. This is not to contend that they acted like children or were otherwise infantilized by colonization; rather, it is to argue that the childhood metaphor, summing up all the very real perils of colonial existence and the need for external imperial support, would independently enforce patterns of thought and action, *in the imperial arena only*, that were modeled after a child's acceptance of and deference to parental authority. The belief in colonial "childhood" thus became ingrained in the colonial American personality, and in so doing erected inhibitions against expressions of dissent or discontent. At least one colonist, as we have seen, understood the power of such inhibitions:

In our infantile indigency and impotent minority [he wrote], we looked with admiration on the comparative greatness and strength of our elder brothers. . . . So great is the force of custom, that it is scarcely possible now, at first blush, to feel ourselves in any degree equal to those, which were once so much our superiors. As a son, or a pupil, seldom loses, even in manhood, those impressions of inferiority, which he received under the culture of his parents, or instructions of his master.[15]

In our terms the objective disparity between English and American power embodied in the notion of the colonies as children had thus created an inner conviction of inferiority, which, quite apart from rational calculations of relative strength, tended to block colonial aggressiveness and to underwrite imperial authority.

HYPOTHESIS TWO: Convinced of their comparative weakness and inferiority within the empire, individual Americans responded with an intense personal affection, even reverence, for English leaders, institutions, and culture. The result was a widespread identification with England and the English that reinforced colonial willingness to accept imperial control. It is possible, too, that colonial Americans were also deeply angered by their dependent status, that the necessary repression of such anger accelerated the process of identification, and that the acceptance of imperial control was thereby rooted still more firmly in the colonial personality.

Having suggested in Hypothesis One that colonial Americans felt themselves weaker than and inferior to Englishmen, let us begin here by recalling that when they tried to describe the ties that bound the "infant" colonies to the "mother country" they returned time and again to words like "affection," "reverence," "devotion," and "love." The colonies accept British authority, James Otis declared, because they sincerely love Britain: "Their affection and reverence for their mother country is unquestionable. They yield the most cheerful and ready obedience to her laws."[16] Or as the Georgian John Zubly put it, so long as England remained "an affectionate parent" her children-colonies would give her their "chearful obedience."[17] Once again, the attribution of such sentiments to the principal symbol of collective colonial identity would have both reflected and induced similar sentiments in the attitudes and behavior of individual colonists.

The explanation for this curious association of affection and obedience can be traced, we think, from the need of colonial Americans to compensate for their sense of childlike helplessness and insufficiency by emulating and incorporating, as best they could, the standards and achievements of the more powerful parent state. Even without reference to symbolic formulations, historians have long been aware of what John Clive and Bernard Bailyn call the pervasive "sense of inferiority" and "sense of guilt regarding local mannerisms" in the colonies.[18] Jack P. Greene speaks of the "frank and usually apologetic admission of colonial cultural inferiority." "Colonial writers and correspondents alike," he notes, "repeatedly found themselves apologizing for the peculiarities in their speech and manners, the crudity of their institutions, the meanness of their architecture, the pallor of their intellectual life, the unimportance of their affairs."[19] The other side of this cultural self-abasement was an insatiable appetite for things British and an oddly stubborn insistence on the wisdom and benevolence of British imperial policy. Americans tirelessly aped the latest English fashions, applauded English literary talent, copied English architecture, mimicked English manners, praised the King, and labored to reproduce English political institutions. "I am almost inclined to believe," William Eddis wrote in amazement, "that a new fashion is adopted earlier by the polished and affluent Americans, than by many opulent persons in the great metropolis."[20] As Greene has shrewdly remarked, the inherent insecurities of colonial life could be resolved "only through a constant reference back to the once certain measure of achievement: the standards of the cultural center."[21]

Yet this insight deserves to be carried further: the very intensity with which the colonists admired and imitated British standards bespeaks a drive to identify with an idealized authority figure that not only boosted colonial self-esteem, but also produced a strong personal affection for Britain and the British that militated against any disruption of the imperial relationship.[22] Among psychoanalytic psychologists, it should be observed, such affection has often been described as a powerful source of political obedience. Fred Weinstein and Gerald Platt, for example, have recently developed at length the idea that a "love" for "nurturant and protective authority figures" promotes dependency and submission more effectively than anything else. Providing only, they argue, that a leader continues to provide his subjects with care and protection, the burdens and inequities of obedience to his authority will be minimized or overlooked altogether.[23] For 150 years, of course, Great Britain did nothing to suggest a lack of goodwill toward the colonies, and the colonists, out of their own need to overcome their lack of self-esteem and strength by becoming as British as they could, responded with an affectionate submission to imperial authority. That finely balanced relationship, deeply imbedded in the colonial consciousness through symbolic representations of kind parents and loving children, gave the empire a stability and harmony that coercion or the threat of coercion would never have achieved.

Affection, however, need not necessarily be the only force at work here. It is almost a commonplace among psychologists that individuals placed in precarious or insecure positions, or situations in which they are made to feel helpless and inferior, will mimic the traits and styles of whoever holds authority over them—not out of affection, but rather out of the unconscious transformation of inexpressible frustration and hostility. As T. W. Adorno and his colleagues explain it, "underlying hostile and rebellious impulses, held in check by fear, lead the subject to overdo in the direction of respect, obedience, gratitude, and the like." Children who resent parental authority, for example, are frequently unable to communicate their resentment openly, and "as a reaction against the underlying hostility, there is often rigid glorification and idealization of the parents."[24] Among some American slaves, to take another example, "dependency and feelings of inadequacy and rejection were accompanied by emotions of anger and rage," but given the danger of expressing those emotions freely they were resolved by intense identification with the master and by self-contempt.[25] The practices of skin-bleaching and hair-straightening among Afro-Americans provide graphic evidence of the same process at work even after the end of slavery.[26] And Albert Memmi, studying the sometimes profound affection which the colonized populations of modern Asia and Africa could maintain for their European rulers, has concluded that "love of the colonizer is subtended by a complex of feelings ranging from shame to self-hate."[27]

Did colonial Americans, too, belittle their own accomplishments and mimic the English because they could not give vent to a secret indignation at dependency? They were not, again, children; neither were they slaves or "colonized" in the contemporary sense of the word. They did not have a pre-colonization culture of their own that had been suppressed and replaced by the foreign culture of a colonizing power, and the authority to which they were subject was certainly far less onerous, far less hostile to the open expression of discontent, than anything experienced by the colonized populations of Africa or Asia. Beyond these obvious qualifications, moreover, there lies the subtler problem of evidence. Repressed anger is, by definition, not only unstated, but out of the range of conscious knowledge as well: any direct testimony to the existence of colonial resentment against British hegemony would mean, *ipso facto*, that such resentment was not repressed.

Even so, it is still not out of the question that repressed anger, in addition to overt affection, promoted American identification with England. One must always keep in mind, after all, that no matter how benignly England ruled America, the colonists did not have full control over their own destinies. The normal development of their economies in particular was checked or manipulated according to imperial necessity, and it would not be inconsistent with what we know of human psychology to suppose them unconsciously resentful at such a state of affairs. Then, too, for all of their parroting of English culture, Americans had constantly to endure the accusation that, as one Englishman put it, they "are remarkably simple, or silly, and blunder eternally."[28] The bitterness this sort of arrogance must have aroused became clear during the Revolutionary controversy, when colonial spokesmen at last began to protest openly that the British "have derided and looked down upon us, with utmost scorn and contempt," often "representing us as savages and barbarians."[29] What would have earlier prohibited the recognition, not to say airing, of this sense of outrage would not have been—and perhaps here emerges a unique feature of the American colonial experience—the fear of physical reprisal, but rather the fear of disrupting that mood of affection between America and England which enabled the colonists to accept the English as a model of their own identity and purpose in the first place. Unable to admit to their anger, then, they would have become even greater admirers of the English, and imperial authority would have become even more firmly entrenched in the colonial mind.

HYPOTHESIS THREE: Over the first century or so of settlement, the structure of both colonial society and the colonial family tended to produce personality types inclined to be acquiescent toward authority and authority-figures. This too contributed to the legitimation of dependency.

Since our aim here is to improve our understanding of why colonial Americans accepted imperial authority it would be well to make the point that individual responses to all kinds of authority are, or have a strong tendency to be, psychologically congruent. There is no special mystery in the phenomenon: obedience or disobedience to state, church, or party is conditioned and regulated by the superego, the result of which is a broad uniformity of attitude toward them.[30] How American colonists responded to imperial authority cannot, therefore, be fully appreciated without reference to the prevailing conceptions of authority in colonial society as a whole.

Evidence on this subject is sketchy at best, but some important recent work in the area suggests that colonial society—in response to the rigorous demands of frontier life, among other things—heavily favored hierarchical organizations and placed a high cultural premium on obedience to all forms of authority. Studying the complex relationship between social structure and personality in colonial Connecticut, for example, Richard L. Bushman found that "the total environment enjoined obedience." The Puritan order, he reported, "produced personalities marked by rigorous moral standards, but even more by a prepossession with authority. Many prominent traits of the Connecticut Puritans were responses to the virtually inescapable authority that dominated [their lives] from childhood until death." It seemed clear, moreover, that patriarchal authority was everywhere the archetype. Every citizen acted the stern father to his inferiors and the dutiful son to his superiors; "petitioners always stood in relation to the Assembly as children to their fathers, a relationship frequently made explicitly."[31]

In tracing the source and transmission of cultural attitudes toward authority special attention must be given to the structure of authority within the family, for it is the child's continuing encounter with parental demands that sets the pattern for the adult's later ideas of command and obedience.[32] That attitudes toward political authority in particular develop out of attitudes toward parental authority is hardly, of course, a modern insight. Bodin, for example, was aware that "children who stand in little awe of their parents, and have even less fear of the wrath of God, readily set at defiance the authority of the magistrates."[33] Only lately, however, have the precise connections between family, polity, and personality been laid out with any degree of precision.[34] Wilhelm Reich, seeking out the psychological roots of fascism, insisted that a close relationship existed between the authoritarian family and the authoritarian state: rigid, tightly organized families stifled the child's individuality and disposed him to accept and support a rigid, tightly organized political order. Sons especially, Reich argued, displayed a strong identification with the domineering father which "forms the basis of the emotional identification with every kind of authority."[35] Erich Fromm has extended and refined the etiology of authoritarianism—most notably in his *Escape from Freedom* (1941), where he suggests that families provide the political system with the personality type it requires.[36] Adorno and his colleagues likewise found that authoritarian personalities most often emerge from households that "base interrelationships on rather clearly defined roles of dominance and submission in contradistinction to equalitarian policies.... Family relationships are characterized by fearful subservience to the demands of the parents and by early suppression of impulses not acceptable to them."[37] And in an important investigation of family psychology in early modern France, David Hunt made the linkages between an authoritarian culture, hierarchical families, and dependent personalities still clearer. Adult Frenchmen, deprived of genuine self-determination in their own youth, could not tolerate their children's strivings toward self-determination; the resulting suppression of infantile autonomy, reinforced by other cultural controls in later stages of growth, lead the child "to doubt his own worth and the possibility of future success." An individual with a personality built on such "sandy foundations," Hunt writes, was an individual who would "never be able to demand what is his due."[38]

Now colonial American society cannot be equated with the relentlessly oppressive societies studied by modern students of the authoritarian personality and its origins. Yet from the evidence assembled in our earlier note on the historical family it seems entirely reasonable to propose that the strength of patriarchal authority in the colonies during the seventeenth and early eighteenth centuries would have been likely, there as elsewhere, to produce individuals inclined to expect and willingly submit to strong political authority—including the authority of the empire to which they belonged.[39]

The Rejection of Dependency

> HYPOTHESIS FOUR: Important changes in the objective conditions of colonial life transformed the collective image of the colonies from one of weakness and inferiority to one of strength and capability. Accordingly, individuals who identified with that image gained in self-respect and self-confidence and began to consider continued imperial control an intolerable constraint.

In the previous section we advanced three distinct but interlocking and overlapping psychological supports for colonial dependency. Here we want to examine the forces that eroded those supports, and the best place to begin is with a consideration of the sustained and comprehensive growth of the colonies after the beginning of the eighteenth century. Between 1700 and 1760 the population of America soared from a meager 223,000 whites and 28,000 blacks to 1,268,000 whites and 326,000 blacks, or six- and twelvefold increases, respectively. Direct exports to England went up from an average £264,000 yearly (1701–1705) to £992,000 (1761–1765), while American prod-

ucts poured into rapidly expanding markets elsewhere, more and more often
carried by American-owned and American-built shipping. American port
cities grew by leaps and bounds, and their prosperity in turn stirred rapid
improvements in transportation, communication, education, medicine, architecture, and the arts. Indeed, after the capture of Louisbourg in 1745 it
looked as though colonial military abilities were also changing for the better,
and after Braddock's defeat on the Monongahela a decade later it looked as
though they equaled, perhaps excelled, those of the British. The truth was,
Franklin said in comparing the two events,

That one ranging captain of a few provincials, Rogers, has harassed the enemy more
on the frontiers of Canada, and destroyed more of their men, than the whole army of
regulars. That it was the regulars who surrendered themselves, with the provincials
under their command, prisoners of war, almost as soon as they were besieged. . . .
That it was the regulars who surrendered Fort William Henry, and suffered themselves to be butchered and scalped with arms in their hands. That it was the
regulars under Braddock, who were thrown into a panic by the "yells of three or four
hundred Indians," in their confusion shot one another, and, with five times the force
of the enemy, fled before them.[40]

The cumulative impact of these manifold transformations on the colonial
American character may be read in the parallel transformation of the symbol
they acknowledged as a representative of their collective identity. What had
been weak and helpless "infants" were becoming, just as British policy toward the colonies stiffened, vigorous and muscular "youths" with minds of
their own. It would thus appear that increasingly large numbers of
colonists—above all, one suspects, those coming of age in the 1750's and
1760's—were thinking more highly of their personal worth and ability than
earlier generations and had correspondingly less tolerance for an inferior and
dependent status within the empire.

Successful resistance to British policy in the Stamp Act crisis toughened
this emerging self-confidence, quickened impatience at restraint, and occasioned, for the first time, extraordinary outbursts of anger against colonial
dependency. Subsequent confrontations, deepening that anger, encouraged
the Americans to find in their material achievements over the previous half-
century a new dignity and a new sense of their possibilities. The idea began
to circulate that England actually envied the swift growth of her "children"
and was bent on suppressing it; indeed, it seemed more and more evident that
England could not survive without the colonies, that, as the Pennsylvania
pamphleteer John Dickinson put it, "THE FOUNDATIONS OF THE
POWER AND GLORY OF GREAT BRITAIN ARE LAID IN AMER-
ICA."[41] The Association movement boldly tested the idea, unthinkable to
an earlier generation, that by cultivating their powers of self-denial and their
respect for their own produce and manufactures the colonists might soon be
able to go it alone. "We may talk and boast of liberty," exclaimed one,
"but after all, the industrious and frugal only will be free."[42] Declared

another: "if we mean still to be free, let us unanimously lay aside foreign superfluities, and encourage our own manufacture."[43] Formerly tolerated restraints on colonial industry—the Woolens Act (1699), the Hat Act (1732), and the Iron Act (1750)—now appeared to be the chains of "a bondaged state" and symptoms of an "abject servility, which . . . disgraces the human nature."[44] Even the original Navigation Acts themselves, John Adams asserted, were "an humiliation, a degradation, a disgrace to my Country and to myself as a native of it."[45]

The more conviction grew that dependency meant painful personal disgrace for a people who no longer needed it, the more clear it became that almost every exertion of British authority over the colonies was a direct assault on American manhood. Thus the exclusive right to tax themselves emerged as a right the colonists could not surrender "without their being degraded, or degrading themselves below the character of men."[46] The institutions of colonial government, not long before regarded as pale and imperfect imitations of British forms, were now prized as evidence of political maturity, and James Otis could write that the ministry's plans for "abolishing all the colony [sic] assemblies" would be the equivalent of "circumcising all the male colonists."[47] Even British cultural arrogance no longer wounded, for the simple manners and morals of America were being transformed from defects into virtues—ultimately, of course, the very virtues which would make republicanism the obvious and immediate choice of the colonists when they determined that only independence would give them the dignity they deserved.[48]

> HYPOTHESIS FIVE: The decline of patriarchalism in both colonial society and the colonial family—brought about by the same social and economic changes that were remaking the collective image of the colonies—tended to produce less authoritarian and more autonomous personality types. For them the arbitrary exercise of imperial authority was likely to be extremely objectionable.

Although, once again, we know far less than we might about the patterns of authority in colonial American culture, there is persuasive evidence that the steady expansion of population and relentless economic growth of the eighteenth century sharply eroded the rigid patriarchalist authority established in the seventeenth. A strong respect for hierarchy and obedience was increasingly more difficult to sustain, let alone justify, as the struggle for sheer survival receded, and as Bushman observed in the case of Connecticut, "after a century of Puritan rule, law and authority were burdens too heavy to bear." Everywhere in Connecticut—in the disintegration of theocratic power, the rise of the money economy and its competitive spirit, the greater self-sufficiency of small farmers, the widening phenomenon of revolt against town proprietors and leaders—were the symptoms of a profound and thoroughgoing movement away from the old ways and the old order. This change did not come without a price, Bushman found, and the price was a pervasive feeling of guilt that did not disappear until the Great Awakening swept through the colony and remitted the sins of contention and acquisitiveness. What the Awakening left behind, in effect, was a new kind of man, acclimated to a freer kind of society and much less disposed to accept authority than his forebears had been.[49]

Once again, too, it is important to focus on the family as an institution which helps to shape individual personalities according to cultural demands. If, as we have previously suggested, the patriarchal family of the seventeenth and early eighteenth centuries was likely to produce individuals with an inclination toward authoritarianism, then it appears equally likely that the breakdown of patriarchal authority in the family around the middle of the eighteenth century—one aspect, of course, of the ebb of traditional authority throughout the culture—would have produced individuals less receptive to authoritarian control. The same generation, in other words, that was gaining new self-confidence from the impressive economic growth of the colonies was also acquiring a larger capacity for personal autonomy and a temperamental dislike for unnecessary, arbitrary, and restrictive authority. This generation, we suggest, would find England's claim to absolute parental sovereignty over her "infant" colonies not merely out of line with their own sense of the rightness of things, but also—because, again, of their close and continuing identification with that symbolic representation of the colonies to which they belonged—deeply, personally, humiliating.

None of this, we should emphasize, is to imply that the Revolution was in any sense inevitable, that the empire was doomed to collapse, no matter what men said or did, simply because there was something in the American psychology less and less hospitable to the tradition of colonial inferiority and subordination. What it does mean is that a rising self-confidence and sensitivity to authority among colonial Americans, each a consequence of the great social and economic changes taking place in colonial life, had together before 1776 begun to eat away at the habit of obedience which had served as one, but only one, of the foundations of imperial stability. And what it prepares us to see, moreover, is that England had the extreme misfortune to embark on a policy of unprecedented severity toward the colonies at precisely the moment when the colonists were ready—economically, politically, and above all emotionally—to fight back. How they came to the realization that they must fight back, on the other hand, is a different matter altogether.

HYPOTHESIS SIX: The unexpected imposition of new imperial controls in the 1760's, then punishment for colonial opposition, shattered the personal trust and affection that Americans had had for the English and their King. A widespread feeling of betrayal aroused still more anger against Britain, and may also have released previously repressed resentments at dependency.

In Hypothesis Two we proposed that colonial Americans were willing to accept dependency because they strongly identified with the English and symbolically construed England and the King as nurturant and protective parents. But the Stamp Act and its successors, as we have seen, revealed that the child-colonies could no longer trust the mother country, and this discovery, as Dickinson put it, left the colonists "filled with grief and anxiety."[50] Desperate appeals for a return of "maternal affection" were heard everywhere. "Can a Woman forget her sucking Child, that she should not have Compassion on the Son of her Womb?" asked "North America" plaintively. "O Britannia! where is your Compassion for the Sons of your Womb, for us Americans[?]"[51] England must not, Allen pleaded, "forget her bowels, as a parent; nor think to be happy in piercing the bosom, and bowels of her own children."[52] British policy had plunged the colonists into an acute emotional crisis. "Repeated acts of unkindness on one side, may by degrees abate the warmth of affection on the other," warned the Massachusetts legislature, "and a total alienation may succeed to that happy union, harmony and confidence, which has subsisted."[53] Yet alienation was not easy to contemplate. "[I]f once *we* are separated from our mother country," Dickinson asked, "what new form of government shall we adopt, or where shall we find another Britain, to supply our loss? Torn from the body, to which we are united by religion, liberty, laws, affections, relation, language and commerce, we must bleed at every vein."[54]

In the years after the Boston Tea Party, and especially after the skirmish at Lexington and Concord, pleas for parental tenderness gave way to the bitter conviction that the mother country had cruelly and irreparably betrayed her trusting offspring. Anxiety at the prospect of separation faded before a rising tide of outrage and hostility. England now appeared as "a parent red with the blood of her children."[55] The loving mother had become a "vile imposter—an old abandoned prostitute—crimsoned o'er with every abominable crime, shocking to humanity!"[56] Troops had been sent by the English "to murder and butcher their own children... that have been so obedient, useful and affectionate."[57] "Trust to Britain, and her flag, no more," Philip Freneau, a patriot poet, cried. "These lands will redden with their children's gore."[58] For a time the colonists continued to look to the King for paternal affection, but he, too, soon proved untrustworthy and became an object of colonial indignation. "King *George* the Third, adieu! No more shall we cry to you for protection," vowed one American writer.[59] "You have totally dissolved our allegiance to the King of England as our King," another writer told General Gage after the battle of Bunker Hill. "We swore allegiance to him as a *King*, not as a *Tyrant*—as a *Protector*, not as a *Destroyer*—as a *Father*, not as a *Murderer*."[60] And as Thomas Paine exclaimed, here as elsewhere capturing the common mood, the King was "a wretch that with the pretended title FATHER OF HIS PEOPLE can unfeelingly hear of their slaughter, and composedly sleep with their blood upon his soul."[61]

The psychological consequences of this anger at an unnatural "parental" betrayal—a betrayal made intimately personal through the continuing inter-

play of individual psyche and the symbol of collective colonial identity—
cannot be underestimated. It swept away once and for all that affection for
England which had been, along with a sense of inferiority and a habitual
deference to authority, a mainstay of imperial order, and it steeled the
Americans to the prospect of separation. Indeed, as John Adams remem-
bered many years later, the outrage with which his countrymen responded to
England's betrayal of their historic affections was the very essence of the
Revolution itself:

> But what do we mean by the American Revolution? Do we mean the American
> War? The revolution was effected before the war commenced. The revolution was in
> the minds and hearts of the people.... The people of America had been educated in
> an habitual affection for England as their mother country; and while they thought her
> a kind and tender parent (erroneously enough, however, for she was never such a
> mother) no affection could be more sincere. But when they found her a cruel Beldam,
> willing like Lady Macbeth, to "dash their brains out," it is no wonder their filial
> affections ceased and were changed into indignation and horror.
>   *This radical change in the principles, opinions, sentiments and affections of the people, was the
> real American Revolution.*[62]

Anger at betrayal was not necessarily, however, the only kind of anger to
make itself felt in the final years before Independence. We had the occasion
in Hypothesis Two, it will be recalled, to speculate on the existence of
repressed anger at dependency in the colonial American personality. Here
we are in a position to see how this anger might have become liberated and
thus propelled the Americans even faster toward revolution, for as Weinstein
and Platt have argued, it is precisely when a sense of betrayal sours the
affection given to a figure of authority that repressed anger at subordination
to him bursts into consciousness. As soon, in other words, as "the moral code
that legitimates and organizes the compliance is violated"—as soon as, from
the colonial perspective, the parent-state no longer appears to cherish and
indulge its "children"—then the habit of obedience is permanently broken
and the old prohibitions against the recognition of latent hostility crumble.[63]
Distinguishing in the historical evidence between expressions of anger at
betrayal and expressions of hitherto repressed anger at dependency is not, to
be sure, a simple matter, and we can do no more at this point than to indicate
the possibility of discovering such a distinction. But consider the spirit in
which John Adams looked back on colonial obedience to British authority.
"They have prevailed on us to consent to many things which were grossly
injurious to us, and to surrender many others, with voluntary tameness, to
which we had the clearest right," he declared bitterly. And think, he went
on, of how badly imperial representatives had treated the Americans:

> Have we not been treated, formerly, with abominable insolence, by officers of the
> navy?... Have not some generals from England treated us like servants, nay, more
> like slaves than like Britons? Have we not been under the most abject submission, the

most supercilious insults, of some custom-house officers? Have we not been trifled with, brow-beaten, and trampled on, by former governors, in a manner which no king of England since James the Second has dared to indulge toward his subjects?

The time had come, Adams announced, for Americans to abandon the habits of mind which had kept them silent and docile for so long. "Believe me, the character of this country has suffered . . . by the pusillanimity with which we have born many insults and indignities from the creatures of power at home and the creatures of those creatures here."[64]

Now Adams, clearly enough, was angry with his countrymen and himself for not having become angry at England in the past. Yet in his insistence on recalling all the old insults and treacheries, in the very contempt he had for the former "pusillanimity" of the Americans, was he not also discharging resentments against British authority that had been accumulating, unconsciously and thus without his own knowledge, for years? If so—and again the entirely speculative nature of such an assumption must always be kept in mind—then the imperial betrayal of colonial affection looms all the larger in the psychology of the Revolution.

The common theme linking Hypotheses Four, Five, and Six is the eruption of intense, personal anger—anger at the maintenance and imposition of restraints that violated a new American sense of strength and worth, anger at the perpetuation of an authority that could only humiliate men accustomed to greater autonomy in their own lives, and anger at the betrayal of a traditional affection for England. Anger was not everything: there remained always, just beneath the surface of hostilities, grave doubts about the colonies' abilities to withstand the power of the empire. "I am often," Adams noted in his diary in 1774, "in Reveries and Brown Studies.—The Objects before me, are too grand, and multifarious for my Comprehension.—We have not Men, fit for the Times. We are deficient in Genius, in Education, in Travel, in Fortune—in every Thing. I feel unutterable Anxiety."[65] And as Josiah Quincy recognized in the same year, it was "love for a *parent*-country, love for a *parent*-king" that still "restrains the career of passion."[66] By March 4, 1776, however, a very different Adams had learned that anger and anger alone was the surest cure for self-doubt and the quickest solvent for deeply ingrained inhibitions:

Resentment is a Passion, implanted by Nature for the Preservation of the Individual. . . . A Man may have the Faculty of concealing his Resentment, or suppressing it, but he must and ought to feel it. It is a Duty. His Person, his Property, his Liberty, his Reputation are not safe without it. He ought, for his own Security and Honour, and for the public good to punish those who injure them. . . . It is the same with Communities. They ought to resent and to punish.[67]

It is just the recognition of this resentment that is so often missing from our accounts of the Revolution, so often buried beneath the weight of competing doctrine and interest that it becomes difficult to imagine the event as much more than a polite disagreement among gentlemen. The fact was, we suggest, that by 1776 most Americans were boiling mad at England for adhering to policies that robbed them of their personal dignity, self-respect, and autonomy—and that if they had not been mad there never would have been a Revolution.

Why the Loyalists Did Not Revolt

HYPOTHESIS SEVEN: Some colonists remained loyal to England because they remained, despite all that had happened, psychologically dependent on England. The prospect of living without a system of external supports and restraints filled them with anxiety, and in the end they chose to fight or flee the rebels rather than accept the emotional burdens of freedom.

Historians of the Revolution have been notoriously unsuccessful in explaining what circumstance or combination of circumstances would explain the Loyalist phenomenon: not all those colonists who opposed Independence, perhaps not even a majority of them, were wealthy, socially prominent, well-educated, politically powerful, agents of the crown, or members of the Anglican Church; nor, for that matter, did all colonists who fell in those categories become Loyalists.[68] Inertia will not do for an explanation, either. By 1776 the pressures to follow the lead of the patriots in Congress and deny allegiance to the King were formidable indeed, and the determination to stand against the popular tide bespeaks a rare and difficult courage. Probably the only thing we do know for certain about the Loyalists is that their image of the imperial relationship never changed: down to the end they continued to think of the colonies as children, emphasizing their many weaknesses and deficiencies and warning always that their mother country was fully capable, if pushed far enough, of crushing the rebels underfoot.

No doubt the Loyalists had a case: England was, after all, a world power, and no one could know for certain that the colonies were capable of winning a fight for their independence, much less preserving order and tranquility among themselves if they did win. Even so, the Loyalists' dogged adherence to the traditional symbols of colonial and imperial identity strongly suggests—and here the sharp contrast with the increasingly self-confident and aggressive patriots is crucial—that they continued to believe themselves too weak and too inferior to Englishmen to risk opposition to imperial policy. "Being still but scions of the parent stock," the Reverend Jonathan Boucher warned, colonial Americans "are in no condition to be torn from that prop and shelter which fosters them with parental tenderness, *ingentique ramorum protegit umbra*."[69] What was more, England remained for the Loyalists a model of perfect parental benevolence. Absolutely nothing had happened, they insisted, to prove that she had betrayed the affections of her American dependencies or in any way ceased to be "a nursing mother to these colonies"; surely, then, to stop "loving and reverencing the mother that bore us" out of a conceit that she no longer cared to "foster and fondle us" was unthinkable.[70] All the blame for disrupting the familial harmony of the empire, rather, fell squarely on the colonists. As another Loyalist clergyman, Charles Inglis, put it, "the present Rebellion is certainly one of the most causeless, unprovoked and unnatural that ever disgraced any Country—a Rebellion marked with peculiarly aggravated Circumstances of Guilt & Ingratitude."[71]

As Independence loomed closer and closer, the Loyalists' insistence on American helplessness grew more and more strident: what had been a generalized conviction of collective and individual inadequacy intensified, as the need to sustain affection and trust between England and the colonies became increasingly urgent, into a consuming anxiety over the prospect of national and personal liberation from external imperial controls. "The Habits of Kindness and Affection, on one Side, and of Respect and Obedience, on the other," Boucher informed the Continental Congress, "are still necessary to [American] Security and Happiness."[72] Remove British protection and restraint, other Loyalists said over and over again, and the colonies would either fall prey to another great power or, likelier yet, fall upon each other in an orgy of unchecked passions and ambitions. "I stand aghast at [the idea of independence]," Inglis exclaimed. "My blood runs chill when I think of the calamities, the complicated evils that must ensue."[73] At the same time, therefore, that the majority of their compatriots were abandoning a close personal identification with English power and influence, the Loyalists remained behind, their fears of going it alone binding them ever more tightly to the mother country. Boucher, for one, might try to remind his fellow colonists of the strength and comfort they had all once derived from their identity as Englishmen—England, he wrote, "is ever ready, to avenge the Cause, of the meanest Individual among us, with a Power respected by the whole World"—but the old order was not to be re-created so easily.[74] By 1776, unable to see any cause for anger and still heavily dependent on the imperial connection for psychological support, the Loyalists had no choice but to fight the patriots as best they could and wait for England to come to their rescue with fire and sword.[75]

It would be enough to conclude that all of what divided Loyalists from patriots was the result of selective perception—that the Loyalists refused to relinquish their belief in the notion of colonial "childhood" because, somewhere along the line, they had not got the message that conditions in the colonies had changed drastically since the beginning of the eighteenth century. But how, then, to account for selective perception? The most obvious answer—although the studies have not yet been done that would confirm or deny it—is that there existed a distinctive Loyalist "personality," marked by a high need for external authority, a fear of autonomy, and a low tolerance for disorder. If American culture was, as we have already speculated, becoming less and less congenial to arbitrary authority and rigid social hierarchy, then the Loyalists might be regarded as those who clung to more traditional styles of interpersonal and political relations. One notes, for example, that Boucher expressed distress not only at unruly children and insubordinate colonies, but also at "the laboring classes," who "instead of regarding the rich as their guardians, patrons, and benefactors, now look on them as so many overgrown colossuses, whom it is no demerit in them to wrong."[76] Such a personality—the product, perhaps, of a vestigial patriarchalism in significant numbers of late eighteenth-century families—would be as little inclined to see the economic development of the colonies as evidence of their movement out of "childhood" as it would be to see any advantages of colonial independence.

Why the British Needed to Suppress Rebellion

HYPOTHESIS EIGHT: Individual Englishmen internalized the image of their country as the imperial parent, and the preservation of parental authority became essential to their sense of identity and self-respect. Colonial revolt was the cause for profound personal anxiety and anger.

A psychological explanation of why England went to war against America might appear superfluous at first glance, given the importance of colonial markets, produce, and trade to the English economy. One of the salient points in the radical critique of Whig and Tory thinking, on the other hand, was that the empire clearly did not need to fight for political control of America: economic control was the only thing that mattered, and it could be preserved far into the foreseeable future on the strength of England's commercial hegemony alone. The real reason Englishmen wanted to fight, the radicals contended, had nothing at all to do with rational calculations of profit and loss, but rather with the fact that every one of them liked to believe he walked a little taller because his country ruled a vast empire. All the talk about the rights of parents and duties of children, the Reverend Richard Price said, merely betrayed an inner desire to preserve the subordination of a people whom "we have a right to order as we please." Was not "the interruption they now give to this pleasure," he asked shrewdly, "the secret spring of our present animosity against them?"[77]

Certainly there was good reason to dispute the radical argument against the need for political as well as economic control of the colonies: the importance of colonies to the national interest was, after all, a staple of mercantilist thought, and the radicals were asking their countrymen to abandon a position they had more than once before gone to war to protect. But what we know of the interaction between collective symbols and individual psyches suggests that Price and the radicals had indeed detected an important component of the desire to maintain imperial hegemony. Many Englishmen, it would appear, did derive deep personal satisfaction from the dependency of America, and America's apparent disregard for their "parental" sacrifices on its behalf caused them genuine pain and dismay. James Stewart, for one, complained that colonial Americans were unfeeling ingrates, "regarding all past Kindness, Care and Affection as nothing."[78] "With more than a mother's fondness," wrote another, Great Britain had nourished and supported her prodigal children, only to be callously and cruelly betrayed.[79] "I feel myself hurt, as I believe every Englishman must," declared still another, while denunciations of "parricides" and those who would "raise the dagger against [England's] breast" filled the press.[80] From a sense of personal betrayal it was a short step to personal anger and the warning that "the dangerous resentment of a great people [is] ready to burst forth."[81] The effect of widespread, popular indignation at the loss of dignity and control was then a groundswell of opinion in favor of swift repression. "There is a spirit rising in this country," William Knox, an administration spokesman, warned the colonies, "which will make you know its strength and your weakness, that will convince you of its authority and of your dependence."[82]

In responding to colonial rebellion as a personal affront—as a challenge to their own individual authority and dignity—eighteenth-century Englishmen were not very different from the citizens of modern imperialist nations. O. Mannoni has observed, for example, that colonialism in our own time promises much more than economic gain: "The 'colonial' is not looking for profit only; he is also greedy for certain other—psychological—satisfactions, and that is much more dangerous."[83] Indeed, the colonial often sacrifices profit for the sake of these satisfactions: "If he has lazy slaves instead of efficient workers it is because he does not particularly want the latter; he derives greater satisfaction from keeping his slaves. Naturally he would prefer it if his slaves worked *like* employees, but he will not sacrifice the satisfaction of being absolute master: he would rather forego the profit."[84] Albert Memmi, writing of French imperialism in Algeria, agreed that while the profit motive was its basis even the poorest of the colonizers took comfort from the thought they could never sink to the level of the colonized masses their nation controlled.[85] And Frantz Fanon, another student of French colonialism in Algeria, found that "the white colonial . . . by assuming the parental role . . . both demeans the native and bolsters his own ego." The inner satisfactions of imperialism, as well as racist assumptions of native inferiority, explain why "a white man addressing a Negro behaves exactly like an adult with a child and starts smirking, whispering, patronizing, cozening."[86]

The sacrifices that men will make to preserve the psychic rewards of domination, even when it openly conflicts with their rational interests, reach of course beyond the colonial situation: the notoriously persistent refusal of poor Southern whites to strike a political alliance with poor Southern blacks, for instance, preserved the satisfactions of racial supremacy but only at the cost of continued exploitation. Surely the Englishmen of the Revolutionary era were neither colonizers in the contemporary sense nor advocates of racial superiority over the Americans. Without recognizing, however, that those Englishmen, too, had more than an economic stake in colonial dependency and inferiority we cannot fully understand the surging indignation which swept them into war.[87]

NOTES

1. "Thoughts on Defensive War," *Pennsylvania Magazine*, July 1775; *Good Humour; or, a Way with the Colonies* (London, 1766), pp. 29–30. [For a biographical-metapsychological view of the parent-child metaphor, see Jordan, "Familial Politics," in Select Bibliography, part 2.]

2. Michael Walzer, "On the Role of Symbolism in Political Thought," *Political Science Quarterly*, 82 (June 1967), 194.

3. Kenneth E. Boulding, *The Image* (Ann Arbor, 1956), p. 64.

4. Clifford Geertz, "Ideology as a Cultural System," in David Apter, ed., *Ideology and Discontent* (Glencoe, 1964), p. 72.

5. Walzer, "Symbolism," p. 196.

6. Geertz, "Ideology," p. 64. Cf. Susanne K. Langer, *Philosophy in a New Key* (Cambridge, Mass.: 1957); Robert Jay Lifton, *History and Human Survival* (New York, 1970), pp. 303–305.

7. Boulding, *The Image*, pp. 109–111.

8. Leonard W. Doob, *Patriotism and Nationalism: Their Psychological Foundations* (New Haven, 1964), p. 181. Cf. Richard L. Merritt, *Symbols of American Community, 1735–1775* (New Haven, 1966), passim; Karl W. Deutsch, *Nationalism and Social Communication: An Inquiry into the Foundations of Nationality* (Cambridge, Mass.: 1953), pp. 170–181.

9. For Freud's thoughts on the personification of authority, see the discussion in Philip Rieff, *Freud: The Mind of the Moralist* (New York, 1961), p. 257. And cf. Robert A. LeVine, "The Role of the Family in Authority Systems: A Cross-Cultural Application of Stimulus-Generalization Theory," *Behavioral Science*, 5 (1960), 292–293, on Chinese and primitive parallels.

Let it be clear that we are not assuming the existence of an "average American," as analysts of the national character school such as Geoffrey Gorer and Margaret Mead have tended to do. For valuable warnings against such generalizations see Walter P. Metzger, "Generalizations about National Character: An Analytical Essay," in Louis Gottschalk, ed., *Generalization in the Writing of History* (1963), and David E. Stannard, "American Historians and the Idea of National Character: Some Problems and Prospects," *American Quarterly*, 22 (May 1971), 202–220.

10. Geertz, "Ideology," p. 58.

11. There has been extensive work done on the reaction of the public to the death of Presidents. See for example Harold Orlansky, "Reactions to the Death of President Roosevelt," *Journal of Social Psychology*, 26 (1947), 235–266; Paul B. Sheatsley and Jacob J. Feldman, "The Assassination of President Kennedy: A Preliminary Report on Public Reactions and Behavior," *Public Opinion Quarterly*, 29 (1964), 189–215; Fred Greenstein, *Personality and Politics* (Chicago, 1969), pp. 175–176.

12. Wilhelm Reich, *The Mass Psychology of Fascism*, trans. Vincent R. Carfagno (New York, 1970), p. 63.

13. Erik H. Erikson, *Childhood and Society*, 2d ed. (New York, 1963), p. 347. See also Lucien Pye's suggestion that there are times when "the search for individual identity hinges on the existence of a national identity." Pye, *Politics, Personality, and Nation Building: Burma's Search for Identity* (New Haven, 1962), p. 4. On the psychology of nationalism, see also Lucien W. Pye, "Personal Identity and Political Ideology," in Bruce Mazlish, ed., *Psychoanalysis and History* (Englewood Cliffs, 1963), pp. 150–173; Hermann Weilmann, "The Interlocking of Nation and Personality Structure," in Karl W. Deutsch and William J. Foltz, eds., *Nation-Building* (New York, 1963), pp. 33–55; Murray Edelman, *The Symbolic Uses of Politics* (New York, 1964); Abram

Kardiner, *The Psychological Frontiers of Society* (New York, 1945); Paul Roazen, *Freud: Political and Social Thought* (New York, 1968), esp. p. 190.

14. Robert Dahl cites research by Hadley Cantril to suggest that "people often judge their own situation by what they perceive to be the direction of change for a larger collectivity with which they identify." (Dahl, *Polyarchy: Participation and Opposition* [New Haven, 1971], pp. 99-101.)

15. "Cosmopolitan," *Massachusetts Spy*, December 1, 1775.

16. Otis, *Rights of the British Colonies Asserted and Proved*, in Bernard Bailyn, ed., *Pamphlets of the American Revolution* (Cambridge, Mass., 1965—) I, 442. Dickinson also insisted that the colonies' "obedience to *Great Britain* is secured by the best and strongest ties, *those of affection.*" (*The Late Regulations*, in Bailyn, *Pamphlets*, I, 690.)

17. John Joachim Zubly, *The Samp-Act Repealed* 2d ed. (Savannah, 1766) p. 25.

18. John Clive and Bernard Bailyn, "England's Cultural Provinces: Scotland and America," *William and Mary Quarterly*, 3d. ser., 11 (1954), 211.

19. Jack P. Greene, "Search for Identity: An Interpretation of Selected Patterns of Social Response in Eighteenth-Century America," *Journal of Social History*, 3 (1970), 209.

20. Clive and Bailyn, "England's Cultural Provinces," p. 209.

21. Jack P. Greene, "Political Mimesis: A Consideration of the Historical and Cultural Roots of Legislative Behavior in the British Colonies in the Eighteenth Century," *American Historical Review*, 75 (1969-70), 344.

22. Here we draw upon the psychoanalytic concepts of the "ego-ideal" and "identification." Very young children combat their powerlessness by fantasizing parental omnipotence, then sharing in that power by identifying with the parents. The child feels that "I am like my parents," and it incorporates parental ideals and ethics. The ego-ideal may be distinguished from superego content—"I have to do what the parents require of me." In the first, parents are loved and admired for their provision of love, protection, comfort, and guidance; in the second, parental restrictions are obeyed out of fear of losing parental love. See Jeanne Lampl-de Groot, "Ego Ideal and Superego," *The Psychoanalytic Study of the Child*, 17 (1962), 94-106; Joseph Sandler, "On the Concept of Super-ego," *ibid.*, 15 (1960), 128-162; Roy Schafer, "The Loving and Beloved Superego in Freud's Structural Theory," *ibid.*, pp. 163-188.

Freud defined identification as the attempt "to mold a person's own ego after the fashion of the one that has been taken as a model." This process often leads to an idealization, an overvaluation, and an avoidance of criticism of the model. Freud, *Group Psychology and the Analysis of the Ego*, Bantam ed. (New York, 1960), pp. 47, 56-59. Sandler et al. similarly define identification as "the changing of the shape of one's self-representation on the basis of another representation as a model," a process that may be either conscious or unconscious. (Joseph Sandler, Alex Holder, and Dale Meers, "The Ego Ideal and the Ideal Self," *Psychoanalytic Study of the Child*, 18 [1963], 139-158.)

23. Fred Weinstein and Gerald M. Platt, *The Wish to Be Free* (Berkeley, 1969), pp. 18, 32-34. Cf. Pye, *Politics, Personality, and Nation Building*, pp. 9, 84; Freud, *Group Psychology*, passim.

24. T. W. Adorno, Else Frenkel-Brunswik, Daniel J. Levinson, R. Nevitt Sanford, *The Authoritarian Personality* (New York, 1950), pp. 231-232, 386, 804. Cf., on identification, Nevitt Sanford, "The Dynamics of Identification," *Psychological Review*, 62 (1955), 106-118; Bruno Bettelheim, "Individual and Mass Behavior in Extreme Situations," *Journal of Abnormal Social Psychology*, 38 (1943), 417-452.

25. James P. Comer, "Individual Development and Black Rebellion: Some Parallels," *Midway*, 9 (1968), 41-42. Cf. Hortense Powdermaker, "The Channeling of Negro Aggression by the Cultural Process," in August Meier and Elliott Rudwick, eds., *The Making of Black America* (New York, 1969), pp. 96-97; Stanley Elkins, *Slavery: A Problem in American Institutional and Intellectual Life*, 2d ed. (Chicago, 1968).

26. See William H. Grier and Price M. Cobbs, *Black Rage* (New York, 1968), passim.

27. Albert Memmi, *The Colonizer and the Colonized*, trans. H. Greenfeld (Boston, 1965), pp. 120-121.

28. Quoted in Franklin's Letter of May 9, 1769, to the *London Chronicle*, in *The Writings of Benjamin Franklin*, ed. Albert H. Smyth (New York, 1905-1907), V, 209.

29. Quoted in Gordon S. Wood, *The Creation of the American Republic, 1776-1787* (Chapel Hill, 1969), p. 105.

30. E. V. Walter, "Power, Civilization and the Psychology of Conscience," *American Political Science Review*, 53 (1959), 641-661. Walter argues that "the responses to domination and subordination are based on prototypes of behavior learned in the family early in life." (*Ibid.*, p. 645.) With Freud, he believes that the family is the bridge between individual and social psychology. For some cautions, see Benson H. Marsten and James C. Coleman, "Specificity of Attitudes Toward Paternal and Non-Paternal Authority Figures," *Journal of Individual Psychology*, 17 (1961), 96-101. Cf. Erik H. Erikson, "Identity and the Life Cycle," as quoted in Weinstein and Platt, *Wish to Be Free*, p. 28n.

31. Richard L. Bushman, *From Puritan to Yankee: Character and the Social Order in Connecticut, 1690-1765* (Cambridge, Mass., 1967), pp. 16-21. Harry Eckstein analyzes the importance of patterns of authority and particularly the consequences of congruent patterns in *Division and Cohesion in Democracy: A Study of Norway* (Princeton, 1966), cited in Dahl, *Polyarchy*, pp. 140-142. Dahl also refers to a study of Amhara children, and the impact on them of the uniform requirement for obedience they face in all areas of the culture. "Family patriarch, parish chieftain, wealthy landlord, ecclesiastical dignitary, political dignitary, military officer—all are perceived in the imagery of fatherhood; all are the objects of comparable attitudes regarding the obeisance which is due them." (Cited in Dahl, *ibid.*, p. 143.) For an extreme cultural case of widespread dependency relationships, one may refer to Madagascar. There a tradition of ancestor-worship provided super-parents for the Malagasy, adults as well as children. "The words Ray aman'dReny, which literally mean 'the father and also the mother,' the parental couple, are those the Malagasy uses to address personages he deems worthy of respect—the administrator or the governor, for instance—and with whom he would be happy to establish a strong bond of dependence." (O. Mannoni, *Prospero and Caliban: The Psychology of Colonization*, trans. P. Powesland [New York, 1956], p. 61.)

32. Cf. Fred I. Greenstein, *Children and Politics* (New Haven, 1969), and James C. Davies, "The Family's Role in Political Socialization," reprinted in Norman Adler and Charles Harrington, eds., *The Learning of Political Behavior* (Glenview, Ill., 1970), pp. 117-123. For some objections to this view, see Lewis Froman, Jr., "Learning Political Attitudes," *ibid.*, pp. 75-81.

33. Quoted in Greenstein, *Children and Politics*, p. 3. Bodin added that "just as the well conducted family is the true image of the republic, and the domestic power similar to the sovereign power, so the governmental right of the household is the true model of the government of the republic. Just as with each individual member doing his duty the whole corps will prosper, so with families being well governed, the republic will thrive." Quoted in David Hunt, *Parents and Children in History; the Psychology of Family Life in Early Modern France* (New York, 1970).

34. Cf. Weinstein and Platt, *Wish to Be Free*, p. 238.

35. Reich, *Mass Psychology of Fascism*, pp. 30-32, 53-58, and passim. Cf. Paul A. Robinson, *The Freudian Left* (New York, 1969), pp. 45-46, and the chapter on Reich, passim.

36. Erich Fromm, *Escape from Freedom* (New York, 1941). Cf. Greenstein, *Personality and Politics*, pp. 100, 112.

37. Adorno et al., *Authoritarian Personality*, p. 385.

38. Hunt, *Parents and Children*, pp. 157-158.

39. It must be emphasized that even our use of Adorno here is not meant to suggest that the colonists exhibited pathologically authoritarian personalities. There is of course a spectrum of possible personality structures, with the classic Adorno type at one end; we are hypothesizing a personality tinctured with authoritarianism, not the "fascist personalities" Adorno and his colleagues analyzed.

40. Here we have relied on the data in the U. S. Bureau of the Census, *Historical Statistics of the United States* (Washington, 1960) and Merrill Jensen, *American Colonial Documents*, pp. 389-

412 and passim. Also informative were Stuart Bruchey, *The Roots of American Economic Growth* (New York, 1965), pp. 16–41; George Rogers Taylor, "American Economic Growth Before 1840: An Exploratory Essay," *Journal of Economic History*, 24 (1964), 427–437; Robert Thomas, "A Quantitative Approach to the Study of the Effects of Imperial Policy Upon Colonial Welfare," *ibid.*, 25 (1965), 615–638; Roger L. Ranson, "British Policy and Colonial Growth: Some Implications of the Burden from the Navigation Acts," *ibid.*, 28 (1968), 427–435. Quotation from Smyth, *Writings of Franklin*, V, 211. Hamilton summed up the sense of transformation when he observed that soon "America will be in no need of protection from Great Britain. She will then be able to protect herself, both at home and abroad." [Alexander Hamilton], *The Farmer Refuted* (New York, 1775), p. 46.

41. Dickinson, *The Late Regulations Respecting the British Colonies . . . Considered* (Philadelphia, 1765), reprinted in Bailyn, *Pamphlets*, I, 687.

42. Quoted in Edmund S. Morgan, "The Puritan Ethic and the American Revolution," *William and Mary Quarterly*, 3d ser., 24 (1967), 10.

43. Quoted *ibid.*, p. 10. Morgan attributes such language to the Puritan ethic, and while that is clearly a source of the rhetoric, we suggest that it should also be seen as a call to reject dependency and develop the basis for autonomy.

44. "Vindex [Sam Adams]," *Boston Gazette*, January 21, 1771, reprinted in *The Writings of Samuel Adams*, ed. H. A. Cushing (New York, 1904–1908), II, 152.

45. [John Adams and Daniel Leonard], *Novanglus and Massachusettensis* (Boston, 1819), p. 269.

46. "Proceedings of the Council," November 29, 1773, quoted in Gipson, *The Coming of the Revolution* (New York, 1954), p. 221.

47. [Otis], "Hampden to Pym," *Boston Gazette*, January 27, 1776. Cf. Bernard Bailyn, *The Origins of American Politics* (New York, 1968), *passim*.

48. See Gordon Wood's perceptive comment that "ultimately the persuasiveness of republicanism for Americans had something to do . . . with a defense of their self-respect." (*Creation of the American Republic*, pp. 106–107.)

49. Bushman, *From Puritan to Yankee*, pp. 194–195.

50. John Dickinson, "Letters from a Farmer" [1768], in *The Writings of John Dickinson*, ed. Paul L. Ford [*Memoirs of the Historical Society of Pennsylvania*, XIV (Philadelphia, 1895)], p. 326.

51. *Essex Gazette*, November 1, 1768.

52. [Allen], *American: Alarm, or the Bostonian Plea* (Boston, 1773), p. 23.

53. "House of Representatives of Massachusetts to Benjamin Franklin," November 6, 1770, in Samuel Adams, *Writings*, II, 55.

54. Dickinson, "Letters from a Farmer," p. 326.

55. "Thoughts on Defensive War," *Pennsylvania Magazine*, July 1775.

56. *New York Journal*, May 25, 1775.

57. John Carmichael, *A Self-Defensive War Lawful* (Lancaster, [1775]), p. 5.

58. *Poems of Philip Freneau*, ed. Fred L. Pattee (Princeton, N.J., 1902), I, 187. Richard Wells demanded to know whether Britain had "trained up her children, like calves in the stall, to fall bloody victims by her own unnatural cruel hands?" (*A Few Political Reflections Submitted to the Consideration of the British Colonies*, pp. 12–13.) Cried John Cleaveland: "*Great Britain*, adieu! No longer shall we honour you as our mother; you are become cruel; you have not so much bowels as the sea monsters towards their young ones. We have cried to you for justice, but behold violence and blood shed! Your sword is drawn offensively, and . . . by this stroke you have broken us off from you, and effectually alienated us from you." ("Johannes in Eremo," April 20, 1775, quoted in Peter Force, comp., *American Archives*, 4th ser. [Washington, 1839], II, 369.

59. Ibid., p. 369.

60. "Letter to General Gage, June 17, 1775," *Boston Gazette*, July 17, 1775.

61. Paine, *Common Sense* (Philadelphia, 1776), reprinted in *The Complete Works of Thomas Paine*, ed. Philip S. Foner (New York, 1945), I, 25.

62. Adams to Hezekiah Niles, February 13, 1818 [Adams and Leonard], *Novanglus and Massachusettensis*, p. 233.

63. Weinstein and Platt, *Wish to Be Free*, pp. 7, 34.

64. Adams, "A Dissertation on the Canon and Feudal Law," reprinted in *The Works of John Adams*, ed. C. F. Adams (Boston, 1850–56), III, 448–64.

65. *Diary and Autobiography of John Adams*, ed. L. H. Butterfield (Cambridge, Mass., 1961), II, 97.

66. Josiah Quincy, *Observations on the Act of Parliament, Commonly Called the Boston Port Bill* (Boston, 1774), p. 14.

67. John Adams, *Diary and Autobiography*, II, 236.

68. The perplexity produced by the attempt to unravel Tory motivation emerges in several works: William H. Nelson's excellent *The American Tory* (New York, 1961); Claude H. Van Tyne, *The Loyalists in the American Revolution* (New York, 1902); Leonard Labaree, "The Nature of American Loyalism," American Antiquarian Society, *Proceedings*, 54 (1944), 15–57; Evarts B. Greene, *The Revolutionary Generation, 1763–1790* (New York, 1950), pp. 198–230; North Callahan, *Flight from the Republic: The Tories of the American Revolution* (Indianapolis, 1967); Wallace Brown, *The Good Americans: The Loyalists in the American Revolution* (New York, 1969); William A. Benton, *Whig-Loyalism: An Aspect of Political Ideology in the American Revolutionary Era* (Rutherford, N.J., 1969); Robert McC. Calhoon, "Critics of Colonial Resistance in the Pre-Revolutionary Debate, 1763–1776" (unpub. PhD diss., Western Reserve, 1964); Paul H. Smith, "The American Loyalists: Notes on their Organization and Numerical Strength," *William and Mary Quarterly*, 3d ser., 25 (1968), 259–277.

69. Boucher, *Reminiscences of an American Loyalist, 1738–1789* (New York, 1967), pp. 87–88.

70. Boucher, "On the Strife Between Abram and Lot," in *A View of the Causes and Consequences of the American Revolution, in Thirteen Discourses* (London, 1797), pp. 360–61.

71. John W. Lydekker, *The Life and Letters of Charles Inglis* (London, 1936), p. 159. Leonard, too, blamed the colonists. "Are we to take up arms and make war against our parent[?]" "The annals of the world have not yet been deformed with a single instance of so unnatural, so causless [sic], so wanton, so wicked a rebellion" ([Adams and Leonard], *Novanglus and Massachusettensis*, p. 217). Peter Oliver's son fretted that Britain might "punish us, according as we deserve it." (Dr. Peter Oliver to Hutchinson, September 2, 1774, in *Diary and Letters of His Excellency Thomas Hutchinson Esq.*, ed. Peter Orlando Hutchinson [Boston, 1884–1886], II, 247.) Thomas Chandler insisted that "our minds are unprincipled, and our hearts disposed for rebellion. Ever since the reduction of Canada, we have been bloated with a vain opinion of our own power and importance. Our ease has produced pride and wantonness. We have been intoxicated with such draughts of liberty, as our constitutions would not bear." ([Rev. Thomas Bradbury Chandler], *A Friendly Address to All Reasonable Americans, On the Subject of Our Political Confusions* [New York, 1774], p. 4.)

72. [Boucher], *A Letter from a Virginian, to the Members of the Congress to be held at Philadelphia on the First of September, 1774* ([New York], 1774), pp. 3–4.

73. [Rev. Charles Inglis], *The True Interest of America Impartially Stated in Certain St[r]ictures on a Pamphlet intitled Common Sense* (Philadelphia, 1776), p. 49. Boucher was every bit as emphatic: "Independency is the forbidden fruit which our tempters hold out to us," he sermonized, and "*in the day we eat thereof we shall surely die.*" ("On the Strife Between Abram and Lot," *View of the Causes and Consequences*, p. 349.)

Repeatedly Loyalists bemoaned the weakness of British control and warned that the colonists, left to their own devices, would fall upon each other. Young Peter Oliver argued that "if the Ministry give way to us, we are an undone people." (Hutchinson, *Diary and Letters*, II, 247.) And Boucher, too, "grumble[d] & complain[ed] of the Strange Inattention of the Mother Country to these Countries! . . . Without seeing, or, at least, without attending to it, She is suffering a strange refractory Spirit to grow up, which, ere long, will work her irremediable Woe." (Boucher to the Rev. Mr. James, November 16, 1773. "Letters of Jonathan Boucher" [*Maryland Historical Magazine*, VII–IX (1912–14)], VIII, 183–84.) Chandler feared that "a final victory would effectually ruin us; as it would necessarily introduce civil wars among ourselves" and America would become "a theatre of inconceivable misery and horror." ([Chandler], *What think ye of the Congress Now?* [New York, 1775], p. 25.) The prevalence of this theme suggests the possibility that the Loyalists were, on some level, aware of the new strength and power of the colonists, and feared that unless that strength were restrained by the mother country, it would erupt into uncontrollable outbursts of destructive fury.

74. [Boucher], *Letter from a Virginian*, p. 26.

75. In another context, Weinstein and Platt speak of "individuals and groups who would not or could not accept the new values, and even disadvantaged elements, who felt themselves more threatened by the attack on traditional morals than by their dependent, subordinate position, [and] could be mobilized to defend the old order." (*Wish to Be Free*, pp. 36, 44.)

76. *View of the Causes and Consequences*, pp. 309–310. Chandler queried "whether some degree of respect be not always due from inferiors to superiors" and "whether it be not a matter both of worldly wisdom, and of indispensible Christian duty, in every *American, to fear the Lord and the King, and to meddle not with them that are Given to Change?*" ([Chandler], *The American Querist; Or, Some Questions* [New York, 1774], not paginated.)

77. Price, *Observations on the Nature of Civil Liberty, the Principles of Government, and the Justice and Policy of the War with America* (London, 1776), p. 53.

78. [Stewart], *A Letter to the Rev. Dr. Price* (London, 1776), pp. 25–26.

79. [James Macpherson], *The Rights of Great Britain Asserted Against the Claims of America* (London, 1776), pp. 24–25.

80. "Distressed Englishman," *Gazetteer and New Daily Advertiser*, January 19, 1775.

81. [Macpherson], *Rights of Great Britain*, p. 85.

82. [Knox], *The Controversy Between Great Britain and her Colonies Reviewed* (London, 1769), p. 204.

83. Mannoni, *Prospero and Caliban*, pp. 32–33.

84. *Ibid.*, p. 203.

85. Memmi, *Colonizer and the Colonized*, pp. 16–17: "All have at least this profound satisfaction of being negatively better than the colonized: they are never completely engulfed in the abasement into which colonialism drives them." "What revenge and what pride for a noncolonized small-time carpenter to walk side by side with an Arab laborer carrying a board and a few nails on his head!"

86. Fanon, *Black Skin, White Masks*, trans. C. L. Markmann (New York, 1967), pp. 60, 84, 31. Another interesting analogy may be drawn to the behavior of twentieth-century bourgeois American parents, among whom a common reaction to the onset of adolescence is a hesitation to give up the satisfactions of parenthood: "Most adults seem to have little tolerance for . . . displays that seem to them to imply a loss of adult prestige and a weakening of their authority." (Paul A. Osterrieth, "Adolescence: Some Psychological Aspects," in Gerard Caplan and Serge Lebovici, eds., *Adolescence: Psychosocial Perspectives* [New York, 1969], p. 17.) Cf. James Anthony, "The Reaction of Adults to Adolescents and Their Behavior," *ibid.*, p. 68; Elizabeth Douvan and Joseph Adelson, *The Adolescent Experience* (New York, 1966), p. 128.

87. See the remarks of Wilhelm Reich on the German lower-middle-class man, who despite his own deplorable condition, perceived himself in the Führer, and was reconciled gladly to his fate: "The wretchedness of his material and sexual situation is so overshadowed by the exalting idea of belonging to a master race and having a brilliant führer that, as time goes on, he ceases to realize how completely he has sunk to a position of insignificant, blind allegiance." (Reich, *Mass Psychology of Fascism*, p. 63.)

4

POLITICS AND PERSONALITY
Loyalists and Revolutionaries in New York

N.E.H. HULL, PETER C. HOFFER, AND STEVEN L. ALLEN

In their seventh hypothesis Burrows and Wallace discuss the problem of division among colonial Americans. Why did some people revolt and others remain persistently loyal to the crown? Answering the call they then make for intensive studies of Loyalist and Revolutionary personality profiles, the authors of the next essay set out to examine empirically the personal characteristics of New York leaders on both sides. The resulting study represents one of the first such attempts on the part of historians. It illustrates both the strengths and weaknesses of this approach. The effort here is to measure the dispositions and values of persons in the sample (scientifically representative or not); but to do so for a group one has to hold time constant, and conceivably such characteristics change when we examine a single subject closely over time: accused of having a "closed mind," one might retort that proof of not having one is a willingness to change it—and go ahead to do so. In any case historians and biographers usually pay attention to personality growth and attitudinal development, growing uneasy when the element of time is suspended. Then again there is something a bit arbitrary and suspect about the categories that sociologists and political scientists—and the authors of the piece below—establish and apply. What real difference, for example, is there between intolerance of dissent and hatred of ambiguity, or between submission to authority and power orientation? Finally, a critic could maintain that trait studies becloud a crucial question: whether personality is cause or effect of these observable tendencies.

Hull, Hoffer, and Allen have anticipated many of these questions. They rely on clinical findings, for example, to strengthen the position that traits change little or not at all in one's adulthood. They quite correctly point out that trait psychology enables historians to explore the psychological makeup of adults—where the evidence is—to do it systematically, and to learn more about group characteristics, thus releasing psychohistory from its frequent preoccupation with biography. Furthermore, their research invites historians to consider habits of thought as well as what people thought

Adapted from *Journal of American History* 65 (September 1978):344–66. Tables 1, 3–7, and 9, copyright © *The Journal of American History* and reprinted with permission.

or how anxious they were. They thus encourage more attention to cognitive psychology in history, and this area of theory could lead to interesting new historical research. It might make clear the newness of such work to describe it not as psychohistory (an informed sense of the unconscious) but as historical psychology, for it amounts to trying to measure the capacities of men and women in the past.

IN THE COURSE of a generation of ideological, political, and military upheaval, almost every American colonist faced a choice between rebellion and obedience. While necessity and accident played their roles in these decisions, human choice should always be viewed in psychological terms as well. As Fred I. Greenstein, a political scientist, puts it, "human action is *never* directly caused by situations; it is invariably mediated by psychological variables." A handful of Loyalists and Revolutionaries have left behind them sufficient evidence for the historian to probe the psychological dimensions of political affiliation in the past.[1]

This essay is a report on the application of modern psychological scaling techniques and quantitative methods to the study of political division between the King's friends and opponents. The colony of New York presents the problem of revolutionary political choice at its most complex. Recent studies agree that Loyalists and Whigs there defy easy categorization. Aristocratic planters, merchants, yeoman farmers, and professional men can be found in both camps. In centers of intense political activity, such as Kings County, partisans regularly switched sides, and on the whole it seems nearly impossible to determine why some New Yorkers revolted and others remained loyal to the Crown.[2] The inconclusiveness of conventional explanations calls for a new approach.

A few American historians have already applied psychological concepts to revolutionary behavior. They have confined themselves to childhood-centered "dynamic" or "ego" psychology to explain the thought of leading figures of both parties. Though these investigations reveal the potential of psychological inquiry, they are by their nature self-limiting. As one spokesman in the field has written, "no childhood, no psychohistory."[3] Dynamic psychology must have specific documentation on the subject's early years to be effective, and material for childhood studies is not available for more than a very few eighteenth-century individuals. What is more, even the most able dynamic psychohistories vary greatly in texture and emphasis according to the particular authors' intuition. Analysis of group affiliation, particularly complex political coalitions like the Loyalists and the Revolutionaries, requires a higher level of consistency and comparability than a simple collation of individual psychobiographies can attain.

This essay introduces a method based upon trait psychology.[4] Our hypothesis is that measurable differences in adult personality distinguished

Loyalists from Whigs in colonial New York. Our first step was to fashion a scale of personality traits linking personal conviction and public conduct. This "LR" (Loyalist-Revolutionary) scale registered traits—mental and emotional attributes more persistent and deeply ingrained than opinions, but never "subconscious" or hidden from the historian's eye. To evaluate the significance of the differences in personality between Loyalists and Patriots which the LR scale measures, the authors also devised a PEF (political-economic-family ties) scale out of the elements historians usually use in explaining why colonists divided as they did on the question of independence. From a long list of colonial New York leaders, we found sufficient biographical data and manuscript materials for 38 Loyalists and 42 Revolutionaries.[5] The only criterion that we used in deciding whether to include a subject in the study was the availability of sufficient biographical and manuscript sources to complete at least one-half of the items of the LR and PEF scales for that individual. The size of the final population, small by comparison with the total number of Loyalists and Revolutionaries in the colony, does not handicap our ability to assess the discriminatory power of LR and PEF hypotheses. These 80 individuals do not make up a representative sample. The goal is to determine whether psychological factors differentiate Tories from Patriots as well as political, economic, and social forces, and not to discover what proportion of either group in the colony as a whole fit any particular socioeconomic or psychological category.

The LR scale is a nine-item personality inventory, designed to investigate adult personality characteristics of public figures in the past. Academic psychologists and social psychologists have developed such scales to test adult cognitive and affective characteristics. Although sophisticated modern personality inventories are too specific for surviving manuscript sources, they have been used here to create a simplified test of traits. With the LR scale, one may measure the personal roots of political choice. Personality is the mental structure that governs the individual's response to external stimuli, including political crisis. We are convinced that "the political, economic, and social convictions of an individual often form a broad and coherent pattern, as if bound together by a 'mentality' or 'spirit,' and that this pattern is an expression of deeply [felt] trends in his personality."[6]

To isolate and evaluate major personality traits in historical figures, one must, as Robert Calhoon has written, find the subjects' "statements of self-consciousness and self-awareness." For many years, political scientists have employed individual attitude scales as indicators of aggregate political motivation. In this essay, the same thing is done using historical manuscripts, public orations, and privately recorded conversations as raw data. Although the authors, who served as scorers of this material, avoided including a person on the scale without an adequate sample of his writing covering a substantial portion of his career, they did accept the principle that scoring could be applied to any kind of surviving document.[7]

The first item on the LR scale measures the need for order, neatness, control of possessions and situations, and the desire for regularity in life experiences. Closely allied to the need for order is a need for definition in expectation, deliberateness, and sobriety. Threats to personal and social stability are magnified by those who have a positive need for order. Pierre Van Cortlandt, for example, expressed this need for order in a report he drafted to the state committee of safety late in 1776: "At a time when the utmost resources of this State were laid open to their [the soldiers'] wants, . . . and after frequent losses of provisions and barracks, to supply two numerous armies, . . . with every article which they required, . . . wherever our troops have marched or been stationed, they have done infinite damage to the possessions and farms, and pilfered the property of the people." In Cadwallader Colden's plea for "as much quietness as could be expected in the present situation" and his demand for suppression of "riots and tumults" during the Stamp Act crisis, there is the same need for order. A negative scorer, like Henry Wisner, required far less order. It did not seem to disturb him that settlers following his directions got lost or that he was not available to sign the Declaration of Independence which he approved the day before.[8]

The next item, intolerance of dissonance, probes the subject's perceptual style. Cognitive dissonance is the product of conflicting cognitive elements within a person's mind, for example, conflicting ideas about what is happening and what ought to be happening. Dissonance is uncomfortable and every individual works to reduce it. For some, dissonance is more unbearable than for others, and this study is based on the belief that "variation in 'toleration for dissonance' would seem to be measurable." An individual's methods of reducing dissonance, such as denial of reality, shifts in group attachment, and selective perception, indicate that individual's ability to handle dissonance. In William Duer's admonition to his untrustworthy apprentice, "be assured I will leave no stone unturned either to confirm what I have strong reason to suspect, or to remove those suspicions," he tried to reduce an intolerable dissonance by seeking new information. Duer showed a low threshold for dissonance on questions that would not have disturbed others, and scored positively on the item. One rarely sees William Smith, Jr., so beset by dissonance. Instead, as he noted in his journal of June 5, 1775, "In times of so much heat, a wise man will set a double guard upon his steps to avoid precipitation." So, too, Beverley Robinson coolly told the state committee for the detection of conspiracies, "Sir, I cant take the oath [of allegiance], but should be exceedingly glad to stay in the country. . . . It is very uncertain who will rule yet for the matter is not determined." Robinson, like Smith, a negative scorer, could have waited out the war, dealing with both sides, without being unduly disturbed by dissonance.[9]

The next four items are loosely derived from the concept of "authoritarianism." Intolerance for ambiguity, item three, is the tendency to see events and issues in black and white terms, to make mechanical judgments, and to be rigid in their application. Charles Inglis' delight that "A perfect harmony has hitherto subsisted between me and my people. Many reigning vices are checked, some quite suppressed" shows an intolerance for ambiguity repeated much later in his castigation of Paine's *Common Sense* as "one of the most virulent, artful, and pernicious pamphlets I have ever met with, and perhaps the wit of man could not devise one better calculated to do mischief." Inglis' fear of Paine may not have been unfounded—many revolutionaries feared Paine's radicalism—but Inglis' reaction to the pamphlet was quick and uncompromising: "At the risk, not only of my liberty, but of my live [*sic*], I drew up an answer, and had it printed here." Others opposed Paine, but listened to both sides of the issue and considered compromise. Among them was Henry Van Schaack, who wrote to his brother Peter, "I told them [the members of the New York delegation to the Continental Congress] that every good man ought to do his endeavors to think of a reconciliation, instead of widening the breach; that perhaps when the House met, some conciliating plan might be suggested and approved. . . ." It should be noted that items two and three are theoretically related.[10]

Item four explores submission to authority. The key concepts here are a need to be dominated, to have visible and rigid rules for dependency, and an affinity for authoritarian leadership. Father figures, a benevolent father-king, for example, are given greater importance by positive scorers on item four than by negative scorers. It is clear where Myles Cooper, president of Kings College, stood on the scale. Comparing rebels to schoolboys in 1775, he rhymed:

So oft the giddy Eton Boys,
Disturb, Oh, Thames, thy peaceful Joys
. . . .
Calling their Comrades, Knaves and Fools,
Who tamely crouch, to College Rules
. . . .
But they cabal, harrangue, resolve,
Rebel, associate, run away;
Exult in Anarchy's short Day.
. . . .
The gen'ral Tenor of its runs,
That Fathers shan't controul their Sons.

James Beekman saw the crisis differently: "But it is impossible that freeborn Englishmen, as we are, . . . should now submit to Parliamentary Taxations, without giving up our Title to Freedom, and become Vassals and Slaves." Beekman's attitude was what Else Frenkel-Brunswik has called "principled independence," the opposite of authoritarian submission.[11]

Power orientation, item five, traces the subject's emphasis upon power relationships in his perceptions of the outside world. Be the situation political, economic, or social, the positive scorer on item five will always be skeptical of idealistic or affective relationships, and instead see interest and advantage as the true motives of others. Positive scorers also tend to divide the world into their own group, family, party, or sect—and "out groups" whose motives and methods are invariably suspect. Robert Livingston, Jr., whose father held vast family estates on the Hudson, saw interpersonal conflicts as power struggles for influence, land, and wealth. He warned his son-in-law, James Duane, against continuing to represent the rival DeLancey family in legal matters, for a "violent spirit still reigned in their hearts." Duane was to join with "men of more sense and honor"—the Livingstons. At the same time, Livingston was writing to Philip Schuyler, "There is a great deal in good management of the votes. Our people are in high spirits, and if there is not fair play shown there will be bloodshed, as we have by far the best part of the bruisers on our side."[12]

Item six, hierarchical thinking and authoritarian aggression, combines two closely related concepts—the subjects' high esteem for those who have power and the subjects' desire to use power themselves. For positive scorers, status confers worth, and they rank other persons according to their power. Positive scorers believe strength and decisiveness good, and weakness bad. John Peters, a transplanted Connecticut Puritan and a Loyalist, illustrated the first of these attributes in his appeal to the crown for recompense: "Some persons, who have commissions, altho very small ones, treated me and other gentlemen very ill by saying that non-commissioned officers should command us... I am a colonel in the militia in Gloucester County, and have my commission with me... I am also one of the judges of the court of common pleas in that county... I am descended from a gentleman who settled in New England and not of the meanest family but one of the best." Alexander Hamilton illustrated the second portion of item six: "... my Ambition is prevalent," he wrote while a youth, "that I contemn [sic] the grov'ling and condition of a Clerk or the like, to which my Fortune &c. condemns me and would willingly risk my life tho' not my Character to exalt my Station." Five years later, in 1774, he expressed the same drives by warning England that military action would be met by bloody, implacable, and obstinate colonial resistance. Where others among the patriot party recoiled from strife, Hamilton embraced it. Samuel Provoost, the assistant rector of Trinity Church, scored negatively on item six, for he believed "my situation perfectly agreeable if it were not for the bigotry and enthusiasm that generally prevail here among people of all denominations.... As I found this to be the case, I made it a point to preach the plain doctrine of religion and morality." Throughout the crisis, Provoost avoided power and shunned status, claiming instead to be guided by conscience.[13]

The last three items concern the social ideas, "schematizations" of values, held by loyalists and revolutionaries. Schematizations are cognitive frameworks, mental lattices of one's values and expectations. They are particularly useful tools for the historian, for they are often the substance of self-descriptive and normative essays. Item seven is concerned with the subjects' views of established institutions, customary ways of thought, and traditions. When Justice Thomas Jones of Long Island, for example, warned the rebels, especially William Livingston, against "pulling down the Church and ruining the constitution," he scored positively on item seven. Of all the items on the scale, this one comes closest to the category of ideology. Positive scorers are conservative and negative scorers welcome change and reform.[14]

Conformity, item eight, evaluates the subject's desire for peer group acceptance and social harmony. The positive scorer tries to fit his behavior and opinion to the current norms of the group in which he happens to belong and demands the same conformity from neighbors. While late eighteenth-century New York had its share of conformists, there were notable exceptions. William Livingston was one. In his October 11, 1753, *Independent Reflector*, he opined "that the word *Orthodoxy*, is a hard equivocal priestly Term, that caused the Effusion of more Blood than all the Roman Emperors put together." Support came from young Schuyler. "I esteem the Church and its liturgy," he wrote in 1753, "but I believe [William Livingston] is right in opposing the ridiculous pretensions of the clergy, who would make it as infallible as the popish church claims to be. I wish liberty of conscience in all things."[15]

The last item in the scale tests the subject's stereotyping of people and events. If the subject labels rather than seeking individual differences, and lumps other individuals together into narrowly defined, demeaning categories, a positive score was assigned on item nine. Merchant Gerard Beekman's descriptions of other groups—"New England men are bad pay," the Irish are "scowbankers," the French are untrustworthy, and Beekman himself "almost Turned Jew" in his business activities—give him a positive score on this item. William Smith, Jr., scored negatively, in part for his willingness to criticize his beloved father for using "an affecting representation of the agonies of the cross" in a speech denying political rights to the Jews of the city of New York. William Smith, Sr.'s, "religious and political creed were [*sic*] both inflamed by the heat . . . of the times. . . . Perhaps," his son suggested, "he was not himself at that time."[16]

The entire LR scale measures individual intolerance for disorder, dissent, independence, equality, change, and nonconformity. A positive score, $+1$, was given for a subject on an item if the subject showed a positive attitude, a -1 if a negative attitude appeared, and no score if the evidence was missing or ambiguous. Although, as is evident from the examples above, not every Revolutionary obtained a negative score nor every Loyalist a positive score on each item, the two groups did tend to score differently. Our hypothesis was that Revolutionaries were likely to be negative scorers on every item and overall, and Loyalists the reverse. Because the results depended so much upon the scoring of the manuscript documents, every effort was made to insure that the scoring would be both sensitive and objective. To guarantee that no systematic bias crept into the scoring, two of the authors scored "blind," that is, without knowing the identity or political affiliation of the subject. Conferences were held after the scoring was completed to discuss disputed results. If the authors could not then agree, the item was not entered for that individual. After a practice session on a small sample of the group, the authors found they tended to agree on their scores.[17]

Throughout the scoring, the authors were aware of the problem of possible personality change after 1776. We assumed that personality differences were the causes of individual decision making in the crisis, yet a small portion of the documentary material came from the period after the Declaration of Independence. Were the traits measured in these cases created by events rather than the reverse? Two recent technical essays were reassuring on this matter. First, Raymond Cattell and his associates have established the fact that personality traits such as "radicalism" and "self-sufficiency"—closely related to the first, fourth, fifth, sixth, seventh, and eighth items—change very little, if at all, between sixteen and sixty. Of course, a stress situation as severe as the Revolutionary crisis might have affected personality—but to what extent? The latest cognitive dissonance experiments suggest that important decisions, far from changing established opinions and attitudes, tend, after a period of regret, to "fix" the pre-decisional state of mind.[18]

Next, a word on the PEF scale, which reflects the sex, age in 1776, education, place of birth, place of residence, officeholding record, religious affiliation, occupation, wealth, travel experience, ethnic background, and military experience of our sample of New Yorkers.[19] Also on this scale are the "F" items relating to family composition, a number of social-psychological hypotheses on the cause of political choice. They proceed from the work of historian Philip Greven and a psychologist, the late Alfred Adler. Greven postulated a causal relationship between the social independence of the fourth and fifth generation and those generations' participation in the rebellion. The children of earlier generations were more dependent upon their parents and tended to live nearer home, marry later, and seek less personal autonomy than the fourth and fifth generations. The latter left the family sooner and were consequently more accustomed to independence. For these individuals, "Thomas Paine's call for independence in 1776 from the mother-country and from the father-king might have been just what Paine claimed it to be—common sense." Following Greven, it was hypothesized that if the subject were fourth generation or later, married before the father's death, and did not live at his place of birth, he should have been a Revolutionary.[20]

The second group of F items expresses in historical terms a facet of Adler's "individual psychology." Adler argued that the "family constellation" had a major impact on the behavioral goals of its members. Older children, after losing the attention of parents to younger siblings, sought to regain adult approval. Middle children lost some but not all of the parents' attention and so wished the approval but not with the same intensity as the eldest child. The youngest child, spurred and tutored by older siblings, while still bathed in the love of parents, could feel secure enough to devote his or her attention to personal goals. Recent experiments show that oldest children indeed require more approval from peer group and parental figures, while children lower in sibling order are more personalized, introspective, and independent in their goals. We hypothesized that older children were more likely to be Loyalists and younger children in the family more likely to be Revolutionaries.[21] While the primary aim of this essay is not to prove or disprove any of the PEF hypotheses so much as to compare their discriminating power with that of the LR scale hypotheses, the quantitative results on the PEF scale are interesting in their own right. In some cases they represent the first numerical test of these theories, and the results are highly informative.

In our effort to assess the comparative validity of the LR and PEF scales— that is, how truly they reflected actual choices—we first determined the percentage of errors each of them made in classifying subjects as Loyalist or Revolutionary. If, under the hypotheses we proposed, the scale score for an individual labelled him as a Patriot (or a Loyalist), and he actually had joined the other side, he was counted as a "classification error" for that item. Every hypothesis was "two-sided." We supposed, for example, that subjects who held executive offices at some time in their careers chose Loyalism, and found that 19 executive officeholders were in fact Loyalists and 12 Revolutionaries, leaving 12 errors or misclassifications out of 31 cases (12 wrong + 19 correct). For the other side of the hypothesis—that non-officeholders would be Revolutionaries—we discovered 27 Whigs and 7 Loyalists, a total of 7 classification errors out of 34 cases. On this item of the PEF scale, there were in all 19 errors for 65 cases or only 29 percent, making clear the value of the hypothesis.

The various LR hypotheses, corresponding to the nine items, were all tested for classification errors in the same manner. The results appear in Table 4.1.

Next, we sought the combination of LR hypotheses that would produce the strongest discrimination between Loyalists and Revolutionaries. Until further study of the scoring of "traditionalism," this item was temporarily excluded. So uniform was the Loyalist scoring on it that we feared it reflected the psychological phenomenon of rationalization rather than the values being tested. The remaining LR hypotheses were tested and combined in the same method used for the PE hypotheses. A short LR scale combining all of the four highly discriminatory hypotheses with "order," one of the marginally discriminatory hypotheses, produced the fewest equivalent classification errors. Table 4.2 displays the distribution of short LR scale scores.

To find the most telling combination of variables on the LR scale, we scored each subject on all nine hypotheses. We assigned a positive score of +1 when a subject fulfilled the Loyalist condition of a hypothesis and a

Table 4.1   Personality Characteristics (LR) Hypotheses

Hypotheses	Percent error	τb percent	λb percent
Highly Discriminatory			
Tradition	20	39	59
Submission	24	25	51
Conformity	30	14	38
Power orientation	37	11	16
Hierarchical thinking/authoritarian aggression	36	9	24
Marginally Discriminatory			
Order	43	4	8
Stereotyping	41	3	10
Non-Discriminatory			
Dissonance	46	1	8
Ambiguity	53	—	

Tau-b and lambda-b are statistical measures of the separating or discriminatory power of the items. They, and not the actual percentage of classification errors, were used to class the items as being highly discriminatory, marginally discriminatory, or non-discriminatory, because they take into account the number of the 80 subjects actually scored for each item. The more who were scored for the item, the more credence one can place in the classifying power of the hypothesis.[22]

negative score of -1 when he met the opposite, Revolutionary criterion, regardless of his actual political affiliation. We then used a form of discriminant analysis to find the best combination of hypotheses by combining each subject's scores on all the hypotheses.[23] The result was that some subjects had high positive scores, others low ones, and a middle group emerged with $+$ and $-$ scores that tended to cancel out one another. An individual with a preponderance of $+$ scores was classified as a Loyalist, and one with a pre-

Table 4.2   Distribution of Scores on Combined Personality Characteristics Hypotheses (Short LR Scale)

Score on short LR scale		Actually loyalist	Actually revolutionary
"High"	5	14	1
	4	5	2
"Middle"	3	4	4
	2	1	3
	1	9	9
	0	2	2
"Low"	−1	2	8
	−2	0	1
	−3	1	10
	−4	0	0
	−5	0	2

ponderance of − scores as a Revolutionary. In cases where the scores tended
to balance each other, the subject was not classified. While the ideal would
have been to classify everyone as either Tory or Whig according to the short
LR scale, we did not wish to do so while amassing a large proportion of
classification errors. To determine how large this middle group would be, we
had to decide what number of classification errors could be committed before
we simply left a group of subjects unclassified. Our decision was to define the
middle group as those subjects with the same score who could not be
classified as either Loyalist or Revolutionary without exceeding 33 percent
classification errors. The end product of our calculations appears in Table
4.3.

The result of this psychohistorical experiment is that, using the LR scale,
we can classify and at least hope to explain the behavior of Loyalists and
Revolutionaries in 1776 with only 13 percent errors in classification. The
question is how these findings compare with the best conventional political,
economic, and familial theories of affiliation. Table 4.4 summarizes the discriminating power of all the PEF items as did Table 4.1 for the LR scale: We
next computed the combination of PE hypotheses that would most strongly
discriminate between Loyalists and Patriots. This short PE scale is equivalent
to the most discriminatory combination of LR hypothesis calculated in Table
4.2. Royal officeholding and age at 1776 were excluded. The former was
omitted because by the time of the arrival of Governor William Tryon, in
1771, royal offices were only given to those men who had already shown
their aversion to dissent. Age at 1776 was dismissed because young Loyalists
did not have the same opportunity to gain political prominence or economic
status, and so leave manuscripts behind them, as did the young Revolutionaries. Had the British won the war, the reverse might have been true.

The several PE hypotheses making the fewest equivalent classification
errors was the combination of all four remaining highly discriminatory
hypotheses and one of the marginally discriminating hypotheses—wealth.
Table 4.5 shows the results of the classification using this short scale. The
combined PE hypotheses have only 13 percent errors on the subjects

Table 4.3   Combined Personality Characteristics Hypotheses (Short LR Scale)

Classifications	Actually loyalist	Actually revolutionary
Loyalist (high combined score)	19	3
Unclassified (middle combined score)	16	18
Revolutionary (low combined score)	3	21

Classification errors, 6; total classified, 46; classification error, 13%.
Equivalent classification errors, 17.2; number of subjects, 80; equivalent classification error,
   22%.

Table 4.4   Political and Economic (PEF) Hypotheses

Hypotheses	Percent error	τb percent	λb percent
Highly Discriminatory			
Royal officeholding	25	24	46
Legislative officeholding	25	23	46
Church affiliation	29	15	35
Place of birth	33	11	30
Executive officeholding	33	10	27
Marginally Discriminatory			
Age at 1776	40	4	12
Generation family in colonies	31[a]	4	12
Wealth	40	3	17
Non-Discriminatory			
European travel	36	2	5
Occupation	42	1	6
Residence	46	0	3
Education	48	0	0
Military service	49	0	0
Travel in American colonies	52	[b]	[b]
Officeholding	53	—	—
Ethnic derivation	59	—	—
Multiple officeholding	60	—	—

[a] Variance caused by difference in number of subjects classified.
[b] Values of τb and λb not meaningful for hypotheses with greater than 50% errors.

classified and 20 percent equivalent errors on all subjects, compared with 25 percent errors on the best of the individual PE hypotheses.

Table 4.3 showed the results of classification of the subjects using the short LR scale. Comparison with Table 4.5 reveals that the combined LR hypotheses yield no more error—13 percent—than the combined PE hypotheses on the subjects classified by each of the short scales, and the former commits only a slightly higher percentage of equivalent classification errors on all subjects than the latter—22 percent versus 20 percent. There is no real difference between the validity of the two scales.[24]

Table 4.5   Combined Political-Economic Hypotheses (Short PE Scale)

Classifications	Actually loyalist	Actually revolutionary
Loyalist (high combined score)	20	3
Unclassified (middle combined score)	14	13
Revolutionary (low combined score)	4	26

Classification errors, 7; total classified, 53; classification error, 13%.
Equivalent classification errors, 15.9; number of subjects, 80; equivalent classification error, 20%.

We performed further tests with F items to determine if there were other ways of explaining political affiliation in the colony. The Greven thesis was nondiscriminatory; of those subjects who fit the Revolutionary prescription, two in fact were Patriots and two were Loyalists. The reverse of the Greven hypothesis, describing conditions leading to Loyalism, fared better, fitting four Tories and one Revolutionary. Sibling order generally agreed with Adlerian theory, but the results were marginally discriminatory. Of eldest children in our sample, ten were Loyalists and seven were Revolutionaries. The thesis that ties to either the Livingston (Patriot) or DeLancey (Loyalist) family determined one's political affiliation did hold almost perfectly for those men who were born or married into the two great families; their numbers were few, however, and when all these subjects were removed from the group we found similar results on the short PE and LR scales as when they were included.

It is clear that the LR scale enables historians to explain with new accuracy past political choice among individuals and groups whose biographical information is scanty or contradictory. The reason is simple: psychological components of political choice are not reducible to political, economic, and social factors. Both scales correctly classify strict Loyalists and ardent Revolutionaries. All twelve subjects in the study who received high scores according to both LR and PEF scales were in fact Loyalists, and all sixteen subjects who received low scores on both scales turned out to be Revolutionaries. For the twenty-eight subjects on whom the psychological and situational factors agreed, no classification error was made. Nevertheless, the LR scale does not merely duplicate the results of analysis obtained using the PEF scale. Subjects with middle level scores on the LR scale were distributed evenly among the PEF high, middle, and low score categories. Across the entire group of subjects, the LR and PEF scale scores show 47 percent agreement, a strong but far from perfect correlation. Finally, the combination of the two scale scores for every subject only slightly decreases the number of equivalent classification errors, from 13 percent to 11 percent, as Table 4.6 shows. The LR scale taps a dimension of historical behavior distinct from political career,

Table 4.6   Summed Short Political and Economic (PE) and Short Personality Characteristics (LR) Scales

Classifications	Actually loyalist	Actually revolutionary
Loyalist (high combined scores)	23	3
Unclassified (middle combined scores)	12	13
Revolutionary (low combined scores)	3	26

Classification errors, 6; total classified, 55; classification error, 11%.
Equivalent classification errors, 14.3; number of subjects, 80; equivalent classification error, 18%.

economic wealth, and family connections.[25] Personality traits, it makes clear, are causes of historical action that historians must explore before completing any account of major political events. This study, the first of its kind, can be no more than an introduction to the personality scaling of historical manuscripts. Nonetheless it has proven promising enough that we are moving ahead to examine Loyalists and Revolutionaries in other colonies. Such research should lead to new perspectives on the larger conflict: the extent to which the two groups differ on the LR scale offers a clue as to their capacity to compromise differences and their tendency to confront one another in the public arena; comparison of the internal psychological nature of the two groups may help to explain why in the crisis of the Revolution one group was more effective than the other in mobilizing public opinion. In short, while the study of personality traits does not replace conventional methods and variables, it does provide insights that traditional approaches miss. Because it is difficult to assemble biographical data on many members of political groups, and since the written thoughts of adults are more accessible to the historian than childhood records, the LR scale provides a means of probing the character and intentions of a wide spectrum of political participants. Personality trait studies permit analyses of group behavior, a claim psychobiography cannot make. Cases of individual and group conduct which may seem puzzling under conventional assumptions may become clear to the student of trait psychology. It is our hope that students of other periods of American political history will find the LR scale useful.

NOTES

1. Fred I. Greenstein, *Personality and Politics: Problems of Evidence, Inference, and Conceptualization* (New York, 1975), xviii.

2. Jacob Judd, "Frederick Philipse III of Westchester County: A Reluctant Loyalist," in Robert A. East and Jacob Judd, eds., *The Loyalist Americans: A Focus on Greater New York* (Tarrytown, N.Y., 1975), 25–28; Bernard Mason, *The Road to Independence: The Revolutionary Movement in New York, 1773–1777* (Lexington, Ky., 1966), 64. [Editor's note: For reasons of readability "Whig" and "Patriot" in this essay occasionally appear as synonyms for Revolutionary, as does "Tory" for Loyalist. By taking this license with the Hull et al. article I do not, I believe, damage their argument or obscure their categories of analysis—though to be sure some friends of the Crown in 1776 did claim to adhere to the Whig tradition in English politics, and "patriot" and "tory" were at the time highly charged terms.]

3. Lloyd deMause to the authors, May, 1975.

4. On the use of trait psychology in history, see David C. McClelland, *The Achieving Society* (New York, 1961), 79; T. W. Adorno, Else Frenkel-Brunswik, Daniel J. Levinson, and R. Nevitt Sanford, *The Authoritarian Personality* (New York, 1950); and Leon Festinger, *A Theory of Cognitive Dissonance* (Evanston, Ill., 1957), 249–51.

The methodological decision to use modern psychological concepts to study eighteenth-century figures, in full cognizance of the "culture-bound" limitations of all psychological theory, proceeded from a number of reasons. In the first place, a great similarity exists between the private concerns of our eighteenth-century subjects and men and women today. In a more technical vein, to view or translate proven modern psychological methods into impressionistic eighteenth-century cultural terms would so weaken the validity of the psychological measures as to render them meaningless. Even if strict and consistent "linkages" were proposed between eighteenth-century cultural, political, and social norms and the subjects' lives, and then these linkages used to revise the terminology of modern personality tests, a criticism would still remain: "Which collectivity should the psychohistorian select as the social context in which the individual personality develops?" See Alfred J. Rieber, "Comment on 'The Psychoanalysis of Groups,'" *Group for the Use of Psychology in History Newsletter* 4 (March 1976):28. The use of potentially anachronistic technical terminology in the LR scales cannot weaken the discriminatory power of the LR scale items—simply because Loyalists and Revolutionaries were scored using the same terms and concepts.

5. For the names of the Loyalists and Patriots who made up the sample of 80 persons, as well as the extensive biographical and secondary sources pertinent to this essay, see its original version, Hull, Hoffer, and Allen, "Choosing Sides: A Quantitative Study of the Personality Determinants of Loyalist and Revolutionary Political Affiliation in New York," *Journal of American History* 65 (September 1978):344-66.

6. Roger Brown, *Social Psychology* (New York, 1965), 422; Adorno et al., *Authoritarian Personality*, 1.

7. Robert M. Calhoon, "The Loyalist Perception," *Acadiensis* 2 (Spring 1973):3. Relevant manuscript collections were consulted at the Albany Institute of History and Art, Columbia University, the New-York Historical Society, the New York Public Library, and the New York State Library (Albany).

8. Henry A. Murray, *Explorations in Personality: A Clinical and Experimental Study of Fifty Men of College Age* (New York, 1938), 80-81, 241-42; *Journals of the Provincial Congress of New York* . . . (2 vols., Albany, 1842), 2:211; "Colden Papers," *Collections of the New-York Historical Society*, 9-10 (1876-1877), 10:66-67; Henry Wisner to William Alexander, April 25, 1767, Alexander Manuscripts, New-York Historical Society. The above and all subsequent quotes are examples to illustrate the definitions of LR items and by no means the sole criterion by which an individual was scored on a particular item.

9. Festinger, *Cognitive Dissonance*, 266-68; Jack W. Brehm and Arthur R. Cohen, *Explorations in Cognitive Dissonance* (New York, 1962), 177; William Duer to Robert Snell, 1773, Duer Papers, New-York Historical Society; Smith to Lewis Morris, June 5, 1775, William W. H. Sabine, ed., *The Historical Memoirs of William Smith, Jr.* (3 vols., New York, 1956), 1:228; Beverley Robinson to Conspiracy Committee, Feb. 22, 1777, *Minutes of the Committee to Detect Conspiracies, Collections of the New-York Historical Society*, 57 (1924):148-49.

10. Else Frenkel-Brunswik, "Further Explorations," in Richard Christie and Marie Jahoda, eds., *Studies in the Scope and Method of "The Authoritarian Personality"* (Glencoe, Ill., 1954), 257; Lydekker, *Life and Letters of Inglis* (London, 1936) 17; Charles Inglis, "State of the Anglo-American Church in 1776," O'Callaghan, ed., *Documentary History of the State of New York*, (Albany, 1847-1851), 3:1059; *Memoirs of the Life of Henry Van Schaack* [ed. Henry C. Van Schaack] (Chicago, 1892), 33.

11. Adorno et al., *Authoritarian Personality*, 223-28, 236-38, 414. [Myles Cooper], *Patriots of North America: A Sketch with Explanation, Notes* (New York, 1775), 13; Philip L. White, ed., *Beekman Mercantile Papers, 1749-1799* (3 vols., New York, 1956), 1:758.

12. Robert Livingston, Jr., to Duane, February 17, 1772, Duane Manuscripts, New-York Historical Society; Benson J. Lossing, *The Life and Times of Philip Schuyler* (2 vols., New York, 1872), 1:236.

13. John Peters to unknown correspondent, October 27, 1780, New York State Library Mss.; Harold C. Syrett, ed., *The Papers of Alexander Hamilton* (26 vols., New York, 1961-), 1:4,54; E. C. Chorley, "Samuel Provoost," *Historical Magazine of the Protestant Episcopal Church* 1 (September 1933), 4.

14. David C. McClelland, *Personality* (New York, 1951), 239-88; Thomas Jones, *The History of New York* . . . , ed. Edward F. DeLancey (2 vols., New York, 1879), 1:6.

15. William Livingston et al., *The Independent Reflector* [1754], ed. Milton M. Klein (Cambridge, Mass., 1963), 391; Lossing, *Schuyler*, 1:78.

16. Philip L. White, ed., *Beekman Mercantile Papers, 1746-1799* (3 vols., New York, 1956), 1:223-224; William Smith, Jr., *History of the Province of New York*, ed. Michael Kammen (2 vols., Cambridge, Mass., 1972), 2:34-35.

17. David C. McClelland, Russell A. Clark, Thornton B. Roby, and John W. Atkinson, "The Effect of the Need for Achievement on Thematic Apperception," in John W. Atkinson, ed., *Motives in Fantasy, Action, and Society* (Princeton, 1958), 80.

18. Raymond B. Cattell, *Personality and Motivation: Structure and Measurement* (Yonkers-on-Hudson, N.Y., 1957), quoted in Allan R. Buss and Wayne Poley, *Individual Differences, Traits and Factors* (New York, 1976), 142; Robert A. Wicklund and Jack W. Brehm, *Perspectives on Cognitive Dissonance* (New York, 1976). See also Leon Festinger, *Conflict, Decision, and Dissonance* (Stanford, 1964), 42-44, 61.

19. On these variables in a later setting, see Stanley Elkins and Eric McKitrick, "The Founding Fathers, Young Men of the Revolution," *Political Science Quarterly* 76 (June 1961):181-216. Alexander C. Flick, ed., *The American Revolution in New York: Its Political, Social and Economic Significance* (Albany, 1926); James Kirby Martin, *Men in Rebellion: Higher Governmental Leaders and the Coming of the American Revolution* (New Brunswick, N.J., 1973); and Carl Lotus Becker, *The History of Political Parties in the Province of New York, 1760-1776* (Madison, Wis., 1960).

20. Philip J. Greven, Jr., *Four Generations: Population, Land, and Family in Colonial Andover, Massachusetts* (Ithaca, 1970), 279-81.

21. Heinz L. Ansbacher and Rowena R. Ansbacher, eds., *The Individual Psychology of Alfred Adler: A Systematic Presentation in Selections from His Writings* (New York, 1956), 379; Salvatore R. Maddi, *Personality Theories: A Comparative Analysis* (Homewood, Ill., 1972), 476-78.

22. For a full discussion of these measures, see Herbert M. Blalock, Jr., *Social Statistics* (New York, 1972), 300-303.

23. Adding together scores on different items to form a single score that provides better discrimination than any of the individual items is called discriminant analysis. In discriminant analysis, one usually multiplies the scores on each item by a weight before adding the scores on the items together. The method used in this essay is equivalent to discriminant analysis with all weights confined to being either 0 or 1. Discriminant analysis with weights was attempted, first using weights assigned by maximizing the ratio of between-groups variance to pooled within-groups variance, and second using weights assigned by dummy regression, where regressands were dichotomous variables. These procedures are discussed in Robert A. Eisenbeirs and Robert B. Avery, *Discriminant Analysis and Classification Procedures: Theory and Applications* (Lexington, Mass., 1972). The scores produced by the two procedures did not have substantially greater discriminatory power than the scores produced without using multiplicative factors. The latter method was used to present the results. For a more detailed comparison of the two kinds of discriminant analysis, see footnote 24 below.

24. Other statistical measures of association confirm that the short PE scale has only slightly better discriminatory power than the short LR scale. Goodman and Kruskal's rb is 36 percent for the short PE and 31 percent for the short LR. Ab is 47 percent for the short PE and 42 percent for the short LR. Kendall's correlation coefficient rb (correlating the rank orderings of the individual subjects' scores with whether they were loyalists or revolutionaries) was 51 percent for the short PE and 48 percent for the short LR. The comparison of the two short scales is presented in terms of equivalent classification errors rather than any of the above statistical measures because these measures place too heavy a penalty upon the number of unclassified individuals. See Blalock, *Social Statistics*, 300-303, 418-20.

25. M. Brewster Smith, "A Map For the Analysis of Personality and Politics," *Journal of Social Issues* 24 (July 1968):18-19.

5

THOMAS JEFFERSON
Self and Society

WINTHROP D. JORDAN

Always reflective of their times, and in many cases participating directly in the movement for racial justice during the past few decades, American historians have labored to deepen our understanding of racial tensions and the black experience in this country. The following two selections examine two especially salient topics, the sources of white prejudice and the effects of antebellum slavery. When the effort to reevaluate existing scholarship on such subjects got under way, cold war unrest led some historians to downplay the role of conflict in our past and to sound an optimistic note. Oscar and Mary Handlin for example, writing in 1950, inferred that white Americans had enslaved blacks in the late seventeenth century only as a last resort and then slowly developed the notion they were inferior because as slaves blacks had no opportunity to demonstrate their full humanity. Prejudice, a reader might have concluded, was as circumstantial as slavery had been, and stood a good chance of extinction as blacks escaped poverty and advanced in American society. Carl Degler's essay on the same subject nine years later voiced doubts that white prejudice was so ephemeral. Then, as if to account for the harsh lessons and ambiguous gains of the equal rights movement, Winthrop Jordan's *White Over Black* (1968)—a prizewinning study of white racial attitudes from the Elizabethan period to 1812—gave further pause.

Jordan argues that white racial prejudice has roots in primordial human fears of darkness, in associations between blackness and evil embedded in the English language, and finally, indirectly, in white Christian ambivalence about the sexual appetite. Prejudice, so far from a reversible judgment based on black poverty or simply "learned behavior," issues from depths that leave everyone susceptible to it and make its eradication highly difficult. Providing a key chapter in this analysis is Thomas Jefferson, whose conflicted thoughts and feelings on race Jordan finds a particularly rich source. Like Bushman on Jonathan Edwards, Jordan on Jefferson uses a single figure to illuminate a larger sociopsychological problem. Yet there are conceptual

From *White Over Black: American Attitudes Toward the Negro, 1550–1812*, by Winthrop D. Jordan. © 1968 The University of North Carolina Press. Published for the Institute of Early American History and Culture, Williamsburg.

diffcrences. While Bushman demonstrates the connection between the themes of Edwards's personality development and social change, between professional career and widespread religious needs, Jordan examines Jefferson's public writings to bring to light a private dilemma which, according to Jordan, was but an articulate version of beliefs that many whites held without expressing them. Because Jefferson's self-deluding devices, his mechanisms of defense, were the same ones that his contemporaries shared (and all of us employ), his private anguish becomes historical material. Edwards's experience provides a personal parallel to socioeconomic change; Jefferson—in Jordan's scheme—a psychological archetype for common prejudice.

The question whether Jefferson did in fact enter into a sexual liaison with Sally Hemings—a point Fawn Brodie accepts in her *Thomas Jefferson: An Intimate History* (1974)—must remain ultimately unanswerable. The evidence is circumstantial. Jefferson was with Hemings nine months before each of her children was born, so far as we know; but so were other possible fathers. He did make special provisions in his will for her and her family; but such attention to house servants was by no means unusual among slaveholders in Jefferson's time and place. It is instructive that two quite different approaches to historical personality yield different answers to the question of Jefferson's tie to Hemings. Dumas Malone, the lifelong student of Jefferson, who is nearing completion of the sixth and final volume of what surely will be the standard biography for years to come, argues that the president had no romantic attachment to this slave woman or any other; having examined virtually every scrap Jefferson ever wrote and having "lived with" the man as his student for over a half-century, Malone finds it inconceivable that Jefferson could have indulged in the miscegenation he condemned so often. The Jefferson Malone has grown to know was incapable of such duplicity, too much in command of his "heart" thus to have indulged himself. This traditional approach to character, emphasizing the bulk of the evidence and a subject's conscious statements, contrasts sharply with that of a psychoanalytic biographer like Brodie, who from theory derives the view that appetites of love and aggression drive us all and that we frequently deny their influence over us. In this light Jefferson most surely did have an "intimate history," circumstantial evidence convicts, and his never writing about this affair makes perfect sense.

Combining such insight with the historian's concern for evidence and deliberate act, Jordan leaves open the matter of Jefferson's relationship with Hemings. Instead this chapter carefully examines Jefferson's texts on slavery and race in a search for the probable roots of his mixed emotions. Jordan's case does not stand or fall on Jefferson's having slept with this slave woman; his sexuality and its connection with shared beliefs about black sexual prowess cannot be denied, however, and help to explain his ambivalence—as well as the widespread doubts of his age—on the issue of black equality.

Finally, in the last paragraph of *White Over Black*, Jordan makes a plea for self-knowledge that parallels the process of psychoanalytic therapy. Only by coming to terms with the energies of the id, by bringing to the level of consciousness what has been unconscious, may we hope to eliminate racism from American life. "If the white man turned to stare at the animal within him," writes Jordan, "if he once admitted unashamedly that the beast was there, he might see that the old foe was a friend as well, that his best and his worst derived from the same deep well of energy. If he once fully acknowledged the powerful forces which drove his being, the necessity of imputing them to others would drastically diminish."

AGAINST THE BACKDROP of changing attitudes and actions concerning Negroes and Negro slavery, the writings of one man become a fixed
and central point of reference and influence. In the years after the Revolution
the speculations of Thomas Jefferson were of great importance because so
many people read and reacted to them. His remarks about Negroes in the
only book he ever wrote were more widely read, in all probability, than any
others until the mid-nineteenth century. In addition to his demonstrable
impact upon other men, Jefferson is important—or perhaps more accurately,
valuable to historical analysis—because he permits (without intending to) a
depth and range of insight into the workings of ideas about Negroes within
one man as he stood in relationship to his culture. Jefferson's energetic facil-
ity with the pen makes it possible, uniquely so in this period of history, to
glimpse some of the inward springs of feeling which supported certain attitudes towards Negroes. It then becomes possible to see the intriciate inter-
lacing of one man's personality with his social surroundings, the values of his
culture, and the ideas with which he had contact. Thomas Jefferson was not a
typical nor an ordinary man, but his enormous breadth of interest and his
lack of originality make him an effective sounding board for his culture. On
some important matters, therefore, he may be taken as accurately reflecting
common presuppositions and sensitivities even though many Americans disagreed with some of his conclusions.

To contemplate any man-in-culture is to savor complexity. It will be
easiest to start with Jefferson's central dilemma: he hated slavery but thought
Negroes inferior to white men. His remarks on the Negro's mental inferiority
helped kindle a revealing public controversy on the subject which deserves
examination. But it will also be necessary to return again to Thomas Jefferson, to his inward world where Negro inferiority was rooted. There it is
possible to discern the interrelationship between his feelings about the races
and his feeling about the sexes and thence to move once again to the problem
of interracial sex in American culture. Finally, by tacking back to Jefferson
and to the way he patterned his perceptions of his surroundings, it becomes
easy to see how he assimilated the Indian to his anthropology and to
America. His solution with the Negro was very different.

Jefferson: The Tyranny of Slavery

Jefferson was personally involved in Negro slavery. On his own plantations he stood confronted by the practical necessity of making slave labor pay
and by the usual frustrating combination of slave recalcitrance and ineffi-
ciency. Keeping the Negro men and especially the women and children clad,
bedded, and fed was expensive, and keeping them busy was a task in itself.[1]
Nor was his load lightened by daily supervision of a system which he
genuinely hated, nor by realization that his livelihood depended on its continuation. This dependence almost inevitably meant that, for Jefferson the

planter, Negroes sometimes became mere objects of financial calculation. "I have observed," he once wrote, "that our families of negroes double in about 25 years, which is an increase of the capital, invested in them, of 4. per cent over and above keeping up the original number." Successful maintenance of several plantations made for a measure of moral callousness: "The first step towards the recovery of our lands," he advised John Taylor, "is to find substitutes for corn and bacon. I count on potatoes, clover, and sheep. The two former to feed every animal on the farm except my negroes, and the latter to feed them, diversified with rations of salted fish and molasses, both of them wholesome, agreeable, and cheap articles of food."[2] For a man of Jefferson's convictions, entanglement in Negro slavery was genuinely tragic. Guiltily he referred to his Negroes as "servants," thus presaging the euphemism of the nineteenth century. His hopes for transforming his slaves into tenants evidenced a desire to seek a way out, but financial considerations perpetually precluded action. In the end he freed a few of them, but more than a hundred remained in slavery.[3] He never doubted that his monetary debts constituted a more immediate obligation than manumission. Most Americans would have agreed.

Jefferson's heartfelt hatred of slavery did not derive so much from this harassing personal entanglement in the practicalities of slavery as from the system of politics in which he was enmeshed mentally. "Enmeshed" seems the appropriate term because the natural rights philosophy was the governing aspect of his theology and his science; it formed a part of his being, and his most original contribution was the graceful lucidity with which he continually restated the doctrine. Yet in Jefferson's hands natural rights took on a peculiar cast, for he thought of rights as being natural in a very literal sense. Rights belonged to men as biological beings, inhering in them, as he said in his draft of the Declaration of Independence, because "all men are created equal and independant" and because "from that equal creation they derive rights inherent and inalienable."[4] The central fact was creation: the Creator, whose primary attribute was tidiness, would scarcely have been so careless as to create a single species equipped with more than one set of rights. If Jefferson's own passion for order was reflected in these phrases, so was his agrarian penchant for solitude. What was reflected most clearly of all, though, was the extent to which the natural world dominated Jefferson's thinking. Creation was the central "fact" because it explained nature. And Jefferson was awed by nature, if "awe" may be used in connection with a man so immensely capable of placid receptivity. While apparently working from a "Supreme Being" to an orderly nature, in fact Jefferson derived his Creator from what He had created—a nature which was by axiom orderly. In the same way, he derived God-given rights from the existence of the class of natural beings known as men. To know whether certain men possessed natural rights one had only to inquire whether they were human beings.[5]

Without question Negroes were members of that class. Hence Jefferson never for a moment considered the possibility that they might rightfully be enslaved. He felt the personal guilt of slaveholding deeply, for he was daily depriving other men of their rightful liberty. With "my debts once cleared off," he wrote with a highly revealing slip of the pen, "I shall try some plan of making their situation happier, determined to content myself with a small portion of their ~~liberty~~ labour."[6] His vigorous antislavery pronouncements, however, were always redolent more of the library than the field. Slavery was an injustice not so much for the specific Negroes held in bondage as for any member of the human species. While he recognized the condition of slaves as "miserable," the weight of Jefferson's concern was reserved for the malevolent effects of slavery upon masters. These effects had always concerned antislavery men of every stripe, but with most of them one is not left wondering what would have remained of their antislavery views had they found slavery beneficial to white society. Fortunately Jefferson went to his grave convinced that slavery was a blight on the white community. With slavery's effect on black men he simply was not overly concerned.[7]

Indicative of Jefferson's approach toward the institution was his horror of slave rebellion. His apprehension was of course shared by most Americans, but he gave it expression at an unusually early date, some years before the disaster in St. Domingo. When denouncing slavery in the Notes on Virginia he gave vent to forebodings of a possible upheaval in America in a passage clouded with dark indirection. "Indeed I tremble for my country," he wrote passionately, "when I reflect that God is just: that his justice cannot sleep for ever: that considering numbers, nature and natural means only, a revolution of the wheel of fortune, an exchange of situation, is among possible events: that it may become probable by supernatural interference! The Almighty has no attribute which can take side with us in such a contest." The depth of his feeling was apparent, for he rarely resorted to exclamation marks and still less often to miracles without skepticism. Later, Negro rebellion in St. Domingo confirmed his fears, the more so because he was utterly unable to condemn it.

As early as the 1780's Jefferson fully recognized the difficulties involved in any practical program for freedom and shrank from publishing his Notes on Virginia because it contained strong antislavery expressions. His friend Charles Thomson agreed that there were just grounds for fearing southern reaction while agreeing too that if the "cancer" was not wiped out "by religion, reason and philosophy" it would be someday "by blood." James Monroe, on the other hand, thought the antislavery sentiments could well be published. They finally did appear, of course, but Jefferson remained pessimistic.[8] He wrote in 1786 concerning possible legislative action in Virginia that "an unsuccessful effort, as too often happens, would only rivet still closer the chains of bondage, and retard the moment of delivery to this oppressed description of men." Later he steadfastly refused to condemn slavery publicly, refused to join antislavery organizations, refused to endorse the publications of abolitionists, in each case because he thought that premature endorsement by a figure of his prominence might easily damage the antislavery cause.[9] It was neither timidity nor concern for reputation which restrained him; in fact he had good reason to think that antislavery pronouncements might solidify the institution. Francis Kinloch wrote him from South Carolina of "the general alarm" which a certain "passage in your Notes occasioned amongst us. It is not easy to get rid of old prejudices, and the word 'emancipation' operates like an apparition upon a South Carolina planter."[10] From wide experience Jefferson had acquired a strong sense of "how difficult it is to move or inflect the great machine of society, how impossible to advance the notions of a whole people suddenly to ideal right." He was acutely conscious of "the passions, the prejudices, and the real difficulties" compounded in American Negro slavery.[11]

Jefferson: The Assertion of Negro Inferiority

His sensitive reaction to social "passions" and "prejudices" was heightened by dim recognition that they operated powerfully within himself, though of course he never realized how deep-seated his anti-Negro feelings were. On the surface of these thoughts lay genuine doubts concerning the Negro's inherent fitness for freedom and recognition of the tensions inherent in racial slavery. He was firmly convinced, as he demonstrated in the Notes on Virginia, that the black man's differences were not only physical but temperamental and mental. Negroes seemed to "require less sleep," for "after hard labour through the day," they were "induced by the slightest amusements to sit up till midnight, or later" though aware that they must rise at "first dawn." They were "at least as brave" as whites, and "more adventuresome." "But," he wrote, withdrawing even this mild encomium, "this may perhaps proceed from a want of forethought, which prevents their seeing a danger till it be present. When present, they do not go through it with more coolness or steadiness than whites." Negroes were "more ardent," their griefs "transient." "In general," he concluded, "their existence appears to participate more of sensation than reflection. To this must be ascribed their disposition to sleep when abstracted from their diversions, and unemployed in labour. An animal whose body is at rest, and who does not reflect, must be disposed to sleep of course." Within the confines of this logic there was no room for even a hint that daily toil for another's benefit might have disposed slaves to frolic and to sleep.[12]

Opinion in the North was distinctly different though far from unanimous. When St. George Tucker addressed queries concerning Negroes in Massachusetts to Jeremy Belknap in 1795, he asked specifically for information concerning mental capacity, and Belknap in turn made enquiries among his prominent friends in Boston. Belknap summarized his little survey by reporting that gentlemen in Massachusetts who had studied the matter "do not scruple to say, that there is no more difference between them and those whites who have had the same education, and have lived in the same habits, than there is among different persons of that class of whites. In this opinion I am inclined to acquiesce. It is neither birth nor colour, but education and habit, which form the human character."[13]

Though it is difficult to judge exactly what most Virginians or other southerners would have thought of this statement, it is clear that only one man in the South felt compelled to take the opposite position publicly. Jefferson alone spoke forth, and this fact in itself suggests, at very least, strong feelings on his part, an uncommon need to discourse upon the subject. It was not that he alone felt need for scientific experiment. George Wythe, Jefferson's much-admired mentor, undertook to give both his own nephew and his mulatto servant boy classical educations as a comparative test of the Negro's ability.[14] On the other hand, Jefferson, who delighted in compiling the facts of the natural world, never attempted any such experiment despite ample opportunity. And the structure of his relevant passage in the *Notes*, where his appeal to science followed lengthy and very definite pronouncements on Negro inferiority, indicated clearly that his appeal to that highest court was not the starting point for his thoughts about Negroes but a safe refuge from them.

Jefferson: Passionate Realities

Jefferson started, in fact, with a brief assertion of the necessity for colonizing Negroes elsewhere once they had been freed.[15] "Why not retain and incorporate the blacks into the state?" Only later did his answer find wide acceptance in Virginia, especially after September 1800. "Deep rooted prejudices entertained by the whites; ten thousand recollections, by the blacks, of the injuries they have sustained; new provocations; the real distinctions which nature has made; and many other circumstances, will... produce convulsions which will probably never end but in the extermination of the one or the other race." His ensuing remarks made evident which factor carried greatest weight with him, for he immediately entered into a long discussion of other "objections" which were "physical and moral." "The first difference which strikes us" he wrote in accurate summary of his countrymen's perceptions, "is that of colour." Accepting the chromatically inaccurate but universally accepted metaphor of the Negro's "black" color, he continued, "Whether the black of the negro resides in the reticular membrane between the skin and scarf-skin, or in the scarf-skin itself; whether it proceeds from the colour of the blood, the colour of the bile, or from that of some other secretion, the difference is fixed in nature, and is as real as if its seat and cause were better known to us." For Jefferson, the overwhelming aspect of the Negro's color was its *reality*; he simply shelved the important scientific question of its cause. Even when he considered the question in a more neutral context, in his discussion of albino Negroes in the section on "Productions

Mineral, Vegetable and Animal," he refused (or perhaps was unable) to offer a word of speculation about a matter on which other scientists speculated freely. Instead he rushed on, spilling forth words which revealed what the "reality" of the "difference" was for Thomas Jefferson. The passionate underpinnings of his feelings were laid bare.

And is this difference of no importance? Is it not the foundation of a greater or less share of beauty in the two races? Are not the fine mixtures of red and white, the expressions of every passion by greater or less suffusions of colour in the one, preferable to that eternal monotony, which reigns in the countenances, that immoveable veil of black which covers all the emotions of the other race? Add to these, flowing hair, a more elegant symmetry of form, and their own judgment in favour of the whites, declared by their preference of them, as uniformly as is the preference of the Oranootan for the black women over those of his own species. The circumstance of superior beauty, is thought worthy attention in the propagation of our horses, dogs, and other domestic animals; why not in that of man?

With this geyser of libidinal energy Jefferson recapitulated major tenets of the American racial complex. Merely on a factual level he passed along several notions which had long been floating about, some since the first years of confrontation in Africa. Red and white were the ingredients of beauty, and Negroes were pronouncedly less beautiful than whites; Negroes desired sexual relations especially with whites; black women had relations with orangoutangs. On a deeper level the pattern of his remarks was more revealing of Jefferson himself. Embedded in his thoughts on beauty was the feeling that whites were subtler and more delicate in their passions and that Negroes, conversely, were more crude. He felt Negroes to be sexually more animal—hence the gratuitous intrusion of the man-like ape. His libidinal desires, unacceptable and inadmissible to his society and to his higher self, were effectively transferred to others and thereby drained of their intolerable immediacy. Having allowed these dynamic emotions perilously close to the surface in the form of the orang-outang, he had immediately shifted to the safe neutral ground of horse-breeding, thus denying his exposure by caricaturing it. Without fully recognizing the adversary within, he continued to flee, taking refuge on higher and higher ground. "They have less hair on the face and body." Not quite safe enough, but he was reaching the safe temple of science. "They secrete less by the kidnies, and more by the glands of the skin," he wrote, carefully placing the rationale before the important fact, "which gives them a very strong and disagreeable odour." Having taken as given the facts of Negro secretion, about which many contemporaries were uncertain, he applied them as proof to a less emotion-laden folk belief. "This greater degree of transpiration renders them more tolerant of heat, and less so of cold, than the whites." He came to rest finally in convoluted speculation. "Perhaps too a difference of structure in the pulmonary apparatus, which a late ingenious experimentalist [Adair Crawford, *Experiments... on Animal Heat*] has discovered to be the principal regulator of animal heat, may have disabled them from extricating, in the act of inspiration, so much of that fluid from the outer air, or obliged them in expiration, to part with more of it."

Yet Jefferson was never completely at rest. His picture of Negroes as crudely sensual beings, which was at once an offprint of popular belief and a functional displacement of his own emotional drives, kept popping up whenever Negroes came to mind. That it did not appear on other, irrelevant occasions indicated that there were limits to its personal importance, yet most of Jefferson's widely-read remarks on the Negro were tinged by it. When discussing the Negro's over-all temperament he wrote, "They are more ardent after their female: but love seems with them to be more an eager desire, than a tender delicate mixture of sentiment and sensation." In the original manuscript he had stated this even more baldly. Elsewhere in the *Notes* he commented in defense of the masculinity of Indian men despite the sparsity of their hair: "Negroes have notoriously less hair than the whites; yet they are more ardent."[16]

Jefferson had framed old beliefs about the Negro's sexuality in newly deprecatory terms, and defenders of the Negro rose in his behalf. Gilbert Imlay laid his finger on the core of Jefferson's argument with acute intuition but faltering analysis:

Were a man, who, with all the ardour of a youthful passion, had just been gazing upon the fair bosom of a loved and beautiful mistress, and afterwards marked the contrast of that paradise of sublunary bliss, to the African or Indian hue, to exclaim in the terms which Mr. Jefferson has used, he might be judged excusable on account of the intoxication of his heated senses—But when a grave philosopher, who has passed the meridian of life, sits down to meliorate, by his writings and opinions, the condition of the slaves of his country, whose fetters have fixed an obliquity upon the virtue and humanity of the southern Americans, I confess it appears to me not a little jejune and inconsistent.

The Reverend Samuel Stanhope Smith of Princeton, however, was affronted by Jefferson's assertions of ardency which kindled "the senses only, not the imagination," and seized the opportunity of reading an environmentalist lecture in morals to slaveowners. "With what fine tints can imagination invest the rags, the dirt, or the nakedness so often seen in a quarter of negro labourers? Besides, to awaken the exquisite sentiments of a delicate love, and to surround it with all the enchantment of the imagination, this passion requires to be placed under certain moral restraints which are seldom formed in the coarse familiarity, and promiscuous intercourse permitted, and too often encouraged among the American slaves." Smith was careful to discharge the other barrel by declaring that he had seen many instances of the highest sentiments of love among Negroes.[17] Jefferson never replied to these attacks.

While the depth of emotional intensity underlying his thinking about the Negro seems sufficiently evident, the sources of his feeling remain obscured by his unsurprising failure to articulate emotional patterns and processes of which he was unaware. As has often been remarked about him, few men have written so much yet revealed so little of themselves. This fact is in itself enormously suggestive, though it has been a disappointment to historians that he did not include in his papers some remarks on parents and childhood, some few letters to his beloved wife. Yet if one draws back the velvet curtain of his graceful style to regard the *pattern* of his life and thought, it is possible to detect certain of the currents running beneath the structure of his intellect.

Jefferson: White Women and Black

Two interrelated currents seem especially relevant to his thoughts on the Negro, the more deep-seated one having to do with his relationships with members of the opposite sex. Jefferson grew up in a world of women. His father, a man of more imposing physique even than Jefferson, died when his son was fourteen. At that critical age he was left with a mother about whom we know almost nothing, four sisters, and one brother. He was never really congenial with his brother, and their infrequent correspondence in later life merely exposed the enormous gulf between them in interests and talents.[18] He never said much concerning his mother and sisters. As a young man, leading a life thoroughly lacking in direction, he filled his letters with talk about girls, but his gay chitchat ended abruptly after a keenly disappointing one-sided romance with Rebecca Burwell, an attractive sixteen-year-old orphan. Consoling himself with outbursts of misogyny, Jefferson turned to the companionship of men. Nearly ten years later he made a level-headed match with Martha Skelton Wayles, a twenty-three-year-old widow whose young son died shortly before the wedding. On the marriage bond he at first inserted the word "spinster" but then corrected himself with "widow."[19] The marriage lasted from 1772 until her death in 1782, but again Jefferson left no picture of the woman sharing his life. She bore him six children: three girls died in infancy, as did their only son (whom Jefferson referred to as such before the birth!),[20] and two daughters survived. His wife's failing health worried him terribly—it was in this period that he wrote the *Notes*—and her death left him shattered with grief, not untinged, as so often happens, with self-pity.[21]

Throughout his life after the Burwell affair, Jefferson seemed capable of attachment only to married women. Several years before his marriage he had made, on his own much later admission, improper advances to the wife of a neighboring friend.[22] In Paris, as a widower, he carried on a superficially frantic flirtation with Mrs. Maria Cosway, a "love affair" in which the "love" was partly play and the "affair" non-existent. The only woman outside his family for whom he formed some attachment was John Adams's remarkable wife, Abigail; with good reason he admired her intellect. With women in general he was uneasy and unsure; he held them at arm's length, wary, especially after his wife's death, of the dangers of over-commitment. Intimate emotional engagement with women seemed to represent for him a gateway into a dangerous, potentially explosive world which threatened revolution against the discipline of his higher self. His famous "Dialogue of the Head and the Heart," written to Maria Cosway, revealed his dim awareness of the struggle within, for beneath its stiltedness one senses a man not naturally cool but thoroughly air-conditioned. Of necessity, the Head emerged victorious in the dialogue, just as it did in real life, declaring pontifically to the Heart, "This is not a world to live at random in as you do."²³ The sentence might have served as a motto for his life.

As Jefferson matured, he seems to have mitigated this inner tension by imputing potential explosiveness to the opposite sex and by assuming that female passion must and could only be controlled by marriage. Not long after the Burwell affair, he wrote or copied a solemn passage which characterized marriage as best founded on a wife's self-restraint and constant attentiveness to the wishes of her husband: "marriage, be a husband what he may, reverses the prerogative of sex." Certainly Jefferson lived in a culture which assumed dutiful wifely submission, but there was a particular urgency in his stress upon the necessity of female decorum. In any age, his strictures on toilet and dress to his unmarried daughter would seem egregiously detailed. "Nothing is so disgusting to our sex," he warned her, "as a want of cleanliness and delicacy in yours."²⁴ It is scarcely surprising, therefore, that when living in Paris, Jefferson dashed off frequent warnings of the sexual corruptions awaiting American youths in Europe: "in lieu of this ["conjugal love"] are substituted pursuits which nourish and invigorate all our bad passions, and which offer only moments of extasy amidst days and months of restlessness and torment." And, he added, characteristically seizing an opportunity to salute republican virtue, "Much, very much inferior this to the tranquil permanent felicity with which domestic society in America blesses most of it's inhabitants."²⁵ If unrestrained sex seemed a dangerous trap to Jefferson, he was deeply certain which sex had set it. On one occasion, in his rough "Notes on a Tour of English Gardens," he jotted down an arresting mental picture, in an otherwise matter-of-fact account, of "a small, dark, deep hollow, with recesses of stone in the banks on every side. In one of these is a Venus pudique, turned half round as if inviting you with her into the recess." It was a revealing description, as much of Jefferson as of the statue. Most revealing of all was a letter to James Madison in 1786. The recent revisal of Virginia laws had included mitigation of criminal punishments, but the *lex talionis* had been preserved in two cases, death for treason or murder and castration for rape and buggery, etc. Jefferson wrote from Paris an interesting commentary. "The principle of retaliation is much criticised here, particularly in the case of Rape. They think the punishment indecent and unjustifiable. I should be for altering it, but for a different reason: that is on account of the temptation women would be under to make it the instrument of vengeance against an inconstant lover, and of disappointment to a rival."[26] Evidently women loomed as threats to masculinity, as dangerously powerful sexual aggressors.

Jefferson's transferal of sexual aggressiveness to women helps explain certain otherwise puzzling aspects of his expressions on the Negro. He was greatly concerned with the Negro's lack of beauty—in his culture a highly feminine attribute—and it was with some justification that a political opponent charged that "The desire of preserving the beauty of the human race predominates... in the mind of our philosopher."[27] Moreover, Jefferson failed to offer even a hint concerning the Negro male's supposedly large organ, and though this failure may have stemmed from an understandable reluctance to broach the matter publicly, he gave no suggestion even indirectly of the sexual aggressiveness of Negro men; nor did he ever do so privately. In fact—and it is an arresting one upon re-reading the passage—his previously quoted remarks concerning beauty and breeding had reference not to Negro men, nor to Negroes in general, but, in implicit yet highly specific fashion, to Negro women!

It is in the light of this emotional pattern that Jefferson's widely discussed relationship with the Hemings family should be considered. The subject is an unpalatable one for many Americans: the assertion that a great national figure was involved in miscegenation—this is the central supposed "fact" of the Hemings matter—is one that Americans find difficult to treat as anything but a malicious accusation. Malice *was*, indeed, the animating force behind the original claim, but we need to brace ourselves into an intellectual posture from which we can see that the importance of the stories about black Sally Hemings and Thomas Jefferson lies in the fact that they seemed—and to some people still seem—of any importance. The facts of the matter require attention not because Jefferson's behavior needs to be questioned but because they are of some (but not very much) help in understanding Jefferson's views about miscegenation and, far more, because they shed light on the cultural context in which he moved and of which we are heirs. Viewed in the context of his feelings about white women, the problem of Jefferson's actual overt behavior becomes essentially irrelevant to the subject of this book; it is to the inner world of his thought and feeling that we must look for significant behavior and, even more, to his culture for the larger significance of the matter.

In 1802 James T. Callender charged in the Richmond *Recorder* that it was "well known" that Jefferson kept Sally, one of his slaves, as concubine and had fathered children by her. The features of "Tom," the eldest offspring, were "said to bear a striking although sable resemblance to those of the president himself."[28] Callender was a notorious professional scandalmonger who had turned upon Jefferson when the President had disappointed his hope for federal office. Despite the utter disreputability of the source, the charge has been dragged after Jefferson like a dead cat through the pages of formal and informal history, tied to him by its attractiveness to a wide variety of interested persons and by the apparent impossibility of utterly refuting it.[29] Ever since Callender's day it has served the varied purposes of those seeking to degrade Jefferson for political or ideological reasons, of abolitionists, defamers of Virginia, the South, and even America in general, and both defenders and opponents of racial segregation. Jefferson's conduct has been attacked from several angles, for in fact the charge of concubinage with Sally Hemings constitutes not one accusation but three, simultaneously accusing Jefferson of fathering bastards, of miscegenation, and of crassly taking advantage of a helpless young slave (for Sally was probably twenty-two when she first conceived). The last of these, insofar as it implies forced attentions on an unwilling girl, may be summarily dismissed. For one thing, indirect evidence indicates that Sally was happy throughout her long period of motherhood, and, more important, Jefferson was simply not capable of violating every rule of honor and kindness, to say nothing of his convictions concerning the master-slave relationship.

As for bastardy and miscegenation, the known circumstances of the situation at Monticello which might support the charges were, very briefly, as follows. The entire Hemings family seems to have received favored treatment. Sally's mother was mulatto and had come to Jefferson with her still lighter children from the estate of his father-in-law, John Wayles, in 1774. Most of Sally's siblings were personal servants; one brother became a skilled carpenter and two of Sally's children were eventually charged to him for training. Sally herself and her mother were house servants, and Sally (described as very fair) was sent as maid with Jefferson's daughter to Paris. All the slaves freed by Jefferson were Hemingses, and none of Sally's children were retained in slavery as adults. She bore five, from 1795 to 1808; and though he was away from Monticello a total of roughly two-thirds of this period, Jefferson was at home nine months prior to each birth. Her first child was conceived following Jefferson's retirement as Secretary of State with nerves raw from political battling with Hamilton. Three others were conceived during Jefferson's summer vacations and the remaining child was born nine months after his very brief return to Monticello for the funeral of his daughter. In short, Jefferson's paternity can be neither refuted nor proved from the known circumstances or from the extant testimony of his overseer, his white descendants, or the descendants of Sally, each of them having fallible memories and personal interests at stake.[30]

If we turn to Jefferson's character we are confronted by evidence which for many people today (and then) furnished an immediate and satisfactory refutation. Yet the assumption that this high-minded man *could not* have carried on such an affair is at variance with what is known today concerning the relationship between human personality and behavior. If the previous suggestions concerning his personality have any validity, Jefferson's relations with women were ambivalent, and in the Hemings situation either tendency could have prevailed.

Assuming this ambivalence in Jefferson, one can construct two reasonable (though not equally probable) and absolutely irreconcilable cases. It is possible to argue on the one hand, briefly, that Jefferson was a truly admirable man if there ever was one and that by the time he had married and matured politically, in the 1770's, his "head" was permanently in control of his "heart." Hence a liaison with a slave girl would have been a lapse from character unique in his mature life. It would have represented, on a deeper level, abandonment of the only grounds on which he was able to maintain satisfactory relations with women, their safe incarceration in the married state. It would have meant complete reversal of his feelings of repulsion toward Negroes and a towering sense of guilt for having connected with such sensual creatures and having given free reign to his own libidinous desires, guilt for which there is no evidence. On the other hand, however, it is possible to argue that attachment with Sally represented a final happy resolution of his inner conflict. This would account for the absence after his return from Paris in 1789 of evidence pointing to continuing high tension concerning women and Negroes, an absence hardly to be explained by senility. Sally Hemings would have become Becky Burwell and the bitter outcome of his marriage erased. Unsurprisingly, his repulsion toward Negroes would have been, all along, merely the obverse of powerful attraction, and external pressures in the 1790's would easily have provided adequate energy for turning the coin of psychic choice from one side to the other. One is left fully persuaded only of the known fact that any given pattern of basic personality can result in widely differing patterns of external behavior.

The question of Jefferson's miscegenation, it should be stressed again, is of limited interest and usefulness even if it could be satisfactorily answered. The *Notes* had been written years before, and Jefferson never deviated from his "aversion," as he wrote just before he died, "to the mixture of colour" in America.[31] One aspect of the history of the Hemings family, however, offers possible clarification on several points. It appears quite probable that Sally and some of her siblings were the children of his father-in-law, John Wayles.[32] It must have been a burden indeed for Jefferson, who probably knew this, to have the Hemingses in the same house with their half-sister and aunt, his beloved wife, who almost certainly was ignorant of the situation. This burden might well have embittered his thoughts on miscegenation in general and have helped convince him to his dying day that it was a social evil.[33] It would also have heightened his conviction that slavery was degrading to white men. And while it does not settle anything concerning his relations with Sally, it would explain the favored treatment the Hemings family received at Monticello.

For many people it seems to require an effort of will to remember that the larger significance of the Hemings matter lay not in Jefferson's conduct but in the charges themselves. Callender's words went echoing through the anti-Jefferson press (with help from Callender) because they played effectively

upon public sentiment. The motivation underlying the charges was undoubtedly political; some of his opponents were willing to seize any weapon,
no matter how crude, for berating Jefferson, but that a white man's sleeping
with a Negro woman should be a weapon at all seems the more significant
fact. It is significant, too, that the charge of bastardy was virtually lost in the
clamor about miscegenation. Hamilton's admission of sexual transgressions
with a white woman had done little to damage *his* reputation. Jefferson's
offense was held to be mixture of the races, and Callender and his fellow
scandalmongers strummed the theme until it was dead tired.

In glaring red, and chalky white,
    Let others beauty see;
Me no such tawdry tints delight—
    No! *black's* the hue for me!

Thick pouting lips! how sweet their grace!
    When passion fires to kiss them!
Wide spreading over half the face,
    Impossible to miss them.

Oh! Sally! hearken to my vows!
    Yield up thy sooty charms—
My best belov'd! my more than spouse,
    Oh! take me to thy arms![34]

The same theme could easily be transformed into ridicule of Jefferson's
equalitarianism.

For make all like, let blackee nab
    De white womans. . . . dat be de track!
Den Quashee de white wife will hab,
    And massa *Jefferson shall hav de black.*
Why should a judge, (him alway white,)
    'Pon pickaninny put him paw,
Cause he steal little! dat no rite!
    No! Quashee say he'll hab no law.[35]

Jefferson's personal transgression could be handsomely enlarged to represent
a threat to society, according to what might be called the law of gross expansion. "Put the case that every white man in Virginia had done as much as
Thomas Jefferson has done towards the utter destruction of its happiness,
that eighty thousand white men had; each of them, been the father of five
mulatto children. Thus you have FOUR HUNDRED THOUSAND
MULATTOES in addition to the present swarm. The country would be no
longer habitable, till after a civil war, and a series of massacres. We all know
with absolute certainty that the contest would end in the utter extirpation
both of blacks and mulattoes. We know that the continent has as many white
people, as could eat the whole race at a breakfast."[36]

Interracial Sex: The Individual and His Society

Callender's grossness should not be allowed to obscure the fact that he was playing upon very real sensitivities. American tenderness on mixture of the races had been unrelieved by the Revolutionary upheaval of thought concerning the Negro. Indeed certain shifts in thought in the latter part of the eighteenth century may have served to deepen objection to intermixture. While conceiving of man's social and political activities as taking place within the ordered realm of nature (most obviously in the natural rights philosophy), Americans also brought biological preconceptions to the consideration of human beings. In nature, likes begat likes in ordered succession. Could Americans be entirely happy, then, with even the superficial confusion of appearances brought about by miscegenation? The "mulatto breed" was an affront to anyone with a sense of tidiness. In the 1790's, too, the Negro rebellions added urgency to all consideration of interracial relationships, and the growing sense of the separateness of Negroes meant more frequent expressions of alarm concerning mongrelization. Given a new nation, with slavery now recognized as a national concern, the omnipresent fact of miscegenation was perforce seen in a somewhat different light than in earlier years. Cases of intermixture once of only local pertinence had now become ingredients in the larger problem of the integrity of the blood of the national community. Hence national councils became forums for denunciation of intermixture. Pennsylvania's James Wilson announced during discussion of the three-fifths clause in the Constitutional Convention that he "had some apprehensions also from the tendency of the blending of the blacks with the whites, to give disgust to the people of Pena." William Loughton Smith, defending slavery in the congressional debate of 1790, declared that any "mixture of the races would degenerate the whites" and that as far as the future of America was concerned if Negroes intermarried "with the whites, then the white race would be extinct, and the American people would be all of the mulatto breed." And a nationalistic President Jefferson remarked concerning the Negro's future that "it is impossible not to look forward to distant times, when our rapid multiplication will expand itself beyond those [present] limits, and cover the whole northern, if not the southern continent, with a people speaking the same language, governed in similar forms, and by similar laws; nor can we contemplate with satisfaction either blot or mixture on that surface."[37]

This theme was to emerge as a dominant one especially in his own state during his presidency; by that time many other important individuals throughout the nation were speculating upon matters concerning the Negro. Important intellectual changes took place during the thirty years after he wrote the *Notes*, but Jefferson grew increasingly silent and depressed about the future of Africans in America. For the moment these individuals and changes may be held aside so as to permit concentration upon the problem of the relationship of one individual's attitudes to those of his society. Beneath all pronouncements on the undesirability of racial mixture lay a substructure of feeling about interracial sex. Jefferson's feelings were of course partially molded by specific beliefs about Negroes which constituted readily visible manifestations of feelings prevailing in his culture not merely about Negroes but about life in general. It seems legitimate and profitable to speak of an entire culture as having feelings, partly because every society demands—and gets—a large measure of the behavior it "wants" (i.e., needs) from individuals and partly because in a literate culture expressions of individual feeling accrete through time, thus forming a common pool of expressed feelings. Usually, but by no means always, these expressions are highly intellectualized, that is, detached from direct functional connection with powerful emotional drives. Sometimes they are not, as they sometimes were not when Thomas Jefferson wrote about Negroes. It seems evident that his feelings, his affective life, his emotions—whatever term one prefers— were being expressed in some of his beliefs or opinions about the Negro. His opinions were thus sometimes quite directly the product of his repressions. And it seems axiomatic, given the assumptions about the nature of culture prevailing in the twentieth century, that variants of his repressions operated in so many individuals that one can speak of deep-seated feelings about the Negro as being social in character, that is, as characterizing an entire society. It seems important to remember that the explicit *content* of social attitudes stemmed not directly from the emotions being repressed but from the mechanisms of repression. The resultant attitudes, moreover, through constant communication within society, acquired autonomous energy and a viability independent of emotional underpinnings. Hence many individuals subscribed to beliefs about Negroes which performed no very vital function in their personality, and these beliefs may be considered as being part of the cultural environment.

It is with this final consideration in mind that such manifestations of attitudes as laws on interracial sexual relations must be considered; it saves us from despair at being unable to obtain much personal information on individual legislators. Again, it constitutes a useful way of looking at sectional differences in attitudes. Differences between North and South concerning interracial sex were not in kind but in vehemence, if vehemence is defined as the product of the degree of individual involvement and proportion of people involved. In New York in 1785, for example, the assembly passed a gradual emancipation bill which would have barred Negroes from the polls and from marrying whites. The senate objected to the intermarriage clause because "in so important a connection they thought the free subjects of this State ought to be left to their free choice." The assembly again voted narrowly to retain the clause and then, after conference with the senate, finally receded on it by a narrow margin, though later for other reasons the entire bill was lost.[38] In

Massachusetts, however, an act of 1786 on the "Solemnization of Marriage" voided marriages between whites and Negroes. Rhode Island passed a similar law in 1798. The Pennsylvania emancipation bill also contained a similar provision which was dropped before final passage.[39] On the whole, this random pattern in the North suggests both the existence of sentiment against intermixture and a lack of great vehemence underlying it.

In the South, on the other hand, where there were more Negroes (wearing fewer clothes)[40] there is evidence suggesting greater tension. For the most part laws prohibiting racial mixture were already on the books and nobody wanted them off.[41] The Virginia legislature's refusal to accept Jefferson's provision in the revisal for banishment of white women bearing mulattoes stemmed more from objection to the harsh penalty than from willingness to countenance interracial matches. One foreign traveler observed that the unusually large number of mulattoes in the state was occasioned only by greater length of settlement and that public opinion was firmly set against interracial unions. Liaisons were carried on in secrecy, he explained, for "no white man is known to live regularly with a black woman."[42] The converse relationship was of course another matter; though white women still occasionally slept with Negro men,[43] southern society was as determined as ever to punish rigorously any Negro sexual attacks on white women. In 1769, Virginia had excluded castration from the penal code except as punishment for that offense. The brutality of castration had become offensive to humanitarian sentiment, however, and the legislature refused to enact Jefferson's revisal bill based on the *lex talionis*. Yet as late as 1792 emasculation was specifically declared by the legislature to be permissible punishment for any slave "convicted of an attempt to ravish a white woman." In practice the courts seem usually to have hanged such offenders but there was at least one case of sentence to castration, in 1797. The penalty was finally abolished in a general amendment to the penal code in 1805. Despite tension on the matter, some Virginians refused to be blinded by their feelings. In the 1800's several petitions to the governor asked clemency for Negroes condemned for rape on grounds that the white woman involved was of low character.[44] Elsewhere in the South, however, there was evidence of smoldering emotion. In North Carolina a tradition was inaugurated at the turn of the century when lynching parties burned a Negro for rape and castrated a slave for remarking that he was going to have some white women. Georgia in 1806 enacted a mandatory death penalty for any Negro raping or attempting to rape a white woman. As late as 1827 a Georgia court sentenced a Negro to castration and deportation for attempted rape, and the *Macon Telegraph* castigated the court for its leniency.[45]

The dynamics of the interracial sexual situation did not, of course, invariably tend toward emotional abandon. For one thing, in regions where slavery was firmly rooted in a high proportion of Negroes, the traditional European double standard for the sexes was subject to caricatural polarization.

More sexual freedom for white men meant less for white women. Throughout the eighteenth century South Carolina had shown the effects of this tendency, though far less than the British West Indian societies. Despite difficulties created by the biases of travelers, it seems clear that the same tendency still operated in the deep South in the early years of the nineteenth century. One American traveler, the prominent ornithologist of Philadelphia, Alexander Wilson, described his unfavorable impressions by first lamenting that the "superabundance of Negroes" had "destroyed the activity of the whites," who "stand with their hands in their pockets, overlooking their negroes." In his letter to William Bartram in 1809 (here given as published much later in the century), Wilson went on to say,

These, however, are not one-tenth of the curses slavery has brought on the Southern States. Nothing has surprised me more than the cold, melancholy reserve of the females, of the best families, in South Carolina and Georgia. Old and young, single and married, all have that dull frigid insipidity, and reserve, which is attributed to solitary old maids. Even in their own houses they scarce utter anything to a stranger but yes or no, and one is perpetually puzzled to know whether it proceeds from awkwardness or dislike. Those who have been at some of their Balls [in Charleston] say that the ladies hardly even speak or smile, but dance with as much gravity, as if they were performing some ceremony of devotion. On the contrary, the negro wenches are all sprightliness and gayety; and if report be not a defamer—(*here there is a hiatus in the manuscript*) which render the men callous to all the finer sensations of love, and female excellence.[46]

While one suspects that the "hiatus" may not have been the author's, the description clearly points to deep alienation on the part of white women. Their rightful consorts were often otherwise engaged, and their resulting shell of "dull frigid insipidity" was hardened by the utter necessity of avoiding any resemblance to women of the other race. Perhaps they sensed, too, that the protection they received against Negro men constituted a very perverse variety of affection. Their proper function, moreover, was to preserve the forms and symbols of civilization—they were, after all, bearers of white civilization in a literal sense—and to serve as priestesses in the temples, performing, in Wilson's perceptive phrase, a "ceremony of devotion."

The relationship between miscegenation and society was intricately reciprocal. While miscegenation altered the tone of society, the social institution of slavery helped reshape the definition of miscegenation from fusion of that which was different to fusion of higher and lower; hence slavery was of course responsible for much of the normative judgment implied in the concept of miscegenation. Yet both slavery and miscegenation rested, in the final analysis, upon a *perception of difference* between the races, a perception founded on physiognomic fact. When Jefferson, for example, set out to prove that emancipated Negroes must be removed from white society he predicated "the real distinctions nature has made," moved immediately into a discussion of appearance, and only then went on to less tangible differences in temperament and intellect. Underlying his discussion of the Negro, and everyone else's, was an axiomatic separation of Negroes from white men based on appearance.

NOTES

1. Since Jefferson's writings are at present available in different editions of varying scope and editorial standards, the following have been used in order of preference: Julian P.Boyd, ed., *The Papers of Thomas Jefferson*, 19 vols. to date (Princeton, N.J., 1950—); Lester J. Cappon, ed., *The Adams-Jefferson Letters: The Complete Correspondence between Thomas Jefferson and Abigail and John Adams*, 2 vols. (Chapel Hill, 1959): Paul L. Ford, ed., *The Works of Thomas Jefferson*, 12 vols. (New York, 1904–1905); Andrew A. Lipscomb and Albert E. Bergh, eds., *The Writings of Thomas Jefferson*, 20 vols. (Washington, D.C., 1903). Material relevant to Jefferson's management of his slaves has been collected in Edwin M. Betts, eds., *Thomas Jefferson's Farm Book, with Commentary and Relevant Extracts from Other Writings* (Princeton, N.J., 1953), especially pp. 5–47 of the Commentary.

2. Notes on Arthur Young's Letter [June 18, 1792], Ford, ed., *Works of Jefferson*, VII, 120; to John Taylor, Monticello, Dec. 29, 1794, Lipscomb and Bergh, eds., *Writings of Jefferson*, XVIII, 197.

3. See especially Boyd, ed., *Papers of Jefferson*, XI, 653, XIII, 607–8, XIV, 492–93. Jefferson was wildly welcomed by his slaves upon his return from Europe: see the editorial note in *ibid.*, XVI, 167–68. Many school books still say that Jefferson freed his slaves.

4. Boyd, ed., *Papers of Jefferson*, I, 423.

5. I am much indebted to certain ideas in the analysis of Jefferson's ideology offered by Daniel J. Boorstin, *The Lost World of Thomas Jefferson* (N. Y., 1948). Jefferson pushed the concept of "natural right" into fields where many of his contemporaries were unwilling to follow in 1790: he described majority rule as "the Natural law of every society" and claimed that "the right to have commerce and intercourse with our neighbors is a natural right," Boyd, ed., *Papers of Jefferson*, XVI, 179, 450. His original draft of the Declaration is in *ibid.*, I, 423-27.

6. To Francis Eppes, Paris, July 30, 1787, Boyd, ed., *Papers of Jefferson*, XI, 653; also to Nicholas Lewis, Paris, Dec. 19, 1786, *ibid.*, X, 615.

7. When confronted with the immediate practicalities of slave ownership Jefferson could more readily imagine its effect upon slaves; he ordered that his nailers not be whipped except in extreme cases, since whipping tended "to degrade them in their own eyes," Jefferson to Thomas Mann Randolph, Washington, Jan. 23, 1801, Lipscomb and Bergh, eds., *Writings of Jefferson*, XVIII, 232.

8. Thomson to Jefferson, N. Y., Nov. 2, 1785, Boyd, ed., *Papers of Jefferson*, IX, 9; Monroe to Jefferson, N. Y., Jan. 19, 1786, *ibid.*, 190.

9. *Ibid.*, VIII, 184, 227, 245, 356–57, X, 63, XII, 577–78; to Dr. George Logan, Washington, May 11, 1805, Ford, ed., *Works of Jefferson*, X, 141–42.

10. Apr. 26, 1789, Boyd, ed., *Papers of Jefferson*, XV, 72.

11. To Walter Jones, Washington, Mar. 31, 1801, Lipscomb and Bergh, eds., *Writings of Jefferson*, X, 256; to St. George Tucker, Monticello, Aug. 28, 1797, Ford, ed., *Works of Jefferson*, VIII, 335; See also Jefferson, *Notes on Virginia*, ed. Peden, 159.

12. Thomas Jefferson, *Notes on the State of Virginia*, ed. William Peden (Chapel Hill, 1955), pp. 138–39.

13. "Queries Respecting the Slavery and Emancipation of Negroes in Massachusetts, Proposed by the Hon. Judge Tucker of Virginia, and Answered by the Rev. Dr. Belknap," Mass. Hist. Soc., *Collections*, 1st Ser., 4 (1795), 209; "Letters and Documents Relating to Slavery in Massachusetts," *Belknap Papers*, 2 vols. (Mass. Hist. Soc. *Collections*, 5th Ser., 3 [1877]), 390, 415.

14. John P. Kennedy, *Memoirs of the Life of William Wirt, Attorney-General of the United States*, rev. ed., 2 vols. (Phila., 1854), I, 141–42; Nathaniel Dwight, *The Lives of the Signers of the Declaration of Independence* (N. Y., 1860), 269–70. For these references I am indebted to Dr. W. Edwin Hemphill of the South Carolina Archives Department. See also his "Examinations of George Wythe Swinney for Forgery and Murder: A Documentary Essay," *Wm. and Mary Qtly.*, 3d ser., 12 (1955), 547; and [B. W. Leigh], *The Letter of Appomattox to the People of Virginia . . .* (Richmond, 1832), 43.

15. The entire passage is in Jefferson, *Notes on Virginia*, ed. Peden, 137–43.

16. *Ibid.*, 138–39, 70–71, 61, and 288*n*: "but love is with them only an eager desire, not a tender delicate excitement, not a delicious foment of the soul."

17. Gilbert Imlay, *A Topographical Description of the Western Territory of North America . . .* (New York, 1793), 192; Smith, *Essay on Variety* (1810), ed. Jordan, 277*n*. Imlay attempted to refute Jefferson's arguments point by point (pp. 192–200), asserting, for example, that whites like Negroes secreted more in hot climates, that Negroes' odor was owing partly to a different manner of living, and that Phyllis Wheatley was indeed a respectable poetess. In the latter years of the 18th century there seems to have been no subsidence of comment on the Negro's smell.

18. Collected in Bernard Mayo, ed., *Thomas Jefferson and His Unknown Brother Randolph . . .* (Charlottesville, Va., 1942).

19. Albert Jay Nock, *Jefferson*, intro. Merrill D. Peterson (N. Y., 1960), 18. The most authoritative biographical information may be found in Dumas Malone, *Jefferson and His Time*, 5 vols. to date (Boston, 1948—).

20. Malone, *Jefferson and His Time*, I, 434.

21. See the revealing description by his daughter in Sarah N. Randolph, *The Domestic Life of Thomas Jefferson . . .* , intro. Dumas Malone (N. Y., 1958), 63.

22. Malone, *Jefferson and His Time*, I, 153–55, 447–51, is a definitive account.

23. Jefferson to Maria Cosway, Paris, Oct. 12, 1786, Boyd, ed., *Papers of Jefferson*, X, 443–53.

24. Marie Kimball, *Jefferson: The Road to Glory, 1743 to 1776* (N. Y., 1943), 166–68; to Martha Jefferson, Annapolis, Dec. 22, 1783, Boyd, ed., *Papers of Jefferson*, VI, 416–17; to Martha Jefferson Randolph, N. Y., Apr. 4, 1790, *ibid.*, XVI, 300. The 1783 letter contained the admonition: "A lady who has been seen as a sloven or slut in the morning, will never efface the impression she then made with all the dress and pageantry she can afterwards involve herself in. Nothing is so disgusting to our sex as a want of cleanliness and delicacy in yours. I hope therefore the moment you rise from bed, your first work will be to dress yourself in such a stile as that you may be seen by any gentleman without his being able to discover a pin amiss, or any other circumstance of neatness wanting."

25. To Charles Bellini, Paris, Sept. 30, 1785, Boyd, ed., *Papers of Jefferson*, VIII, 568–69, also 636–37; Jefferson's theme of sexual promiscuity as the ultimate corruption is noted in a perceptive portrayal by Bernard Bailyn, "Boyd's Jefferson: Notes for a Sketch," *New Eng. Qtly.*, 33 (1960), 386–87.

26. Boyd, ed., *Papers of Jefferson*, IX, 372, X, 604. This comment accurately but fortuitously forecasts later incidents in the 19th and 20th centuries where the charge of rape was used by white women against Negro men.

27. [William L. Smith], *Pretensions of Jefferson to the Presidency Examined; and the Charges Against John Adams Refuted . . .* (Philadelphia, 1796), 6.

28. Sept. 1, 1802.

29. By far the best account is Merrill D. Peterson, *The Jefferson Image in the American Mind* (N. Y., 1960), 181–87, though a complete history would require a volume. For more recent rehabilitations of the charge see the pseudo-scholarly article, Pearl N. Graham, "Thomas Jefferson and Sally Hemings," *Jour. Negro Hist.*, 44 (1961), 89–103, and the even less excusable tale in Raymond L. Bruckberger, *Image of America*, trans. C. G. Paulding and Virgilia Peterson (N. Y., 1959), 76–77.

30. This is a highly telescoped account; a full and *unexcited* discussion of the matter is needed.

A possible earlier daughter supposedly born in France can be quite safely ruled out. For the timing of the births and certain blood relationships, see Betts, ed., *Jefferson's Farm Book, passim*, points which the fine brief discussion by Peterson does not consider. See also Rayford W. Logan, ed., *Memoirs of a Monticello Slave, As Dictated to Charles Campbell in the 1840's by Isaac, One of Thomas Jefferson's Slaves* (Charlottesville, Va., 1951), *passim*; Waverly, Ohio, *Pike County Republican*, Mar. 13, 1873; Hamilton W. Pierson, *Jefferson at Monticello: The Private Life of Thomas Jefferson* ... (N. Y., 1862), 110–11; Henry S. Randall to James Parton, Courtland Village, N. Y., June 1, 1868, in Milton E. Flower, *James Parton: The Father of Modern Biography* (Durham, N.C., 1951), 236–39; codicil to Jefferson's will, Mar. 17, 1826, Lipscomb and Bergh, eds., *Writings of Jefferson*, XVII, 469–70.

31. Jefferson to William Short, Monticello, Jan. 18, 1826, Ford, ed., *Works of Jefferson*, XII, 434.

32. Logan, ed., *Memoirs of a Monticello Slave*, 13; Waverly *Pike County Republican*, Mar. 13, 1873; Peterson, *Jefferson Image*, 184.

33. The bizarre development in his household may have accounted for both an absence of strong feeling in his description of miscegenation, in a lawyer's brief *before* his marriage, as "that confusion of species, which the legislature seems to have considered as an evil," and the alteration, for which he may have been responsible, of the legal definition of a mulatto from one-eighth to one-fourth Negro in the Virginia revisal, five years *after* his marriage. Ford, ed., *Works of Jefferson*, I, 471; Boyd, ed., *Papers of Jefferson*, II, 476; William Waller Hening, ed., *The Statutes at Large Being a Collection of All the Laws of Virginia*, 13 vols. (Richmond, New York, and Philadelphia, 1809–23), XII, 184.

34. Reprinted from *Boston Gazette* in Richmond *Recorder*, Dec. 1, 1802.

35. *Ibid.*, Sept. 1, 1802.

36. *Ibid.*, Sept. 22, 1802.

37. Max Farrand, ed., *Records Federal Convention of 1787*, rev. ed., 4 vols. (New Haven, 1937), 1st Cong., 2d sess., 1455, 1458 (Smith had just finished reading aloud the relevant excerpts from the *Notes on Virginia*); Jefferson to Gov. James Monroe, Washington, Nov. 24, 1801, Ford, ed., *Works of Jefferson*, IX, 317.

38. Quote is from Charles Thomson to his wife, Harriet, Mar. 22, 1785, Charles Thomson Papers, Misc., Lib. Cong.; *Journal Assembly N.-Y.* (1785), 77, 86; also McManus, "Antislavery Legislation in New York," *Jour. Negro Hist.*, 46 (1961), 208–10.

39. *Acts and Laws of the Commonwealth of Massachusetts (1780–1805)*, 13 vols. (Boston, 1890–98), 1786–87, 10; *Public Laws of the State of Rhode-Island* ... 1798 (Providence, 1798), 483; Phila. *Pa. Packet*, Mar. 4, 1779; James T. Mitchell *et al.*, eds., *Statutes at Large of Pennsylvania from 1682 to 1809*, 18 vols. (Harrisburg, 1896–1915), X, 67–73. In the year 1800 Rhode Island cleared up ambiguity in an earlier law by declaring that no paternity suits could be brought by Negro women against white men. *Public Laws of the State of Rhode-Island and Providence Plantations, Passed Since* ... 1798 (Newport, [1813?]), 41.

40. Lida Tunstall Rodman, ed., *Journal of a Tour to North Carolina, by William Attmore, 1787* (Chapel Hill, 1922), 25, 44; Annapolis *Md. Gaz.*, Sept. 16, 1790; John Davis, *Travels of Four Years and a Half in the United States of America during 1798, 1799, 1800, 1801, and 1802*, ed. A. J. Morrison (New York, 1901), 97, 422; Robert Sutcliff, *Travels in Some Parts of North America*, ... 1804 ... 1806 ... (Phila., 1812), 51–52, 97; Louis B. Wright and Marion Tinling, eds., *Quebec to Carolina in 1785–1786: Being the Travel Diary and Observations of Robert Hunter, Jr., a Young Merchant of London* (San Marino, Calif., 1943), 267; Charles William Janson, *The Stranger in America*, ed. C. S. Driver (New York, 1935), 381–82; James O'Kelly, *Essay on Negro Slavery* (Phila., 1789), 26; "Extract from a Diary Kept by the Hon. Jonathan Mason of a Journey from Boston to Savannah in the Years 1804–1805," Mass. Hist. Soc., *Proceedings*, 2d Ser., 2 (1885–86), 22.

41. Delaware banned intermarriage in 1807 and repealed the ban in 1808, owing to confusion over other matters in the law. *Laws of the State of Delaware*, 4 vols. (New Castle and Wilmington, 1797–1816), IV, 112, 221.

42. *Report of the Committee of Revisors* in Boyd, ed., *Papers of Jefferson*, II, 471; Duc de La Rochefoucauld-Liancourt, *Travels through the United States of North America . . . 1795, 1796, and 1797 . . .* , 2 vols. (London, 1799), II, 82. Other foreign travelers reported specific (though anonymous) instances of masters or their sons sleeping with their slaves; Davis, *Travels in the United States*, 56, 414; Sutcliff, *Travels in North America*, 53. Cases of sexual relations came to light in curiously different ways. Rev. James Fowles of Virginia admitted fathering mulattoes; a Virginia man appealed to the legislature for permission to free his mulatto child; a North Carolina law confirmed a planter's leaving property to his bastard children by "his negro slave Hester" and freed her and the children (1789—ten years later legislators would probably have been less lenient); and in Wilmington, N.C., a Dr. Nesbitt killed a Negro whose mulatto wife the doctor had previously been keeping. James H. Johnston, "Race Relations in Virginia and Miscegenation in the South, 1776-1860" (Ph.D. dissertation University of Chicago, 1937) 178, 175; Walter Clark, ed., *The State Records of North Carolina*, 26 vols. (Goldsboro, 1886-1907), XXV, 36-37; *Raleigh Register*, Aug. 10, 1802.

43. Ten petitions (1798-1808) for divorce by white men on grounds of the wife's adultery with a Negro slave are cited in Johnston, *Race Relations in Virginia*, 199-202, 206-7, 211, 221. Other instances of the same combination are in Annapolis *Md. Gaz.*, July 31, 1794; Edgar J. McManus, "Negro Slavery in New York" (Ph.D. diss., Columbia University, 1959), 262; John Melish, *Travels through the United States of America, . . . 1806 . . . 1811 . . .* 2d ed. (London, 1818), 49; John Hope Franklin, *The Free Negro in North Carolina, 1790-1860* (Chapel Hill, 1943), 37-39.

44. Hening, ed., *Statutes Va.*, VIII, 358; Samuel Shepard, ed., *The Statutes at Large of Virginia, from October Session 1792, to December Session 1806, Inclusive, New Ser., continuation of Hening*, 3 vols. (Richmond, 1835-36), I, 125, III, 119; Troy, N.Y., *Farmer's Oracle*, Oct. 3, 1797 (for reference to which I am indebted to McManus, "Negro Slavery in New York," 97); the petitions in Johnston, *Race Relations in Virginia*, 206-7.

45. Janson, *Stranger in America*, ed. Driver, 386-87; *A Compilation of the Laws of the State of Georgia, Passed by the Legislature Since the Political Year 1800, to the Year 1810, Inclusive . . .* (Augusta, 1813), 334-35; Ralph B. Flanders, *Plantation Slavery in Georgia* (Chapel Hill, 1933), 267.

46. Wilson to Bartram, Savannah, Mar. 8, 1809. Alexander B. Grosart, ed., *The Poems and Literary Prose of Alexander Wilson, the American Ornithologist*, 2 vols. (Paisley, Scotland, 1876), I, 167-68. A foreign traveler remarked on a concomitant phenomenon in 1819: "The ladies of Carolina, it is said, prefer a fair effeminate kind of man to one of a robust habit, and swarthy dark complexion. This preference of delicate complexions originates in their antipathy to any colour approaching to that of the negro or mulatto, or yellow man, whom it is sometimes difficult to distinguish from a white or brown person." William Faux, *Memorable Days in America, Being a Journal of a Tour to the United States [1818-1820] . . .* (London, 1823), in Reuben G. Thwaites, ed., *Early Western Travels, 1748-1846 . . .* , 32 vols. (Cleveland, 1904-07), XI, 100.

6

SLAVERY AND PERSONALITY

STANLEY M. ELKINS

One of the most controversial passages in American historiography, Stanley Elkins's chapter on the slave personality has made the "Sambo thesis" a familiar point of departure in debates—whether classroom or street—over the residual impact of slavery on black Americans. Elkins's *Slavery: A Problem in American Institutional and Intellectual Life* (1959), relying exclusively on secondary sources, argued for a reinterpretation of American slavery keying on institutions or their absence. A peculiarly closed system, American slavery compared unfavorably with regimes in Latin America, Elkins wrote, because there Catholic Church teachings and protections originating in Roman law allowed the slave to retain a measure of his manhood; the lack of these structures—indeed the dearth of mediating national organizations in Jacksonian America—not only gave the money-minded slaveholder free rein but provided no means of discourse between Northern and Southern moderates on the subject of slavery.

As comparative and black history, Elkins's study generated considerable opposition. One historian went so far as to collect the many rebuttals to *Slavery* and make a book of them. Slavery may have duplicated the misery and fear of the concentration camp—actually Elkins said that features of the concentration camp resembled slavery—but, said critics, perhaps such other institutions as armies, prisons, and asylums do so more closely. In addition historians of slavery since 1959 have found abundant evidence that blacks were far more resilient and resourceful in the slave community than Elkins's "Sambo" interpretation would permit and that the black family was much stronger than his thesis suggested it was or could have been. The figures after whom young slaves could have modeled their behavior apparently were more numerous (and therefore various) than were those in control of the concentration camp inmates; among authority figures in the slave experience were blacks who held responsibility and exercised leadership. Recent works—John Blassingame's *Slave Community* (1970) and Eugene Genovese's *Roll, Jordan, Roll* (1974)—offer strong evi-

142   STANLEY M. ELKINS

dence that to understand the slave's psychology one must study the give and take
strategies inherent in the master-slave relationship. In many respects, Elkins's *Slavery*
is "classically wrong"—that is, valuable in teaching primarily for its flaws.

Still, as psychological analysis—remember that it pioneered in this approach—the
book raises at least three interesting questions. The first involves the value of role
theory. It is unclear whether Elkins meant to say that blacks adopted the role of
Sambo as so much protective coloring or that they were helplessly confined to it. Did
they, in other words, deliberately choose the role and polish it or did they play it
despite themselves? By now most historians probably would agree that slaves were
quite deliberate in this role, that they wrote their own script when they "put on ol'
massa." But if the nub of the issue is whether blacks were cognizant of a ploy or were
victims in a psychological straitjacket, role theory finally fails to offer an answer
because it deals with behavior rather than intentions. Secondly, Elkins's chapter asks
whether it makes sense to speak of group personality or "character type" at all. To
what degree, for example, is there an American character or a middle-class personality? Though many such attempts at generalization are of doubtful importance—
telling how people are alike at an almost useless level of abstraction—several pieces in
this collection defend a less exposed position. Members of carefully defined groups,
they suggest, often do share personality characteristcs that their common experience
"draws out" or emphasizes. Third, one wonders how Elkins's chapter would have
fared had he chosen cognitive psychology over role theory. Slave conditions, the
courage and resourcefulness of black parents notwithstanding, hardly lent themselves
to the development of the cognitive skills necessary even in nineteenth-century society. How easily such deficiencies can be overcome and where such development takes
place—at home or school—remain open questions, as does the ability of the state to
help citizens of any race or creed to acquire those skills.

AN EXAMINATION of American slavery, checked at certain critical points
against a very different slave system, that of Latin America, reveals that a
major key to many of the contrasts between them was an institutional key:
The presence or absence of other powerful institutions in society made an
immense difference in the character of slavery itself. In Latin America, the
very tension and balance among three kinds of organizational concerns—
church, crown, and plantation agriculture—prevented slavery from being
carried by the planting class to its ultimate logic. For the slave, in terms of the
space thus allowed for the development of men and women as moral beings,
the result was an "open system": a system of contacts with free society
through which ultimate absorption into that society could and did occur with
great frequency. The rights of personality implicit in the ancient traditions of
slavery and in the church's most venerable assumptions on the nature of the
human soul were thus in a vital sense conserved, whereas to a staggering
extent the very opposite was true in North American slavery. The latter
system had developed virtually unchecked by institutions having anything
like the power of their Latin counterparts; the legal structure which sup-

ported it, shaped only by the demands of a staple-raising capitalism, had defined with such nicety the slave's character as chattel that his character as a moral individual was left in the vaguest of legal obscurity. In this sense American slavery operated as a "closed" system—one in which, for the generality of slaves in their nature as men and women, *sub specie aeternitatis*, contacts with free society could occur only on the most narrowly circumscribed of terms. The next question is whether living within such a "closed system" might not have produced noticeable effects upon the slave's very personality.

Personality Types and Stereotypes

The name "Sambo" has come to be synonymous with "race stereotype." Here is an automatic danger signal, warning that the analytical difficulties of asking questions about slave personality may not be nearly so great as the moral difficulties. The one inhibits the other; the morality of the matter has had a clogging effect on its theoretical development that may not be to the best interests of either. And yet theory on group personality is still in a stage rudimentary enough that this particular body of material—potentially illuminating—ought not to remain morally impounded any longer.

Is it possible to deal with "Sambo" as a type? The characteristics that have been claimed for the type come principally from Southern lore. Sambo, the typical plantation slave, was docile but irresponsible, loyal but lazy, humble but chronically given to lying and stealing; his behavior was full of infantile silliness and his talk inflated with childish exaggeration. His relationship with his master was one of utter dependence and childlike attachment: it was indeed this childlike quality that was the very key to his being. Although the merest hint of Sambo's "manhood" might fill the Southern breast with scorn, the child, "in his place," could be both exasperating and lovable.

One searches in vain through the literature of the Latin-American slave systems for the "Sambo" of our tradition—the perpetual child incapable of maturity. How is this to be explained? If Sambo is not a product of race (that "explanation" can be consigned to oblivion) and not simply a product of "slavery" in the abstract (other societies have had slavery), then he must be related to our own peculiar variety of it. And if Sambo is uniquely an American product, then his existence, and the reasons for his character, must be recognized in order to appreciate the very scope of our slave problem and its aftermath. The absoluteness with which such a personality ("real" or "unreal") had been stamped upon the plantation slave does much to make plausible the ante-bellum Southerner's difficulty in imagining that blacks anywhere could be anything but a degraded race—and it goes far to explain his failure to see any sense at all in abolitionism. It even casts light on the peculiar quality of abolitionism itself; it was so all-enveloping a problem in human personality that our abolitionists could literally not afford to recognize it. Virtually without exception, they met this dilemma either by side-tracking it altogether (they explicitly refused to advance plans for solving it, arguing that this would rob their message of its moral force) or by countering it with theories of infinite human perfectibility. The question of personality, therefore, becomes a crucial phase of the entire problem of slavery in the United States, having conceivably something to do with the difference—already alluded to—between an "open" and a "closed" system of slavery.

If it were taken for granted that a special type existed in significant numbers on American plantations, closer connections might be made with a growing literature on personality and character types, the investigation of which has become a widespread, respectable, and productive enterprise among our psychologists and social scientists.[1] Realizing that, it might then seem not quite so dangerous to add that the type corresponded in its major outlines to "Sambo."

Let the above, then, be a preface to the argument of the present essay. It will be assumed that there were elements in the very structure of the plantation system—its "closed" character—that could sustain infantilism as a normal feature of behavior. These elements, having less to do with "cruelty" per se than simply with the sanctions of authority, were effective and pervasive enough to require that such infantilism be characterized as something much more basic than mere "accommodation." It will be assumed that the sanctions of the system were in themselves sufficient to produce a recognizable personality type.[2]

It should be understood that to identify a social type in this sense is still to generalize on a fairly crude level—and to insist for a limited purpose on the legitimacy of such generalizing is by no means to deny that, on more defined levels, a great profusion of individual types might have been observed in slave society. Nor need it be claimed that the "Sambo" type, even in the relatively crude sense employed here, was a universal type. It was, however, a plantation type, and a plantation existence embraced well over half the slave population.[3] Two kinds of material will be used in the effort to picture the mechanisms whereby this adjustment to absolute power—an adjustment whose end product included infantile features of behavior—may have been effected. One is drawn from the theoretical knowledge presently available in social psychology, and the other, in the form of an analogy, is derived from some of the data that have come out of the German concentration camps. It is recognized in most theory that social behavior is regulated in some general way by adjustment to symbols of authority—however diversely "authority" may be defined either in theory or in culture itself—and that such adjustment is closely related to the very formation of personality. A corollary would be, of course, that the more diverse those symbols of authority may be, the greater is the permissible variety of adjustment to them—and the wider the margin of individuality, consequently, in the development of the self. The question here has to do with the wideness or narrowness of that margin on the ante-bellum plantation.

The other body of material, involving an experience undergone by several million men and women in the concentration camps of our own time, contains certain items of relevance to the problem here being considered. The experience was analogous to that of slavery and was one in which wide-scale instances of infantilization were observed. The material is sufficiently detailed, and sufficiently documented by men who not only took part in the experience itself but who were versed in the use of psychological theory for analyzing it, that the advantages of drawing upon such data for purposes of analogy seem to outweigh the possible risks.

Shock and Detachment

We may suppose that every African who became a slave underwent an experience whose crude psychic impact must have been staggering and whose consequences superseded anything that had ever previously happened to him. Some effort should therefore be made to picture the series of shocks which must have accompanied the principal events of that enslavement.

The majority of slaves appear to have been taken in native wars, which meant that no one—neither persons of high rank nor warriors of prowess—was guaranteed against capture and enslavement.[4] Great numbers were caught in surprise attacks upon their villages, and since the tribes acting as middlemen for the trade had come to depend on regular supplies of captives in order to maintain that function, the distinction between wars and raiding expeditions tended to be very dim. The first shock, in an experience destined to endure many months and to leave its survivors irrevocably changed, was thus the shock of capture. It is an effort to remember that while enslavement occurred in Africa every day, to the individual it occurred just once.

The second shock—the long march to the sea—drew out the nightmare for many weeks. Under the glaring sun, through the steaming jungle, they were driven along like beasts tied together by their necks; day after day, eight or more hours at a time, they would stagger barefoot over thorny underbrush, dried reeds, and stones. Hardship, thirst, brutalities, and near starvation penetrated the experience of each exhausted man and woman who reached the coast. One traveler tells of seeing hundreds of bleaching skeletons strewn along one of the slave caravan routes. But then the man who must interest us is.the man who survived—he who underwent the entire experience, of which this was only the beginning.

The next shock, aside from the fresh physical torments which accompanied it, was the sale to the European slavers. After being crowded into pens near the trading stations and kept there overnight, sometimes for days, the slaves were brought out for examination. Those rejected would be abandoned to starvation; the remaining ones—those who had been bought—were branded, given numbers inscribed on leaden tags, and herded on shipboard. The episode that followed—almost too protracted and stupefying to be called a mere "shock"—was the dread Middle Passage, brutalizing to any man, black or white, ever to be involved with it. The holds, packed with squirming and suffocating humanity, became stinking infernos of filth and pestilence. Stories of disease, death, and cruelty on the terrible two-month voyage abound in the testimony which did much toward ending the British slave trade forever.

The final shock in the process of enslavement came with the Negro's introduction to the West Indies. Bryan Edwards, describing the arrival of a slave ship, writes of how in times of labor scarcity crowds of people would come scrambling aboard, manhandling the slaves and throwing them into panic. The Jamaica legislature eventually "corrected the enormity" by enacting that the sales be held on shore. Edwards felt a certain mortification at seeing the Negroes exposed naked in public, similar to that felt by the trader Degrandpré at seeing them examined back at the African factories. Yet here they did not seem to care. "They display . . . very few signs of lamentation for their past or of apprehension for their future condition; but . . . commonly express great eagerness to be sold."[5] The "seasoning" process which followed completed the series of steps whereby the African Negro became a slave.

The mortality had been very high. One-third of the numbers first taken, out of a total of perhaps fifteen million, had died on the march and at the trading stations; another third died during the Middle Passage and the seasoning. Since a majority of the African-born slaves who came to the North American plantations did not come directly but were imported through the British West Indies, one may assume that the typical slave underwent an experience something like that just outlined. This was the man—one in three—who had come through it all and lived and was about to enter our "closed system." What would he be like if he survived and adjusted to that?

Actually, a great deal had happened to him already. Much of his past had been annihilated; nearly every prior connection had been severed. Not that he had really "forgotten" all these things—his family and kinship arrangements, his language, the tribal religion, the taboos, the name he had once borne, and so on—but none of it any longer carried much meaning. The old values, the sanctions, the standards, already unreal, could no longer furnish him guides for conduct, for adjusting to the expectations of a complete new life. Where then was he to look for new standards, new cues—who would furnish them now? He could now look to none but his master, the one man to whom the system had committed his entire being: the man upon whose will depended his food, his shelter, his sexual connections, whatever moral instruction he might be offered, whatever "success" was possible within the system, his very security—in short, everything.

The thoroughness with which African Negroes coming to America were detached from prior cultural sanctions should thus be partly explainable by the very shock sequence inherent in the technique of procurement. But it took something more than this to produce "Sambo," and it is possible to overrate—or at least to overgeneralize—this shock sequence in the effort to explain what followed. A comparable experience was also undergone by slaves coming into Latin America, where very little that resembled our "Sambo" tradition would ever develop. We should also remember that, in either case, it was only the first generation that actually experienced these shocks. It could even be argued that the shock sequence is not an absolute necessity for explaining "Sambo" at all.

So whereas the Middle Passage and all that went with it must have been psychologically numbing, and should probably be regarded as a long thrust, at least, toward the end product, it has little meaning considered apart from what came later. It may be assumed that the process of detachment was completed—and, as it were, guaranteed—by the kind of "closed" authority-system into which the slave was introduced and to which he would have to adjust. At any rate, a test of this detachment and its thoroughness is virtually ready-made. Everyone who has looked into the problem of African cultural features surviving among New World Negroes agrees that the contrast between North America and Latin America is immense. In Brazil, survivals from African religion are not only to be encountered everywhere, but such carry-overs are so distinct that they may even be identified with particular tribal groups. "The Negro religions and cults," Arthur Ramos adds, "were not the only form of cultural expression which survived in Brazil. The number of folklore survivals is extremely large, the prolongation of social institutions, habits, practices and events from Africa." Fernando Ortiz, writing of Cuba in 1905, saw the African witchcraft cults flourishing on the island as a formidable social problem. On the other hand the anthropologist Melville Herskovits, despite much dedicated field work, has been put to great effort to prove that in North American Negro society any African cultural vestiges have survived at all.

Adjustment to Absolute Power in the Concentration Camp

A certain amount of the mellowness in Ulrich Phillips' picture of ante-bellum plantation life [in his classic *American Negro Slavery* (1918)] has of necessity been discredited by recent efforts not only to refocus attention upon the brutalities of the slave system but also to dispose once and for all of Phillips' assumptions about the slave as a racially inferior being. And yet it is important—particularly in view of the analogy about to be presented—to keep in mind that for all the system's cruelties there were still clear standards of patriarchal benevolence inherent in its human side, and that such standards were recognized as those of the best Southern families. This aspect, despite the most drastic changes of emphasis, should continue to guarantee for Phillips' view more than just a modicum of legitimacy; the patriarchal quality, whatever measure of benevolence or lack of it one wants to impute to the regime, still holds a major key to its nature as a social system.

Introducing, therefore, certain elements of the German concentration-camp experience involves the risky business of trying to balance two necessities—emphasizing both the vast dissimilarities of the two regimes and the essentially limited purpose for which they are being brought together, and at the same time justifying the use of the analogy in the first place. The point is perhaps best made by insisting on an order of classification. The American plantation was not even in the metaphorical sense a "concentration camp"; nor was it even "like" a concentration camp, to the extent that any standards comparable to those governing the camps might be imputed to any sector of American society, at any time; but it should at least be permissible to turn the thing around—to speak of the concentration camp as a special and highly perverted instance of human slavery. Doing so, moreover, should actually be of some assistance in the strategy, now universally sanctioned, of demonstrating how little the products and consequences of slavery ever had to do with race. The only mass experience that Western people have had within recorded history comparable in any way with Negro slavery was undergone in the nether world of Nazism. The concentration camp was not only a perverted slave system; it was also—what is less obvious but even more to the point—a perverted patriarchy.

The system of the concentration camps was expressly devised in the 1930's by high officials of the German government to function as an instrument of terror. The first groups detained in the camps consisted of prominent enemies of the Nazi regime; later, when these had mostly been eliminated, it was still felt necessary that the system be institutionalized and made into a standing weapon of intimidation—which required a continuing flow of incoming prisoners. The categories of eligible persons were greatly widened to include all real, fancied, or "potential" opposition to the state. They were often selected on capricious and random grounds, and together they formed a cross-section of society which was virtually complete: criminals, workers, businessmen, professional people, middle-class Jews, even members of the aristocracy. The teeming camps thus held all kinds—not only the scum of the underworld but also countless men and women of culture and refinement. During the war a specialized objective was added, that of exterminating the Jewish populations of subject countries, which required special mass-production methods of which the gas chambers and crematories of Auschwitz-Birkenau were outstanding examples. Yet the basic technique was everywhere and at all times the same: the deliberate infliction of various forms of torture upon the incoming prisoners in such a way as to break their resistance and make way for their degradation as individuals. These brutalities were not merely "permitted" or "encouraged"; they were pre-scribed. Duty in the camps was a mandatory phase in the training of SS guards, and it was here that particular efforts were made to overcome their scruples and to develop in them a capacity for relishing spectacles of pain and anguish.

The concentration camps and everything that took place in them were veiled in the utmost isolation and secrecy. Of course complete secrecy was impossible, and a continuing stream of rumors circulated among the popula-tion. At the same time so repellent was the nature of these stories that in their enormity they transcended the experience of nearly everyone who heard them; in self-protection it was somehow necessary to persuade oneself that they could not really be true. The results, therefore, contained elements of the diabolical. The undenied existence of the camps cast a shadow of name-less dread over the entire population; on the other hand the *individual* who actually became a prisoner in one of them was in most cases devastated with fright and utterly demoralized to discover that what was happening to *him* was not less, but rather far more terrible than anything he had imagined. The shock sequence of "procurement," therefore, together with the initial phases of the prisoner's introduction to camp life, is not without significance in assessing some of the psychic effects upon those who survived as long-term inmates.

The arrest was typically made at night, preferably late; this was standing Gestapo policy, designed to heighten the element of shock, terror, and unre-ality surrounding the arrest. After a day or so in the police jail came the next major shock, that of being transported to the camp itself. "This transporta-tion into the camp, and the 'initiation' into it," writes Bruno Bettelheim (an ex-inmate of Dachau and Buchenwald), "is often the first torture which the prisoner has ever experienced and is, as a rule, physically and psychologically the worst torture to which he will ever be exposed."[6] It involved a planned series of brutalities inflicted by guards making repeated rounds through the train over a twelve- to thirty-six-hour period during which the prisoner was prevented from resting. If transported in cattle cars instead of passenger cars, the prisoners were sealed in, under conditions not dissimilar to those of the Middle Passage.[7] Upon their arrival—if the camp was one in which mass exterminations were carried out—there might be sham ceremonies designed to reassure temporarily the exhausted prisoners, which meant that the fresh terrors in the offing would then strike them with redoubled impact. An SS officer might deliver an address, or a band might be playing popular tunes, and it would be in such a setting that the initial "selection" was made. The newcomers would file past an SS doctor who indicated, with a motion of the forefinger, whether they were to go to the left or to the right. To one side went those considered capable of heavy labor; to the other would go wide categories of "undesirables"; those in the latter group were being condemned to the gas chambers.[8] Those who remained would undergo the formalities of "registration," full of indignities, which culminated in the marking of each prisoner with a number.

There were certain physical and psychological strains of camp life, especially debilitating in the early stages, which should be classed with the introductory shock sequence. There was a state of chronic hunger whose pressures were unusually effective in detaching prior scruples of all kinds; even the sexual instincts no longer functioned in the face of the drive for food. The man who at his pleasure could bestow or withhold food thus wielded, for that reason alone, abnormal power. Another strain at first was the demand for absolute obedience, the slightest deviation from which brought savage punishments. The prisoner had to ask permission—by no means granted as a matter of course—even to defecate. The power of the SS guard, as the prisoner was hourly reminded, was that of life and death over his body. A more exquisite form of pressure lay in the fact that the prisoner had never a moment of solitude: he no longer had a private existence; it was no longer possible, in any imaginable sense, for him to be an "individual."

Another factor having deep disintegrative effects upon the prisoner was the prospect of a limitless future in the camp. In the immediate sense this meant that he could no longer make plans for the future. But there would eventually be a subtler meaning: it made the break with the outside world a *real* break; in time the "real" life would become the life of the camp, the outside world an abstraction. Had it been a limited detention, whose end could be calculated, one's outside relationships—one's roles, one's very "personality"—might temporarily have been laid aside, to be reclaimed more or less intact at the end of the term. Here, however, the prisoner was faced with the apparent impossibility of his old roles or even his old personality ever having any future at all; it became more and more difficult to imagine himself resuming them. It was this that underlay the "egalitarianism" of the camps; old statuses had lost their meaning. A final strain, which must have been particularly acute for the newcomer, was the omnipresent threat of death and the very unpredictable suddenness with which death might strike. Quite aside from the periodic gas-chamber selections, the guards in their sports and caprices were at liberty to kill any prisoner any time.[9]

In the face of all this, one might suppose that the very notion of an "adjustment" would be grotesque. The majority of those who entered the camps never came out again, but our concern here has to be with those who survived —an estimated 700,000 out of nearly eight million. For them, the regime must be considered not as a system of death but as a way of life. These survivors did make an adjustment of some sort to the system; it is they themselves who report it. After the initial shocks, what was the nature of the "normality" that emerged?

A dramatic species of psychic displacement seems to have occurred at the very outset. This experience, described as a kind of "splitting of personality," has been noted by most of the inmates who later wrote of their imprisonment. The very extremity of the initial tortures produced in the prisoner what actually amounted to a sense of detachment; these brutalities went so beyond his own experience that they became somehow incredible—they seemed to be happening no longer to him but almost to someone else. "[The author] has no doubt," writes Bruno Bettelheim, "that he was able to endure the transportation, and all that followed, because right from the beginning he became convinced that these horrible and degrading experiences somehow did not happen to 'him' as a subject, but only to 'him' as an object."[10] This subject-object "split" appears to have served a double function: not only was it an immediate psychic defense mechanism against shock, but it also acted as the first thrust toward a new adjustment. This splitting-off of a special "self"—a self which endured the tortures but which was not the "real" self— also provided the first glimpse of a new personality which, being not "real," would not need to feel bound by the values which guided the individual in his former life. "The prisoners' feelings," according to Mr. Bettelheim, "could be summed up by the following sentence: 'What I am doing here, or what is happening to me, does not count at all; here everything is permissible as long and insofar as it contributes to helping me survive in the camp.'"[11]

One part of the prisoner's being was thus, under sharp stress, brought to the crude realization that he must thenceforth be governed by an entire new set of standards in order to live. Mrs. Lingens-Reiner puts it bluntly: "Will you survive, or shall I? As soon as one sensed that this was at stake everyone turned egotist."[12] "I think it of primary importance," writes Dr. Cohen, "to take into account that the superego acquired new values in a concentration camp, so much at variance with those which the prisoner bore with him into camp that the latter faded."[13] But then this acquisition of "new values" did not all take place immediately; it was not until some time after the most acute period of stress was over that the new, "unreal" self would become at last the "real" one.

"If you survive the first three months you will survive the next three years." Such was the formula transmitted from the old prisoners to the new ones,[14] and its meaning lay in the fact that the first three months would generally determine a prisoner's capacity for survival and adaptation. "Be inconspicuous": this was the golden rule. The prisoner who called attention to himself, even in such trivial matters as the wearing of glasses, risked doom. Any show of bravado, any heroics, any kind of resistance condemned a man instantly. There were no rewards for martyrdom: not only did the martyr himself suffer, but mass punishments were wreaked upon his fellow inmates. To "be inconspicuous" required a special kind of alertness—almost an animal instinct—against the apathy which tended to follow the initial shocks. To give up the struggle for survival was to commit "passive suicide"; a careless mistake meant death. There were those, however, who did come through this phase and who managed an adjustment to the life of the camp. It was the striking contrasts between this group of two-and three-year veterans and the perpetual stream of newcomers which made it possible for men like Bettelheim and Cohen to speak of the "old prisoner" as a specific type.

The most immediate aspect of the old inmates' behavior which struck these observers was its *childlike* quality. "The prisoners developed types of behavior which are characteristic of infancy or early youth. Some of these behaviors developed slowly, others were immediately imposed on the prisoners and developed only in intensity as time went on."[15] Such infantile behavior took innumerable forms. The inmates' sexual impotence brought about a disappearance of sexuality in their talk;[16] instead, excretory functions occupied them endlessly. They lost many of the customary inhibitions as to soiling their beds and their persons. Their humor was shot with silliness and they giggled like children when one of them would expel wind. Their relationships were highly unstable. "Prisoners would, like early adolescents, fight one another tooth and nail . . . only to become close friends within a few minutes."[17] Dishonesty became chronic. "Now they suddenly appeared to be pathological liars, to be unable to restrain themselves, to be unable to make objective evaluation, etc."[18] "In hundreds of ways," writes Colaço Belmonte, "the soldier, and to an even greater extent the prisoner of war, is given to understand that he is a child. . . . Then dishonesty, mendacity, egotistic actions in order to obtain more food or to get out of scrapes reach full development, and theft becomes a veritable affliction of camp life."[19] This was all true, according to Elie Cohen, in the concentration camp as well.[20] Benedikt Kautsky observed such things in his own behavior: "I myself can declare that often I saw myself as I used to be in my school days, when by sly dodges and clever pretexts we avoided being found out, or could 'organize' something."[21] Bruno Bettelheim remarks on the extravagance of the stories told by the prisoners to one another. "They were boastful, telling tales about what they had accomplished in their former lives, or how they succeeded in cheating foremen or guards, and how they sabotaged the work. Like children they felt not at all set back or ashamed when it became known that they had lied about their prowess."[22]

This development of childlike behavior in the old inmates was the counterpart of something even more striking that was happening to them: "*Only very few of the prisoners escaped a more or less intensive identification with the SS.*"[23] As Mr. Bettelheim puts it: "A prisoner had reached the final stage of adjustment to the camp situation when he had changed his personality so as to accept as his own the values of the Gestapo."[24] The Bettelheim study furnishes a catalogue of examples. The old prisoners came to share the attitude of the SS toward the "unfit" prisoners; newcomers who behaved badly in the labor groups or who could not withstand the strain became a liability for the others, who were often instrumental in getting rid of them. Many old prisoners actually imitated the SS; they would sew and mend their uniforms in such a way as to make them look more like those of the SS—even though they risked punishment for it. "When asked why they did it, they admitted that they loved to look like . . . the guards." Some took great enjoyment in the fact that during roll call "they really had stood well at attention." There were cases of nonsensical rules, made by the guards, which the older prisoners would continue to observe and try to force on the others long after the SS had forgotten them.[25] Even the most abstract ideals of the SS, such as their intense German nationalism and anti-Semitism, were often absorbed by the old inmates—a phenomenon observed among the politically well-educated and even among the Jews themselves. The final quintessence of all this was seen in the "Kapo"—the prisoner who had been placed in a supervisory position over his fellow inmates. These creatures, many of them professional criminals, not only behaved with slavish servility to the SS, but the way in which they often outdid the SS in sheer brutality became one of the most durable features of the concentration-camp legend.

To all these men, reduced to complete and childish dependence upon their masters, the SS had actually become a father-symbol. "The SS man was all-powerful in the camp, he was the lord and master of the prisoner's life. As a cruel father he could, without fear of punishment, even kill the prisoner and as a gentle father he could scatter largesse and afford the prisoner his protection."[26] The result, admits Dr. Cohen, was that "for all of us the SS was a father image. . . ."[27] The closed system, in short, had become a kind of grotesque patriarchy.

The literature provides us with three remarkable tests of the profundity of the experience that these prisoners had undergone and the thoroughness of the changes that had been brought about in them. One is the fact that few cases of real resistance were ever recorded, even among prisoners going to their death. Even upon liberation, when revenge against their tormentors at last became possible, mass uprisings very rarely occurred. A second test of the system's effectiveness was the relative scarcity of suicides in the camps. The third one lies in the very absence of hatred toward the SS among the prisoners. This is probably the hardest of all to understand. Yet the burning spirit of rebellion that many of their liberators expected to find would have had to be supported by fierce and smoldering emotions; such emotions were not there. "It is remarkable," one observer notes, "how little hatred of their wardens is revealed in their stories."[28]

Three Theories of Personality

The immense revelation for psychology in the concentration-camp literature has been the discovery of how elements of dramatic personality change could be brought about in masses of individuals. And yet it is not proper that the crude fact of "change" alone should dominate the conceptual image with which one emerges from this problem. "Change" per se, change that does not go beyond itself, is productive of nothing; it leaves only destruction, shock, and howling bedlam behind it unless some future basis of stability and order lies waiting to guarantee it and give it reality. So it is with the human psyche, which is apparently capable of making terms with a state other than liberty as we know it. The very dramatic features of the process just described may upset the nicety of this point. There is the related danger, moreover, of unduly stressing the individual psychology of the problem at the expense of its social psychology.

These hazards might be minimized by maintaining a conceptual distinction between two phases of the group experience. The process of detachment from prior standards of behavior and value is one of them, and is doubtless the more striking, but there must be another one. That such detachment can, by extension, involve the whole scope of an individual's culture is an implication for which the vocabulary of individual psychology was caught somewhat unawares. Fluctuations in the state of the individual psyche could formerly be dealt with, or so it seemed, while taking for granted the more or less static nature of social organization, and with a minimum of reference to its features. That such organization might itself become an important variable was therefore a possibility not highly developed in theory, focused as theory was upon individual case histories to the invariable minimization of social and cultural setting. The other phase of the experience should be considered as the "stability" side of the problem, that phase which stabilized what the "shock" phase only opened the way for. This was essentially a process of adjustment to a standard of social normality, though in this case a drastic *re*adjustment and compressed within a very short time—a process which under typical conditions of individual and group existence is supposed to begin at birth and last a lifetime and be transmitted in many and diffuse ways from generation to generation. The adjustment is assumed to be slow and organic, and it normally is. Its numerous aspects extend much beyond psychology; those aspects have in the past been treated at great leisure within the rich provinces not only of psychology but of history, sociology, and literature as well. What rearrangement and compression of those provinces may be needed to accommodate a mass experience that not only involved profound individual shock but also required rapid assimilation to a drastically different form of social organization, can hardly be known. But perhaps the most conservative beginning may be made with existing psychological theory.

The theoretical system whose terminology was orthodox for most of the Europeans who have written about the camps was that of Freud. It was necessary for them to do a certain amount of improvising, since the scheme's existing framework provided only the narrowest leeway for dealing with such radical concepts as out-and-out change in personality. This was due to two kinds of limitations which the Freudian vocabulary places upon the notion of the "self." One is that the superego—that part of the self involved in social relationships, social values, expectations of others, and so on—is conceived as only a small and highly refined part of the "total" self. The other is the assumption that the content and character of the superego is laid down in childhood and undergoes relatively little basic alteration thereafter.[29] Yet a Freudian diagnosis of the concentration-camp inmate—whose social self, or superego, did appear to change and who seemed basically changed thereby—is, given these limitations, still possible. Elie Cohen, whose analysis is the most thorough of these, specifically states that "the superego acquired new values in a concentration camp."[30] The old values, according to Dr. Cohen, were first silenced by the shocks which produced "acute depersonalization" (the subject-object split: "It is not the real 'me' who is undergoing this"), and by the powerful drives of hunger and survival. Old values, thus set aside, could be replaced by new ones. It was a process made possible by "infantile regression"—regression to a previous condition of childlike dependency in which parental prohibitions once more became all-powerful and in which parental judgments might once more be internalized. In this way a new "father-image," personified in the SS guard, came into being. That the prisoner's identification with the SS could be so positive is explained by still another mechanism: the principle of "identification with the aggressor." "A child," as Anna Freud writes, "interjects some characteristic of an anxiety-object and so assimilates an anxiety-experience which he has just undergone.... By impersonating the aggressor, assuming his attributes or imitating his aggression, the child transforms himself from the person threatened into the person who makes the threat."[31] In short, the child's only "defense" in the presence of a cruel, all-powerful father is the psychic defense of identification.

Now one could, still retaining the Freudian language, represent all this in somewhat less cumbersome terms by a slight modification of the metaphor. It could simply be said that under great stress the superego, like a bucket, is violently emptied of content and acquires, in a radically changed setting, new content. It would thus not be necessary to postulate a literal "regression" to childhood in order for this to occur. Something of the sort is suggested by Leo Alexander. "The psychiatrist stands in amazement," he writes, "before the thoroughness and completeness with which this perversion of essential superego values was accomplished in adults... [and] it may be that the decisive importance of childhood and youth in the formation of [these] values may have been overrated by psychiatrists in a society in which allegiance to these values in normal adult life was taken too much for granted because of the stability, religiousness, legality, and security of the 19th Century and early 20th Century society."[32]

A second theoretical scheme is better prepared for crisis and more closely geared to social environment than the Freudian adaptation indicated above, and it may consequently be more suitable for accommodating not only the concentration-camp experience but also the more general problem of plantation slave personality. This is the "interpersonal theory" developed by the late Harry Stack Sullivan. One may view this body of work as the response to a peculiarly American set of needs. The system of Freud, so aptly designed for a European society the stability of whose institutional and status relationships could always to a large extent be taken for granted, turns out to be less clearly adapted to the culture of the United States. The American psychiatrist has had to deal with individuals in a culture where the diffuse, shifting, and often uncertain quality of such relationships has always been more pronounced than in Europe. He has come to appreciate the extent to which these relationships actually support the individual's psychic balance—the full extent, that is, to which the self is "social" in its nature. Thus a psychology whose terms are flexible enough to permit altering social relationships to make actual differences in character structure would be a psychology especially promising for dealing with the present problem.[33]

Sullivan's great contribution was to offer a concept whereby the really critical determinants of personality might be isolated for purposes of observation. Out of the hopelessly immense totality of "influences" which in one way or another go to make up the personality, or "self," Sullivan designated one—the estimations and expectations of others—as the one promising to unlock the most secrets. He then made a second elimination: the *majority* of "others" in one's existence may for theoretical purposes be neglected; what counts is who the *significant* others are. Here, "significant others"[34] may be understood very crudely to mean those individuals who hold, or seem to hold, the keys to security in one's own personal situation, whatever its nature. Now as to the psychic processes whereby these "significant others" become an actual part of the personality, it may be said that the very sense of "self" first emerges in connection with anxiety about the attitudes of the most important persons in one's life (initially, the mother, father, and their surrogates—persons of more or less absolute authority), and automatic attempts are set in motion to adjust to these attitudes. In this way their approval, their disapproval, their estimates and appraisals, and indeed a whole range of their expectations become as it were internalized, and are reflected in one's very character. Of course as one "grows up," one acquires more and more significant others whose attitudes are diffuse and may indeed compete, and thus "significance," in Sullivan's sense, becomes subtler and less easy to define. The personality exfoliates; it takes on traits of distinction and, as we say, "individuality." The impact of particular significant others is less dramatic than in early life. But the pattern is a continuing one; new significant others do still appear, and theoretically it is conceivable that even in mature life the personality might be visibly affected by the arrival of such a one— supposing that this new significant other were vested with sufficient authority and power. In any event there are possibilities for fluidity and actual change inherent in this concept which earlier schemes have lacked.

The purest form of the process is to be observed in the development of children, not so much because of their "immaturity" as such (though their plasticity is great and the imprint of early experience goes deep), but rather because for them there are fewer significant others. For this reason—because the pattern is simpler and more easily controlled—much of Sullivan's attention was devoted to what happens in childhood. In any case let us say that unlike the adult, the child, being drastically limited in the selection of significant others, must operate in a "closed system."

Such are the elements which make for order and balance in the normal self: "significant others" plus "anxiety" in a special sense—conceived with not simply disruptive but also guiding, warning functions.[35] The structure of "interpersonal" theory thus has considerable room in it for conceptions of guided change—change for either beneficent or malevolent ends. One technique for managing such change would of course be the orthodox one of psychoanalysis; another, the actual changing of significant others.[36] Patrick Mullahy, a leading exponent of Sullivan, believes that in group therapy much is possible along these lines.[37] A demonic test of the whole hypothesis is available in the concentration camp.

Consider the camp prisoner—not the one who fell by the wayside but the one who was eventually to survive; consider the ways in which he was forced to adjust to the one significant other which he now had—the SS guard, who held absolute dominion over every aspect of his life. The very shock of his introduction was perfectly designed to dramatize this fact; he was brutally maltreated ("as by a cruel father"); the shadow of resistance would bring instant Death. Daily life in the camp, with its fear and tensions, taught over and over the lesson of absolute power. It prepared the personality for a drastic shift in standards. It crushed whatever anxieties might have been drawn from prior standards; such standards had become meaningless. It focused the prisoner's attention constantly on the moods, attitudes, and standards of the only man who mattered. A truly childlike situation was thus created: utter and abject dependency on one, or on a rigidly limited few, significant others. All the conditions which in normal life would give the individual leeway—which allowed him to defend himself against a new and hostile significant other, no matter how powerful—were absent in the camp. No competition of significant others was possible; the prisoner's comrades for practical purposes were helpless to assist him. He had no degree of independence, no lines to the outside, in any matter. Everything, every vital concern, focused on the SS: food, warmth, security, freedom from pain, all depended on the omnipotent significant other, all had to be worked out within the closed system. Nowhere was there a shred of privacy; everything one did was subject to SS supervision. The pressure was never absent. It is thus no wonder that the prisoners should become "as children." It is no wonder that their obedience became unquestioning, that they did not revolt, that they could not "hate" their masters. Their masters' attitudes had become *internalized* as a part of their very selves; those attitudes and standards now dominated all others that they had. They had, indeed, been "changed."

There still exists a third conceptual framework within which these phenomena may be considered. It is to be found in the growing field of "role psychology." This psychology is not at all incompatible with interpersonal theory; the two might easily be fitted into the same system.[38] But it might be strategically desirable, for several reasons, to segregate them for purposes of discussion. One such reason is the extraordinary degree to which role psychology shifts the focus of attention upon the individual's cultural and institutional environment rather than upon his "self." At the same time it gives us a manageable concept—that of "role"—for mediating between the two. As a mechanism, the role enables us to isolate the unique contribution of culture and institutions toward maintaining the psychic balance of the individual. In it, we see formalized for the individual a range of choices in models of behavior and expression, each with its particular style, quality, and attributes. The relationship between the "role" and the "self," though not yet clear, is intimate; it is at least possible at certain levels of inquiry to look upon the individual as the variable and upon the roles extended him as the stable factor. We thus have a potentially durable link between individual psychology and the study of culture. It might even be said, inasmuch as its key term is directly borrowed from the theater, that role psychology offers in workable form the long-awaited connection—apparently missed by Ernest Jones in his *Hamlet* study—between the insights of the classical dramatists and those of the contemporary social theorist.[39] But be that as it may, for our present problem, the concentration camp, it suggests the most flexible account of how the ex-prisoners may have succeeded in resuming their places in normal life.

Let us note certain of the leading terms.[40] A "social role" is definable in its simplest sense as the behavior expected of persons specifically located in specific social groups.[41] A distinction is kept between "expectations" and "behavior"; the expectations of a role (embodied in the "script") theoretically exist in advance and are defined by the organization, the institution, or by society at large. Behavior (the "performance") refers to the manner in which the role is played. Another distinction involves roles which are "pervasive" and those which are "limited." A pervasive role is extensive in scope ("female citizen") and not only influences but also sets bounds upon the other sorts of roles available to the individual ("mother," "nurse," but not "husband," "soldier"); a limited role ("purchaser," "patient") is transitory and intermittent. A further concept is that of "role clarity." Some roles are more specifically defined than others; their impact upon performance (and, indeed, upon the personality of the performer) depends on the clarity of their definition. Finally, it is asserted that those roles which carry with them the clearest and most automatic rewards and punishments are those which will be (as it were) most "artistically" played.

What sorts of things might this explain? It might illuminate the process whereby the child develops his personality in terms not only of the roles which his parents offer him but of those which he "picks up" elsewhere and tries on. It could show how society, in its coercive character, lays down patterns of behavior with which it expects the individual to comply. It suggests the way in which society, now turning its benevolent face to the individual, tenders him alternatives and defines for him the style appropriate to their fulfillment. It provides us with a further term for the definition of personality itself: there appears an extent to which we can say that personality is actually made up of the roles which the individual plays.[42] And here, once more assuming "change" to be possible, we have in certain ways the least cumbersome terms for plotting its course.

It is hoped that the very hideousness of the concentration camp has not disqualified it as a test for certain features of a far milder and more benevolent form of slavery. But it should still be possible to say, with regard to the individuals who lived as slaves within the respective systems, that just as on one level there is every difference between a wretched childhood and a carefree one, there are, for other purposes, limited features which the one may be said to have shared with the other.

Both were closed systems from which all standards based on prior connections had been effectively detached. A working adjustment to either system required a childlike conformity, a limited choice of "significant others." Cruelty per se cannot be considered the primary key to this; of far greater importance was the simple "closedness" of the system, in which all lines of authority descended from the master and in which alternative social bases that might have supported alternative standards were systematically suppressed. The individual, consequently, for his very psychic security, had to picture his master in some way as the "good father,"[43] even when, as in the concentration camp, it made no sense at all. But why should it not have made sense for many a simple plantation Negro whose master did exhibit, in all the ways that could be expected, the features of the good father who was really "good"? If the concentration camp could produce in two or three years the results that it did, one wonders how much more pervasive must have been those attitudes, expectations, and values which had, certainly, their benevolent side and which were accepted and transmitted over generations.

For the Negro child, in particular, the plantation offered no really satisfactory father-image other than the master. The "real" father was virtually without authority over his child, since discipline, parental responsibility, and control of rewards and punishments all rested in other hands; the slave father could not even protect the mother of his children except by appealing directly to the master. Indeed, the mother's own role loomed far larger for the slave child than did that of the father. She controlled those few activities—household care, preparation of food, and rearing of children—that were left to the slave family. For that matter, the very etiquette of plantation life removed even the honorific attributes of fatherhood from the Negro male, who was addressed as "boy"—until, when the vigorous years of his prime were past, he was allowed to assume the title of "uncle."

From the master's viewpoint, slaves had been defined in law as property, and the master's power over his property must be absolute. But then this property was still human property. These slaves might never be quite as human as *he* was, but still there were certain standards that could be laid down for their behavior: obedience, fidelity, humility, docility, cheerfulness, and so on. Industry and diligence would of course be demanded, but a final element in the master's situation would undoubtedly qualify that expectation. Absolute power for him meant absolute dependency for the slave—the dependency not of the developing child but of the perpetual child. For the master, the role most aptly fitting such a relationship would naturally be that of the father. As a father he could be either harsh or kind, as he chose, but as a *wise* father he would have, we may suspect, a sense of the limits of his situation. He must be ready to cope with *all* the qualities of the child, exasperating as well as ingratiating. He might conceivably have to expect in this child—besides his loyalty, docility, humility, cheerfulness, and (under supervision) his diligence—such additional qualities as irresponsibility, playfulness, silliness, laziness, and (quite possibly) tendencies to lying and stealing. Should the entire prediction prove accurate, the result would be something resembling "Sambo."

Might the process, on the other hand, be reversed? It is hard to imagine its being reversed overnight. The same role might still be played in the years after slavery—we are told that it was—and yet it was played to more vulgar audiences with cruder standards, who paid much less for what they saw. The lines might be repeated more and more mechanically, with less and less conviction; the incentives to perfection could become hazy and blurred, and the excellent old piece could degenerate over time into low farce. There could come a point, conceivably, with the old zest gone, that it was no longer worth the candle. The day might come at last when it dawned on a man's full waking consciousness that he had really grown up, that he was, after all, only playing a part.

NOTES

1. Among such studies are Robert K. Merton, "Bureaucratic Structure and Personality," *Social Forces*, XVIII (May, 1940), 560–68; Erich Fromm, *Man for Himself* (New York: Rinehart, 1947); David Riesman, *The Lonely Crowd* (New Haven: Yale University Press, 1950); and Theodore Adorno and Others, *The Authoritarian Personality* (New York: Harper, 1950)—a work which is itself subjected to examination in Richard Christie and Marie Jahoda (eds.), *Studies in the*

Scope and Method of "The Authoritarian Personality" (Glencoe, Ill.: Free Press, 1954); and H. H. Gerth and C. Wright Mills, *Character and Social Structure: The Psychology of Social Institutions* (New York: Harcourt, Brace, 1953). For a consideration of this field in the broadest terms, see Alex Inkeles and Daniel J. Levinson, "National Character: The Study of Modal Personality and Sociocultural Systems," *Handbook of Social Psychology,* ed. Gardner Lindzey (Cambridge, Mass.: Addison-Wesley, 1954), II, 977-1020.

2. The line between "accommodation" (as conscious hypocrisy) and behavior inextricable from basic personality, though the line certainly exists, is anything but a clear and simple matter of choice. There is reason to think that the one grades into the other, and vice versa, with considerable subtlety. In this connection, the most satisfactory theoretical mediating term between deliberate role-playing and "natural" role-playing might be found in role-psychology.

3. Although the majority of Southern slaveholders were not planters, the majority of slaves were owned by a planter minority.

4. As to "character types," one might be tempted to suppose that as a rule it would be only the weaker and more submissive who allowed themselves to be taken into slavery. Yet it appears that a heavy proportion of the slaves were in fact drawn from among the most warlike.

5. L. Degrandpré, *Voyage à la côte occidentale d'Afrique, fait dans les années 1786 et 1787* (Paris, 1801), II, 55-56.

6. Bruno Bettelheim, "Individual and Mass Behavior in Extreme Situations," *Journal of Abnormal Psychology,* XXXVIII (October, 1943), 424.

7. A description of such a trip may be found in Olga Lengyel, *Five Chimneys: The Story of Auschwitz* (Chicago, 1947), pp. 7-10. See also Eugen Kogon, *The Theory and Practice of Hell* (New York: Farrar, Straus, 1946), p. 67.

8. Elie Cohen, *Human Behavior in the Concentration Camp* (New York: Norton, 1953), pp. 118-22; Ella Lingens-Reiner, *Prisoners of Fear* (London: Victor Gollancz, 1948).

9. Kogon, *Theory and Practice,* p. 274; Cohen, *Human Behavior,* p. 155; Hilde O. Bluhm, "How Did They Survive?" *American Journal of Psychotherapy,* II (January, 1948), 5.

10. Bettelheim, "Individual and Mass Behavior," p. 431.

11. *Ibid.,* p. 432.

12. Lingens-Reiner, *Prisoners of Fear,* p. 23.

13. Cohen, *Human Behavior,* p. 136. The "superego," Freud's term for the "conscience," is discussed in the following section of this chapter.

14. Bettelheim, "Individual and Mass Behavior," p. 438.

15. *Ibid.,* p. 141.

16. Says Dr. Cohen, "I am not asserting that sex was never discussed; it was, though not often. Frankl also states 'that in contrast to mass existence in other military communities . . . here (in the concentration camp) there is *no smut talk.'* " *Human Behavior,* p. 141.

17. Bettelheim, "Individual and Mass Behavior," p. 445.

18. *Ibid.,* p. 421.

19. Quoted in Cohen, *Human Behavior,* p. 176.

20. *Ibid.*

21. *Ibid.,* p. 174.

22. Bettelheim, "Individual and Mass Behavior," pp. 445-46. This same phenomenon is noted by Curt Bondy: "They tell great stories about what they have been before and what they have performed." "Problems of Internment Camps," *Journal of Abnormal and Social Psychology,* XXXVIII (October, 1943), 453-75.

23. Cohen, *Human Behavior,* p. 177. Italics in original.

24. Bettelheim, "Individual and Mass Behavior," p. 447.

25. *Ibid.,* pp. 448-50. "Once, for instance, a guard on inspecting the prisoners' apparel found that the shoes of some of them were dirty on the inside. He ordered all prisoners to wash their shoes inside and out with water and soap. The heavy shoes treated this way became hard as stone. The order was never repeated, and many prisoners did not execute it when given. Nevertheless there were some old prisoners who not only continued to wash the inside of their

shoes every day but cursed all others who did not do so as negligent and dirty. These prisoners firmly believed that the rules set down by the Gestapo were desirable standards of human behavior, at least in the camp situation." *Ibid.*, p. 450.

26. Cohen, *Human Behavior*, pp. 176–77.

27. *Ibid.*, p. 179. On this and other points I must also acknowledge my indebtedness to Mr. Ies Spetter, a former Dutch journalist now living in this country, who was imprisoned for a time at Auschwitz during World War II. Mr. Spetter permitted me to see an unpublished paper, "Some Thoughts on Victims and Criminals in the German Concentration Camps," which he wrote in 1954 at the New School for Social Research; and this, together with a number of conversations I had with him, added much to my understanding of concentration-camp psychology.

28. A. Hottinger, *Hungerkrankheit, Hungerödem, Hungertuberkulose*, p. 32, quoted in Cohen, *Human Behavior*, p. 197. "After the liberation many writers were struck by the callousness of the onetime prisoners, and particularly by their apathy when relating their experiences, even the most horrible." *Ibid.*, p. 144.

29. "For just as the ego is a modified portion of the id as a result of contact with the outer world, the super-ego represents a modified portion of the ego, formed through experiences absorbed from the parents, especially from the father. The super-ego is the highest evolution attainable by man, and consists of a precipitate of all prohibitions and inhibitions, all the rules of conduct which are impressed on the child by his parents and by parental substitutes. The feeling of *conscience* depends altogether on the development of the super-ego." A. A. Brill, Introduction to *The Basic Writings of Sigmund Freud* (New York: Modern Library, 1938), pp. 12–13. "Its relation to the ego is not exhausted by the precept: 'You *ought to be* such and such (like your father)'; it also comprises the prohibition: 'You *must not be* such and such (like your father); that is, you may not do all that he does; many things are his prerogative.'" Sigmund Freud, *The Ego and the Id* (London: Hogarth Press, 1947), pp. 44–45. ". . . and here we have that higher nature, in this ego-ideal or super-ego, the representative of our relation to our parents. When we were little children we knew these higher natures, we admired them and feared them; and later we took them into ourselves." *Ibid.*, p. 47. "As a child grows up, the office of father is carried on by masters and by others in authority; the power of their injunctions and prohibitions remains vested in the ego-ideal and continues, in the form of conscience, to exercise the censorship of morals. The tension between the demands of conscience and the actual attainments of the ego is experienced as a sense of guilt. Social feelings rest on the foundation of identification with others, on the basis of an ego-ideal in common with them." *Ibid.*, p. 49.

30. *Human Behavior*, p. 136.

31. Anna Freud, *The ego and the Mechanisms of Defence* (London: Hogarth Press, 1948), p. 121. "In some illustrative case reports, Clara Thompson stresses the vicious circle put in motion by this defense-mechanism. The stronger the need for identification, the more a person loses himself in his omnipotent enemy—the more helpless he becomes. The more helpless he feels, the stronger the identification, and—we may add—the more likely it is that he tries even to surpass the aggressiveness of his aggressor. This may explain the almost unbelievable phenomenon that prisoner-superiors sometimes acted more brutally than did members of the SS. . . . Identification with the aggressor represented the final stage of passive adaptation. It was a means of defense of a rather paradoxical nature: survival through surrender; protection against the fear of the enemy—by becoming part of him; overcoming helplessness—by regressing to childish dependence." Bluhm, "How Did They Survive?" pp. 24–25.

32. Leo Alexander, "War Crimes: Their Social-Psychological Aspects," *American Journal of Psychiatry*, CV (September, 1948), 173. "The superego structure is . . . in peril whenever these established guiding forces weaken or are in the process of being undermined, shifted, or perverted, and becomes itself open to undermining, shifting, or perversion even in adult life—a fact which is probably more important than we have been aware of heretofore." *Ibid.*, p. 175.

33. My use of Sullivan here does not imply a willingness to regard his work as a "refutation" to that of Freud, or even as an adequate substitute for it in all other situations. It lacks the

imaginative scope which in Freud makes possible so great a range of cultural connections; in it we miss Freud's effort to deal as scientifically as possible with an infinite array of psychological and cultural phenomena; the fragmentary nature of Sullivan's work, its limited scope, its cloudy presentation, all present us with obstacles not to be surmounted overnight. This might well change as his ideas are elaborated and refined. But meanwhile it would be too much to ask that all connections be broken with the staggering amount of work already done on Freudian models.

34. Sullivan refined this concept from the earlier notion of the "generalized other" formulated by George Herbert Mead. "The organized community or social group [Mead wrote] which gives to the individual his unity of self may be called 'the generalized other.' The attitude of the generalized other is the attitude of the whole community. Thus, for example, in the case of such a social group as a ball team, the team is the generalized other in so far as it enters—as an organized process or social activity—into the experience of any one of the individual members of it." George H. Mead, *Mind, Self and Society: From the Standpoint of a Social Behaviorist* (Chicago: University of Chicago Press, 1934), p. 154.

35. The technical term, in Sullivan's terminology, for the mechanism represented by these two elements functioning in combination, is the individual's "self-dynamism." David Riesman has refined this concept; he has, with his "inner-directed, other-directed" polarity, considered the possibility of different kinds of "self-dynamisms." The self-dynamism which functions with reference to specific aims and which is formed and set early in life is characterized as the "gyroscope." On the other hand the self-dynamism which must function in a cultural situation of constantly shifting significant others and which must constantly adjust to them is pictured as the "radar." See *The Lonely Crowd, passim.* The principles summarized in this and the preceding paragraphs are to be found most clearly set forth in Harry Stack Sullivan, *Conceptions of Modern Psychiatry* (Washington: William Alanson White Psychiatric Foundation, 1945). Sullivan's relationship to the general development of theory is assessed in Patrick Mullahy, *Oedipus Myth and Complex: A Review of Psychoanalytic Theory* (New York: Hermitage House, 1948).

36. Actually, one of the chief functions of psychoanalysis as it has been practiced from the beginning is simply given more explicit recognition here. The psychiatrist who helps the patient exhibit to himself attitudes and feelings systematically repressed—or "selectively ignored"— becomes in the process a new and trusted significant other.

37. "Indeed . . . when the whole Sullivanian conception of the effect of significant others upon the origin and stability of self-conceptions is pushed farther, really revolutionary vistas of guided personality emerge. If the maintenance of certain characteristic patterns of interpersonal behavior depends upon their support by significant others, then to alter the composition of any person's community of significant others is the most direct and drastic way of altering his 'personality.' This can be done. Indeed, it is being done, with impressive results, by the many types of therapeutic groups, or quasi-families of significant new others, which have come up in the past few years." Patrick Mullahy (ed.), *The Contributions of Harry Stack Sullivan* (New York: Hermitage House, 1952), p. 193.

38. An outstanding instance of authorities who are exponents of both is that of H. H. Gerth and C. Wright Mills, whose study *Character and Social Structure* ranges very widely in both interpersonal theory and role psychology and uses them interchangeably.

39. In the resources of dramatic literature a variety of insights may await the "social scientist" equipped with both the imagination and the conceptual tools for exploiting them, and the emergence of role psychology may represent the most promising step yet taken in this direction. A previous area of contact has been in the realm of Freudian psychology, but this has never been a very natural or comfortable meeting ground for either the analyst or the literary critic. For example, in Shakespeare's *Hamlet* there is the problem, both psychological and dramatic, of Hamlet's inability to kill his uncle. Dr. Ernest Jones (in *Hamlet and Oedipus*) reduces all the play's tensions to a single Freudian complex. It should be at once more "scientific" and more "literary," however, to consider the problem in terms of role-conflict (Hamlet as prince, son, nephew, lover, etc., has multiple roles which keep getting in the way of one another). Francis Fergusson, though he uses other terminology, in effect does this in his *Idea of a Theater.*

40. In this paragraph I duplicate and paraphrase material from Eugene and Ruth Hartley, *Fundamentals of Social Psychology* (New York: Knopf, 1952), chap. xvi. See also David C. McClelland, *Personality* (New York: Sloane, 1951), pp. 289–332. Both these books are, strictly speaking, "texts," but this point could be misleading, inasmuch as the whole subject is one not normally studied at an "elementary" level anywhere. At the same time a highly successful effort has been made in each of these works to formulate the role concept with clarity and simplicity, and this makes their formulations peculiarly relevant to the empirical facts of the present problem. It may be that the very simplicity of the roles in both the plantation and concentration-camp settings accounts for this coincidence. Another reason why I am inclined to put a special premium on simplicity here is my conviction that the role concept has a range of "literary" overtones, potentially exploitable in realms other than psychology. For a recent general statement, see Theodore R. Sarbin, "Role Theory," *Handbook of Social Psychology*, I, 223–58.

41. Hartley, *Fundamentals of Social Psychology*, p. 485.

42. "Personality development is not exclusively a matter of socialization. Rather, it represents the organism's more or less integrated way of adapting to *all* the influences that come its way—both inner and outer influences, both social and nonsocial ones. Social influences, however, are essential to human personality, and socialization accounts for a very great deal of personality development.

"From this point of view it would not be surprising to find that many personality disturbances represent some sort of breakdown or reversal of the socialization process." Theodore M. Newcomb, *Social Psychology* (New York: Dryden Press, 1950), p. 475.

43. In a system as tightly closed as the plantation or the concentration camp, the slave's or prisoner's position of absolute dependency virtually compels him to see the authority-figure as somehow really "good." Indeed, all the evil in his life may flow from this man—but then so also must everything of any value. Here is the seat of the only "good" he knows, and to maintain his psychic balance he must persuade himself that the good is in some way dominant. A threat to this illusion is thus in a real sense a threat to his very existence. It is a common experience among social workers dealing with neglected and maltreated children to have a child desperately insist on his love for a cruel and brutal parent and beg that he be allowed to remain with that parent. The most dramatic feature of this situation is the cruelty which it involves, but the mechanism which inspires the devotion is not the cruelty of the parent but rather the abnormal dependency of the child.

7

CONTROL, SEXUAL ATTITUDES, SELF-MASTERY, AND CIVILIZATION:
Abolitionists and the Erotic South

RONALD G. WALTERS

Psychological theory and abolitionism have not enjoyed a blissful relationship. But then American historians seem commonly to make their first pass at reformers an exploration of deviance. For example, if the Civil War was a "needless" conflict, as some students of the period contended in the 1930's and 1940's, one large reason for the outbreak of war was the emotionalism that irresponsible demagogues like William Lloyd Garrison aroused. In this scheme such oddballs cried out for psychologizing, and frequently got it. While any attempt to pry back layers of a reformer's motives eventually will yield mixed or unattractive—certainly personal—ones, recent biographies of antebellum activists have tried to place them in their socio-intellectual setting. Northerners Catharine Beecher and John Humphrey Noyes or the Virginia proslavery radical Beverley Tucker, rather than oddballs or deviants from their society, turn out to be highly representative of the concerns and conflict within it. Even farther along this line of approach is Ronald G. Walters's study of the themes that tied together all abolitionists, despite their personal or tactical differences.

Slavery and power evoked fearsome images in the minds of Jacksonian Americans. The abolitionist call for an end of Southern slavery raised the specter of civil war; behind the question of federal-state authority and debates over the powers of banks and corporations was the realization that being vulnerable to an outside power brought with it helplessness and therefore a form of slavery. Power could easily mean dominance. As Walters points out in the chapter excerpted below, these apprehensions—which we usually consider in a political context—could in sexual terms also shape the charges reformers made against moral targets; the South, bellowed one abolitionist, was "one great Sodom." Connections between pointed anger and sexual imagery invite the observation that after a certain level is reached the worst one can say about or to an enemy always seems to draw on sexual allusions, to

Reprinted from *The Anti-Slavery Appeal: American Abolitionism after 1830* (Baltimore: The Johns Hopkins University Press, 1976), pp. 70-87.

ascribe perversion. One might rest content here: obscenity by one definition misuses the beautiful or intermixes it with the ugly.

Another view is that slur or epithet also provides—since one's guard is down—a hint of the reasons for the anger or fear. "Why," asks David Brion Davis in an article studying anti-Mason, anti-Catholic, and anti-Mormon rhetoric, "did nativist literature dwell so persistently on themes of brutal sadism and sexual immorality? Why did its authors describe sin in such minute detail, endowing even the worst offenses of their enemies with a certain fascinating appeal?" Every observer of Jacksonian America stood amazed at its pace of development, its social dislocations. In such a society, Davis argues, and Walters would agree, the most sensitive pressure points lay with changing sexual roles and the apparent rise of vice: with growing cities threatening established standards of morality and women working in factories for the first time, there was every reason for anxiety, and it was far easier for the dissatisfied to find blameworthy objects than to turn back time. The literature of countersubversion, Davis continues, "could serve the double purpose of vicariously fulfilling repressed desires, and of releasing the tension and guilt arising from rapid social change and conflicting values." The Walters chapter explores a similar pattern of attributed sin, which, besides suggesting that abolitionists saw in the license of slavery what they unconsciously wished to enjoy, demonstrates their concern for self-control as a protection in a distressing world. The conclusion is not that abolitionists were insincere or wicked, but that what one sees in an enemy can say something about oneself, that reform can be highly illuminating of cultural restrictions and social tensions.

MORALITY was self-evident to the abolitionist. Other people found it much less obvious and evaded its demands with little difficulty. Although reformers sought human liberation they, as citizens of a sinful society, could not believe that mankind should be left to the claims of the flesh. Just as the potential for moral behavior seemed to lie in human nature, so did some of the forces preventing that potential from being realized.

Charles K. Whipple described slavery as "absolute, irresponsible power on one side, and entire subjection on the other." Like virtually all abolitionists he grounded his objections to bondage on this relationship of utter submission and total dominance between slave and master. There were, of course, other kinds of emphases possible. Earlier humanitarian reform had stressed the suffering of slaves, but, no matter how useful examples of inhuman treatment might be in stirring sentiment against slavery, most post-1830 abolitionists denied that cruelty was what made the institution so terrible. After combing Southern newspapers and exhausting eye-witnesses for horror stories about slavery, Theodore Dwight Weld declared that these were not the basic fact of the institution. The "combined experience of the human race," he thought, proved that such "cruelty is the spontaneous and uniform product of arbitrary power." Abuse was only an effect of submission and dominance. Even those who began by looking at slavery in still another way, in terms of "the chattel principle," came around (like Weld) to a definition which was neither economic, nor institutional, nor based on specific kinds of treatment. "Slavery is the act of one holding another as property," a correspondent to the *Philanthropist* declared, adding "or one man being wholly subject to the will of others." In his mind slavery (as a property relationship) resolved itself into a matter of power just as surely as it did for Whipple or Weld.[1]

A. A. Phelps constructed an imaginary state of nature to show how it came to be acceptable to hold some humans as property. Phelps' original man "loves, and is grasping after power," and the white Southerner was his direct descendant. So driving was this urge to dominate, abolitionists believed, that it outdistanced all other possible motives, including greed. When Garrison assessed "the master-passion in the bosom of the slaveholder" he found it to be "not the love of gain, but the possession of absolute power, unlimited sovereignty." His words echoed those of Angelina Grimké shortly after her arrival in the North. "There are hundreds of thousands at the South, who do *not* hold their slaves, by any means, as much 'for purposes of gain,' as they do from the *lust of power*," Miss Grimké exclaimed. "This is the passion that reigns triumphant there."[2]

Achievement of authority brought destructive results for its possessor as well as for his victim. Having helped her husband compile the material for *American Slavery as It Is*, Angelina Grimké (by this time Mrs. Weld), told a sister that these stories were designed "to show the awful havock which arbitrary power makes in human hearts, and to excite a holy indignation against an *institution* which degrades the oppressor as well as the oppressed." William Goodell gave it as "an old maxim that the exercise of unlimited power will make any man a tyrant." "It is," he noted "no slander to say that the slaveholder is a man!"[3] Goodell's phraseology was not just an accident. Abolitionists did not maintain that slaveholders were somehow peculiar in their failings but rather that they demonstrated what all people should beware of.[4] After having detailed in their different ways the devastating effects of slavery, C. K. Whipple and Theodore Dwight Weld each reminded his readers that the danger was a general one, not confined to white Southerners. "No human being is fit to be trusted with absolute irresponsible power," Whipple claimed. "If the best portion of our own community were selected to hold and use such authority [as masters possess], they would very soon be corrupted." Weld believed "arbitrary power is to the mind what alcohol is to the body; it intoxicates."[5] Man might have an innate moral sense, he might at times be moulded by his race or environment; but abolitionists, not obligated to cling to any theory to the end, were at the bottom certain that mankind also had a deeply implanted drive to dominate others—a drive that required constant vigilance and suppression.

Enslavement of blacks was not the only kind of coercion and "arbitrary power" disturbing to abolitionists. Slavery was a special case because of its magnitude, but the principle behind it appeared in countless places, many of them closer to home. Few abolitionists were so extreme as Abby Kelley who—lest she be a tyrant—was "very conscientious not to use the least worldly authority over her child."[6] But even abolitionists less dogmatic (or foolhardy) than she were outraged by the tyranny of preachers, politicians, public opinion, and institutions.[7] Quite early William Goodell perceived that slavery served a symbolic function as the extreme example of what happened when man's drive for power ran rampant. "We acknowledge that there is a propriety in holding up 'NEGRO SLAVERY' from age to age, as the perfect image of oppression personified," he wrote, "so that everything insufferably dreadful, and superlatively hateful in despotism, to the end of time, may be branded with infamy simply by showing its affinity with SLAVEHOLD-ING."[8]

Americans of an earlier generation had been just as suspicious as Goodell was of man's ability to wield authority. Such wariness was epidemic at the time of the American Revolution, and it had affected the way individuals saw slavery, just as it would again after 1830. Almost a lifetime before Garrison's career began, John Woolman argued against the institution because "so long as men are biassed by narrow self-love, so long an absolute power over other men is unfit for them." In 1765 John Adams wrote of "the love of power, which has been so often the cause of slavery."[9] Fear of power has always been an appealing perception of reality in times when the political system seems unrepresentative and unresponsive. It took on new vitality in the antebellum period as moralistic whites saw political and economic affairs increasingly dominated by ambitious, uncouth men.

There was, in addition, a subtle cultural shift between the Revolutionary and antebellum periods. The concept of "power" was coming by the 1830s to fit into a web of associations that ensnared some of the deepest and most mysterious forces that abolitionists believed to be in all men. This included the deepest, most mysterious, most fearful force of all: human sexuality. By 1831 there was not a great distance from the concept of lust for power to that of mere lust.

Abolitionists did not dwell "excessively" on sexual misconduct in the South—their writings have little merit as pornography. From the beginning whites perceived (and cultivated) an erotic potential in interracial contact. Nevertheless, this potential could be organized into more than one pattern of perception and post-1830 antislavery propaganda directly reversed a prevalent assumption by presenting white men, not black men, as the sexual aggressors. Early in his career Garrison set the tone. He was accosted by a slaveholder who posed the classic question of American racism: "How should you like to have a black man marry your daughter?" Garrison replied that "slaveholders generally should be the last persons to affect fastidiousness on that point; for they seem to be enamoured with amalgamation."[10] The retort was unanswerable, and it survived down to the Civil War. It was, in part, simply fine strategy, pointing both to an obvious hypocrisy and a very real condition of slavery.

But abolitionists did not stop with this simple and expedient formula. They did not argue that erotic activity always was at the instigation of white males. Gerrit Smith believed planters would not fight an insurrection effectively because they would be too "busy in transporting their wives and daughters to places where they would be safe from that worst fate which husbands and fathers can imagine for their wives and daughters." George Bourne pondered, "What may be the awful consequences, if ever the colored men by physical force should attain the mastery?" "If," he decided, "no other argument could be adduced in favor of immediate and universal emancipation, that single fact is sufficient. Delay only increases the danger of the white women and augments the spirit of determined malignity and revenge in the colored men." Abolition would lead to forgiveness and to sexual security for the white woman as well as for the female slave.[11]

Rape was only one form of sexual retribution abolitionists foresaw slaves exacting upon the master class. Louisa Barker believed black women lured young slaveholders into illicit attachments with female slaves as a way of lessening the chance that the slave might be sold—and to destroy the constitution of the master through physical overindulgence. Still another writer argued that "women who have been drawn into licentiousness by wicked men, if they retain their vicious habits, almost invariably display their revenge for their debasement, by ensnaring others into the same corruption and moral ruin." This placed on female slaves much of the responsibility for stirring the sensuality of their masters, thus degrading the slaveholder as they had been degraded. But there were even more horrifying prospects— lasciviousness did not stop with white men and black women enticing each other. "Were it necessary," John Rankin stated primly, "I could refer you to several instances of slaves actually seducing the daughters of their masters! Such seductions sometimes happen even in the most respectable slaveholding families." It was impossible for daughters of slaveholders always to "escape this impetuous fountain of pollution."[12] Comments like these touched the white South at a sensitive point—its image of itself and of its women.[13] Furthermore, they moved the argument from the idea that whites were sexual aggressors over to the more comfortable position (for whites) that blacks represented sensuality after all.

Emotional associations concerning miscegenation undoubtedly played their part, but the horror of Southern sexuality for abolitionists was not in its interracial nature. At work was a more generalized sense that the South represented a society in which eroticism had no checks put upon it. "Illicit intercourse" was embedded in the very conditions of Southern life, abolitionists believed. For the master "the temptation is always at hand—the legal authority absolute—the actual power complete—the vice a profitable one" if it produced slaves for market, "and the custom so universal as to bring no disgrace." One author, using the apt pseudonym, "Puritan," was appalled that

not only in taverns, but in boarding houses, and the dwellings of individuals, boys and girls verging on maturity altogether unclothed, wait upon ladies and gentlemen, without exciting even the suffusion of a blush on the face of young females, who thus gradually become habituated to scenes of which delicate and refined Northern women cannot adequately conceive.

To make matters worse, the free and easy association between slave children and white children spread the depravity of the back cabins to the big house. "Between the female slaves and the misses there is an unrestrained communication," Southern-born James A. Thome explained to the American Anti-Slavery Society. "As they come in contact through the day, the courtesan feats of the over night are whispered into the ear of the unsuspecting [white] girl and poison her youthful mind."[14]

In its libidinousness the South could only be compared to other examples of utter depravity and dissolution. Thome informed an audience of attentive young ladies that "THE SOUTHERN STATES ARE ONE GREAT SODOM," and his account was seconded by another abolitionist, who had lived in Virginia and Maryland. In 1834 the *Pennsylvania Freeman* spoke of the "great moral lazarhouse of Southern slavery." Thomas Wentworth Higginson decided that, compared to the South, "a Turkish harem is a cradle of virgin purity." Henry C. Wright preferred a comparison with the notorious Five Points district in New York—much to the latter's advantage, of course.[15] Like Sodom, brothels, or a harem, the South appeared to be a place in which men could indulge their erotic impulses with impunity.

Yet, in the nature of things, there must be retribution. It could be physiological since—nineteenth-century moralists assumed—sexual excesses ultimately destroyed body and mind. Planters, according to Mrs. Louisa Barker, exemplified the "wreck of early manhood always resulting from self-indulgence." They were "born with feeble minds and bodies, with just force enough to transmit the family name, and produce in feebler characters a second edition of the father's life." Mrs. Barker's comments were consistent with the way other abolitionists viewed the South and with the way her times viewed sexuality, but they were almost unique in antislavery literature—although the character of the languid but erratic planter was not.[16] The more usual form of retribution predicted from Southern licentiousness was social and demographic.

At the beginning of the antislavery crusade there was a sense among some abolitionists, that (in the words of James G. Birney) "from causes now operating, the South must be filled in a few years with blacks and, it may be, that in our lives it will be given up to them." Birney, in the letter that marked his public renunciation of colonization, detailed the "alarming rapidity" with which the process was operating in his native Kentucky. In a similar vein, John Rankin warned that slavery will "increase their [blacks'] numbers, and enable them to overpower the nation. Their enormous increase beyond that of the white population is truly alarming." Liberation, however, would disperse them and make their population growth "proportionate to the rest of the nation." LaRoy Sunderland quantified the increase, using censuses through 1830, and explained why he thought it was occurring. "That the blacks should increase faster than the whites, is easily accounted for," he remarked dryly, "from the fact, that the former class are increased by the latter, but the blacks cannot increase the whites."[17] Such statements seem to have decreased in time and with additional censuses (although complaints about licentiousness persisted), but they and fears of imminent insurrections glare luridly from early abolitionist propaganda—they were twin expressions of a belief that the South faced an overwhelming chastizing event and that white dominance might soon become submission. In both cases— insurrection and the fruits of unchecked sexuality—the only security rested with abolition.

There were wonderful propaganda advantages here. The issue of miscegenation forever dogged the antislavery movement and by stressing Southern licentiousness abolitionists turned the tables. They could both speak of the "dreadful amalgamating abominations" of the slave system and argue that they would "experience, in all probability, a ten fold diminution" with emancipation. Elijah Lovejoy went so far as to state the "one reason why abolitionists urge the abolition of slavery is, that they fully believe it will put a stop, in a great and almost entire measure to that wretched, and shameful, and polluted intercourse between the whites and blacks, now so common, it may be said so universal, in the slave states."[18] Yet the propaganda advantages—if they were the only consideration—would have been greater had abolitionists not also insisted, as they did at times, that "the right to choose a partner for life is so exclusive and sacred, that it is never interfered with, except by the worst of tyrants." Garrison, with his usual boldness and lack of tact, asserted the perfect equality of the races and drew the conclusion that "intermarriage is neither unnatural nor repugnant to nature, but designed to unite people of different tribes and nations."[19] Such assaults on antimiscegenation sentiment, if nothing else, show that abolitionists were not just saying what they thought their audience wanted to hear when they spoke out on sexual matters. Instead, what abolitionists wrote about Southern sexuality must be put in relation to nineteenth-century assumptions, to conditions in the North that gave urgency to concern for licentiousness, and to the other reform interests of antislavery men and women.

Abolitionists did not perceive the South as lustful simply because unhallowed sex occurred under slavery. Erotic activity between master class and bondsmen, after all, did not originate in 1831 (nor did disgust with Southern morals; New England Federalists had that in abundance a generation earlier). Miscegenation itself may well have been decreasing at the very time it became a staple of antislavery propaganda.[20]

Abolitionists were especially sensitive to Southern eroticism because, like most middle-class moralists of the day, they saw a certain interchangeability between power and sexuality. Sexuality, as far as they were concerned, was not a peculiarly Southern problem: it was intrinsic to any situation in which one person's arbitrary will could rule over others. Abolitionist revulsion at Southern sensuality was, to be sure, very much in line with Victorian morality; but it was also in large measure part of a more general abolitionist revulsion against domination and possession. The abolitionists' association of sexuality with power and dominance had some validity, and it was unique neither to them nor to the antebellum period. But such an association did have much wider currency and more fearsome connotations in nineteenth-century America than in previous centuries or in our own day. To take an extreme but revealing example, Victorian pornography exploited situations of power and powerlessness more than the contemporary variety does (despite some noteworthy exceptions) and probably more than ancient bawdy literature did. In one nineteenth-century classic the action took place in a harem where "The Lustful Turk," a darkly sensual being, reduced women (even good English women!) to sexual slaves. His power was both political and erotic, and his desires were as unchecked as they were varied. This was strikingly similar to antislavery images of the South and the slaveholder—a similarity increased when one of the lustful Turk's victims made a speech in which she attacked slavery as "the most powerful agent in the degradation of mankind," a charming bit of abolitionism amidst depravity. In more respectable Victorian circles it was thought that servants, another class of underling, were both sexually corrupted and agents of corruption, a matter which later attracted the attention of Sigmund Freud.[21] Anti-Catholic diatribes likewise played to a sense that subordination led to debauchery. George Bourne, an early and important abolitionist, doubled as a professional Catholic baiter, and he found the two careers quite easily reconciled. He pictured the South as an erotic society where whites "have been indulged in all the vicious gratifications which lawless power and unrestrained lust, can amalgamate." Much the same, he believed, prevailed in the convent, another kind of closed society. There the absolute power and unchecked erotic energy of the priest replaced that of the planter (in Bourne's imagination) and the seduction and seductiveness of nuns replaced female slaves.[22]

Enough licentiousness existed under slavery to fuel the minds of men like Bourne; but as much as anything, Southern sensuality illustrated a general principle which abolitionists held to be true about man and what possession of power did to him. "We know what human nature is; what are its weaknesses, what its passions," the *Philanthropist* asserted confidently, as it remarked upon the potential for depravity on the plantation.[23] Certainly abolitionists saw what was actually there—erotic encounters did occur—but they were able to do so because culturally determined associations of power with sexual domination prepared them to see and to react strongly to it.

Southern licentiousness took on further meaning for abolitionists because it intersected some typically nineteenth-century judgments about what mankind and society ought to be. In 1839, unconsciously forecasting a later and more famous Victorian moralist—Sigmund Freud—Theodore Dwight Weld wrote that "restraints are the web of civilized society, warp and woof." James G. Birney, musing to his diary in 1850, decided

the reason that savage & barbarous nations remain so—& unrighteous men, too—is that they manage their affairs by passion—not by reason. Just in proportion as reason prevails, it will control & restrain passion, & just in proportion as it prevails, & passion diminishes nations emerge from ignorance & darkness and become civilized.

Here was a feeling that civilization, if not its discontents, depended on curbing what another abolitionist called "the fatal anarchy of the lowest passions."[24]

Of course, these passions were not exclusively sexual. Birney would not have argued that "savage & barbarous nations" governed themselves by erotic means. But in the minds of abolitionists sex was clearly among the most formidable components of the "animal nature" that had to be subdued before humans or society could be counted as civilized. Henry C. Wright gave as a general principle that "it is for man to keep himself in the image in which he was made, with a power to grasp and control, for the welfare of the race, every element of his own nature and the external world." Yet the specific element that concerned Wright was the reproductive, the husband's "natural propensities" to indulge himself sexually. Theodore Parker decided when a man "is cultivated and refined, the sentiment [of love] is more than the appetite [of sex]; the animal appetite remains but it does not bear so large a ratio to the whole consciousness of the man as before." Sarah Grimké agreed with Parker's estimate. It was impossible for men and women to enjoy the relationship God intended until "our intercourse is purified by the forgetfulness of sex."[25] This resonated almost as a linguistic pun with a biblical tradition, restated by Beriah Green, holding that "all visable slavery is merely a picture of the invisable sway of the passions."[26] Slavery had long borne with it imputations of sin and human willfulness, but nineteenth-century American culture transferred the sin from the slave to the master and combined its suppression with a drive for civilization and self-control. In antislavery propaganda the plantation was less a real place than an imaginary one where the repressed came out of hiding.

Slavery was a guidepost, marking the outer limits of disorder and debauchery; but abolitionists consistently defined their own moral responsibilities and those of fellow Northerners in the same terms they applied to

Southerners. "And how is slavery to be abolished by those who are slaves themselves to their own appetites and passions?" Beriah Green asked. William Goodell informed the American Health Convention that "no efforts of yours, nor mine, nor of those who labor with us for the enfranchisement of the enslaved, will ever raise human beings, of any complexion to the true dignity of freemen, so long as they permit themselves to be the slaves of their own appetites, the panders of their own lusts, the forgers of their own fetters." Some years before, the *Emancipator* had noted "the common acceptance of things" in which "men deem themselves the most happy when they can the most easily set aside known prohibitions and indulge in certain propensities." It contrasted this with the "early propagators of the religion of the cross" who had "no animal passions to gratify" as they were led to martyrdom. The lesson was unmistakable: the person who would do good must first conquer himself.[27]

The courtship of Theodore Dwight Weld and Angelina Grimké, a veritable orgy of restraint, revealed that reformers were willing to practice what they preached. Weld regarded the intensity of his emotions for Miss Grimké as a challenge to be overcome, and it was with triumph that he wrote her in March 1838. "It will be a relief to you," he assured Angelina, "to know that I have acquired *perfect self control*, so far as any *expression* or *appearance* of deep feeling is visable to others." Angelina earlier chided him for carrying things too far. "Why this waste of moral strength?" she asked. But she too thought of civilization as a repression of the deeper and more mysterious forces in mankind. She responded ecstatically upon finding how elevated Weld's views of courtship were—how similar to her own, how unsensual. "I have been tempted to think marriage was *sinful*, because of what appeared to me almost invariably to prompt and lead to it," she wrote.

Instead of the higher, nobler sentiments being first aroused, and leading on the lower passions *captive* to their will, the *latter* seemed to be *lords* over the *former*. Well I am convinced that men in general, the vast majority believe most seriously that women were made to gratify their appetites, *expressly* to minister to *their* pleasure.

The couple's control extended beyond the awkwardness of courtship. A few years after their marriage James G. Birney visited them, remarking to his diary, with a touch of envy, "their self-denial—their firmness in principles puts me to shame."[28] For abolitionists like the Welds the goal was self-mastery and the reward was an orderly life in which affection, even spontaneous joy, had a place—but only after the animal passions were subdued.

Abolitionists saw restraint as a problem for all Americans, not just for themselves and for Southerners. The mass of humanity, Thomas Wentworth Higginson proclaimed, was mired "deep in sensual vileness." William Lloyd Garrison attacked an opponent for refusing to believe that "licentiousness pervades the whole land." Somewhat later Garrison bemoaned the large number of human beings "caring for nothing but the gratification of their lusts and appetites, and dead in trespasses and sins!" William Goodell felt that licentiousness "pollutes the atmosphere of our splendid cities, and infects the whole land with the leprosy of Sodom." Less metaphorical, Stephen Pearl Andrews flatly stated that "prostitution, in Marriage and out of it, and solitary vice characterize Society as it is."[29]

A great many factors lay behind the sexual jeremiads of people like Higginson, Garrison, Goodell, and Andrews. Their warnings echoed the rumblings of nineteenth-century spiritual and medical authorities, who counseled erotic restraint and spoke gloomily of the dangers of erotic excess for body and soul. For some reformers complex psychological impulses also figured in—Henry C. Wright and Stephen Pearl Andrews mingled the rhetoric of control with fantasies of transcendental sexual rapture. Yet the significant thing for antislavery men and women was that antebellum culture defined loss of moral control and a consequent growth of licentiousness as major threats to civilization. At that point perception and real conditions converged. Southern sensuality forecast growing Northern sensuality and Southern "barbarism" confirmed abolitionists in their fears about unbridled human nature. The South led the way in debauchery, but prostitution in America's growing cities and a seeming nation-wide moral breakdown demonstrated to abolitionists that the sin of licentiousness jeopardized the North as well.

Abolitionism began, and ended, with mankind: it began with a call for individual outrage and repentance and ended with the Yankee schoolmarm in the South. It sought to liberate slaves and, at the same time, to control all human beings, to make them moral, to direct their most fearful energies toward their salvation. When it drew upon the moral sense and upon environmentalism, it casually used the assumptions of its time, and it echoed the language of an earlier reform tradition. When it drew upon its sense of mankind's physical nature (and, unfortunately, when it drew upon belief in innate racial differences), it looked toward the future. To its credit, antebellum reform was too optimistic—and perhaps too naïve—to see mankind, even at its most beastly, imprisoned by biology. There was hope among abolitionists that human nature could be overcome, that civilization depended on a struggle within human beings, not on struggle among men.

NOTES

1. Charles K. Whipple, *The Family Relation, as Affected by Slavery* (Cincinnati, [1858], p. 17; [Theodore Dwight Weld], *American Slavery As It Is: Testimony of a Thousand Witnesses* (New York, 1839), p. 117; the *Philanthropist*, April 14, 1840.

2. Amos A. Phelps, *Lectures on Slavery and Its Remedy* (Boston, 1834), p. 60; the *Liberator*, March 1, 1850; A. E. Grimké, *Letters to Catherine E. Beecher in Reply to an Essay on Slavery and Abolitionism, Addressed to A. E. Grimké*, rev. ed. (Boston, 1838), p. 8.

3. Angelina Grimké Weld to Anna R. Frost, [August, 1839], in *Letters of Theodore Dwight Weld, Angelina Grimké Weld, and Sarah Grimké, 1822–1844*, ed. Gilbert H. Barnes and Dwight L.

Dumond, 2 vols. (New York, 1934), 2: 789; Goodell, "Lectures on Anti-Slavery," part 5 (most conveniently reprinted in the *Liberator*, June 21, 1839).

4. J. Elizabeth Jones, *The Young Abolitionists, Or Conversations on Slavery* (Boston, 1848), p. 54; [Beriah Green], *The Chattel Principle the Abhorrence of Jesus Christ and the Apostles; Or, No Refuge for American Slavery in the New Testament* (New York, 1839), p. 17.

5. Whipple, *Family Relations*, p. 23; [Weld], *American Slavery As It Is*, p. 115.

6. John White Chadwick, ed., *A Life for Liberty: Anti-Slavery and Other Letters of Sallie Holley* (1899; reprint, New York, 1969), p. 123.

7. Even abolitionists who were not nonresistants had difficulty determining where authority and power should be used. See, for example, Weld's *American Slavery As It Is* and the speech of Nathaniel Colver, as reported in *Proceedings of the General Anti-Slavery Convention . . . Held in London, from Friday, June 12th, to Tuesday, June 23rd, 1840* (London, 1841), pp. 278-79. Lewis Perry, *Radical Abolitionism: Anarchy and the Government of God in Antislavery Thought* (Ithaca, 1973), shows how attacks on slavery easily became attacks upon authority. John L. Thomas, *The Liberator: William Lloyd Garrison* (Boston, 1963), pp. 327, 45, argued that "Garrison distrusted politics not simply because he feared power but because he wanted it." This seems to me to brush past the very real—and diverse—concern of Garrison and other abolitionists about power. Lewis Perry, "Versions of Anarchism in the Antislavery Movement," *American Quarterly* 22 (Winter 1968): 772, seems more nearly correct in giving it as the goal of the Garrisonians "to renounce all authoritarian relationships among men."

8. The *Emancipator*, July 21, 1836; January 28, 1834. Also L. Maria Child, *An Appeal in Favor of Americans Called Africans* (1836; reprint, New York, 1968), p. 101.

9. Bernard Bailyn, *The Origin of American Politics* (New York, 1968), p. 56; Woolman conveniently quoted in *The Antislavery Argument*, ed. William H. Pease and Jane H. Pease (Indianapolis, 1965), p. 7; Adams quoted in Ernest Lee Tuveson, *Redeemer Nation: The Idea of America's Millennial Role* (Chicago, 1968), p. 21.

10. The *Liberator*, February 5, 1831. For another early example see LaRoy Sunderland, *Anti-Slavery Manual, Containing a Collection of Facts and Arguments on American Slavery*, 2nd ed. (New York, 1837), pp. 132-33.

11. Gerrit Smith to the Jerry Rescue Committee, August 27, 1859, in Octavius Brooks Frothingham, *Gerrit Smith: A Biography*, 2nd ed. (New York, 1879), p. 240; [George Bourne], *Slavery Illustrated in Its Effects upon Woman and Domestic Society* (Boston, 1837), p. 73. Cf. Thomas Wentworth Higginson, *Black Rebellion* (New York, 1969), pp. 126-27, 175-76.

12. [Mrs. Louisa J. Barker], *Influence of Slavery upon the White Population* (American Anti-Slavery Tracts no. 9, 1855-56), p. 6; [Bourne], *Slavery Illustrated*, p. 71; John Rankin, *Letters on American Slavery, Addressed to Mr. Thomas Rankin, Merchant at Middlebrook, Augusta Co., Va.* (1838; reprint, New York: 1969), xi.

13. Abolitionists seldom assaulted the image of the pure Southern white woman so directly, although they often blamed the women of the South for cruelty, idleness, and for maintaining the system. For one of the few open (and vicious) attacks on the image see [Bourne], *Slavery Illustrated*, p. 77, in which a young slaveholder explains why he will not marry any Southern lady: "Do you think that I am going to marry a young woman with a vitiated constitution, the remains of her attachment for her father's niggers?"

14. Whipple, *Family Relation*, p. 8; "Influence of Slavery on Slaveholders," *Quarterly Anti-Slavery Magazine* 1 (July 1836): 326; Rankin, *Letters on Slavery*, pp. 62-63; Puritan, *The Abrogation of the Seventh Commandment by the American Churches* (New York, 1835), p. 5; Thome quoted in the *Liberator*, May 17, 1834. Thomas F. Harwood, "The Abolitionist Image of Louisiana and Mississippi," *Louisiana History* 7 (Fall 1966): 298, 299-300, notes abolitionist concern for Southern sexuality.

15. The *Liberator*, May 10, 1834 (comments on Thome's address by "G. B.," undoubtedly George Bourne); January 29, 1858; the *Pennsylvania Freeman*, July 4, 1834; Higginson quoted in Tilden G. Edelstein, *Strange Enthusiasm: A Life of Thomas Wentworth Higginson* (New Haven, 1968), p. 100; the *Liberator*, October 8, 1858. Also see Parker Pillsbury, *Acts of the Anti-Slavery Apostles* (Boston, 1884), p. 491; and Sarah M. Grimké, *Letters on the Equality of the Sexes, and the*

Condition of Woman: Addressed to Mary S. Parker, President of the Boston Female Anti-Slavery Society (Boston, 1838), p. 51.

16. [Barker], *Influence of Slavery*, p. 6. William R. Taylor, *Cavalier and Yankee: The Old South and American National Character* (New York, 1961), p. 139, notes that the planter, as a literary figure, was often depicted as lacking vitality and manliness. Taylor felt (I think correctly) that this may reflect the image of John Randolph as well as a nineteenth-century fascination with Hamlet. In the case of Mrs. Barker's planter—and perhaps in the case of the languid and erratic and unstable Southerner of other antislavery writings—the implications are sexual: the worn-out, enfeebled planter is not Hamlet but the age's concept of the man who has committed sexual excesses.

17. Birney to R. R. Gurley, December 3, 1833 (also, Birney to Gurley, September 24, 1833), in *Letters of James Gillespie Birney, 1831-1857*, ed. Dwight L. Dumond, 2 vols. (New York, 1938), I: 97, 90; James G. Birney, *Letter on Colonization, Addressed to the Rev. Thornton J. Mills, Corresponding Secretary of the Kentucky Colonization Society* (New York, 1834), p. 44; Rankin, *Letters on Slavery*, p. 108; Sunderland, *Anti-Slavery Manual*, pp. 11-12. The *Liberator*, August 13, 1841, noted that by the Census of 1840 blacks showed less than "a fair rate of increase." It was then impossible to maintain that the South was in danger of being overwhelmed. The *Liberator*, alert to an argument, explained that the new figures now proved that slavery had murdered a quarter of a million people who might otherwise have lived.

18. The *Emancipator*, September 14, 1833; August 1837. See also "Humanitas," in *The National Era*, September 7, 1854; and George Thompson, *Prison Life and Reflection . . .* (Hartford, Connecticut, 1849), p. 251. Leonard L. Richards, *"Gentlemen of Property and Standing": Anti-Abolition Mobs in Jacksonian America* (New York, 1970), pp. 31-32, notes the intense fear of miscegenation which anti-abolitionists fastened onto antislavery men and women.

19. Sunderland, *Anti-Slavery Manual*, p. 132; the *Liberator*, May 7, 1831 (also, November 17, 1832); see also Child, *Appeal*, p. 133; Phelps, *Lectures on Slavery*, p. 236; and Gerrit Smith, *Letter of Gerrit Smith to Hon. Henry Clay* (New York, 1839), p. 36. Bertram Wyatt-Brown, *Lewis Tappan and the Evangelical War Against Slavery* (Cleveland, 1969), p. 177, quotes a passage which he interprets as showing a belief on the part of Tappan that miscegenation was inevitable. I suspect that Tappan may instead have been assuming the climatic theory of race. But under either interpretation it is obvious that Tappan believed that in several generations Americans would all be the same skin color—and that that color would be dark.

20. Winthrop D. Jordan, *White Over Black: American Attitudes toward the Negro, 1550-1812* (Chapel Hill, 1968), p. 137. Also Robert W. Fogel and Stanley L. Engerman, *Time on the Cross*, 2 vols. (Boston, 1974).

21. Anonymous, *The Lustful Turk . . .* (1893 ed.; reprint, New York, 1967), p. 71; Bernard Wishy, *The Child and the Republic: The Dawn of Modern American Child Nurture* (Philadelphia, 1968), p. 40, notes the belief that servants were corruptors, and he cites George Combe, an author respected and personally known by many abolitionists; Philip Rieff, *Freud: The Mind of the Moralist* (New York, 1959), p. 166. On Victorian pornography generally, see Steven Marcus, *The Other Victorians: A Study of Sexuality and Pornography in Mid-Nineteenth Century England*, rev. ed. (New York, 1967). Marcus relates the cult of sensibility to sexuality, which certainly appeared among antislavery writers (*Other Victorians*, p. 211). *The Lustful Turk* seems to have been written sometime around 1828.

22. Bourne, letter to the Rhode Island Anti-Slavery Society, in the *Liberator*, February 6, 1836. [Bourne], *Lorette, The History of Louise, Daughter of a Canadian Nun, Exhibiting the Interior of Female Convents*, 3rd ed. (New York, 1834), pp. 37-40, 45, stresses the absolute power of the priest—a theme, actually, of the whole novel. Bourne was also a supporter of the notorious Maria Monk. This aspect of his career is brushed by in what is otherwise the best work on him, the introduction to John W. Christie and Dwight L. Dumond, *George Bourne and the Book and Slavery Irreconcilable* (Wilmington, Del., 1969), pp. 1-101.

23. The *Philanthropist*, quoted in the *Emancipator*, December 6, 1838.

24. [Theodore Dwight Weld], *The Bible Against Slavery. An Inquiry into the Patriarchal and Mosaic Systems on the Subject of Human Rights*, 4th ed. (New York, 1838), p. 7; James G. Birney Ms

Diary, May 9, 1850, Birney Mss, Library of Congress; Gilbert Haven, *National Sermons. Sermons, Speeches and Letters on Slavery and Its War . . .* (Boston, 1869), p. 3. Daniel Walker Howe, *The Unitarian Conscience: Harvard Moral Philosophy, 1805-1861* (Cambridge, Massachusetts, 1970), p. 60 observes that "Unitarians were led to espouse the view that sin consisted of a breakdown in the internal harmony, an abdication by the higher faculties of their dominion over the lower." The theme of control clearly was not confined to antislavery. Wishy, *Child and the Republic*, p. 17 sees an attempt to balance individualism and control in nineteenth-century child-raising. Clifford S. Griffin, *Their Brother's Keepers: Moral Stewardship in the United States, 1800-1865* (New Brunswick, New Jersey, 1960), sees this as an impulse behind "moral stewardship," but is overly unsympathetic and covers too broad a range of people really to be able to get at its roots. J. A. Banks, *Prosperity and Parenthood: A Study of Family Planning among the Victorian Middle Classes* (London, 1954), p. 198, notes that about 1830 the English middle class began "applying the theme of control to their own way of life." They did this, in part, by advocating sexual self-restraint. I am aware that the word "passions" had a rather technical, psychological sense which lingered on into the nineteenth century. But both the context of comments and a check of the *Oxford English Dictionary* have convinced me that the abolitionists generally used the word in its more modern sense of "intense emotions," largely sexual. There is information on topics discussed on following pages, as well as on Victorian sexuality, in John R. Betts, "Mind and Body in Early American Thought," *Journal of American History* 54 (March 1968): 787-805; and in Charles E. Rosenberg, "Sexuality, Class and Role in 19th-Century America," *American Quarterly* 25 (May 1973): 131-53. John C. Burnham, "American Historians and the Subject of Sex," *Societas* 2 (Autumn 1972): 307-16, is a good bibliographical essay. See also Ronald G. Walters, ed., *Primers for Prudery: Sexual Advice to Victorian America* (Englewood Cliffs, N.J., 1974).

25. Henry C. Wright, *Marriage and Parentage: Or, the Reproductive Element in Man, as a Means to His Elevation and Happiness*, 5th ed. (Boston, 1866), p. 271; Parker to Robert White, October 7, 1849, in John Weiss, *Life and Correspondence of Theodore Parker, Minister of the Twenty-Eighth Congregational Society, Boston*, 2 vols. (New York, 1864), 1: 386; the *Liberator*, January 12, 1838. I realize that Miss Grimké could have simply been referring to distinctions based on sex, but in the antebellum period attempts to deny social distinctions based on sex were often coupled with attempts to deny sexuality itself. Miss Grimké's views, parts of which will appear below, were strongly pointed toward subduing erotic impulses.

26. Green to Weld, July 11, 1841, in Dumond, *Weld-Grimké Letters*, 2: 868. On the religious meaning of slavery, sin, and bondage see David Brion Davis, *The Problem of Slavery in Western Culture* (Ithaca, 1966), and Jordan, *White Over Black*.

27. The *Radical Abolitionist* 1 (July 1856): 101; Goodell quoted in the *Graham Journal, of Health and Longevity* 2 (1838): 214; the *Emancipator*, August 24, 1833. Bertram Wyatt-Brown, "Prophets Outside Zion: Career and Commitment in the Abolitionist Movement," unpublished paper, delivered at the American Historical Association annual convention, December 30, 1970, notes many abolitionists recalled childhood struggles with self-control. Professor Wyatt-Brown has recast his ideas in slightly different form in "The New Left and the Abolitionists: Romantic Radicalism in America," *Soundings* 44 (Summer 1971): 147-63; and in "New Leftists and Abolitionists: A Comparison of American Radical Styles," *Wisconsin Magazine of History* 53 (Summer 1970): 256-68.

28. Weld to Angelina Grimké, March 12, 1838; Angelina Grimké to Weld, February 21, March 4, 1838 (see also Weld to Angelina and Sarah M. Grimké, February 16, 1838; and Weld to Angelina Grimké, February 18, 1838), in Barnes and Dumond, *Weld-Grimké Letters*, 2: 602, 565, 587, 556, 560; Birney Ms Diary, March 14, 1840, Birney Mss, LC. Katherine Du Pre Lumpkin's *The Emancipation of Angelina Grimké* (Chapel Hill, 1974) is a very good account of Miss Grimké and her marriage to Weld. It appeared after I had written these passages.

29. Higginson, "Holiness Unto the Lord," the *Harbinger* 3 (1847): 28; the *Liberator*, September 17, 1836; Garrison to Helen Garrison, May 28, 1840, Ms Am 1.1, v. 3, no. 46, Boston Public Library; the *Emancipator*, January 14, 1834; Stephen Pearl Andrews, *Love, Marriage and Divorce, and the Sovereignty of the Individual . . .* (New York, 1853), p. 17.

8

ABRAHAM LINCOLN AND THE
MELODRAMA OF THE HOUSE DIVIDED

GEORGE B. FORGIE

"The fact of being born too late to experience the Revolution," notes George B. Forgie, "but in time to be raised by the generation that had fought it, informed the way that many members of this later generation identified and thought about themselves." Historians have agreed for many years that public figures in the early republic and the Jacksonian period were terribly conscious of the origins of the republic, its peculiar requirements of virtue and vigilance, and the illustrious example of men like Washington.

In *Patricide in the House Divided* (1979), Forgie uses these themes to build a new interpretation of the coming of the Civil War. Framing it in father-son conflict (while denying that nations undergo oedipal crises), he observes that the Founding Fathers' legacy carried benefits and burdens alike. One burden was the oft-discussed debt of gratitude to the Revolutionary heroes; another was the delicate balance of union, an admonition to the "sons" not to quarrel despite regional differences. Forgie's thesis is that men of Lincoln's generation faced the problem of venerating the Founding Fathers while somehow winning fame for themselves: preserving the Republic was hardly as exciting as the earlier challenge of establishing it; searching for something "heroic" to do, they nonetheless had to be careful that their ambition, like the Founding Fathers', be selfless. Here was a problem Lincoln himself hinted at in speaking before the Springfield Lyceum in 1836. Though by the 1850s some Americans were growing weary under this weight of tradition, Forgie says that Senator Stephen A. Douglas's "popular sovereignty" plan—allowing settlers in the western territories to decide the issue of slavery for themselves—dangerously departed from the Fathers' example of compromise. Douglas's "repudiation" was a sign that a "bad son" had arisen in the Fathers' "house," according to Forgie, and Lincoln's fury resulted from his projecting onto Douglas the ambition that he could not face in himself.

Conceptually, Forgie's work contributes to this collection because it makes use of the generation as a psychologically and historically definable group. "Generation" can

Selection is reprinted from *Patricide in the House Divided* by George B. Forgie, with permission of W. W. Norton & Company, Inc. Copyright © 1979 by W. W. Norton & Company, Inc.

make sense only if a set of people—their individual life histories notwithstanding—do indeed share a critical experience, as Forgie says, and are aware of sharing it. In his scheme, Lincoln and other early- and mid-nineteenth-century Americans were a psychologically unified group because they shared growing up in the afterglow of the Revolution, learning the lessons of early-republican educators, and imbibing the mythology of George Washington. But by this view everyone from Henry Clay (born in 1777) to Jefferson Davis (1808) and conceivably even to Henry Adams (1838) was a member of the same "post-heroic" generation.

Perhaps a less expansive sample would have sharpened the analysis. People are born all the time; one might go on to say that a generation as something historically significant forms when an event of disturbing, shaping, or memorable import occurs at the time during which a group of young persons faces the problem of identity formation—when, we know, they make an effort to meld together their past and their possibilities in the political, economic, and social world they are moving into. Thus the men who came of age during the Revolutionary crisis and won independence clearly comprised a distinct generation. The young men who came to political power in 1812, and who were so conscious of assuming the reins of government, might have made up a true post-revolutionary or "preserving" generation with Clay, Daniel Webster, and John C. Calhoun representative of it. Then, more weakly—like the third ripple after a splash in water—a less discrete generation might have been made up of men, like Lincoln, Douglas, and Davis, who came of age in Jacksonian America and for whom not merely preserving but building and even experimenting provided the stuff of life and career. After all, Davis and other Southerners tried to win their own independence—an act that both copied the Founding Fathers and repudiated the preservers who followed them; though Lincoln led the effort to preserve the Union he was really building a new nation.

Interesting as Forgie's thesis is, it rests partly on the premise that psychoanalytic oedipal theory would posit competition between or among brothers as they challenged the father—an assumption clinicians may or may not accept. In any case, one may well ask whether formulating generations or playing with metaphors like "sons" and "killing" Founding Fathers really helps to account for sectional crisis in 1860. Did being in a generation actually influence anyone politically or did political realities, in retrospect, create generations?

> Aggressive conflict between the generations [can]
> be "solved" by . . . finding an enemy outside the
> group who could be dominated or killed.
>
> MARTIN WANGH, 1972

THE RITUALISTIC CUSTOM of sectional compromise, which permitted the acting out of fratricidal wishes while also containing them, had helped to preserve the Union for more than half a century before it collapsed with the passage of the Kansas-Nebraska bill. As though attempting to find another peaceable way of achieving exactly the same result, Abraham Lincoln between 1854 and 1860 moved to create a substitute ritual. In the original one, the brothers would begin with extreme demands, would threaten to divide the house, and then, seeming to heed the warnings that a house divided must lead to fratricide, would discover, and then acquiesce in, a middle formula. In Lincoln's new version all the good brothers would band together to direct their angry passions upon a scapegoat brother and, by throwing him from power (symbolically killing him), actively rid themselves of the only danger to their Union at the same time that they psychologically returned to the world of the fathers who had created it. This ritual was ultimately as sentimental as the one it replaced. Unlike the one it replaced, however, it never demonstrated that it had any power to save the Union. On the contrary, it led directly to the result it sought to avoid—civil war.

Even in his lifetime it was well known that Abraham Lincoln was a close and frequent reader of Shakespeare.[1] The interest became almost intense during the Civil War years, when he would sometimes spend hours at a stretch reading from Shakespeare's tragedies—often aloud to the people about him. According to his own testimony and the memories of others, Lincoln was evidently drawn to three passages in particular, for he kept returning to them. The first, from *Hamlet*, was a speech by Claudius, who usurps the throne of Denmark after murdering his brother, the king. Overwhelmed with guilt, he says:

O, my offence is rank, it smells to heaven;
It hath the primal eldest curse upon't,
A brother's murther!

He longs to pray for pardon, but he cannot,

            since I am still possess'd
Of those effects for which I did the murther—
My crown, mine own ambition, and my queen,

and he does not intend to give them up.[2]

Lincoln told a Shakespearean actor in 1863 that he preferred this soliloquy to the one by Hamlet that begins, "To be or not to be."[3] He told Francis B. Carpenter, an artist, in 1864 that Claudius's speech "always struck me as one of the finest touches of nature in the world." He then proceeded to recite it "with a feeling and appreciation," Carpenter thought, "unsurpassed by anything I ever witnessed upon the stage." After this Lincoln fell into a silence during which his mind made the connection to the second of his favorite passages, the opening speech of *Richard III*. Here the future king speaks of his own ugliness and regrets the "weak piping time of peace" he lives in. Hindered by both from more noble pursuits, "to entertain these fair well-spoken days, I am determined to prove a villain." Lincoln told Carpenter that actors did not deliver the lines with any sign of awareness of the force of the man's ambition.

Richard, you remember, had been, and was then, plotting the destruction of his brothers, to make room for himself. Outwardly, the most loyal to the newly created

182   GEORGE B. FORGIE

king, secretly he could scarcely contain his impatience at the obstacles still in the way
of his own elevation. He appears upon the stage . . . burning with repressed hate and
jealousy.

At this point, according to Carpenter, Lincoln "unconsciously" assumed the
character of Richard and repeated the speech from memory. The artist was
again greatly moved at "the force and power" of Lincoln's acting, and jok-
ingly suggested to him that he had missed his calling.[4] Obviously, what
Lincoln was showing him was that he had not missed it at all.

The third passage was from *Macbeth*, Lincoln's favorite among all Shakespeare's plays. "I think nothing equals Macbeth," he once said. "It is wonderful."[5] Another witness to his recitations recalled hearing Lincoln read from
the play five days before he was murdered. He was particularly drawn to the
scenes in which Macbeth "falls a prey to moral torment." After he replaces
Duncan, whom he has slain, as king, Macbeth says:

                    Better be with the dead,
Whom we, to gain our peace, have sent to peace,
Than on the torture of the mind to lie
In restless ecstasy. Duncan is in his grave;
After life's fitful fever he sleeps well.

After reading these lines aloud, Lincoln "paused to expatiate on how exact a
picture Shakespeare here gives of a murderer's mind when, the dark deed
achieved, its perpetrator already envies his victim's calm sleep. He read the
scene over twice."[6] How could Lincoln have been certain that Shakespeare's
picture of the murderer's mind was exact?

Of all Shakespeare's creations, Lincoln was drawn to the plays, characters,
and indeed the very scenes that most vividly dramatize fratricidal ambition.
In all three of these plays, ambitious and envious men kill members of their
own families to reach and keep power. Claudius and Richard kill brothers
and Macbeth kills his cousin. Each becomes king as a result. Each reflects
powerfully upon his own guilt and alienation from all that is good—and then
goes on killing. Lincoln was not only fascinated with these characters. He
evidently identified with them. Carpenter's memoir indicates that Lincoln
did more than imitate Richard III: he became Richard III, the man he understood to be consumed with "repressed hate and jealousy."

How could Lincoln have identified with the mentality of men consumed
with fratricidal guilt? Was there any sense in which he also burned with
repressed hate and jealousy and then committed a "brother's murther" in
order to get to power? Between 1854 and 1860, the years in which Lincoln
sought (using again his own words about Richard) to "make room for himself," it would seem that he was headed in the opposite direction by attempting to avoid fratricide in the form of the civil war that he and many others
considered possible. But there was an intensely personal aspect to Lincoln's
politics in the 1850s, for there was one man in his way who had to be pushed

aside; that man, of course, was Stephen A. Douglas. The rivalry between these two men was one of the most extraordinary in background, as well as one of the most fateful in result, in the history of American politics. Douglas after 1854 represented all that Lincoln opposed, and he sat in the Senate seat that Lincoln coveted in 1858. One reason this rivalry has been so intriguing to historians is the problem of scale it presents. On the one hand, the man who stood in Lincoln's way was not just any American, but probably the most famous politician in the nation. On the other, Lincoln had known Douglas since the days when both men were equally obscure. He could scarcely have avoided developing powerful feelings about Douglas personally before he found himself opposing Douglas on grounds of political principle.

The two politicians had begun their careers at about the same time in the 1830s—young lawyers in the center of Illinois, serving together in the state legislature, and debating against each other even then. But between the 1830s and the 1850s events carried Douglas to national and even international renown. The prominence Lincoln attained was far narrower in scope. Thus to the obscurity he endured was added the humiliation of Douglas's success. In a private fragment, Lincoln wrote to himself in 1856:

Twenty-two years ago Judge Douglas and I first became acquainted. We were both young then; he a trifle younger than I. Even then, we were both ambitious; I, perhaps, quite as much so as he. With *me*, the race of ambition has been a failure—a flat failure; with *him* it has been one of splendid success. His name fills the nation; and is not unknown, even, in foreign lands. I affect no contempt for the high eminence he has reached. So reached, that the oppressed of my species, might have shared with me in the elevation, I would rather stand on that eminence, than wear the richest crown that ever pressed a monarch's brow.[7]

In addition to the factors inherent in a contest fought upon major issues for high office, this one contained the emotional charge of a long-sustained and unbalanced rivalry.

Initially it was not to Shakespeare especially but more to the structure and the language of drama generally that Lincoln turned in order to give a single scale to a personal rivalry that had become a public contest involving the very principles on which the nation was founded. He compared his debates with Douglas in 1858 to "the successive acts of a drama" whose audience was not just the attending crowd, or even the nation, but (because of Douglas's fame) the entire world.[8] The analogy is revealing. Lincoln learned his politics at the village level, where affairs were managed through the interaction of a few individuals one knew personally. Anyone who reads the accounts of the way, as president, he dealt with the public to a striking degree on an individual, personal basis is likely to surmise that he never really got beyond the sense, which after all his generation largely shared, that politics was an extension of personal relationships. His ancient habits did adjust to his stature, however, and it is just here that theater provided an opening to the wider world. It was as though he thought of himself as moving from a narrow, private realm to a public stage. He continued always to think of politics as the interaction of political leaders. To the extent that he could comprehend mass society at all, it seems to have been as an audience that watched the struggles of the great in order to be moved by and choose between them. The people were acted upon, rather than actors, in politics. This is not to say that the audience was either passive or infinitely manipulable. On the contrary, it brought to the drama feelings and opinions that were decidedly fixed and that set the boundaries of political action. In this conception it was more the task of the actors through their speeches to arouse and exploit preexisting feelings than to change them.

It was on this "stage" that Lincoln cornered and "killed" his rival Douglas. As if trying to prevent disunion and fratricidal war, Lincoln between 1854 and 1860 staged a ritual in which the fratricidal emotions of Americans (not excluding the South) could be satisfied by heaping upon this scapegoat responsibility for all their problems and then symbolically murdering him. The accumulated tensions of many years might thereby be peaceably relieved. Lincoln's rivalry with Douglas might be interpreted in these terms, but it must be said that the effect did not fully match his apparent intent. Lincoln did manage eventually to cast Douglas aside and rise to power; the good son did defeat the bad one. But the social and psychological purposes of the ritual were not achieved. Not only did the fratricidal play fail to prevent actual fratricide, but Lincoln's pursuit and defeat of Douglas actually contributed to the bringing of fratricidal war.

It might seem that guilt was an inappropriate reaction to a murder that was symbolic and committed with the best of filiopietistic intent. That civil war followed soon upon it was an ironic, for it was an unintended, development that might have occurred had Lincoln not existed. But Lincoln's emotional identification with ambitious men who became conscience-stricken murderers makes more sense when we recall that [in the Springfield Lyceum address] he did wish to "kill" the fathers, whose memory blocked his own chances for immortality, and that in order to banish this unacceptable desire he projected it onto a mythical patricidal figure whom he must be prepared to slay in order to save the fathers' work. Now the figure at last appeared and was slain according to expectation.[9] But surely no sensitive person could have failed entirely to see that the symbolic murder, which led to power but also to war, was required more by displaced homicidal wishes than by any objective danger Douglas and his friends posed to republican institutions.

From the late 1830s, when he made the Lyceum speech, until 1854, the year of the Kansas-Nebraska Act, Lincoln was on the edge of the history that was being made. To be sure, he served a term in Congress from 1847 to 1849, but to note it only calls attention to the peripheral role he played in the politics of the time. Unlike Douglas, he was not identified with territorial expansion, real estate speculation, railroad promotion, or the other quests that constituted "the spirit of the age." Outwardly he lived the live of respectable middle-class Whiggery, rising to prominence and prosperity in Springfield, Illinois; marrying well, raising a family, and buying a house at the corner of Eighth and Jackson streets, which he expanded through the years in accordance with his needs and rising status. Every outward sign indicated that the national political situation would keep his life on that course. He seemed resigned to this, declaring in 1852 that "the nation has passed its perils, and is free, prosperous, and powerful."[10]

The events of 1854 and afterward changed the course of Lincoln's life. They gave him a role to play that comported with—and allowed him to exploit—his filiopiety, his ambition, and his prophecy of the emergence of the bad son. They gave him an opportunity to mediate between the conflicting desires of Americans—toward the restoration of the security of childhood on the one hand and the achievement of democratic manhood on the other. They put him in position to attempt to resolve simultaneously the crisis of the Union, the post-heroic problem, and his own psychological dilemma. He succeeded ultimately in all of these efforts, although not in the way that he intended.

By inspiring the creation of the Republican party, the Kansas-Nebraska Act gave Lincoln a vehicle to ride to power. In their opposition to the extension of slavery and in their policies generally, the Republicans appealed to the diverse psychological needs of the American people in a way that the Whigs—and for that matter the post-Jackson Democrats—had never been able to do. The Whigs had presented themselves as the party of preservation. The Republicans presented themselves as the party of restoration. They claimed to stand "precisely on the ground upon which . . . Washington and Jefferson stood."[11] They sought to "roll back the governments of the nation and the States to the principles and policy of our revolutionary fathers."[12] Like preservation, restoration denotes conservative goals. Unlike preservation, restoration requires activist means. Preservation and action seemed to many Americans to be incompatible desires. Republicans now argued that they were complementary.

A debate that occurred in 1858 between Rufus Choate, a sentimentalist who had moved from the moribund Whigs to become a Buchanan Democrat, and James Russell Lowell, a Young America spokesman who had joined the Republican camp, illustrates the matter. Countering an assertion made by Choate that the new party was guilty of irreverence for the past, Lowell repeated the by-then familiar party line that "the object of the Republicans is to bring back the policy and practice of the Republic to some nearer agreement with the traditions of the fathers." But the lesson Lowell found in those traditions was hardly the sentimental one of "forbearance, submission, and waiting for God's good time." Rather the "tradition is rebellion," he claimed, bringing into conjunction two words that sentimentalists saw as opposites.

The past to which the Republicans would return was not the domesticated past of conservative fantasy, but one resembling the masculine past Emerson summoned to mind when he gazed at the portrait of Washington. "That is the America which the Fathers conceived, and it is that to which the children look forward." The difference Lowell saw between the sentimentalists and the Republicans was that for the former the Revolution was to be remembered. For the latter it was a set of principles that the sons must act out and translate into policy.[13]

Thus, to put the matter in more personal terms, the Republicans presented a formula that taught people how to be both men and good sons. The dictates of filiopiety required that the nation, now in great danger, be saved. In the process the needs of ambition could simultaneously be fulfilled. The object of the Republicans was regeneration—to give birth in accordance with tradition. Since giving birth had been the act of the fathers that had originally marked off the generations, the act that had made their fame both possible and permanent, and since the sons had worried that they could never play a similar role, the Republicans offered nothing less than the resolution of a central dilemma of the age. Manhood and fulfilled ambition for this generation could be achieved by saving the nation and restoring it to the original republican purity from which it had departed—by giving it, to anticipate here, "a new birth of freedom."

Of all Republicans, Lincoln was in the best position, in terms of his own political beliefs, his personality, and his geographical location, to exploit the opportunities that generated the party. Richard Hofstadter once showed how Lincoln was able simultaneously to appeal to people who were hostile to slavery (he said it was wrong and must someday die) and to people who were hostile to blacks (he said he opposed their becoming socially or politically equal to whites) by insisting with regard to slavery and implying with regard to blacks that the territories not be ruined by either.[14] Lincoln was similarly able to appeal to Young America types who wanted action and manhood, and to sentimentalists who wanted the restoration of, and regression to, a supposedly more secure past. It is true that he sometimes disparaged both casts of mind. He derided Young America for its "great passion—a perfect rage— for the 'new.'"[15] He believed the sentimentalists overestimated or at least talked too much about the danger to the Union. He regretted their willingness to make almost any concession to avoid the conflict they feared, thereby "reversing the divine rule, and calling, not the sinners, but the righteous to repentence—such as invocations to Washington, imploring men to unsay what Washington said, and undo what Washington did." Certainly he counted himself among the Union savers. "But when I go to Union saving, I must believe . . . that the means I employ has some adaptation to the end."[16] Sentimentalist encouragement of regression alone was not an effective means because it represented the search for security and order that Lincoln believed contributed to a climate hospitable to a tyrant. Sentimentalists tended only to prolong the crisis. Moreover, Lincoln always insisted that it was not enough merely to save the Union; it must be "worthy of the saving."[17]

Yet, if he identified with neither, in many ways Lincoln's character combined traits that the two mentalities considered antagonistic. He was the masculine, rugged rail-splitter of the West and (to some people) he would become the bearded patriarch. But the beard was offset by the shawl, and Herndon's picture of Lincoln going to market wearing that garment, carrying a basket and with children in tow, casts up a domesticated image indeed.[18] Horace White said that Lincoln's nature was "one of almost child-like sweetness,"[19] and Seward observed that he had "a curious vein of sentiment running through his thought which is his most valuable mental attribute."[20] Francis Parkman also noticed these qualities, although not with favor. According to one of Parkman's contemporaries, Lincoln failed to meet his standard that men should be masculine and women feminine. "This wish always to keep the two types, mutually complementary, separate and apart, lay at the bottom of his putting Washington so much higher than Lincoln as a hero; for the womanly tenderness of Lincoln seemed to him out of place."[21] But as the changing image of Washington suggests, many people in the 1850s welcomed a blending of "the two types." If Lincoln had consciously set out to fit his persona to the androgynous tendencies of the time, he could scarcely have done better than he did.

In his words and personality he merged the cult of domesticity with the mainly Republican theory that a conspiracy existed to extend slavery, a process that modified both cult and theory. People like Harriet Beecher Stowe and Edward Everett were counterpolitical sentimentalists uncomfortable with ideology. People like Salmon P. Chase and, much of the time, William Henry Seward were political ideologues uncomfortable with sentiment. Lincoln was at ease with both. Originating little, he borrowed from, adapted, and mixed both strains to express his own understanding of the danger to the nation and how to end it forever. As if sensing the regressive desires present among members of his generation, he encouraged them by creating a public fantasy that corresponded not only with the reality of political developments and his own needs, but also with the child's fantasy of the monster coming into the house—a monumental case of "regression in the service of the ego." That is, unlike the sentimentalists who cast up images of terror as warnings, Lincoln seemed to understand that they could be used to reach and to work through adult problems. By a ritualistic working out of what we may call the fantasy of the besieged house, Americans could exploit their regressive urges to get beyond the problems that had set them on that course in the first place.[22]

Lincoln agreed with other Republicans that the Kansas-Nebraska Act represented a repudiation of the slavery policy of the fathers, which he insisted had remained essentially intact until the mounting of this assault. His own version of the fathers' record on slavery was that they generally abhorred it and placed it on the road to eventual extinction. They made to the institution only such concessions (protecting it in the Constitution, permitting it in some territories) as necessity (the need to create and preserve the Union, or the existence of slavery already in a given area) dictated. It was the duty of the sons, Lincoln went on to say, to follow both parts of the fathers' policy. Although the abolitionists might deplore it, they must follow the fathers in upholding the arrangements they made to protect slavery in the states that chose to have it. Although slaveholders and advocates of popular sovereignty, among others, might deplore it, they must also follow the fathers in pursuit of their ultimate goal. This meant, in practical terms, that they must keep slavery out of areas into which it had not already spread.[23]

Until 1854, according to Lincoln, the policy of the fathers had been successfully working in two different ways. First, it was achieving its goal. The "public mind" assumed that slavery was "in course of ultimate extinction." The second result followed from the first. Because the public mind so assumed, "all was peace and quiet. . . . A long course of peace and prosperity seemed to lie before us." The Kansas-Nebraska Act marked a great and mistaken departure from this course, a departure that defined the task of Lincoln and all other good sons: slavery must be placed again where the fathers left it. But the Kansas-Nebraska Act was not just a case of bad judgment, although it was that. Nor was it only an example of degeneration from "the high republican faith of our ancestors," although it was that too.[24] In addition to both, and much more to be feared than either, the Kansas-Nebraska legislation was an insidious act that could be explained only as a deliberate assault on republican institutions.

Opponents of the Kansas-Nebraska bill argued from the start that it was the brainchild of a "slave power conspiracy" which sought to extend the sway of the despotic institution.[25] Lincoln, too, eventually adopted a conspiratorial explanation for the law, but it is important to realize that his version of conspiracy differed in important respects from the prevailing one, which focused on the machinations of the slaveholding class. He asserted that a cabal of mainly Northern Democrats, which dominated the federal government and counted Stephen A. Douglas, Franklin Pierce, James Buchanan, and Roger B. Taney among its leaders, was plotting to transform slavery from an institution that was transitory, sectional, and limited to blacks, into one that would become perpetual, national, and perhaps even biracial. The Kansas-Nebraska Act was the first blow. When the nation after three years got more or less used to that, the cabal delivered the second: the opinion of the Supreme Court in the *Dred Scott* decision, which stated that Congress could not bar slavery from the territories. The third and worst blow, Lincoln said in 1858, "*is* probably coming, and will soon be upon us." He expected that once the American people had learned to live with the *Dred Scott* decision, the Supreme Court would then move to strike down the antislavery constitutions of the free states, thereby making slavery in effect a national institution.[26]

In legalistic terms, the case for the existence of a conspiracy began with the construction of what Lincoln considered to be superfluous language in the Kansas-Nebraska Act. The law stated that its "true intent and meaning" was "not to legislate slavery into any Territory or State, nor to exclude it therefrom, but to leave the people thereof perfectly free to form and regulate their domestic institutions in their own way, subject only to the Constitution of the United States."[27] Lincoln asserted that the reference to "State" in this clause was suspicious since no state was the object of the legislation, and in any case the power of states over slavery had never before been seriously questioned. The second superfluous passage was "subject only to the Constitution," since no one could have doubted it. Lincoln saw the entire section of the law as the herald of eventual Supreme Court decisions interpreting the Constitution to say that the people in neither territories *nor states* were free to prohibit slavery.[28]

Popular sovereignty, according to Lincoln, was a superficially appealing phrase that was actually a hideous misnomer, for it was designed to provide an ideological curtain behind which the plotters schemed. Contrary to its claims, popular sovereignty had nothing to do with government by the consent of the governed, which Lincoln always considered to be the "leading principle... of American republicanism."[29] It pointed instead toward tyranny. The application of the doctrine to the problem of slavery in the territories demonstrated the point. People who wished to carry slaves into the territories did not propose to ask their consent either to be slaves or to go to the territories.

Lincoln's conspiracy theory, which was central in his political thought at perhaps the crucial point in his career, has usually been an object of puzzlement and even embarrassment to scholars, because it seems to have so little to do with the events it purported to explain.[30] His analysis virtually ignored and by implication ruled out two other dangerous possibilities that loomed much more obviously and were far more often stressed by nearly everyone else. First, of course, was the fear of disunion and subsequent civil war that we have already considered. The second usually receives far less attention for the simple reason that, unlike the first, it was not eventually realized. This was the possibility that acquiescence in popular sovereignty would revive expansionist pressures, leading the South (or the "slave power" in some formulations) to demand the acquisition of new territories—Cuba for example—hospitable to slavery. This was an obvious prospect and a prevalent concern throughout the 1850s. Douglas himself made the possibility credible with his repeated insistence that further territorial expansion to the south was certain. He thereby left himself open to the charge, which some of his opponents did not fail to push, that he was a lackey in the service of an expansionist slavocracy.

These prevailing formulations of danger stressed the sectional nature of the crisis. Lincoln's analysis did not. Indeed, of all the major actors in the politics of the 1850s, Lincoln was the least inclined to interpret the recurrent crises in sectional terms. Born in a slave state and married to a woman born and raised in a slave state, he always had great empathy for the South. He seemed to go out of his way to stress that geography and economics, rather than a superior character, distinguished the Northern record on slavery from that of the Southern. "We are not better... than they." He said that the people of the South were "just what we would be in their situation" and that there were no more "tyrants... in the slave States than in the free."[31] He also avoided appearing to take seriously the danger of secession. Several times after 1854 he dismissed, occasionally with derision, the possibility of disunion. "All this talk about the dissolution of the Union is humbug—nothing but folly," he said at one point. "The people of the South," he said at another, "have too much of good sense, and good temper, to attempt the ruin of the government, rather than see it administered as it was... by the men who made it." Even after secession had occurred, he insisted in public that "the crisis is... artificial" and he evidently underestimated the danger of war between the sections until the American Civil War itself was actually upon him.[32]

For all that, Lincoln was not oblivious to the possibility of disunion and civil war, although like many Northerners he tended to take the double prospect less seriously with each passing year that it was threatened but never came to pass. He said in 1854 that the failure to restore the Missouri restriction would signify the end of the compromise spirit "which first gave us the constitution, and which has thrice saved the Union." Without that spirit, the sections would rapidly become polarized. It was easy to envision "the South flushed with triumph and tempted to excesses; the North, betrayed, as they believe, brooding on wrong and burning for revenge. One side will provoke; the other resent. The one will taunt, the other defy; one [aggresses], the other retaliates"—and so events would move, to their oft-predicted calamitous end.[33] In 1855 Lincoln seemed at least briefly to despair that the slavery problem could ever be resolved peaceably. He came to think that "there is no peaceful extinction of slavery in prospect for us"—a prediction that, if not the same thing as an expectation of civil war, is certainly consistent with such an expectation and with few others.[34] Lincoln was not unaware, either, of the possibility of renewed expansion. It is true that not until after his election as president in 1860 did he show much interest in the prospect that popular sovereignty could lead to the acquisition of new territory for slavery. But at that point this seemed to surpass the danger of the northward spread of slavery in his thinking about the effects of Douglas's doctrines.[35]

If Lincoln understood these dangers, why did he neglect to stress them? A plausible answer is that they did not share one crucial factor with his analysis of passing events. Regardless of the connection it did or did not bear to the politics of the 1850s, Lincoln's interpretation comported with his preexisting needs and ideas and the others did not. He had been disposed throughout his adult life to expect a certain kind of crisis. The Kansas-Nebraska Act brought events into phase with his expectations. He clearly sensed this: his charges against Douglas accorded precisely with the dangers predicted in the Lyceum speech. It was, after all, "Douglas and his friends" who moved the slavery question "from the position in which our fathers originally placed it."[36] This move was not made in good faith. By his policies and his arguments for them, which were "the van-guard—the miners, and sappers—of returning despotism,"[37] Douglas had proven himself to be an enemy of the true meaning of the Revolution. The bad son of the Lyceum prophecy had at last appeared to make his assault upon the fathers' institutions.

Stephen A. Douglas—a man Lincoln knew even before he made the prophecy, and a proven spokesman for the majoritarian ethos: this was a potential despot? He may not seem particularly tyrannical or even dangerous to us, but we must recall that the despot's role, a projection of Lincoln's own wishes, existed and needed to be played. The emotional charge from within shaped what Lincoln came to see in Douglas as much as or more than Douglas's actions or character shaped Lincoln's attitude toward him. Douglas needed to do little more than pass across Lincoln's established field of vision in order to be recognized as the long-threatened danger and cast into the well-delineated image. A rough congruence sufficed. There was one difference between Douglas and the tyrant of prophecy, and it made Douglas all the more dangerous: his methods were covert. The imagined figure of 1836 would tear down the fathers' temple of liberty. Douglas "shirks the responsibility of pulling the house down, but he digs under it that it may fall of its own weight."[38] It was his burrowing method that made Douglas, who seemed so genial and even jolly, so fearsome in fact. He was "the most dangerous enemy of liberty, because the most insidious one."[39] That Douglas did not seem to present a threat to republican institutions was no obstacle to conspiracy theories. Conspirators, of course, go out of their way to hide their real purposes, which suggests, paradoxically, that Douglas could have avoided Lincoln's charge only by agreeing with it.

Like the possible success of the tyrant in Lincoln's prophecy, so now the results of the conspiratorial effort would depend heavily on a gathering indifference to the principles and safeguards of liberty. Douglas's famous claim of indifference to whether or not slavery spread was a cloak that covered "*real* zeal" for the expansion of the blight. The strategy behind popular sovereignty was the "debauching of public sentiment"—to wear down the love of liberty and make people indifferent to it by blurring the distinction between liberty and despotism. Popular sovereignty was "calculated to break down the very idea of a free government, even for white men, and to undermine the very foundations of a free society." People who became indifferent to the principle of liberty in one context were on the way to indifference to liberty generally, which opened the way to tyranny.[40]

Douglas's interpretation of the Declaration of Independence was meant to assist this downward process. He took the position that when the fathers had written "all men are created equal," they had in mind only the equality of Americans and Englishmen and were not referring to American blacks, most of whom they continued to hold as slaves.[41] To Lincoln, who interpreted the words "all men" to mean "*all* men," the passage was the statement of an ideal. Movement toward the ideal was the very purpose of a free society. Moreover, the principle of equality was placed in the founding document as an obstacle in the path of later would-be tyrants, "a stumbling block to those who in after times might seek to turn a free people back into the hateful paths of despotism." Douglas knew this, which meant that one of his first needs was to trivialize the passage.[42]

Douglas shrewdly attacked liberty at its most vulnerable point and its most vulnerable time. He and other enemies of liberty understood (as Lincoln had prophesied in the Lyceum speech) that prosperity dulled sensitivity to encroachments upon political rights—particularly abstract, piecemeal, and seemingly distant encroachments upon the rights of others. Lincoln worried that "now when we have grown fat," Americans would be unable to appreciate—let alone act against—the dangers they faced.[43] Douglas and others like him began with blacks and with the remote territories because they thought they could count on a racist society to acquiesce in a move that did not obviously, directly, and immediately affect them.

Sufficient numbers of white Americans could not be roused to a sustained resistive effort by telling them that the issue in the territories was whether or not a small number of slaves might go there, nor even by telling them that the question of the extension of slavery into the territories was the skirmish line in the encompassing struggle over the future of black slavery in the entire Republic. They could be aroused only if they were made to feel that their own liberty and prosperity were at stake. It was precisely here that Lincoln reworked the slave power conspiracy idea to fit his own structure of thought. Concede one exception to the meaning of the Declaration of Independence, he argued, and there would no longer be any barrier to others. "It does not stop with the negro," he warned. "Is the white man quite certain that the tyrant demon will not turn upon him too?" Successful in their immediate quest, Douglas and his friends would soon besiege the white man's house.

Our defense is in the preservation of the spirit which prizes liberty. . . . Destroy this spirit, and you have planted the seeds of despotism around your own doors. Familiarize yourselves with the chains of bondage, and you are preparing your own limbs to wear them. Accustomed to trample on the rights of those around you, you have lost the genius of your own independence, and become the fit subjects of the first cunning tyrant who rises.[44]

Nowhere did Lincoln more effectively vivify this set of perceptions and fears than in the famous opening passage of the House Divided speech of 1858. More than that, his words at this point revealed his strategy for involving the people generally in his own struggle. "We are now far into the *fifth* year," he began,

since a policy was initiated, with the *avowed* object, and *confident* promise, of putting an end to slavery agitation.

Under the operation of that policy, that agitation has not only, *not ceased*, but has *constantly augmented*.

In *my* opinion, it *will* not cease, until a *crisis* shall have been reached, and passed.

"A house divided against itself cannot stand."

I believe this government cannot endure, permanently half *slave* and half *free*.

I do not expect the Union to be *dissolved*—I do not expect the house to *fall*—but I *do* expect it will cease to be divided.

It will become *all* one thing, or *all* the other.

Either the *opponents* of slavery, will arrest the further spread of it, and place it where the public mind shall rest in the belief that it is in course of ultimate extinction; or its *advocates* will push it forward, till it shall become alike lawful in *all* the States, *old* as well as *new—North* as well as *South*.

Have we no *tendency* to the latter condition?[45]

The passage says that the agitation that began with the Kansas-Nebraska Act in 1854 will not continue indefinitely. It will move toward a crisis that will be resolved in one of two ways. Either slavery will thrive and become legal everywhere, or the spread of slavery will be halted, leading to a consensus that the institution is on the way to eventual disappearance. The present tendency of events is toward the former result. Once the crisis is resolved, agitation will cease. The course of events will seem so firmly set that there will be no cause for agitation to continue. The quoted passage is more pessimistic than otherwise, but the tenor of the entire speech is actually optimistic, reflecting Lincoln's confidence in the outcome of the conflict. "The result is not doubtful," he says in closing. "*Wise councils* may *accelerate* or *mistakes delay* it, but, sooner or later the victory is *sure* to come."[46] That is, good and evil are engaged in a desperate struggle. There will be suspense about the outcome for a time, but good will triumph in the end. This formulation is unmistakably melodramatic, as was the ritual it implied. In order to make his ideas available to the public and involve it in his own concerns, Lincoln dramatized the demons of his mind according to the dictates of popular culture.

Thus Douglas in many ways resembled the villains of melodrama, who smilingly attempted to get people within their clutching powers by cloaking their evil motives under sacred principles. Lincoln cast himself into the representative role of the good son who attempted to do no more than defend the fathers' house against usurpation by tyranny. In exploiting the popularity of melodrama in this way he was hardly unique. The lines between drama and

oratory were never clearly fixed in the nineteenth century.[47] Some of the
most popular plays contain long set speeches that were indistinguishable
from oratory. Some politicians, who after all had as much need to hold
popular attention as playwrights did, cast complex political and constitutional questions into the stock situations and stock language of popular theater.[48]

In his important study of ancient Greek drama, Gerald Else has argued
that the genre of tragedy developed out of oratory as the result of an attempt
to revivify the epic tradition, which was losing its hold on a society given over
to the making of money. In successive steps, Solon, Thespis, and Aeschylus
invented the new form to keep the people of Athens in emotional contact
with their ancient myths.[49] I have been arguing here that American orators
and other writers experienced similar apprehensions and made similar efforts
to keep Americans in emotional contact with their own already mythic origins. In the American case the attempt to restore the past through art did not
lead to the invention of a new genre but to the exploitation of an existing one.
In their effort to involve the American people emotionally in their own
restorationist desires, American politicians increasingly tended verbally to
structure the crisis according to the conventions of melodrama. Indeed, it is
only a slight exaggeration to say that by the end of the 1850s, the crisis of the
Union not only imitated, but had become, a work of art, with the paradoxical
result that as the crisis grew more serious its seriousness grew more difficult
to measure. For the crisis grew to resemble drama at a time when drama was
itself far gone into what the age referred to negatively as theatricality. "Nobody now, on entering one of our theatres, expects to see the mirror held up
to nature, or society," a critic observed with regret in 1856. Attacking "the
false and the forced" on the stage, he continued: "All men do not growl and
frown their emotions in private life; but upon the stage, they all must do so.
All women do not gasp and shriek their joy or sorrow by the domestic hearth;
but upon the stage they all must do so."[50]

Emerging early in the nineteenth century, melodrama was tragedy that
had been reworked (some would say debased) by sentimentality. It grabbed
and held the attention of its audience by developing ordinary situations into a
series of sensational incidents linked together by sentimental dialogue. The
juxtaposition of the plausible and the implausible permitted the audience the
luxury of sympathetic feelings unrestrained by the reality of personal responsibility or danger. Freed from any burden of involvement, they could be
moved to weep delicious (and surely communing) tears for misfortunes that,
although perfectly recognizable, were not theirs.

Plots of melodramatic plays typically involve a dastardly assault on familial
ties or the sanctity of the home. All evil in the world is embodied in a stock
villain whose malevolence, highlighted by his strenuous pretenses to virtue,
is obvious throughout to everyone but his should-be antagonists. He praises
the values of his victims in order to put them off guard. But he always fails

ultimately, when the hero blocks, though barely in time, his wicked designs. Melodrama is a celebration both of virtue, which can be counted on to prevail, and of its audience, which is assumed to possess already the values represented by the protagonist. That the outcome is known in advance does nothing to diminish either suspense or the emotional nature of the course to the result. Indeed, it is the very certainty that the threatened calamity will not materialize that permits the temporary sway (and surely the vicarious enjoyment) of evil and danger. At the same time this certainty implies that evil, although the focus of everyone's concern, is not to be taken too seriously. Melodrama strikes an implied bargain with its audience based on the premise of escape from the real world; part of the suspense it engineers is the suspension of reality itself. Play and audience agree: we know that the world is not like this, but it suits us for the moment to pretend that it is.

Because for us the chaos of political events in the 1850s is structured into coherence by the Civil War that followed, we tend to forget that people witnessing the occurrence of those same events had to turn elsewhere for structuring devices. Melodrama helped to perform that function; it also could organize emotions and provide some of the satisfactions of action without the dangers. Yet in the act of imposing structure on the seeming randomness of events, melodrama distorted the passing scene in crucial ways. In seeing the world as a contest between virtue and vice, it grossly simplified complex problems and lent support to the idea that all adverse change was ultimately caused by the malevolence of a few individuals rather than anything grander, less personal, or beyond the control of the will and efforts of good men. In seeing virtue as unfailingly triumphant, it encouraged an optimistic view of events that permitted people to take a passive stance toward them, and to doubt that the crisis must be taken altogether seriously.

Lincoln in the House Divided passage and elsewhere took these risks with the plainly calculated hope that the crisis of the Union would be redefined—and ended. He repeatedly suggested that the locus of the problem facing the Republic was "the public mind" and that the solution he sought was to put that mind at "rest."[51] If he could move public opinion to a certain kind of expectation, events would then take care of themselves. Thus in Lincoln's view two issues dominated the crisis of the Union as he challenged Douglas for the Senate in 1858. Whether slavery would in fact expand—its *actual* future—was one of them, but more immediately pressing was the question of public opinion on whether slavery should or should not expand. To settle the second would (he believed) settle the first. Thus to Lincoln the crisis ultimately involved a question of sensibility.

In an undated fragment found among his papers he wrote that American prosperity (by which he evidently meant well-being in a very broad sense) rested on the Constitution and the Union, but these in turn rested on the love of liberty "entwining itself more closely about the human heart." It was this sentiment, and not simply the desire for independence, that drove "our fathers" to fight.[52] It was this sentiment that Douglas was seeking to destroy. Lincoln did not disagree with the sentimentalists' central idea that feeling was the great conservative social force, and he sought, as they did, a solution that was fundamentally emotional. "To the salvation of this Union, there needs but one single thing," he told an audience in Indiana in 1861: "the hearts of a people like yours."[53] The people must be emotionally involved. What better way to achieve this than to evoke and dramatize the powerful fantasy of the besieged house?

To Lincoln, as to others, the house metaphor was a conventional way of (as he put it) "figuratively expressing the Union." In his rhetoric after 1854 he often spoke of political matters in the language of domesticity. Government was "national house-keeping," the nation, "our national homestead." Cast into domestic terms the problem of class conflict proved to be no problem at all: "Let not him who is houseless pull down the house of another; but let him labor diligently and build one for himself, thus by example assuring that his own shall be safe from violence when built." Slavery he called "an element of division in the house." "By the Nebraska bill, a door has been opened for the spread of slavery in the Territories."[54] Like Harriet Beecher Stowe, Lincoln used domestic imagery to bring complex political issues to people in their own ancient and daily language, thereby enabling and finally compelling them to feel the slavery problem as their problem.

Although he agreed with the Union-saving sentimentalists that "the Union is a house divided against itself," Lincoln reworked their image for his own purposes.[55] In his hands it ceased to be a warning of disunion to be inevitably followed by civil war. It became instead a warning that Douglas and his allies were conspiring to destroy liberty—a very different danger. The sentimentalists warned of separating brothers who would end up fighting each other. As if sensing that this prospect was almost as attractive as it was horrible (and thus truly dangerous in a political situation where the brake of compromise no longer worked), Lincoln reimagined the danger so as to divest it of all possible appeal. He invoked the deeper, primordial fear of the monster trying to get into the house.

To convey an adequate sense of the danger he saw, Lincoln on more than one occasion associated Douglas, the Kansas-Nebraska Act, and slavery generally with the imagery of monsters. Douglas's position on slavery in the territories was "monstrous" and a "serpent." When Douglas asserted that despite the *Dred Scott* decision the people of a territory could keep slavery out by passing unfriendly legislation, Lincoln responded that "there has never been so monstrous a doctrine uttered from the mouth of a respectable man." "When it came upon us," Lincoln said of the predatory Kansas-Nebraska legislation, "all was peace and quiet." The idea of extending slavery was "the great Behemoth of danger." Slavery itself was a "monstrous injustice." Lincoln once compared the institution to a "venomous snake" which if found "in bed with my children,"—his image for the existing situation in the South—

he would treat with surpassing caution. But if the snake were found out on the prairie, no one would *"put it in bed with other children,* I think we'd *kill* it!"[56]

Lincoln thus set up a confrontation between good and evil, but good did not correspond to North, nor evil to South. Because the metaphor of the house divided has almost always been used in this historical context to refer to the conflict between the sections, it was and is natural, although incorrect, to assume that like everyone else Lincoln was talking about disunion. Nothing about the reaction to the House Divided speech so perplexed him as the prevalent interpretation that he was talking about coming civil war. "I said no such thing and . . . I thought of no such thing," he insisted. The famous passage is clear on the point: "I do not expect the Union to be *dissolved*—I do not expect the house to *fall.*"[57] People who thought the way Lincoln did, and evoked an image of the Republic as a besieged house, quite naturally did not tend to be preoccupied with the possibility of secession. The man who believes that his brother is trying to take all of the inheritance they were meant to share is not likely to spend time supposing that his brother is going to disappear altogether. Moreover, from the standpoint of arousing Northern emotions, the melodramatic formulation made strategic sense. It was easier to arouse people to the prospect of the house being taken over than to the less horrific, and progressively less plausible, prospect that the South would move out of it.

From the start of the political conflict over slavery, it was obvious that the stakes of the sections in its outcome were very different. It was a commonplace for Southerners to say, as one did to a Northerner at its climax, that "with us the question at issue involves our property, our lives, and those of our families, while with you it is but a political abstraction." Southerners claimed that they were defending homes and firesides "as if . . . hordes of insatiable desperadoes threatened domestic security."[58] Henry Clay reminded Northerners in 1850 that they were "safely housed, enjoying all the blessings of domestic comfort, peace, and quiet in the bosom of their own families." Southerners, on the other hand, lived with a sense of siege, a fear that as a result of antislavery agitation, their dwellings would be attacked and burned.[59] Lincoln appreciated the way that the fire-eaters were able to "maintain apprehension among the Southern people that their homes, and firesides, and lives, are . . . endangered" by the abolitionist- and Black Republican-inspired monster of slave insurrection.[60]

It was precisely because there was no plausible way any longer to argue that Northern homes were in any sense similarly endangered by prosecessionists that Lincoln attempted to restructure the conflict along party rather than sectional lines.[61] Except for Taney, who came from Maryland, the men Lincoln named as conspirators were all Northerners. They were also all Democrats. Partisan conflict adhered to a ritual of its own that promised to move toward a resolution that was both decisive (which sectional conflict had never been) and peaceful (which sectional conflict was no longer so likely to be). Thus to place the struggle on a party basis was to take advantage of the built-in and well-practiced ways that parties handled aggressive tensions, channeling them toward the climax of an election which produced a result that normally dissipated those tensions rather than escalated them to violence.

Lincoln set up a conflict that implicitly defined its own resolution—the defeat of the villain or, in more prosaic electoral terms, the defeat of Douglas, the Democrats, and popular sovereignty, and the triumph of the principle of the federal prohibition of slavery extension. The purpose of the formulation of the besieged but rescuable house was not to solve intractable problems of race relations. It was not intended to solve the problem of slavery for the slave or for the slaveholder, but to solve it for Northern whites in psychological terms by permitting their minds to rest in the belief that slavery was back where it had been in the beginning days of the Republic. This was what Lincoln meant by the restoration of the house. Thus in meeting the danger of the possible extension of slavery by popular sovereignty and, even more, the triumph of despotism, the good (but up to now passively preserving) sons were given a chance to act at last by rescuing and restoring the fathers' work.

Countless times after 1854 Lincoln made statements to the effect that Republican policy "is exactly the policy of the men who made the Union. Nothing more and nothing less."[62] He sought only to "reinaugurate the good old 'central ideas' of the Republic," and to "restore the government to the policy of the fathers."[63] In broad terms, the Republicans, once in office, would "treat you... like Washington, Jefferson, and Madison treated you."[64] As for the slavery question in particular, "All I have asked or desired anywhere is that it should be placed back again upon the basis that the fathers of our government originally placed it upon."[65] Placing slavery "where our fathers originally placed it" meant treating it in such a way that the public mind would conclude that the institution was on the road to eventual extinction.[66] In New York City in 1860 he insisted that

this is all Republicans ask—all Republicans desire—in relation to slavery. As those fathers marked it, so let it be again marked, as an evil not to be extended, but to be tolerated and protected only because of and only so far as its actual presence among us makes that toleration and protection a necessity.[67]

Restoration involved change at the level of policy, but more importantly it also involved emotional regeneration. "Let me entreat you to come back," Lincoln once pleaded in words that received wide distribution. "Return to the fountain whose waters spring close by the blood of the Revolution."[68]

Resolving the crisis in this ritualistic way promised also to solve the problem of the post-heroic generation—at least for some of its members. Action in the service of restoring slavery to the place it had held in the paternal vision would be a deed of heroic quality. "If we do this," Lincoln believed, "we shall not only have saved the Union; but we shall have so saved it . . . that the succeeding millions of free happy people, the world over, shall rise up, and call us blessed, to the latest generations."[69] He, of course, received the immortality he desired, although hardly in the way he intended or expected. The melodramatic ritual he created led not to a psychological solution to the crisis of the Union, but to secession and civil war. Thus it failed, and the failure was anything but innocuous.

The results of the rivalry between Lincoln and Douglas are perhaps as well known as any other sequence of events in American political history. Lincoln narrowly lost to Douglas in the contest for the latter's Senate seat in 1858. The formal result may have served briefly to hide, but it did not retard, the increasing erosion of Douglas's centrist political base, a process that Lincoln assisted with effect. Douglas won reelection to the Senate at the cost of exacerbating his tense relationship with the Southern, proslavery wing of the Democratic party, which had been growing increasingly wary of him ever since he decided to oppose the proslavery Lecompton constitution in Kansas on the grounds that it did not represent the will of the people there.[70] Strained as it was, however, this relationship in 1858 was not necessarily any further beyond repair than was Douglas's relationship with the Northerners who burned him in effigy in 1854 only to talk four years later of supporting him for president after he took his anti-Lecompton stand. There was nothing preordained about the Southern rejection of his candidacy in 1860. Indeed, as Harry Jaffa has plausibly supposed, if Douglas in 1860 had seemed headed for victory, Southern Democrats probably would not have deserted the party.[71] Repudiating him would not bring them Kansas, but tolerating him might well bring them Cuba. By leading Douglas repeatedly to emphasize his belief that popular sovereignty was a means to free soil, Lincoln prevented Douglas from taking the steps to repair his standing with the South that this endlessly resourceful man might otherwise have been able to initiate.

The second isolating effect of Lincoln's pursuit was to prevent the offsetting of Douglas's Southern losses by Northern gains. As he approached his showdown with Lincoln, Douglas was attempting to win the backing both of Northerners who were willing to accept free soil in the territories as long as it did not threaten the Union, and of Northerners who very much wanted free soil but were not overly fastidious about the means of getting it. He was making gains in this direction, and by 1858 Douglas represented to many Northerners the prospect of free soil neither tainted by abolitionism nor accompanied by the danger of disunion. He was not without potentially expanding attraction, after all, to the vast middle of the electorate—many of them still wandering homelessly in search of political calm and security after the decay of the Whigs and the Know-Nothings—the very people, in other words, who were responding to appeals of the sort made by Edward Everett. In a famous *Harper's Weekly* article, published late in 1859, Douglas tried hard to enhance his own restorationist credentials. But by evoking in vivid language the fear that Douglas offered neither calm nor free soil but continuing agitation, expanding slavery, and ultimately despotism, Lincoln reduced his opponent's acceptability to the political center, probably by a decisive degree. It is hardly fanciful to suppose that if Lincoln had not opposed him in 1858, Douglas might have been able not only to retain but also to expand his centrist base and win the presidency in 1860. At the very least, this result would certainly have had the effect of postponing disunion and civil war, for with slavery restrictionists held at bay, Southern Democrats would have been (nominally at any rate) on the winning side of the electoral contest.

In his struggle with Douglas, Lincoln sought to restructure and help resolve the crisis of the Union and also to win election to the United States Senate. He achieved neither object. Instead, within little more than two years, he became president and led the Union into a civil war with the eleven Southern states that seceded from it. One of the three other candidates Lincoln defeated in the election of 1860 was Stephen A. Douglas, the candidate of the Northern wing of the Democratic party, whose Southern leaders left it rather than march behind him. He had long since lost any control over the current of political events; now he lost even the ability to ride it. In 1861, after watching helplessly as the country fell into the war he had both tried to prevent and helped to bring, Douglas became one of its first casualties. A combination of maladies not then or since clearly diagnosed carried him off in the first spring of the war. He was forty-eight years old.

There are two ways then, opposite sides of the same coin so to say, in which the events of 1858 contributed to the coming of civil war. Everyone knows the first: the prominence Lincoln achieved in 1858 put him on the course (a winding one, to be sure) that led to his election to the presidency, which in turn led to secession, which in turn led to civil war. The second way is the other side of the first: the victory that Douglas won in 1858 ironically narrowed his base and weakened his power, which led to the split of the Democratic party in 1860, which led to Lincoln's election and to the subsequent disasters. There is a subtle difference in the nature of Lincoln's role in these two formulations, and his moral stature is perhaps affected by whether one emphasizes the first or the second. In the first, he appears to be almost a passive figure who happened to be in a crucial position when he was struck by the historical lightning from a long-darkening sky. In the second, he appears in a much more active role, as the man who set in motion a sequence of events that might not otherwise have occurred.

In 1860, the year of Lincoln's election, a writer calling himself "Procrustes, Jr." analyzed the long-term effects on a nation's history of a heroic age and great men. One of the results of their sway was that their successors attempted to imitate them whether or not the times required imitation. "Such men create war for the purpose of showing their heroism. It is like setting a house on fire for the purpose of showing our skill in putting it out."[72] People who live in dull ages cast up imaginary challenges, so that they can meet them and demonstrate to themselves and others that they are not, after all, degenerate sons of heroic sires. Procrustes was writing about the national situation generally, and gave no sign that he had Lincoln in mind. Even if he had, one might respond that the challenge that preoccupied Lincoln was hardly imaginary, and that the house was already on fire when he came upon it. But to concede this is still to leave room for the possibility—which is what the writer evidently had in mind—that when an ambitious man perceives that because the house exists he cannot satisfy his ambition by building it, and that the only way he can rise is defensively, by saving it—that these circumstances increase the likelihood that he will tend, consciously or not, to create or contribute to a situation that will put the house in danger, thereby permitting him to act not only defensively but also heroically to save and restore it.

If Lincoln had not played the role that he did, would the Republican party in Illinois in its first years have been more moderate than it was, thereby permitting the practical Douglas to avoid either breaking with the Buchanan administration or alienating the South? Would the Republicans in 1860 have nominated someone perceived to be more radical than Lincoln—say, William H. Seward of New York, who might have lost the election, thereby electing Douglas and blunting the secessionist drive? Would the Republicans have nominated someone perceived to be more moderate—say, Edward Bates of Missouri, whose election might not have inspired a secession movement that could not be peaceably contained? Would some other president have abandoned Fort Sumter? Would peaceable reunion have eventually taken place if Fort Sumter had been abandoned? Of course we cannot know the answers to these questions, but that fact suggests the point: Abraham Lincoln, who had every reason to ask them and others, could not have known the answers to these questions either. What the questions reveal is that, step by barely perceptible step, symbolic fratricide edged over into the real thing, that there is a straight line from the melodrama of the house divided to the tragedy of the house divided.

NOTES

1. Abraham Lincoln to James H. Hackett, August 17, 1863, in Roy P. Basler, ed., *The Collected Works of Abraham Lincoln*, 8 vols. (New Brunswick, N.J.: Rutgers University Press, 1953), 6:392–93. On Lincoln and Shakespeare, see Don E. Fehrenbacher, "Lincoln and the Weight of Responsibility," *Journal of the Illinois State Historical Society* 68 (1975): 45–56; David Chambers Mearns, *Largely Lincoln* (New York: St. Martin's Press, 1961), pp. 126–33; Roy P. Basler, *A Touchstone for Greatness: Essays, Addresses, and Occasional Pieces about Abraham Lincoln* (Westport, Conn.: Greenwood Press, 1973), pp. 206–27.

2. Act 3, sc. 3.

3. Lincoln to Hackett, in Basler, *Works of Lincoln*, 6:392.

4. F[rancis] B. Carpenter, *Six Months at the White House with Abraham Lincoln: The Story of a Picture* (New York: Hurd and Houghton, 1867), pp. 49–52. See also John Hay, August 23, 1863: Lincoln "read Shakespeare to me, the end of Henry VI and the beginning of Richard III, till my heavy eyelids caught his considerate notice." Tyler Dennett, ed., *Lincoln and the Civil War in the Diaries and Letters of John Hay* (New York: Dodd, Mead & Co., 1939), p. 82.

5. Lincoln to Hackett, in Basler, *Works of Lincoln*, 6:392.

6. Adolphe de Chambrun, *Impressions of Lincoln and the Civil War: A Foreigner's Account*, trans. Aldebert de Chambrun (New York: Random House, 1952), p. 83. The *Macbeth* passage is in Act 3, sc. 2.

7. Basler, *Works of Lincoln*, 2:382–83.

8. Ibid., 3:252–53.

9. "Aggressive conflict between the generations [can] be 'solved' by externalization, that is, by finding an enemy outside the group who could be dominated or killed." Martin Wangh, "Some Unconscious Factors in the Psychogenesis of Recent Student Uprisings," *Psychoanalytic Quarterly* 41 (1972): 221.

10. Basler, *Works of Lincoln*, 2:122.

11. Lyman Trumbull, *Congressional Globe*, 36 Cong., 1 Sess. (December 7, 1859), p. 39.

12. E. P. Walton, ibid., 35 Cong., 1 Sess. (March 31, 1858), appendix, p. 331. On the early Republican party generally, see Eric Foner, *Free Soil, Free Labor, Free Men: The Ideology of the Republican Party before the Civil War* (New York: Oxford University Press, 1970).

13. Rufus Choate, Boston *Daily Advertiser*, July 7, 1858; [James Russell Lowell], "The Pocket-Celebration of the Fourth," *Atlantic Monthly* 2 (1858): 378–79. See also [idem], "The Election in November," ibid. 6 (1860): 499–500. Lowell's formulation was precisely the same as the one secession-minded Southerners were reaching at the same time: rebellion and tradition were not antagonistic but synonymous.

14. Richard Hofstadter, *The American Political Tradition and the Men Who Made It* (New York: Alfred A. Knopf, 1948), pp. 106–19.

15. Basler, *Works of Lincoln*, 3:357.

16. Ibid., p. 550; 2:270.

17. Ibid., 2:276.

18. Emanuel Hertz, ed., *The Hidden Lincoln: From the Letters and Papers of William H. Herndon* (New York: Viking Press, 1938), pp. 414–15.

19. Horace White, Introduction to William H. Herndon and Jesse W. Weik, *Abraham Lincoln: The True Story of a Great Life*, 2 vols. (New York: D. Appleton and Co., 1892), 1:xxiii.

20. Quoted in Glyndon G. Van Deusen, *William Henry Seward* (New York: Oxford University Press, 1967), p. 251.

21. Henry Dwight Sedgwick, *Francis Parkman* (Boston: Houghton Mifflin Co., 1904), pp. 310–11.

22. Cf. D. W. Winnicott, *Through Paediatrics to Psycho-Analysis* (New York: Basic Books, 1975), pp. 278–94.

23. Lincoln's views on the fathers and slavery pervade his speeches and other writings from 1854 to 1860. In particular see Basler, *Works of Lincoln*, 2:230–31, 235, 240–41, 248–50, 266–67, 274, 405–7, 452, 492, 501, 514, 520, 551; 3:18, 77–78, 276, 307, 464–66, 522–35.

24. Ibid., 3:439; 2:270, 242.

25. See the "Appeal of the Independent Democrats," in J. W. Schuckers, *The Life and Public Services of Salmon Portland Chase, United States Senator and Governor of Ohio; Secretary of the Treasury, and Chief-Justice of the United States* (New York: D. Appleton and Co., 1874), pp. 140–47.

26. Basler, *Works of Lincoln*, 2:375, 385, 453, 461–69, 518, 525–26, 541; 3:18, 95; 4:16. The quotation is from 2:467.

27. U.S., *Statutes at Large*, 10:283.

28. Basler, *Works of Lincoln*, 2:466–67. As late as December 1860, Lincoln was still fearful of "an early Supreme court decision, holding our free-state constitutions to be unconstitutional." Lincoln to John D. Defrees, December 18, 1860, in ibid., 4:155.

29. Ibid., 2:266.

30. J. G. Randall, *Lincoln the President*, 4 vols. (New York: Dodd, Mead & Co., 1945–55), 1:107–8; Allan Nevins, *The Emergence of Lincoln*, 2 vols. (New York: Charles Scribner's Sons, 1950), 1:361–63. But see Harry V. Jaffa, *Crisis of the House Divided: An Interpretation of the Issues in the Lincoln-Douglas Debates* (New York: Doubleday & Co., 1959), pp. 275–301; and Don E. Fehrenbacher, *Prelude to Greatness: Lincoln in the 1850's* (Stanford: Stanford University Press, 1962), pp. 79–82.

31. Basler, *Works of Lincoln*, 4:3; 2:255, 264.

32. Ibid., 2:354–55; 4:95, 238. "Mr. Lincoln entered Washington the victim of a grave delusion. . . . He fully believed that there would be no civil war,—no serious effort to consummate Disunion. . . . I infer that Mr. Lincoln did not fully realize that we were to have a great civil war till the Bull Run disaster." Horace Greeley, *Recollections of a Busy Life* (New York: J. B. Ford & Co., 1868), pp. 404–5.

33. Basler, *Works of Lincoln*, 2:272.

34. Lincoln to George Robertson, August 15, 1855, in ibid., p. 318. But the letter in which he said this reveals that he had already formulated the question ("Can we, as a nation, continue together *permanently* . . . half slave, and half free?") that he would answer in the House Divided speech without even considering the possibility of civil war.

35. Ibid., 4:154, 155, 172.

36. Ibid., 3:117.

37. Lincoln to Henry L. Pierce and others, April 6, 1859, in ibid., p. 375.

38. Ibid., p. 205.

39. Lincoln to Samuel Galloway, July 28, 1859, in ibid., p. 394.

40. Ibid., 2:255; 3:469; 4:16.

41. Ibid., 3:113.

42. Ibid., 2:405–7.

43. Lincoln to Robertson, in ibid., p. 318.

44. Ibid., pp. 500, 553; 3:95.

45. Ibid., 2:461–62. On the speech generally, see the analysis in Fehrenbacher, *Prelude to Greatness*, pp. 70–95.

46. Basler, *Works of Lincoln*, 2:468–69.

47. Thus, for example, "The lyceum is the American theatre." "Lectures and Lecturers," *Putnam's Monthly* 9 (1857): 317. See also "Percival's Poems," *Southern Quarterly Review* 5 (1844): 213. Henry T. Tuckerman wrote that "orations constitute our literary staple by the same law that causes letters and comedies to attain such perfection in France, domestic novels in England, and the lyrical drama in Italy." "Edward Everett," *Graham's Magazine* 38 (1851): 74.

48. Almost all of my statements about nineteenth-century American drama owe something to David Grimsted, *Melodrama Unveiled: American Theater and Culture, 1800–1850* (Chicago: University of Chicago Press, 1968), which is an excellent book in all scholarly respects, and witty besides.

49. Gerald F. Else, *The Origin and Early Form of Greek Tragedy* (Cambridge, Mass.: Harvard University Press, 1965).

50. "The World of New York," *Putnam's Monthly* 7 (1856): 446.

51. This is most conspicuously the case in the House Divided speech. Basler, *Works of Lincoln*, 2:461.

52. Ibid., 4:168–69. See also 2:271.

53. Ibid., 4:193.

54. Ibid., 3:309; 4:13; 5:529; 7:259–60; 3:18; 2:362–63. See also 2:237, 238, 241, 258; 3:211, 213.

55. Ibid., 3:18.

56. Ibid., 2:237; 2:500; 3:317; 2:270; 2:255; 4:10–11. See also 3:306; 4:5.

57. Lincoln to Oliver P. Hall, Jacob N. Fullinwider, and William F. Correll, February 14, 1860, in ibid., 3:520; 2:461.

58. Henry T. Tuckerman, *The Rebellion: Its Latent Causes and True Significance* (New York: James G. Gregory, 1861), pp. 35, 22.

59. *Congressional Globe*, 31 Cong., 1 Sess. (January 29, 1850), p. 246. See also A. G. Brown, ibid., 31 Cong., 1 Sess. (January 30, 1850), p. 257; Abraham W. Venable, ibid., 31 Cong., 1 Sess. (February 19, 1850), appendix, p. 161; Clement C. Clay, Jr., ibid., 36 Cong., 1 Sess. (December 13, 1859), p. 121; James D. Richardson, ed., *A Compilation of the Messages and Papers of the Presidents*, 10 vols. (Washington: Government Printing Office, 1897), 5:627.

60. Basler, *Works of Lincoln*, 4:142.

61. Ibid., 2:385.

62. Ibid., 3:502.

63. Ibid., 2:385; 3:93. See also 3:118, 538.

64. Ibid., 3:453.

65. Ibid., p. 117.

66. Ibid., 2:515, 492, 501, 513, 514.

67. Ibid., 3:535. The entire statement is italicized in the original.

68. Ibid., 2:547.

69. Ibid., p. 276.

70. Robert W. Johannsen, *Stephen A. Douglas* (New York: Oxford University Press, 1973), pp. 576–613, 685–705.

71. Harry V. Jaffa and Robert W. Johannsen, eds., *In the Name of the People: Speeches and Writings of Lincoln and Douglas in the Ohio Campaign of 1859* (Columbus: Ohio State University Press, 1959), pp. 45–46.

72. "Great Men, a Misfortune," *Southern Literary Messenger* 30 (1860): 312.

9

THE HYSTERICAL WOMAN
Sex Roles and Role Conflict in Nineteenth-Century America

CARROLL SMITH-ROSENBERG

No one would deny that medicine and psychology go together. Physical disabilities are sometimes exacerbated, if not caused, by psychological stress, and healing partakes of both body and will. Historians have discovered in this relationship important source material: physical ailments and "mental illness" in the past tell us much about their social setting and the formulas—theoretical, folk, religious—that people used in dealing with them. Even the patient's "role" as one who was sick (especially in discussing "madness") reveals what a society considered acceptable and unacceptable behavior and may offer a clue as to how and why these parameters were established. Disease, the anthropologist Ruth Benedict wrote, is a cultural artifact.

The next two essays demonstrate the value of Benedict's theorem by tracing the definition and "style" of illness in nineteenth-century America and thereby help us to know more of the tensions within it. First Carroll Smith-Rosenberg explores a pattern of behavior among women that makes clear how limited the social roles of women were in those years. Like Stanley Elkins's chapter on the "slave personality," Smith-Rosenberg's article serves as a methodological example of group analysis, where evidence and hypothesis recommend that one look for a common psychological experience. It, in turn, can lead to conclusions about the peculiar life circumstances of the group and thereby to an understanding of the society as a whole.

Both this piece and the one following highlight conceptual questions that are especially visible in psychohistory. Smith-Rosenberg works from our historical vantage point and uses current clinical concepts. But if our concepts are as much a part of our culture as those of our subjects were of theirs, does the use of our categories of analysis distort the historical artifact?

Reprinted, with author's revisions to section III, from *Social Research: An International Quarterly of the Social Sciences* 39 (Winter 1972):652–78, with permission of the publisher.
This project was supported in part by grants from the National Institutes of Health and the Grant Foundation, New York.

HYSTERIA was one of the classic diseases of the nineteenth century. It was a protean ailment characterized by such varied symptoms as paraplegia, aphonia, hemi-anaesthesia, and violent epileptoid seizures. Under the broad rubric of hysteria, nineteenth-century physicians gathered cases which might today be diagnosed as neurasthenia, hypochondriasis, depression, conversion reaction, and ambulatory schizophrenia. It fascinated and frustrated some of the century's most eminent clinicians; through its redefinition Freud rose to international fame, while the towering reputation of Charcot suffered a comparative eclipse. Psychoanalysis can historically be called the child of the hysterical woman.

Not only was hysteria a widespread and—in the intellectual history of medicine—significant disease, it remains to this day a frustrating and ever-changing illness. What was diagnosed as hysteria in the nineteenth century is not necessarily related to the hysterical character as defined in the twentieth century, or again to what the Greeks meant by hysteria when they christened the disease millennia ago. The one constant in this varied history has been the existence in virtually every era of Western culture of some clinical entity called hysteria; an entity which has always been seen as peculiarly relevant to the female experience, and one which has almost always carried with it a pejorative implication.

For the past half century and longer, American culture has defined hysteria in terms of individual psychodynamics. Physicians and psychologists have seen hysteria as a "neurosis" or character disorder, the product of an unresolved oedipal complex. Hysterical women, fearful of their own sexual impulses—so the argument went—channeled that energy into psychosomatic illness. Characteristically, they proved unable to form satisfying and stable relationships.[1] More recently psychoanalysts such as Elizabeth Zetzel have refined this Freudian hypothesis, tracing the roots of hysteria to a woman's excessively ambivalent preoedipal relation with her mother and to the resulting complications of oedipal development and resolution.[2] Psychologist David Shapiro has emphasized the hysterical woman's impressionistic thought pattern.[3] All such interpretations focus exclusively on individual psychodynamics and relations within particular families.

Yet hysteria is also a socially recognized behavior pattern and as such exists within the larger world of cultural values and role relationships. For centuries hysteria has been seen as characteristically female—the hysterical woman the embodiment of a perverse or hyper femininity.[4] Why has this been so? Why did large numbers of women "choose" the character traits of hysteria as their particular mode of expressing malaise, discontent, anger, or pain?[5] To begin to answer this question, we must explore the female role and role socialization. Clearly not all women were hysterics; yet the parallel between the hysteric's behavior and stereotypic femininity is too close to be explained as mere coincidence. To examine hysteria from this social perspective means necessarily to explore the complex relationships that exist between cultural norms and individual behavior, between behavior defined as disease and behavior considered normal.

Using nineteenth-century America as a case study,[6] I propose to explore hysteria on at least two levels of social interaction. The first involves an examination of hysteria as a social role within the nineteenth-century family. This was a period when, it has been argued, social and structural change had created stress within the family and when, in addition, individual domestic role alternatives were few and rigidly defined. From this perspective hysteria can be seen as an alternate role option for particular women incapable of accepting their life situation. Hysteria thus serves as a valuable indicator both of domestic stress and of the tactics through which some individuals sought to resolve that stress. By analyzing the function of hysteria within the family and the interaction of the hysteric, her family, and the interceding—yet interacting—physician. I also hope to throw light upon the role of women and female-male relationships within the larger world of nineteenth-century American society. Secondly, I will attempt to raise some questions concerning female role socialization, female personality options, and the nature of hysterical behavior.[7]

I

It might be best to begin with a brief discussion of three relatively well known areas: first, the role of women in nineteenth-century American society; second, the symptoms which hysterical women presented and which established the definition of the disease, and lastly, the response of male physicians to their hysterical patients.

The ideal female in nineteenth-century America was expected to be gentle and refined, sensitive and loving. She was the guardian of religion and spokeswoman for morality. Hers was the task of guiding the more worldly and more frequently tempted male past the maelstroms of atheism and uncontrolled sexuality. Her sphere was the hearth and the nursery; within it she was to bestow care and love, peace and joy. The American girl was taught at home, at school, and in the literature of the period, that aggression, independence, self-assertion, and curiosity were male traits, inappropriate for the weaker sex and her limited sphere. Dependent throughout her life, she was to reward her male protectors with affection and submission. At no time was she expected to achieve in any area considered important by men and thus highly valued by society. She was, in essence, to remain a child-woman, never developing the strengths and skills of adult autonomy. The stereotype of the middle-class woman as emotional, pious, passive, and nurturant was to become increasingly rigid throughout the nineteenth century.[8]

There were significant discontinuities and inconsistencies between such ideals of female socialization and the real world in which the American woman had to live. The first relates to a dichotomy between the ideal woman and the ideal mother. The ideal woman was emotional, dependent, and gentle—a born follower. The ideal mother, then and now, was expected to be strong, self-reliant, protective, an efficient caretaker in relation to children and home. She was to manage the family's day-to-day finances, prepare foods, make clothes, compound drugs, serve as family nurse—and, in rural areas, as physician as well.[9] Especially in the nineteenth century, with its still primitive obstetrical practices and its high child mortality rates, she was expected to face severe bodily pain, disease, and death—and still serve as the emotional support and strength of her family.[10] As S. Weir Mitchell, the eminent Philadelphia neurologist wrote in the 1880's, "We may be sure that our daughters will be more likely to have to face at some time the grim question of pain than the lads who grow up beside them.... To most women... there comes a time when pain is a grim presence in their lives." Yet, as Mitchell pointed out, it was boys whom society taught from early childhood on to bear pain stoically, while girls were encouraged to respond to pain and stress with tears and the expectation of elaborate sympathy.[11]

Contemporaries noted routinely in the 1870's, 1880's, and 1890's that middle-class American girls seemed ill-prepared to assume the responsibilities and trials of marriage, motherhood, and maturation. Frequently women, especially married women with children, complained of isolation, loneliness, and depression. Physicians reported a high incidence of nervous disease and hysteria among women who felt overwhelmed by the burdens of frequent pregnancies, the demands of children, the daily exertions of housekeeping and family management.[12] The realities of adult life no longer permitted them to elaborate and exploit the role of fragile, sensitive, and dependent child.

Not only was the Victorian woman increasingly ill-prepared for the trials of childbirth and child-rearing, but changes were also at work within the larger society which were to make her particular socialization increasingly inappropriate. Reduced birth and mortality rates, growing population concentration in towns, cities, and even in rural areas, a new, highly mobile economy, as well as new patterns of middle-class aspiration—all reached into the family, altering that institution, affecting domestic relations, and increasing the normal quantity of infrafamilial stress.[13] Women lived longer; they married later and less often. They spent less and less time in the primary processing of food, cloth and clothing. Increasingly, both middle- and lower-class women took jobs outside the home until their marriages—or permanently if unable to secure a husband.[14] By the post–Civil War years, family limitation—with its necessary implication of altered domestic roles and relationships—had become a real option within the decision-making processes of every family.[15]

Despite such basic social, economic and demographic changes, however, the family and gender role socialization remained relatively inflexible. It is quite possible that many women experienced a significant level of anxiety when forced to confront or adapt in one way or another to these changes. Thus hysteria may have served as one option or tactic offering particular women otherwise unable to respond to these changes a chance to redefine or restructure their place within the family.

So far this discussion of role socialization and stress has emphasized primarily the malaise and dissatisfaction of the middle-class woman. It is only a covert romanticism, however, which permits us to assume that the lower-class or farm woman, because her economic functions within her family were more vital than those of her decorative and economically secure urban sisters, escaped their sense of frustration, conflict, or confusion. Normative prescriptions of proper womanly behavior were certainly internalized by many poorer women. The desire to marry and the belief that a woman's social status came not from the exercise of her own talents and efforts but from her ability to attract a competent male protector were as universal among lower-class and farm women as among middle- and upper-class urban women. For some of these women—as for their urban middle-class sisters— the traditional female role proved functional, bringing material and psychic rewards. But for some it did not. The discontinuity between the child and adult female roles, along with the failure to develop substantial ego strengths, crossed class and geographic barriers—as did hysteria itself. Physicians connected with almshouses, and later in the century with urban hospitals and dispensaries, often reported hysteria among immigrant and tenement house women.[16] Sex differentiation and class distinctions both play a role in American social history, yet hysteria seems to have followed a psychic fault line corresponding more to distinctions of gender than to those of class.

Against this background of possible role conflict and discontinuity, what were the presenting symptoms of the female hysteric in nineteenth-century America? While physicians agreed that hysteria could afflict persons of both sexes and of all ages and economic classes (the male hysteric was an accepted clinical entity by the late nineteenth century), they reported that hysteria was most frequent among women between the ages of 15 and 40 and of the urban middle and upper middle classes. Symptoms were highly varied. As early as the seventeenth century, indeed, Sydenham had remarked that "the frequency of hysteria is no less remarkable than the multiformity of the shapes it puts on. Few maladies are not imitated by it; whatever part of the body it attacks, it will create the proper symptom of that part."[17] The nineteenth-century physician could only concur. There were complaints of nervousness, depression, the tendency to tears and chronic fatigue, or of disabling pain. Not a few women thus afflicted showed a remarkable willingness to submit to long-term, painful therapy—to electric shock treatment, to blistering, to multiple operations, even to amputations.[18]

The most characteristic and dramatic symptom, however, was the hysterical "fit." Mimicking an epileptic seizure, these fits often occurred with shocking suddenness. At other times they "came on" gradually, announcing their approach with a general feeling of depression, nervousness, crying, or lassitude. Such seizures, physicians generally agreed, were precipitated by a sudden or deeply felt emotion—fear, shock, a sudden death, marital disappointment—or by physical trauma. It began with pain and tension, most frequently in the "uterine area." The sufferer alternately sobbed and laughed violently, complained of palpitations of the heart, clawed her throat as if strangling, and, at times, abruptly lost the power of hearing and speech. A death-like trance might follow, lasting hours, even days. At other times violent convulsions—sometimes accompanied by hallucinations—seized her body.[19] "Let the reader imagine," New York physician E. H. Dixon wrote in the 1840's,

the patient writhing like a serpent upon the floor, rending her garments to tatters, plucking out handsful of hair, and striking her person with violence—with contorted and swollen countenance and fixed eyes resisting every effort of bystanders to control her...[20]

Finally the fit subsided; the patient, exhausted and sore, fell into a restful sleep.

During the first half of the nineteenth century physicians described hysteria principally though not exclusively in terms of such episodes. Symptoms such as paralysis and contracture were believed to be caused by seizures and categorized as infraseizure symptoms. Beginning in mid-century, however, physicians became increasingly flexible in their diagnosis of hysteria and gradually the fit declined in significance as a pathognomonic symptom.[21] Dr. Robert Carter, a widely-read British authority on hysteria, insisted in 1852 that at least one hysterical seizure must have occurred to justify a diagnosis of hysteria. But, he admitted, this seizure might be so minor as to have escaped the notice even of the patient herself; no subsequent seizures were necessary.[22] This was clearly a transitional position. By the last third of the nineteenth century the seizure was no longer the central phenomenon defining hysteria; physicians had categorized hysterical symptoms which included virtually every known human ill. They ranged from loss of sensation in part, half, or all of the body, loss of taste, smell, hearing, or vision, numbness of the skin, inability to swallow, nausea, headaches, pain in the breast, knees, hip, spine, or neck, as well as contracture or paralysis of virtually any extremity.[23]

Hysterical symptoms were not limited to the physical. An hysterical female character gradually began to emerge in the nineteenth-century medical literature, one based on interpretations of mood and personality rather than on discrete physical symptoms—one which grew closely to resemble twentieth-century definitions of the "hysterical personality." Doctors commonly described hysterical women as highly impressionistic, suggestible, and narcissistic. Highly labile, their moods changed suddenly, dramatically, and for seemingly inconsequential reasons. Doctors complained that the hysterical woman was egocentric in the extreme, her involvement with others consistently superficial and tangential. While the hysterical woman might appear to physicians and relatives as quite sexually aroused or attractive, she was, doctors cautioned, essentially asexual and not uncommonly frigid.[24]

Depression also appears as a common theme. Hysterical symptoms frequently followed a death in the family, a miscarriage, some financial setback which forced the patient to become self-supporting; or they were seen by the patient as related to some long-term, unsatisfying life situation—a tired school teacher, a mother unable to cope with the demands of a large family.[25] Most of these women took to their beds because of pain, paralysis or general weakness. Some remained there for years.

The medical profession's response to the hysterical woman was at best ambivalent. Many doctors—and indeed a significant proportion of society at large—tended to be caustic, if not punitive towards the hysterical woman. This resentment seems rooted in two factors: first, the baffling and elusive nature of hysteria itself, and second, the relation which existed in the physicians' minds between their categorizing of hysteria as a disease and the role women were expected to play in society. These patients did not function as women were expected to function, and, as we shall see, the physician who treated them felt threatened both as a professional and as a rejected male. He was the therapist thwarted, the child untended, the husband denied nurturance and sex.

During the second half of the nineteenth century, the newly established germ theory and discoveries by neurologists and anatomists for the first time made an insistence on disease specificity a *sine qua non* for scientific respectability. Neurology was just becoming accepted as a speciality, and in its search for acceptance it was particularly dependent on the establishment of firm, somatically-based disease entities.[26] If hysteria *was* a disease, and not the imposition of self-pitying women striving to avoid their traditional roles and responsibilities—as was frequently charged, it must be a disease with a specific etiology and a predictable course. In the period 1870 to 1900, especially, it was felt to be a disease rooted in some specific organic malfunction.

Hysteria, of course, lacked all such disease characteristics. Contracture or paralysis could occur without muscular atrophy or change in skin temperature. The hysteric might mimic tuberculosis, heart attacks, blindness, or hip disease, while lungs, heart, eyes, and hips remained in perfect health.[27] The physician had only his patient's statement that she could not move or was wracked with pain. If concerned and sympathetic, he faced a puzzling dilemma. As George Preston wrote in his 1897 monograph on hysteria:

In studying the . . . disturbances of hysteria, a very formidable difficulty presents itself in the fact that the symptoms are purely subjective. . . . There is only the bald

statement of the patient.... No confirming symptoms present themselves... and
the appearance of the affected parts stands as contradictory evidence against the
patient's word.[28]

Equally frustrating and medically inexplicable were the sudden changes in
the hysteric's symptoms. Paralysis or anaesthesia could shift from one side of
the body to the other, from one limb to another. Headaches would replace
contracture of a limb, loss of voice, the inability to taste. How could a
physician prescribe for such ephemeral symptoms? "Few practitioners desire
the management of hysterics," one eminent gynecologist, Samuel Ashwell,
wrote in 1833. "Its symptoms are so varied and obscure, so contradictory and
changeable, and if by chance several of them, or even a single one be relieved,
numerous others almost immediately spring into existence."[29] Half a century
later, neurologist Charles K. Mills echoed Ashwell's discouraging evaluation.
"Hysteria is pre-eminently a chronic disease," he warned. "Deceptive remis-
sions in hysterical symptoms often mislead the unwary practitioner. Cures
are sometimes claimed where simply a change in the character of the
phenomena has taken place. It is a disease in which it is unsafe to claim a
conquest."[30]

Yet physicians, especially newly established neurologists with urban practices, were besieged by patients who appeared to be sincere, respectable
women sorely afflicted with pain, paralysis, or uncontrollable "nervous fits."
"Looking at the pain evoked by ideas and beliefs," S. Weir Mitchell, America's leading expert on hysteria wrote in 1885, "we are hardly wise to stamp
these pains as non-existent."[31] Despite the tendency of many physicians to
dismiss the hysterical patient contemptuously when no organic lesions could
be found, neurologists such as Mitchell, George M. Beard, or Charles L.
Dana sympathized with these patients and sought to alleviate their symptoms.

Such pioneer specialists were therefore in the position of having defined
hysteria as a legitimate disease entity, and the hysterical woman as sick,
when they were painfully aware that no organic etiology had yet been found.
Cautiously, they sought to define hysteria formally in terms appropriately
mechanistic. Some late-nineteenth-century physicians, for example, still
placing a traditional emphasis on hysteria's uterine origins, argued that hysteria resulted from "the reflex effects of utero-ovarian irritation."[32] Others,
reflecting George M. Beard's work on neurasthenia, defined hysteria as a
functional disease caused either by "metabolic or nutritional changes in the
cellular elements of the central nervous system." Still others wrote in terms
of a malfunction of the cerebral cortex.[33] All such explanations were but
hypothetical gropings for an organic explanation—still a necessity if they
were to legitimate hysteria as a disease.[34]

The fear that hysteria might after all be only a functional or "ideational"
disease—to use a nineteenth-century term—and therefore not really a disease

at all, underlies much of the writing on hysteria as well as the physicians' own attitudes toward their patients. These hysterical women might after all be only clever frauds and sensation-seekers—morally delinquent and, for the physician, professionally embarrassing.

Not surprisingly, a compensatory sense of superiority and hostility permeated many physicians' discussions of the nature and etiology of hysteria. Except when called upon to provide a hypothetical organic etiology, physicians saw hysteria as caused either by the indolent, vapid, and unconstructive life of the fashionable middle- and upper-class woman, or by the ignorant, exhausting, and sensual life of the lower- or working-class woman. Neither were flattering etiologies. Both denied the hysteric the sympathy granted to sufferers from unquestionably organic ailments.

Any general description of the personal characteristics of the well-to-do hysteric emphasized her idleness, self-indulgence, her deceitfulness and "craving for sympathy." Petted and spoiled by her parents, waited upon hand and foot by servants, she had never been taught to exercise self-control or to curb her emotions and desires.[35] Certainly she had not been trained to undertake the arduous and necessary duties of wife and mother. "Young persons who have been raised in luxury and too often in idleness," one late-nineteenth-century physician lectured, "who have never been called upon to face the hardships of life, who have never accustomed themselves to self-denial, who have abundant time and opportunity to cultivate the emotional and sensuous, to indulge the sentimental side of life, whose life purpose is too often an indefinite and self-indulgent idea of pleasure, these are the most frequent victims of hysteria."[36] Sound education, outside interests such as charity and good works, moral training, systematic outdoor exercise, and removal from an overly sympathetic family were among the most frequent forms of treatment recommended. Mothers, consistently enough, were urged to bring up daughters with a strong sense of self-discipline, devotion to family needs, and a dread of uncontrolled emotionality.[37]

Emotional indulgence, moral weakness, and lack of willpower characterized the hysteric in both lay and medical thought. Hysteria, S. Weir Mitchell warned, occurred in women who had never developed habitual restraint and "rational endurance"—who had early lost their power of "self rule."[38] "The mind and body are deteriorated by the force of evil habit," Charles Lockwood wrote in 1895, "morbid thought and morbid impulse run through the poor, weak, unresisting brain, until all mental control is lost, and the poor sufferer is . . . at the mercy of . . . evil and unrestrained passions, appetites and morbid thoughts and impulses."[39]

In an age when will, control, and hard work were fundamental social values, this hypothetical etiology necessarily implied a negative evaluation of those who succumbed to hysteria. Such women were described as weak, capricious and, perhaps most important, morbidly suggestible.[40] Their intellectual abilities were meager, their powers of concentration eroded by years of self-indulgence and narcissistic introspection.[41] Hysterical women were, in effect, children, and ill-behaved, difficult children at that. "They have in fact," Roger Carter wrote, "all the instability of childhood, joined to the vices and passions of adult age....[42]

Many nineteenth-century critics felt that this emotional regression and instability was rooted in woman's very nature. The female nervous system, doctors argued, was physiologically more sensitive and thus more difficult to subject to the will. Some physicians assumed as well that woman's blood was "thinner" than man's, causing nutritional inadequacies in the central nervous system and an inability to store nervous energy—a weakness, Marty Putnam Jacobi stressed, women shared with children. Most commonly, a woman's emotional states generally, and hysteria in particular, were believed to have the closest ties to her reproductive cycle.[43] Hysteria commenced with puberty and ended with menopause, while ailments as varied as menstrual pain and irregularity, prolapsed or tipped uterus, uterine tumor, vaginal infections and discharges, sterility, could all—doctors were certain—cause hysteria. Indeed, the first question routinely asked hysterical women was "are your courses regular?"[44] Thus a woman's very physiology and anatomy predisposed her to hysteria; it was, as Thomas Laycock put it, "the natural state" in a female, a "morbid state" in the male.[45] In an era when a sexual perspective implied conflict and ambivalence, hysteria was perceived by physician and patient as a disease both peculiarly female and peculiarly sexual.

Hysteria could also result from a secret and less forgivable form of sexuality. Throughout the nineteenth century, physicians believed that masturbation was widespread among America's females and a frequent cause of hysteria and insanity. As early as 1846, E. H. Dixon reported that masturbation caused hysteria "among females even in society where physical and intellectual culture would seem to present the strongest barriers against its incursions...." Other physicians concurred, reporting that harsh public and medical reactions to hysterical women were often based on the belief that masturbation was the cause of their behavior.[46]

Masturbation was only one form of sexual indulgence. A number of doctors saw hysteria among lower-class women as originating in the sensuality believed to characterize their class. Such tenement-dwelling females, doctors reported, "gave free reign to... 'passions of the baser sort,' not feeling the necessity of self-control because they have to a pitiably small degree any sense of propriety or decency." Hysteria, another physician reported, was found commonly among prostitutes, while virtually all physicians agreed that even within marriage sexual excess could easily lead to hysteria.[47]

Expectedly, conscious anger and hostility marked the response of a good many doctors to their hysterical patients. One New York neurologist called the female hysteric a willful, self-indulgent and narcissistic person who cynically manipulated her symptoms. "To her distorted vision," he complained, "there is but one commanding personage in the universe—herself—in comparison with whom the rest of mankind are nothing." Doctors admitted that they were frequently tempted to use such terms as "willful" and "evil," "angry" and "impatient" when describing the hysteric and her symptoms.[48] Even the concerned and genteel S. Weir Mitchell, confident of his remarkable record in curing hysteria, described hysterical women as "the pests of many households, who constitute the despair of physicians, and who furnish those annoying examples of despotic selfishness, which wreck the constitutions of nurses and devoted relatives, and in unconscious or half-conscious self-indulgence destroy the comfort of everyone about them." He concluded by quoting Oliver Wendell Holmes' acid judgment that "a hysterical girl is a vampire who sucks the blood of the healthy people about her."[49]

Hysteria as a chronic, dramatic and socially accepted sick role could thus provide some alleviation of conflict and tension, but the hysteric purchased her escape from the emotional—and frequently—from the sexual demands of her life only at the cost of pain, disability, and an intensification of woman's traditional passivity and dependence. Indeed a complex interplay existed between the character traits assigned women in Victorian society and the characteristic symptoms of the nineteenth-century hysteric: dependency, fragility, emotionality, narcissism. Hysteria, after all, has been called in that century and this a stark caricature of femininity. Not surprisingly the hysteric's peculiar passive aggression and her exploitive dependency often functioned to cue a corresponding hostility in the men who cared for her or lived with her. Whether father, husband, or physician, they reacted with ambivalence and in many cases with hostility to her aggressive and never-ending demands.

II

What inferences concerning woman's role and female-male relationships can be drawn from this description of nineteenth-century hysteria and of medical attitudes toward the female patient? What insights does it allow into patterns of stress and resolution within the traditional nuclear family?

Because traditional medical wisdom had defined hysteria as a disease, its victims could expect to be treated as sick and thus to elicit a particular set of responses—the right to be seen and treated by a physician, to stay in bed and thus be relieved of their normal day-to-day responsibilities, to enjoy the special prerogatives, indulgences, and sympathy the sick role entailed. Hysteria thus became one way in which conventional women could express—in most cases unconsciously—dissatisfaction with one or several aspects of their lives.

The effect of hysteria upon the family and traditional sex role differentiation was disruptive in the extreme. The hysterical woman virtually ceased to function within the family. No longer did she devote herself to the needs of others, acting as self-sacrificing wife, mother, or daughter. Through her hysteria she could and in fact did force others to assume those functions. Household activities were reoriented to answer the hysterical woman's importunate needs. Children were hushed, rooms darkened, entertaining suspended, a devoted nurse recruited. Fortunes might be spent on medical bills or for drugs and operations. Worry and concern bowed the husband's shoulders; his home had suddenly become a hospital and he a nurse. Through her illness, the bedridden woman came to dominate her family to an extent that would have been considered inappropriate—indeed shrewish—in a healthy woman. Taking to one's bed, especially when suffering from dramatic and ever-visible symptoms, might also have functioned as a mode of passive aggression, especially in a milieu in which weakness was rewarded and in which women had since childhood been taught not to express overt aggression. Consciously or unconsciously, she had thus opted out of her traditional role.

Women did not accomplish this redefinition of domestic roles without the aid of the men in their family. Doctors commented that the hysteric's husband and family often, and unfortunately, rewarded her symptoms with elaborate sympathy. "The hysteric's credit is usually first established," as one astute mid-century clinician pointed out, "by those who have, at least, the wish to believe them."[50] Husbands and fathers were not alone in their cooperation; the physician often played a complex and in a sense emotionally compromising role in legitimizing the female hysteric's behavior. As an impartial and professionally skilled observer, he was empowered to judge whether or not a particular woman had the right to withdraw from her socially allotted duties. At the same time, these physicians accepted as correct, indeed as biologically inevitable, the structure of the Victorian family and the division of sex roles within it. He excused the woman only in the belief that she was ill and that she would make every effort to get well and resume her accustomed role. It was the transitory and unavoidable nature of the sick role that made it acceptable to family and physician as an alternate mode of female behavior.[51]

The doctor's ambivalence toward the hysterical woman, already rooted as we have seen in professional and sexual uncertainties, may well have been reinforced by his complicitory role within the family. It was for this reason that the disease's erratic pattern, its chronic nature, its lack of a determinable organic etiology, and the patient's seeming failure of will, so angered him. Even if she were not a conscious malingerer, she might well be guilty of self-indulgence and moral delinquency. By diagnosing her as ill, he had in effect created or permitted the hysterical woman to create a bond between himself and her. Within the family configuration he had sided with her against her husband or other male family members—men with whom he would normally have identified.[52]

The quintessential sexual nature of hysteria further complicated the doctor's professional stance. As we have already seen, the hysterical patient in her role as woman may well have mobilized whatever ambivalence towards sex a particular physician felt. In a number of cases, moreover, the physician also played the role of oedipal father figure to the patient's child-woman role, and in such instances his complicity was not only moral and intellectual but sexual as well. These doctors had become part of a domestic triangle—a husband's rival, the fatherly attendant of a daughter. This intra-family role may therefore go far to explain the particularly strident and suspicious tone which characterized much of the clinical discussion of hysteria. The physician, by his alertness to deception and self-indulgence and by his therapeutic skills, had to prevent the hysterical woman from using her disease to avoid her feminine duties—and from making him an unwitting accomplice in her deviant role. While tied to her as physician and thus legitimizer of her sick role, he also had to preserve his independence.

Although much of this interpretation must remain speculative, both the tone and substance of contemporary medical reaction to the female hysteric tends to confirm these inferences. Physicians were concerned with—and condemned—the power which chronic illness such as hysteria gave a woman over her family. Many women, doctors noted with annoyance, enjoyed this power and showed no inclination to get well: it is hardly coincidental that most late-nineteenth-century authorities agreed that removal from her family was a necessary first step in attempting to cure the hysterical patient.[53]

Not only did the physician condemn the hysteric's power within her family, he was clearly sensitive to her as a threat to his own prestige and authority. It is evident from their writings that many doctors felt themselves to be locked in a power struggle with their hysterical patients. Such women, doctors claimed, used their symptoms as weapons in asserting autonomy in relation to their physician; in continued illness was their victory. Physicians perceived hysterical women as unusually intractable and self-assertive. Although patients and women, they reserved the right to judge and approve their male physician's every action. Indeed, much of the medical literature on hysteria is devoted to providing doctors with the means of winning this war of wills. Physicians felt that they must dominate the hysteric's will; only in this way, they wrote, could they bring about her permanent cure. "Do not flatter yourselves . . . that you will gain an easy victory," Dr. L. C. Grey told a medical school class in 1888:

On the contrary, you must expect to have your temper, your ingenuity, your nerves tested to a degree that cannot be surpassed even by the greatest surgical operations. I maintain that the man who has the nerve and the tact to conquer some of these grave cases of hysteria has the nerve and the tact that will make him equal to the great emergencies of life. Your patient must be taught day by day . . . by steady resolute, iron-willed determination and tact—that combination which the French . . . call "the iron hand beneath the velvet glove."[54]

"Assume a tone of authority which will of itself almost compel submission," Robert Carter directed. "If a patient . . . interrupts the speaker, she must be told to keep silence and to listen; and must be told, moreover, not only in a voice that betrays no impatience and no anger, but in such a manner as to convey the speaker's full conviction that the command will be immediately obeyed."[55]

Much of the treatment prescribed by physicians for hysteria reflects, in its draconic severity, their need to exert control—and, when thwarted, their impulse to punish. Doctors frequently recommended suffocating hysterical women until their fits stopped, beating them across the face and body with wet towels, ridiculing and exposing them in front of family and friends, showering them with icy water. "The mode adopted to arrest this curious malady," a physician connected with a large mental hospital wrote,

consists in making some strong and sudden impression on the mind through... the most potent of all impressions, fear.... Ridicule to a woman of sensitive mind, is a powerful weapon... but there is no emotion equal to fear and the threat of personal chastisement... They will listen to the voice of authority.[56]

When, on the other hand, the hysterical patient proved tractable, gave up her fits or paralyses and accepted the physician as saviour and moral guide, he no longer had to appear in the posture of chastising father. He could respond to his hysterical patient with fondness, sympathy, and praise. No longer was she thwarting him with "temper, tears, ticks, and tantrums"—as one doctor chose to title a study of hysteria.[57] Her cure demonstrated that he had mastered her will and body. The successful father-like practitioner had restored another wayward woman to her familial duties. Thomas Addis Emmett, pioneer gynecological specialist, recalled with ingenuous candor his mode of treating hysterics:

the patient... was a child in my hands. In some respects the power gained was not unlike that obtained over a wild beast except that in one case the domination would be due to fear, while with my patient as a rule, it would be the desire to please me and to merit my approval from the effort she would make to gain her self-control. I have at times been depressed with the responsibility attending the blind influence I have often been able to gain over the nervous women under my influence.[58]

Nor surprisingly, S. Weir Mitchell ended one of his treatises on hysteria with the comment that doctors, who knew and understood all women's petty weaknesses, who could govern and forgive them, made the best husbands.[59] Clearly the male physician who treated the hysterical woman was unable to escape the sex role relations that existed within nineteenth-century society generally.

III

The hysterical female emerges from the essentially male medical literature of the nineteenth century as a "child-woman," highly impressionable, labile, superficially sexual, exhibitionistic, given to dramatic body language and grand gestures, with strong dependency needs, a masochistic or self-punishing behavior pattern, and decided ego weaknesses. She resembles in many ways the hysterical personality described in the 1968 *Diagnostic and Statistical Manual of Mental Disorders* of the American Psychiatric Association: a personality characterized, that is, by "excitablity, emotional instability, over-reactivity, self-dramatization, attention seeking, immaturity, vanity, and unusual dependence." Her symptoms correspond closely to those Otto Kernberg describes as an "infantile personality" or Samuel B. Guze as a "hysterical personality."[60] Thus we find the child-woman a person who, filled with self-doubt, constantly needs the reassurance and attention of others. In fact, these characteristics are merely hypertrophied versions of traits and behavior routinely reinforced throughout the nineteenth century in girls, female adolescents, and adult women.

In attempting to understand hysteria, then, it might be best not only to look at stress and dysfunction within the hysteric's particular psychic background but also to examine the correspondence between this personality pattern and the literature to which a young woman was exposed. This method means discussing normative cultural values or prescription rather than actual behavior. Yet what women were supposed to do and be provides the historian with a valuable source. Prescriptive values—almost universally accepted in a culture and actively fostered by its authority figures—undoubtedly influence the child-rearing practices of mothers and the behavior of children, especially during the early years of life when gender identity is formed. From this perspective, then, the historian is justified in exploring the possible ways in which female gender role socialization affected the development of ego strengths and weaknesses in nineteenth-century women.

At a time when American society accepted egalitarian democracy and free will as transcendent social values, women were routinely socialized to fill a weak, dependent, and severely limited social role. There is evidence from children's books, child-rearing manuals, marriage guides, and books of etiquette that women were sharply discouraged from expressing competition or mastery in such "masculine" areas as physical skill, strength, and courage, or in academic, scientific, or commercial pursuits. Instead they were encouraged to be coquettish, entertaining, nonthreatening, and nurturant. Overt anger and violence were forbidden as unfeminine and vulgar. Women were not rewarded for curiosity, intrusiveness, or exploratory behavior. Indeed when such characteristics conflicted with the higher feminine values of cleanliness, proper deportment, unobtrusiveness, and obedience, women were criticized or punished—yet these same habits of mind are now deemed essential to the development of autonomy and identity in children. Most children's literature asserted that boys were brave, active, lively. Girls, on the other hand, were taught that their greatest happiness lay in an unselfish routine of caring for the needs of others.[61]

Nineteenth-century American society provided but one socially respectable, nondeviant role for women—that of loving wife and mother. Thus women, who presumably came in assorted psychological and intellectual shapes and sizes, had to find adjustment in only one prescribed social role— one that demanded continual self-abnegation and a desire to please others. Children's literature and genteel women's magazines in every case required of women an altruistic denial of their own ambition and a displacement of their wishes and abilities onto the men in their lives. We may assume that for a certain percentage of women such sacrifice led to a form of what Anna Freud and Edward Bibring defined as "altruistic surrender."[62] In other cases training to fit a narrowly defined role must have resulted in significant ego restriction—the ego choosing not to develop in certain directions because the pain of punishment or of being defined as deviant was too costly. "When the ego is young and Plastic," Anna Freud wrote,

its withdrawal from one field of activity is sometimes compensated for by excellence in another, upon which it concentrates. But, when it has become rigid or has already acquired an intolerance of "pain" and so is obsessionally fixated to the method of flight, such withdrawal is punished by impaired development. By abandoning one position after another it becomes onesided, loses too many interests and can show but a meagre achievement.[63]

Significant differences appear to lie as well in the ways in which boys and girls were punished in the nineteenth century. It is true that disciplinary patterns were changing then, and that corporal punishment seems to have decreased in frequency for boys as well as girls. Nevertheless, sociological studies offer evidence that even until fairly recently boys received far more physical punishment than did girls, who commonly were punished by being made to feel guilty and by being threatened with withdrawal of love or actually being separated from parents. Social psychologists and sociologists such as Uri Brofenbrenner and Judith Bardwick have argued that while such "love-oriented punishment" produced obedient and docile children, it also made children timid, anxious, dependent, and sensitive to rejection.[64] Other psychologists have recently argued that love-oriented punishment and girls' more socialized behavior in early childhood tend to delay their forming an independent identity until late adolescence—if then—and lead them to be overly dependent upon the approval and support of significant others in their lives.[65] To put it differently, women in nineteenth-century society necessarily restricted their ego functions to low-prestige areas, remaining dependent on others and altruistically wishing worldly success not for themselves but for their husbands, fathers, or brothers. The effect of this socialization may well have been to impede ego development significantly in many women and—if there is an aggressive drive in the id—to repress it. The behavioral result appears to have been to limit opportunities for conflict-free ego growth, or to neglect that form of ego development.

Thus one finds suggestive parallels between the "hysterical" woman of the

nineteenth century and the "masochistic" female personality that Karen
Horney described in *New Ways to Psychoanalysis* (1949). The masochistic woman, argued Horney, suffered from "free floating anxiety," a deep-rooted
sense of inferiority, and an absence of adequate aggression, by which Horney
meant the ability to take initiative, to make efforts, to carry things through to
completion, and to form and express autonomous views. Insecure, afflicted
with anxieties, she demanded constant attention and expressions of affection,
which she sought to secure by appealing to pity and displaying inferiority
feelings, weakness, and suffering. Such a self-image and pattern of object
relations necessarily "generated hostile feelings, but feelings which the
masochistic woman was unable to express directly because they would have
jeopardized her dependency relationships." Weakness and suffering, Horney
continued, "already serving many functions, now also act as a vehicle for the
indirect expression of hostility." While both men and women develop
masochistic personalities, Horney hypothesized that far larger numbers of
women than men would do so in cultures in which women more than men (1)
"manifest[ed]... inhibitions in the direct expression of demands and aggres-
sions; (2) regard[ed]... themselves as weak, helpless, or inferior and implicitly or explicitly demand[ed] considerations and advantages on this basis;
(3) [became] emotionally dependent on the other sex; (4) show[ed]... tendencies to be self-sacrificing, to be submissive, to feel used or to be exploited, to
put responsibilities on the other sex; (5) us[ed]... weakness and helplessness
as a means of wooing and subduing the other sex."[66]

In short, many nineteenth-century women reached maturity with major
ego weaknesses and narrowly limited compensatory ego strengths, all of
which implies a relationship between this pattern of socialization and one's
adoption of hysterical behavior. The reasons why each individual displayed
the pattern of behavior that nineteenth-century physicians called "hysteria"
must remain moot. It seems plausible to suggest that a certain percentage of
nineteenth-century women, faced with stress developing out of their own
peculiar personality needs or out of situational anxieties, might well have
defended themselves against such stress by regressing towards the childish
hyperfemininity of the hysteric. The discontinuity between the roles of
courted young woman and pain-bearing, self-sacrificing wife and mother, the
realities of an unhappy marriage, the loneliness and chagrin of spinsterhood
may all have made the petulant infantilism and narcissistic self-assertion of
the hysteric a necessary alternative to women who felt unfairly deprived of
their promised social role and who had few strengths with which to adapt to a
more trying one. Society had indeed structured this regression by consistently reinforcing those very emotional traits characterized in the stereotype
of the female and caricatured in the symptomatology of the hysteric. At the
same time, the nineteenth-century female hysteric also exhibited a significant
level of hostility and aggression-rage—which may have led in turn to her
depression and to her self-punishing psychosomatic illnesses. In all these

ways, then, the hysterical woman was both product and indictment of her culture. This paper has sought to suggest why certain symptoms were available and why women, in particular, tended to resort to them. It has sought as well to use the reactions of contemporaries to illuminate the realities of female-male and intrafamilial role. As such it has dealt with hysteria as a psychological role produced by and functional within a specific set of social circumstances.

Finally, there is a conceptual point that is important to make. Nothing is more tempting for the woman historian than to treat the Victorian physician as the spokesman, and hence the scapegoat, of his age. The chauvinistic comments of male medical doctors provoke the militant in us all. But we have no evidence that they were more arrogant in their attitude towards women than any other husband or father: Male physicians simply belonged to a group that made formal and in-depth comments on women and whose writings are readily available to us. Perhaps historians use this evidence to best advantage when we see the doctor not only as a man but as a practitioner—one who needed a framework of rationale and hypothesis within which to explain the health and disease of his patients as well as to conduct the doctor-patient relationship. The interaction of a male physician and a female patient can thus be seen—and used by the historian—as a cultural artifact: the physician stood at the junction where cultural definitions of femininity, the needs of his individual female patient, and masculinity met.

NOTES

1. For a review of the recent psychiatric literature on hysteria see Aaron Lazare, "The Hysterical Character in Psychoanalytic Theory: Evolution and Confusion," *Archives of General Psychiatry*, XXV (August, 1971), pp. 131-137; Barbara Ruth Easser and S. R. Lesser, "Hysterical Personality: A Reevaluation," *Psychoanalytic Quarterly*, XXXIV (1965), pp. 390-405, and Mare H. Hollander, "Hysterical Personality," *Comments on Contemporary Psychiatry*, I (1971), pp. 17-24.

2. Elizabeth Zetzel, *The Capacity for Emotional Growth. Theoretical and Clinical Contributions to Psychoanalysis, 1943-1969* (London: Hogarth Press, 1970), Chap. 1-f, "The So-Called Good Hysteric."

3. David Shapiro, *Neurotic Styles* (New York: Basic Books, 1965).

4. The argument can be made that hysteria exists among men and therefore is not exclusively related to the female experience; the question is a complex one, and I am presently at work on a parallel study of male hysteria. There are, however, four brief points concerning male hysteria that I would like to make. First, to this day hysteria is still believed to be principally a female "disease" or behavior pattern. Second, the male hysteric is usually seen by physicians as somehow different. Today it is a truism that hysteria in males is found most frequently among homosexuals; in the nineteenth century men diagnosed as hysterics came almost exclusively from a lower socio-economic status than their physicians—immigrants, especially "new immigrants," miners, railroad workers, blacks. Third, since it was defined by society as a female disease, one may hypothesize that there was some degree of female identification among the men who assumed a hysterical role. Lastly, we must recall that a most common form of male hysteria

was battle fatigue and shell shock. I should like to thank Erving Goffman for the suggestion that the soldier is in an analogous position to women regarding autonomy and power.

5. The word choose, even in quotes, is value-laden. I do not mean to imply that hysterical women consciously chose their behavior. I feel that three complex factors interacted to make hysteria a real behavioral option for American women: first, the various experiences that caused a woman to arrive at adulthood with significant ego weaknesses; second, certain socialization patterns and cultural values which made hysteria a readily available alternate behavior pattern for women, and third, the secondary gains conferred by the hysterical role in terms of enhanced power within the family. Individual cases presumably each represented their own peculiar balance of these factors, all of which will be discussed in this paper.

6. Nineteenth-century hysteria has attracted a good number of students: two of the most important are Henri F. Ellenberger, *The Discovery of the Unconscious* (New York: Basic Books, 1970), and Ilza Veith, *Hysteria: The History of a Disease* (Chicago: University of Chicago Press, 1965). Ellenberger and Veith approach hysteria largely from the framework of intellectual history. For a review of Veith see Charles E. Rosenberg, "Historical Sociology of Medical Thought," *Science*, CL (October 15, 1965), p. 330. For two studies which view nineteenth-century hysteria from a more sociological perspective see Esther Fischer-Homberger, "Hysterie und Misogynie: Ein Aspekt der Hysteriegeschichte," *Gesnerus*, XXVI (1969), pp. 117–127, and Marc H. Hollander, "Conversion Hysteria: A Post-Freudian Reinterpretation of Nineteenth-Century Psychosocial Data," *Archives of General Psychiatry*, XXVI (1972), pp. 311–314.

7. I would like to thank Renée Fox, Cornelia Friedman, Erving Goffman, Charles E. Rosenberg, and Paul Rosenkrantz for having read and criticized this paper. I would also like to thank my clinical colleagues Philip Mechanick, Henry Bachrach, Ellen Berman, and Carol Wolman of the Psychiatry Department of the University of Pennsylvania for similar assistance. Versions of this paper were presented to the Institute of the Pennsylvania Hospital, the Berkshire Historical Society, and initially, in October 1971, at the Psychiatry Department of Hannehmann Medical College, Philadelphia.

8. This summary of woman's role and role socialization is drawn from a larger study of male and female gender roles and gender role socialization in the United States from 1785 to 1895 on which I am presently engaged. This research has been supported by both the Grant Foundation, New York City and the National Institute of Child Health and Human Development, N.I.H. It is difficult to refer succinctly to the wide range of sources on which this paragraph is based. Such a role model appears in virtually every nineteenth-century woman's magazine, in countless guides to young women and young wives and in etiquette books. For a basic secondary source see Barbara Welter, "The Cult of True Womanhood," *American Quarterly*, XVIII (1966), pp. 151–174. For an excellent over-all history of women in America see Eleanor Flexner, *Century of Struggle* (Cambridge, Mass.: Harvard University Press, 1959).

9. For the daily activities of a nineteenth-century American housewife see, for example, *The Maternal Physician: By an American Matron* (New York: Isaac Riley, 1811. Reprinted New York: Arno Press, 1972); Hugh Smith, *Letters to Married Ladies* (New York: Bliss, White and G. & C. Carvill, 1827); John S. C. Abbott, *The Mother at Home* (Boston: Crocker and Brewster, 1833); Lydia H. Sigourney, *Letters to Mothers* (New York: Harper & Brothers, 1841); Mrs. C. A. Hopkinson, *Hints for the Nursery or the Young Mother's Guide* (Boston: Little, Brown & Company, 1836); Catherine Beecher and Harriet Beecher Stowe, *The American Woman's Home* (New York: J. B. Ford & Company, 1869). For an excellent secondary account of the southern woman's domestic life see Anne Firor Scott, *The Southern Lady* (Chicago: University of Chicago Press, 1970).

10. Nineteenth-century domestic medicine books, gynecological textbooks, and monographs on the diseases of women provide a detailed picture of women's diseases and health expectations.

11. S. Weir Mitchell, *Doctor and Patient* (Philadelphia: J. B. Lippincott Company, 1887), pp. 84, 92.

12. See among others Edward H. Dixon, *Woman and Her Diseases* (New York: Charles H. Ring, 1846), pp. 135–136; Alice Stockham, *Tokology: A Book for Every Woman* (Chicago: Sanitary

Publishers, 1887), p. 83; Sarah A. Stevenson, *Physiology of Women*, 2nd edn. (Chicago: Cushing, Thomas & Co., 1881), p. 91; Henry Pye Chavasse, *Advice to a Wife and Counsel to a Mother* (Philadelphia: J. B. Lippincott, 1891), p. 97. A Missouri physician reported the case of a twenty-eight-year-old middle-class woman with two children. Shortly after the birth of her second child, she missed her period, believed herself to be pregnant for a third time and succumbed to hysterical symptoms: depression, headaches, vomiting, and seizures. Her doctor concluded that she had uterine disease, exacerbated by pregnancy. He aborted her and reported a full recovery the following day. George J. Engelmann, "A Hystero-Psychosis Epilepsy Dependent upon Erosions of the Cervix Uteri," *St. Louis Clinic Record* (1878), pp. 321–324. For similar cases, see A. B. Arnold, "Hystero-Hypochondriasis," *Pacific Medical Journal*, XXXIII (1890), pp. 321–324, and George J. Engelmann, "Hystero-neurosis," *Transactions of the American Gynecological Association*, II (1877), pp. 513–518.

13. For a study of declining nineteenth-century American birth rates see Yasukichi Yasuba, *Birth Rates of the White Population in the United States, 1800–1860* (Baltimore: The Johns Hopkins University Press, 1962) and J. Potter, "American Population in the Early National Period," in *Proceedings of Section V of the Fourth Congress of the International Economic History Association*, Paul Deprez, ed., (Winnipeg, 1970), pp. 55–69.

14. For a useful general discussion of women's changing roles see Eleanor Flexner, *op. cit.*

15. For a discussion of birth control and its effect on domestic relations see Carroll Smith-Rosenberg and Charles E. Rosenberg, "The Female Animal: Medical and Biological Views of Woman and Her Role in Nineteenth-Century America," *Journal of American History*, LX (September, 1973), pp. 332–56.

16. William A. Hammond, *On Certain Conditions of Nervous Derangement* (New York: G. P. Putnam's Sons, 1881), p. 42; S. Weir Mitchell, *Lectures on the Diseases of the Nervous System, Especially in Women*, 2nd edn. (Philadelphia: Lea Brothers & Co., 1885), pp. 114, 110; Charles K. Mills, "Hysteria," in *A System of Practical Medicine by American Authors*, William Pepper, ed., assisted by Louis Starr, vol. V, "Diseases of the Nervous System" (Philadelphia: Lea Brothers & Co., 1883), p. 213; Charles E. Lockwood, "A Study of Hysteria and Hypochondriasis," *Transactions of the New York State Medical Association*, XII (1895), pp. 340–351. E. H. Van Deusen, Superintendent of the Michigan Asylum for the Insane, reported that nervousness, hysteria, and neurasthenia were common among farm women and resulted, he felt, from the social and intellectual deprivation of their isolated lives. Van Deusen, "Observations on a Form of Nervous Prostration," *American Journal of Insanity*, XXV (1869), p. 447. Significantly most English and American authorities on hysteria were members of a medical elite who saw the wealthy in their private practices and the very poor in their hospital and dispensary work. Thus the observation that hysteria occurred in different social classes was often made by the very same clinicians.

17. Thomas Sydenham, "Epistolary Dissertation," in *The Works of Thomas Sydenham, M.D. . . . with a Life of the Author*, R. G. Lathan, ed., 2 vols. (London: New Sydenham Society, 1850), II, p. 85.

18. Some women diagnosed as hysterics displayed quite bizarre behavior—including self-mutilation and hallucinations. Clearly a certain percentage of these women would be diagnosed today as schizophrenic. The majority of the women diagnosed as hysterical, however, did not display such symptoms, but rather appear from clinical descriptions to have had a personality similar to that considered hysterical by mid-twentieth-century psychiatrists.

19. For three typical descriptions of such seizures, see Buel Eastman, *Practical Treatise on Diseases Peculiar to Women and Girls* (Cincinnati: C. Cropper & Son, 1848), p. 40; Samuel Ashwell, *A Practical Treatise on the Diseases Peculiar to Women* (London: Samuel Highley, 1844), pp. 210–212; William Campbell, *Introduction to the Study and Practice of Midwifery and the Diseases of Children* (London: Longman, Rees, Orme, Brown, Green & Longman, 1833), pp. 440–442.

20. E. H. Dixon, *op. cit.*, p. 133.

21. For examples of mid-nineteenth-century hysterical symptoms see Colombat de L'Isère, *A Treatise on the Diseases and Special Hygiene of Females*, trans. with additions by Charles D. Meigs

(Philadelphia: Lea and Blanchard, 1845), pp. 522, 527–530; Gunning S. Bedford, *Clinical Lectures on the Diseases of Women and Children* (New York: Samuel S. & W. Wood, 1855), p. 373.

22. Robert B. Carter, *On the Pathology and Treatment of Hysteria* (London: John Churchill, 1853), p. 3.

23. See, for example, F. C. Skey, *Hysteria* (New York: A. Simpson, 1867), pp. 66, 71, 86; Mary Putnam Jacobi, "Hysterical Fever," *Journal of Nervous and Mental Disease*, XV (1890), pp. 373–388; Landon Carter Grey, "Neurasthenia: Its Differentiation and Treatment," *New York Medical Journal*, XLVIII (1888), p. 421.

24. See, for example, George Preston, *Hysteria and Certain Allied Conditions* (Philadelphia: P. Blakiston, Son & Co., 1897), pp. 31, 53; Charles E. Lockwood, *op. cit.* p. 346; Buel Eastman, *op. cit.*, p. 39; Thomas More Madden, *Clinical Gynecology* (Philadelphia: J. B. Lippincott, 1895), p. 472.

25. See W. Symington Brown, *A Clinical Handbook on the Diseases of Women* (New York: William Wood & Company, 1882); Charles L. Dana, "A Study of the Anaesthesias of Hysteria," *American Journal of the Medical Sciences* (October, 1890), p. 1; William S. Playfair, *The Systematic Treatment of Nerve Prostration and Hysteria* (Philadelphia: Henry C. Lea's Son & Co., 1883), p. 29.

26. For a discussion of the importance of creating such organic etiologies in the legitimization of an increasingly large number of such "functional" ills, see Charles E. Rosenberg, "The Place of George M. Beard in Nineteenth-Century Psychiatry," *Bulletin of the History of Medicine*, XXXVI (1962), pp. 245–259. See also Owsei Temkin's discussion in his classic history of epilepsy, *The Falling Sickness*, 2nd edn., rev. (Baltimore: The Johns Hopkins University Press, 1971), of the importance placed by neurologists in the late nineteenth century upon the differentiation of epilepsy and hysteria.

27. William Campbell, *op. cit.*, pp. 440–441; Walter Channing, *Bed Case: Its History and Treatment* (Boston: Ticknor and Fields, 1860), pp. 41–42, 49; Charles L. Mix, "Hysteria: Its Nature and Etiology," *New York Medical Journal*, LXXII (August, 1900), pp. 183–189.

28. George Preston, *op. cit.*, pp. 96–97.

29. Samuel Ashwell, *op. cit.*, p. 226.

30. Charles K. Mills, *op. cit.*, p. 258.

31. S. Weir Mitchell, *Lectures on the Diseases of the Nervous System*, *op. cit.*, p. 66.

32. Thomas More Madden, *op. cit.*, p. 474. The uterine origin of hysteria was by far the most commonly held opinion throughout the eighteenth and nineteenth centuries. Some believed it to be the exclusive cause, others to be among the most important causes. For three typical examples see: Alexander Hamilton, *A Treatise on the Management of Female Complaints and of Children in Early Infancy* (Edinburgh: Peter Hill, 1792), pp. 51–53. George J. Engelmann, "Hysteroneurosis," *op. cit.*, note 12; Augustus P. Clarke, "Relations of Hysteria to Structural Changes in the Uterus and its Adnexa," *American Journal of Obstetrics*, XXXIII (1894), pp. 477–483. The uterine theory came under increasing attack during the late nineteenth century. See Hugh J. Patrick, "Hysteria; Neurasthenia," *International Clinics*, III (1898), pp. 183–184; F. C. Skey, *op. cit.*, p. 68.

33. Robert Barnes, *Medical and Surgical Diseases of Women* (Philadelphia: H. C. Lea, 1874), p. 101; S. D. Hopkins, "A Case of Hysteria Simulating Organic Disease of the Brain," *Medical Fortnightly*, XI (July, 1897), p. 327; C. K. Mills, *op. cit.*, p. 218; J. Leonard Corning, *A Treatise on Hysteria and Epilepsy* (Detroit: George S. Davis, 1888), p. 2; August A. Eshner, "Hysteria in Early Life," read before the Philadelphia County Medical Society, June 23, 1897.

34. For examples of such concern and complexity, see A. A. King, "Hysteria," *The American Journal of Obstetrics*, XXIV (May, 1891), pp. 513–515; Marshall Hall, *Commentaries Principally on the Diseases of Females* (London: Sherwood, Gilbert and Piper, 1830), p. 118; C. L'Isère, *op. cit.*, p. 530.

35. Robert B. Carter, *op. cit.*, p. 140; J. L. Corning, *op. cit.*, p. 70; Mills, *op. cit.*, p. 218.

36. Preston, *op. cit.*, p. 36.

37. See, for example: Mitchell, *Lectures on the Diseases of the Nervous System*, p. 170; Rebecca B.

Gleason, M.D., of Elmira, New York, quoted by M. L. Holbrook, *Hygiene of the Brain and Nerves and the Cure of Nervousness* (New York: M. L. Holbrook & Company, 1878), pp. 270–271.

38. S. Weir Mitchell, *Fat and Blood* (Philadelphia: J. B. Lippincott, 1881), pp. 30–31.

39. Lockwood, *op. cit.*, pp. 342–343; virtually every authority on hysteria echoed these sentiments.

40. Alexander Hamilton, *op. cit.*, p. 52; Dixon, *op. cit.*, pp. 142–143; Ashwell, *op. cit.*, p. 217; Mills, *op. cit.*, p. 230.

41. Walter Channing, *op. cit.*, p. 28.

42. Robert B. Carter, *op. cit.*, p. 113.

43. Mary P. Jacobi, *op. cit.*, pp. 384–388; M. E. Dirix, *Woman's Complete Guide to Health* (New York: W. A. Townsend & Adams, 1869), p. 24; E. B. Foote, *Medical Common Sense* (New York: Published by the author, 1864), p. 167.

44. Reuben Ludlum, *Lectures, Clinical and Didactic, on the Diseases of Women* (Chicago: C. S. Halsey, 1872), p. 87; Robert Barnes, *op. cit.*, p. 247. In 1847, the well-known Philadelphia gynecologist Charles D. Meigs had asked his medical school class the rhetorical question: "What is her erotic state? What the protean manifestations of the life force developed by a reproductive irritation which you call hysteria." Meigs, *Lectures on the Distinctive Characteristics of the Female*, delivered before the Class of Jefferson Medical College, January 5, 1847 (Philadelphia: T. K. & P. G. Collins, 1847), p. 20.

45. Thomas Laycock, *Essay on Hysteria*, pp. 76, 103, 105. See also Graham J. Barker-Benfield, "The Horrors of the Half-Known Life" (unpublished Ph.D. thesis, University of California at Los Angeles, 1969) and Ann Douglas Wood, "The 'Fashionable Diseases': Women's Complaints and Their Treatment in Nineteenth Century America," *Journal of Interdisciplinary History*, IV (Summer, 1973), pp. 25–52, for a speculative psychoanalytic approach to gynecological practice in nineteenth-century America.

46. Dixon, *op. cit.*, p. 134; J. L. Corning, *op. cit.*, p. 70; William Murray, *A Treatise on Emotional Disorders of the Sympathetic System of the Nerves* (London: John Churchill, 1866). An extensive nineteenth-century masturbation literature exists. See, for example, Samuel Gregory, *Facts and Important Information for Young Women on the Self-Indulgence of the Sexual Appetite* (Boston: George Gregory, 1857), and Calvin Cutter, *The Female Guide: Containing Facts and Information upon the Effects of Masturbation* (West Brookfield, Mass.: Charles A. Mirick, 1844). Most general treatises on masturbation refer to its occurrence in females.

47. Preston, *op. cit.*, p. 37; Carter, *op. cit.*, pp. 46, 90. Nineteenth-century physicians maintained a delicate balance in their view of the sexual etiology of hysteria. Any deviation from moderation could cause hysteria or insanity: habitual masturbation, extended virginity, over-indulgence, prostitution, or sterility.

48. Skey, *op. cit.*, p. 63.

49. Mitchell, *Lectures on the Diseases of the Nervous System*, p. 266; S. Weir Mitchell, *Fat and Blood*, *op. cit.*, p. 37.

50. Carter, *op. cit.*, p. 58.

51. For an exposition of this argument see Erving Goffman, "Insanity of Place," *Psychiatry*, XXXII (1969), pp. 357–388.

52. Such complaints are commonplace in the medical literature. See Mitchell, *Lectures*, p. 67; Mitchell, *Doctor and Patient*, *op. cit.*, p. 117; Robert Thornton, *The Hysterical Women: Trials, Tears, Tricks and Tantrums* (Chicago: Donohue & Henneberry, 1893), pp. 97–98; Channing, *op. cit.*, pp. 35–37; L'Isère, *op. cit.*, p. 534.

53. The fact that the physician was at the same time employed and paid by the woman or her family—in a period when the profession was far more competitive and economically insecure than it is in mid-twentieth century—implied another level of stress and ambiguity.

54. Channing, *op. cit.*, p. 22; Thomas A. Emmett, *Principles and Practices of Gynecology* (Philadelphia: H. C. Lea, 1879), p. 107; L. C. Grey, "Clinical Lecture," p. 132.

55. Carter, *op. cit.*, p. 119; Ashwell, *op. cit.*, p. 227.

56. Skey, *op. cit.*, p. 60.

57. Robert Thornton, *op. cit.*

58. Thomas A. Emmett, *Incidents of My Life* (New York: G. P. Putnam's Sons, 1911), p. 210. These are Emmett's recollections at the end of a long life. It is interesting that decades earlier Emmett, in discussing treating hysterical women, had confessed in hostile frustration that "in fact the physician is helpless. . . ." Emmett, *Principles and Practices, op. cit.*, p. 107.

59. Mitchell, *Doctor and Patient*, pp. 99-100.

60. *Diagnostic and Statistical Manual of Mental Disorders*, 2d ed. (Washington, D.C.: American Psychiatric Association, 1968), p. 43. Otto Kernberg, "Borderline Personality Organization," *Journal of the American Psychoanalytical Association*, XV (July, 1967), pp. 641-85; Samuel B. Guze, "The Diagnosis of Hysteria: What are We Trying to Do?" *American Journal of Psychiatry*, CXXIV (October, 1967), pp. 491-98.

61. These conclusions are based on an analysis of American children's books, 1760-1890, that I am currently completing.

62. Anna Freud, *The Ego and the Mechanisms of Defense*. Revised ed. (New York: International Universities Press, 1966), pp. 122-37.

63. Ibid., pp. 102-3. See chapter 8 for Freud's discussion of ego restriction.

64. Judith Bardwick and Elizabeth Douvan, "Ambivalence: the Socialization of Women," in Vivian Gornick and Barbara K. Moran, eds., *Women in a Sexist Society* (New York: Basic Books, 1971).

65. Elizabeth Douvan, "Sex Differences in Adolescent Character Processes," *Merrill-Palmer Quarterly*, VI (1958), pp. 203-11.

66. Karen Horney, "The Problem of Female Masochism," in *Feminine Psychology* (New York: W. W. Norton and Co., 1967), pp. 214-33 and especially pp. 228-29.

10

THE USE AND ABUSE OF ILLNESS
IN THE JAMES FAMILY CIRCLE
A View of Neurasthenia as a Social Phenomenon

HOWARD M. FEINSTEIN

Smith-Rosenberg's article makes clear how firmly late-nineteenth-century Americans believed in strong family ties and in the doméstic sphere as the place for women. Another prominent cultural theme was the value of hard work and the self-discipline that it required. While conventional restrictions on women produced Smith-Rosenberg's middle- and upper-middle-class hysterics, the standard concern for work, Howard Feinstein argues on the basis of his research on the James family, led to a disability that more often afflicted men of the same social strata. Known then as invalidism—or as we now describe it, neurasthenia—this malady seems to have developed among members of those New England families whose formal manners made open conflict unthinkable and whose concern with striking a balance between work and play made for considerable anxiety. Feinstein's study of travel and exercise as therapies, and of therapeutic theory itself, sheds new light on the imperatives of the male role in Victorian society and the behavioral suggestions of romanticism. Like hysteria among women, invalidism also provided a socially acceptable excuse for idleness and vented hostility that otherwise was inexpressible.

All the same, one may well wonder about the pieces of the puzzle that do not seem to fit. Smith-Rosenberg argues that hysteria, deriving from repressed impulses, growing out of restricted roles, divided women from men more than it did women of different classes. Yet Victorian proscriptions against "improper" womanly sexuality apparently held no fear for the prostitutes she mentions, and they too suffered from hysterical symptoms. In like manner the search for meaningful work may have been a central difficulty revealed in invalidism, but surely men like William Dean Howells and Louis Agassiz—sufferers from neurasthenia—were involved in work that they found absorbing and engaging. One may also ask what it was that prevented the indomitable Mary James from becoming an hysteric of the sort Smith-Rosenberg writes about.

Reprinted, with slight revisions, from *The Psychohistory Review* 8 (Summer–Fall 1979):6–14, courtesy of the publishers.

IT IS STARTLING for a twentieth-century reader of the James family letters to discover how many of its members and friends suffered from "invalidism," or what the contemporary student of the illness, Dr. George Beard, first called neurasthenia.[1] William James was a semi-invalid from the time he was eighteen and a freshman at the Lawrence Scientific School at Harvard, in 1860, until he joined the faculty there as an instructor, thirteen years later. The illness recurred throughout his life. Intermittently his brothers Henry and Robertson and sister Alice were invalids themselves, as was their aunt, Catherine Walsh, who lived in the same household. In 1862 Ralph Waldo Emerson good-naturedly complained to Henry James, Sr., about the "dyspeptic habit" of his own son Edward, who believed that if he went away to college he would only "pine away as before."[2] William Morris Hunt, James's painting teacher, and John La Farge, a fellow art student, also fell victim to neurasthenia, La Farge reportedly suffering "quite a breakdown" in 1867.[3] William Dean Howells, editor of the *Atlantic Monthly*, complained of so much mysterious trouble with his wrist that in 1870 his wife had to write for him.[4] Louis Agassiz, professor of natural history at Harvard, suffered a "collapse" in the spring of 1871; two years later his son Alexander and a friend, Gurney, became, in William's words, "the last two brain collapsers."[5]

One might dismiss invalidism either as too technical for historians or, in this case, as a biographical matter uniquely tied to William James's personal uncertainties. But clearly he was not alone in his neurasthenic struggles. Moreover psychoanalysis provides a framework for viewing this disease as a meaningful act rather than a fateful accident. Just as disease can offer access to the inner life of an individual, so can widespread illness of doubtful physical origin enable the historian to explore patterns of stress in a society: neurasthenia—whether in James, his family, or in post–Civil War New England—had at its root the problem of work.

I

Dr. Beard's preliminary papers were published in the late 1860s, when William's nervous symptoms reached their peak.[6] He noted that patients suffering from nervous exhaustion, or "neurasthenia," were typically in their late teens to mid-forties. One out of ten, like William, was a physician. Beard described a variant of the disease that affected the eyes, causing weakness and difficulty reading—William's symptoms—and reported that it had a "contagious" quality. There had been a spread of these symptoms "through many of the colleges and seminaries of the country—in some instances compelling young men to abandon their plans of a liberal education."[7] Beard disapproved of the fashionable treatment for functional disorders that involved treating "nervous disease by recommending a trip to Europe."[8] Furthermore, he recognized that work was therapeutic for many of his patients. "Very rarely indeed do I advise a patient to change profession or occupation, whatever it may be, provided he is happy and successful in it." He was convinced that work was particularly important for young men suffering from the disease. "In a large number of cases I urge, especially upon young men, the necessity of obtaining some occupation; and I would rather have them work too hard than not work at all."[9]

While Dr. Beard was of the opinion that insufficient work, or at least insufficiently gratifying work, contributed to the development and persistence of neurasthenia, there were those who argued that too much work was the core of the problem. On a visit to the United States, Herbert Spencer, philosopher of evolution and James's philosophic antagonist, took a traveler's privilege to comment on the malaise he saw about him: "In every circle I have met men who had themselves suffered from nervous collapses, due to stress of business, or named friends who had crippled themselves by overwork." Spencer thought that the danger of overwork was the outcome of too much evolutionary development. Americans had moved too far beyond the savage. The savage, in his view, was incapable of monotonous daily toil, but "it is otherwise with the more developed man. The stern discipline of social life has gradually increased the aptitude for persistent industry until among us and still among you, work has become with many a passion." And it was a passion with disastrous consequences for health. "Exclusive devotion to work has the result that amusements cease to please; and when relaxation becomes imperative, life becomes dreary from lack of its sole interest—the interest in business." Spencer preached a new gospel for the over-routinized, over-worked American. "In brief, I may say that we have had somewhat too much of 'the gospel of work.' It is time to preach the gospel of relaxation."[10] Both the American doctor and the English philosopher agreed that whether too much or too little, the phenomenon of neurasthenia was connected with work.

The James family correspondence reflects both poles of the discussion. The elder Henry spoke decisively for the benefits of leisure. He set the dominant tone for the James household, blending the romantic ideal of work expressive of selfhood with a religious ideal of holy rest. "I am determined," he told his friend J. J. Garth Wilkinson, in 1852, "to take holiday for the rest of my life [he was forty-one], and make all my work sabbatical, and expressive only of irrepressive inward health and impulsions."[11] Though he applied himself steadfastly to his literary labors, he maintained a lifelong suspicion of the dangers of too much work. Mary James, following her husband's lead as she did in most intellectual matters, shared the same suspicion. Of La Farge's breakdown she said, "He ascribed it to the cold rainy weather, but perhaps he had worked too hard in New York."[12] When William was abroad and undertook to write some reviews for publication as a gesture of self-support, she lamented, "I fear he is working himself to death to meet his expenses."[13] When Professor Agassiz fell ill, she offered the same explanation. "He was attacked a day or two ago with a paralysis of the larynx. . . . His condition is thought very critical. He has been overworking very much of late."[14] Of William's friend Oliver Wendell Holmes, Jr., she remarked, "His whole life, soul and body, is utterly absorbed in his *last* work upon his Kent. He carries about his manuscript in his green bag and never loses sight of it for a moment.... His pallid face and this fearful grip upon his work, makes him a melancholy sight."[15]

A corollary to her belief in the dangers of overwork was Mary James's conviction that physical exertion should be avoided by her frail children. Thus, to Henry, who was enjoying an exhilarating walking trip in the Alps, she cautioned, "Of course I know you would not attempt any dizzy heights or any but well beaten tracks without a guide—But you might easily over estimate your strength and sink down with sudden exhaustion."[16] Again to Henry, who was enjoying horseback riding in Rome and finding it salutary, "Do not run any risks darling Harry, by staying too long in Rome, and do not overdo the horse-back exercise."[17]

This fearful view of work and exertion rested upon an assumption that many Americans seemed to share about human energy. They were convinced that human energy was scarce, had to be expended parsimoniously, and was easily exhausted. Capital and the laws that governed it seemed an unconscious metaphor that structured human action. It had to be saved rather than spent. If the principal was invaded and reduced, it might no longer adequately support life. Scarcity rather than abundance, weakness instead of strength, ill health rather than health was their natural expectation. And effort was an extravagance that depleted already strained resources. In the summer of 1867, Mary James wrote a letter to William, who was in Europe recovering from back trouble. It rested upon this assumption of scarcity. "I feared very much that you might be the worse for all the fatigue of your journey, and getting settled in Dresden—Your letter was delightful. You were evidently in excellent spirits, but no word about your back—from which I infer you were about the same—You have had no time since you left us for rest, and we ought not to look for improvement, until you get that."[18]

William made the energy supply problem even more explicit in a letter to his friend Tom Ward, who was momentarily reconciled to his business career and was working well. "How I envy you your fund of energy. I have a little spoonful ready for each day and when that's out, as it usually is by 10 o'clock A.M., I'm good for nothing."[19] Henry James used the capitalist metaphor when he was in Europe enjoying a vigorous grand tour in search of health. He had discovered that walking made him feel better and feared that the hot Italian summer would prevent this kind of exercise. "I have laid in such a capital stock of strength and satisfaction in Switzerland," he told his sister, "that I shall be sorry to be compelled to see it diminished and if I find it is melting away beneath the southern sun I shall not scruple... to cross over from Verona into southern Germany."[20] Both brothers obviously shared the view by which many in their social group lived.

Since work depleted energy, it followed that it was bad for health. William did not hold to this view consistently, since he often came upon evidence to the contrary. In Germany, the sight of hardworking peasant women led him to urge hard work on his sister Alice. "The sight of the women here has strengthened me more than ever in my belief that they ought to be made to do the hard labor of the community—they are far happier and better for it. I only wish I had that pampered Alice here to see these little runts of peasant women stumping about with their immense burdens on their back... they are as active and strong as little lionesses, and work from morning til night. Seriously there is a great deal of good in it—and the ideal German woman of poetry (see Goethe, for instance) is a working woman."[21] It was not until the 1880s, when he became a spokesman for the strenuous outdoor life, that William James acted upon that advice himself.

To subscribe to the conception of limited energy was to embrace the belief that rest was a logical cure. But William was skeptical of the value of extreme rest cures. When a friend was undergoing treatment that virtually amounted to sensory deprivation, he remarked, "She seems to be suffering from a general nervous debility[,] for the treatment they are now pursuing is one of absolute quiet and non-stimulation. She may not even talk much. Poor girl! I should think it would prey on her spirits more than it would rest her nerves."[22] He favored rest, especially from undesirable labor, but leisure without literature, repose without responsive conversation was out of the question.

Mary James shared her husband's belief that work was dangerous to health, and she cultivated that attitude in her children. Yet she operated under different laws herself. An 1873 letter to William, for example, reads like a list of wounded from the front. She reported the current status of "our invalids." Alice, "poor child," had one of her fainting attacks "from a little overexertion"; father had an attack of eczema of the face [apparently Herpes Zoster or "shingles"] and is "nervous and sleepless"; Aunt Kate "is progressing slowly" under Dr. Munro's care and "certainly bears well much more fatigue." But she, like a surviving heroine surveying the slain minions strewn about her, proclaimed, "The poor old mater wears well I am happy to say; strong in the back, strong in the nerves, and strong in the legs so far, and equal to her day."[23]

Her strength and endurance were the more remarkable when repeatedly juxtaposed to the weakness of the rest. It was apparently worthy of comment in 1873 that Alice returned from visiting a friend in Beverly for three days and "came home with her nervous system unimpaired." It was also notable that father was "remarkably well." Others were expected to be short of energy, but she remained stalwart and ever ready to shoulder her caretaking tasks. It is not surprising that this attitude extended to household servants as well. She complained of the unreliability of that "race by whom unfortunately we live," but even when she did have someone she could count on she did not dare do so because she expected the worst. "I'm glad to say that Mary in the kitchen still proves reliable, but I am afraid almost to lean upon her, least she too prove a broken reed."[24] William reported that sickness did not keep *her* from her household tasks. "Mother is recovering from one of her indispositions, which she bears like an angel, doing any amount of work at the same time, putting up cornices and raking out the garret-room like a little buffalo."[25] Obviously, each Victorian household where invalidism flourished required a strong caretaker who would nurture the weak and defer to the mythology of scarce resources yet remain a fount of energy that miraculously never gave out. Among the Jameses, Mary James was that "protecting spirit." She was the "household genius" upon whom Henry James, Sr., rested "with the absolute whole of his weight."[26] It is not surprising that the children followed his lead.

II

Though work was unappealing to these New Englanders, pleasure was also suspect. There was a noticeable waning of puritanical zeal in mid-nineteenth-century New England, but the suspicion that pleasure was evil lingered on. Sabbatarian scrupulosity over game-playing or singing would have been unthinkable in Mr. James's liberal household. Yet they showed a subtle lack of hospitality for pleasure. In Mary James's correspondence, puritanism often masqueraded as humor. This was particularly true when writing to her daughter Alice. In the summer of 1872, Alice was abroad enjoying a grand tour. She found France especially to her liking, and Mary James reacted with a mocking jibe. "My daughter a child of France! What has become of that high moral nature, on which I have always based such hopes for her for this world and the next? That you should so soon have succumbed to this assault upon your senses, so easily have been carried captive by the mere delights of eating and drinking and seeing and dressing [unclear], I should not have believed."[27] Mary James was bantering, but it was humor that cut deep.

Work that was supposed to be sabbatical and leisure that was supposed to be uplifting both required money. Capital, not as a metaphor for human energy but as a limited supply of cash, was an important ingredient of the neurasthenic phenomenon. No matter how extensive the resources of a family, if it shared in a distrust of pleasure and leisure, money could not easily be spent on traveling for amusement. It was far simpler to justify travel for reasons of health. The elder Henry had been amply provided for by his inheritance (his income was about $10,000 a year), but numerous family trips abroad had cut into his capital. Furthermore, he invested heavily in a Florida plantation using hired black labor, which was run by his younger sons Robertson and Wilkie, and the plantation failed. The family was still well off but there was not enough money to maintain parents and children in leisured extravagance. Between 1866 and 1873 sickness became a means by which the James children struggled for a lion's share of the family resources.

If both Henry and William wanted to go abroad but there was only money enough for one, then surely the sicker of the two should go. If both were equally ill, then the one who had most recently had his turn at the cure should remain behind. This required careful balancing on the part of the invalid. If he were too sick, then the effort of travel was out of the question. If he were not sick enough, then he might not need the cure as much as another member of the household. If he responded too quickly when abroad to the benefits of the cure, or seemed to be enjoying himself too much, then his travel might be cut short because it was using limited family resources for pleasure while others required "treatment." Both Henry and Mary James kept a sharp eye on the letters written by their traveling invalid children to monitor expenditure and healthful returns.

A most revealing exchange took place between Henry and his parents in 1869. Since William had returned from his quest for health in the European spas, it was Henry's turn. He traveled in England, France, Switzerland, and Italy and, violating the precept of limited energy, found delight in walking, climbing, and horseback riding. He seemed to be enjoying himself too much, however, and was criticized by his Cambridge-bound parents. He wrote a defense to his father, whose side of the exchange can easily be inferred from the son's remarks. "To have you think that I am extravagant with these truly sacred funds sickens me to the heart, and I hasten in so far as I may to reassure you. When I left Malvern, I found myself so exacerbated by immobility and confinement that I felt it to be absolutely due to myself to test the impression which had been maturing in my mind, that a certain amount of regular lively travel would do me more good than any further repose. As I came abroad to try and get better, it seemed inexcusable to neglect a course which I believed for various reasons to have so much in its favor." Having made show of concern for limited funds and the evils of idle pleasure, Henry deftly concluded that what he needed for *really* good health was *more* pleasurable travel. "I have now an impression amounting almost to a conviction that if I were to travel steadily for a year I would be a good part of a well man."[28]

Seven weeks later, he replied to a remonstrance against extravagance from his mother's pen. Here too he balanced carefully between accepting parental injunction against pleasure and insisting upon his need, as one weak in body, to cater to the pleasures of the spirit. He wisely commended the play for its utility in increasing his capacity to work.

I duly noted your injunction to spend the summer quietly and economically. I hope to do both—or that is, to circulate in so far as I do, by the inexpensive vehicle of my own legs. When you speak of your own increased expenses, etc., I feel very guilty and selfish in entertaining any projects which look in the least like extravagance. My beloved mother, if you but knew the purity of my motives! Reflection assures me, as it will assure you, that the only economy for me is to get thoroughly well and into such a state as that I can work. For this consummation, I will accept everything—even the appearance of mere pleasure-seeking.[29]

That Henry had learned well the puritanical judgment of selfishness and mere pleasure-seeking was clear. He had also learned that illness and the need for treatment made divine what might otherwise have been labeled diabolical—even in his parents' liberal household. Energy and capital flowed freely for healing, while the sluices were clanged decisively shut for pleasure and idleness.

"When I think that a winter in Italy is not as you call it a winter of 'recreation,'" Henry wrote, "but an occasion not only of physical regeneration, but of serious culture too (culture of the kind which alone I have now at twenty six any time left for) I find the courage to maintain my proposition even in the fact of your allusions to the need of economy at home. It takes a very honest conviction thus to plead the cause of apparently gross idleness against such grave and touching facts. I have trifled so long with my trouble that I feel as if I could afford now to be a little brutal. My lovely mother, if ever I am restored to you sound and serviceable you will find that you have not cast the pearls of your charity before a senseless beast, but before a creature with a soul to be grateful and a will to act.[30]

A month later his mother reassured Henry that he could do what he wished. He was so successful at the politics of invalidism that he got her to apologize for having questioned his motives. The coffers were wide open, with Mary James urging Henry to let your "prudent old mother" take care of everything. She added, "If you were only here for an hour, and we could talk over this subject of expense, I could I know exorcise all these demons of anxiety and conscienciousness that possess you, and leave [you] free as air, to enjoy to the full all that surrounds you, and drink in health of body and of mind in following out your own safe and innocent attractions." The only promise that she wished to extract was that henceforth he would, "throw away prudence and think only of your own comfort and pleasure, for our sakes as well as your own."[31] Henry remained in Europe and traveled as he saw fit, gathering impressions for his literary career. He was intermittently plagued by back and bowel complaints, so that repeated convalescence was necessary.

Not all the children were equally adept or as intensely driven to succeed at the manipulative politics of invalidism. A note from Alice James canceling a visit to her friend Sara Darwin shows one way that a "prudent old mother" could manage limited funds. If she decided to give money to support the illness of one child, it meant depriving another. Alice openly recognized illness to be a tactic of family politics, although on this occasion she rejected using illness to get her own way. "Poverty reminds me of my visit to New York, or rather my non-visit," she wrote.

You must not mention this on your return in Quincy St. A vague rumour reached number 20 a few days ago. A package of dynamite suddenly introduced into the midst would have produced a less shattering effect on the family circle—parent and child torn literally limb from limb, but its true nevertheless if I go to New York I shall have to buy some duds [unclear], which in these rural districts I can do very well without. Mother is constantly throwing out dark mysterious hints upon the necessity of economy and now I am economizing? (is it spelt with an s or a z?) *I am in a very robust condition of health so that I cannot wriggle out there, but I am strongly tempted to abandon virtue when I think of thee as a companion in vice and of the little parental encouragement which I receive* [my italics]. But I shall be rewarded, I have quite determined elsewhere.

As an apology for not answering Sara's letter sooner she pleaded, "Original sin is my only refuge; I was born bad and I never have recovered."[32] She had, as the letter reveals, learned her mother's trick of participating in the abstemious atmosphere of Calvinism yet rejecting it, through humor. But virtue and vice, sin and redemption were familiar points of the compass whether called in a stern voice or softened with a chuckle.

III

Within this familial and social context, illness could be seen in either a negative or a positive light. Illness was an unfortunate consequence of overwork, yet it justified the pleasure of travel and leisure to a carping conscience. It caused pain and suffering, yet to the romantically influenced it marked the sufferer as one possessed of unique sensibility like a poet or a saint. Not just a physical evil, illness was to be cultivated as a romantic sign of grace. Alice James's diary provides an ironic illustration of this attitude. She had taken to her bed and required perpetual nursing care for "sick headaches." While her nurse was dressing her one morning, Alice was "suddenly flooded by one of those luminous waves that sweep out of consciousness all but the living sense and overpower one with joy in the rich, throbbing complexity of life." She was so taken with her own sensitivity compared with the "primitive rudimentary expression" of the nurse that she announced, "Oh! Nurse, don't you wish you were inside of *me!*" But the nurse disclaimed, "Inside of you, Miss, when you have just had a sick head-ache for five days!" The caretakers in the serving class apparently looked upon the enterprise of invalidism with different eyes. Alice wryly noted, "Nurse and I had a good laugh but I must allow that decidedly she 'had' me."[33]

IV

In a work-centered, pleasure-phobic culture, invalidism made idleness socially acceptable. It also provided social definition, particularly to the young, who felt keenly the need to *do* something but found other social options unattractive. In the time of his youth, Henry, Jr., recalled, "Just staying at home when everyone was on the move couldn't in any degree show the right mark: to be properly and perfectly vague one had to be vague *about* something."[34] Invalidism was to show "just the right mark" for him for the next decade and even beyond. Henry injured his back fighting a fire at Newport in the autumn of 1861. His recollection of that experience is most revealing, alluding, as it does, to the embarrassing yet useful aspects of being ill in that early Civil War period. He admitted obliquely to his intent: "To have trumped up a lameness at such a juncture could be made to pass in no light for graceful." He was vague about the nature of his injury but was convinced, from the outset, that the disability would last a long time. He continued to suffer from back trouble for years, but medical examinations after he had recovered from the initial injury revealed no lasting physical damage.

Physicians were unpredictable supporters of the invalid role. Dr. Bigelow, the medical "oracle" Henry consulted, said that there was "nothing to speak of the matter." Without the doctor's support, Henry's invalidism could not flourish. He quite rightly reasoned that the work of a law student could also offer "in the public eye, a season of some retirement." He extolled the virtues of that position. "The beauty was—I can fairly see it now, through the haze of time, even as beauty! that studious retirement and preparatory hours did after all supply the supine attitude, did invest the ruefulness, did deck out the cynicism of lying down book in hand with a certain fine plausibility."[35]

In addition to protecting leisure, invalidism served admirably to convey feelings that would have been difficult to express directly without ruffling the surface calm called for by the social ideal of the Victorian family. In our post-Freudian age, we live more easily with ambivalence between intimates than would have been conceivable in the social setting of William James's youth. That one might hate the parent whom one also loved, resent the caretaker whose nurturing made invalidism possible, loathe the domestic scene whose apparent peace shielded one from worldly struggles, was unthinkable—or at least unmentionable. But an invalid could refuse to improve, bemoan his long list of complaints, and inflict pain on his anxious relatives as if to say, "I hate you for what you have done *to* me by doing *for* me." The perplexed caretaker felt the impact of the blow yet was unable to strike back at another so weak and helpless. Once again, Mary James's letters provide vivid illustration. When William returned from a voyage of recovery, she was frankly irritated by the assaulting quality of his complaints. She told Henry, Jr., "Well, he seems *as yet* too much the old story to give us all the pleasure that we expected. Of course we make every allowance for the fatigue of the voyage; and his broken sleep, and know he *must* have made great gains, and we shall presently see it. He looks *well*. The trouble with him is that he *must express* every fluctuation of feeling, and especially every unfavorable symptom; without reference to the effect upon those about him."[36] Though she was an acute observer, Mary James could not admit what must have been patently obvious to others—that William's unhappiness at being home had something to do with the jibes she received in the form of physical complaints.

Henry James, Sr., also received his share of barbs through illness. Whenever they were unhappy with him, William and Henry mocked his ideas. Alice occasionally felt the urge to be more outspoken but could not do this directly. She could play the part of adoring child to perfection, but when angry feelings threatened to erupt, sickness became her way of expression. In 1867–68, William and Henry were both actively nursing their backs, and she became overwhelmed with "violent turns of hysteria" that left her prostrate like her admired older brothers. There was no hint of cause for her fainting spells in the family correspondence. It was blamed, as usual, on overexertion. But a diary entry written after reading William's essay on the "Hidden Self" more than twenty years later exposed what she had been trying to hide. She had felt barely repressed rage pushing her toward murder or suicide. She was flooded with waves of anger toward her father. She recalled that she had had to police her patricidal impulses and was terrified that her moral powers would be overwhelmed. "I saw so distinctly that it was a fight simply between my body and my will," she confided in her diary, "a battle in which the former was to be triumphant to the end. Owing to some physical weakness, excess of nervous susceptibility, the moral power *pauses*, as it were for a moment, and refuses to maintain muscular sanity, worn out with the strain of its constabulary functions."[37] She was not weak from overwork but from the strain of holding her deepest emotions back. The diary entry gave a graphic description of her inner conflict but offered no clue as to the source of her anger with her father. It is likely that it had something to do with the vocational struggles of the family. Her older brothers were stalled in invalidism while making a show of seeking vocation. Her younger brothers were off working the plantation in Florida backed by a substantial portion of the family estate. She was trapped in what she felt to be a rural backwater in order to keep her parents company as they passed into old age. There is virtually no mention of education for her in the family correspondence, save what she might learn from medical treatment, nor of efforts to introduce her to young men, except physicians for healing. She joked with her girl friend Sara well into the 1870s about looking for a husband, but family interest and resources were committed to the boys. If one were casting about for omens, it would have been disturbing to note, as Mary James did in 1869, that the occasion of Alice's majority was ushered in by a solar eclipse.[38]

The limited options of a woman from her social class were rapidly closing for her during the 1860s. It is easy to see how she might have been infuriated with her father. He promised glorious spiritual fulfillment but did little to help her in any practical ways, and he paid close attention to his four sons' education and careers while making no provisions for her future. But how could she dare express animosity toward a "benignant pater" who made brotherhood the test of redemption and ideal fatherhood a model for himself and God? She stifled the rage and became ill. This gave her father the discomfort of witnessing her invalidism. When her rage intensified, she had to use all of her powers of restraint to keep from killing him—or doing what Freud has taught us amounts to the same thing symbolically—killing herself. Her rage combined with her moral rectitude produced her neurasthenic condition. Alice experienced the intrusion of violence into her consciousness as a physical defect, a "breakdown in her machinery," or "muscular insanity," rather than her own emotional response to her plight. "As I used to sit immovable reading in the library," she noted in her diary, "with waves of violent inclination suddenly invading my muscles taking some one of their myriad forms such as throwing myself out of the window, or knocking off the head of the benignant pater as he sat with his silver locks, writing at his table, it used to seem to me that the only difference between me and the insane was that I had not only all the horrors and suffering of insanity but the duties of doctor, nurse, and strait-jacket imposed upon me, too."[39]

Though an astute clinician, George Beard shared the same family ideal as did his patients. He showed little comprehension of the love-hate relationship between parents and children. Violence toward loved ones was "insane" by definition, he wrote. "The sane man murders those whom he hates, from whose death he expects to gain something; the insane man murders those whom he most loves—from whose death he can gain nothing."[40] It was a comforting distortion to banish evil into the realm of unreason. Freud had to remind the Victorian world that murder was a family affair in real life as well as in gothic novels.

V

If invalidism had obvious social and interpersonal utility, it was at best a compromise. The invalid might enjoy the leisure that illness provided, but he also shared in the social judgment of that enjoyment and felt guilty. If illness served as a niche for social participation, it was one that the sufferer judged to be inferior, and as a result he felt shame. The quest for health was a lever for prying loose family funds, but the beneficiary knew that others were being deprived and was torn by a sense of responsibility to them. Sickness could express the unmentionable but the sufferer judged his own feelings as evil. In sum, cultivating illness may have aided transgressions against society, family, and self, but it also levied penalties for those acts. Invalidism was a compromise between crime and punishment.

Henry James's letters from Italy provide an illustration of the way that illness helped the sufferer do penance for the advantages he enjoyed. Henry had successfully argued for including Italy in his itinerary, pleading its salutary effects for health and its enriching influences for general culture. But, having overcome parental opposition, he found himself strangely hampered

in his enjoyment of the prize. "It's as if," he complained to William, "I had
been born in Boston: I can't for my life frankly surrender myself to the
Genius of Italy, or the Spirit of the South—or whatever one may call the
confounded thing; but I nevertheless *feel* it in all my pulses."[41] He did
eventually unbend and wrote excitedly, "If I might talk of these things I
would talk of more and tell you in glowing accents how beautiful a thing this
month in Italy has been and my bosom aches with memories."[42] Unfortunately, as he opened himself to Italy, his health began to fail. "I'm very sorry
to say that I am anything but well," he complained to his father. "Not that I
have any new and startling affliction, but . . . Ever since I have been in Italy I
have been rapidly losing ground. . . . It makes a sad trouble of what ought to
be a great pleasure."[43] True, Henry James was not a Bostonian by birth, but
to his chagrin, he was prey to the very attitudes that he mocked. Invalidism,
though useful, proved a restricted visa for such a traveler.

Doctors were important in the structure of invalidism. Sometimes unwit-
tingly, but often with consummate skill, they matched illness with treatment, as a judge might match a crime with a suitable sentence. It would take
us too far afield to describe in detail the entire range of treatments mentioned
in the James family correspondence. Lifting, hot irons, icepacks, blistering,
galvanism, the water cure—each justified by some medical theory, each
translated into the exchange of pain for pleasure, and all tried in their turn by
the members of the family in their search for health. Several illustrations
connected to the problem of work will suffice. If illness justified work-
avoidance in a work-centered culture, logic dictated that the sanction for
ill-gotten leisure should be hard labor. Whether the doctors understood this
relationship or not, their invalid patients saw it that way. Too simply stated,
treatment turned leisure into labor, either through prescribing rest to a degree that became a test of one's endurance or by recommending physical
exertion to a degree that seemed like work. When Mary James reported on
Alice's attempts at a rest cure, for example, she described it as labor. "Alice is
busy trying to idle, and it is always very hard depressing work, this to her,
but I think it will tell in the end."[44] There was more self-conscious irony in
the younger Henry's description of sight-seeing in Rome as labor. "I have
buckled down to my work with a fair amount of resolution. . . . The Vatican,
the Museum of the Capitol, the Colisium [*sic*] and the Baths of Caraculla, the
Pantheon, the forum, and the churches of the Lateran and St. Maria
Maggiore—such are my special acquisitions."[45]

But Rev. William James (brother of Henry James, Sr.) was not attempting
humor when he described the water cure at Clifton Springs as work. Doctors
reassured him that his headaches were not a sign of impending apoplexy (his
father's fatal illness); they were due to "torpidity" of the glands, stomach, and
nervous system, which the doctors claimed could be relieved by prolonged
water treatment. No matter what pathophysiology the physician used, it
could be translated into the language of industry by the invalid. The daily

regimen at Clifton Springs was characterized in a letter to his daughter. "Let me give you each days work." And work it was, at least enough to satisfy a puritan conscience for the leisure enjoyed. The day began at 5:30 A.M. Besides baths of total and partial immersion in water ranging from tepid to very hot, there were two required periods of exercise—bowling in the morning, "which brings streams of perspiration from every pore of my body," and a walk of "4 to 5 miles" in the afternoon.

Henry James had an intuitive grasp of the relationship between leisure and pain. Witness his playful query to a friend, "Have you ever a superstitious sense of having to give some *quid pro quo* for your particular pleasure?"[46] A good-humored judge, he condemned his correspondent to describing her travels to him in person when they met again. However magical he felt such an exchange to be, he along with other invalids bartered in that economy. The full cooperation of the medical profession was readily obtained. Supported by the theory of counter-irritation—which hypothesized that therapeutically induced pain could relieve the underlying cause of existing pain—patients were shocked and blistered and boiled. When Alice James subjected herself to galvanism (the application of electric current to the skin), she wrote graphically of the painful experience to a friend. She was being treated, she said, "by Dr. N——, of whom I have heard great things & who certainly either in spite or because of his quackish quality had done me a great deal of good in many ways. . . . His electricity however has the starching properties of the longest Puritan descent."[47] Like so many other remedies that she tried, its effects were only temporary.

One of the many therapies William tried on himself was blistering. Blisters were produced by making chemical burns on the skin. They were supposed to help relieve back pain. He described the process in detail and urged it upon his brother as he often did with other nostrums. "I have been trying blisters on my back and they do undeniable good. Get a number about the size of a 25 cents piece, or of a copper cent. Apply one every night on alternate sides of the spine over the diseased muscles. In the morning prick the bubbles; and cover then with a slip of rag with cerate, fastened down by cross straps of sticking plaster. Try a dozen in this way at first. Then wait two weeks and try ½ doz. more & so on . . ."[48] A year later, blistering was still in his therapeutic armamentarium, and he assured Henry, "The application is uncomfortable, but *will pay*."[49] But the beneficial effects, like those from Alice's galvanism, were short-lived at best.

Indeed, all of the cures were doomed to failure, though they succeeded admirably in supporting the structure of invalidism. No matter what the theoretical basis for their therapeutics, experienced healers have always known that invalidism is a complex creation. In mid-nineteenth-century New England, it coalesced from a Romantic and puritanical matrix into a durable social role. Salvation through work, condemnation of idleness, suspicion of pleasure, and a belief that suffering leads to grace flowed from the

Puritan source. Insistence upon self-expression, a high valuation of leisure, and the admiration of delicacy and acute sensibility issued from the Romantic. In such vigorous crosscurrents, illness had considerable utility. It provided social definition, sanctioned pleasure, prescribed leisure for health, protected from premature responsibility, forced others to care, and expressed inadmissible feelings while protecting vital personal ties. For the patient, it was a compromise between the attainment of forbidden goals and punishment for that accomplishment. With the cooperation of their physicians, patients balanced pain against pleasure, crime against punishment, and maintained an uneasy equilibrium.

NOTES

1. Neurasthenia, in Alice James' phrase, was the "life-long occupation of improving." Quoted in F. O. Matthiessen, *The James Family* (New York: Alfred A. Knopf, 1947), p. 271 n. For Beard's book, see note 6 below.

2. Emerson quoted in Anna Robeson Burr, ed., *Alice James, Her Brothers; Her Journal* (Cornwall, N.Y.: Dodd, Mead & Co., 1934), p. 17.

3. Mrs. Henry James, Sr., to William James, May 27, 1867 (The James Family Papers, Houghton Library, Harvard University. Hereinafter referred to as James Papers).

4. Mrs. Henry James, Sr., to Henry James, Jr., April 5, 1870 (James Papers).

5. William James to Henry James, Jr., May 11, 1873 (James Papers).

6. George Miller Beard, *A Practical Treatise in Nervous Exhaustion, Neurasthenia, Its Symptoms, Nature; Sequences, Treatment* (New York: William Ward and Company, 1880).

7. *Ibid.*, p. 20.

8. *Ibid.*, p. 184.

9. *Ibid.*, p. 180.

10. *Boston Evening Transcript*, November 10, 1882.

11. Ralph Barton Perry, *The Thought and Character of William James*, 2 vols. (Boston: Little, Brown and Company, 1935), I:23.

12. Mrs. Henry James, Sr., to William James, May 27, 1867 (James Papers).

13. Mrs. Henry James, Sr., to Alice James, January 14, 1870 (James Papers).

14. Mrs. Henry James, Sr., to Henry James, Jr., December 8, 1873 (James Papers).

15. Perry, *William James*, I:519.

16. Mrs. Henry James, Sr., to Henry James, Jr., August 8, 1869 (James Papers).

17. Mrs. Henry James, Sr. to Henry James, Jr., April 1, 1873 (James Papers).

18. Mrs. Henry James, Sr., to William James, June 10, 1867 (James Papers).

19. Perry, *William James*, I:373.

20. Leon Edel, ed., *Henry James Letters*, Vol. I, 1843–1875 (Cambridge, Mass.: Harvard University Press, 1974), p. 131.

21. Perry, *William James*, I:239–40.

22. William James to Mrs. Henry James, Sr., June 12, 1867 (James Papers).

23. Leon Edel, *Henry James: The Untried Years 1843–1870* (Philadelphia: J. B. Lippincott Company, 1953), p. 44. [In an article noted in part 2 of the Select Bibliography, James William Anderson conducts a search for the elusive Mary James.]

24. Mrs. Henry James, Sr., to Henry James, Jr., September 22, 1873 (James Papers).

25. Henry James, *The Letters of William James*, 2 vols. (Boston: The Atlantic Monthly Press, 1920), p. 80.

26. Edel, *Henry James*, pp. 47, 49.

27. Mrs. Henry James, Sr., to Alice James, July 18, 1872 (James Papers).

28. Edel, *Letters*, I:115.

29. *Ibid.*, p. 124.

30. *Ibid.*, pp. 124–25.

31. Mrs. Henry James, Sr., to Henry James, Jr., July 24, 1869 (James Papers).

32. Alice James to Sara Darwin, March 23, 1874 (James Papers).

33. Leon Edel, ed., *The Diary of Alice James* (New York: Dodd, Mead & Co., 1964), p. 48.

34. Henry James, *Notes of a Son and a Brother* (New York: Charles Scribner's Sons, 1914), p. 292.

35. *Ibid.*, pp. 299–301.

36. Mrs. Henry James, Sr., to Henry James, Jr., March 17, 1874 (James Papers).

37. Edel, *Alice James*, p. 149.

38. Mrs. Henry James, Sr., to Henry James, Jr., August 8, 1869 (James Papers).

39. Edel, *Alice James*, p. 149.

40. George Miller Beard, *The Psychology of the Salem Witchcraft Excitement of 1692 and its Practical Affiliation to Our Own Time* (New York: 1892), pp. 94–95.

41. Edel, *Letters*, I:136.

42. *Ibid.*, p. 142.

43. *Ibid.*, pp. 155–56.

44. Mrs. Henry James, Sr., to Henry James, Jr., July 24, 1869 (James Papers). A vivid description of rest turned into a trial of sensory deprivation is to be found in Charlotte Perkins Gilman's, "The Yellow Wall Paper." It is an indictment of the Weir Mitchell rest cure.

45. Edel, *Letters*, I:163.

46. *Ibid.*, p. 256.

47. Alice James to Sara Darwin, May 5, 1883 (James Papers).

48. William James to Henry James, Jr., December 26, 1867 (James Papers).

49. William James to Henry James, Jr., September 22, 1868 (James Papers).

11

PERSONALITY AND CULTURAL
HISTORY IN THE NOVEL
Two American Examples

CUSHING STROUT

Any future history of psychology-in-history would have to discuss the impetus given this genre by the American Studies scholars who, mostly in the 1950s and 1960s, published books on cultural themes. These volumes had in common the discovery of opposites or tensions within popular American beliefs, and exploring them called for a preeminently (though always implicitly) psychoanalytic regard for paradox, ambivalence, conflict. Americans—culturally speaking—held contradictory views of themselves (Cavalier or Yankee?), of nature (better accommodated or exploited?), and of the West (wilderness or garden?); Jacksonian Democrats could not decide whether to look forward or backward. American studies thus explored what deep down may be understood as the push/pull between high regard for the pristine newness of America and aroused appetite for material gain. These monographs searched for surface and subsurface themes in magazines, ceremonial orations, and literature.

Descending from the mythic and symbolic heights where such studies dwell, Cushing Strout in the following essay tries to show that literary sources can be of more specific value to historians. Closely and carefully read fiction, he argues, besides offering hints about the author's private life, may reveal the experiences of particular peoples—their conflicts with prevailing values and attitudes—and therefore suggest how in real life personality, society, and culture intersected. Using a work of the imagination, the historian thereby gains a "feel" for the analysis his conventional primary sources buttress with harder evidence. Henry Adams's fictional account of Esther's personal strivings brings vividly to life the male-female tensions that Smith-Rosenberg introduced above; Abraham Cahan's Jewish immigrant in late-nineteenth-century New York City serves, by dint of Cahan's experience but also his powers of imagination, to answer questions about ethnic identity, social mobility, and

Reprinted, with minor alterations, from *New Literary History* (Spring 1970):423–37 by permission.

the psychic costs of making it in a pluralistic society. Novels can therefore be "historical," Strout concludes in a longer version of this article, in the sense that, through art, they "openly explore a middle range of identity problems that occur when an individual's emotional life, representative in part of a group, class, or movement, entangles itself in cultural patterns that are subject to the deeper tides of historical change."

Finally, a valuable point that Strout repeats is that historians who use psychological or social scientific jargon might take a lesson from the novelist: we can best relate the richness of the interplay between mind and society by letting a novelist's narrative line absorb it.

IN A CRITICAL review of contemporary directions in the study of American cultural history, David Davis has pointed out that the American Studies movement has characteristically produced works that "expose a contradiction or cluster of tensions embedded within the culture itself as the result of an interplay between past choices and commitments and new ideas or situations." Many of these literary studies have been alert to the way in which symbols and myths have concealed or accommodated conflicts in belief and value: the myths of the West or of the American Adam; the pastoral ideal of the middle landscape between primitive nature and urban civilization; the image of Europe as the Old World; and the contrary types of Cavalier and Yankee as stand-ins for the American character. But Davis properly notes that "one must guard against relegating all conflict to the world of symbol and myth," and he adds that it is still necessary to find some means of seeing how cultural patterns find "internalization and adaptation within individual personalities." Pointing to Erik Erikson's *Young Man Luther*, he suggests that biography, "by showing how cultural tensions and contradictions may be internalized, struggled with, and resolved within actual individuals," offers "the most promising key to the synthesis of culture and history."[1]

It is no longer unusual to hear scholars refer to identity-crises, any more than it is for students to speak of having them. I have done it myself at length in a study of William James, using the psycho-historical concepts of Erikson,[2] but I know there are those who would say that such analyses express what they describe—identity-diffusion. They ask, "Who is the fellow anyway, a psychoanalyst or a historian?" What I shall propose may provoke a further accusatory query: "Who is he anyway, a literary historian or a social psychologist?" The only proper reply is that to see some things clearly you must have binocular vision, especially in matters of the historical and cultural meaning of personality.

Strictly speaking, the identity-crisis concept is a semi-clinical description of the emotional turmoil characteristic of late adolescence and early manhood facing decisive choices of mate and vocation. Erikson has expanded its usefulness by his own sensitivity to the historical elements that enter into such dramas, particularly in the lives of creative men whose development is marked by intense and disruptive difficulties in the very measure that the problems which they generate and suffer have a wide relevance to the major intellectual, cultural, or political problems of their time. Erikson's revision of Freud has its own framework, a schedule of opposing emotional tendencies for each of his eight stages of the lifecycle. It mediates between the deterministic view that men do not know the psychosexual process that has made them what they are and the voluntaristic view that a historical process is one in which the mind knows itself to be living. Erikson finds in the search for vocation and the experience of work a neglected clue to the meaning of psychic conflict; his theoretical concept of identity, nevertheless, makes it largely unconscious, or pre-conscious at most, in any case not to be confused with "social roles, personal traits, or conscious self-images."[3] His limiting definition is meant to be a useful warning against loosely using the concept of identity to apply to whatever we happen to be investigating.

Certainly the clinical context of Erikson's concept is necessary when the presence of inorganic disabilities, inappropriate feelings, or paradoxical behavior is striking enough (as with Martin Luther or William James) to compel the analyst to become a part-time alienist in order to make sense of the bizarre data. But there are few people now at work in academic life who can confidently follow the path that he has charted by virtue of his unusual training and experience in clinical and anthropological study, and the number of cases where extensive appropriate evidence is available for depth-analysis, though greater than we thought before we began to look for it, is still small enough to act as a deterrent for most scholars against straying from more traditional scholarly routes.

Yet many of Freud's terms—repression, ambivalence, projection, compensation, and displacement—have been exploited out of their original context in his specific theory of the individual's psychosexual etiology because contemporary historians need a vocabulary to explore a broad range of more or less conscious strategies for dealing with powerful feelings generated by the conflicts of group-life, conflicts not reducible to "the family romance" that both Freud and Erikson have emphasized. Similarly, Erikson's concern for identity-formation tends to appear nowadays in sociological formulations of historical problems that are usually much more matters of the conscious assertion of group ideologies, interests, and images than they are of unconscious feelings and assumptions, for example, the movement for "black power," for various anti-imperial nationalisms, or for woman's liberation. For the purpose of bringing together culture and history in the analysis of individual or group conflicts there will be a range of formulations between the terms appropriate to Freud's vocabulary and the terms of "habits, opinions, usages, and beliefs" that have been characteristic of sociology ever since Tocqueville used them in *Democracy in America*.[4] It would seem to be a major problem that we do not have a vocabulary of analysis as specific as either Freud's, Erikson's, or Tocqueville's for the difficult, shifting middle ground between egopsychology and sociology.

I would like to suggest that we can be compensated to some degree for the missing vocabulary by the narrative method of certain novelists whose imagined characters, drawn indirectly from experience, dramatize in their lives the sort of intellectual, cultural, and psychological interplay that has attracted Erikson's attention. The novel tends to focus on the growth of personality through conflict and crisis, and if the novelist has a strong sense of time and place, combined with perception into the individual motivations of his characters, those changes will resonate with the historical and cultural issues that enter into them. I want to illustrate this proposition with two neglected novels, *Esther* and *The Rise of David Levinsky*, one closer to the psychoanalytic end of the spectrum, the other closer to the sociological, though both incorporate shades of meaning at the complementary opposite pole.

Over a decade ago Edward N. Saveth found an ambivalence towards women in Henry Adams's work that led Adams to lament the historical decline of the Virgin as force, while dooming his fictional heroines to be without husbands or children. Saveth speculates that Adams's expectation of a coming cataclysm is masochistically linked to his guilt for quarreling with the "dynamo" as an embodiment of the male principle, like the fantasy of killing the father. Adams's doomed heroines are seen as revenge-fantasies against the mother, aggressive dreams harbored by "meek children and impotent men."[5] In this Freudian interpretation Saveth reduces the novels to projections of Adams's inner tensions, and merely deduces their origin from psychoanalytic theory rather than tracing them to a specific historical-biographical contest. Saveth's treatment of Adams needs to be revised in the light of a post-Freudian psychology that can do justice to the historical situation to which Adams addressed himself in his reflections on women. Whatever his own conflicts, he was, as a novelist, seeking to comprehend those of his characters, drawn from his experience of the women he knew well, and the cultural limits of their problems found an echo in his own personal sense of the limitations of contemporary masculine attitudes.

Adams's own psycho-history must remain elusive because he destroyed his private diaries and many of his letters after the suicide of his wife in 1885. There is one unnoticed clue, however, in his autobiography: "the fourth [child], being of less account, was in a way given to his mother, who named him Henry Brooks, after a favorite brother just lost."[6] According to Henry's brother Charles Francis, their mother delighted in the dark side of anticipation, in "the forecast of evil."[7] This trait became a notorious one of her fourth child, reflecting his own incorporation of an aspect of his mother's personality. His mother probably had on her side a special feeling for the child she had named for her recently-lost brother, and Adams's fascination with women was probably in part rooted in his response to this relation. More important for the historian (if not for the biographer) is the point that Adams's empathy with his heroines, his cult of the Virgin, and his role as an avuncular mentor to his flock of "nieces" can be seen as ways of expressing

certain aspects of himself traditionally designated in his culture as more
"feminine" than "masculine," qualities of sympathy, artistic feeling, and
flirtatious wit not favored by men in the hard, power-oriented capitalist
world of his age.

Despite his success as an editor, scholar, and teacher, his autobiography
monotonously laments his "failure" from the point of view of a person who
sees himself as a passive spectator rather than as a participant "playing the
game" of life. This sense of his own displacement from that world of aggressive power, which "sensitive and timid natures" could not regard "without a
shudder," gave him an unusual and penetrating sympathy with women. By
analogy he could understand with particular keenness the plight of women
who for whatever reason did not find their destiny adequately summed up in
the image of meekness or of frivolity. In a lecture given in Boston in 1876 on
"The Primitive Rights of Women," Adams used Lewis Henry Morgan's
findings about American Indians to show that primitive peoples did not treat
women as property, and he blamed the Church for having "stimulated or
permitted" woman's degradation, which it later softened by idealizing the
image of woman as "the meek and patient, the silent and tender sufferer, the
pale reflection of the Mater Dolorosa."[8]

Adams's *Esther* exploits his own personal knowledge of such American
figures as his cousin Phillips Brooks, pastor of Boston's Trinity Church; John
La Farge, who painted its murals and decorated St. Thomas Church in New
York; Clarence King, the geologist and explorer of the West; Elizabeth
Cameron, wife of a senator; and Adams's own wife.[9] But the novel's value is
not that of a *roman à clef*; it hovers instead about the competing values of
religion, science, and art as they bear on an intellectual woman's search for
herself.

The heroine of *Esther* has artistic interests, does charity work, and is not
conventionally religious. She complains of her "feminine want of motive in
life" (273), confessing that she wished that she earned her living. Two weeks
after her father dies, Esther submits to a minister's passionate insistence that
they be engaged. It is clear that she finds her geologist cousin's scientific
naturalism and devotion to abstract truth far more congenial than the minister's sensuous and passionate supernaturalism, but she loves him and not her
cousin. Her mother is dead and, as her father says, she has been " 'brought up
among men, and is not used to harness,' " and " 'a woman who rebels is lost' "
(231). Hearing the minister preach of love, she feels that the privacy of her
own love has been violated by his public expression of passion. He is persuasive, but she "could no more allow him to come into her life and take charge
of her thoughts than to go down into her kitchen and take charge of her cook"
(306). Her aunt, trying to break up what she knows is a bad match, appeals to
Esther's feminine pride by pointing out that a woman cannot afford to be
" 'thrown over by a man, not even if he is a clergyman.' " Esther should
therefore make it clear to him that she is jealous of the church, which she can

never accept as a minister's wife should. In the climax she is determined to turn their relationship into a mere friendship, "even if it cost her a lover as well as a husband" (364). But the minister confesses that he wants her soul for his church and demands that she share his faith, which she cannot feel. "'It is not my fault if you and your profession are one,'" Esther protests; "'and of all things on earth, to be half-married must be the worst torture'" (366). Threatened by "the thunders of the church" that are "already rolling over her head," she confesses that to her he always had seemed to be an archaic "priest in a Pagan temple" (368). The minister then loses his case forever by appealing to her to accept the hope of resurrection and immortality on the ground that "the natural instincts" of her sex should lead her to want to meet once more the relatives she loves. This appeal to her weakness revolts her: "I ask for spiritual life and you send me back to my flesh and blood as though I were a tigress you were sending back to her cubs" (370). She has succeeded in driving the minister away, and she knows that "the romance of her life was ended" (371). In this light Esther's integrity prevents her from succumbing to the great pressure put upon her by both the scientist and the minister to "have" a faith that she does not have.

Adams's conception of Esther gives her the dignity of principled rejection as well as the pathos of troubled identity. But a careful reading shows that there is another level to her story. It is parallel, incidentally, in this respect to Adams's other novel, *Democracy*, in which the cultivated heroine eventually rejects a powerful amoral senator and is unable to respond emotionally to a powerless but honorable statesman because of her loyalty to her first husband and child, whose deaths have left her with the fire of her emotional and sexual life "burned out."

There is a powerful undercurrent to Esther's conflicts connecting her story with the biographical fact that when Adams's wife lost her father, she went into a depression that ended in suicide. That Adams saw the connection, as his biographer Ernest Samuels observes, is evident from his own suppression of the novel after the tragedy had happened. Esther's father scorns clergymen and jokes about his hatred for Esther's potential suitors whom in fantasy he has hated all his life and twice a year "treacherously stabbed . . . in the back" (229). Esther's inability to accept the minister has another dimension suggested by the intensity of her outburst: "'I despise and loathe myself, and yet you thrust self at me from every corner of the church as though I loved and admired it!'" (369). The church, she complains, cries "flesh-flesh-flesh' at every corner." When Catherine Brooke at Niagara Falls compares the fall to a pretty, self-conscious woman like herself, Esther "vehemently" protests that the roaring cataract is really "a man," too powerful to be a woman (352). Adams's comment on the minister has a psychological resonance: "To have Niagara for a rival is no joke" (349). In one sense the fall is for Esther a "huge church," thundering its naturalistic gospel before her eyes, suggesting the traditional attributes of God, "eternity, infinity, and onmipotence," reducing her fret about her love affair to an "impertinence." In another, unconscious sense, her image of it may express a wish to be a man. In a strange passage she "feverishly" proposes to "elope together" with Catherine on a "wedding journey" (332) as a flight from the problems of their suitors. Her language is appropriate to a fantasy-role as a man. These intense reactions on her part, in their range of possible meanings, compel the attentive reader to look for a deeper trouble in her feelings than any rational disagreement with the minister can account for. Her self-revulsion and horror of the flesh suggest a deep-seated difficulty in accepting her own body, her sexual identity. Her aunt, who understands Esther, the minister, and the geologist better than anyone else in the story, believes that "if Esther is sensible she will never marry" (231).

These psychological considerations should lead us back to historical ones. Something in the culture of these women has prediposed them to unhappy histories. Esther's friend, Catherine Brooke, rebukes the dominating, erratic painter who loves her: " 'Men are always making themselves into ideals and expecting women to follow them' " (359). Esther is conventionally expected to accept the preacher's faith if she is to marry him. The best option in the judgment of Esther's tart-tongued aunt is for women to fall in love with clever men and then "marry dull, steady men in Wall Street, without any manners, and with hands in their pockets," using the rest of their lives for the business of "educating their husbands" (351). But at bottom, in her view, the situation is much worse than that. She tells Esther's father, who is worried that Esther will make a mistake in her marriage: " 'Marriage makes no real difference in their lot. All the contented women are fools, and all the discontented ones want to be men. Women are a blunder in the creation, and must take the consequences' " (231). Woman's identity could hardly be more problematical than her aunt's bleak-jest would have it. At the end of the story the heroine and her female companion flee to Europe to escape the pressures put upon them by rejected men.

Popular writers, Adams wryly observes in *Democracy*, "have decided that any woman will, under the right conditions, marry any man at any time, provided her 'higher nature' is properly appealed to" (158). Both heroines, Madeline and Esther, come to the verge of illustrating Adams's aphorism that "the capacity of women to make unsuitable marriages must be considered as the corner-stone of our society" (159). These characters hold Adams's interest because ultimately they refuse to surrender. But such women, who challenge the ordinary rules, are themselves scarred and troubled by earlier family life. Their curiosity and conviction are isolated from their sexuality, and they can see themselves as active agents only in their agonized refusals. They purchase their self-respect at the price of alienating their suitors. In so presenting them, Adams dramatized the effects on female character of a cultural definition of women as beings assumed to be irrelevant to politics and to rational thought. The depth of the educated American woman's trouble in this era was that she herself, to a painful extent, internalized the definition that cramped her. Their own previous roles have not fitted them for new beginnings. Esther's identification with her anti-clerical father has confused her own sexual identity. If the men demand too much of the heroines of both novels because of their interest in power—political or spiritual—the women are more attracted to them than to the available suitors who do not threaten their individuality. To some extent their suffering is self-inflicted.

In his autobiography, published twenty-three years after *Esther*, Adams's view of women shifts in two ways. He expands his vision downward in the social scale of women to include "telephone and telegraph-girls, shop-clerks, factory hands, running into millions of millions, and, as classes, unknown to themselves as to historians."[10] But he sees this new "free" woman as "sexless" and bound like the man, to "marry machinery."[11] He also looks far backward to the time when woman was a historical force by virtue of her power of sex, expressed in her role as beauty and as mother, as Venus and as Virgin. Traces of this power of woman remain in France, but in America, he laments, "an American Virgin would never dare command; an American Venus would never dare exist." Both symbols represent energy, and woman in this sense is "animated dynamo," or the power of reproduction—"the greatest and most mysterious of all energies; all she needed was to be fecund." The Middle Ages charmed him because the combination of Venus and Virgin, evident at the Louvre and at Chartres, had exercised "vastly more attraction over the human mind than all the steam-engines and dynamos ever dreamed of; and yet this energy was unknown to the American mind."[12] This myth-making was a lament for the historical passivity of women in an age of the machine, and a criticism of merely "masculine" images of power and energy. If he had the good sense to see that "the Marguerite of the future could alone decide whether she were better off than the Marguerite of the past," he was afraid that she would substitute for submission to the man or the church, submission to the machine.[13] He is at his best on women in the autobiography, however, when he speaks without mythologizing:

The study of history is useful to the historian by teaching him his ignorance of women; and the mass of this ignorance crushes one who is familiar enough with what are called historical sources to realize how few women have ever been known. The woman who is known only through a man is known wrong.... The American woman of the nineteenth century will live only as the man saw her; probably she will be less known than the woman of the eighteenth ... and all this is pure loss to history, for the American woman of the nineteenth century was much better company than the American man; she was probably much better company than her grandmothers.[14]

If some women were not able to be happy in the passive roles that their culture had invented for them, neither was Adams, as a reformer, a historian, and a poet, content to be judged by the dominant standards of economic and political power. Every reader of the autobiography knows that Adams was ambivalent about what William James called "the bitch-goddess SUCCESS" if only because the author so monotonously insisted on his own "failure." A self-styled "pilgrim of power," Adams knew that he did not have the power that his illustrious ancestors had wielded, but he "saw no office that he wanted."[15] He could therefore sympathetically understand his heroine's ambivalence about submitting to masculine power or defying it:

"I want to submit!" cried Esther piteously, rising in her turn and speaking in accents of real distress and passion. "Why can't some of you make me? For a few minutes at a time I think it done, and then I suddenly find myself more defiant than ever" [319].

Looking backward in his autobiography through a poetic haze of nostalgia, Adams could celebrate the time when the Virgin had the power over men to make them want to build Chartres Cathedral. But that celebration was flawed by its reduction of woman's humanity to a symbol of maternity, transcending sex, his own version of the characteristic misogyny of his class and culture. Elegant, witty, and penetrating, his novel tells another story, however, and proves the force of D. H. Lawrence's advice to trust the artist's tale and not his opinions.

As a novelist, Adams was more sympathetic to Esther than Freud was to Dora, one of his most famous cases. What Freud missed in her, as Erikson has pointed out, was a "vital identity fragment" of "the woman intellectual which had been encouraged by her father's delight in her precocious intelligence, but discouraged by her brother's superior example as favored by the times."[16] Freud's blindness to certain aspects of the Dora case, as Philip Rieff has suggested, reflected a common type of nineteenth-century misogyny that depreciated the intellectual aspects of woman's personality: "the child-bearing female represents the natural heritage of humanity, while the male carries on in spite of her enticements the burden of government and rational thought."[17] If Adams tended to approach the same view in his myth of the Virgin, he could transcend it as a novelist, finding sympathy for a woman's agnosticism and rebellion against male domination, even if, like Freud with Dora, he suspected that all was not well with Esther's sexual identity, as it was not with his own wife's relation to her father. For himself he valued *Esther* more than his nine-volume history. Though it has remained largely neglected by American scholars, it is one of the few American novels, after *The Scarlet Letter*, whose heroine has a similar name, that sympathetically portrays an intellectual woman outside the church.

With *The Rise of David Levinsky* we must shift our focus towards the sociological without losing sight of the individual personality of its hero, who undergoes the representative experience of an immigrant encountering what Tocqueville saw as "a virtuous materialism" that might in the future "not corrupt, but enervate the soul and noiselessly unbend its springs of action," unfitting men for public responsibility.[18] Abraham Cahan's novel, published in 1917, is set in the same time period of the 1880's as *Esther*, but it deals with the other end of the social scale.[19] It brings us into intimate knowledge of the inner meaning of the cultural strain implied in the movement of a Russian Jew to America, and it modulates our understanding of that process in a way that dramatization can achieve better than any sociological generalization. At the same time it links up certain ideological currents with the social pattern of economic upward-mobility and clarifies the function of Jewish religion in the life of immigrants. Just as Adams's novel circles over the intellectual issue of the conflict of science and faith to probe at a less rationalistic level, so also Cahan's story in all its "thick" social detail goes much deeper than the conventional literature of economic success ever did.

The usual history of a religious group that breaks in a reformist spirit from its institutional tradition is characterized by sociologists as the development of a "sect" in tension with its surrounding society in contrast to a "church" that accepts it. But America had already blurred this distinction in the history of the Puritans who became the established church in New England. The American Reform Jews illustrated another variation by splitting off from the tradition of Orthodoxy in order to have *less* tension with the larger society. But the Jews, like both Protestants and Catholics in the American world of the late nineteenth century, experienced a common process of accommodation to the secular, rationalistic, and middle-class ethos of a modernizing industrial and urban society with democratic traditions. In this sense Jewish history was not an anomaly, and it produced its own version of this process in *The Rise of David Levinsky*. Cahan himself represented the new immigration of Jews from eastern Europe, a great influx that was markedly different from the earlier German middle-class emigrants. Its grimmer circumstances of ghetto life had made for a more traditional piety, a stronger sense of peoplehood among different nationalities, or a more radical passion for secular social justice. The small group of American Jews who had in 1885 formed the Jewish Theological Seminary Association in New York as a protest against the sacrifice of tradition by the reform movement would find its opportunity for influence in the flood of the new immigration. Cahan himself was a Russian Jew with a passion for Russian literary culture and for socialism. Emigrating to America in 1882 as a political exile, he mastered both English and Yiddish, edited the *Jewish Daily Forward* in the language of its readers, and worked as an organizer in Jewish labor unions. By the turn of the century his literary work had earned the praise of William Dean Howells, and *The Rise of David Levinsky* was, in one sense, a Russian-Yiddish study in "realism" to match the American's *The Rise of Silas Lapham*.

Howells's Yankee hero finally forsakes the material advantages which complicity with sharp practices could have brought him and abandons Beacon Street for his native Vermont. More faithful to representative social actuality of its period, Cahan's novel portrays the slow economic rise in the garment industry of the lower East Side of a Jewish immigrant from Russia. Levinsky begins as a rabbinical student in the Russian ghetto, steeped in the

Talmud, but distracted by guilty sexual desires. Stricken when anti-Semites cause his mother's death, he is comforted and rescued from desperate poverty by an educated and prosperous Russian girl who is close to Gentile culture. Subsidizing his exodus, she resolves to achieve her vision of him as an educated man. On American shores the process of his adaptation to the economic and social conditions of his new world completes his alienation from Orthodoxy. Levinsky begins to see Americanization as the "tangible form of becoming a man of culture," because he regards even the most learned and refined Europeans as "greenhorns." Yet at the same time he retains an ambivalent feeling that American education is a "cheap machine-made product." All the outward earmarks of his conventional earlier identity as a rabbinical student, his earlocks and beard, disappear in his struggle for economic advancement and for sexual satisfaction in the teeming world of the East Side. The hope of going to City College, occasional lectures on ethical culture, the Darwinism of Herbert Spencer's *Sociology*, and the dream of a close family life come to take the place of his training in rabbinical studies. Evading union regulations, thereby winning the support of big manufacturers, and copying his rivals' designs, Levinsky becomes increasingly prosperous, able to donate to the Antomir Synagogue, which is a sentimental link for him to the world of his mother. If he studies poetry it is as a strategy to get to the poet's daughter. But he is as out of place in her Hebrew-speaking milieu of advanced literature, socialism, and Zionism, as he is among pious traditionalists. Both ends of the eastern European spectrum of Jewish life are distant from his new life.

Levinsky fashions for himself a new identity as a highly successful leader in the women's ready-made cloak and suit business, but his doggedly honest account of his rise is also a recurrent lament for his lost ambition, his disappointments in love, and his aching, distorted feeling that the Talmudic student he was in Russia has more in common with his "inner identity" than the self he has made in America. His autobiography is the only way he can express his wistful vision of himself as a person "born for a life of intellectual interest." But his own story also shows that even as a schoolboy he had a vengeful dream of becoming rich and influential so as to punish his tormentors and that after his mother's death he had lost his interest in the Talmud and was looking for "some violent change, for piquant sensations." It is in this mood that the image of America seized his imagination. His divorced Russian-speaking patron had made it clear to him that she found his piety and his Jewish look equally ridiculous. She prophetically expects America to make "another man" of him. Shaved and outfitted in his first American clothes, Levinsky mentally parades his "modern" make-up before his patroness. In America his reading of the Talmud at the Antomir Synagogue is only a stay against homesickness and a refuge from the strains of his struggles as a push-cart operator. Levinsky feels that his rigid native religion cannot be bent to the spirit of his new surroundings without breaking. But what makes the most critical difference in his development is the shame reflected in his decision to shave: he cannot bear to be called a "green one." His teacher in a public evening school, an American-born Reform Jew of German descent, devoted to the English Bible, to Dickens' novels, and the Democratic Party, is his instructor in accommodation to the new world, a midwife to the immigrant's representative experience of a second birth.

Cahan himself, though equally alienated from Orthodoxy, had a quite different development in the new world, preserving his ties to Russian literature, to socialism, and to the Yiddish culture of the East Side Jews. The artfulness of his novel is not so much its documentation of a closely observed world as its exposure of the psychology of a Jew whose successful adaptation to American life of the late nineteenth century leaves him with a melancholy sense that his past and his present "do not comport well." David Levinsky is not destroyed but successfully made over in a businessman's role that only fitfully troubles him in retrospect. His wistful feelings are derived from the ideals that his mother and his patron have fostered in his youthful imagination. Despite his adaptation, however, Levinsky knows that he cannot marry a Gentile woman to whom he is attracted, and he is still enough of a Jew to know that he is not really an educated man, that he has not served the cause of social justice and that his connection with a fashionable synagogue is quite external. Levinsky earns our sympathy for his plain prosaic honesty in accounting for his success. If he has missed much in achieving it, he knows, as his creator does, that it has been a representative experience in a country testifying to the power of worldliness.

That power has been able to exert its force over him so thoroughly because a process of change had already begun in him before he crossed the sea. In Levinsky's life Cahan dramatized the portentous fact that Judaism in America, like Catholicism, would be intimately connected with the problem of ethnic identity, thus complicating the problem of religious belief in America to the benefit of sociologists, if not to believers. Tocqueville had observed a peculiar mingling in America of patriotism and religion. If he had returned at the turn of the century, he would have had to add a missing chapter on immigration, Even in 1835 he had briefly noted with his usual keenness that economic success in America often forced the European emigrant "to unlearn the lessons of his early education."[20] Cahan's novel refines that observation by making it clear that for many of those who found the motive and the means to emigrate, the unlearning had already begun before the crossing.[21]

These novels, as I have read them, are not so much "a mirror set up in the roadway" as they are small lasers with a focussed beam that is very penetrating. They demonstrate the power of the novelist's imagination to collapse into a narrative unity elements of psychology, history, and sociology that have also challenged the talents of scholars who seek to make the kind of integration that modern psycho-history demands but rarely achieves. What they provide is an invaluable resource for advancing our understanding of the complex transactions between the self and its culture in a historical moment. But only if we bring to them a curiosity and a knowledge informed by these concerns will they answer in kind to our questions.

NOTES

1. David Brion Davis, "Some Recent Directions in American Cultural History," *American Historical Review*, LXXIII (February, 1968), 700, 704, 705.

2. Cushing Strout, "William James and the Twice-Born Sick Soul," *Daedalus, No. 97* (Summer, 1968), 1062–82. The research was done in collaboration with a psychiatrist, Dr. Howard Feinstein.

3. I have discussed the methodological advantages and limits of psycho-biography in "Ego Psychology and the Historian," *History and Theory*, VII (1968), 281–97. For Erikson's warning about the over-extension of the identity concept see his "The Concept of Identity in Race Relations: Notes and Queries," *Daedalus*, No. 95 (1966), 146, 151, 155.

4. Alexis de Tocqueville, *Democracy in America*, ed. Phillips Bradley (New York, 1945), II, 322. I have discussed Tocqueville's method in "Tocqueville's Duality: Describing America and Thinking of Europe," *American Quarterly*, XXI (Spring, 1969), 87–99.

5. Edward N. Saveth, "The Heroines of Henry Adams," *American Quarterly*, IX (Fall, 1956), 231–42.

6. *The Education of Henry Adams*, Modern Library Edition (New York, 1931), p. 23.

7. Quoted in Ernest Samuels, *The Young Henry Adams* (Cambridge, Mass., 1948), p. 93.

8. *Ibid.*, p. 264.

9. *Democracy and Esther: Two Novels by Henry Adams*, intro. Ernest Samuels (Garden City, N.Y., 1961), pp. xvi–xviii.

10. *The Education of Henry Adams*, p. 445.

11. *Ibid.*, p. 447.

12. *Ibid.*, pp. 384–85.

13. *Ibid.*, p. 447.

14. *Ibid.*, p. 353.

15. Adams asks "why had no President ever cared to employ him?" and suggests that it would require "a volume of intricate explanation." Yet he concludes that "from his own point of view, in the long run, he was likely to be a more useful citizen without office." The missing "volume" is eloquent by its absence. Similarly, in estimating his success he says that he and John Hay could look out their window "with the sense of having all that any one had; all that the world had to offer; all that they wanted in life. . . ." But he concludes, "this was not consideration, still less power in any of its concrete forms, and applied as well or better to a comic actor." *Ibid.*, pp. 322–23; 326–27.

16. Erik H. Erikson, *Insight and Responsibility* (New York, 1964), p. 172.

17. Philip Rieff, *Freud: The Mind of the Moralist*, rev. ed. (Garden City, N.Y., 1961), p. 201.

18. *Democracy in America*, II, 128, 133.

19. I have used the Harper Torchbook Edition (New York, 1960) with a valuable introduction by John Higham.

20. *Democracy in America*, II, 298.

21. My reading of Cahan's novel agrees with the analysis of David Singer, "David Levinsky's Fall: A Note on the Liebman Thesis," *American Quarterly*, XIX (Winter, 1967), 696–706. He points out that Charles Liebman's recent work confirms Cahan's story by emphasizing the prior secularization of Orthodoxy before its emigration to America.

12

WERE POPULISTS IRRATIONAL?
An Adlerian Approach
to the Watershed of the 1890s

James M. Youngdale

Few problems in American history offer a more attractive test case for the use of psychological theory on the nonbiographical scale than does late-nineteenth-century Populism. With a capital "P" the term refers to an outburst of ordinary people, mostly farmers and ranchers in the south and west, who were caught in the sharp depression of the 1890s. Banding together in the short-lived People's Party, seeking economic relief and social justice in an increasingly integrated economy, they demanded government ownership of railroads, telephone, and telegraph; they called for a graduated income tax and freer circulation of silver money.

The stated purposes of the Populists help to shape the treatment historians have given them. An early historical view, represented in the work of Vernon Louis Parrington in the 1920s, was that Populists spoke for the "progressive" impulse in the American experience; for Parrington the people waged continuing, slowly successful war on special interests as American progressed inexorably toward a more just and democratic state. The closest student of the Populists before 1950, John D. Hicks, saw their revolt as the climactic chapter in the story of western challenges to eastern dominance and as part of the democratic-liberal theme that finally produced the New Deal. Writing in the 1960s, Norman Pollack emphasized the role of rational self-interest in the Populist crusade, as have more recent scholars like Sheldon Hackney.

Emphasis on reason and economic motive aims to undercut a rival interpretation, based more on intangibles and the emotional, by which Populism betrayed deep ambivalence about changing values in American society. According to the late Richard Hofstadter, in *The Age of Reform* (1955), Populists belonged to an American tradition, not of progress, but of fear and provincialism. While voicing a belief in the natural superiority of the small farmer, Populism fostered less noble traits like prejudice, suspicion, and a conspiracy theory of history. Populism was "retrogressive,"

Reprinted in revised form from *Populism: A Psychohistorical Perspective* by James M. Youngdale by permission of Kennikat Press Corp. Copyright 1975 by Kennikat Press, Port Washington, N.Y.

Hofstadter argued; it was nostalgic and a bit foolish. At bottom the Populist was irrational.

In the next selection, a shortened chapter from a book-length "psychohistorical perspective" on Populism, James M. Youngdale challenges Hofstadter's irrationality thesis while applying his own analysis of the Populists. They reacted, he says, with an "offensive" rather than merely "defensive" strategy—one that makes most sense within the framework of Alfred Adler's theory of social adaptation and search for community. Youngdale incorporates Adlerian ideas with the theory of paradigms, which he borrows from the history of science. Paradigms are overarching, all-encompassing views of reality that people discard when they no longer appear to be true to the facts, as for example when the theory that the world was flat gave way to the realization that it was neither flat nor the center of the universe. In the case of the Populists the large belief passing into disrepute was of limitless American land and the individual's guarantee of reaping its rewards. Growing awareness that facts did not indeed square with this theory, Youngdale says, brought disillusionment that recalls Leon Festinger's writings in social psychology. Disenchanted, unconsciously trying to minimize dissonance, Americans desperately searched for a new paradigm. "Bryanism," after the pro-silver Democrat from Nebraska, explained disappointment as being the result of selfish monopolists and special interests in government; "mug-wumpism" was the prevailing attitude among middle- and upper-class persons whom change served to render less important than they had once been in public life; so-cialism, for some of the disgusted, looked ahead to an improved and more equitable community. Youngdale's view is that Populism represents an interim or transitional paradigm in the gradual movement from individualistic or laissez faire assumptions to a socialistic, cooperationist one.

Just as Youngdale's book lumps together disaffected groups in American society running from members of the People's Party in 1892 to the Minnesota Farmer-Laborites of the 1920s, and beyond, his chapter below says less than one would wish about the Populists themselves: Why did some Americans join the Populist Party and others not? Vulnerable for this reason, Youngdale's essay nonetheless raises useful questions about how one treats disenchantment in rapidly changing circumstances and explores psychological as well as "objective" reasons why the 1890s were so critical a period in American history. Finally, by working with the concepts of Adler and Festinger, he offers an example of the ways in which psychological theory can help bring order to apparent disarray in the historical sources.

A STUDY of Populism quickly forces one into that area of cultural criticism known as psychohistory. In using such terms as "zany fringe," "much that was comic," and "sour, illiberal and ill tempered" in referring to Populists, Richard Hofstadter, especially, focuses attention both on matters that fall under the rubric of psychology and on the problem of evaluating the gap between the subjective evaluation of reality by the actors in history and the objective paradigm imposed by the historian for understanding reality. The implied charge of irrationality in Hofstadter's analysis has drawn heavy fire from Norman Pollack, who suggests that the responsibility for discontent has been wrongly shifted from society to the Populists. "The result has been that the extent of oppression has been increasingly minimized and finally glossed over. And because the basis for discontent has been almost totally denied, Populism became subject to the charge of double irrationality; not only was it regressive, but it also responded to non-existent grievances."[1] The debate between Hofstadter and Pollack dramatizes the problem of evaluating myth versus reality. Here is a central concern for the historian who wishes to move from "factual," or narrative, history into the realm of motivation and interpretation, to ask "why" as well as "who, what, where and when."

It is fitting to observe, however, that all historical writing, even the so-called scientific history, is value-laden and based on certain assumptions about human nature. For example, the filiopietistic historians of the nineteenth century, who often dealt with "great" events and "great" people as heroes, were in effect portraying role models with whom, it was assumed, ordinary people could feel a sense of identity; these historians also ascribed "proper" normative values to mythic heroes as a response to such large moral questions as slavery or the growth of economic institutions like banks or trusts. In heroes like Franklin and Jackson, one could find such qualities as honesty, industry, and self-reliance, often with the touch of avarice that made up the positive image of the nineteenth-century rugged individualist. The later progressive historians, working with a dualism of "the people" versus "the interests," were committed to a view of inner human nature as inherently "good" but subject to corruption by "evil" social institutions, which at times led them paradoxically to imagine an escape from society—as if, like Huck Finn, they could strike out for the territories.

When instead one deals with Populism as a formal psychological problem, the first point to be made is the inadequacy of the psychoanalytic point of view. Freud was a medical doctor, looking always for a physiological remedy for "mental illness." He attempted to reduce neurotic phenomena to a conflict between instincts and cultural prohibitions; but, of course, culture itself was a product of instinctual sublimation. Caught up in this circular logic, Freud overvalued the importance of deep impulses and by the same token ignored the middle level (between instincts and paradigms) of social reality. There is barely a sense of history in Freud's outlook, only the notion of oedipal conflict repeated as generational conflict. At best, this is a highly truncated sense of history; at worst, it is hopelessly irrelevant and misleading. Freudians who subscribe literally to this model ignore the realities of changing social systems and of conflicting world-views as sources of individual and collective discord.

It is also possible to discern within the Freudian scheme a highly elitist and conservative bias in a social sense, derived from identifying the superego as a necessary guardian of the status quo. The id in the model, with its animallike aggressive drives, is analogous to Calvin's concept of human depravity as the inner core of human nature. For both men, a highly ordered society was essential to control and channel the inner irrationality or depravity in man; and thus social elitism came easily to both Calvin and Freud. Rollo May is perceptive in describing Freudianism as "Calvinism in Bermuda shorts."

In much social science analysis, "neo-Freudians" (like Erik Erikson) are more directly significant than Freud himself. The problem with this group is that they try to ride two horses at once; they retain some version of instinctualism while spinning theories about the ways in which social reality impinges on individual consciousness. Erich Fromm, for example, spoke of the internalization of external reality with his observation that "the social character internalizes external necessities and thus harnesses human energy for the task of a given economic and social system."[2] Fromm's emphasis is on external reality; in his analytical scheme society determines personality without reference to the creative role of the individual in forming or choosing new paradigms for viewing reality. Not only does Fromm subscribe to a version of social determinism, but he retains from Freud the notion of instinctual determinism. This is evident when he digresses to excoriate Alfred Adler in *Escape from Freedom.*

And while we think of the wish for power as an irrational impulse to rule over others, Adler looked entirely at it from the rational side and speaks of the wish for power as an adequate reaction which has the function of protecting the person against dangers springing from his insecurity and inferiority. Adler, here, as always, cannot see beyond purposeful and rational human determinations of human behavior; and though he has contributed valuable insights into the intricacies of motivation, he remains always on the surface and never descends into the abyss of irrational impulses as Freud has done.[3]

More recently, in *The Crisis in Psychoanalysis*, Fromm criticizes Freud on several counts, especially for his social conservatism. Yet he hails him for founding the "science of human irrationality" in developing psychoanalytic theory.[4] As will be more fully evident after we turn to Adler, it is less than helpful to speak as Fromm does of the "abyss of irrational impulses." For this point of view denies or obscures the social basis for ambivalence and tension caused by conflicting conceptual frameworks. Furthermore, Fromm grossly oversimplifies Adler's outlook in suggesting that his views reduce themselves to a "wish for power" that is the controlling factor in human life.

In addition to the psychoanalytic view of psychology, there is a body of theory that falls under the heading of social behaviorism. At one end of this spectrum is the Stimulus-Response point of view developed by J. B. Watson and later by B. F. Skinner. S-R psychology has been widely criticized for failing to include either human organism or ideology as intervening factors between stimulus and response. This psychology is perhaps useful for studying habit formation and behavior reinforcement; even so, S-R theory does not take into account ambivalence in ideology as an element complicating the choice-making process and cannot explain the basis for a new choice as it is made. Certain neobehaviorists have developed more sophisticated theoretical outlooks in such areas as learning theory and group process; however, by virtue of the assumptions they work within, they too fail to examine macroprocesses in history in terms of overlapping paradigms.

In a certain fundamental way, Karl Marx reflects an adherence to S-R psychology in his dictum that social being determines social consciousness and in his view that exploitation and/or deprivation produces responses toward reform and revolution. There is a tendency in Marx to deprecate anomalies with such terms as "lumpen proletariat," for example, rather than to develop a more adequate explanation of the varieties of psychological strategies that people employ in striving to overcome dissonance and alienation and to achieve a sense of harmony between life expectations and life settings.

Another variant in behaviorist psychology comes from the progressives of the twentieth century, from such persons as George Herbert Mead and John Dewey, whose outlooks cast a long shadow on the present. Building upon William James's ideas about the individual relativity of truth, these men developed systems involving situational psychology and morality. Necessarily, they came to view "human nature" as being highly elastic and variable in its potential for responding to widely differing, socially defined situations, and thus they have departed from the Freudian notion of an unchanging inner personality. Their difficulty arises with a tendency to define "social situation" in terms of small groups—for example, the family, the peer group, or the immediate community—a view that has led to the development of transactional analysis. The result of this definition of "social" has been the exclusion of changing social systems and conflicting ideologies as facets of the social situation. Even though these progressives and their followers have developed new theories about the significance of symbolic and nonverbal means of communication as forms of transactional interaction, they tend to accept the large status quo as a given and have failed to get at the root of ambivalence and ambiguity in paradigm conflict.

Alfred Adler's outlook, when coupled with the notion of history as overlapping paradigms in a changing social reality, produces a special version of psychohistory. Adler not only rejected the Freudian notion of internalized personality structure, but also developed a positive theory emphasizing social environment as the factor accounting for variations in personality types or life-styles. In some ways, Adler is close to Mead, who viewed psychology in the context of social interaction; but Adler himself saw individuals interacting in a wider world of communities rather than the more narrow world of dyadic interaction stressed by Mead. It is noteworthy, too, that Adler is not truly open to the charge leveled against behavior modificationists that they would have the individual conform to existing norms; for Adler was consciously a socialist and saw various kinds of social reform as a precondition to successful individual therapy.

For Adler, all inherited capabilities, the physical as well as the so-called instinctual ones, are employed strategically by persons to accomplish certain goals they set before themselves: human activities, thoughts, and personality types can best be understood in the context of people carrying out general tasks and striving for specific goals. Adler speaks of three tasks—work, love, and friendship—around which human activities are deployed. Later, I should like to add a fourth task; however, let us persist for the present in defining more fully the Adlerian model. Around the general tasks of work, love, and friendship, individuals develop specific goals in terms of occupation, marriage involving sexual gratification, and developing a circle of friends. Thus a typical individual committed to the nineteenth-century rugged individualist or laissez faire paradigm might strive to become a successful independent farmer or businessman, to marry and live in a patriarchal family structure, and to enjoy friends primarily within a community defined by church membership; and such a typical person would adopt strategies for reaching these goals, strategies that become reflected in personality traits, which in turn define an individual's overt identity or life-style.

For Adler, personality types emerge as kinds of strategies available for meeting the problems a person encounters in social reality, problems defined variously depending on a person's cognitive view of reality (which again is at variance with Freud's anal and oral types arising from instinctual repression). In one essay in his early writing, Adler catalogues a number of types, each in effect describing a tactical approach in social relations. He lists the following complexes: Inferiority (submissiveness, sense of failure); Superiority (will to power, domineering attitudes, egocentricity, godlike self-image); Oedipus (not universal as with Freud, but a part of the pampered-child syndrome); Redeemer (messianic); Proof (perfectionism); Predestination (chosen people); Polonius (the "as if" illusion); Exclusion (withdrawal, flight from community); Leader (king of the mountain); Spectator (passivity, apathy); and No (rebellion, negativism).[5]

It should be noted that Adler later reduced this list to the two mechanisms involving superiority and inferiority and to the interplay of these complexes. Adler holds that every individual, by virtue of dependency as an infant, tends to have a feeling of inferiority and that the process of growing up involves a constant striving to overcome this inferiority. Depending on the total situation from which an individual emerges, his degree of success in overcoming inferiority will range from total failure to total egocentricity. In this view, a neurotic person can be defined as one who is insecure and overly bound to social norms, thus denying individual perceptivity, whereas a psychotic person moves into a private world of egocentricity, operating with insufficient social feeling or consideration of social norms of any kind. Adler speaks of the superiority complex as overcompensation for inferiority, as a kind of masked inferiority which in men is often seen as masculine superiority. Adler's definition of democracy in interpersonal relations involves a balance between becoming meekly submissive and powerfully autocratic. The democratic individual is one who enjoys a feeling of community with fellow human beings, both drawing support from others and also playing a creative role in social relations, for which Adler uses the term *Gemeinschaftsgefühl* (community feeling) as an ideal or normative value.

Adler's stress on the primacy of community in human life is central to his general outlook. His idea of *Gemeinschaftsgefühl* can be translated variously as social feeling, social solidarity, sense of fellowship in the human community, or as the emotional counterpart of movements.

What we call justice and righteousness, and consider most valuable in all human character, is essentially nothing more than the fulfillment of the conditions which arise in the social needs of mankind. These conditions give shape to the soul and direct its activity; responsibility, loyalty, frankness, love of truth, and the like virtues which have been set up and retained only by the universally valid principle of communal life. . . . In the course of our demonstrations it will become increasingly evident that no adequate man can grow up without cultivating a deep sense of his fellowship in humanity and practicing the art of being a human being.[6]

The need and feeling for community pervades all facets of society, according to Adler.

The compulsion toward the community and communal life exists in institutions whose forms we need not entirely understand, as in religion, where the sanctification of communal formula serves as a bond between members of the community. . . . The communal life of man antedates the individual life of man. In the history of human civilization no form of life whose foundations were not laid communally can be found. No human being ever appeared except in a community of human beings.[7]

The emphasis in Adler on the inseparability of the individual and the community runs counter to Freud's vision of the individual with internal tensions that are discharged externally through sublimation. Rudolph Dreikurs has compared the two viewpoints:

For Freud, all human conflicts are intra-personal, caused by opposing conflicts within the personality structure. . . . For Adler, all problems are inter-personal. This implies a different emphasis on both the origin of conflicts and on therapeutic procedure. For Freud, the maladjustment with its consequent disturbance of human relationships originates in the inner-personal conflicts, while for Adler the inner conflicts express disturbed human relationships. Freud emphasized the inner needs, while Adler emphasized the significance of the attitude toward others.[8]

For the historian the Adlerian point of view, with its emphasis on community as a central aspect of human experience, offers a special perspective on movements and associations; and at the same time, the relative sterility of psychologies based on Freud or Erickson is evident in their tendency to focus on the internal tension of individuals.

Making goals and aspirations the cornerstone of thought and behavior, Adlerians see much of the anxiety in our culture as deriving from the failure to fulfill aspirations, a failure that might result from our expecting too much.

Whether this apparent overambition is due to unrealistic aspirations on the part of individuals or too few possibilities within the social structure is always a matter for investigation; but regardless of one's judgment on this matter, individuals suffer from anxiety and frustration. Somewhat as Freud theorized that people develop defense mechanisms to allay tensions, Adler saw individuals adopting strategies (reflected as personality types) to blunt feelings of anxiety. But in Adler's view these measures are always related to the larger goals of the individual. The adaptive measures in the Adlerian model can better be seen as offense mechanisms, strategies either for realizing present goals or for achieving success (even as a successful criminal) within a new version of reality and a new sense of ego-identity.

According to Adler, an initial response to anxiety involves either choosing new personality traits or accentuating present traits, as the case may be. Adler preferred to view these traits as complexes. Terminology seems unimportant as long as the function of personality types is understood as an offense mechanism for confronting the world, including even "withdrawal" as a paradoxical tactic of confrontation. Furthermore, these complexes do not exist in the abstract, simply as psychic mechanisms; but rather, they filter through and attach themselves to social institutions and provide norms for life-styles and personality patterns, often becoming attached to particular cognitive views of the world. Thus family, church, or political party tend in their concrete manifestations (1) to provide the individual with a commitment to a paradigm and (2) to institutionalize norms for life-styles that reflect a deployment of one or more offense mechanisms or personality strategies.

Earlier, we noted Adler's definition of the primary tasks in life as work, friendship, and love, the essential human tasks around which specific goals are formed. To this list one must add the task of achieving an intellectual view of the world, a cognitive version of reality. In the case of inarticulate or uneducated people, the world view may be expressed in simple terms organized around prevailing symbols and myths; but a simple view (low culture) may be no different qualitatively from a sophisticated *weltanschauung* (high culture), in that both may express affinity for the same paradigm. To deny that groping for a world view is an essential task for every person is to ignore the distinction between man and lower animals or between thinking man and man the idiot.

An additional assumption, implicit in Adler but developed more fully by Leon Festinger, is that man strives for consonance in life, or that there exists in man a tendency toward homeostasis. The concept of homeostasis is widely employed in such disparate fields as cell biology and economics; but it is especially useful in psychology to describe man's quest for psychic harmony. Using the situation of the cigarette smoker who knows that smoking causes cancer, Festinger notes that the alternatives facing such a person range from stopping smoking to developing various kinds of rationalizations that neutralize the knowledge about cancer and thereby permit continued smoking.

The rationalizing smoker illustrates the dissonance that can lead to paradigm revolutions. As discrepancies or contradictions appear in an existing paradigm, new strategies come into play, either as new forms of behavior or new theories about reality, or both, to create a new sense of harmony. In developing a new theory of reality, a given person, for the sake of harmony, must repress or reject his previous belief structure or alter previous behavior patterns.

Taking into account repression and/or rejection of a social outlook defines a version of the unconscious (or barely conscious) that is at variance with the Freudian concept of instinctual drives as the core of the unconscious. In addition, combining Festinger and Adler enables us better to understand ideological ambivalence: emotional ties often exist with a repressed paradigm, so that it is possible for a person to switch his commitment or "flip-flop" from one outlook to another as life experience changes. Striving for consonance at times produces an effect other than making a clear choice between paradigms and repressing the rejected outlook. That alternative takes the form of rationalizing opposing views into some form of ambiguity to obscure conflict and to create a semblance of harmony—even though such ambiguity is less a resolution of conflict than an intellectual obfuscation aimed at papering over anomalies in the social system.

While this study is concerned primarily with a macromovement in American history, we must be aware that larger anomalies and contradictions are reflected in minute ways as crises in an individual's life-style or identity, as tensions in immediate relations with others, or as problems in finding meaning in work. While helpers (counselors, psychiatrists, etc.) may help people find practical expedients in these kinds of crises, the larger meaning of such crises can be fully understood only in terms of the state of paradigm conflict at a given time. Thus, a theory of social process that links the social structure and the individual in a symbiotic relationship makes it possible to move back and forth from macro- to micro-levels of human experience.

A typical person must live in both a micro- and a macrosociety, striving for homeostasis and/or ego esteem[9] in personal relationships and yet trying to adjust to changing social reality and paradigm conflict. Thus personality strategies adopted at one point in life may prove to be ill-suited at another stage. The temper-tantrum tactic children employ for attention and control over others gives way when one grows to adulthood; the "boss" who at work adopts an authoritarian personality may face a double crisis if his business goes bankrupt, for he may be forced to take a job in which his personality does not "fit." Obviously the range of human responses to defeat and frustration or to the need for change is varied and finally unique to each individual.

Yet to the extent that members of a society share goals and personality traits and significant portions of a population adhere to a pattern, it is possible to understand the emergence of the Populists in terms of those shared experiences and shared offensive mechanisms. When massive changes in economy or social structure cause a shift from one paradigm to another, a revolution in social consciousness occurs, a general reevaluation or transformation in the meaning of social and individual problems and in the meaning of received myths and symbols. This process was at work as Populism struggled to emerge as a new paradigm in America. Populists were pulled between a tendency to look back to a restoration of the laissez faire world and to look ahead in the direction of a socialist restructuring of social life.

Because old values and personality traits persisted even as Populists shifted from one paradigm to another, they produced ambiguous language and eclectric personalities. Among the small number of men who made the leap from laissez faire individualism to socialism, many continued to exhibit messianic or ascetic character traits; when disputes arose among socialists and efforts to organize a new movement failed, there were tendencies to revert to laissez faire cultural patterns in search of a new psychic harmony. Examples are legion of attempts to recapture the old outlook of Jacksonian individualism, with Populist leaders, having angrily discarded the socialist paradigm, often becoming tormentors of their former comrades. A well-known example was Tom Watson of Georgia, a tolerant Populist in the 1890s who later turned savagely on blacks, Catholics, and Jews in the pages of the monthly magazine he ironically called *The Jeffersonian*. Watson's case often goes to prove that Populism had its dark side. More accurately, the Georgian's changes of mind spoke to the persistent attractions of the individualist paradigm—a source of values (many of them nativist) that divided the hearts and minds of many Populists. Another example of internal division was the career of Algie Simons, a Milwaukee socialist who in World War I left the party to join the official witch-hunt for his ex-friends.

Obviously not all people who were disillusioned or anxious over their life circumstances in an emerging industrial America became Populists as the first step in the process of cognitive reorientation. Indeed, the American Dream was not given up easily, and the first reaction of most people was to retain hope in it. Adler's complexes describe almost without elaboration the strategies middle-class Americans employed—strategies that implied formation of personality types as well as social movements. There was the "no," or negativistic reaction, often associated with mugwumpism and with Bryanism. There was the "withdrawal" reaction into family and private concerns ("children, kitchen, and church") among persons hoping that social conflict would go away. Some persons, notably members of certain religious sects, adopted a "messianic" or "chosen people" attitude as a source of psychic support. Still others become rigidly perfectionist, a mechanism linked with a sense of superiority and a dogged determination to live with the Dream.

Although Populists tended to be "mixed up" and their movement "schizophrenic" in its blend of conflicting social paradigms, it is less than helpful to look for causes in Freud's unconscious. Erich Fromm speaks of a "pathology of normalcy" in the modern world as a part of a "chronic, low-grade schizophrenia that is endemic to the cybernated, technological society of today and tomorrow."[10] Following Freud, Fromm speaks of an "underworld of the unconscious" as the source of irrationality. Yet it seems unwise and unnecessary to settle on so mystical an explanation for the "low-grade schizophrenia" that Fromm finds. Instead one might say that one or another conflicting world view becomes repressed and remains unexamined as a source of values and as a basis for contradictory aspirations and seemingly confused behavior. Certainly it is never easy to discover the basis for behavior, thought, and emotions; all these manifestations emerge partly from repressed or unadmitted world views and values that stand in the way of understanding. But the potential for insight is greater when, ferreting out the motives of individuals and examining the roots of movements, we consider the lessons of Adlerian psychology and the fact of paradigm revolutions.

To see Populism in light of Adler and Festinger is to question the simplicity of Hofstadter's irrationality thesis. The social psychological approach also adds a much-needed corrective to the idealization of Populists on the part of Norman Pollack. Once we introduce the theory of overlapping paradigms for understanding history, it is possible to understand the ambivalence and vacillation of the Populists along with the schismatic tendencies that appeared in the movement. One finds examples of frustrated petty capitalists, as Hofstader did, and of proto-socialists, as did Pollack. It is possible to search out unattractive traits of persons within Populist movements who turned sour and intolerant because continued commitment to their world view brought only frustration; and it is possible to find large numbers who worked with courage and tolerance toward reforms and who almost succeeded in achieving a paradigm revolution of their own before the Progressives co-opted some of their specific reforms and deflected their revolutionary momentum.

A final observation on the function of psychological mechanisms among Populists is in order. While such "subjective" attributes as courage, love, hate, honesty, and dishonesty are rarely mentioned in "objective" analyses of social movements, these qualities deserve greater stress since they necessarily play a part among those involved in reform movements. Granting that such qualities can perhaps be sensed only as impressions, it is my view that courage has been one of the most important forces to sustain reform movements. The literature of Populism along with my own observations suggest that Populists generally tended to fight against the mechanism of "withdrawal" into a private world of apparent aimlessness and apathy; and by this tendency they perforce became advocates of courage to face a new reality and to pursue a new course of behavior. The story is told that A. C. Townley, president and charismatic leader of the Farmers Nonpartisan League, was asked by an irate farmer, "What good am I getting for the sixteen dollars dues I paid the League?" Townley's reply was sharp and incisive: "You got the courage to ask that question. You got your money's worth."

The IWW sympathizer and poet Morris Chaflin wrote these lines deploring apathy and lack of courage in facing the evils of society.

Mourn not the dead that in the cold earth lie
But rather mourn the apathetic crowd
The cowed and the meek
Who see the world's great anguish and its wrong
And dare not Speak!

By preaching courage as a heuristic device and by showing courage themselves, many reform leaders acted out the social psychology described in this chapter. They sensed that certain psychological mechanisms stood in the way of anyone's adopting a new outlook on reality, and they implicitly understood that personality is plastic, that people can and do change.

NOTES

1. Norman Pollack, *The Populist Response to Industrial America* (Cambridge, Mass.: Harvard University Press, 1962), p. 7.

2. Erich Fromm, *Escape from Freedom* (New York: Avon Books, 1967), p. 311.

3. Ibid., pp. 171–72.

4. Erich Fromm, *The Crisis in Psychoanalysis* (New York: Holt, Rinehart and Winston, 1970), p. 36.

5. Heinz L. Ansbacher and Rowena R. Ansbacher, eds., *Superiority and Social Interest*, Collected later writings of Alfred Adler (London: Routledge and Kegan Paul Ltd., 1965), chapter 7, pp. 71–80, "Complex Compulsion as a Part of Personality and Neurosis."

6. Ibid., p. 32.

7. Ibid., pp. 27–28.

8. Rudolph Dreikurs, *Fundamentals of Adlerian Psychology* (Chicago: Alfred Adler Institute, 1950), p. 31.

9. The concept of "ego esteem," implying a tendency for satisfaction based on a consistent and coherent life-style, flows from Adler. He is often criticized by Freudians for being an "ego psychologist" and for ignoring the unconscious; however, both Freud and Anna Freud finally devoted more attention to the ego and the development of defense mechanisms somewhat in the Adlerian manner.

10. Fromm, *Crisis in Psychoanalysis*, p. 29.

13

WHY AMERICA LOVED TEDDY ROOSEVELT
Or, Charisma Is in the Eyes of the Beholders

KATHLEEN DALTON

Theodore Roosevelt has never wanted for talented biographers. Henry Pringle, William H. Harbaugh, and John Morton Blum all have written enduring studies of Roosevelt, and more recently Edmund Morris has published yet another book on this incredible figure who, sickly in boyhood, rose above all infirmities to become a boxer, cowboy, soldier, New York governor, president, and big game hunter. Everyone who has written about him marvels at the energy and enthusiasm he took to every physical stunt and political challenge. Teddy—his face set with determination, his big stick at the ready—remains, like Paul Bunyan, a folk hero, the quintessential American.

Historians have noted for some time that Roosevelt's personal prejudices and reformist politics captured nicely the ambiguities of the Progressive Era—its racial antipathies and urges for order and efficiency. Now, in a book soon to be published, Kathleen Dalton has set out to trace the connections between his personality and the governing assumptions of late Victorian American society. By her interpretation Roosevelt represented an ultimate example of the masculine ideals that Americans, formally and informally, strove to realize in young men. Roosevelt's preoccupation with masculine prowess and his need to exert his will on other persons, countries, and even nature itself illustrated the highest values of late-nineteenth- and early-twentieth-century America. Focusing on this point, the next essay shows how TR's popular appeal demonstrated the tensions between the ideals Roosevelt personified and the realities of twentieth-century life. Dalton's attempt to examine this appeal from the ground up—working with the letters Roosevelt received from admirers—is interesting and innovative; though her typology of four leader-follower bonds may not satisfy every political scientist or student of "mass psychology," it does help to make clear the nature of Roosevelt's representativeness. The more characteristic Teddy's behavior, the more independent and blustering he grew as a "Bull Moose," the greater his popularity among Americans whose "virility" seemed stifled at a time of growing cities and expanding factories.

Reprinted in revised form from *The Psychohistory Review* 8, no. 3 (Winter 1979):16–26, courtesy of the publishers.

ADORING contemporaries called Theodore Roosevelt a "great American hero" and "the ideal man and statesman."[1] When in 1913 his countrymen were asked by *American Magazine* who was the "greatest man in the United States," Roosevelt won hands down.[2] He shared the spotlight of public affection in the first thirty years of this century with Woodrow Wilson, William Jennings Bryan, Robert M. LaFollette, Henry Ford, and Charles Lindbergh, but Roosevelt's relationship with grass-roots America was not quite like the others'. Unlike the Great Commoner he was not born a man of the people, so he had to work hard to build egalitarian bonds with them. Though, like Wilson, Bryan, and LaFollette, Roosevelt's moral style of leadership had religious overtones, he preached a distinctive manly gospel of the strenuous life, which hit home with unmatched aptness among the pious and the secular. Lone Eagle Lindbergh's flight and Flivver King Ford's inventions appealed to a populace still marveling at the wonders of science, but Roosevelt's heroism, shown first in his childhood triumph of willpower over asthma, was an everyday psychological heroism that touched people more deeply because it was exactly the kind of bravery they needed in their own lives if they were to survive unburned by the "acids of modernity."[3]

Roosevelt stands above the other cultural heroes of his age in one astounding particular—all the rest have fallen from grace. LaFollette became irrelevant; Wilson committed infanticide by killing his brainchild, the Treaty of Versailles; Bryan died a martyr to fundamentalism; anti-Semitism ruined Ford; and Lindbergh made a fool out of himself by putting America First. Roosevelt alone remains a vital folk hero today. Almost sixty years after his death the New York *Times* ran a cartoon of Mount Rushmore showing God's light shining down through the clouds onto TR's eternal stone face. Underneath, a tourist says, "Teddy is my favorite, too."[4] Today Roosevelt's active fan club holds spirited celebrations to commemorate his birth—the affection that progressive America felt for Roosevelt lives on.[5]

One obvious yardstick of TR's popularity during the Progressive Era was his landslide victory in the 1904 presidential election. Even in 1912, when he came out of "retirement" to wage a long-shot third-party fight against Republican incumbent Taft and Democratic hopeful Wilson, Roosevelt made electoral history. No other third party candidate has whipped an incumbent vote for vote. Though he lost to Wilson in 1912 he did not sink to defeat because of an inadequately narrow base of support. Running best among Republicans, easterners, and the urban middle classes, he won votes from every corner, class, and allegiance around the country. Despite his left-of-center rhetoric and the slim chance of success in any third party race, Roosevelt proved by his strong showing in the election that he had diversified nationwide appeal.[6]

Votes, of course, are not the only measure of popular devotion. Fan mail, eulogies, songs, poetry, cartoons, and records of passionate crowds attest to America's love for TR more vividly than election tallies. From these varied sources emerges an undeniable fact: many Americans were deeply attached to Theodore Roosevelt. Such popular outpourings reveal a hitherto unexplored "underside" of public consciousness. Just as social historians study mobility patterns and labor conditions as clues to the external social circumstances average people faced, psychohistorians, by studying popular emotions, can find clues to the ways in which plain people made those circumstances meaningful, to what they valued, and to what transformed and excited their daily lives.

Charisma is usually thought of as a magical charm inherent in the personality of a popular leader. Roosevelt had that charm. He exuded energy. His powerful electric presence and flamboyant stage-stealing drew public attention. He was entertaining. Crowds loved his boyish playfulness and humor, and were uplifted by his gift for moral leadership. But these traits did not make TR charismatic. His relationship with the public did. Indeed, all charismatic leadership arises out of the interaction between the leader and the led. Followers are not passive in the relationship. By their responsiveness they speak approval and lend guidance to the leader. The "charisma in the eyes of the beholders" is the public's emotional need for a special kind of leader at a particular moment in history. Instead of taking the all-too-familiar tack of focusing solely on the leader to understand charisma, I will explore the four bonds of charismatic love by doing "psychohistory-from-the bottom-up," that is, looking into the lives and feelings of the common and uncommon people in whose eyes Theodore Roosevelt was lovable.

I

How did love spring up in the hearts of Americans for this man? Why did it matter so much to so many people that he spoke out for certain ideals? Why should crowds embrace, cheer, and in many cases, worship a leader who was, after all, a mere mortal? Why should love, a uniquely powerful and private emotion, be given at all to a stranger?

To find answers let us look at love itself. Love is an emotion that may emerge out of need, fantasy, stress, identification, and mature altruism. Love may be narcissistic or it may come from the desire to reach out and give to another person. It may be blind or it can be filled with insight into the loved object (person). A person's developmental level shapes why and how he loves. For instance, infants love blindly and selfishly. They cannot distinguish between the self and the loved object. They take but cannot give. Typically they feel a primitive narcissistic love filled with fantasy about the all-encompassing power of the loved object. Later, the person works to build an independent identity, i.e., to complete the separation-individuation process. The person gradually learns to distinguish between the self and the loved object by identifying with people against whose image his worth is measured. Thus, adolescents often idealize and identify with the people they love. After a separate identity is formed a person may become capable of mature love. The loved object is finally evaluated realistically. The boundaries between the self and the loved object are at long last clear. Mature love, like other styles of love, grows out of need for another person. But need is no longer a one-way street. Mutual dependency and altruistic giving to the loved object become possible.[7]

These developmental styles of private love or object relations are parallel to the four styles of political love. Political object relations evolve from early, wishful, fantasied attachments to seemingly all-powerful leaders. Wishful love for a leader is primarily dependent and naively adoring. Ego-ideal love emerges from the admirer's identification with a heroic leader. As the capacity for somewhat more realistic relations develops, a person may love a charismatic leader symbolically for seeming to manage both politics and larger social forces. Finally, illusion may disappear altogether. The admirer may see the leader for what he is and love him for the real work he can do. This is reality-oriented love, the most mature political object relation. Wishful, ego-ideal, symbolic, and reality-oriented relations with leaders may represent stages a person passes through like infancy, childhood, adolescence and adulthood.[8] Or they may be styles of emotional attachment that emerge simultaneously in response to a leader. The most wishful attachments still may have a place in the life of adults who normally relate to leaders on reality-oriented grounds. As with private relations, stress or crisis may cause a person to regress to an earlier or less developed style of love. For example the imminent threat of foreign invasion or nuclear holocaust might prompt a person who typically formed reality-oriented relations to give in to a wishful belief that a leader might resolve the crisis.

Charismatic bonds arise out of public emotional needs. Need for leadership, like need in the private realm, affects the style of political object relation a person forms. Desperation and deprivation, for instance, usually make for wishfulness. In personal relationships, however, wishful or inaccurate perceptions will be tested sooner or later by the reality of direct experience with the loved object. Political object relations are too distant for such testing. Admirers learn about leaders through intermediaries—through press agents, political commentators, newspapers, and television, or by word-of-mouth. Some leaders use the distance to create false impressions. Thus inaccurate and idealized images of leaders and unrealistically high public expectations crop up easily. Even in the absence of national crises the public expects a great deal. Leaders are asked not only to offer tangible solutions to political problems, but often are expected to grapple through symbolic gestures with troublesome social forces as well. Followers frequently need to admire the leader's personal qualities, to have him serve as a heroic representation of culturally valued ideals. They also seek to build in their own minds an emotive relationship with him, no matter how wishful that bond might be.

Theodore Roosevelt became a charismatic leader by responding to all of these public emotional needs—from the most realistic to the most wishful.

II

Reality-oriented charismatic bonds, unlike the other three, were formed rather simply between Roosevelt and his admirers. Some people perceived in a realistic fashion how well TR met their needs for political leadership, and their perception was not inflated by exaggerated and ungrounded images of his power or by desperate wishfulness. People who rationally evaluated his actions in terms of their political philosophies or commitment to issues—and found him acceptable—grew to love him. Letters from his supporters tell that they commonly judged his foreign policy and domestic reform initiatives to be sound. Accordingly, a Los Angeles civics teacher sent in a list of issues in the 1912 campaign which had made him decide to give his allegiance to Roosevelt.[9] Others loved TR because he had a more "modern" political philosophy than his predecessor, William McKinley. While it seems in retrospect mistaken, if not irrational, for many radicals to have become attached to a moderate reformer like Roosevelt, some did so quite realistically on the basis of the information intermediaries offered them. Though it now seems incorrect to perceive TR as a champion of blacks, especially in light of the Brownsville incident of August 1906, it was reasonable for one 1912 supporter to become attached to TR because he perceived his leader as pro-black for giving them a "fair chance" in federal appointments.[10] Issues and facts, not fantasy, created this kind of bond.

Similarly, self-interest and pressure-group membership provided bases for reality-oriented love for Roosevelt. Many Civil War veterans, for instance, viewed President Roosevelt as their defender because he had removed an unpopular commissioner of pensions. In consequence, their verdict was that the "Grand Army will waver not one hair's breadth in its devotion" to him.[11] A Washington, D.C., man came into the Bull Moose camp in 1912 because he disliked Wilson and the Democratic party's traditional "jealously of the Federal government," and as a federally employed conservationist he had reason to believe his job would be more secure in a Roosevelt administration.[12]

Roosevelt won reality-oriented love in one last, less obvious way. Leaders are expected to address the troubles their followers face as individuals and as a nation. Leaders who reach the public on a deep emotional level usually do so by laying out a path for them to take, by offering them a new vision of their society. By capturing and mobilizing the public's capacity for mature, altruistic giving a leader can unite people behind a new vision. When John F. Kennedy in his inaugural address called for his countrymen to set aside selfish interests and "ask what you can do for your country" he tapped an emotional reserve—a widespread public desire to participate in making a better society.[13] What James MacGregor Burns calls "transforming" leadership is the ability to provide a vision that mobilizes public altruism and helps people unite behind a common purpose.[14]

Theodore Roosevelt offered his followers a vision of an efficient, progressive society organized on principles of social justice and collective moral endeavor. He also offered them a vision of America as an interventionist world power. Elting Morison described how Roosevelt's visionary leadership worked: "He had the hold of a hero. By his words and deeds he gave a defining and supporting frame for the aspirations of those insufficiently clear or strong to support their aspirations by their own endeavor. Men, in hope of finding their better selves, attached themselves to him. In doing so, they transferred some of the responsibility for themselves to him and in turn created in themselves a compensating sense of responsibility for his own actions."[15] When Roosevelt stood at Armageddon in 1912 he hailed his followers as the men who "have come together to spend and be spent in the endless crusade against wrong . . . who strive in the spirit of brotherhood for the betterment of our nation."[16] Just as other "transforming" leaders urged their followers to abandon politics-as-usual, Roosevelt called upon Progressives to muster up their selflessness and idealism for the work ahead. Bobby Kennedy in the 1968 campaign used George Bernard Shaw's words to stir the same public emotions. "Some people see things as they are and say: why? I dream things that never were and say: why not?"[17] "Transforming" leaders inspire idealistic dreams, and in doing so change the lives of their followers—sometimes permanently. Stanley Isaacs, four decades after the Bull Moose campaign, said, "I doubt if anyone today can realize the personal inspiration that came from direct contact with TR or can appreciate the fervor that animated those of us who shared in the early Progressive Party years."[18] William Allen White's life was altered forever, as TR "poured into my heart such visions, such ideals, such hopes, such a new attitude toward life and patriotism and the meaning of things, as I had never dreamed men had." As he found himself transformed White began to share Roosevelt's vision of a "new order" awaiting their collective creation.[19] Of course, providing followers with a new vision or "language of ideology" can appeal to sources of public emotion that are far from reality-oriented.[20] "Transforming" leaders invite fantasy and identification as well as reality-oriented love.

III

A charismatic leader also serves as an exemplar, as a person with whom the public can identify. The public turns to leaders to find models of virtue, embodiments of cultural ideals, spokesmen for values and cultural themes of emotional significance to them. Personal characteristics—strength, determination, optimism—take on greater weight than political factors in the public's judgment of a leader when an ego-ideal bond is formed. When one Anti-saloon Leaguer confessed to TR his "supreme faith in you as a man, and the things for which you stand" he emphasized personality, not issues.[21] One man, though he disagreed with Roosevelt on the issues, wrote that he was beginning to favor the Bull Moose in 1912 because "you come nearer my ideals than either of the other candidates."[22]

Leaders, as anthropologist Waud Kracke put it, not only serve as a "model for identification and aspiration," but they help "reinforce" followers' "inner control over impulses."[23] In some people's minds leaders stand for the "shoulds" and "oughts"—the moral boundaries as well as the highest ideals—of a culture. Thus, love for the leader is tied to the cultural values he represents. For example, a sixteen-year-old Chicago worker named Hyman Skolnick wrote that he constantly looked at a quotation from TR that he kept on his wall. It read: "It is only through strife, through hard labor and painful effort, by grim energy and resolute courage, that we move on to better things." Skolnick told Roosevelt that these lines helped him when he was "discouraged and downhearted," and they inspired "new life, new grit" in him as he toiled, "striving to succeed."[24] Roosevelt had become an impor-tant person in Skolnick's life, for he encouraged the young man to keep pushing himself to seek his goals. TR stood for persistence, the work ethic, masculine stoicism, and the belief that just rewards would be forthcoming. Skolnick's need to use TR as an external conscience was the foundation for his ego-ideal attachment to his leader. Many Americans were fond of Roosevelt in a similarly personal way: he egged them on as they sought their "better selves."

For many Americans Roosevelt served as more than a personal reminder of cultural values. He was to them the personification of Victorian willpower and manliness—two emotionally significant cultural themes during the Pro-gressive Era. TR appealed to the populace as a strenuous, moralistic, and public-spirited Alger hero, and his fan mail is filled with admiring references to his pluck. He hammered home to his listeners in speech after speech that he detested moral flabbiness and weak-willed passivity, the bugaboos of his own emotional past.[25] His public discussions of his life and his campaign biographies stressed his childhood triumph of will over asthma.[26] Thus he was offered to the public as a model of willpower to be emulated. Progressive Americans were newly uneasy about how on earth they would contend with the unknown powers of the giant industrial combines and large organizations that had begun to dominate the country. Struggling with what seemed like an increasingly closed system managed by experts and industrial magnates, Roosevelt's listeners eagerly grasped his message that individual free will could still win just rewards in an environment each person could understand and manipulate. Roosevelt asserted: "If there is any lesson to teach a boy from my life . . . it is that a man of common place and ordinary attributes can achieve a measure of success, *if he will only use to the utmost, and develop to their limit*, these ordinary qualities, so that they become reasonably good instruments for his purpose. Then he may do the work of the halfgods."[27] In order to play upon the cultural theme of will as the key to success Roosevelt lied about his "commonplace" origins, denying that he had begun the race for success with the head start of being born into the most privileged caste of Edith Wharton's old New York.[28]

Nevertheless, the public responded eagerly to the imagery of Roosevelt's self-improvement through willpower, of his difficult upward struggle to conquer illness, and of the eventual just rewards when he became strong—and later president. Americans were especially receptive to this cultural theme because they had reason to be anxious about their prospects for success in the new century. The old frontiers of opportunity seemed to be closing. As Peter Filene has written, success seemed harder to achieve and, worse yet, harder now to define.[29] The Pandora's box of industrialism had produced ominous creatures—uncontrollable corporations and the no longer "respectable" working class; furthermore, the new, organizational society encroached daily upon the individual's belief that he controlled his destiny.[30] Roosevelt could not banish these frightful new forces. He could, however, reassure the public by optimistically reminding them that old ideals would get them through. Jacob Riis spoke for countless people when he wrote: "It was one of the things that early attracted me to Theodore Roosevelt, long before he became famous, that he was a believer in the gospel of will. Nothing is more certain, humanly speaking, than this, that what a man wills himself to be, that he will be. Is he willing to put in all on getting rich, rich he will get."[31] All around them was upheaval. America's relations with the rest of the world, the ethnic makeup of the population, class relationships, the economic order, sex roles, and the power of the individual in a reorganized society were changing.[32] Drastic social change like this may evoke object loss in the people who endure it, according to Fred Weinstein and Gerald Platt, for the disappearance of old verities and landmarks, as well as symbolic cultural codes, may disrupt ego functioning as the loss of a loved one often does.[33] Americans sought mastery of the change and their own loss through the ideology of will that Roosevelt expounded.

TR also defended another emotionally significant cultural theme, masculinity. As he lectured Americans on the dangers of "national emasculation" he touched a responsive nerve.[34] Men had derived their feelings of maleness—their male gender identity—from varied sources in the Victorian age—from pride in their self-control and steadfast character, from their toughness and physical prowess, from their freedom to express romantic individualism by creating their own opportunities, from their aggressive conquests in enterprise and on the frontier, from their procreative and sexual performance, or from their place in the family and their dominance over women.[35] Some of these anchors of male gender identity were unsettled in the new century. Would feminist cries for equality mean the end of male dominance or even the destruction of family life? Where in factory work was the adventure of manly conquest? Where in white-collar work was romantic individualism? Where was manliness to be found in soft, compartmentalized city living? Many men wondered how their manliness would survive intact through the changing times.[36] Roosevelt reaffirmed the possibilities of manliness by preaching to them the strenuous life. Nothing was worse in TR's mind than the "over-civilized man, who has lost the great fighting, masterful virtues."[37] He insisted that masculinity could be revived if men cultivated, as he did, the "stern and virile virtues which move the men of stout heart and strong hand who uphold the honor of their flag in battle."[38] As a vivid symbol of masculinity thriving undaunted in the machine age, Roosevelt widely advertised his exploits as a Rough Rider charging up San Juan Hill. A Dakota cowboy and big game hunter, too, TR served the public as an exemplary male ego-ideal.

The response from his public was overwhelmingly enthusiastic. Poets acclaimed him for his "vital, virile, warrior soul." They admired him because "if force were needed, he exalted force."[39] Frank Crane wrote in tribute to Roosevelt's masculine strength, "He conceived of life, of duty, and even love in terms of conflict. His make-up was militant. . . . For he was a man's man . . . no man has ever been more a part of every man in the United States than Theodore Roosevelt."[40] Admirers declared that in their eyes he embodied the "virile spirit of progressive political action."[41] One man said he had joined the Bull Moose's party because Woodrow Wilson lacked "a kernal of aggressiveness."[41] Roosevelt's "immense virility" was hailed by eulogists, who reminded their audiences that there was a big difference between TR's muscular Christianity and modern masculine sexual permissiveness, for "in his maleness was the virility of the athlete, not the excessive sexuality of the degenerate."[42]

Today TR lives on as a popular symbol of masculinity, not only in movies like *The Wind and the Lion* but in the minds of people born long after the Progressive Era. A retired navy captain, a thoroughgoing military man like Douglas MacArthur, told an oral history interviewer recently that Roosevelt was his favorite president. Though he could not recall any political specifics, the captain admired TR more than any other president because "he was rough and ready."[43] A gay Republican Club in San Francisco has taken Roosevelt as its mascot because the Rough Rider continues to stand firm as a symbol of uncompromising and occasionally overacted traditional masculinity, an image that haunts gay men in their choice of sexual identity.[44] Roosevelt's leadership was linked in the minds of many progressive Americans with their varied personal needs to have the cultural themes of will and manliness exemplified and defended. Though the world had changed around them, many people maintained a sense of personal continuity by reaffirming through their leader reassuring, emotionally significant cultural themes.

Many, like Hyman Skolnick, loved TR for helping them face life in the new century.

One of Bernard Malamud's characters in *The Natural* explained public enthusiasm for baseball stars by declaring that "without heroes, we're all plain people and don't know how far we can go."[45] Public affection for charismatic political leaders is the same. Heroes define a culture's aspirations and hopes. They offer people dreams and magic to enhance everyday life. Leaders become heroic to the public when they transcend normal mortal limitations of self. Leaders' apparent superhuman feats, although they have nothing to do with politics, win popular love. After Andrew Jackson's duel with Charles Dickinson—when Old Hickory stood still, accepting a bullet in his chest before fatally shooting his opponent in the groin—observers remarked in awe that Jackson's "self-command appeared almost superhuman."[46] In a similar heroic scene in the 1912 campaign TR was shot in an assasination attempt just before he was scheduled to speak to well-wishers in Milwaukee. Refusing to go to a hospital, Roosevelt insisted on speaking for an hour and a half despite bleeding from the bullet wound in his chest.[47] His supporters were profoundly moved. Earlier, in 1901, days after McKinley's murder and TR's assumption of the presidency, one man had written to approve the Rough Rider's refusal of secret service protection: "I admire that kind of pluck, and so do the American people."[48] TR's boundless energy and courage made him seem like a "physical marvel." Supporters queried, "What leader has so powerful a personal equipment? . . . Show us someone who is Roosevelt's equal as a warrior, a man close to the people, a true-hearted captain of our hopes before you ask us to give him up."[49] A woman in Wyoming also saw Roosevelt as a transcendent hero; she wrote that he had "always been to me a modern 'Sir Galahad.'"[50] According to Freud's *Group Psychology and the Analysis of the Ego*, our craving for a hero, a model of virtue to emulate, a romantic, adventurous, but distant alter ego to enliven our sense of self, is not so different from falling in love with a role model.[51] The blurring of ego boundaries in crowds or in charismatic bonds can be, as Freud suggested, dangerous. Hitler and his followers come to mind as frightening examples of the power of non-rational identification with a leader and the excesses of popular emotions. Nevertheless, in many other cases ego-ideal attachments to leaders, like adolescent infatuation with idealistic causes or religious movements, can be a useful part of growing up. A leader can serve as a role model, an image of what we might become as we struggle to define ourselves. Leaders who serve as ego-ideals, like certain types of loved objects, can make us want to be better people, and they can make life more worth living. In modern mass society where instrumental, impersonal social relations predominate, heroes also have become a means for people to build much-needed personal bonds with society at large. Superstars—in fact the phenomenon of "celebrity" which predates even radio—are not so much the products of the mass media as they are creatures of an impersonal and emotionally isolating modern society. Love for a hero personalizes life in the masses for the average citizen by affirming his belonging to and identity within the crowd. Cultural leadership and availability for identification, then—not practical, political work—are central to ego-ideal love.

IV

American politics does more than provide the people with appealing heroes. Our elections and political hoopla can be viewed, not merely as part of political decision-making, but as revealing cultural rituals. Thomas Scheff, in reminding anthropologists that rituals are filled with emotional meaning for the participants, offered an overstated but useful definition of ritual: "the distanced reenactment of situations of emotional distress that are virtually universal in a given culture."[52] Americans distance themselves from excruciating cultural tensions, inter-group hostilities, and other shared distress by dramatically expunging and symbolically resolving common troubles through the "deep play" of ritual in the open political arena.[53] When populist candidates reach out in their speeches to crowds of mixed class and ethnic backgrounds, they are serving as the central actors in a unifying ritual drama of egalitarian social integration. Demagogues like Huey Long come right out and say through politics all class distinctions can be shed and "every man" can become "king." Of course, rituals change as culture evolves. Elections in America today are no longer invested with quite the same emotion as in the past. In TR's day, however, elections were such meaningful rituals that reformers frequently tampered with the election machinery—its ballots, primaries, referendum, initiative, and direct election of senators. If they perfected the ritual, they believed, America would become more democratic.

Charismatic leaders, stars of the ritual political show, capture public emotion by making symbolic gestures.[54] Like Greek tragedy, symbolic gestures can be emotionally cathartic for followers because the leader brings to the public stage a conflictual issue and then resolves it through symbolic gestures. For example, trusts justifiably frightened many people at the turn of the century, for the growth of big business seemed to promise a future corporate oligarchy. American attitudes toward big business were changing throughout the Progressive Era, according to Louis P. Galambos in *The Public Image of Big Business in America, 1880–1940* (1975). Roosevelt hastened public acceptance of big business by symbolically seeming to bring it under the control of government by regulation and anti-trust cases.[55] When he confronted J. P. Morgan in the Northern Securities Case, TR in fact did virtually nothing to undermine the economic and political power of big business; yet to a large segment of the public it looked as if Roosevelt had been their champion in a clear-cut popular defeat of the moneyed interests. Many midwestern farmers trusted TR to tame the "small group of purse-proud and

arrogant plutocrats" who had dominated the economy.[56] Prevailing progressive beliefs about the broad-ranging effects of reform fed their faith in
Roosevelt's ability to achieve mastery over the social order. But belief and
formal ideas are not sufficient explanations in this case. Part of grass-roots
America, on emotional grounds, needed to see Roosevelt as its powerful
surrogate in a symbolic battle against trusts. Roosevelt won a landslide electoral victory in 1904 as cartoonists began to portray him as the man who
wielded the Big Stick, not just at foes overseas, but against trusts at home.[57]

Similarly in the 1912 campaign Roosevelt used symbolic gestures of anti-
establishment rhetoric to win popular support. He attacked bosses, party
leaders, trust magnates, and all entrenched privilege. Verbal barrages did
little to redistribute power in the society, but such attacks relieved emotional
tension and convinced many people that Roosevelt was involved in an actual
fight. As one supporter put it, TR seemed to be warring "in the interest of all
the people against the bosses."[58] The hatred of privilege runs deep in the
hearts of grass-roots Americans, especially when the extremes of wealth and
poverty seem to be growing. One spirited supporter proudly told TR that the
"despisable people" were on their way out because "we have got all of the old
'bosses' treed in both parties and they dasen't back out."[59] Perhaps
Roosevelt's admirers did not imagine total abolition of economic and social
distinctions, but their letters are nonetheless filled with hope that he could
somehow eliminate "special privilege . . . looking to the welfare of the people
at large."[60] They thanked him for awakening them to "the fact that in the
past we have been governed by a handful of designing politicians representing corrupt interests." Letter after letter complimented him for being the
"champion of the people's cause."[61] They turned over to him their responsibility to act, and expected him magically to bring about social equality and
economic justice. Roosevelt's symbolic gestures of combat ritually relieved
some of the distressful emotions produced by class and other inequalities.
But political ritual and charismatic leadership can change public consciousness faster than they can change social and economic conditions. If Roosevelt
had won in 1912, America would have remained a stratified and unjust
society.

In Roosevelt's 1912 campaign attacking privilege went hand in hand with
symbolic gestures toward social integration. Within cities, he remarked,
threatening "lines of social cleavage are far more deeply marked" than in the
country. Roosevelt lectured his audiences repeatedly on the danger of America's becoming a "polyglot boarding house" of people who share nothing but
economic interdependence.[62] Instead, national purpose and common moral
moral goals should unite a diverse people. "Each group of men has its special
interests," he insisted, "and yet the higher, the broader, and deeper interests
are those which apply to all men alike."[63] Along with William James,
Roosevelt believed that "all the qualities of a man acquire dignity when he
knows that the service of the collectivity that owns him needs him."[64] Both

men had the Civil War in mind as a model of shared national purpose. James sought to arouse in the public the "moral equivalent of war"—building a spirit of community and public service through national reform. Roosevelt, on the other hand, saw war as the best way to pull people into public-mindedness.[65]

On a symbolic level his talk about brotherhood touched his countrymen's needs for affiliation, community, and shared moral purpose. As the twentieth century pulled asunder an already factious, individualistic people, these needs were especially urgent. By bringing Booker T. Washington into the White House and Jane Addams onto the Progressive Party podium Roosevelt began the work of symbolic integration that his distant cousin, Franklin Delano Roosevelt carried on later. By encouraging labor and management to arbitrate during the Anthracite Coal Strike, TR symbolically told the public no longer to fear the class warfare between militant workers and recalcitrant capitalists that had seemed imminent since Haymarket days. He was a man who brought people together peaceably.

Roosevelt understood that the symbolism of harmonious social unity and equality drew the public to him. When he first gained fame as a Spanish-American War hero, Roosevelt portrayed himself in his book *The Rough Riders* as a leader who could unite an odd assortment of American types—cowboys, polo-players, derelicts, football stars, Indians, and Wall Street lawyers. Achievement and brotherhood counted, not ascribed status and class distinctions. TR boasted that under his command "we had men of every grade socially... each of them glad to get in on his worth as a man only, and content to be judged purely by what he could show himself to be."[66]

Plain people knew what Roosevelt was suggesting. Recognizing the symbolic promise TR made to bring more equality and social cohesion, one semi-literate man, who lived in poverty in Alabama, wrote that he hoped the Bull Moose would bring "a government by the people and for the people." He believed so fervently in this hope that he was willing to "do all I can for the cause.... My plan is to work among the common people of the country and among my own class... I do not care to go among the high class as I am a poor man." He told TR that before he died he wanted to see change.[67] Like the man from Alabama, a black woman from New York City had in mind an image of Roosevelt as the guiding spirit of social integration when she wrote that "all races" should support him. She confessed she was "unidentified" with other blacks but she felt a kinship with TR, adding that "according to my humble judgment, I love the good and the great, that's why I admire you."[68] One Bull Mooser summed up the public's image of Roosevelt as a force for social inclusiveness: "Strangers meet in the crowds of the street, and in a moment they find they are brothers facing the same way.... The cause counts. It calls to Republicans, to Democrats, to Socialists, to Independents, to Jew, to Catholic, to Protestant, to men of the South and men of the North, to native born, to foreigner become American—to all who are brothers and

who want to march on and up to better, squarer, more equal dealings between man and man."[69] Many Americans loved Theodore Roosevelt because
they needed so badly to see themselves as potential social equals and because
they longed to join together in a national community of shared purpose. Love
built on symbolic gestures is based on the people's need to see their society
unified and managed. They ask the leader to stand at the center of social and
cultural conflict as the agent of public will, resolving tensions with symbolic
gestures. Roosevelt won popular affection by fighting grass-roots Americans'
battles for them.

V

A 1912 campaign song, to be sung to the tune of "Just Before the Battle
Mother," began:

Farewell Teddy, we may never
Grasp your hand or see your face;
Those remote are proud to hail you,
Leader of the human race.[70]

People who would never see Roosevelt, who would never be anything but
"remote" from him, felt intimate with him. They looked at him as their
friend. They invited him to their houses for dinner, asked him to join in
church or community activities, and wrote him for personal advice. Ignoring
the distance that in reality existed between them and their leader, admirers of
TR fantasized that he was a part of their lives. Some imagined that they were
married to him and that together they constituted "one happy family."[71] An
immigrant wrote TR that after listening to his recent speech he felt as if he
had had a "heart to heart talk" with his leader.[72] Admirers of Henry Ford
developed similar wishful attachments to him. Total strangers wrote asking
him to stop by to help them churn the butter or to loan them money. A
farmer from Louisiana told Ford "I have seen so much of your life recorded
in the papers that it just seems I have known you all my life."[73]

Wishful attachments, the least emotionally developed or reality-oriented
form of follower-leader bond, arise out of extravagant fantasies about the
leader. An admirer may have trouble distinguishing himself from the leader
or he may assume that the leader is a god who watches over him and knows
all about him. Wishful love for a leader often has less to do with a need for
political leadership than it does with private unmet needs. Downright loneliness may bring about wishful love for a leader, as does a crying need for
connectedness with a parental figure who seems larger or more powerful.
Fantasies about leaders may also emerge because of ignorance, miseducation,
creative imagination, or religious impulses. Distorted and fanciful images
have been implanted in people's minds by leaders or intermediaries. In any

case, wishful love is necessarily related to the same social pressures that inspire love based on symbolic gestures. National troubles—e.g., war, depression, or social change drastic enough to inspire object loss—may coincide with or cause severe personal stress. The result is often disorientation or strong wishful attachments to a charismatic leader.

National crises are not always easily pinpointed or evaluated. Certainly the Civil War and the Great Depression were crises. But was the bustling and prosperous Progressive Era an equivalent time of crisis? Probably not, but a crisis atmosphere pervaded public consciousness more than it did later, during the twenties. Robert H. Wiebe insisted in *The Search for Order, 1877–1920* that the depression of the 1890s "worked on men's nerves" so much that "some resolution to the general crisis became imperative."[74] Roosevelt's generation faced the perplexing social disruption of the Gilded Age as their first order of business in the new century. The word "crisis" appears over and over again in the letters Roosevelt received from the public. One Progressive Party member wrote that "at this crisis in our national affairs" Roosevelt's leadership was badly needed.[75] A man who described himself modestly as the "average type of plain American citizen, unpolitic and unpolitical" called for Roosevelt's help in the national emergency. He wrote that America faced a "crisis unparalleled since the decade prior to the Civil War."[76] Though the feeling of urgency was widespread among the people who wrote to TR, people disagreed about the nature of the crisis. Many of them cited political corruption and bosses as the main threats. Big business, railroads, slums, and religious tolerance also troubled some people. Others talked in general terms about moral decay and sin. An antisuffragist blamed the emergency on "aliens" who had upset the "ship of state." Indeed, she wrote, suffragists and female "usurpers of authority" were also the source of the crisis.[77] To one citizen it made sense for government to become "so much less a *political* and so much more a *social* agency" in the emergency; another worried about the potentially threatening expansion of federal power, because "no one can see what is ahead of us within the next few years."[78]

Public uneasiness about the crisis, regardless of how it was diagnosed, brought calls for strong leadership. Many of those calls were somewhat fanciful. A Bull Moose supporter from western New York told TR: "I will devote my life to this cause because you have been so abused, and are the *only* man to rescue us at this crisis . . . you are Napoleon when it comes to action. I *know* you will cut this Gordian knot."[79] An eighty-six-year-old bookseller wrote Roosevelt that the crisis was so serious that "we need a Dictator." The "social disturbances," machine politics, "labor troubles," and "war scares" had put the country in turmoil. He wished that TR could manage it all.[80] Wallace Battle, claiming to voice the "feeling of all the thoughtful Negroes in Mississippi," wrote TR that he hoped the Bull Moose would "thwart *every* evil that is now so deceitfully working at the very taproot of the nation."[81] The fantasy that Roosevelt would purify the nation and master all "oppression, wrong and evil" appears repeatedly in his fan mail and in popular songs and poetry.[82] One supporter wrote TR that he regarded Progressive policies "as a revelation from God in the heart of men to relieve the people of a national sin."[83]

Roosevelt's political return as a Bull Moose looked like the second coming of Christ to some wishful admirers, who loved him as a "Savior." In June 1912, when he came to Chicago to fight for the Republican presidential nomination, ten thousand handbills announced to credulous readers that TR would soon walk on the waters of Lake Michigan.[84] Such wishfulness may be akin to folklore, a colorful embellishment of reality that is only half-believed. Educated, scientific minds were equally susceptible to such fantasies. When TR died, in 1919, naturalist John Burroughs could not believe that his hero had actually succumbed, for "I must have unconsciously felt that his power to live was unconquerable."[85]

Roosevelt was asked not only to resolve national crises, but also to fulfill private longings. The wish that an all-powerful distributor of justice, a mortal god, could save them from the random cruelties endemic to human life cropped up frequently in the letters written to TR. For example, a widow struggling haplessly to support a child on her salary as a stenographer asked him to find a job for her.[86] A railroad conductor who had lost his job pleaded with Roosevelt to get him reinstated, promising that if he could be returned to work he would "give the rail road company a square deal."[87] A New York City resident who had been wronged by Congressman Frank Greene asked TR to kick Greene out of office: "I want you to tell me if you will see that he is put out if you are elected to the Presidency."[88] A traveling salesman for a piano company wrote TR to request that he help free the man's son from Sing-Sing. Trying to cajole Roosevelt into aiding him, the man wrote that "if you will put yourself out to aid us I will guarantee you that I will add many votes to your election."[89] Though such pleas may simply have represented an overevaluation of TR's power or naiveté about the boundaries of social interactions, they also expressed universal wishes for justice and for help with the trials of life.

A poem an Italian-American sent to TR began with a tribute to "Ted a da Rose de man wid a heart."[90] The public turned to him with wishful needs because of his compassion. Roosevelt had conveyed warmth and concern to his audiences, and many people loved him for it. Emulating his boyhood hero Abraham Lincoln, TR talked about "the need of broad human sympathy, and the need of lofty and generous emotion in the individual."[91] But he did not always practice what he preached. Neither capable of paternal, reassuring fireside chats nor the tenderhearted responsiveness that made Lincoln so beloved, TR became a lesser hero of compassion to the people than FDR and Honest Abe were. Though he romped through White House pillow fights with his rambunctious young sons, and was moved deeply when Jacob Riis took him to see slum life first-hand, Roosevelt's public image was not built primarily on his effusiveness and nurturance. He met some, but not all, public emotional needs, and he met the needs that best suited his personality. TR's personal trademarks were vitality and morality. Between Roosevelt and his public, therefore, the moral chords of "Onward Christian Soldiers" and the exciting rhythms of "There'll Be a Hot Time in the Old Town Tonight" played best.

VI

Americans loved Theodore Roosevelt because he knew how to be "the voice of America," as one contemporary put it: "All of us found that he but uttered the thought, the aspirations and dreams that we had unawares entertained but needed the notes of his clarion voice to flower into speech."[92] Listeners filtered out Roosevelt's voice to hear his words as balms for their own personal troubles. Thus, people from all walks of life took TR to heart to use him for their own purposes. At the appropriate time of need they pressed him into service wishfully, realistically, symbolically, or as an ego-ideal. In consequence, they made him serve variously as their champion, their god, their politician, their friend, their savior, or even as their conscience. Roosevelt, as we have seen, played as many roles as the people required. As the public discovered more and more ways for him to meet their private needs, Roosevelt looked increasingly charismatic in the "eyes of the beholders." This was charisma suited to the public's personal concerns.

By exploring the four styles of public love for TR we have exposed some of the emotional undercurrents of American life during the Progressive Era. In particular, we have looked at many of the predominant cultural and social tensions of the day and the personal anxieties they engendered. When the events and trends of their times weighed too heavily upon them and a crisis threatened them, the American people naturally looked for a leader. As Roosevelt preached his progressive gospel of will, manliness, equality, and social cohesion many people were reassured. His cures appeared to hit the spot. This was charismatic leadership suited to the shared cultural dilemmas of the Progressive Era. Americans loved Teddy Roosevelt, then, because he simultaneously tapped the private longings and the shared cultural roots of his contemporaries' "charisma-hunger," their special need for inspirational leadership in the first years of the twentieth century.

NOTES

1. T. Harrison Cummings, *Memorial Exercises, Commemorating the Sixty-Fourth Anniversary of the Birth of Theodore Roosevelt.* Held at the Cambridge City Hall, Oct. 27, 1922 (Cambridge: privately printed, 1922); Ferdinand C. Inglehart to TR, July 11, 1912, Reel 149, Theodore Roosevelt Papers, Library of Congress, Washington, D.C. All letters and manuscript refer-

ences, unless otherwise designated, are to this collection. The author wishes to thank E. Anthony Rotundo, John H. Gable, Dom Cavallo, Bruce Mazlish, Stephen Beamon, Brett Williams, Kenneth S. Lynn, John Higham, Joseph Herzberg, Robert M. Kvarnes, Louis P. Galambos, and Barbara Finkelstein for their useful comments on my efforts to do "psychohistory-from-the-bottom-up." The work that inspired this article is Reynold M. Wik, *Henry Ford and Grassroots America* (Ann Arbor, Mich.: University of Michigan Press, 1972).

2. Nathan G. Hale, Jr., *Freud and the Americans: The Beginnings of Psychoanalysis in the United States, 1876–1917* (New York: Oxford University Press, 1971), p. 45. On TR as a cultural hero and symbol: Richard H. Collin, "The Image of Theodore Roosevelt in American History and Thought, 1885–1965," dissertation, New York University, 1966; David Francis Sadler, "Theodore Roosevelt: A Symbol to Americans," dissertation, University of Minnesota, 1955. On heroes in America: Theodore P. Greene, *America's Heroes: The Changing Models of Success in America's Magazines* (New York: Oxford University Press, 1970); Dixon Wecter, *The Hero in America; A Chronicle of Hero-Worship* (New York: Charles Scribner's Sons, 1972); Marshall W. Fishwick, *American Heroes, Myth and Reality* (Washington, D.C.: Public Affairs Press, 1954); Ray B. Browne, Marshall W. Fishwick, and Michael T. Marsden (eds.), *Heroes of Popular Culture* (Bowling Green, Ohio: Bowling Green University Popular Press, 1972).

3. Lawrence W. Levine, *Defender of the Faith: William Jennings Bryan; The Last Decade, 1915–1925* (New York: Oxford University Press, 1965), p. 256. For background on the other cultural heroes: Paul W. Glad, *McKinley, Bryan, and the People* (Philadelphia: Lippincott, 1964); Louis W. Koenig, *Bryan* (New York: Putnam, 1971); Paolo E. Coletta, *William Jennings Bryan* (Lincoln: University of Nebraska Press, 1964–1969), 3 vols.; Belle Case LaFollette and Fola LaFollette, *Robert M. LaFollette* (New York: Hafner Publishing Co., 1971), 2 vols.; David P. Thelen, *Robert M. LaFollette and the Insurgent Spirit* (Boston: Little, Brown and Co., 1976); Robert S. Maxwell (ed.), *LaFollette* (Englewood Cliffs, N.J.: Prentice-Hall, 1969); Arthur S. Link, *Wilson* (Princeton: Princeton University Press, 1947-), 4 vols.; Arthur S. Link, *Woodrow Wilson and the Progressive Era, 1910–1917* (New York: Harper and Row, 1954); John Morton Blum, *Woodrow Wilson and the Politics of Morality* (Boston: Little, Brown and Co., 1956); John Braeman (ed.), *Wilson* (Englewood Cliffs, N.J.: Prentice-Hall, 1972); Kenneth S. Davis, *Charles A. Lindbergh and the American Dream* (Garden City, N.Y.: Doubleday and Co., 1959).

4. *New York Times*, July 10, 1977, Section 10, p. 5. Folk heroes do not always fall from grace, but they have cycles of resurgent popularity. Roosevelt's reputation and salience as a hero declined after his death, only to have later revivals.

5. The Theodore Roosevelt Association, "dedicated to perpetuating the memory" of TR, publishes quarterly the Theodore Roosevelt *Journal*. Popular interest in TR continues: he appeared on the cover of *Newsweek*, Aug. 6, 1979, under the caption "Where Have All the Heroes Gone?" See also Alan Havig, "Presidential Images, History, and Homage: Memorializing Theodore Roosevelt, 1919–1967," *American Quarterly*, 30, no. 4 (Fall 1978), pp. 514–32; and George Neavoll, "T.R.'s Ghost and the Land," *Washington Post*, Feb. 12, 1977.

6. Allan J. Lichtman and Jack B. Lord II, "Party Loyalty and Progressive Politics: Quantitative Analysis of the Vote for President in 1912," paper presented at the annual meeting of the Organization of American Historians, April 1979; John H. Gable, *The Bull Moose Years: Theodore Roosevelt and the Progressive Party 1912–1916* (Port Washington, N.Y.: Kennikat Press, 1978).

7. See for the theoretical background to this summary: Gertrude and Rubin Blanck, *Ego Psychology: Theory and Practice* (New York: Columbia University Press, 1974); Margaret S. Mahler, *On Human Symbiosis and the Vicissitudes of Individuation* (New York: International Universities Press, 1968); G. H. Pollack, "Mourning and Adaptation," *International Journal of Psychoanalysis* 42 (1961), pp. 341–61; Edith Jacobson, *The Self and the Object World* (New York: International Universities Press, 1964); Heinz Hartmann, *Ego Psychology and the Problem of Adaptation* (New York: International Universities Press, 1958); D. W. Winnicott, *The Maturational Processes and the Facilitating Environment* (New York: International Universities Press, 1965); Harry Stack Sullivan, *The Interpersonal Theory of Psychiatry* (New York: W. W. Norton and Co., 1953).

8. These four styles of political object relations or leader-follower attachments are categorized on the basis of the developmental level of the affect felt for the leader. My new theoretical formulation emerged from several sources of influence: Joseph H. Herzberg, M.D., "Coalitions and Other Political Object Relationships: A Psychodynamic Conceptional Scheme," unpublished paper presented to the Political Psychology Study Group at the Washington School of Psychiatry; conversations with Joseph H. Herzberg, M.D., and Robert Kvarnes, M.D., and other members of the study group; conversations with Fred Weinstein and Gerald M. Platt and their theories presented in *The Wish to Be Free* (Berkeley: University of California Press, 1969) and *Psychoanalytic Sociology* (Baltimore: Johns Hopkins University Press, 1973); Murray Edelman, *The Symbolic Uses of Politics* (Urbana, Ill.: University of Illinois Press, 1976); James MacGregor Burns, *Leadership* (New York: Harper and Row, 1978); Bruce Mazlish, *The Revolutionary Ascetic* (New York: Basic Books, 1976).

9. Charles Edward Locke to TR, July 20, 1912, Reel 149.

10. William Maxwell to TR, July 28, 1912, Reel 150.

11. James Tanner to TR, March 31, 1902, Reel 25.

12. Philip P. Wells, July 22, 1912, Reel 149.

13. *Inaugural Addresses of the Presidents of the United States* (Washington, D.C.: U.S. Government Printing Office, 1974), p. 269.

14. See James MacGregor Burns, *Leadership*.

15. Elting E. Morison, *Turmoil and Tradition: A Study of the Life and Times of Henry L. Stimson* (Boston: Houghton Mifflin Co., 1960), p. 188.

16. Theodore Roosevelt, "A Confession of Faith," address before the national convention of the Progressive Party in Chicago, August 6, 1912, in *The Works of Theodore Roosevelt*, National Edition, vol. 17 (New York: Charles Scribner's Sons, 1926), p. 299.

17. Theodore H. White, *The Making of the President, 1968* (New York: Atheneum Publishers, 1969), p. 171.

18. William H. Harbaugh, *The Life and Times of Theodore Roosevelt* (New York: Oxford University Press, 1975), p. 414.

19. William Allen White, *The Autobiography of William Allen White* (New York: Macmillan Co., 1946), p. 297.

20. Gerald M. Platt, "Thoughts on a Theory of Collective Action: Language, Affect and Ideology in Revolution," in Mel Albin (ed.), *New Directions in Psychohistory, The Adelphi Papers in Honor of Erik H. Erikson* (New York: Lexington Press, 1980).

21. Ferdinand C. Inglehart to TR, July 11, 1912, Reel 149.

22. Horatio King to TR, July 10, 1912, Reel 149.

23. Waud H. Kracke, "Leader-Follower Relationship in Small Local Groups: A Psychoanalytic Perspective From the Amazon," paper presented to the International Society of Political Psychology, September, 1978, p. 7. Ego-ideal attachments were described by Sigmund Freud in *Group Psychology and the Analysis of the Ego* (London: The International Psycho-Analytical Press, 1922); see also Mazlish, *The Revolutionary Ascetic*.

24. Hyman A. Skolnick to TR, Aug. 17, 1912, Reel 151.

25. See Kathleen Dalton, "The Early Life of Theodore Roosevelt," dissertation, Johns Hopkins University, 1979, and "Theodore Roosevelt: Morality and Manliness in the Progressive Era," unpublished manuscript.

26. Offering TR as a model of will were: Charles Eugene Banks and Leroy Armstrong. *Theodore Roosevelt: 26th President of the United States, A Typical American* (Chicago: American Citizen Co., 1901); *Our Patriotic President: His Life in Pictures, Famous Words and Maxims, Anecdotes, Biography* (New York: Columbia Press, 1904); Charles Morris, *Battling For the Right: The Life Story of Theodore Roosevelt, Including His Early Life Struggles and Victorious Public Career* (Philadelphia: privately printed, 1910); John Matthew Chappel, *Theodore Roosevelt; What He Has Achieved and What He Stands For* (Chicago: The John M. Chappel Organization, 1912). On the problem of individualism and free will: Allen Wheelis, *The Quest for Identity* (New York: W. W. Norton and Co., 1958); William H. Whyte, Jr., *The Organization Man* (Garden City, N.Y.:

Doubleday and Co., 1956); Wiebe, *The Search for Order*; David Riesman et al., *The Lonely Crowd: A Study of Identity in America* (New York: Nelson, 1964).

27. TR to Fanny Parsons, Dec. 3, 1912; Theodore Roosevelt Collection, Houghton Library, Harvard University, Cambridge, Mass.

28. On TR's class background and its psychological ramifications: Kathleen Dalton, "The Education of Theodore Roosevelt: Formal Learning and its Informal Messages," paper presented at the Annual Meetings of the American Educational Research Association, March, 1979.

29. Peter Gabriel Filene, *Him/Her Self: Sex Roles in Modern America* (New York: New American Library, 1975), p. 72.

30. For the origins and disturbing decline of "the image of the respectable worker," see Carl Siracusa, *A Mechanical People: Perceptions of the Industrial Order in Massachusetts, 1815–1880* (Middletown, Conn.: Wesleyan University Press, 1979); also on economic and social trends and their relationship to changing consciousness see Louis P. Galambos, *The Public Image of Big Business in America, 1880–1940* (Baltimore: Johns Hopkins University Press, 1975) and James B. Gilbert, *Work Without Salvation: America's Intellectuals and Industrial Alienation 1880–1910* (Baltimore: Johns Hopkins University Press, 1977).

31. Riis is quoted in David W. Noble, *The Progressive Mind, 1890–1917* (Chicago: Rand McNally and Co., 1970), p. 162.

32. See Wiebe, *The Search For Order*.

33. Weinstein and Platt, *Psychoanalytic Sociology*, pp. 16–17; on the ways that will and ego control go together, see Weinstein and Platt, *The Wish to Be Free* (Berkeley: University of California Press, 1969): "attacks on traditional authority" are often "characterized by doctrines of self-discipline; self-denial; systematic, practical activity; objectivity; and rationality. Such doctrines are in fact psychological techniques for the maintenance of personal control" (p. 204). Weinstein and Platt define "object loss" as "the normatively perceived passing or failing of, disappointment in, abandonment or betrayal by loved or otherwise valued persons, institutions, symbols, and even aspects of self" (*Psychoanalytic Sociology*, p. 92). Object loss, stated more simply, can be understood as the feelings of grief and the disorientation that may follow the death of a loved person or the "death" of loved cultural forms such as family, work patterns, or religious customs.

34. TR, *The Great Adventure*, vol. 19 of *Works*, p. 324. On masculinity and related issues: Filene, *Him/Her Self*; James R. McGovern, "David Graham Phillips and the Virility Impulse of Progressivism," *New England Quarterly*, 29, no. 3 (Sept. 1966), pp. 334–55; John Higham, "The Reorientation of American Culture in the 1890s," in John Weiss (ed.), *The Origins of Modern Consciousness* (Detroit: Wayne State University Press, 1965); Joseph F. Kett, *Rites of Passage: Adolescence in America 1790 to the Present* (New York: Basic Books, 1977); Gerald F. Roberts, "The Strenuous Life: The Cult of Manliness in the Era of Theodore Roosevelt," dissertation, Michigan State University, 1970; Pete Hamill, "A Farewell to Machismo," in Leonard Kriegel (ed.), *The Myth of American Manhood* (New York: Dell Publishing Co., 1978); Elizabeth H. Pleck and Joseph H. Pleck (eds.), *The American Man* (Englewood Cliffs, N.J.: Prentice-Hall, 1980); Joe L. Dubbert, *A Man's Place: Masculinity in Transition* (Englewood Cliffs, N.J.: Prentice-Hall, 1979); E. Anthony Rotundo, "Manhood in America: Middle Class Ideals 1780–1920," unpublished manuscript.

35. Filene, *Him/Her Self*, pp. 68–94.

36. Roberts, "The Strenuous Life: The Cult of Manliness in the Era of Theodore Roosevelt"; Filene, *Him/Her Self*.

37. TR, *The Strenuous Life*, vol. 13 of *Works*, p. 322.

38. Ibid., p. 406.

39. Clinton Scollard, "A Man," in Hilah Paulmier and Robert Haven Schauffler (comp. and eds.), *Roosevelt Day* (New York: Dodd, Mead, and Co., 1932), p. 125.

40. Frank Crane, "Theodore Roosevelt," in Paulmier and Schauffler (eds.), *Roosevelt Day*, p. 121; see also Charles Hanson Towne (ed.), *Roosevelt As the Poets Saw Him* (New York: Charles Scribner's Sons, 1923); Leslie Chase, *Rooseveltiana* (New York: The Grafton Press,

1908); William W. Peavyhouse, *A Tribute in Rhyme to Theodore Roosevelt, also other Patriotic Poems and Tributes to Our War Heroes...* (Hazard, Ky.: printed privately, 1919); Rudyard Kipling, *Great-Heart* (Garden City, N.Y.: Doubleday, Page, and Co., 1919); George Willis Patterson, *Our Strong Man: An Appreciation of Theodore Roosevelt* (Washington, D.C.: published by the author, 1923); Russell J. Wilbur, *Theodore Roosevelt: A Verse Sequence in Sonnets and Quatorzains* (Boston: Houghton Mifflin Co., 1919).

41. Fred A. Johnson to TR, Aug. 8, 1912, Reel 150.

42. William Eleazar Barton, *Theodore Roosevelt, An Address by the Reverend William E. Barton, delivered in the First Congregational Church of Oak Park, Illinois, on Jan. 12, 1919* (Oak Park, Ill.: Advance Publishing Co., 1920). Other memorial addresses: Buffalo Citizens, *Theodore Roosevelt, born Oct. 27, 1858, died Jan. 6, 1919* (Buffalo: J. W. Clement Co., 1919); Columbia Club, Indianapolis, *An Expression of Its Appreciation of the Life and Character of Theodore Roosevelt* (Indianapolis: Levey Printing Co., 1919); William Hard, *Theodore Roosevelt: A Tribute* (Portland, Me.: T. B. Mosher, 1919); Charles Evans Hughes, *Address of Honorable Charles E. Hughes at the Memorial Service in Honor of Theodore Roosevelt at the Republican Club of the City of New York* (New York: privately printed, 1919); Illinois State Historical Society, *Memorial Service, State Arsenal, Springfield, Ill.* (Springfield, Ill.: privately printed, 1919); Henry Cabot Lodge, *Address of Senator Henry Cabot Lodge of Massachusetts in Honor of Theodore Roosevelt, Ex-President of the United States, Before the Congress of the United States, Feb. 9, 1919* (Washington, D.C.: Government Printing Office, 1919); Milford B. Martin, *In Memoriam... Theodore Roosevelt* (Spokane: M. B. Martin, 1919); George Henry Payne, *Roosevelt the Moralist in Action* (New York: Eastern and Middle West Travelers' Association, 1919); Alexander Hamilton Reid, *Theodore Roosevelt* (Wausau, Wis.: printed for distribution by the Wausau Rotary Club, 1919); *The Roosevelt Pilgrimage of 1922, Being a Record of Certain Friends of Theodore Roosevelt's Visit to His Grave and To His Home on the Third Anniversary of His Death.* (New York: privately printed, 1922).

43. David G. Gottlieb, Oral History Interviews, Capitol Institute of Technology, interviewee to remain anonymous, Sept. 10, 1979.

44. The Theodore Roosevelt Republican Club of San Francisco is known as the "Teddys."

45. Bernard Malamud, *The Natural* (New York: Farrar, Straus and Giroux, 1952), p. 154.

46. John William Ward, *Andrew Jackson: Symbol for an Age* (New York: Oxford University Press, 1969), p. 164.

47. For details of the assassination attempt: Harbaugh, *Life and Times of Theodore Roosevelt*, pp. 421–22; Henry F. Pringle, *Theodore Roosevelt: A Biography* (New York: Harcourt Brace and Co., 1956), pp. 398–99. For a psychological explanation of Roosevelt's insistence upon speaking, see Dalton, "Theodore Roosevelt: Morality and Manliness in the Progressive Era."

48. A. C. Mathews to TR, Sept. 24, 1901, Reel 19.

49. *Memorial Exercises, Commemorating the 64th Anniversary of the Birth of Theodore Roosevelt* (Cambridge, Mass.: privately printed, 1922); Eugene Twing to TR, July 10, 1912, Reel 149.

50. Mrs. Yorick Nichols to Edith Roosevelt, Oct. 18, 1912, Reel 153.

51. Freud, *Group Psychology;* Reynolds Price, "The Heroes of Our Times," *Saturday Review*, December, 1978, pp. 16–17.

52. Thomas J. Scheff, "The Distancing of Emotion in Ritual," *Current Anthropology*, 18, no. 3 (Sept. 1977), pp. 483–505, 408.

53. Clifford Geertz, *The Interpretation of Cultures* (New York: Basic Books, 1973), "deep play" is the social tensions of underlying meaning which Geertz finds in culturally significant events such as cock-fighting in Bali.

54. Edelman, *The Symbolic Uses of Politics;* Edelman's excellent work is slightly flawed by his emphasis on the deceptive power of symbols—they are also a means for bringing out into the open, in metaphoric terms, the most painful subjects in a society. While symbolic gestures are not the most direct way of dealing with difficult problems, they do serve to wash out a culture's dirty laundry without open conflict. David O. Sears, Carl P. Hensler, and Leslie K. Speer, "Whites' Opposition to 'Busing': Self-Interest or Symbolic Politics?" *American Political Science Review*, 73, no. 2 (June 1979), pp. 369–84, is a recent use of the symbolic politics idea, but

the authors' deterministic "oversocialized conception of man" and their ontogenetic psychological model of behavior—political attitudes being the result of "residues of preadult socialization"—produce a shallow analysis.

55. Galambos, *Public Image of Big Business*, pp. 119–56.

56. Ibid., p. 126.

57. Albert Shaw, *A Cartoon History of Roosevelt's Career* (New York: The Review of Reviews Co., 1910); John T. McCutcheon, *T.R. in Cartoons* (Chicago: A. C. McClurg and Co., 1910); Raymond Gros, *T.R. in Cartoons* (New York: The Saalfield Publishing Co., 1910).

58. Walter Graham to TR, July 11, 1912, Reel 149.

59. Leroy Tobey to TR, July 17, 1912, Reel 149.

60. A. W. Pattiani to TR, July 19, 1912, Reel 149.

61. E. L. Flanagan to TR, Aug. 13, 1912, Reel 151: W. F. Axton to TR, July 20, 1912, Reel 149.

62. TR, *American Problems*, vol. 16 of *Works*, p. 63; TR, *The Foes of Our Own Household*, vol. 19 of *Works*, p. 30.

63. TR, *The Strenuous Life*, vol. 13 of *Works*, pp. 481–82.

64. William James, "The Moral Equivalent of War," *Memories and Studies* (New York: Longmans, Green and Co., 1911), p. 285; George M. Fredrickson, *The Inner Civil War* (New York: Harper and Row, 1968); Robert Kvarnes, M.D. "What is the Moral Equivalent of War?" unpublished draft and Dalton, "Moral Equivalents in America's Past," unpublished draft, working papers in the Political Psychology Study Group at the Washington School of Psychiatry.

65. Richard T. Fry, "Community Through War: A Study of T.R.'s Rise and Fall as a Prophet and Hero in Modern America," dissertation, University of Minnesota, 1969; Thomas C. Leonard, *Above the Battle: War-Making in America From Appomattox to Versailles* (New York: Oxford University Press, 1978); Harbaugh, *Life and Times of Theodore Roosevelt*, pp. 450–54. For a psychological explanation see Dalton, "The Early Life of Theodore Roosevelt."

66. TR, *The Rough Riders*, vol. 11 of *Works*, p. 177. See also on this topic: Hermann Hagedorn, *Roosevelt, Prophet of Unity* (New York: Charles Scribner's Sons, 1924); on social differentiation and value change: Weinstein and Platt, *Wish to Be Free*; Thomas Bender, *Community and Social Change in America* (New Brunswick, N.J.: Rutgers University Press, 1978); Robert H. Wiebe, *The Segmented Society* (New York: Oxford University Press, 1975).

67. D. Davidson to TR, Sept. 7, 1912, Reel 152, spelling corrected.

68. Lauren Bruce to TR, Aug. 2, 1912, Reel 150.

69. Eugene Twing to TR, July 10, 1912, Reel 149.

70. Campaign song, "Just Before the Election, Teddy," Reel 153.

71. Alice Folger to TR, July 21, 18, 11, 1912, Reel 149.

72. David Carver to TR, Aug. 26, 1912, Reel 152.

73. Wik, *Henry Ford and Grassroots America*, p. 214.

74. Wiebe, *The Search For Order*, p. 91.

75. William O. Lynch to TR, July 10, 1912, Reel 149.

76. Ernest A. Bigelow to TR, July 22, 1912, Reel 149.

77. Anna C. Fay to TR, Aug. 10, 1912, Reel 151.

78. Charles F. Amidon to TR, July 24, 1912, Reel 150.

79. W. S. Wright to TR, July 16, 1912, Reel 149.

80. H. C. Bowers to TR, Aug. 13, 1912, Reel 151.

81. Wallace Battle to TR, Aug. 8, 1912, Reel 150.

82. Vivian Alexander, "Armageddon," typescript poem, Reel 151.

83. J. E. Sistrunk to TR, Aug. 5, 1912, Reel 150.

84. William Allen White, *Autobiography*, p. 464.

85. Century Association, New York. *Theodore Roosevelt; Memorial Addresses Delivered Before The Century Association, Feb. 9, 1919* (New York: printed for the Century Association, 1919).

86. Lillian Scharf to TR, Sept. 6, 1912, Reel 152.

87. N. P. Pangborn to TR, Aug. 9, 1912, Reel 151.

88. Sarah Le Ponero to TR, n.d., Reel 150.
89. W. H. Kinsman to TR, Aug. 19, 1912, Reel 151.
90. Lawrence Griffith, "Ted a da Rose," poem, Reel 149.
91. William H. Harbaugh, *Power and Responsibility* (New York: Farrar, Straus and Cudahy, 1961), p. 456.
92. James B. Diggs, *Theodore Roosevelt, The Voice of America: Address of James B. Diggs, Jan. 12, 1919 at Roosevelt Memorial Services, Tulsa, Okla.* (Tulsa: Privately printed, 1919).

14

OEDIPUS AND AMERICA
Historical Perspectives on the Reception
of Psychoanalysis in the United States

JOHN DEMOS

The sudden influence of psychoanalysis among American psychologists and others after 1909 was a cause for comment then and remains a historical curiosity now. Especially since Freud's fortunes in Europe at the same time greatly disappointed him, one wonders why he was so quickly accepted as an authority in the United States.

In the next essay John Demos asks that question. In suggesting an answer he tries to link by-now familiar patterns of family life and sex roles to this chapter in twentieth-century American intellectual history. He admits that the essay does not address a number of related issues: among whom, for example, was psychoanalysis particularly important? How well were Freud's ideas understood, and what changes did Americans tend to make in them? But the article does mount an effort to relate ideas—a cluster of psychological theories—to the social setting that helped them to appear plausible. Conceptually the piece resembles the Burrows and Wallace essay on patterns of child-rearing and the argument for independence: How do social circumstances—in both cases the structure of family relations—interact with unconscious dispositions to make one ideology more attractive than another? Finally, if the psychoanalytic paradigm now receives sharp criticism as a therapeutic approach, it may be worth asking whether such hostility reflects structural changes in the American family or shifting patterns of intimate relations in contemporary life.

THERE IS a famous remark attributed to Freud by Ernest Jones: "America is a mistake: a gigantic mistake, it is true, but nonetheless a mistake."[1] Jones

Reprinted with permission of the author from *Annual of Psychoanalysis* 6 (1978):23–39.

does not say when the remark was made, or in what specific context; however, Freud's skepticism about most things American is well known. It is tempting to think that the founder of psychoanalysis referred, perhaps just half-consciously, to the reception accorded his ideas in the early decades of this century. The issue, in that case, was the very success achieved by psychoanalysis in the United States—a success which seemed to Freud surprising, ill-founded, and in some ways quite unwelcome. Eager as he clearly was to associate himself with the finest traditions of scientific and humanitarian concern in Europe, he saw his ideas criticized or (worse) ignored by the great majority of his cultural peers. And yet, an ocean away, psychoanalysis was taking firm root in the shallow cultural soil of upstart, bourgeois America. There was indeed a "mistake" here—and of quite unsettling proportions.[2]

In fact, the passage of psychoanalysis from Europe to the United States has long intrigued intellectual historians.[3] It presents a singularly vivid instance of the transmission of ideas from one cultural setting to another. Viewed from the American side these ideas were indisputably "foreign" in origin; though American psychologists and psychiatrists had, like their European counterparts, previously reconnoitered some parts of the same intellectual territory, no one questioned Freud's primacy as its true "discoverer." Moreover, the arrival of the Freudian system in the United States was carefully planned and highly visible. The famous conference at Clark University in 1909, the founding of the American Psychoanalytic Association a few years later, the translation and publication of Freud's early writings: all this was stage-managed by a small circle of psychoanalytic pioneers, both here and abroad; and the master himself, despite his ambivalence in relation to America, lent a hand at various critical junctures. Indeed the history of this process has acquired some of the trappings of legend: picture, for example, the great William James moving solemnly down the aisle after the Clark conference to announce to the lecturer, "Yours is the psychology of the future"—or asking Freud, on a walking trip a few days later, to carry his briefcase for a while.[4]

But such anecdotal flourishes aside, there is no doubting the impression made by psychoanalysis in the United States beginning about 1910. Freud himself wrote, looking back years later on the Clark conference: "In Europe I felt as though I were despised; but over there I found myself received by the foremost men as an equal. . . . [Furthermore] psychoanalysis has not lost ground since our visit; it is extremely popular among the lay public and is recognized by a number of psychiatrists as an important element in medical training." Paul Roazen expresses the common verdict of scholars, in affirming "the extraordinary nature of the success of Freud's doctrines in one country in particular—the United States. This is true medically as well as among the general public."[5] And Nathan G. Hale, Jr., author of the almost-definitive study *Freud and the Americans*, measures this success through detailed analysis of press and magazine coverage:

Within six years of the Clark conference psychoanalysis had eclipsed all other psychotherapies in the nation's magazines. . . . Psychoanalysis received three-fifths as much attention as birth control, more attention than divorce, and nearly four times more than mental hygiene between 1915 and 1918. The figures are impressive: between 1910 and 1914 eleven articles about Freud and psychoanalysis were published, most of them favorable; between 1915 and 1918, about thirty-one, of which twenty-five were favorable. Perhaps one-fourth reviewed psychoanalytic books, more than another fourth were full-dress popularizations; the rest were serious short expositions or criticisms, sometimes summarized from medical journals. In 1915 psychoanalysis reached the mass circulation women's magazines, and the first American psychoanalytic novel, *Mrs. Marden's Ordeal*, was published two years later.[6]

Of course, there was opposition indeed bitter hostility—in some quarters, and those early years marked the beginning of a long and arduous struggle.[7] But, whether as converts or antagonists, Americans *engaged themselves* with psychoanalysis on a scale unparalleled elsewhere in the world. And is it not true even now that there are more analysts, and presumably more analysands, in the United States than in all other countries combined?

So here is the nub of a genuine historiographic problem: psychoanalysis has won its widest and most favorable hearing where least expected to do so by its creator.[8] And the question, of course, is *why?* Professor Hale has explored, and perhaps exhausted, a broad range of possible answers from the standpoint of intellectual history. Briefly, he has focused on a pair of professional and cultural "crises" confronting Americans just after the turn of the century. The first was specific to psychiatric medicine: the so-called "crisis of the somatic style." There was, Hale argues, growing disaffection with the organic theory on which treatment of mental and nervous disorders had rested theretofore. The second crisis was much broader in scope; it involved nothing less than a wholesale revision of accepted mores and customs—what Hale terms the "crisis of civilized morality." This was, of course, the twilight—if not the late evening—of Victorian culture, the time when the great "sexual hush" began finally to lift. Hale contends that psychoanalysis fell right into line as these trends unfolded, replacing the somatic style with a new, radically different *psycho*therapy, and confronting civilized morality with a franker, freer view of human sexuality. In addition, he argues the importance of other psychotherapies (just beginning to hatch after 1900) in paving the way for Freud, and finds certain points of congeniality between psychoanalytic ideas and the social ethos of American progressivism. In short, there was in this country a *readiness* for psychoanalysis, which Freud and his followers skillfully exploited.[9]

Now this interpretation is persuasive up to a point—but it does not settle all questions. For even by Hale's own account there were significant countertendencies—trends and influences that would seem to have qualified

American "readiness" for psychoanalysis. The somatic style, for example, was still the dominant force in American neurology and psychiatry at large; its critics were only a small, albeit resourceful, band until at least 1910.[10] And civilized morality was less attacked than readjusted during the same period; the cutting edge here was a new frankness about sex, in the service of suppressing its least attractive manifestations. So-called "purity campaigns" were organized by leading progressives to oppose prostitution and reduce veneral disease, and increasingly their spokesmen deplored the polite facade of reticence that had veiled such problems from public scrutiny.[11] However, the larger point is that candor in sexual matters was advocated in the service of ever-greater "purity"; except for a tiny minority of cultural radicals, American progressives reaffirmed the central core of traditional mores.

But there is no reason to argue at length with Hale's work—which remains a signal contribution over-all. It permits us to follow some enormously complex and elusive lines of intellectual transmission; indeed it constitutes a historical map which helps considerably to locate the development of psychoanalysis in time and space. More, the specific arguments for "cultural readiness" retain at least some of their importance, even after allowance has been made for the various *caveats* and qualifications. The aim of this paper is to propose an alternative line of explanation for the "mistake" of psychoanalytic success in America. Perhaps it should not even be called an alternative, but simply a complement. After all, as historians no less than psychoanalysts will agree, "mistakes" are notoriously overdetermined.

I

It is necessary in what follows to redirect the focus toward certain different areas of American life and culture, during the period preceding the arrival of psychoanalysis. This will mean a shift, broadly speaking, from intellectual to social history. More specifically, it will entail some extended consideration of the subject of family life in the American past. We should recognize at the outset that this subject has been "legitimated" for historians only during the past decade or so. Previous generations of scholars avoided such seemingly mundane and personal matters—preferring instead to concentrate on politics, diplomacy, commerce, and other manifestly "public" themes. Thus the field of "family history," as we are coming to call it, is quite new and in some respects unexplored. Still, many historians are now busily at work in this and related areas, and the sum-total of results so far is quite substantial. Certain of these results seem fairly surprising, others may well be completely *un*surprising; but in any case they do bear on the question from which this paper began.[12]

To summarize the central point in several anticipatory sentences: it will be argued that a family system developed in these United States, during the last several decades of the nineteenth century, which involved significant departures from the dominant modes of family life in still earlier historical periods. In fact, these changes were *so* significant and encompassing that it is reasonable to speak of a "critical period" in the history of the American family. The result was the flowering of a kind of "hothouse family," which did indeed lay the cultural and psychological ground in which Freudian ideas would subsequently take root. To some extent, the themes that we will emphasize could be explored in terms of other Western countries as well; to that same extent, therefore, this discussion will embrace the historical context of Freud's life and work in the very broadest sense. However, it appears that the family system described in what follows was more widely and deeply normative in this country than anywhere else. If so, perhaps it supplies that additional element of "cultural readiness" which finally escaped Professor Hale.

Let us proceed now with an overview of central conclusions in recent historical scholarship on nineteenth-century American family life. These conclusions will be presented in summary form and virtually without documentation. Considerations of space preclude any systematic effort to sample the voluminous evidence which might otherwise flesh out our rough and skeletal outline.

In the first place: by at least 1850 (perhaps earlier) Americans had developed a view of the family that assumed its radical disjunction from all other aspects of their culture. The individual household, and the world at large, were pictured as contrasting "spheres," and the relation between them was that of adversaries. Community life—epitomized by the growth of the modern city—seemed agitated, disordered, unpredictable, and insidiously conducive to the expression of the worst of human instincts.[13] To all this, family life stood as a deeply necessary foil. The evocative significance of "home"—the word itself became highly sentimentalized—is manifest through an enormous range of literary and personal artifacts of the period. Home became the abiding source of all the tender virtues in life. Love, kindliness, altruism, peace, harmony, good order: these were among the leading qualities attributed exclusively to the domestic environment.[14] It should be emphasized that there was something very new here. In the colonial period of American history, family and community had been experienced as complementary to one another; indeed the household unit was typically viewed as a "little commonwealth" which prepared the individual in a wholly natural way for social and political roles in the wider world.[15] In sum: we can view the changes of the nineteenth century as involving the establishment of a sharp social boundary, where previously things had been open, and free, and relatively undivided. The effects of this dichotomy were profound—for many aspects of popular culture—but one that deserves special emphasis here is the equation of home-life with the development of individual character. Whereas, in a still earlier period, responsibility for character-training was shared among a variety of people and institutions (parents, other kin, neighbors; churches, courts, and local government), from henceforth this responsibility belonged to the family alone.

Even as the family was progressively marked off from other networks of human interaction, it underwent a process of *in*ternal sub-division as well. There developed, for example, a massive system of sex-role stereotyping, whereby maleness and femaleness were set apart as never before. Men and women were thought to occupy entirely different "spheres"—indeed they were presumed to have essentially different *characters*.[16] Women were charged with maintaining the sanctity of the home, while men became the representatives of individual families in the wide and dangerous world at large. This contrast was explicitly pejorative: women were supposed to be "pure" in all things, while men, alas, were necessarily tainted by their contact with life outside the home. Once again we must recognize the historical novelty of these trends. In the colonial era men and women had shared a broad range of everyday experience, easily and informally; and within the household the roles of husband and wife had overlapped at many points.[17]

As the nineteenth century progressed, a further splitting of roles and statuses within the family developed along *generational* lines. This was the era of what has been called "the discovery of childhood."[18] For the first time in Western history children emerged from the larger social backdrop as distinctive creatures with their own needs and tendencies; no longer were they viewed simply as "miniature adults." From here on children would have their own patterns of work and play; or rather, to put it more accurately, some children would have no meaningful work at all, while others would be steered into very special work. (Consider, for example, the phenomenon of child labor in the factories.)[19]

Now this is a very large and complex historical process, impossible to discuss in a few sentences, but clearly the main engine of change was the movement from a local, rural, agrarian culture, to the increasingly urban, industrial, "mass society" of modern times. It is *easy* enough to see that in a farm household work and recreation are everywhere joined—and *shared* by men and women, young and old, pretty much alike. But take that same household and transplant it in the city—and experience is so profoundly divided that *people* come perforce to occupy a range of distinct positions. (The formal term for this process, in the language of academic sociology, is "structural differentiation.") There were, moreover, demographic trends which reinforced the process of differentiation. Throughout the nineteenth century the birth rate was falling steadily, so that by 1900 the number of children born to an average couple had been reduced almost by half.[20] For the first time large numbers of parents were attempting to control their own fertility, and this meant not only fewer children, but also the compression of reproductive activity into a much shorter time span. Whereas in colonial America a household might contain as many as ten children, ranging from one or two who were virtually adult down to toddlers and even a babe at the breast, a typical middle-class family of the late nineteenth century would consist of parents and two, three, or four children relatively close to one another in age. In a sense, therefore, families were becoming more visibly two-generational; in the parlance of our own time, there was the basis here for a "generation gap."[21]

These powerful long-term trends, both the narrowly demographic ones and the broader transformations of economic and social structure, converged in their effects on family life—and particularly on the lives of children. What seems most important is the way the whole process of individual maturation became disjunctive and problematic. No longer could growth and development be taken for granted—that is, assumed as a natural concomitant of universal social processes. Instead, it became increasingly difficult to believe that the experience of the older generation would directly prefigure the life of the younger one.

As one result of these altered circumstances, there sprang into being a new genre of popular literature—the literature of child-rearing advice. Since the care of children had become a self-conscious activity, full of unexpected risks and dangers, a variety of self-appointed "experts" busied themselves with the production of books and essays designed to resolve the questions of increasingly troubles parents. The line of these authors descends, in virtually unbroken continuity, from a nucleus of Protestant clergymen and "scribbling ladies" (writing in the 1820s and 1830s) to our own Dr. Spock.[22] We will undertake in the next few pages to focus more sharply on the question of child-rearing, and in doing so will be obliged to rely heavily on these early advice books. The use of such materials is open to question—the gap between advice and behavior being, in many instances, quite substantial—but there is, on balance, enough supporting and confirming evidence from other sources to make this a worthwhile inquiry. From all we can tell about nineteenth-century America, children were raised in new and different settings, according to altered goals and precepts, and with distinctive effects on their adult lives later on. So, herewith some brief observations about the dominant strain of child-rearing advice:

1. All authorities agreed on the extreme urgency of careful, responsible parenting. In the brave new world of nineteenth-century America there was no alternative to home life for the proper rearing of children. If parents did not perform effectively, no one else would do the job for them. Furthermore, the stakes were so high and initial trends so hard to reverse, that the rearing process should begin when children were very young. The Rev. Horace Bushnell, a Congregational minister whose enormously influential book *Christian Nurture* was published in 1843, declared flatly: "Let every Christian father and mother understand, when the child is three years old, that they have done more than half of what they will do for his character."[23] The resonance between this particular statement and views which would subsequently be derived from psychoanalysis is so obvious as hardly to need mentioning.

2. In speaking of parental responsibility for raising children, Americans of

the nineteenth century actually meant *maternal* responsibility. Father simply vanished from the domestic stage, and mother's role was correspondingly enlarged. Her influence would be absolutely decisive for the character of her children—especially her *male* children, for these issues were formulated most conspicuously in terms of mothers of sons. In the words of a favorite period cliché: "All that I am, I owe to my angel mother." This relationship, as typically described, had literal qualities of symbiosis. "Every look, every movement, every expression"—wrote one authority—"does something toward forming the character of the little heir to immortal life." And the same pattern prevailed even in embryo; thus, for example, a mother is supposed to have spent leisure hours during her pregnancy gazing at engravings of handsome buildings, in order to destine her child to greatness as an architect. (In some cases, it appears, this strategy was fully vindicated by the results; the instance cited here involved the mother of Frank Lloyd Wright.[24]

3. The *goals* of child-rearing, as expressed in the advice literature, were somewhat divided and confused. On the one hand, there was much emphasis on encouraging qualities of independence, resourcefulness, initiative—a whole expressive mode. Only thus would a young person be prepared to seize the main chance and "get ahead" in the open society of modern America. On the other hand, the same authorities also stressed the development of inner discipline and self-control. For, without a moral compass—and that was a favorite metaphor—a child might go wildly astray as soon as he ventured beyond the threshold of home. These twin goals, of expressiveness and control, seem to have constituted a kind of double message from parents; and one wonders how the balance was struck in the day-to-day experience of average households.

4. The authorities spoke with a clearer voice on the subject of methods and procedures. Discipline, they agreed, must be based on the good example of parents—and on repeated appeals to *conscience* in the child. Important values and standards must be *in*ternalized, as early and as fully as possible. Just as the American nation was founded on a principle of "self-government" in its public affairs, so the young person must develop a similar capacity to guide his private life.[25] In our own terms, the touchstone of this disciplinary regime was guilt; the child's inner feelings became the chief agency of punishment. It is in the materials from this era, incidentally, that one first encounters that remarkable bit of domestic sophistry—the parent who says, as he bends a whimpering child over his knee, "It hurts me to spank you, more than it hurts you to be spanked." But this notion, that the wrong one does causes distress and dismay for others, is the inner foundation of a "guilty" orientation to the world. And here, once again, is a sharp contrast with the norms of an earlier time. In colonial America, child-rearing (and social control, more generally) had been based on a principle of *shame*—that is, the exposure of wrongdoing to the ridicule and contempt of others.[26]

5. These different themes join at one important point: together they imply a massive intensification of the parent-child bond. I have already underscored

the burden of responsibility which the culture assigned to parents for the welfare and future prospects of the young, but sometimes the case was turned the other way around: children, for *their* part, had the power to blight the happiness of parents by falling into paths of wickedness. Nineteenth-century fiction plays endless variations on this theme. A virtuous couple anxiously rears their beloved son for a life of decent respectability (if not of greatness); the son grows up and goes out into the world, is exposed to the influence of "evil companions," takes to drink and gambling or whatever; his misdeeds are reported back to his parents, who in turn are so literally "heart-broken" that they may sicken and die. Seen in this light, domestic bonding had become a matter of life and death.[27]

So much for the child-rearing literature; we must now try to integrate certain additional considerations reflecting the shape and substance of the culture at large. It is well known that sexual behavior in this "Victorian" era was hedged about with uniquely restrictive ideas and values. There is no point in attempting to cover this familiar ground in detail; we should, however, notice one aspect of nineteenth-century sexual conventions for its specific relevance in the present context. For the first time in Western history the idea was propounded, and widely accepted, that women are passionless—not merely chaste, but literally devoid of sexual feelings.[28] Sometimes this idea appeared as a prescribed standard, and sometimes as an experiential reality; and where reality diverged from the standard, women (literally by the thousands) resorted to a drastic remedy—the surgical procedure of clitoridectomy.[29] One way or another, feminine "purity" would be sustained and "sensual wishes" repudiated. What, then, may we infer about the role of such women as mothers? Recall that the advice literature was essentially a body of morality tales about mothers and sons. Is it too much to suppose that many nineteenth-century women—faced with overbearing cultural constraints on their sexuality in relation to sweethearts and husbands—proved to be rather "seductive" in their maternal function? This was, after all, the period when the great American tradition of "Mom-ism" began to flourish;[30] an early and extraordinary manifestation was the vast corpus of folksongs and ballads spawned by the experience of the country in fighting a terrible Civil War.[31] The preeminent figure in this Civil War music is Mother—Mother for whose sake the war must be won. Mother whose influence keeps her soldier-son from yielding to various forms of camp-life temptation. Mother whose past self-sacrifices justify the supreme sacrifice of life itself, and so forth. There is, of course, no overtly sexual reference in all this; Mother is sentimentalized, not erotized; but perhaps in the world of unconscious process the distance from sentiment to Eros was not so great after all.

And what about fathers, in this same framework of psycho-cultural circumstance? Fred Weinstein and Gerald Platt have developed an ingenious argument around this question in their book *The Wish to Be Free*.[32] The success of psychoanalytic theory, they contend, was made possible by long-term changes in the role of *paterfamilias*. The traditional father of pre-modern times was able to assert a variety of "patriarchal" claims, because of the many immediate and personal services he performed, for other members of his household. Beginning with the Industrial Revolution, however, he was increasingly drawn out of the home (especially by his work), and his relation to his children became less nurturant and more instrumental. In a sense this amounted to a loss of legitimacy; at any rate, in Weinstein and Platt's own words, "the father had become available at last for conscious examination."[33] This argument seems substantially persuasive; perhaps, though, we may add to it one element deriving from specifically American circumstances. The "success creed" that took hold in this country during the nineteenth century strongly urged that young men should aspire to continual improvement of their social and economic rank—and, more, that the position of their own fathers should serve as their chief criterion of measurement. In short, success in America meant surpassing one's father. Here was a covert inducement to competition in the relation of fathers and sons; and it was one of the truly new things that blossomed under the American sun.[34]

Certainly, too, these ideological tendencies were reinforced from the direction of life experience and life history. Mobility of two sorts—social and geographic—was notoriously characteristic of American society in the nineteenth century. Immigrants from the Old World poured into the country in a gathering tide after about 1840. Meanwhile another *internal* migration brought vast numbers of the native-born from farms and villages in the rural countryside to the burgeoning life of Metropolis. Americans of this period were truly "men in motion"—to borrow an apt phrase from a recent study of migration.[35] Presumably this quality of motion reorganized the inner—no less than the outward—frame of their experience.

The immigrants who left the blighted heaths of Ireland, or the mountain sheepfolds of Greece, or the teeming ghettos of central Europe, were fellow-travelers in a long existential journey. Wrenched from the encasing web of traditional culture, they sought a highly individualized fulfillment in a new and volatile setting. Irrevocably, they were parted from "the land of their fathers"—not to mention *the living presence* of those same fathers. Uprooted, they were also liberated; anxious and sometimes guilt-ridden, they tasted as well the rewards of *self*-improvement.[36] And the farm-boys who made good in the city traced a similar, if less dramatic, course. They, too, exchanged one world for another, and emerged profoundly transformed.

The central myths and metaphors of American experience conveyed, at least by implication, the *filial* meaning of all this. The "man in motion" was physically separated from his father's influence. The "self-made man" declared that he owed his father nothing. The "successful man" demonstrated, in his very success, a superiority over his father. These natural and adopted "sons" of America had not, of course, done away with fathers altogether;

indeed, in some respects they had only complicated their entanglement. But from henceforth the relation of father and son was on a substantially new footing. Much that had been taken for granted hitherto was now open to question. Bonds of blood and tuition that seemed wholly "natural" in traditional settings became problematic, self-conscious, and infused with chronic tension.

II

That completes our panoramic survey of the history of American family life; it is necessary now to pull these ideas more closely together, so as to rejoin the issue from which our inquiry began. And let us adopt the metaphor of *theater* as a way of epitomizing the changes that transformed the family during the period under consideration. Note, in the first place, that the domestic stage itself has been more sharply articulated; lifted whole from out of the general cultural backdrop, it now encompasses a distinct and consciously realized portion of social space. The cast of characters has been reduced in number; declining birth rates have meant fewer children among whom to divide (and diffuse) the action of this familial drama. Moreover, the roles themselves have been more sharply differentiated than was even true before. The Husband-Father, the Wife-Mother, and the Child: here was a central, structural triangle around which all else revolved. Within the triangle, culture prescribed a delicate balance of exchange. The Child—we might as well say, the Son—derived from the Mother both everyday nurturance and the shape of his character in years to come; all this was framed in lavish hues of sentiment—which may perhaps have covered "earthly" feelings as well. The relation of the Father and the Son was quite different. There was affection, to be sure, but there was also distance; there was modeling, but also rivalry. Each of the actors and actresses aspired to "self-government," and the Parents tried especially hard to stimulate the Child's capacity to experience inner guilt. At the same time, each one was made to feel responsible for all the others. Last but not least, a mood of urgency and intensity, of ultimate (and potentially dire) consequence, suffused the entire script. Each scene led on to the next with inexorable certainty; missed cues and bungled lines would be lasting in their effects.[37]

At some point much earlier we spoke of the group which typically played out this drama as the "hothouse family." But let us change the frame of reference a bit, and adopt a psychoanalytic terminology; and the hothouse family may also be called the "oedipal family." If the Oedipus complex was indeed a *sine qua non* of the theoretical system devised by Freud, then we may surmise that its importance—and the response it evoked in others—was rooted in historically specific patterns of domestic relationship. People accepted and endorsed the Freudian system, or alternatively they resisted and denounced it, because at some level they *recognized* its correspondence to basic aspects of their own experience. This kind of implicit recognition is, in fact, an underlying dynamic of social response to all significant intellectual and scientific "discoveries."

Now at this point we can anticipate a possible source of misunderstanding. We need not argue that fresh intrapsychic patterns were created *de novo* by the historical process itself, or that at some point in the nineteenth century large numbers of people suddenly began to have Oedipus complexes where before there was nothing of the kind. It is, of course, sometimes maintained that Freudian theory applies only to modern Western society; but that is another issue, substantially at variance with what is proposed here. Almost by definition, the Oedipus complex has *multiple* points of origin—which presumably encompass biology, psychology, sociology, and history, in intricate combination. To put it another way, the Oedipus complex is a significant developmental potential in all persons, no matter what their location in time and space. However, particular patterns of historical and cultural circumstance have much to do with the way this potential is realized—whether it is highlighted, or muted, or neutralized, or whatever. Now the main line of historical change in the nineteenth century did, we suggest, create a situation in which oedipal issues become highly charged for many people. And among all the Western countries, this situation was most fully elaborated in the United States.

Which brings us back to the starting point—namely, the tricks played, and the "mistakes" made, by the historical process. The mistake is not that Freud created psychoanalysis; nor is it that America responded to psychoanalysis so fully and on the whole so favorably. Instead, as we can now clearly see, the mistake is that Freud himself was not an American! He should by all rights have been born and raised in some bustling new metropolis, surrounded by "hothouse families," egged on by the peculiarly American and patricidal cult of success. But, then, there are some mistakes which even historians cannot account for.

NOTES

1. Ernest Jones, *The Life and Work of Sigmund Freud*, vol. 2 (New York: Basic Books, 1955), p. 60.

2. In his "Autobiographical Study" (1925) Freud complained that in America psychoanalysis "has suffered a great deal from being watered down. Moreover, many abuses which have no relation to it find a cover under its name" (Sigmund Freud, "An Autobiographical Study," *Standard Edition*, vol. 20 [London: Hogarth Press, 1959], p. 52). For additional comment on Freud's skepticism about the reception accorded his work in the United States, see Nathan G. Hale, Jr., *Freud and the Americans* (New York: Oxford University Press, 1971), p. 331. On Freud's general disenchantment with American life and culture, see Jones, *Life and Work*, pp. 59–60.

304   JOHN DEMOS

3. Hale, *Freud and the Americans;* J. C. Burnham, "Psychology, Psychoanalysis, and the Progressive Movement." *American Quarterly* 12 (1960):457–65, and *Psychoanalysis in American Medicine: 1894–1918: Medicine, Science, and Culture* (New York: International Universities Press, 1967); F. Matthews, "The Americanization of Sigmund Freud," *Journal of American Studies* 1 (1967):39–62.

4. Jones, *Life and Work*, p. 57; Freud, "Autobiographical Study," p. 52.

5. Freud, "Autobiographical Study," p. 52; Paul Roazen, *Freud: Political and Social Thought* (New York: Knopf, 1968), p. 96.

6. Hale, *Freud and the Americans*, p. 397.

7. On early opposition to psychoanalysis among Americans, see Jones, *Life and Work*, pp. 110ff, and Hale, *Freud and the Americans*, chap. 11. Some of this opposition itself implies the growing strength of the movement; for example, the psychologist Boris Sidis, speaking at a meeting of the American Psychological Association in 1909, attacked "the mad epidemic of Freudism now invading America."

8. Admittedly, this broad formulation glosses over certain important historical questions: e.g., by *what groups*, in particular, were psychoanalytic ideas so well received: And *which* psychoanalytic ideas? And *how* were these ideas understood, and perhaps transformed, in the course of their passage into American culture? For the purposes of this essay the significant reception is that associated with the educated middle class (not the literary and/or intellectual leadership). Furthermore, psychoanalysis is considered primarily as a belief system (not as a form of therapeutic treatment). And, finally, some modification of the system, under the influence of American norms and values, is simply assumed. (On this issue, see Hale, *Freud and the Americans*, passim.) Each of these points deserves extended treatment in itself, but none is directly germane to the argument presented here. Another matter that lies beyond the scope of this essay is the cultural readiness for psychoanalysis of the various countries of Europe. Ideally, the trends examined here should be tested on a comparative basis, i.e., alongside parallel materials from European history. But detailed investigation of such materials will have to await another time and a different hand.

9. Hale, *Freud and the Americans*, chaps. 1–9.

10. Ibid., pp. 17, 172, 277ff.

11. R. Lubove, "The Progressive and the Prostitute," *Historian* 24 (1961):308–25; E. Feldman, "Prostitution, the Alien Woman, and the Progressive Imagination," *American Quarterly* 19 (1967):29–51.

12. For a summary of recent historical scholarship on American family life, see the author's "The American Family in Past Time," *American Scholar* 43 (1974):422–46, and "Reflections on the History of the Family: A Review Essay," *Comparative Studies in Society and History* 15 (1973):493–503. A number of valuable essays appear in two collections: P. Laslett, ed., *Household and Family in Past Time* (Cambridge: Cambridge University Press, 1973) and M. Gordon, ed., *The American Family in Social-Historical Perspective* (New York: St. Martin's Press, 1973). The seminal work that began the current vogue of family history is Philippe Ariès, *Centuries of Childhood*, trans. R. Baldick (New York: Knopf, 1960). A major contribution (though touching only slightly on American materials) is E. Shorter, *The Making of the Modern Family* (New York: Basic Books, 1975).

13. R. Sennett, "Middle-Class Families and Urban Violence: The Experience of a Chicago Community in the Nineteenth Century," in *Nineteenth-Century Cities: Essays in the New Urban History*, ed. S. Thernstrom and R. Sennett (New Haven: Yale University Press, 1969), pp. 386–420, and *Families against the City: Middle-Class Homes of Industrial Chicago, 1872–1890* (Cambridge: Harvard University Press, 1970); K. Jeffrey, "The Family as Utopian Retreat from the City: The Nineteenth Century Contribution," *Soundings* 55 (1972):21–41.

14. Popular fiction from the mid-nineteenth century displays this viewpoint most forcibly. See, for example, C. M. Sedgewick, *Home* (Boston, 1854).

15. John Demos, *A Little Commonwealth: Family Life in Plymouth Colony* (New York: Basic Books, 1970); E. Morgan, *The Puritan Family* (New York: Harper & Row, 1966); B. Bailyn,

Education in the Forming of American Society (Chapel Hill: University of North Carolina Press, 1960).

16. B. Welter, "The Cult of True Womanhood: 1820–1860," *American Quarterly* 18 (1966):151–74; G. J. Barker-Benfield, *The Horrors of the Half-Known Life: Male Attitudes toward Women and Sexuality in Nineteenth-Century America* (New York: Harper & Row, 1976).

17. Demos, *Little Commonwealth*, chap. 5.

18. The classic study of "the discovery of childhood" is Ariès, *Centuries of Childhood.* Ariès traces the beginnings of this development to the experience of elite groups in sixteenth- and seventeenth-century Europe. For average people, both in Europe and in the United States, the sequence seems to have occurred considerably later. See, for example, B. Wishy, *The Child and the Republic* (Philadelphia: University of Pennsylvania Press, 1968); J. Kett, "Growing Up in Rural New England, 1800–1840," in *Anonymous Americans: Explorations in Nineteenth-Century Social History*, ed. T. Hareven (Englewood Cliffs, N.J.: Prentice-Hall, 1971), pp. 1–16; and John Demos and V. Demos, "Adolescence in Historical Perspective," in *Journal of Marriage and Family* 31 (1969):632–38.

19. For instances of child labor in nineteenth-century America see R. Bremner, J. Barnard, T. K. Hareven, and R. M. Mennell, *Children and Youth in America: A Documentary History*, vol. 1 (Cambridge: Harvard University Press, 1970).

20. The timing and steepness of this trend are reflected in a demographic measure which compares the number of children less than five years old in a given population with the number of women of child bearing age (16–44 years). The figures for the United States in the nineteenth century are as follows: *1800*—976 per 1,000; *1850*—699 per 1,000; *1900*—541 per 1,000. There has been a further drop, in our own century, to approximately 425 per 1,000. Interestingly enough, from the standpoint of the present argument, the process of declining fertility seems to have begun much earlier, and to have been substantially more dramatic over-all, in this country than in Europe. (The starting point, however, was a higher American level of fertility.) On these points the standard works are Y. Yasuba, *Birth Rates of the White Population in the United States, 1800–1860* (Baltimore: The Johns Hopkins University Press, 1962) and B. Okun, *Trends in Birth Rates in the United States Since 1870* (Baltimore: The Johns Hopkins University Press, 1958).

21. Demos and Demos, "Adolescence."

22. Wishy, *Child and the Republic;* R. Sunley, "Early Nineteenth-Century American Literature on Child Rearing," in *Childhood in Contemporary Cultures*, ed. M. Mead and M. Wolfenstein (Chicago: University of Chicago Press, 1963).

23. Horace Bushnell, *Christian Nurture* (New York: 1843), p. 248.

24. L. M. Child, *The Mother's Book* (Boston, 1832), p. 8; Frank Lloyd Wright, *An Autobiography* (New York: Longmans Green, 1932), p. 8.

25. Note, for example, this comment from one of the earliest of the advice books: "The child must be his own chief disciplinarian through life, and the art of self-government must be taught him, as a regular point of his education, and that both by precept and example" (T. Dwight, *The Father's Book* [Springfield, 1834], p. 113).

26. Two brief quotations may serve to exemplify this change. For the earlier period, consider the following advice attributed to the Rev. John Ward (a New England minister of the seventeenth century): "Whatever you do, be sure to maintain shame in [children]; for if that be gone, there is no hope that they'll ever come to good" (C. Mather, *Magnalia Christi Americana* [Hartford, 1953], 1:522). For the nineteenth century, note the opinion of Mrs. Child: "Punishments which make a child ashamed should be avoided. A sense of degradation is not healthy for the character" (Child, *Mother's Book*, p. 37). (For a similar vein of comment, see Bushnell, *Christian Nurture*, pp. 300, 332.) For a brief discussion of the colonial pattern see Demos, *Little Commonwealth*, pp. 138–39.

27. See, for example, the plot line in Sedgewick, *Home*—one of the most popular works of fiction in the mid-nineteenth century. The child-rearing literature displayed a similar viewpoint, e.g., this comment from J. S. C. Abbott, *The Mother at Home* (Boston, 1833): "How entirely is your earthly happiness at the disposal of your child. His character is now in your hands, and you

are to form it for good or evil. If you are consistent in your government, and faithful in the discharge of your duties, your child will probably, through life, revere you—to be the stay and solace of your declining years. If, on the other hand, you cannot summon resolution to punish your child when disobedient; if you do not curb his passions; if you do not bring him to entire and willing subjection to your authority, you must expect that he will be your curse" (p. 25).

28. N. F. Cott, "In the Bonds of Womanhood: Perspectives on Female Experience and Consciousness in New England, 1780–1840," Ph.D. diss., Brandeis University, 1974, chap. 6; Barker-Benfield, *Horrors of the Half-Known Life*, pp. 113–16, 275.

29. Barker-Benfield, *Horrors of the Half-Known Life*, pp. 120ff.

30. Erik H. Erikson, *Childhood and Society* (New York: Norton, 1950), pp. 288–97.

31. F. Moore, Ed., *The Civil War in Song and Story* (New York, 1889).

32. Fred Weinstein and Gerald Platt, *The Wish to Be Free: Society, Psyche, and Value Change* (Berkeley: University of California Press, 1969), chap. 5.

33. Ibid., p. 147.

34. M. Rischin, ed., *The American Gospel of Success* (Chicago: Quadrangle, 1965); J. G. Cawelti, *Apostles of the Self-Made Man* (Chicago: University of Chicago Press, 1965); K. Lynn, *The Dream of Success: A Study of the Modern American Literary Imagination* (Boston: Little, Brown, 1955); J. Tebbel, *From Rags to Riches: Horatio Alger, Jr., and the American Dream* (New York: Macmillan, 1963); I. G. Wyllie, *The Self-Made Man in America: The Myth of Rags to Riches* (New Brunswick, N.J.: Rutgers University Press, 1954).

35. S. Thernstrom and P. Knights, "Men in Motion: Some Data and Speculations about Urban Population Mobility in Nineteenth-Century America," in *Anonymous Americans*, ed. Hareven, pp. 17–47.

36. Oscar Handlin, *The Uprooted* (Boston: Little, Brown, 1973).

37. Although it has been impossible to give any systematic consideration to the same issues in European history, some brief speculations may prove useful. In certain respects European and American trends seem to have been roughly similar: e.g., the bounded quality of nineteenth-century family life; the sharpened definition of sex roles; the "Victorian" culture of sexual repressiveness; and the "discovery" of childhood. In other respects European developments had the same direction as American ones, but not the same intensity: e.g., the cult of motherhood; the shift to a child-rearing regime based on guilt more than shame; the declining birth rate; the sense of exclusive responsibility among the family members for one another. In still other ways the American pattern found no significant parallel in Europe whatsoever: e.g., the "cult of success," and the transforming effects of vast in-migration. Europe, in short, experienced some, but not all, of these influences which created the "hothouse" (or "oedipal") family in America. Thus, from a cumulative standpoint, her "readiness" for psychoanalysis was less—though hardly nil.

15

NOTHING TO FEAR
Notes on the Life of Eleanor Roosevelt

JOAN M. ERIKSON

It is easy to think of Eleanor Roosevelt as the niece of Theodore Roosevelt who married her cousin Franklin Delano and then served as first lady during the twelve years of her husband's presidency. Yet in her lifetime she developed a stature that indisputably was all her own. She championed the cause of the needy and forgotten in the Depression years and after, speaking on behalf of blacks, women, immigrants, the aged, and the handicapped; an outspoken champion of organized labor—then an exposed position to take—she endured a barrage of criticism for her politics, even ridicule for her appearance. She was by any measure a strong and courageous person. She also was unusually, notoriously, needy of support and affection, and her close relationships with several women were the subject of considerable gossip in the 1930s and 1940s. Doris Faber's recent biography of one of these intimates, the news reporter Lorena Hickock, has led to renewed discussion (see the *New Republic*, April 26, 1980) of the evidence that these friendships may have been physical.

In the following sketch of Eleanor Roosevelt's life, written not long after her autobiography appeared in 1961, Joan M. Erikson demonstrates the sensitivity and powers of insight that her own husband has made the standard in psychobiography. This portrait of Eleanor offers a negative of Theodore Roosevelt's, in chapter 13: his niece suffered from all the restrictions and slights that allowed him and men generally to flourish—or, to put it differently, that placed high demands on men and women alike. Her life experience refers us back to the Smith-Rosenberg essay and to Adams's *Esther*; all the same, Roosevelt's insistence on a voice for women also makes her an illustration of one of the impulses that led to the women's movement of our day. She helped to bring about that revolution despite the constraints of the society she grew out of, and the reasons for her irrepressibility remain a bit mysterious. On that account Erikson's article reminds us that the psychobiographer needs to be a humanist whose effort to bring a subject back to life avoids formulaic or pat answers to questions of personality.

Reprinted by permission of *Daedalus*, Journal of the American Academy of Arts and Sciences, Boston, Massachusetts. Spring 1964, *The Women in America*.

THE FOREIGN visitor to this country in the 1930's might well have
been astounded by the portrayal in newspapers and magazines of the First
Lady of the land. Eleanor Roosevelt was featured prominently in the press as
the butt of jokes and anecdotes. Much of this humor was kindly, some of it
was cruel, and upon occasions it became vicious. Cartoonists were never at a
loss with the assignment of portraying Mrs. Roosevelt. She smiled often and
broadly, displaying prominent front teeth. The caricatures were cruel and
repetitious, combined with such taunting remarks as, "Eleanor can bite an
apple through a picket fence." That she continued to smile frequently,
broadly and unaffectedly in spite of consistent lampooning attests to unusual
fortitude, perhaps especially in a woman.

What were the characteristics which offered themselves for this ridicule?
The more kindly humor focused on her soft-hearted and sometimes deep
involvement in any cause which supported the improvement of conditions for
the underprivileged. She was moved by any tale of woe, often using private
funds to alleviate an individual financial problem, but she also espoused
wholeheartedly and without cautionary hesitation the more debatable large-
scale official measures for dealing with employment.

But the most savage ridicule was focused on her phenomenal energy. This
ability of Eleanor Roosevelt to go on when all companions were falling by the
wayside, to travel extensively, to write reams about seemingly insignificant
daily affairs, to talk enthusiastically about the issues that concerned her, to
entertain in the White House as if it were a public museum—all exposed her
constantly to the suspicion of others less endowed. Her critics suggested that
this drive could be maintained only in the service of an extraordinary hunger
for power and that she was a flagrant busybody on the national scale; that she
was in love with the sound of her own voice and the sight of her own words in
print. This kind of energy might be admirable in a man. It was applauded
among the qualities of her uncle, Theodore Roosevelt, whom in some ways
she was said to resemble. But it was said to be unseemly in a woman who
after all belonged at home, even if home happened to be the White House and
her children for that very good reason were all away in school or college.
Moreover, these activities were the more disconcerting to her critics because
it gradually became evident that they were not merely a kind of innocuous
busywork on the part of the President's wife. She was, in fact, unquestionably effective as a voice urgently enlisting the responsible participation of
women in public affairs and in the support of the various humanitarian causes
which she promoted; and she was a successful ambassadress to the countries
that she visited. Perhaps the only weapon against such formidable enterprise
was ridicule.

How does a person, especially a woman, who is kept prominently in the
public eye, survive such attack? Close friends of Mrs. Roosevelt report that
she deliberately avoided reading what the papers printed about her. When
her attention was called to particularly ugly criticism she would reply, "They

mean my husband; they are only getting at him through me." On a trip to Puerto Rico a cartoonist in a local paper produced a cruel cartoon featuring her teeth and expression. When her friends objected and clamored that he be fired, she defended his right to draw her as he wished and invited him to tea. Westbrook Pegler, in his column, often attacked her viciously. When this was pointed out to her, she said, "I think he must be a very unhappy man."

But avoid what she might, the venom must to some degree have penetrated through her defenses. She made no effort, however, to fend off the negative reaction and to make her image more effective. She smiled as usual, her daily schedule remained a source of wonder to friend and foe alike, and she continued to plunge with earnest enthusiasm into the causes which interested her. Her name was a byword for the soft touch. (The number of daily requests for personal help which came to her by mail are legendary.) In fact, instead of reacting to personal criticism by letting it interfere with the work at hand, she seemed to open herself to it with apparently naïve abandon.

Her first book of memoirs is a touchingly self-revealing story of the little girl who grew up to be Eleanor Roosevelt. She wrote in the conclusion that her purpose was to give "as truthful a picture as possible of a human being." This she tried to do in the honest, straightforward prose of a schoolgirl. In her "My Day" column, she continued this self-exposure of her actions and thoughts. Perhaps she felt that in this kind of intimate sharing of the banal elements of a woman's life she could reach more women and draw them into sympathetic support of the causes she sponsored. Perhaps, too, she hoped to impart some of her discipline and her energy into lives grown sluggish in the constant coping with household chores.

Her memoirs reveal, I think, the sources of her courage and her discipline, her enthusiasm and her serenity. One of her favorite quotations was "Back of tranquillity lies always conquered unhappiness," and her unassuming autobiographic writings offer a better and more intuitive account of such conquest than do many more ambitious self-revelations. She records her memories with a feminine concreteness and closeness to people, reminiscing with critical sympathy about the little girl and the young woman whose life is being described. Her later writings lose some of this quality. They read as though the events reported had initially been more self-consciously recorded in a diary and later assembled to continue a history. There is little self-observation. In them we find Mrs. Roosevelt in action and history taking form around her, but we are given few glimpses of the inner development of the maturing woman.

This account, then, will follow her life only as far as she reveals some hints of her inner experience of growth to us. It will attempt to let Eleanor Roosevelt speak, underlining with commentary only such insights as may otherwise escape the reader. Her own words are, in fact, often so naïve and without humor that the dynamic truths they express can be overlooked in what might be considered an amateurish and superficial style. Let us

review briefly some of the most critical and telling experiences of her childhood as she has recorded them, seeking possible sources for her outstanding
qualities—for she was no stranger to adversity.

Anna Eleanor Roosevelt was born in 1884 in New York. Her mother was
Anna Hall Roosevelt, then twenty-one years old and according to the *New
York Times*, "one of the most beautiful and popular women in New York
Society." Her father was Elliot Roosevelt, aged twenty-four, at the time of
her birth a dashing, handsome and adventurous man, brother of Theodore
Roosevelt and also a member of one of New York's socially elite families.

Eleanor was not a pretty baby. As she grew older it became apparent that
she would be an unattractive little girl and that she had inherited none of the
acclaimed charm and good looks of the women in her mother's family. This
seems to have estranged her from Anna, who lavished her affection on the
two sons who followed Eleanor. "I felt a curious barrier between myself and
these three," she writes.

... and still I can remember standing in the door, very often with my finger in my
mouth—which was, of course, forbidden—and I can see the look in her eyes and hear
the tone of her voice as she said: "Come in, Granny." If a visitor was there she might
turn and say: "She is such a funny child, so old-fashioned, that we always call her
'Granny.'" I wanted to sink through the floor in shame, and I felt I was apart from the
boys.

And again,

I must have been very sensitive, with an inordinate desire for affection and praise—
perhaps brought on by the fact that I was fully conscious of my plain looks and lack of
manners. My mother was always a little troubled by my lack of beauty, and I knew it
as a child senses those things. She tried very hard to bring me up well so my manners
would in some way compensate for my looks, but her efforts only made me more
keenly conscious of my shortcomings.

But if the little girl Eleanor's relationship with her mother was uncomfortable and cool, her delight in and closeness to her father provided warmth and
tenderness to grow on. He had welcomed her as "a miracle from Heaven,"
later nicknaming her "Little Nell," and he seemed to find her in all ways
charming, amusing, and companionable.

I remember my father acting as gondolier, taking me out on the Venice canals, singing
with the other boatmen, to my intense joy. I think there never was a child who was
less able to carry a tune and had less gift for music than I. I loved his voice, however,
and above all, I loved the way he treated me. He called me "Little Nell," after the
Little Nell in Dickens' "Old Curiosity Shop." Later he made me read the book, but at
that time I only knew it was a term of affection, and I never doubted that I stood first
in his heart.

One senses that Eleanor's relationship to her father was never as uncompli-
cated as she describes it, and soon one stark complication became critical: this
delightful father began to drink heavily and later became a confirmed al-

coholic. He was banished from the family to visit European spas in search of a cure, and later to live in a small Virginia town. The little girl, then eight years old, was told that her father was sick, which puzzled her, for sick people need to be taken care of, not to be exiled.

In simple terms Eleanor Roosevelt then described a series of traumatic events. The year after her father's departure, her mother died very suddenly of diphtheria, and very shortly afterward Elliott, Jr., also died. Eleanor and her younger brother Hall were moved into their Grandmother Hall's house, and it was in this household and in their summer residence at Tivoli that she grew up.

After we were installed, my father came to see me, and I remember going down into the high ceilinged, dim library on the first floor of the house in West 37th Street. He sat in a big chair. He was dressed all in black, looking very sad. He held out his arms and gathered me to him. In a little while he began to talk, to explain to me that my mother was gone, that she had been all the world to him, and now he had only my brothers and myself, that my brothers were very young, and that he and I must keep close together. Some day I would make a home for him again, we would travel together and do many things which he painted as interesting and pleasant, to be looked forward to in the future together.

This experience remained etched on her memory and guided her life through many years. The following statement, however, could have been written only by an individual of remarkable psychological innocence:

Somehow it was always he and I. I did not understand whether my brothers were to be our children or whether he felt that they would be at school and college and later independent.

There started that day a feeling which never left me—that he and I were very close together, and some day would have a life of our own together. He told me to write to him often, to be a good girl, not to give any trouble, to study hard, to grow up into a woman he could be proud of, and he would come to see me whenever it was possible.

When he left, I was all alone to keep our secret of mutual understanding and to adjust myself to my new existence.

He came occasionally to see his children that year in New York, and these visits were joyous ones for his lonely little daughter.

Though he was so little with us, my father dominated all this period of my life. Subconsciously I must have been waiting always for his visits. They were irregular, and he rarely sent word before he arrived, but never was I in the house, even in my room two long flights of stairs above the entrance door, that I did not hear his voice the minute he entered the front door. Walking down stairs was far too slow. I slid down the banisters and usually catapulted into his arms before his hat was hung up.

But Eleanor was to learn that no happiness was secure, and that security itself was an illusion. Even this period of existing hopefully from one visit to the next was short-lived, for within the year her father was killed in a riding accident.

On August 14, 1894, just before I was ten years old, word came that my father had died. My aunts told me, but I simply refused to believe it, and while I wept long and went to bed still weeping, I finally went to sleep and began the next day living in my dream world as usual.

My grandmother decided that we children should not go to the funeral, and so I had no tangible thing to make death real to me. From that time on I knew in my mind that my father was dead, and yet I lived with him more closely, probably, than I had when he was alive.

The years in Grandmother Hall's New York house and in Tivoli with her aunts and uncles must have been dreary ones by any standard. Granted that one has a tendency to remember injustices and sorrows more vividly than pleasures, the list of Eleanor's deprivations and discomforts is still unnerving. She was forbidden sweets and therefore stole them, lied, got caught and was disgraced and shamed. She was made to wear a steel brace to improve her posture which was "vastly uncomfortable and prevented my bending over." To keep her from catching colds, she alone of the family was obliged to take a cold bath every morning. Her clothes were a source of constant embarrassment to her. She was tall, thin and shy and was dressed in skirts which were above her knees while other girls of her size wore them half way down their legs. Grandmother believed in warm clothing, and long thick underwear was prescribed and worn according to set dates of the calendar rather than as made reasonable by the temperature. Mrs. Roosevelt later recalls, "All my clothes seem to me now to have been incredibly uncomfortable." In addition to these physical discomforts and deprivations, this young girl was kept very much to herself under the surveillance of governesses and maids.

They always tried to talk to me, and I wished to be left alone to live in a dream world in which I was the heroine and my father the hero. Into this world I retired as soon as I went to bed and as soon as I woke in the morning, and all the time I was walking or when anyone bored me.

The companionship of children her own age was also denied her during the long summers at Tivoli because her Uncle Vallie had also become alcoholic and no guests were welcome at the house. Her grandmother, who was strict with her in every way, also refused to let her visit her Roosevelt relations with any frequency and denied her the opportunity to travel with a young friend and her family.

My grandmother was adamant and would not allow me to go. She gave me no reasons, either. It was sufficient that she did not think it wise. She so often said "no" that I built up the defense of saying I did not want things in order to forestall her refusals and keep down my disappointments.

Yet life was not all black. Her aunts and uncles led interesting, even somewhat wild lives, in spite of Grandmother's efforts at restraint, and Eleanor took vicarious pleasure in their exploits. And there was always time for reading, for walking and for dreaming—these three lonely occupations which she loved.

When she was fifteen, however, a friend and mentor came into her life from outside the family, a woman who was destined to sponsor what was strongest and most forward-looking in Eleanor. Grandmother Hall decided to send her to England to a private school for girls under an excellent head-mistress. Intellectually, Mlle. Souvestre "shocked me into thinking," she writes. She had "an active keen mind" and she conveyed her vital interest in public affairs to her pupils. She expressed indignation at the judgment against Dreyfus, announced her total lack of sympathy with Britain during the Boer War, in fact taking the position that war was no solution to international problems—certainly a bold opinion to hold in the early 1900's. Beyond stimulating young Eleanor to independent thinking, she also undertook to increase her limited knowledge of the world by traveling with her on the continent during the holidays. They traveled widely, off the more beaten paths, Eleanor finding both advantage and enrichment in learning languages. She did learn French, German and Italian. She was allowed to remain three years under the tutelage of this gifted and inspiring teacher. Then, after having glimpsed new vistas of freedom, she was called home to be introduced to New York society. She was eighteen.

In decisive and "formative" years, then, Eleanor learned that the spirit can count for more than appearance and social form. However, she was as yet too young to sustain such insight, and the ways of her social class decreed that she must try to conform. Coming out was a gruelling experience for this shy, still rather awkward girl, and she gives us this account of her misery:

> My aunt, Mrs. Mortimer, had bought my clothes in Paris, and I imagine that I was well dressed, but there was absolutely nothing about me to attract anybody's attention. . . . I do not think I quite realized beforehand what utter agony it was going to be or I would never have had the courage to go. . . . I knew I was the first girl in my mother's family who was not a belle, and though I never acknowledged it to any of them at the time, I was deeply ashamed. . . . Gradually I acquired a few friends . . . and finally going out lost some of its terrors; but that first winter, when my sole object in life was society, nearly brought me to a state of nervous collapse.

Whatever tensions contributed to Eleanor's nervous state, it is clear that she suffered not only from strenuous and incompatible activity, but also from an inner conflict between socially approved goals and her own aspirations and emerging potentialities. The rules of her class, however, aligned her activities at first with the customary contribution of a lady to social problems: charity.

During this period of her life in New York with her Aunt Pussie she turned her attention to all kinds of charitable endeavors. From her childhood on she had been taught that people of wealth and social standing should engage in philanthropy. There was an obligation to be kind to the poor and to give to those who had less, she had always been told. Therefore, she could remember that when she was still quite a little girl she had played her part in fulfilling this obligation by aiding her father in serving Thanksgiving dinner to the poor little boys at the Newsboys Club, and he had told her of the hard life they led. And she had spread the season's cheer by helping her grandmother decorate a Christmas tree for a children's ward in the hospital. She had visited the Orthopaedic Hospital with Auntie Grace and The Bowery Mission with Aunt Maud and Aunt Pussie. So it seemed appropriate that at nineteen she should offer her services to teach fancy dancing and calisthenics at the Rivington Street Settlement House and to investigate working conditions in garment factories and department stores for the Consumers League. Later she would turn indignantly against a system that offered mere charity where it should provide the underprivileged with the right of equal opportunity to help themselves. For the time being, however, she learned to work and to care deeply.

I had painfully high ideals and a tremendous sense of duty at that time, entirely unrelieved by any sense of humor or any appreciation of the weaknesses of human nature. Things were either right or wrong to me with very few shades, and I had had too little experience to know as yet how very fallible human judgments are.

In 1903 she became engaged to her distant cousin Franklin Roosevelt. There must have been general astonishment then, even as this betrothal now in retrospect astonishes. Franklin expressed himself in a letter to his mother as being "the happiest man just now in the world; likewise the luckiest." Mrs. Roosevelt, Sr., promptly sent him off on a Caribbean tour. Eleanor later wrote about her engagement with touching candor:

I had a great curiosity about life and a desire to participate in every experience that might be the lot of woman. There seemed to me to be a necessity for hurry; without rhyme or reason I felt the urge to be a part of the stream of life, and so in the autumn of 1903 when Franklin Roosevelt, my fifth cousin once removed, asked me to marry him, though I was only nineteen, it seemed an entirely natural thing and I never even thought that we were both rather young and inexperienced. I came back from Groton, where I had spent the weekend, and asked Cousin Susie whether she thought I cared enough, and my grandmother, when I told her, asked me if I was sure I was really in love. I solemnly answered "yes" and yet I know now that it was years later before I understood what being in love was or what loving really meant.

A year later, after Eleanor had met Franklin's side of the family, the engagement was announced and the wedding set for March 17. Theodore Roosevelt had been elected President. He was, in fact, inaugurated on March 4, and his first visit to New York following this ceremony was made in order to give his niece away in marriage. It followed naturally that he became the star of the festivities, with crowds forming to catch a glimpse of the President and large groups gathering around him at the reception. It was a memorable wedding and it should have warned Eleanor that her life would not be her own—until she would eventually make it her own.

For their honeymoon the young couple went to Hyde Park and thus a new era began for the bride, of a kind of upper-class captivity. Holidays would be spent at Hyde Park with mother-in-law; in summer they would move to Campobello with her and in winter they would live in a house bought for them, furnished for them, staffed with servants for them by her, and right next door to her.

Sarah Delano Roosevelt was a domineering woman who had devoted years of widowhood to the upbringing of her only son. His marriage in no way decreased her sense of responsibility and she took over the training and management of her daughter-in-law with a conviction and dedication which trapped the young wife in a sense of helplessness. Upon moving into the newly built, furnished and staffed house on East 65th Street, Eleanor felt so submerged in the strong personalities of her husband and mother-in-law that she at one point burst into tears, a self-indulgence she permitted herself only twice throughout her adult life. When Franklin asked her what might be the matter she confessed that she did not like living in a house which was not in any way hers, one that she had in no way planned and which did not represent the way she wanted to live. But her young husband, who was also a devoted son, just teased her and told her not to be silly.

Since Eleanor, during these years, was going through one pregnancy after another—Anna, 1906; James, 1907; Franklin, Jr., 1908 (died at eight months); Elliot, 1910; Franklin, Jr., II, 1914; John, 1916—and was very occupied with her unsuccessful efforts to manage the nurses and servants who were the experts called in to care for her babies, she could do little to express her own wishes, nor did she have the physical strength to combat the formidable team of husband and mother-in-law. Although she was for ten years "always just getting over having a baby or about to have one," she was not unaware of what was happening to her own personality. She recognized that she was in danger of developing "into a completely colorless echo," that she "was not developing any individual taste or initiative," and that something within her craved to be an independent individual.

As F. D. R. became involved in politics and was sent first to Albany and then to Washington, Eleanor undertook the duties appropriate to the wife of a New York senator and later those incumbent on her when he became the Assistant Secretary of the Navy. The social round of duties in Washington was strenuous but she had the advantage of the advice of her practiced Auntie Bye, who had advised Theodore Roosevelt when he held the same post, regarding the complications of procedure and protocol. During the war years she plunged into activities with other women in the Navy League providing comforts for seamen or visiting naval hospitals, talking to sick and wounded men and cooking in a Red Cross canteen.

The war years in Washington were hectic and demanding for the Roosevelts. Probably it was during this period that Eleanor's capacity for dicipline, endurance and energetic undertaking were first really challenged and confirmed. She says of this experience, too, that the exposure to all kinds of people and to the confidences of the boys in the naval hospitals provided her with "a liberal education." Out of these contacts with human beings, she writes, "I became a more tolerant person—far less sure of my own beliefs and methods of action, but I think more determined to try for certain ultimate objectives." Then, once again, her horizon was widened by travel. The trip with President and Mrs. Wilson to the Paris Peace Conference, where she could feel herself a part of historic decision-making, no doubt also added to her status as a mature woman. During F. D. R.'s unsuccessful campaign for the Vice-Presidency in 1920 she had her first taste of traveling around the country on the campaign train, and she later referred to this experience as "the start of my political education."

Then a crisis occurred which threatened to contract her life space and that of her husband and to preshadow a future of severe restriction. In the summer of 1921, F. D. R. contracted infantile paralysis at Campobello. Eleanor became his day and night attendant and nursed him with efficient dedication.

Almost everything we have noted about Eleanor Roosevelt's development up to this point would seem to suggest that she was now offered a potentially absorbing role. Needing to be needed, eager to please, dedicated to service—how appropriate that she should now devote herself to an invalid husband's care. An amazing transformation, however, took place slowly but irrevocably, for it was at this point in her life that the woman who as a girl had bowed to domination by mother, grandmother, husband and mother-in-law, firmly stood her full height and took over the responsibility not only for her husband's care and her family's well-being, but also for their joint right to manage their own future. Mrs. Roosevelt, Sr., was the first to record the change. In a letter to her brother about the sickroom at Campobello, she wrote the simple truth. "Eleanor is the lead."

How true this was she perhaps did not quite realize at the time. When it became clear that F. D. R. would not recover the use of his legs and that he would be permanently crippled, his mother demanded that he be brought to Hyde Park, where he could have rest and complete quiet. There, she said, he could write as he always wanted to and "he can keep busy doing that or reading books or collecting stamps." But she had not counted with her daughter-in-law. "That's the last thing he should do," Eleanor told her. "And I won't let him."

This was the beginning of a determined struggle between the two women, between two generations who "knew what was best" for a stricken man. Eleanor by then had found a firm ally in the person of F. D. R.'s friend Louis Howe, who was also intent on not allowing him to become a dispirited invalid. Together they contrived to bring rewarding activities, interesting people and stimulating ideas to F. D. R. Howe searched the bookstores for rare old books and studied stamps so that he could talk intelligently about them. But Eleanor and Howe agreed that hobbies would not be enough for their charge, and even when he added a work schedule it was clear to them that his real interest was politics. So it was decided that Eleanor should become active in politics and in this way involve F. D. R. in current issues. She turned her attention and amazing energy to the work of the Women's Trade Union League and brought some of her co-workers home with her to meet her husband. She joined the Women's Division of the Democratic State Committee and began a round of public speaking, which, though frightening for her initially, proved most successful. (She had a habit of giggling which infuriated Louis Howe, and he reproved her severely.) And she traveled extensively all over the state organizing women voters into the Democratic party.

All of this activity came to a head when Al Smith, in 1924, asked F. D. R. to take charge of his preconvention campaign and to nominate him as presidential nominee for the Democratic party. F. D. R. agreed, and though his candidate ran unsuccessfully, he showed a triumphant courage by facing the Democratic convention on his own feet, even though his legs had to be supported by braces, and by giving his now famous "Happy Warrior" speech. F. D. R. was back in the public eye. He was back in politics.

The rest is well known. From the childhood and young womanhood sketched here, the woman emerged who more than any other woman in American history played a leading role in public affairs, the woman who gave to the position of the President's wife an entirely new force, the woman who was to become chairman of the committee which drew up the United Nations Declaration of Human Rights. We shall not here discuss in any detail these later developments which proved that the time was ripe for the emergence of a woman like Eleanor Roosevelt, even as she had now become adequate to and ready for her historical role. But let us ask ourselves whether it is possible to trace any inner logic in this story.

Eleanor Roosevelt's account of her early life highlights a lesson often lost in the study of biographies. This record of her childhood experiences could, if it were offered as a case history, account for a total failure to accept the challenge of participation in an active and productive life. Such documentation could be used trauma for trauma to "explain" failure. Yet Eleanor Roosevelt "succeeded," in many ways triumphantly, in other ways not without tragic overtones. Victory of this caliber should be kept before us to contribute to a better understanding of the intimate history accompanying great events.

Reviewing, then, the traumatic aspects of her childhood, can we bring into focus the qualities, the strengths that were pitted against failure—and that won? What became of the shame of "Granny," the deep sadness of "Little Nell," the pervading sense of inferiority and fear of the small girl Eleanor? The inner tranquillity of the Mrs. Roosevelt that the world knew and honored was indeed the fruit of actively "conquered unhappiness," of deprivation transcended. But, in addition, she became an individual who manifested such transcendance in what Woodrow Wilson called "activity on a large scale."

She seems to have settled her account with her unlucky childhood by a determined rebalancing of the scales and by projecting this shift onto an almost global screen. Once deeply ashamed of her own unattractiveness, she spent her entire life developing her capacity for empathizing with people. She listened with compassion. Her response to any demonstrable need was immediate and generous to a fault. Indignation was by no means foreign to her, but she transformed it into strong feelings in the service of causes. Such empathizing requires the capacity to be self-effacing. Having set her own needs aside, as it were, her relationships with others could be immediate and warm. She became one of the most attractive and charming women in public life.

The little girl Eleanor had been ashamed about her physical cowardice. She had been afraid of the dark and of burglars, of water, of horses, of physical exploits of many kinds. Her reckless and dashing father had chided her about this and had tried to encourage his timid daughter. Her Uncle Ted had teased her, and her Hall aunts and uncles had made fun of her fears. This same child became renowned as a grown woman for her endurance and her fearlessness in meeting danger. It was not a courage lightly won. Perhaps it grew out of her determination to accept all challenges actively in order to avoid that fate worse than death—public shaming. Green with seasickness on a battleship one day, the suggestion was made to her that she climb the 100-foot ladder of the skeleton mask. She did, and in time she slowly overcame her fear of height and of seasickness.

Even more than physical apprehension of danger she suffered from fear of the disapproval of those from whom she needed love. In her loneliness and perplexity she lied and she stole.

I could bear with swift punishment of any kind far better than long scoldings. I could cheerfully lie anytime to escape a scolding, whereas if I had known that I would simply be put to bed or be spanked I probably would have told the truth. This habit of lying stayed with me for a number of years. I now realize I was a great trial to my mother. She did not understand that a child may lie from fear; I myself never understood it until I reached the age when I suddenly realized that there was nothing to fear.

One may note here that this realization came to her only when she left her grandmother's house for school in England, for she writes, "this was the first time in all my life that all my fears left me."

She did later lead a fearless public life, disregarding petty criticism and caricature and striking out boldly for charity in issues both big and small. And it was she who selected for her husband's tombstone the depression-conquering slogan, "The only thing we have to fear is fear itself."

Having suffered from certain psychological deprivations as a child, she responded with immediate concern to the support of any oppressed group. She championed the cause of educating and freeing women so that they

might become responsible citizens. She did not address herself to this problem by joining groups working explicitly for women's rights. Instead she set
herself the task of demonstrating in her own person how the rights already
gained could be made use of to greatest advantage. She wasted no breath on
battle-cries—she simply rearranged the furniture, as it were, placing her desk
in an advantageous position in the living room and getting up an hour earlier
to make time for her correspondence. Her devotion to the cause of the
underprivileged found its crowning achievement in her magnificent work for
the Committee on Human Rights of the United Nations.

Deprived in her childhood of the people she loved most, of the possibly
compensatory sweets, of trips and of friends, and being exposed so often to
"no" as the answer to her requests, she learned early not to ask for things, and
better still not to want or hope for them, in order to avoid disappointment.
But she was an observant child and noted that the grandmother who disciplined her so sternly had no discipline whatsoever where her own children
were concerned. She spoiled them unrestrainedly and was helplessly outraged with their misbehavior, especially when her sons began their heavy
drinking. Mrs. Roosevelt speaks of this drinking as having made a deep
impression on her:

This was my first [really her second] contact with anyone who had completely lost
power of self-control and I think it began to develop in me an almost exaggerated idea
of the necessity of keeping all of one's desires under complete subjugation.

Actively then she began to impose on herself the controls, the discipline to
which she had been passively subjected as a little girl. She became extraordinarily self-disciplined. Her workday was strenuous, but organized to the
minute, for with the proverbial energy went control, the capacity both for
renunciation and for complete relaxation. She exercised every morning without fail and she could sleep anywhere sitting up in a chair.

This life-sustaining strength came somehow from the few people whom
she loved and admired and with whom she identified. Who were these important people? Her relationship with her mother, at least in later childhood,
was certainly not one of loving mutuality. The little Eleanor admired this
glamorous mother and loved to watch her as she dressed to go out in the
evening, and she was content to rub her mother's head by the hour when she
complained of a headache. However, she also knew her as a stern judge who
found a child who could lie despicable, but who nevertheless "made a great
effort for me" obviously out of a sense of duty. One is tempted to wonder
how much of the onus of this mother's disappointment in her "uncontrolled"
husband was projected onto the little daughter who looked so much like him.

Be that as it may, the daughter could not learn from this mother how to
become the loving and caring mother of her own children. She writes of her
own mothering, "I never had any interest in dolls or in little children and I
knew absolutely nothing about handling or feeding a baby." No wonder,

then, that she felt incompetent and awkward with her own babies and turned them over to nurses and governesses. Writing later in life, she deplores this lack of training and understanding and expresses the wish that she had taken over the upbringing of her children herself. "Had I done this," she says,

... my subsequent troubles would have been avoided and my children would have had far happier childhoods. As it was, for years I was afraid of my nurses, who from this time on were usually trained English nurses who ordered me around quite as much as they ordered the children.

Eleanor Roosevelt's role as a mother is both fascinating and disturbing. Motherhood seems to have happened to her as an inexorable fate, before she could grasp its meaning. In her story she emphasizes how strongly she felt her responsibilities for her children's welfare, how dutifully she cared for them when ill or injured, but little joy or even satisfaction in mothering shines through.

The mother surrogate appointed by Anna Hall to take over the upbringing of her children was also unable to provide the little Eleanor with warm mothering. Grandmother Hall, according to the story we are told, apparently had just decided to mend her previously all too permissive ways with children when it devolved on her to bring up her daughter's child. No doubt this responsibility was unwelcome. She had already brought up a family of five children, widowed as she was, with rather questionable success. Perhaps she also saw in her granddaughter the child of her tragically intemperate son-in-law, and determined to control her with a firm hand. She is mentioned with sympathy and understanding in Mrs. Roosevelt's account of her life with her, but with neither admiration nor love. She speaks of one lesson, however, which she took to heart:

My grandmother's life had a considerable effect on me, for even when I was young I determined that I would never be dependent on my children by allowing all my interests to center in them. The conviction has grown through the years. In watching the lives of those around her, I have felt that it might have been well in their youth if they had not been able to count on her devotion and her presence whenever they needed her.... [I]t might have been far better ... had she insisted on bringing more discipline into their lives simply by having a life of her own.

Whether or not, in the end, Eleanor Roosevelt's "life of her own" benefited her children is not a matter to be discussed here, although the hostile press during her lifetime did not shirk suggestive remarks. What must be said, however, is that this whole question of a mother's "life of her own" and her children's lives is a matter demanding concrete study free from prejudice and from unpleasant eagerness to draw general (and negative) conclusions from the lives of pioneers and innovators.

One figure stands out in the story of young Eleanor who is described by her in only the happiest and most admiring terms. This was Mlle. Souvestre, the principal of the English school where she spent three wonderfully happy years. Mlle. Souvestre was apparently the epitome of what a fine teacher should be, both intelligent and wise, dignified and motherly, disciplined in her thinking but independent. Though she did not flout convention, she remained honest and nonconforming in her attitudes. She must also have been a fine judge of character, for she took the shy awkward American girl under her wing, called her "ma chère petite" and set herself the task of developing in her pupil a sense of self-confidence and also of opening her mind to intellectual interests. She discovered Eleanor's remarkable capacity to memorize, to listen to and remember conversation, and she gave her ample opportunity to use and develop this gift, of which she made such admirable use in later life.

In her Eleanor found a thoughtful and intelligent woman of strong convictions, who was unafraid to represent what she believed. Under the tutelage of this devoted teacher, then, Eleanor absorbed principles which could give her commitment to her American heritage new impetus and later enlist her uncompromising involvement in the struggle for human dignity. Here was a woman to love, admire and deeply respect, and Eleanor writes of her that she "exerted the greatest influence, after my father, on this period of my life."

"After my father," What influence did her father have on the life of Eleanor Roosevelt? For the little girl who loved him so devotedly it would be almost impossible to exaggerate his role. He was her life, her *raison d'être*. Her life was dominated by his presence even after his death, and his wish became her will. When she went off to school she took the "letters of my father's which I always carried with me" and these were read and reread. She habitually bit her fingernails, but one day "I came across one in which he spoke of always making the most of one's personal appearance, and from that day forward my nails were allowed to grow."

When she was forty years old and the wife of the President of the United States, she wrote:

On the other side of my family, of course, many people whom I have mentioned will be described far better and more fully by other people, except in the case of my father, whose short and happy life was so tragically ended. With him I have a curious feeling that as long as he remains to me the vivid, living person that he is, he will, after the manner of the people in the "Blue Bird," be alive and continue to exert his influence which was always a very gentle, kindly one.

Could one not say that the young Eleanor and the mature woman she became were the product of an act of will—the will to be the daughter that her father had lovingly preordained, the daughter that would make him proud? This deep love for her father and her conviction that she was beloved and that much was expected of her was surely the source of the inner strength which upheld her and made it possible for her to transcend her misfortunes.

And she married Franklin Roosevelt. It is impossible to judge what mixture of conventionality and of affection marked the beginnings of this relationship. One has the impression that in this instance two emotionally immature people found one another whose needs for intimacy may have remained atuned to the demands of a more remote destiny. Hindsight, at any rate, makes it seem probable that these two people sensed potentialities which in each could only be realized with the help that each could offer the other.

In her autobiography Eleanor Roosevelt gives us little information and only few hints about her relationship with her husband. Perhaps this is just reticence, but one is tempted to conjecture that only by deliberately barring this scene-stealing actor from the stage could she highlight herself in the setting of her early married life. There are known facts, however, and her own words to consider. At eighteen years of age Eleanor was not a promising and popular debutante. To become at nineteen the fiancée of one of the socially most outstanding young bachelors of New York must have been in itself both a pleasant development and one which promoted her personal and social security. To be chosen, to be wanted in spite of Mrs. Roosevelt, Sr.'s obvious reluctance to give her approval, surely must have warmed her heart and supported her wavering self-confidence. And his name was Roosevelt, a loved name for the daughter of a Roosevelt who had grown up in a family of Halls. He was also her own father's godson.*

What does Eleanor's story tell us of F. D. R.'s role in her development? Speaking of an annoying fault in her character, Eleanor describes how as a young wife she was given to moods and would retreat into wordless martyrdom and limelight self-effacement: "my Griselda mood," she called it. Franklin was the antidote for this. He could tease her out of her gloom, and she was grateful. She was also very inept as a housekeeper and knew little about wifely duties, and she writes appreciatively, "I marvel now at my husband's patience, for I realize how trying I must have been in many ways." She mentions too that he talked history endlessly on their honeymoon, that he was informed about the government of his country (which she was not and vowed to become) and that he taught her how to keep track of money; "my husband educated me in the question of accounts." And she learned things because it is a wife's duty to be interested in whatever interests her husband. "You so obviously must want that which you ought to do," she wrote. "So I took an interest in politics."

She also made a heroic effort to take part in the sports which he loved, golf, sailing, and swimming; but she was inept and he finally discouraged her efforts. He was a collector of books, stamps, and anything pertaining to the American Navy. Of these interests she says only that she wasted time trying to restrain him.

In a remark evaluating her own development at the time of the First World War, she makes an astonishing statement—astonishing because the tribute to

---

*The Roosevelts had met Elliot on a world cruise and had become so devoted to him that they had asked him to be their son's godfather.

her husband is so casual. She describes an argument with her grandmother about her brother Hall's enlistment and adds: "This was my first outspoken declaration against the accepted standards of the surroundings in which I had spent my childhood, and marked the fact that either my husband, or an increasing ability to think for myself, was changing my point of view." Perhaps F. D. R.'s outstanding contribution to Eleanor's development was to foster that "increasing ability to think for myself."

From these sources, then, and undoubtedly from other interesting and exemplary figures of her wider family and her time, such as Uncle Ted and Auntie Bye, Eleanor gradually built up that personality which was to become the legendary figure—the "Great Lady" of our country and the world. This slow unfolding withstood a number of crises. The self-confidence that had been nourished at school abroad apparently suffered a considerable set-back when she became a debutante. A constant round of gaieties and parties was inconsistent with any of the goals for which her education had prepared her, and surely her image of herself was not that of a social butterfly. Her early engagement to F. D. R. seems to have been a relationship that she almost drifted into; and her first years of married life, with the problems of getting along with mother-in-law and the perplexities of bearing and caring for children, seem almost to have inundated her with demands. Obviously these were years of tremendous importance in her development—obviously she grew in stature and gained poise through her experience.

But a moment came in her life which again brought near tragedy—her husband's serious illness. Once before, as a little girl, she had been the helpless observer of the tragic destruction of a beloved person. This time she was not helpless. This time she responded with a will of iron, the patience and endurance, the love necessary to rehabilitate the man, now stricken, whom she had married. An extraordinary consolidation of her capacities seems to have taken place so that she could even take a firm stand against the pronouncements of the overprotective mother-in-law who had always dominated her. She became F. D. R.'s champion against invalidism and resignation, thereby actively redeeming her own father's tragedy. She became Eleanor Roosevelt.

For almost twelve years Eleanor Roosevelt was the First Lady of the land, the wife of the President of the United States. In truly growing into the role of her great husband's wife, she found her stature as a citizen and a leader. History had called her husband to a high office, and although she had undertaken her role as mistress of the White House with misgiving and reluctance, she nevertheless became the most outstanding wife of a president that this country has produced. The historical setting both challenged and supported the development of her unusual potentialities, and her position gave her scope to fulfill them in a grand manner.

This is our image of Mrs. Roosevelt during her years in the White House. But how does she herself describe this period of her life? "I think I lived those years very impersonally. It was almost as though I had erected someone a little outside of myself who was the president's wife. I was lost somewhere deep down inside myself." Briefly but poignantly reviewing her life when she was sixty-four years of age, she summarized: "In my early married years the pattern of my life had been largely my mother-in-law's pattern. Later it was the children and Franklin who made the pattern. When the last child went to boarding school I began to want to do things on my own, to use my own mind and abilities for my own aims. When I went to Washington I felt sure that I would be able to use opportunities which came to me to help Franklin gain the objectives he cared about—but the work would be his work and the pattern his pattern. . . . I was one of those who served his purposes."

The final volume of her autobiography is entitled "On My Own." What were her "own aims"? Though warmly supporting many causes, essentially she was dedicated to two utopian ideals—Equality: equality of women in their responsible involvement in public affairs; human equality between individuals in a classless society; equality of rights and opportunities for all races, classes and creeds—for all mankind—these to be won in the service of human dignity; and Peace: a precept learned in her youth remained her conviction—that war is no solution to problems between nations or between people. Her appointment to the United Nations after F. D. R.'s death provided an ideal setting for activities directed toward these aims. She believed deeply in world government and she was eminently fitted to become the chairman of the Committee on Human Rights.

Transcendence of the human condition through activity on a large scale, then, could characterize Eleanor Roosevelt's career. In the final paragraph of her book, written when she was seventy-four years old, however, we can still hear the voice of a younger Eleanor, an echo from the past:

> It seems to me that we must have the courage to face ourselves in this crisis. We must regain a vision of ourselves as leaders of the world. We must join in an effort to use all knowledge for the good of all human beings.
> When we do that, we shall have nothing to fear.

16

TOWARD A PSYCHOHISTORICAL INQUIRY
The "Real" Richard Nixon

BRUCE MAZLISH

With the possible exception of Woodrow Wilson, no American political leader lends himself more auspiciously to psychological inquiry than Richard Nixon. His quirks, frets, spites, retirements and resurrections contain all the sharp outlines of an inviting classic study. Regardless what one thinks of his achievements when he finally did win the presidency in 1968 or of the justice of his near-impeachment in 1974, questions about his career invariably become psychological: Why the vitriol of his early campaigns, or the frenzy of his search for Communists in government in the 1950s? Why the awkwardness of his relationship with Eisenhower, particularly in the 1960 presidential campaign? Why his celebrated trouble with reporters or his self-conscious association with Lincoln while defending himself against corruption charges? Why, finally, did Nixon—virtually a certain victor—overdo his reelection effort in 1972 to the point where his underlings believed that anything was justified to win? Might it be, in short, that Nixon's personality made Watergate predictable?

The next essay, written during Nixon's first year in the White House and published in 1970, offers a unique example of psychohistory as attempted foresight. Bruce Mazlish's article makes no pretense of being fully biographical; indeed as if Nixon deliberately hides his "real" self, Mazlish points out in the longer version of this article, the source materials for such a study are remarkably scarce. Instead of paying strict attention to chronology and developing an integrated picture of conscious and unconscious, Mazlish draws out what he sees as a few critical themes in Nixon's personality. He tries to trace the course of these lines of development and to show how they influenced Nixon in both private and public life.

Though Mazlish works within the psychoanalytic framework, the interpretation he relies on to show the relevance of Nixon's personality is the "projection screen" approach associated with Harold D. Lasswell, a political scientist whose studies of political leaders—most notably Hitler—began in the 1930s. Lasswell put into

Reprinted, in abbreviated form, from *The Journal of Interdisciplinary History* 1 (1970):49–105, by permission of *The Journal of Interdisciplinary History* and the M.I.T. Press, Cambridge, Massachusetts. Copyright © 1970 by Bruce Mazlish.

scholarly form the perhaps commonplace observation that politicians use the public stage to act or play out their personal anxieties. This relationship between a politician and the limelight of public life recalls Erikson's talk of the intersection of life history and history—wherein private issues carry wide appeal because they speak to historical circumstances. The essay on Theodore Roosevelt in this volume illustrates the slight difference in emphasis between Lasswell and Erikson. Roosevelt reflected the concerns or "answered" the calls of his admirers, while in Lasswell's scheme politicians are driven to public life for the resolutions of neuroses that then give shape to political history. In 1956, using Lasswell as a departure, Alexander and Juliette George wrote an excellent political-psychological portrait of Wilson and his intimate advisor, Colonel Edward House. Mazlish, like Lasswell and the Georges, argues here that Nixon's disorders urged him onstage, where, exaggerated for effect (and often to his political advantage), they promised in 1970 eventually to bring him down.

If one were to weave a whole cloth of the threads Mazlish pulls in this article, the result would be illuminating not only of Nixon but of several themes in twentieth-century American life. One is the longstanding suspicion or self-reproaching envy of westerners looking back to the Eastern Establishment—that citadel of old manners and true distinctions. Nixon's struggle to win acceptance there illustrates the rural-urban conflict that the Youngdale and Dalton essays hint at and that if anything grew sharper as transportation and telephone ties drew regions together in the years of Nixon's boyhood. His experience also suggests the impact of the Depression on the men and women who reached adulthood in that period of severe trial and economic deprivation, which historians have yet to study as a problem in generational trauma. Finally, this outline of Nixon's biography raises questions about loyalty in postwar America: How have Americans defined loyalty, what does it mean psychologically to have many (or few) loyalties, and how does a sense of what is worth being loyal to change as one grows older or as the society in which an individual feels he belongs grows either "smaller" or "larger" in his perception?

WHEN RICHARD NIXON became the thirty-seventh President of the United States, friends and foes alike conceded that they did not know who the "real" Nixon was, and how he might be expected to behave. Typical of innumerable comments was Tom Wicker's: "In fact, the career and personality of Richard Nixon defy confident analysis, and what he will do in the White House is by no means easy to divine."

Wicker, of course, was right. Yet, the power of the American president is such that "analysis" of his "personality" seems requisite and justified. In so far as his personality may affect his decisions and actions, it is incumbent upon us to seek the best possible understanding of his character. Most commentators, however, have flitted like moths around this subject; thus, as Richard H. Rovere correctly points out, "Nixon's leanings, we know, are mostly conservative. But a politician is not a tree that must incline as the twig was bent a long while back." Having said this, Rovere then unconsciously undercuts his own observation by remarking that "To my mind, the greatest and most distressing revelation of this period has been the President's politi-

cal ineptitude . . . some *kind of perversity* [my italics] or some failure of calculation seems to make everything go wrong."[1]

Without taking "perversity" too seriously and abandoning Rovere's ambivalence, we can ask: what is the inter-play between Nixon's fundamental
character traits—the way in which the twig was bent for the *young boy*—and
the demands of his situation as a *politician?* To answer the first part of this
question, our main preoccupation here, we can usefully turn to the body of
theory and fact that concentrates most deeply on this problem:
psychoanalysis. In its classic form, however, psychoanalysis is oriented to
clinical data, about a patient in therapy. It is necessary, therefore, to bypass
orthodox psychoanalysis and to approach a political subject who is *not* a
patient in therapy in terms of the new discipline, variously described as
"psychohistory," or "psychological history." Such an approach emphasizes
strengths and abilities, creative and adaptive powers, as much as if not more
than the usual difficulties pictured in psychotherapy.[2]

A true psychobiography would approach Nixon chronologically, seeking
to study his personal development in the context of the changing times.
Another approach deals with themes or patterns discernible throughout Nixon's life; and it is this approach that I shall take, attending to Nixon's
chronological personal development when possible.

Both theme and chronology indicate that Nixon's family upbringing
should be our first topic. According to Mazo and Hess, "his family intimates
see Richard Nixon as a composite of his father, mother and grandmother."[3]
We need, however, to see how this "composite" is formed and interrelated.
Nixon's own account of his grandmother is that she "set the standards for the
whole family. Honesty, hard work, do your best at all times—humanitarian
ideals. She was always taking care of every tramp that came along the road,
just like my own mother, too. She had strong feelings about pacifism and
very strong feelings on civil liberties. She probably affected me in that respect" (M-H, 16).

Nixon's mother, Hannah Milhous, was much like his grandmother, a
pious Quaker and a strong, hard worker. Clearly, it is from her (and his
grandmother) that Nixon seems to have acquired the traits of the "Protestant
Ethic" that predominate so forcefully in his make-up. As Nixon's brother
Donald recalls, "Dick always planned things out. He didn't do things accidentally . . . he had more of Mother's traits than the rest of us" (M-H, 18).

Richard Nixon was the second son, born January 9, 1913, to Hannah
Milhous Nixon. His brother, Harold, was born four years before him, and
after Richard, came Donald in 1914. Arthur in 1918, and Edward in 1930.
What effect did these siblings have on Richard, and on his relations to his
mother? The Mazo-Hess account gives us only the following data, without
interpretation. The oldest boy, Harold, contracted tuberculosis. Mrs. Nixon
took him to Arizona in hopes of a cure, and stayed there for two years. The

rest of the family stayed in California, with the boys and their father taking turns at preparing the meals. "It was a period of extreme hardship for the whole family." Meanwhile, we are told, "Arthur, the fourth son, became seriously ill, and a week or so later died of tubercular meningitis. He was seven." Worse was to come, for Harold, returned from Arizona, was not cured. One morning, after Richard had driven his brother to town and back home, and then headed off for school, a message came to him, "Come home. Your brother has died" (M-H, 16–17).

How old was Richard when his mother "deserted" him? If Arthur was seven or so at the time, it would make Richard about twelve or thirteen. What effect did these "traumatic" events have on him? We can only speculate. First there is the strong possibility that he unconsciously perceived his beloved mother's leaving him for two years as a "betrayal." Consciously, he obviously understood the necessity.[4] If I am right about the unconscious feeling of "betrayal," this might affect his later attitudes on the subject of "traitors" in high places, preparing him emotionally for such a belief. Whatever the effect, we can be sure of one thing: his mother's absence for two years must have had a crucial impact on the young Richard. (I suspect it turned him back to his father, but more of this later.) We can also postulate that the birth of his brother Donald, only a little over a year after Richard's birth, must have been perceived as "taking" his mother away from him, thus laying the first seeds of his feelings of the precariousness of life and love. Of course, this perception must have been balanced by the loving concern for all her children that the hard-working, admirable Mrs. Nixon seems to have exhibited.

What of the death of Harold and of Arthur? We can speculate on at least two effects. The first is the arousal of strong unconscious guilt feelings. It would be only natural that Richard, the second son, would have rivalrous feelings toward the earlier sibling, and an unconscious desire to "replace" him (especially in the affection of the mother); all this, of course, would be accompanied by feelings of love toward his brother. The death of his brother would awaken all the feelings of "survivor guilt" so well described by analysts, such as Robert Lifton.[5] It is not at all clear, however, how Richard Nixon coped with his ambivalent feelings. It is a subject that will arise again, when we examine Nixon's relationship with President Eisenhower.

The second effect would be to arouse in him the threat and fear of death. We are told by Mazo-Hess that Nixon narrowly escaped death, at age three, in an accident that has left him with a still-existent "ugly scar" (hidden, physically, "by hair always parted on the right"). They continue, "Nixon has always been susceptible to illnesses of one kind or another since that childhood experience. When he was four he nearly died of pneumonia" (M-H, 13). More than most children, then, we can assume a death anxiety in Nixon, accentuated by the actual death of his brother Harold, and compounded by the death of his brother Arthur. It may be, therefore, that Nixon's need for "crises," as we shall see later, is partly motivated by the need to confront his death fears, repeatedly and constantly.

The paucity of our information leaves us only with these speculations: a possible sense of betrayal by the beloved mother; guilt over death wishes; and anxiety over death fears. Out of these feelings, Richard Nixon could draw either strengths or weaknesses, or both.

What of his father? Here the picture seems even more complicated. Francis (Frank) Nixon seems to have been a good man in a family dominated by strong women. In spite of his efforts, however, he seems also to have been a "failure," who drifted from enterprise to enterprise: the American who did not "make it rich." Frank Nixon, we are told, first emigrated to Whittier, California, for reasons of health, having suffered severe frostbite while running an open trolley in Columbus, Ohio. When he met Hannah Milhous in 1908 in southern California, he was still the motorman of a trolley. Since grandmother Milhous, we are told, had "a big house on the boulevard," we can assume that Frank Nixon had married above his station. In any case, he tried to improve himself. Speculating that Whittier would grow rapidly, he opened a gasoline station (in 1922 moving, in fact, from nearby Yorba Linda, where Richard was actually born, to Whittier proper; in Yorba Linda, Frank Nixon had planted a lemon grove that failed). He also converted an abandoned meeting house nearby into a general store (where Richard worked at the counter and pumped gas as well). In none of these enterprises did he seem to have great success. As one commentator puts it, the elder Nixon was "a rolling stone and man of many jobs."

My theory is that Richard Nixon, who was so like his mother in her traits of hard work and persistence, eventually turned those traits to use in terms of an *identification* with the father. In this identification, he also sought to redeem his father, by being successful. I suspect the full identification took place shortly after what I have called the mother's "betrayal," around age twelve or thirteen, when young Richard would have been moving into the swift currents of feelings that we call the reawakened Oedipus complex. All in all, he seems to have navigated these currents with relative success, being able to "let go" of his mother and to take on the role of his father. There was, of course, a price to be paid, psychically, if not outwardly. For one thing, he must always have been haunted by the sense that he, too, might fail.

What is the evidence in back of such speculation? Mazo and Hess tell us how Richard's father served as inspiration for his decision to become a lawyer and to go into politics. Incensed by the Teapot Dome Scandal, Frank Nixon "became increasingly livid over each new disclosure in the sensational theft of government oil reserves through the connivance of principles [*sic*] in President Harding's administration. His diatribes against 'crooked politicians' and 'crooked lawyers' dominated the family conversation for weeks and provoked 12-year-old Richard to abandon the romance of railroading for a more idealized road to greatness. His mother was the first to be told of the decision. She recalls that the boy declared 'I will be an old-fashioned kind of lawyer, a lawyer who can't be bought.' Donald, the third Nixon boy and Richard's junior by two years, believes his brother 'made up his mind to political life then and there, whether he realized it or not' " (M-H, 11). From our vantage point, we can also see that the father's diatribes against "crooked politicians" correspond closely to the mature Richard Nixon's attacks on "corruption."

More revealing than the Mazo-Hess account are Richard Nixon's own statements in *Six Crises*. Noting that "the last thing my mother, a devout Quaker, wanted me to do was go into the *warfare of politics*" [my italics],[6] Nixon explains that there were "two major reasons for my competitive drive. . . ." One was economic (the necessity to win a scholarship in order to go to college), the other personal:

The personal factor was contributed by my father. Because of illness in his family he had had to leave school after only six years of formal education. Never a day went by when he did not tell me and my four brothers how fortunate we were to be able to go to school. I was determined not to let him down. My biggest thrill in those years was to see the light in his eyes when I brought home a good report card. He loved the excitement and the battles of political life. During the two years he was bedridden before his death (which came just at the start of the 1956 campaign) his one request of me was that I send him the *Congressional Record*. He used to read it daily, cover-to-cover, something I never had the patience to do. I have often thought that with his fierce competitive drive and his intense interest in political issues, he might have been more successful than I in political life had he had the opportunity to continue his education [N, 318]

In many ways, this is perhaps the most revealing of the rare revelations of Richard Nixon in *Six Crises*. We have honest affect. Let us analyze it. "I was determined not to let him down." Here we have Nixon redeeming his unsuccessful father. There are also strong guilt feelings in this account. The father awakens guilt in his sons by telling them how fortunate they are to have what he did *not* have: education. Yet, Richard can overcome this guilt (and the resentment he must have felt at the accusation), as well as the natural guilt at doing better than his father, by offering excuses for the latter's failure. Frank Nixon had had to leave school because of family illness, and *this* had kept him from being successful. Moreover, Nixon concludes that *if* his father had had the same educational opportunities as he, Richard, his fierce competitive "drive and interest" in political issues would have made him even more successful than the future president of the United States. Hence, Nixon was not really displacing and exceeding his father—the dangerous fantasied Oedipal victory—but, by identification with him, merely doing in his person what his father would have accomplished, given the opportunities. As a result, Nixon could, with a good heart, follow his father, forsaking his mother in this crucial matter, into the "warfare of politics."

Hannah Milhous, as we have noted, was a dedicated Quaker, strongly pacifist. Her psychological dominance over her husband manifested itself here, too, it would seem, when he gave up his forebears' "Bible-pounding" Methodism and, once married, embraced her faith. The children then were all raised as Quakers, and this fact had great influence in Richard Nixon's life. His attitudes toward political "warfare" and feelings about aggressive impulses were obviously influenced by his religious background (and this will require special study in itself later). So were many of his friendships and personal relations.

Initially, Nixon was most influenced by his mother's version of Quakerism, presumably akin in its idealism and pacificism to that found among Philadelphia Quakers. Gradually, it appears, he swung over to his father's watered-down version, which corresponded much more to the "informality and emotionalism" of the frontier Quakerism generally to be found in California.[7] In this form, it was hardly distinguishable from a sort of fundamentalism. Interestingly enough, Nixon definitely cast his lot with his father's reversion to "Bible-pounding," in a conversion episode at which his mother was not present. As Nixon tells it, "I remember vividly the day just after I entered high school, when my father took me and my two brothers to Los Angeles to attend the great revival meetings being held there by the Chicago evangelist, Dr. Paul Rader. We joined hundreds of others that night in making our personal commitments to Christ and Christian service."[8]

It is also interesting to note that Nixon revealed this episode (unmentioned by Mazo and Hess) in the November 1962 issue of Billy Graham's monthly magazine *Decision*, thus showing that his fundamentalist "commitment" still held. Such a commitment would drastically color not only Nixon's emotional life, but his cognitive beliefs. That Billy Graham was Nixon's first preacher in the White House, that he preached at the funeral of Nixon's mother, Hannah, in 1967 (had she changed her views? would she have approved?), that Nixon was one of his original sponsors in 1965 for his New York rally, and that Nixon has appeared at a number of Graham rallies, including the grande finale of his last New York "crusade" are all facts which support the contention.

Yet Nixon, in general, has not worn his religion on his sleeve. Although we are told that as a boy "he and his family attended one form of service or another four times on Sunday and several times during the week" (M-H, 17), the mature Nixon, at least before becoming president, did not attend church regularly. Religion, if we judge by his account in *Six Crises*, seems not to have played a role, except as a general ethical inspiration, during his crucial encounters. In short, outwardly, Richard Nixon is not a deeply religious man.

What is the inward significance of his religious training and convictions? We have almost no data here. I would suggest, however, that what little we have can allow us to postulate that a significant attitude toward authority (along with the ambivalence about aggressive impulses mentioned earlier) emerged from Nixon's religious background. Let us deal with this attitude toward authority now.

Our clue comes from his relationship with and approval of Billy Graham. Graham's views on "authority" are apparent in such quotations as: "Man rebelled against God, and so he was separated from God by sin" and "The human race was made for the control of God, and young people are made for the control of their parents"; and in his statement, made to an organization of Protestant policemen in New York, paraphrasing a section from Romans 13 on the obligation to submit to authority (and substituting the word "policeman" for "authorities"): "the Bible teaches that the policeman is an agent and servant of God, and the authority that he has is given to him not only by the city and the state but is given to him by Almighty God."[9]

I am not suggesting that Nixon and Graham are totally alike, although there are a number of unusual similarities in their background. Both came from deeply religious families, with the mother being most devout; both had fathers (Graham's, incidentally, though named William Franklin Graham, Sr., was also known as "Frank") who had less education and "breeding" than their wives and sons; both had "conversion" episodes in their high school years, etc. The key difference seems to be that Billy Graham strenuously rebelled in his early years and then, in adolescence, gave in *completely* to "God the Father." Nixon neither rebelled nor, as a result, bowed so totally before authority. It seems, in fact, that he never questioned it. (Or has all the data on his rebellion simply been passed over in silence?)

There is one curious line in the Mazo-Hess account that further relates to this problem of attitude toward authority. "Richard," they tell us, "took his spankings without a whimper" (M-H, 10). I would certainly have passed by this line without a second thought—after all, parents were less inhibited about physical punishment in Nixon's generation—except for my attention being drawn to the role of whippings in Graham's life. Autobiographical information about Graham is filled with stories of the harsh whippings given him by his father. "If I broke a rule," Graham reports, "believe me, Father never hesitated. Off came his belt. Mother preferred a long hickory switch. I had literally hundreds of whippings until I was thirteen or fourteen."[10] Billy Graham's powerful spirit, and physique, ultimately buckled to the "rightness" of punishing authority. What of Nixon? Was he, at any time, a rebellious child who needed repeated spankings? Who exercised this "authority," his father or mother? Until what age? The impression we are given is that Nixon's "tussle" with authority was never, at any point, traumatic. He simply accepted the structure of things as they were. But we cannot be sure.[11]

Nevertheless, I am suggesting that Nixon's Quaker-fundamentalist religious background is undoubtedly important in explaining his attitude toward authority, though it must be placed in the context of his family's general mode of upbringing. While the picture is shadowy, we seem to see the

outlines of a fairly placid development, with an easy and unrebellious identification with the father, and thus authority.[12]

Nixon's Quakerism also figures, dramatically, in the Hiss case, which first
brought him to prominence. He became convinced that Chambers was telling the truth about Hiss when Nixon "happened to mention the fact" that he
was a Quaker. Chambers acknowledged that he was as well, and said that
Mrs. Hiss had also been a Friend when he had known the Hisses. Priscilla
Hiss had even used the "plain speaking" (using "thee" and "thou") in talking
to Alger at home, Chambers remembered. Nixon recalled how his mother, at
home with the family, had herself spoken in the Quaker mode. "I recognized," Nixon wrote in *Six Crises*, "that someone else who knew Priscilla Hiss
could have informed Chambers of this habit of hers. But the way he told me
about it, rather than what he said, gave me an intuitive feeling that he was
speaking from first-hand rather than second-hand knowledge. [N, 24]

I cannot help suspecting that part of the intensity of Nixon's involvement
in the case was his identification with Chambers. Thus Nixon describes him
as "a thoughtful introspective man, careful with his words, speaking with what
sounded like the ring of truth" (N, 3–4); and "like most men of quality, he
made a deeper impression personally than he did in public" (N, 32). This
sounds much like Nixon's vision of himself. In any event, in defending
Chambers' "truthfulness," Nixon was attesting to his own belief in his
Quaker past—and thus his own "truthfulness."

The setting in which family and religion exercised their influence on
Nixon was rural and Californian. The attraction of the big city and the East
became the counter pull to his life, and throughout, I believe, he manifested
great ambivalence toward it. In this respect he mirrored the attitude of many
of his fellow Americans.

The farming village in which Nixon was born, Yorba Linda, was about
thirty miles inland from Los Angeles. Whittier, where he moved at about
nine, was thirteen miles from Los Angeles. By 1937, when Nixon returned to
Whittier to practice law, it had become a suburb of Los Angeles, with a
population of about 25,000. As Mazo and Hess tell it, at that time "Nixon
confided to a few intimates that he aimed sooner or later to get into a big city
law practice" (M-H, 31).

Nixon's goal was not simply a "big city law practice"; it was, really, an
Eastern city law practice. Thus, after graduation from Duke Law School,
Nixon and two fellow seniors went job-hunting in New York. "They applied
at practically all the well-known law offices," we are told. Nixon's "highest
hope was to find a place with Sullivan and Cromwell, of which John Foster
Dulles was a senior partner. Nixon recalls that he was attracted more by the
'thick, luxurious carpets and the fine oak paneling' of the Sullivan and
Cromwell reception room than by the possibility of being a low-echelon
associate of Dulles, however. 'If they had given me a job,' he said in 1958,

'I'm sure I would have been there today, a corporation lawyer instead of Vice-President'" (M-H, 22).

Nixon's two friends landed New York jobs, one with a distinguished law firm and the other with a large oil corporation, "Nixon got only an 'iffy' response from the Donovan firm" (M-H, 22). Then, after waiting for an FBI job that did not materialize, Nixon returned to Whittier to practice law. Nixon, clearly, had not made it on his first try. Psychologically, he must have perceived himself, as like his father, a failure. There was, therefore, much to atone for when he finally succeeded in his initial ambition, to be a big corporation lawyer, and took his place in 1963 as a senior partner in the Wall Street firm of Mudge, Stern. Ironically, it was only through his second choice, politics, that Nixon realized his boyhood dream.

Rural vs. urban, this has been a perennial tension in American political life. As for Nixon (like his wife Pat), he was a "farm boy" who made good in the city. Yet, the values which he started with, and are strongest in him, are rural values (especially Protestant), and it is these that he brings into confrontation with his urban desires. We see this ambivalence (it reminds one, in many ways, of Henry Ford's) still present in Nixon's presidential acceptance speech of 1968, when he says, "I see a day when life in rural America attracts people to the country, rather than driving them away (N, xiv).

So, too, Nixon is a "Westerner," who finally made good in the East. (How good he was and how careful to hew to the pattern, we see in Nixon's sending his daughters to Finch and to Smith College, and presenting them to society in a Debutante Ball, as well as in his own joining of prestigious New York men's clubs, such as the Metropolitan and the Links.)

Yet, ambivalence about the Eastern Establishment undoubtedly runs deep in Nixon (as it did, incidentally, in Eisenhower). Some of this feeling must have been present in the encounter with Alger Hiss, who was everything Nixon was not: in Nixon's own words, Hiss "had come from a fine family, had made an outstanding record at Johns Hopkins and Harvard Law, had been honored by being selected for the staff of a great justice of the Supreme Court" (N, 19), and so forth. Hiss, the embodiment of Eastern values, treated Nixon, the thirty-five-year-old freshman congressman, like dirt. Nixon's chapter on the Hiss Case is filled with statements about Hiss, such as: "His manner was coldly courteous and, at time, almost condescending" (N, 7); "He was rather insolent toward me" (M-H, 48); and "his manner and tone were insulting in the extreme" (M-H, 52). Obviously, Nixon had straightforward legal and political reasons for attacking Hiss as he did; I am only suggesting here that the passion and tenaciousness came from deeper sources.

There is a strange irony in the fact that, in the end, Nixon was rejected by his own state of California, in his traumatic defeat for governor in 1962 (and largely on the grounds that he had deserted California and its interests for larger, more Eastern-oriented spheres). Only after finally succeeding in the East was he able to mount his winning campaign of 1968 for president.

To understand Nixon fully, one would need carefully to analyze the turbulent currents of Californian life, values, and politics. Its mixed Republican-Democratic politics, its evangelical setting in Los Angeles, its extremes of right-wing Birchites and left-wing Bohemians, all of this and more have shaped Richard Nixon's perceptions and feelings.[13] Thus, in many ways, Nixon is a "typical" southern Californian, only with a heightened ambivalence toward the Eastern Establishment.

One wonders, therefore, at the significance of Nixon's acquisition, after his election, of a luxurious house in San Clemente, California. In this heavily Birchite county, in the exclusive Cyprus Shore community, Nixon bought himself a ten-room house and five acres for $340,000. Has he, figuratively speaking, finally returned "home," successful? It is interesting to note that his new house is only four miles away from his favorite restaurant at San Juan Capistrano where, we are told, "he dines at least once each time he comes here. It is a setting that evokes memories for the president and First Lady who dined there during their dating days thirty years ago." It is interesting, too, that there is a railroad track along the beach, below the house, "on which six trains pass daily between Los Angeles to San Diego to the South."[14] Does it remind the president of his boyhood dreams, associated with the Santa Fe Railroad line that ran past his house in Yorba Linda? As Mazo and Hess describe it, "Long freight trains rumbled past at all hours. The Nixon homestead shook and the throbbing stirred in Richard visions of faraway places" (M-H, 10).

Having gone far, Nixon could now afford to return home. Yet his comparable house in Key Biscayne, Florida, must check our thesis here, and remind us that Nixon still retains his ambivalence about the East. Part of his political strength and appeal, one suspects, is that he is a composite of the American dream, or at least the middle-class dream, about East and West. In Nixon the two have met, even if they have not necessarily fused psychologically.

Let us return now to the young Nixon. What strengths and weaknesses, of body and spirit, did he bring to his "socialization" process? The picture we are given is of a boy prone to illness and physically rather clumsy. We have already quoted Mazo and Hess to the effect that "Nixon has been susceptible to illnesses of one kind or another" since infancy and nearly died of pneumonia when he was four. In addition, "During his senior year at high school he had a severe attack of undulant fever. . . . He was absent much of that school year" (M-H, 10). He tended to "motion" sickness; he had hay fever; and he was constantly afraid of getting fat.

Once in college, Nixon worked hard to make the football team—unsuccessfully. "A classmate," Mazo and Hess tell us, "recalled that Dick had two left feet. He couldn't coordinate." At meal time he was "too tensed up" to eat (M-H, 18-19). His wife, Pat Nixon, reminiscing about their courtship, remarked that "We liked to do active things like sports of different kinds. We were taking up ice skating, the artificial ice rinks had just opened up and it was the gay thing to do. But it was awful for Dick. He almost broke his head two or three times, but he still kept going" (M-H, 30).

In fact, Nixon seems to have made up in persistence and drive what he lacked in native ability. We have here almost a classic case (in Adlerian theory) of "compensation for inferiority"—especially as that insight has been taken up by the political scientist Harold D. Lasswell.[15] Quiet, shy, Nixon became a source of inspiration to others. He seems to have been well liked by everybody. He became an "organizer" and a "doer": he helped form a new fraternity at Whittier College, was elected president of his freshman class, as a junior became chairman of a traditional undergraduate escapade, and so on in the typical pattern of "campus leaders." As Pat Nixon recalled, "He was always president of some group . . . so I knew that he would be successful in whatever he undertook" (M-H, 30).

Nixon's real ability was verbal. He was a debater at Whittier, and this became his primary skill as a politician. Not very good at physical "warfare," he could release his aggressive feelings successfully in oratory. His other strength was the use of caution and planning. Lacking spontaneous coordination and the ability to react properly without thought, Nixon turned his weaknesses into strengths. As numerous observers have testified, Nixon "always played it cautious" (M-H, 33). This trait was combined with the decision to succeed where his father had drifted and failed, and we see the result in the comment of a wartime friend that Nixon "was one guy who knew where he was going. Most of us had big, grandiose schemes. Dick's plans were concise, concrete and specific" (M-H, 33).

Thus, the mature Nixon compensated for the physical awkwardness and the propensity to sickness of the young Nixon by careful planning and reliance on verbal and organizing skills. In times of crisis, as he admits on numerous occasions, he experienced all the physical symptoms of tension: edginess, short-temper, inability to eat and to sleep (N, 115). Are these symptoms especially prominent in Nixon, building on his earlier stresses and strains? Or are they normal to anyone in time of crisis? In any case, as Nixon tells us in Six Crises, he learned, painstakingly, to cope with his tensions and, as he sees it, to use them as a source of strength. The pattern throughout is constant: weakness and failure turned into strength and success by dint of sheer persistence and hard work.

On the way to becoming a successful lawyer-politician, Nixon claims to have started as a "liberal" and ended as a "conservative." According to Mazo and Hess, "Nixon classified himself as 'liberal' in college, 'but not a flaming liberal.' Like many law students of that period, his public heroes were Justice Brandeis, Cardozo and Hughes . . ." (M-H, 22). Once in Washington, D.C., however, working for the Office of Price Administration, Nixon apparently experienced a "conversion" (though Nixon's immediate superior recalls he was "very quiet, self-effacing, conservative" [M-H, 32], from the beginning). Nixon's own account is as follows:

"I came out of college more liberal than I am today, more liberal in the sense that I thought it was possible for government to do more than I later found it was practical to do. . . . I became more conservative first, after my experience with OPA. . . . I also became greatly disillusioned about bureaucracy and about what the government could do because I saw the terrible paper work that people had to go through. I also saw the mediocrity of so many civil servants. And for the first time when I was in OPA I also saw that there were people in government who were not satisfied merely with interpreting the regulations, enforcing the law that Congress passed, but who actually had a passion to get business and used their government jobs to that end. There were of course some of the remnants of the old, violent New Deal crowd. They set me to thinking a lot at that point." In the OPA, Nixon said, he learned first-hand how "political appointees at the top feathered their nests with all kinds of overlapping and empire building." [M-H, 32]

How can we explain what happened? On the most obvious level, Nixon had come to identify the "corrupt politicians" of his father's wrath with the "old, violent New Deal crowd." Is there anything more to this episode? Further research will probably help answer this question. At the moment, however, I can only suggest a psychological line of inquiry to use in weighing future information. It emerges from a consideration by a psychologist, Lawrence F. Schiff, of a number of case studies of what he calls "Dynamic Young Fogies—Rebels on the Right." Schiff studies the conversion to conservatism as it occurs at adolescence, and sets up two categories: (1) where the conversion occurs immediately following puberty (between twelve and seventeen), and (2) in late adolescence (beyond seventeen).

We shall concentrate on this second category. I quote Schiff:

The late converts—whom I call "the obedient rebels"—were the ones most representative of campus conservative activists. Typically they were from homes very much concerned with high status and achievement. In almost all cases their early experiences were dominated by a determined parent, or parents, with detailed and ambitious expectations for their children. All but one were eldest or only sons and the burden of parental ambition fell on them. The obedient rebels (at least in the early years and again after conversion) were usually considered the "good boys" of their families.

Each "rebelled"—sometimes because he felt he could not live up to or realize himself under such pressure—or departed to some degree from the path set out for him. But the revolt was not without peril. Suddenly he would be horrified to discover (on the campus, in the armed services, or among the lower-classes) that he was surrounded by "radicalism," "immorality," or personal hardship—something for which his comfortable background had not prepared him. He would reject the new environment totally and become converted to a conservatism not much different from the one he had left in the first place—but which, superficially at least, he had accepted on his own initiative and conviction.

Psychologically, in essence, his conversion was a reaction to the threat of genuine personality change—which allows great creative possibilities, but also involves dangers. In effect he had come to the pit of change, looked down into it, and turned back, rejecting all alternatives beyond the reaffirmation of obedience.[16]

Did something comfortable to this pattern happen to Nixon in Washington, D.C.? Do we recognize a familiar note in Schiff's account of one of his case studies: "Herron's conversion took place while he was stationed abroad in the Navy. Disturbed by the 'slothfulness' and 'self-indulgent habits' of the local citizenry, he had a sudden realization of 'the consequences of not subscribing to a strict moral code.'"[17] Is this where any potential "rebellion" against authority became grounded and harmless in the case of Richard Nixon? Only time and future research, as already suggested, will answer such questions. All we can now say with certainty is that Nixon experienced some sort of significant reassertion of conservative beliefs while in the big city of Washington, D.C.

We are used to anthropologists studying the courtship patterns of small societies; surely, with even more justification, psychologists ought to study the courtship pattern of individuals. Above all, a man's marriage tells us much about him, as well as helping to shape what he will be in the future. Thus, Richard Nixon's courtship and marriage to Pat Ryan reveal more than might appear at first glance.

Before he met his future wife, we are told, Nixon had neither time nor money to be a ladies' man. According to Mazo and Hess, "He dated the daughter of the local police chief steadily before going east to law school [if only *her* memoirs were available], and at Duke he attended occasional dances as a stag" (M-H, 26). Once back in Whittier, as a struggling lawyer, he attended a tryout for a Little Theatre play. There he met Catherine Patricia Thelma Ryan, a new school teacher of commercial subjects.

Pat Ryan, two months younger than Nixon, had been born in Plymouth, Nevada. Her father was a miner, who moved his family to California (about eighteen miles ·from Los Angeles) and took up farming. Everyone in the family worked together, and the picture we have of their life then is a very pleasant one. When Pat was twelve, her mother died, and the young girl took on the responsibility for the house. Her father died five years later. Graduating from high school, Pat worked in the local bank for a year, went East with relatives for a year or so (working during that time in a hospital near New York), and returned to Los Angeles to attend the University of Southern California. To earn money, she took bit parts in movies, though her real love was the field of merchandising. More money in a teaching job unexpectedly caused her to shift vocation, and to come to Whittier in 1937. A friend trying out for a Little Theatre play persuaded her to come along. Here occurred her "fated" meeting with Richard Nixon.

That very night Nixon proposed. Mazo and Hess report Pat as saying "I thought he was nuts or something. I guess I just looked at him. I couldn't imagine anyone ever saying anything like that so suddenly. Now that I know Dick much better I can't imagine that he would ever say that, because he is very much the opposite, he's more reserved" (M-H, 27). Though she admired Nixon from the beginning, she was in no mood to settle down; she had visions of travel, she tells us. But Richard Nixon persisted. We have already seen how he was prepared to break his neck ice skating. He took up dancing. While Pat kept dating, Nixon gave up all other dates (no real sacrifice on his part). We are given the extraordinary information by Mazo and Hess that "He hung around dutifully even when she had other dates and would drive her to Los Angeles if she was to meet someone there, and wait around to take her home" (M-H, 29) (what did her other swains think of that?). Finally, in the spring of 1940, Pat said yes and they were married on June 21, 1940.

What is the significance and meaning of Nixon's courtship? The first thing to notice is his unusual impulsive behavior: proposing to Pat Ryan on their first meeting. It seems, as it did later to Pat, "out of character." I suspect that it was not, and that it just appears impulsive and out of character. Given the general pattern of Nixon's behavior—cautious, planned, and contrived—we are on better ground postulating his proposal to Pat not as an impulsive exception, but as part of a "plan," even though perhaps an unconscious one, as to the girl he wished to marry. I suspect this romantic plan and daydreams of ultimate success—a favorite Nixon pastime—came together in the person of Pat Ryan, and Nixon acted accordingly, with complete deliberation. Persistence did the rest.

The second thing to notice about his conquest of Pat Ryan is that it was his first real success. At about the time of meeting Pat, Nixon had helped set up the Citra-Frost Co. to market frozen orange juice, which, apparently through no fault of his, folded after a year and a half. Earlier, as we have seen, he had failed to secure a job in an Eastern law firm. Failure to have won Pat Ryan would have been a tremendous blow on top of the others; success undoubtedly gave him a great uplift. As Freud has remarked (and I paraphrase), "To win the girl of one's dream is to have the feeling that all of nature is on one's side."

Moreover, and this is the third point to notice, Pat Nixon undoubtedly brought Nixon real strength. In the pattern of his own parents, in fact, she seemed the stronger of the two. Loyally, she stood by him through failure and success. Patiently, she worked in his campaigns. There is some evidence that she would have preferred some other life than the political—attacks on the Nixons, culminating in the "Checkers Speech" of 1952, especially, seems to have soured her, and she even prevailed upon Nixon to write out a decision to retire from politics after his term as vice president ended in 1957 and to pack this note into his wallet—but always she followed where he led. Yet, even Nixon admitted that she was the more decisive and stronger of the two. It was Pat who insisted, in the 1952 Fund controversy, that Nixon could not resign under fire. Three minutes before he was to make his famous talk, Nixon tells us, he turned to Pat and said, " 'I just don't think I can go through with this one,' 'Of course you can,' she said, with the firmness and confidence in her voice that I so desperately needed" (N, 120). In the campaign of 1960, Nixon informs us that "Her physical stamina had been even greater than mine. In the long hand-shaking sessions, it was I, rather than she, who would first have to ask for a break in the line" (N, 404). In Caracas and in Moscow, Pat Nixon showed similar coolness and decisiveness.

Thus, in marrying Pat, Nixon gained great strength, both in her and in the affirmation of his own possibilities for success that lay in her acquiescence in his persistence and determination. Moreover, insofar as Pat would embody some of the qualities of his mother (and we assume a certain amount of transference here, as in all such relations), it also meant approval and acceptance of his decision to enter the "warfare of politics."

Before we have the years of Nixon's youthful and young manhood character formation and enter into a consideration of his political patterns of behavior and belief, we need to look briefly at another element in his make-up: acting. Nixon's career as an actor began at Whittier College. We are told that he collaborated in writing his fraternity's first play, a "shocker" entitled *The Trysting Place*, and was its director and male lead. And we already know that he met Pat Ryan at a Little Theatre tryout. Such facts make us look twice at the picture of Nixon as a shy, introspective boy.

There is a most interesting comment on his acting ability made by one of his Whittier teachers, on seeing Nixon weeping on Senator Knowland's shoulder after the Checkers Speech: " 'I taught him how to cry,' said Dr. Upton, 'in a play by John Drinkwater called *Bird in Hand*. He tried conscientiously at rehearsals, and he'd get a pretty good lump in his throat and that was all. But on the evenings of performance tears just ran right out of his eyes. It was beautifully done, those tears' " (M-H, 19).[18]

Nixon obviously learned his lesson well, and in later life rose to the occasions. For a "strong" man, it is strange how often he breaks down in tears. Thus, we are told that on the evening of his Checkers Speech, "when a 'Have Faith' message was handed him from his mother, Nixon stepped into a vacant room to hide his tears" (M-H, 109) (how, one wonders, was this observed?). After the speech itself—one of the most sentimental political appeals in all of American history, embarrassing even to many of Nixon's partisans— "when he reached the dressing room, Nixon turned away from his friends and let loose the tears he had been holding back" (M-H, 120). When Eisenhower put his arm around Nixon, "Nixon turned his head to the window and tried to keep back the tears" (M-H, 123). Nixon explained his various effusions by saying that he cried because he had exhausted all his "emotional reserve" (N, 132). In the Introduction to *Six Crises*, he claims that "I have found leaders are subject to all the human frailties. . . . Sometimes even strong men will cry" (N, xxvii).[19]

Nixon is right in his analysis of leaders. But the words of Dr. Upton, "It was beautifully done, those tears," cast a strange light on Nixon's Rousseau-like performances. Certainly Nixon himself believes he is an authority on when other people were acting, and this "intuition" on his part seems to play an important role in much of his political activity. For example, he frequently talks about the Hiss case as if it were a sort of stage play, a momentous soap opera. The stage itself is set for the Hiss-Chambers confrontation at the Commodore Hotel in New York. Nixon even remembers the "decor": "The living room was decorated with Audubon prints," and, he concludes, "We then proceeded to set up the room" (M-H, 51–52).

The "actors" play out their roles. In an earlier interview, Nixon tells how he became convinced that Chambers was telling the truth: "His [Chambers'] voice broke and there was a pause of at least 15 to 20 seconds during which he attempted to gain control of his emotions before he could proceed. This one incident was to have a considerable bearing upon my own attitude toward him because I did not feel that it was an *act*.... On the contrary, I felt he indicated deep sincerity and honesty" (M-H, 45–46, my italics). Hiss, on the contrary, now comes through as a ham actor: "I felt he had *put on a show* when he was shown a picture of Chambers... his statement 'This might look like you, Mr. Chairman,' seemed to me to be *overacted...*" (M-H, 48, my italics). According to Nixon, this hearing "showed the committee the *real* Hiss because, except for a few minutes at the beginning and... end... he *acted* the part of a liar who had been caught, rather than the part of the outraged innocent man, which he had so successfully portrayed before then" (M-H, 52, my italics).

Nixon's own "performances" were obviously far more professional. After his emotional Checkers Speech, he received a phone call from Darryl Zanuck, the Hollywood producer: "The most tremendous performance I've ever seen," was the comment of this professional (M-H, 120). Now one does not have to equate Nixon with Hiss—I, for one, have no doubt that Nixon was "clear" of the corruption charges leveled against him, while the evidence against Hiss is very strong—to realize that Nixon's training in acting must have stood him in good stead during his performance. Nixon seemed to have sensed this himself, when he remarked in disgust about the televised Army-McCarthy hearings: "I prefer professionals to amateur actors" (M-H, 137–138).

Even in the international arena, with foreign-speaking politicians, Nixon felt he could distinguish between acting and sincerity. Speaking of Khrushchev's reaction to the Captive Nations Resolution, asking for prayer for the liberating of "enslaved people," passed by Congress just before Nixon's trip, he says, "I was sure that he was going through an *act*—that he was using the resolution as a pretext for taking the offensive against me..." (N, 271, my italics). Nixon also told of speaking to Zhukov about the behavior of the Soviet police and crowds: "'Mr. Zhukov,' I said, 'this little game you've been playing with me through your planted hecklers for the past few days has not been going well with the press, and in my opinion it is backfiring even among your own people. You underestimate their intelligence. They aren't dumb. They know when somebody is acting and when it is the real thing—particularly when the acts have been so amateurish' " (N, 299–300).

Constantly, then, Nixon was concerned with acting. At one point, he informs us that, during the 1960 campaign, his problem was to hold the Republican vote (the minority party) and then persuade five to six million Democrats to leave their own candidate and vote Republican. "I recognized that I could accomplish this only as President Eisenhower had—by *acting* [Nixon means this in the sense of "action," but the other meaning inheres in it] and speaking not just as a Republican partisan but as a representative of all the people. My trips to Caracas and Moscow had provided an opportunity for me to appear in this *role*" (N, 326, my italics). Nixon's highest praise for the campaigning of his wife, Pat, is that she was "a good trouper" (N, 137).

Of course, all American politicians must play many "roles," and "act" many parts. Moreover, Nixon's own Thespian experiences may have given him greater empathy for the "acts" of the Hisses and Khrushchevs whom he encountered on the political stage. However, Nixon's empathy may also carry a good deal of projection with it. The one thing we can be sure of is that Nixon's attitude to acting is more significant and more conscious than that of most politicians. It does give rise, in fact, to a suspicion that the "real" Richard Nixon may by now have been lost in the variety of "roles" in which he has acted. As with other professional actors, the man becomes his roles—and that is his character.

With this postulated, one would then have to add that Nixon's acting probably serves extremely important political functions. A leader must communicate effectively with his followers: Nixon obviously "reaches," by means of TV spots and news coverage, a large segment of the American population, especially the middle class. His ability to play a role lends itself to the pragmatic politics so typical of America; Nixon, unlike Sir Thomas More, is, in fact, a "man for all seasons." Thus, whatever ideological commitments belong in Nixon's personality development, they are severely tempered by his devotion to "acting."

A word must also be said of a close cousin of Nixon's acting abilities: his skill as a debater. As with his acting experience, this, too, seems to have started in college. It first became politically important for Nixon in his 1946 congressional campaign against the incumbent Jerry Voorhis. In all, the two men had five debates, and, according to Mazo and Hess, Nixon believed "the turning point for him, as the underdog, was the first debate. 'It was tough,' Nixon says. 'I was the challenger, and he was the experienced incumbent. Once that debate was over, I was on my way to eventual victory' " (M-H, 39).

In the light of this debate, we must look at his more famous debates with John F. Kennedy in the 1960 election. Why did Nixon, then, so to speak, in

Voorhis' position as an "incumbent," agree to debate the relatively unknown Kennedy? " 'He [Nixon] had no reason to help build up an audience for Kennedy,' Sorenson wrote" (M-H, 234). The explanation Nixon gave—that the other people wanted the debates—is weak. Mazo and Hess grasp the truth when they write that Nixon "*was convinced he could win*" (M-H, 234). I believe another reason is that Nixon is the sort of person who constantly has to test himself, in order to quiet his self-doubts and the continuous threat of failure. In the *Six Crises* he offers us his reason for accepting the Kennedy debates. "Had I refused the challenge, I would have opened myself to the charge that I was *afraid* to defend the Administration's and my own record" [N, 348, my italics]. It is interesting, too, to note that in his unneccessary and disastrous press conference after his 1962 gubernatorial defeat, Nixon placed his relations with the press on an antagonistic basis, saying . . . "you've had an opportunity to attack me and I think I've given as good as I've taken. I have welcomed the opportunity *to test wits with you*" (M-H, 281–282, my italics). Thus, in his formal debates, as well as reports and encounters, Nixon could give way to his aggressive impulses at the same time as he was testing himself. Making full use of his verbal and acting skills in debate provided a wonderful release, with an extremely high chance of a successful outcome. It is no wonder that Nixon fancied himself as a debater and a performer.

What was the content of Nixon's political debates? His reputation, as we know, was based on his "anti-Communist" positions, and these need now to be examined. We must start with a paradox: Though Congressman Nixon came from an isolationist district, he quickly showed himself an internationalist in orientation. Thus, he worked on the Herter Committee, whose report led to the Marshall Plan, and considered this the most important service of his congressional career. From the very beginning of his political life, Nixon showed his inclination toward the Eastern Establishment and its internationalist position.

But Nixon gave it a very special twist, combining it with a Western fundamentalist attack on Communism. In vehemently attacking Communism, Nixon was defending Americanism. Indeed, one could then define the latter by the former action. It allowed for the luxury of polarizing feelings, so that total hate could flow out to the enemy and total love to one's "own" people. Yet, as we shall see at the end, there is a certain strange identification with the "enemy," the "Devil," which must be strenuously denied.

We must remember throughout this discussion, however, the context in which Nixon operated. The late 1940s saw the beginning of the Cold War. Although *domestic* Communism was not an issue in the 1948 election, it became one thereafter, and was linked, by Nixon and others, with the sensitive theme of corruption—in the Fund controversy, for example, Nixon defended himself by saying, "I was warned that if I continued to attack the Communists and crooks in this [Truman's] Government, they would continue to smear me" (M-H, 103). After 1948, threats of recession, the outbreak of the Korean War, and all of the other Russo-American developments supplied the background of fear in which anti-Communism flourished. Nixon was merely a "typical" American in much of his position.

Nixon's anti-Communism first publicly manifested itself in his debates with Congressman Voorhis. Nixon attacked him as a front-man for the "Communist-dominated PAC" [i.e., the Political Action Committee of the CIO] and suggested that he was one of those "lip-service Americans . . . who front for un-American elements, wittingly, or otherwise, by advocating increasing federal controls over the lives of the people" (M-H, 39, 40). (Here, incidentally, we see a trace of Nixon's OPA "conversion" experience, now linked to anti-Communism.) In opposition to Voorhis' "un-Americanism," Nixon resorted to the sentimental promise "to preserve our sacred heritage in the name of my buddies and your loved ones, who died that these might endure." One wonders whether Nixon believed his own statement following his victory: "Our campaign was a very honest debate on the issues" (M-H, 40,41).

In any case, the pattern of Nixon's "warfare of politics" was set. He tried to narrow his senatorial campaign of 1950, against Mrs. Helen Gahagan Douglas, to one issue, "simply the choice between freedom and state socialism" (M-H, 65), and implied that the latter also meant pro-Russian Communism. Nixon, of course, pictured himself as the warrior preserving the American way of life. It was a rough campaign, and, on top of the Voorhis contest, left Nixon with the image of "Tricky Dicky," the rabid anti-Communist who did not hesitate to use the same tactics of smear and simplification that he accused the Communists of using. Indeed, one wonders if mammoth projection were not at work in Nixon. Was he in fact defending against his own evil impulses by imputing them all to some other?

Did Nixon believe in what he said, or was his anti-Communism largely a matter of practical politics, a convenient way to win? One suspects a good deal of both. In any case, there was strong personal feeling in Nixon's view of the "enemy." On his Latin American trip in 1958, he talked of the "Communist bully" (N, 223) and described his reaction to the Caracas attack on him as "a feeling of *absolute hatred* for the rough Communist agitators who were driving children to this irrational state" (N, 235, my italics). He further talked about "the ruthlessness and determination, the fanaticism of the enemy that we face. That was what I saw in the faces of the mob. *This is really Communism as it is*" (M-H, 177, my italics).

One cannot help asking what Nixon actually knew about Marxism. Should we take seriously his comment that "I do not presume to be an expert, and only the experts on Communism, who are sprouting up all over the landscape these days, have single, simple solutions for the problem" (N, 311), even though Nixon then betrayed his own words by offering rather simple solutions to, and simplifications of, Communism? Did he ever meet any of the leading Marxist theoreticians of Latin-America? Did he ever think of comparing lynch mobs in the American South with the Caracas mob he faced, and realize that one cannot characterize a whole political setting by such incidents, or, if one can, that both must be characterized equally? Nixon's view of Communism, of course, was primarily "dramatic" and thus did not allow for such subtleties. His attitude toward Communism is best shown when, in relation to the Hiss case and the meeting in the Commodore Hotel, he told his television audience, "let me describe the room for you, because it is here that you can see the Communist conspiracy in action . . . twisting and turning and squirming . . . evading and avoiding" (M-H, 59).

Nixon could not, at least in this stage of his life, envision Communism as anything *but* mob action and individual conspiracy. Can we, however, place this attitude in a larger context? Social scientists have tried to isolate the characteristics of what they have called an "authoritarian personality," and to analyze the belief-system of a hater, such as Adolf Hitler.[20] It is worth looking at Nixon's anti-Communism in such terms. What are the images that he uses? We have seen him talking constantly about the threat of the Communist "conspiracy." Whatever the reality (and there was some), the extreme concentration on this aspect of Communism bears with it traces of paranoid fear. For Nixon, Communism is also an "infection," which can reach almost everyone. It is like the plague, hidden and unsuspected, but capable of striking anyone. As Nixon says of Chambers and Hiss, "They were both idealists. Yet, here are two men of this quality who became infected with Communism, infected with it to the degree that they were willing to run the risk, as they did, of disgrace in order to serve the Communist conspiracy. The fact that this could happen to them shows the potential threat that Communism presents among people of this type throughout the world" (M-H, 62).

Communism, of course, is "aggressive international Communism . . . on the loose in the world." It is "an insidious evil." It is engaged in "infiltration of the American government" (N, 2, 3, 4). Communists are "a bunch of rats," and Nixon's only objection to Joe McCarthy's question, "Why worry about being fair when you are shooting rats?" is that you must shoot straight because wild shooting means some of the rats will get away (M-H, 1937). And rats carry plague, and plague means infection. The adjective "Communist" is different, but the images of infection and conspiracy are the same images used by many in Nazi Germany to describe the international and domestic "influence" of the Jews.

How much of the paranoic fears that some members of the Nazi movement defended against by these projections and displacements of their own impulses onto the Jews Nixon shares (though, needless to say, not against the Jews) is a question to be decided only by the prior decision as to how much of his rhetoric was motivated "purely" by political factors. However, we have already seen Nixon, who constantly smeared *his* political opponents, accusing his enemies—Communists and crooks—of smearing him. So, too, we wonder about his accusation that his Democratic opponents are "a group of ruthless, cynical seekers after power. . ." (M-H, 66). The pattern of projection in Nixon ran strong, at least in these early years.[21]

Yet, we must balance this knowledge with the knowledge that Nixon began to have a different view of Communism, based on his visit to Moscow and his encounters with *Russian* Communists. While he still insisted that "the Communist threat is indivisible. . . universal" (N, 312), by 1968 he was prepared to say that "The Communists are a very pragmatic people" (M-H, 312). This is an especially interesting statement in the light of Nixon's concluding remark, in the Mazo-Hess biography, based on an interview with him on May 5, 1968: "I'm a pragmatist with some deep principles that never change" (M-H, 316).

The solution to the puzzle of how Nixon can have such "extreme" feelings about Communism, as exemplified above, and yet cordon them off by his pragmatism is explained to a large extent, I believe, by his subordination of feeling to what he perceives to be the "national interest." Nixon is constantly involving the good of his party (usually identified with the good of his country) and the good of mankind as a justification for his own activities. In the Hiss case, he tells us that "more important by far than the fate of the [House Un-American Activities] Committee the national interest required that this investigation go forward" (N, 15). It is interesting to note Nixon's analysis of Chambers' motives: "He had come forward out of necessity, he said, as a kind of duty to warn his country of the scope, strength and danger of the Communist conspiracy in the United States. It would be a great pity if the nation continued to look upon this case as simply a clash of personalities between Hiss and himself. Much more was at stake than what happened to either of them as individuals. Turning to me, he said with great feeling, 'This is what you must get the country to realize'" [N, 24]). The claim widens further in his writing, when Nixon says, "It [the Hiss case] involved the security of the whole nation and the cause of free men everywhere" (N, 40). Similarly, in discussing the Fund case in 1952, and his decision to stay on as Eisenhower's vice president, Nixon claims that "most important of all, I believed that what I did would affect the future of my country and the cause of peace and freedom for the world" (N, 102).

Is this hyperbole mere rhetoric, or did Nixon sincerely believe what he said? I have no doubt whatever that the latter interpretation is correct. Like most politicians, only more so, Nixon believed in his misson and identified his own self and fortunes with the success of his country. It is part of the secret of *his* political success, since total belief in himself is a means by which a politician convinces others to believe in him.

We can see Nixon's sublime belief in the identification of his own interests with the national interest, and indeed, the interests of all mankind, in his comments, such as the following: "The Hiss case was the first major crisis of my political life. . . [it was] not only an acute personal crisis but. . . a vivid

case study of the continuing crisis [i.e., Communism] of our times" (N, 12);
"While my meeting with Khrushchev might be a personal crisis for me, I
recognized that in perspective it was only one episode in the continuing crisis
that Mr. Khrushchev and his Communist colleagues are determined to per-
petuate through our lifetime" (N, 264); "I recognized the obvious strategy of
the Soviets to probe for any weakness that might be within me, not unlike
their international strategy of probing for soft spots around the world" (N,
298); "I believe in the American dream, because I have seen it come true in
my own life" (N, 344); and lately, Nixon's boastful comment in his acceptance speech of 1968 to the Republican National Committee, "My fellow
Americans, we make history tonight—not for ourselves alone but for the
ages" (N, v). For better or for worse, Nixon's last claim, and identification,
now has the ring of truth about it. His behavior as president of the United
States does, in fact as well as in fantasy, affect the behavior of much of the
world.

Thus, the "crises" of Richard Nixon take on a vastly more important
character than the merely personal, though his "crisis syndrome" is of crucial
significance for Nixon himself. Nixon's one sustained piece of writing is his
own *Six Crises*. Throughout that book, he is obsessed with the problems of
"crisis." Nixon's crisis, however, is far from the psychologist's or psychohistorian's concern with "identity crisis"; for Nixon, it is not a question of
"finding" himself, but of "testing" his already formed self. The orientation is
largely to public events.

Nixon's own initial definition of "crisis" is rather lame. "Life for everyone
is a series of crises," he informs us. "A doctor performing a critically difficult
operation involving life and death, a lawyer trying an important case, an
athlete playing in a championship contest, a salesman competing for a big
order, a worker applying for a job or a promotion, an actor on the first night
of a new play, an author writing a book—all these situations involve crises for
the individuals concerned" (N, 12). Nixon raises the significance of crisis,
however, when he continues, "Only when I ran for Congress in 1946 did the
meaning of crisis take on sharply expanded dimensions" (N, 13). At this
point, Nixon jumps personal crises to the hyperbolic level we have discussed
before, where, for example, his "Fund" crisis became critical to the national
interest. In neither of his definitions do we rise above the ordinary, to the sort
of real national crisis embodied in one of Nixon's own inspirations: Tom
Paine's pamphlet of 1776, *The American Crisis*, with its famous line, "These
are the times that try men's souls" (N, xvii).

Nixon's own account of how he came to write his *Six Crises* is worth
recounting, especially since the book itself is one of our main "autobiographical" sources. "Shortly after the election [1960]," he informs us,

I had the honor of sitting by Mrs. Eisenhower at a White House dinner. I told her that
one of the reasons I had decided against writing a book was my belief that only the
President could write the story of his Administration and that, by comparison, any

other account would be incomplete and uninteresting. She answered, "But there are exciting events like your trips to South America and to Russia which only you can tell, and I think people would be interested in reading your account of what really happened."

In April, I visited President Kennedy for the first time since he had taken office. When I told him I was considering the possibility of joining the "literary" ranks, of which he himself is so distinguished a member, he expressed the thought that every public man should write a book at some time in his life, both for the mental discipline and because it tends to elevate him in popular esteem to the respected status of an "intellectual." [N, xxiii]

The reference to Kennedy is particularly interesting. Throughout his political career, Nixon, one has the feeling, was measuring and testing himself against this self-assured scion of Eastern wealth and position. The famous television debate was undoubtedly partly motivated by a desire to best Kennedy personally. Moreover, Kennedy was a war hero who had shown remarkable personal courage. It is no accident, then, that Nixon wished to match Kennedy's *Profiles in Courage* with his own *Six Crises*. He would prove there not only that he had pretensions to being an "intellectual," but that he, too, like Kennedy, had courage.

In the introduction, Nixon makes his gesture toward intellectuality. He does so with an air of humility: "I do not presume to suggest that this is a scholarly treatise on conduct in crisis. The experts will have to judge what contribution my observations may make to a better understanding of that intriguing and vitally important subject" (N, xxiv–xxv). Nixon then proceeds to offer some generalizations on the topic. There are two points of particular concern to us.

The first is Nixon's conviction that crisis behavior is primarily a "learned" action, and thus available to him. "These attributes [quickness, smartness, boldness] are for the most part acquired and not inherited. . . . Confidence in crisis depends in great part on adequacy of preparation—where preparation is possible" (N, xxvi, xxvii). Thus, Nixon's pattern of careful planning and caution works even in the area of personal courage.

The second is even more revealing. Over and over again, Nixon repeats his main insight about crisis: it is the *aftermath*, not the crisis itself, that is critical for him. At one stage of the Hiss account, he remarks:

The next morning I learned a fundamental rule of conduct in crises. The point of greatest danger is not in preparing to meet the crisis or fighting the battle; it occurs after the crisis of battle is over, regardless of whether it has resulted in victory or defeat. The individual is spent physically, emotionally, and mentally. He lets down. Then if he is confronted with another battle, even a minor skirmish, he is prone to drop his guard and to err in his judgment. [N, 40]

Nixon lamented that he had gone "soft" on Priscilla Hiss, who, on the witness stand, had played on the Quaker background she and Nixon shared. "I should have remembered that Chambers had described her as, if anything, a more fanatical Communist than Hiss. . . . that even a woman who happens to be a Quaker and then turns to Communism must be a Communist first and a Quaker second. But I dropped the ball," Nixon wrote, using a favorite football metaphor, "and was responsible for not exploiting what could have been a second break-through in the case." [N, 40–41] Moving from the personal to the political, Nixon insists he "was never to make that same error again."

In the years ahead I would never forget that where the battle against Communism is concerned, victories are never final so long as the Communists are still able to fight. There is never a time when it is safe to relax or let down. When you have won one battle is the time you should step up your effort to win another—until final victory is achieved. [N, 41]

Since we are mainly interested in the personal aspect, Nixon's most important remark comes when he says, "I experienced a sense of letdown which is difficult to describe or *even to understand*" (N, 39–40, my italics). Can we understand what happened better than Nixon himself?

We must begin by asking what function crisis performed for Nixon. On the public or political level, as he perceived it, the successful handling of what he calls a crisis enhances a leader in the eyes of his followers. For example, the Caracas "crisis" boosted Nixon's popularity greatly. As he put it, "in June 1958, just one month after my return from South America, the Gallup Poll showed me leading Adlai Stevenson for the first time, and running neck-and-neck against John F. Kennedy. It was the high point of my political popularity up to that time" (N, 249). Nixon's generalization is that "It is the crisis, itself, more than the merits of the engagement which rallies people to a leader. Moreover, when the leader handles the crisis with success, the public support he receives is even greater" (N, 248).

It ought not to surprise us that Nixon projects some of his own attitudes, in this area as in others, on to the Communists. At the head of the chapter on Khrushchev, he informs us that "Communism creates and uses crisis as a weapon" (N, 253). In the body of the chapter, Nixon elaborates: "They [Communists] use crisis as a weapon, as a tactic in their all-front, all-out struggle" (N, 313).

As we know, Nixon defines a leader as one able to act in a crisis. He also stresses the fact that a leader without crisis is almost a contradiction in terms. For example, as he remarks about Eisenhower: he "demonstrated a trait that I believe all great leaders have in common: they thrive on challenge; they are at their best when the going is hardest. When life is routine, they become bored; when they have no challenge, they tend to wither and die or to go to seed" (N, 181–182). One of Nixon's concluding remarks to his chapter on the Campaign of 1960 is even more revealing: "But probably the greatest magnet of all is that those who have known great crisis—its challenge and tension, its victory and defeat—can never become adjusted to a more leisurely and orderly pace. They have drunk too deeply of the stuff which really makes life exciting and worth living to be satisfied with the froth" (N, 461). In the light of all the foregoing, can one help but conclude that Nixon, like the Communists, "uses crisis as a weapon, as a tactic" and will so create and use it in the future, when "tactics" call for it?

The above gives us the "public" dimension of Nixon's crisis. We need to go deeper, however, to try to understand his "let down" feeling. I believe that we begin to approach a fuller understanding if we look at "crisis" in relation to decisiveness. The latter is obviously a serious problem for Nixon. In discussing Eisenhower's heart attack, Nixon makes two revealing statements:

This was far different from any other crisis I had faced in my life and had to be handled differently. I had always believed in meeting a crisis head-on. The difficult period is reaching a decision, but once that has been done, the carrying-out of the decision is easier than the making of it. In meeting any crisis in life, one must either fight or run away. But one must do something. Not knowing how to act or not being able to act is what tears your insides out. [N, 152]

A few pages later, he reiterates: "For me . . . this period continued to be one which drained my emotional as well as physical energies, for it was, above all, a period of indecision" (N, 166).

Interestingly enough, Nixon accused Stevenson of being "a man plagued with indecision who could speak beautifully but could not act decisively" (N, 102). As for Eisenhower, Nixon had ambivalent feelings which he was hard put to suppress. For example, Nixon says that "what had happened during the past week had not shaken my faith in Eisenhower. If, as some of my associates thought, he appeared to be indecisive, I put the blame not on him but on his lack of experience in political warfare" (N, 102). Further on, he declares emphatically:

Eisenhower was a man of decision. As General Walter Bedell Smith had pointed out in his book, *Eisenhower's Six Great Decisions* [another inspiration for Nixon's *Six Crises?*], he never did anything rashly. Sometimes he took more time to decide an issue than some of his eager lieutenants thought necessary, but invariably, when the line was drawn and the lonely responsibility for making the right decision rested solely with him, he came up with the right answer. [N, 116]

After his television program about the Fund, Nixon said to Eisenhower, "if you think I should stay on or get off, I think you should say so either way. The great trouble here is the indecision" (N, 106).

Nixon, however, had to wrestle not only with the problem of indecisiveness, his own and others (his constant attention to this problem is an indication of its importance for him), but with the problem of holding fast to a decision once taken. We have already noted his "decision" to retire from politics after his term as vice president ended in 1957, a decision which was reinforced by being put on paper and tucked into his wallet—and then was repudiated promptly in 1960. Earlier, in 1956, during the "Dump Nixon" movement, we are told that "On a Wednesday he told two or three friends he would call a press conference the next day to make an announcement of retirement from public life" (M-H, 146); naturally, he was talked out of this "decision." The high spot in this pattern was his 1962 "retirement" speech to the Press (after his gubernatorial defeat), and then his Lazarus-like resurrection in 1968. Clearly, the really decisive member of the Nixon family was Pat.

Plagued with the torments of decision and indecision in a "crisis" situation, we can begin to see why Nixon felt "let down" after his emotional fight was over. Nevertheless, I believe that there is an even more important reason for his feeling let down and this is related to Nixon's attitudes about aggression. My thesis here is that Nixon has enormously ambivalent feelings, probably dating back to his mother's injunctions, about the release of hostile emotions, and consequently experiences strong, though unconscious, feelings of guilt after their release. Moreover, because of the tremendous effort of control needed to fight effectively and to harden himself for a struggle (*which does not come naturally to him*, even though events and his party have cast him in this role) and because of his constant personal need to "test" himself, Nixon runs the danger of going "soft." This moment of weakness is, then, additionally threatening to him.

What is the evidence for this combined thesis? One of Nixon's most revealing comments is when he says:

the most difficult period in one of these incidents is not in handling the situation at the time. The difficult task is with your reactions after it is all over. I get a real let down after one of these issues. Then I begin to think of what bums they are. You also get the sense that you licked them . . . though they really poured it on. Then you try to catch yourself . . . in statements and actions . . . to be a generous winner, if you have won. [M-H, 183]

Here, again, we have the use of the term "let down." If one's opponents are "bums," then one is clearly justified in fighting them without quarter. But, the guilt sets in, and one catches oneself and tries to be a generous winner. To sum up, before the fight there is the agony of indecision: whether or not to release the aggressive impulses. Then there is the blessed release. "As I had learned in the Hiss case," Nixon says typically, "the period of indecision, of necessary soul-searching was the hardest. Now the emotions, the drive, the intense desire to act and speak decisively which I had kept bottled up inside myself could be released and directed to the single target of winning a victory" (N, 103). In short, there is the fight, followed by the let down, guilt, and self-justification.

Nixon alternates between denial of aggressive intent and glorification of the hard struggle. Typically, he identifies himself with the nation, and denies for both any aggressive desires. Thus, he tells us that "Khrushchev does not need to be convinced of our good intentions. He knows we are not aggressors and do not threaten the security of the Soviet Union" (N, 260). Again, "It was my belief that Khrushchev knew that our intentions were peaceful" (N, 263). The fact that Khrushchev, and the Russians, might remember the American intervention in the Russian Civil War, the American willingness, in part, to have Germany invade Russia, the American ring of nuclear bases around Russia, and so forth was all written off by Nixon as merely an "act" on Khrushchev's part. In this denial of his own aggressive intent, and a refusal to recognize his opponent's real fears of it, Nixon seems at one with much of America's recent self-image.

Yet, while denying aggressive intent, Nixon could glorify fighting and the hard masculine qualities necessary for it. Thus, Nixon could compare Khrushchev and Eisenhower in an interesting conjunction of adjectives: "Men like you and President Eisenhower," he told Khrushchev, are "tough, reasonable men who are not soft or frightened . . ." (M-H, 199). Nixon spoke in praise of the average Russian: "there was a steel-like quality, a cold deter-mination, a tough, amoral ruthlessness which somehow had been instilled into every one of them" (N, 304). Nixon constantly asked himself, "How did we stack up against the kind of fanatically dedicated men I had seen in the past ten days?" (N, 305). We can see how Nixon wished to answer this question for himself, as well as for the American people, in the following, most revealing, comment about his career in New York after the 1962 defeat:

"New York is very cold and very ruthless and very exciting, and, therefore, an interesting place to live," he observed to Robert J. Donovan of the Lost Angeles *Times.* "It has many great disadvantages but also many advantages. The main thing, it is a place where you can't slow down—a fast track. Any person tends to vegetate unless he is moving on a fast track. New York is a very challenging place to live. You have to bone up to keep alive in the competition here." [M-H, 285]

Such a statement must be placed in the context of Nixon's parental models: the mother who did not wish him to enter the "warfare of politics," and the father with "his fierce competitive drive." Is it any wonder that Nixon has a problem making the decision to fight, to release *his* competitive drive, and that he feels let down after the semi-forbidden impulses have been un-leashed? Yet, having indicated Nixon's ambivalence in this matter, we must conclude with the observation that Nixon did, indeed, gain strength from his difficulties. Like his Russian foes, he learned to "steel" himself, and to reject the softer, debilitating, and feminine impulses that threaten him so fearfully—for the simple reason that they are so strongly contained within him. Once again, out of "weakness," Nixon can be said to have drawn "strength."[22]

There is one particular crisis in Nixon's life that we must briefly discuss a bit further. It is a continuous crisis, involving his relationship to President Eisenhower, which unfolds in terms of half of Nixon's six crises in his book: "The Fund," "The Heart Attack," and "The Campaign of 1960." Much of

Nixon's mature life, until the present, has circled about Eisenhower: it was Eisenhower who picked him out of obscurity to be his running mate in 1952, almost dumped him in the Fund controversy that erupted then, allowed a "Dump Nixon" movement to spread in 1956, almost presented Nixon with the presidency itself because of his heart attacks in 1955 and 1957, and played an ambiguous role in Nixon's own campaign for president in 1960. On a more intimate level, the two families were united by the marriage of Ike's grandson, David, to Nixon's daughter, Julie. On the deepest personal level, Eisenhower presented Nixon with a crisis of feeling, involving emotions about Ike as a father-figure, to whom death wishes as both father and president became attached. These, we need hardly add, would be on the unconscious level.

The evidence for Eisenhower as the father-figure is strong. At one point, discussing the fund, Nixon says of Eisenhower's attitude, "I must admit that it made me feel like the little boy caught with jam on his face" (N, 98). Further on, he says that "Chotiner [his adviser], particularly, insisted that I not allow myself to be put in the position of going to Eisenhower like a little boy to be taken to the woodshed, properly punished, and then restored to a place of dignity" (N, 129) (and we, of course, remember Nixon's possible "spankings" at home). On a slightly different note, Eisenhower is a commanding authority figure, and Nixon remarks that "Despite his great capacity for friendliness, he also had a quality of reserve which, at least subconsciously, tended to make a visitor feel like a junior officer coming in to see the commanding General" (N, 81). Given Nixon's feelings of "little boy" and "junior officer" (Nixon was, in fact, a Lt. Commander at the end of World War II), we can understand better his tears when, in 1952, Eisenhower, the "father," finally accepted him back on the team:

"General, you didn't need to come out to the airport," was all I could think to say. "Why not?" he said with a broad grin, "you're my boy."
We walked to the head of the ramp, posed for photographers, and then rode together to the Wheeling stadium. I was still so surprised by his unexpected gesture of coming to meet me that I found myself riding on his right as the car pulled away from the airport. I apologized for what I, with my Navy training, knew was an inexcusable breach of political as well as military protocol, and tried to change places with him. He put his hand on my shoulder and said, "Forget it. No one will know the difference with all the excitement out there." [N, 131]

No one "out there" might know, but Nixon "knew" inwardly that he had usurped Eisenhower's place, and fulfilled a forbidden, though perfectly natural, wish. Nixon would have had to be inhuman not to have mixed feelings toward the man who placed him one heart beat away from the highest office in the land. The fact that Nixon behaved with exemplary restraint during Ike's incapacity suggests nothing besides shrewd political judgment on the conscious level, and tremendous ambivalence on the unconscious level. Death wishes are generally compounded of many parts: love for the potential victim and anticipation of great loss, secret satisfaction at his removal, guilt for this suppressed feeling and the gladness one experiences at surviving him, etc. Nixon's reaction, for example, to the news of Eisenhower's heart attack shows, first, denial and, then, numbing. According to Mazo and Hess, he reacted as follows when told of Eisenhower's condition:

"My God!" Nixon whispered horsely. He caught his breath, then proceeded to tell Hagerty that heart attacks are not necessarily serious any more, that victims frequently recover completely.

"I don't see how I could describe those first few minutes except as a complete shock," he recalls. "I remember going into my living room and sitting down in a chair and not saying anything or really thinking of anything for at least five or ten minutes. For quite a while I didn't even think to tell Pat, who was upstairs."

The numbness receded gradually. Nixon went back to the telephone and called Deputy Attorney General William P. Rogers. [M-H, 159]

The alternating love-hate relationship really put Nixon through the emotional wringer. First, Eisenhower had taken Nixon for his chosen heir by picking him for vice president in 1952. Then, he had shown no faith in his choice and seemed willing to drop him before the Checkers speech. Worse, he awakened all of Nixon's problems about indecision, compounded by the fact that Nixon had to inhibit almost all his aggressive feelings toward Eisenhower. We can see how strong these were by Nixon's one outbreak, when Eisenhower stated that he did not think that he, Eisenhower, should make the decision about Nixon staying on the ticket. According to Mazo and Hess, "At this Nixon stiffened and said sternly, 'There comes a time in a man's life when he has to fish or cut bait.' (Actually, his words were stronger.)" (M-H, 110). We can certainly guess at Eisenhower's reaction to such a statement (possibly anal in the actual words) coming from his "junior officer." One can speculate that his enthusiasm for his "boy," Nixon, was always tempered by the memory of that phrase.[23]

Shortly thereafter Eisenhower took Nixon back into his good graces, and the praise pushed Nixon all the way over to the other side of his feelings. After the Checkers speech, we are told, Eisenhower said that "As a 'warrior,' he had never seen 'courage' to surpass that shown by Nixon . . . and in a showdown fight he preferred 'one courageous, honest man' at his side to 'a whole boxcar full of pussy-footers'" (M-H, 121). It must have been music to Nixon's ears, in view of his concern for courage and his desire to be a warrior in politics, according to his father's inspiration.

But Nixon's emotional ordeals with Eisenhower were far from over. The heart attack imposed the next strain. There is an unsuspected psychological aspect to the story Nixon tells about Ike's grandson: "David, the President's oldest and favorite grandchild, provided a pleasant interlude when he came into the room. Hagerty introduced me as 'the Vice President of the United

States.' David took a second look and said, 'The Vice President, wow!' Then he turned to his grandfather and said, 'Ike, I didn't know there were two Presidents' " (N, 167). Obviously, there was room for only one president, and as soon as Eisenhower recovered he resumed the full powers of his office. At that point, he expressed no appreciation to Nixon for being the second president. As Nixon remarks, "He had also spoken or written to me personally of his appreciation after each of my trips abroad. But after this most difficult assignment of all—treading the tightrope during his convalescence from the heart attack—there was no personal thank you" (N, 162). That Nixon was hurt is clear, even though he quickly adds, "Nor was one needed or expected. After all, we both recognized that I had only done what a Vice President should do when the President is ill" (N, 163). (If that is so, why does Nixon mention it?)

There was one last twinge of the filial nerve. In 1960, Nixon was at last about to be his own man, running for the presidency himself. At this point, Eisenhower, advertently or inadvertently, made a major blooper. Asked at a presidential press conference on August 24 "to give us an example of a major idea of his [Nixon's] that you adopted... ," he replied, "If you give me a week, I might think of one" (M-H, 238). Then, at an October 31 White House luncheon to plan Eisenhower's participation in Nixon's campaign, the president buoyantly declared his willingness to campaign for the "new commander," Nixon, like a "soldier in the ranks." The vice president's campaign manager had begun to outline Eisenhower's schedule of speaking engagements when Nixon interrupted him.

Quietly, he expressed gratitude for all Eisenhower already had done in his behalf, said he believed the American people were well aware of his role as the President's associate and deputy for eight years and the continuing closeness of the Eisenhower-Nixon team, and suggested the President now could be most helpful by concentrating during the remaining campaign days on a couple of previously scheduled appearances and election-eve broadcast to the nation. As virtually everyone in the room gasped, Nixon added that he had given considerable thought to the idea of a massive politicking drive by Eisenhower and concluded it might not be proper for the President. Nixon said he and all his associates appreciated beyond words Eisenhower's willingness to barnstorm the country for the Nixon-Lodge ticket, expecially since no one knew better than the President how exhausting that sort of intensive campaigning would be. It was difficult to resist Eisenhower's offer, Nixon concluded, but on reflection he felt (and hoped) the President and his other friends in the room would appreciate Nixon's decision [M-H, 239–240]

Mazo and Hess expect us to believe that it was a telephone call the night before from Mrs. Eisenhower, and a talk that morning with General Snyder, Eisenhower's physician, cautioning Nixon about the strain on Eisenhower's health of a vigorous campaign, that made Nixon indulge in his strange behavior. Without doubting the facts (though it would be interesting to check them), in order to accept this interpretation we would have to put aside all of

Snyder's previous advice that a vigorous life and schedule for Eisenhower was the best possible medicine, and Eisenhower's failure to speak out for Nixon *before* October 31 and the luncheon meeting. In any case, given Nixon's feelings about being the "junior officer," Eisenhower's "soldier in the ranks" offer must have awakened strange, disturbing feelings in Nixon, and the memory of the inept "give me a week" response must have left him with some trepidation as to how Eisenhower might behave in his "lowly" role.

There is little need for further speculation. Nixon's victory, on his own, in 1968 undoubtedly was a successful achievement of the position of primacy, without the replacement of the father implicit in the 1960 campaign. There was, also, no need for death wishes—or fears. In this sense, I believe, we do have a "new Nixon," released from old emotions. I suspect that part of his nomination of the unknown Spiro Agnew was a replaying, in reversal, of his own nomination from obscurity by Eisenhower. The assignment of Agnew to the "low road" of hatchet man, while Nixon strolled along the "high road," offers some confirmation of this hypothesis. Although Mazo and Hess do not tell us when Nixon's father died, other sources indicate the date as 1956. In any case, Nixon was no longer Eisenhower's or anybody else's "little boy." We can postulate that he had passed through this "crisis" in his life—in this unsuspected sense, an "identity crisis"—and finally come to maturity.

What, then, are the characteristics of the mature Nixon? Many of the elements in his personality have already been suggested; but before we attempt a summary, we need directly to confront the question: What is Nixon's own image of himself? His first self-image is that he is a "big," a "great" man. In the introduction to *Six Crises*, he says, "We often hear it said that truly 'big' men are at their best in handling big affairs, and that they falter and fail when confronted with petty irritations—with crises which are, in other words, essentially personal." A few paragraphs further on, Nixon comments: "No one really knows what he is capable of until he is tested to the full by events over which he may have no control. That is why this book is an account not of great men but rather of great events—and how one man responded to them" (N, xxvi). Nixon's "great events" include the Fund controversy, Eisenhower's heart attacks, the visit to Caracas, and his encounter with Khrushchev—hardly events that will figure in future history books—yet implicit is his belief that, having handled these "big affairs" well, he is a "big" man.

Nixon makes an explicit comparison of himself, during the 1960 campaign, with a great president, Abraham Lincoln, and suggests that the great events confronting him, Nixon, are even greater than those of 1860: "One hundred years ago, in this very city, Abraham Lincoln was nominated for President. . . . The question then was freedom for the slaves and survival of the nation. The question now is freedom for all mankind and the survival of civilization" (M-H, 228). The hyperbole, as to the survival of civilization, is partly the usual political rhetoric, but partly a reflection of Nixon's self-confidence, a vital ingredient for any politician.

Overwhelmingly, what emerges from a reading of Nixon's own writings, as well as the Mazo-Hess biography, is Nixon's ability to think well of himself, to believe he is always acting fairly, and to deny to himself almost any of his nasty, aggressive feelings. For example, he makes one statement, demonstrating considerable psychological insight, but then fails to see its applicability to himself. "From considerable experience in observing witnesses on the stand," he tells us, "I had learned that those who are lying or *trying to cover up something* generally make a common mistake—they tend to overact, to overstate their case" (N, 8, my italics). And this comes from the man who could say about his vicious campaign against Voorhis, "Our campaign was a very honest debate on the issues." This is the same Nixon who could say throughout the 1940s, 1950s and early 1960s that Communism was indivisible and monolithic, and then say, without blushing, in a 1968 interview that "I don't see the Communist world as one world. I see the shades of gray. I see it as a multicolor thing" (M-H, 316). So, too, Nixon, who used the smear against Voorhis, Mrs. Douglas, and Adlai Stevenson could complain about a *New York Post* story insinuating wrong-doing in a Nixon political fund, and say innocently, "After all, I had come into this 1952 campaign well prepared, I thought, for any political smear that could be directed at me. After what my opponents had thrown at me in my campaigns for the House and Senate, and after the almost unbelievably vicious assults I had survived during the Hiss case, I thought I had been through the worst" (N, 85–86). Nixon, one of the most pragmatic and expedient of politicians—witness his 1968 alliance with the Southern politicians, such as Strom Thurmond—could sincerely state:

My philosophy has always been: don't lean with the wind. Don't do what is politically expedient. Do what your instinct tells you is right. Public opinion polls are useful if a politician uses them only to learn approximately what the people are thinking, so that he can talk to them more intelligently. The politician who sways with the polls is not worth his pay. And I believe the people eventually catch up with the man who merely tells them what he thinks they want to hear. [N, 152]

And Nixon, who appointed Agnew as his running mate in 1968, could state in 1961, when writing *Six Crises*, that the vice president should be selected as a real deputy, able to be president if necessary: "This being true," he informs us, "it will also bolster the new political trend of selecting capable men as vice presidential nominees, men to whom the presidential nominee would be willing to turn over his duties during a period of disability, rather than the selection of men solely on geographical, factional, or party appeasement considerations" (N, 194). One can argue that changing circumstances make for changing views, and Nixon has merely adapted, as in his views on Communism, to reality. I cannot accept this explanation. Nixon's ability to believe in the rightness, and *total* rightness, of whatever he is saying at the moment is so pervasive, and so in tune with what is expedient, that I see no grounds for believing in any real change of principles or perception of reality. For example, Nixon really believed what he said in the 1960 campaign:

On this and every other issue, the admonition I gave to some of those who had a tendency to let their eagerness to appeal to voters overrule their judgment on the substance of issues went something like this: "We must always assume that we are going to win this election. And I do not want to say anything or do anything during the campaign that I will not be able to live with as President." [N, 359–360]

Fundamentally, Nixon is an uncritical man. Thus Mazo and Hess tell us that Nixon "never shared the belief of some in the Eisenhower administration that 'Communism to McCarthy was a racket.' Nixon felt that the Senator 'believed what he was doing very deeply'" (M-H, 132). Yet Nixon knew that McCarthy had exhibited no knowledge of, or antipathy toward, Communism before his West Virginia "numbers" speech of February, 1950. Similarly, Nixon mentioned that the House Un-American Activities Committee

had been widely condemned as a "Red-baiting" group, habitually unfair and irresponsible, whose investigations had failed to lead to a single conviction of anyone against whom charges had been made at its hearings. It was, the critics said, doing more of a disservice to the country because of its abridgment of civil liberties than any alleged services it might be rendering in uncovering Communist subversives. [N, 14]

But at no point did he admit the justice of the charges.

The uncritical Nixon, however, sees himself in a very different light from the one I have cast on him. For example, he commented about his performance in his first television debate with Kennedy:

I had concentrated too much on substance and not enough on appearance. I should have remembered that "a picture is worth a thousand words." I would be the first to recognize that I have many weaknesses as a political candidate, but one of my strengths is that I try to be my own severest critic. [N, 367]

Obviously, Nixon's concept of criticism is in no way related to my use of the term criticism.

In general, Nixon's basic vision of himself is as a high-principled, fair-minded man (of greatness), who is constantly being unfairly attacked and smeared by his opponents (mainly Communists and crooks), and who is his own severest critic. Much of this self-image, we must admit, corresponds to the image of self-righteousness projected by America as a whole; and this correspondence is undoubtedly a part of Nixon's political success.[24]

Who, then, is the "real" Richard Nixon, and how will he act as president? Our evidence regarding the first part of this question relates primarily to Nixon until about 1962; after that, we must speculate about changes in him. Nixon, we have said, is a man torn between his mother's dislike of warfare and his father's sharp competitiveness; thus, he is extremely ambivalent about his aggressive impulses and tends to deal with them by projection onto others. He is a man haunted by his father's "failure," and driven to avoid that failure for himself and to redeem it for his parent. He compensates for lack of native abilities, where this is the case, by enormous hard work and persistence. He is racked by indecision and by the question of his own courage, especially in a crisis. He has had a serious problem with death wishes and anxiety: in relation to his brothers, himself, and Eisenhower. He is an "actor," in the theatrical sense, and releases himself verbally in debates. He is a fundamentalist in religion, with a passive acceptance of authority.

These are the psychological banalities of Nixon's character. More important is what he has done with them. No man reaches his position without a good deal of ability, and Nixon, in fact, starts with strong cognitive powers: he is quick, shrewd, and possessed of a good memory. Moreover, he has turned his problems and weaknesses into challenges and strengths. Racked by indecision, he has learned how to plan and contrive ahead of time. Constantly having to test himself, he has shown real courage on a number of occasions. His aggressive projections are in tune with those of many of his fellow Americans. His quiet fundamentalism accords with the uses of religion of a large segment of the American people. His acting is so good, that he has become his roles.

Since 1962, I would speculate, he has matured in the sense of coming to grips with his fear of failure and his death wishes toward the father-figure, Eisenhower. The nadir for Nixon was the gubernatorial defeat of 1962. After that, he returned to success via his first ambition: to be a big Eastern corporation lawyer. When he finally won the presidency in 1968, he won it on his own, owing nothing to Eisenhower. By this time, too, Nixon had solidified his method of meeting "crises." His control of impulse, his planning and deliberation were greater than ever.

If the description above gives us some of the traits of the "real" Nixon, how will he act from now on? The memory of Shakespeare's Henry IV must give us pause, as we seek to predict the behavior not of kings, but of presidents as they reach their new office. Prince Henry, as King Henry IV, confounded Falstaff and all his former companions by his totally changed behavior. Will Nixon be another Henry IV, a "new" Nixon?

My belief is that he will not.

We can expect Nixon's policy as president to correspond closely to the aspects of his personality mentioned earlier. In line with them, and his character as a pragmatic and expedient politician, the demands of the office, and of political necessity, ought largely to determine his actions. Walter Lippmann, for example, has written persuasively that the actual situation of the United States demands a "deflationary" policy. "Because of the objective situation, the task imposed on President Nixon has become one of deflating the economy, of reducing the political promises, of cutting down the commitments to the realities of the human scale (e.g., Vietnam and similar commitments).

The role of the deflator is never glamorous. Has there ever been a 'charismatic' deflator?"[25] Nixon, surely, is not charismatic. Perhaps, as Lippmann suggests, it is Nixon's destiny to have his "pragmatic" character exactly fit the needs of his time and the mood of the American people.

What of the needs and aspirations of America and its people that lie outside the "deflationary" situation? These, unfortunately for Nixon, may grow larger. The problems of blacks, of youth, of possible recession and uncontrollable inflation, of wars and commitments cannot easily be collapsed. Will Nixon's sort of non-charismatic leadership succeed in such circumstances, or might he tend to lose his "cool"? I confess to a haunting sense of doubt as to Nixon's ability to rise to such challenges.

If Lippmann is right, then Nixon will not be severely "tested." In that case, we need only be on the lookout for certain fundamental features of Nixon's character, especially his "pragmatism," continuously to assert themselves. He will continue to anguish over decisions, but will eventually make them, often with a good sense of timing. At requisite moments, he will *create* crises, as a means of testing himself and assuring himself greater public support. I am positive that he will continue to make irreconcilable statements, such as promising not to embroil America in future Vietnams at the same time as he pledges similar assistance to Thailand. He will do this because, in the presence of any given audience, Nixon believes implicitly in the "lines" he is uttering. I emphasize that he is an "actor," not an "ideologue."

Above all, I would stress Nixon's belief in his own goodness and morality. Un-selfconsciously, he quotes in *Six Crises* the faith in him expressed—by Whittaker Chambers. "Almost from the first day we met (think, it is already 12 years ago)," Chambers wrote to him, "I sensed in you some quality, deep-going, difficult to identify in the world's glib way, but good, and meaningful for you and multitudes of others" (N, 460). This is the same Nixon, however, who seems always to *act* in an amoral way, and who constantly asserts, for example, that "American foreign policy must always be directed by the security interests of the United States and not by some vague concept of 'world public opinion'" (M-H, 253). Granted that there is some truth to this latter remark, one must question whether "world public opinion" does not point to a morality, or immorality, that can lie hidden in a nation's or an individual's pursuit of power under the name of protection and self-defense, and should also be taken into account in formulating policy.

In short, I am suggesting that there is a "blindness" to his own drives and desires—and those of America—exhibited by Richard Nixon. If we have difficulty in discovering the "real" Nixon, I believe that our president has even greater difficulty. Socrates counsels that "Know Thyself" is the right adage for a successful philosopher. Should a politician also "know himself"? Time, and events, alone will tell us whether Nixon has correctly "analyzed" his American Dream, or whether a deeper interpretation would be better for the health and well-being of America and the world.

NOTES

1. The Wicker comment is in the *New York Times Magazine*, January 19, 1969, 21; Rovere's is in *ibid*, July 20, 1969, 4.

2. There is a growing literature in this field, most of it stemming from the pioneering work by Erik H. Erikson, *Childhood and Society* (New York, 1950). My own position is put forth in the introduction to Bruce Mazlish (ed.), *Psychoanalysis and History* (Englewood Cliffs, 1963), and "Clio on the Couch: Prolegomena to Psychohistory," *Encounter*, XXXI (September 1968), 46–54. Compare Cushing Strout, "Ego Psychology and the Historian," *History and Theory*, VII (1968), 281–297.

3. Earl Mazo and Stephen Hess, *Nixon: A Political Portrait* (New York, 1968), 15. References to this book hereinafter will be indicated in the text of the article by M-H, followed by pages.

4. Nixon spent one summer—Mazo and Hess give his age as fourteen (M-H, 12)—during the two years with his mother and brother in Prescott, Arizona, putting his nascent oratorical skills to work as a barker at a concession in the Slippery Gulch Rodeo (see William Costello, *The Facts About Nixon: An Unauthorized Biography* [New York, 1960], 23). I do not believe, however, that this would much affect the feeling that I postulate for Nixon of perceiving, on the unconscious level, his mother as "deserting" him. (Incidentally, existing published sources do not allow me to establish with certainty the precise dates involved. James Keogh, *This Is Nixon* [New York, 1956], 25, for example, claims Harold got tuberculosis at age eighteen, and died five years later. On the face of it, Mazo and Hess' dates are more acceptable.)

5. See, for example, Robert Lifton, "On Death and Death Symbolism" and "The Hiroshima Bomb," reprinted in *History and Human Survival* (New York, 1970), and *Death in Life: Survivors of Hiroshima* (New York, 1967). For Nixon's own account of his feelings about his brother Arthur, see the composition that, at age seventeen, he wrote about his sibling; it is reproduced in Bela Kornitzer, *The Real Nixon: An Intimate Biography* (New York, 1960), 61–66.

6. Richard M. Nixon, *Six Crises* (New York, 1968), 317. References to this book hereinafter will be indicated in the text of the article by N, followed by pages.

7. Compare Edward Fiske's article in the *New York Times*, January 26, 1969, 54.

8. *New York Times Magazine*, June 8, 1969, 108.

9. *Ibid*, 111.

10. "Billy Graham's Own Story: 'God Is My Witness,'" Part One," *McCall's*, XCI (April, 1964), 124. Cf. John Pollock, *Billy Graham: The Authorized Biography* (London, 1966), 18.

11. There is general agreement that the father, Frank Nixon, was given to fits of anger and irritability, and spanked his sons. Whether Hannah also spanked them is unclear, though doing so would seem out of character for her. Whether his father actually whipped Richard is also unclear, as the following passages from Kornitzer indicate: "Frank's rigid and uncompromising attitude, not only towards politics but toward life in general, made life hard for his family. 'He would not hesitate using the strap or rod on the boys when they did wrong,' Hannah says, 'although I don't remember that he ever spanked Richard.'" When asked directly, Richard Nixon told Kornitzer "'Dad played no favorites with us . . . when you got into mischief, you had to be pretty convincing to avoid punishment. . . . He had a hot temper, and I learned early that the only way to deal with him was to abide by the rules he laid down. Otherwise, I would probably have felt the touch of a ruler or the strap as my brothers did.'" (*The Real Nixon*, 78–79.)

12. On a less psychological level, Nixon's Quaker background must be viewed in connection with his entrance to Whittier College, a small Quaker institution, which played a strong role in his development, and with such figures in his later political life as Herbert Hoover, a fellow Californian and Quaker, who from early on seems to have taken a special interest in Nixon.

13. See Mazo and Hess, *Nixon*, 258, for a beginning analysis.

14. Marie Smith, "Nixon's California Home," *Boston Sunday Globe*, July 6, 1969.

15. See, for example, Harold D. Lasswell, *Psychopathology and Politics* (Chicago, 1930).

16. Lawrence F. Schiff, "Dynamic Young Fogies—Rebels on the Right," *Trans-Action*, IV (November 1966), 32.

17. *Ibid.*, 32–33.

18. In another account Dr. Upton reportedly added, "But it was a sincere performance, and there is nothing perfidious or immoral about being a good actor" (Kornitzer, *The Real Nixon*, 107); however, this addition does not undercut the point I am making.

19. It is interesting to note that Nixon's foreign policy adviser, Henry A. Kissinger, in his psychological study of Bismarck, points out that "the apostle of the claims of power was subject to fits of weeping in a crisis." ("The White Revolutionary: Reflections on Bismarck," *Daedalus*, XCVII [1968], 890.) A reading of this article opens up fascinating speculations as to the comparisons and "transferences" Kissinger may be making between Bismarck and Nixon; for example, compare also the observation that "It was not that Bismarck lied—this is much too self-conscious an act—but that he was finely attuned to the subtlest currents of any environment and produced measures precisely adjusted to the need to prevail. The key to Bismarck's success was that he was always sincere" (898). (In all fairness, I ought to indicate that some of my "transferences," though in a different context, may be spotted in my own article, "James Mill and the Utilitarians," *ibid.*, 1036–1061.) Aside from "transferences," a close reading of Kissinger's article might shed light on some of his, and therefore perhaps President Nixon's, fundamental foreign policy attitudes.

20. See T. Adorno, *et al.*, *The Authoritarian Personality* (New York, 1950), and, on Hitler, for example, Robert G. L. Waite, "Adolf Hitler's Anti-Semitism, A Study in History and Psychoanalysis," in Benjamin B. Wolman (ed.), *Psychoanalytic Interpretations of History*. Foreword by William L. Langer (New York: Basic Books, 1971), and "Adolf Hitler's Guilt Feelings: A Problem in History and Psychology," *Journal of Interdisciplinary History* 1 (Winter 1971): 229–49.

21. Clearly, much of Nixon's behavior, even in the area of "smearing" and feeling "smeared," is typical behavior of *all* politicians (which poses some interesting questions as to the nature of politics). The problem is in deciding whether the degree of feeling raises it to another level, and justifies the term "projection."

22. A well-known analysis of the Soviet Politburo in the terms that I have been using is, of course, Nathan Leites, *A Study of Bolshevism* (Glencoe, 1953).

23. Quite a while after writing this paragraph, I came across some confirmation of my guess as to the actual phrase used by Nixon. Steward Alsop, *Nixon and Rockefeller: A Double Portrait* (Garden City, 1960), 63, claims "three people who should know" have Nixon saying "pee or get off the pot." My own hunch is still that the language was even stronger than this. After all, one of Nixon's triumphs in college was bringing in a "four holer" to his fraternity.

24. The entire discussion of the last few pages raises again the issue of what is characteristic of all politicians and what is particularly personal to Nixon, a sticky issue for all psychohistorical work. The need to believe well of oneself, to think of oneself as principled and fair, and to avoid self-examination seems to be a characteristic necessity of politicians as a group; a minimum requirement of their egos to sustain them, as the journalist David Broder suggested to me, against "the terrific competitive pressures of their profession." So, too, simple political necessity forces them often to take public positions during a campaign diametrically opposed to what they know to be right and truthful. Once again, then, the question of "degree" arises (as in fn. 21 above). More than this, however, the question of "fit" also arises: the way in which an individual's personality allows him to be a "typical" politician (Adlai Stevenson obviously had difficulties in this respect), and the ways in which the behavior of politicians "fits" the expectations of their constituents.

25. Walter Lippmann, in *The Boston Globe*, February 16, 1969.

17

AMERICA'S NEW SURVIVORS
The Image of My Lai

ROBERT JAY LIFTON

Psychohistory, Fred Weinstein and Gerald Platt argue in a recent interdisciplinary text, can be of only limited value as long as it confines itself to biography. In their effort to wed psychoanalysis, a preeminently "personal" body of theory, to group dynamics, Weinstein and Platt in *Psychoanalytic Sociology* make a sophisticated effort to show links between Freud's ideas of identification and internalization, and Tallcott Parson's theory of social structure and equilibrium. Without doing that book justice, one might introduce it as setting out to demonstrate how sociopolitical change can interrupt or frustrate the pattern of life and meaning of symbols that people have come to expect. Weinstein and Platt are interested in explaining why, at a particular time, large numbers and different kinds of people (by age, class, personality structure) all join the same movement. While many pieces in this collection deal suggestively with nonbiographical topics, no one has yet tried to apply Weinstein and Platt's theoretical formulations to a historical study. One essay that comes close is Robert Jay Lifton's analysis of the soldiers who were involved in a massacre of civilians during the Vietnam War. Why, he asks, did so many dissimilar young men suddenly act as one—as if they were a single, insane animal—in committing the documented atrocity at My Lai?

Lifton's chapter first appeared in a 1973 book recounting his interviews and therapy sessions with Vietnam veterans who were experiencing serious trouble readjusting to civilian life. Whether or not he began his work expecting to find similarities between these men and the subjects of his earlier, famous research on the victims of the first atom bomb blast on Japan, he soon recognized in the ex-GI's a familiar pattern of shock and dislocation. Lifton argues that understanding these veterans—helping them to come to terms with their own war experience—requires the concept of the survivor syndrome. According to this theory, which Lifton applied in his Hiroshima book, persons who survive a massively destructive experience commonly feel a vague unease

Reprinted with minor alterations from *Home From the War; Vietnam Veterans: Neither Victims Nor Executioners* (New York: Simon and Schuster, 1973), pp. 35–71, 452–53, by permission of Simon and Schuster and Wildwood House Limited.

about being "spared," a guilt that can oppress, give rise to questions about one's destiny, paralyze, or—says Lifton—can contribute while one is in combat to an atrocity-producing situation. Welding the men of Company C together the morning they attacked My Lai, aside from their vengeful anger, was their guilt for escaping earlier losses. Moreover, Lifton says, they realized that they had not been called upon to become "heroes"; they were victimized, to some extent at least, having expected something else, enraged over the "unheroic" conflict they were thrust into. Thus Lifton's chapter resembles Stanley Elkins's concentration camp analogy in its efforts to use clinical evidence in answering historical questions. Because in therapy Vietnam vets showed symptoms of the survivor syndrome, Lifton argues that survivor guilt enables us to understand more fully what went wrong at My Lai.

Lifton's finding that in one sense nothing did go wrong—the troops acted predictably given the nature of the war and the shock they survived—was designed to raise its own questions. Offering an example of clinical work that provides a framework for historical study, Lifton's analysis of My Lai also shows how important that history can be to the discussion of public issues. If we can learn from our past, and if psychotherapy attempts humane healing, it is but a short step from psychohistory to political activism.

THERE IS something special about Vietnam veterans. Everyone who has contact with them seems to agree that they are different from veterans of other wars. A favorite word to describe them is "alienated." Veterans Administration reports stress their sensitivity to issues of authority and autonomy. This group of veterans is seen as having "greater distrust of institutions and unwillingness to be awed by traditional authorities," so that "they are less willing to be passive recipients of our wisdom." The individual Vietnam veteran, it is said, "feels an intense positive identification with his own age group" and is part of "an unspoken 'pact of youth' which assures mutual safety from threats to their sense of individual identity."[1]

Even when sufficiently incapacitated to require hospitalization on a VA psychiatric ward, Vietnam veterans tend to stress the issue of the generation gap and of larger social problems rather than merely their own sickness. And there is evidence, confirmed by my own observations, that large numbers of them feel themselves to be "hurting" and in need of psychological help but avoid contact with the Veterans Administration. They associate it with the war-military-government establishment, with the forces responsible for a hated ordeal, or with their suspicion (whether on the basis of hearsay or personal experience) that VA doctors are likely to interpret their rage at everything connected with the war as no more than their own individual problem. The result has been (again in the words of VA observers) "degrees of bitterness, distrust, and suspicion of those in positions of authority and responsibility."

To be sure, these patterns can occur in veterans of any war—along with restless shifting of jobs and living arrangements, and difficulty forming or maintaining intimate relationships. These precise tendencies among World War II veterans, men who had "lost a sense of personal sameness and historical continuity," led Erik Erikson to evolve his concepts of "identity crisis" and "loss of 'ego identity.' "[2]

But these men give the impression of something more. Murray Polner, who interviewed more than two hundred Vietnam veterans of diverse views and backgrounds concluded that "not one of them—hawk, dove, or haunted—was entirely free of doubt about the nature of the war and the American role in it." As a group they retain the "gnawing suspicion that 'it was all for nothing.' " Polner concluded that "never before have so many questioned as much, as these veterans have, the essential rightness of what they were forced to do."[3] Beyond just being young and having been asked to fight a war, these men have a sense of violated personal and social order, of fundamental break in human connection, which they relate to conditions imposed upon them by the war in Vietnam.[4]

Some of the quality of that war experience is revealed in the following recollection of My Lai by a GI who was there, and whom I shall henceforth refer to as "the My Lai survivor":

The landscape doesn't change much. For days and days you see just about nothing. It's unfamiliar—always unfamiliar. Even when you go back to the same place, it's unfamiliar. And it makes you feel as though, well, there's nothing left in the world but this. . . . You have the illusion of going great distances and traveling like hundreds of miles . . . and you end up in the same place because you're only a couple of miles away. . . . But you feel like it's not all real. It couldn't possibly be. We couldn't still be in this country. We've been walking for days. . . . You're in Vietnam and they're using real bullets. . . . Here in Vietnam they're actually shooting people for no reason. . . . Any other time you think, it's such an extreme. Here you can go ahead and shoot them for nothing. . . . As a matter of fact it's even . . . smiled upon, you know. Good for you. Everything is backwards. That's part of the kind of unreality of the thing. To the grunt [infantryman] this isn't backwards. He doesn't understand. . . . But something [at My Lai] was missing. Something you thought was real that would accompany this. It wasn't there. . . . There was something missing in the whole business that made it seem like it really wasn't happening.*

The predominant emotional tone here is all-encompassing absurdity and moral inversion. The absurdity has to do with a sense of being alien and profoundly lost, yet at the same time locked into a situation as meaningless

---

*Note a similar passage from a description of World War I: "How long has it been? Weeks—months—years? Only days. We see time pass in the colourless faces of the dying, we cram food into us, we run, we throw, we shoot, we kill, we lie about, we are feeble and spent, and nothing supports us but the knowledge that there are feebler, still more spent, still more helpless ones there who, with staring eyes, look upon us as gods that escaped death many times."[5]

and unreal as it is deadly. The moral inversion, eventuating in a sense of evil, has to do not only with the absolute reversal of ethical standards but with its occurrence in absurdity, without inner justification, so that the killing is rendered naked.

This overall emotional sense, which I came to view as one of *absurd evil*, is conveyed even more forcefully by something said in a rap group by a former "grunt." He had been talking about the horrors of combat and told how, after a heavy air strike on an NLF [Viet Cong] unit, his company came upon a terrible scene of dismembered corpses. Many of the men then began a kind of wild victory dance, in the course of which they mutilated the bodies still further. He recalled wondering to himself:

What am I doing here? We don't take any land. We don't give it back. We just mutilate bodies. What the fuck are we doing here?

Whatever the element of retrospective judgment in this kind of recollection, the image was characteristic. During another rap group discussion about how men felt about what they were doing in Vietnam, a man asked: "What the hell *was* going on? What the fuck *were* we doing?"

These questions express a sense of the war's total lack of order or structure, the feeling that there was no genuine purpose, that nothing could ever be secured or gained, and that there could be no measurable progress. We may say that there was no genuine "script" or "scenario" of war that could provide meaning or even sequence or progression, a script within which armies clash, battles are fought, won, or lost, and individual suffering, courage, cowardice, or honor can be evaluated. Nor could the patrols seeking out an elusive enemy, the ambushes in which Americans were likely to be the surprised victims, or the "search-and-destroy missions" lashing out blindly at noncombatants achieve the psychological status of meaningful combat ritual. Rather, these became part of the general absurdity, the antimeaning. So did the "secret movements" on this alien terrain, since, as one man put it, "Little kids could tell us exactly where we would set up the next night." The men were adrift in an environment not only strange and hostile but offering no honorable encounter, no warrior grandeur.

Now there are mutilations, midst absurdity and evil, in any war. Men who fight wars inevitably become aware of the terrible disparity between romantic views of heroism expressed "back home" and the reality of degradation and unspeakable suffering they have witnessed, experienced, and caused. One thinks of the answer given by Audie Murphy, much-decorated hero of World War II, to the question put to him about how long it takes a man to get over his war experiences. Murphy's reply, recorded in his obituary, was that one never does. What he meant was that residual inner conflicts—survivor conflicts—stay with one indefinitely. These conflicts, as I was able to generalize from my Hiroshima work, have to do with anxiety in relationship to an indelible death imprint, death guilt inseparable from that imprint, various forms of prolonged psychic numbing and suppression of feeling, profound suspicion of the counterfeit (or of "counterfeit nurturance"), and an overall inability to give significant inner form—to "formulate"—one's war-linked death immersion. This impaired survivor formulation undoubtedly was a factor in Murphy's repeated difficulties and disappointments after his return from his war, as it has been in the unrealized lives and premature deaths of many war heroes.*

Yet veterans have always come to some terms with their war experiences through some formulation of their survival that permits them to overcome much of their death anxiety and death guilt, diffuse suspiciousness and numbing. Crucial even to this partial resolution of survivor conflict is the veteran's capacity to believe that his war had purpose and significance beyond the immediate horrors he witnessed. He can then connect his own actions with ultimately humane principles, and can come to feel that he had performed a dirty but necessary job. He may even be able to experience renewed feelings of continuity or symbolic immortality around these larger principles, side by side with his residual survivor pain and conflict.

But the central fact of the Vietnam War was that no one really believed in it. The larger purposes put forth to explain the American presence—repelling outside invaders, or giving the people of the South an opportunity to choose their own form of government—were directly contradicted by the overwhelming evidence a GI encountered that *he* was the outside invader, that the government he had come to defend was justly hated by the people he had come to help, and that he, the American helper was hated by them most of all.[6] Even those who seemed to acquiesce to these claims did so, as Polner's findings suggest, with profound inner doubt, and in response to tenuous and defensive "psychological work."

Nor did many actually fighting the war take seriously the quasi-religious impulse to "fight the communists." Rather, their gut realization that some-

---

*A more extreme parallel is the case of Sergeant Dwight W. Johnson, who won a Medal of Honor in Vietnam for racing through heavy crossfire to rescue a close buddy from a burning tank, and then, when the tank had exploded killing the rest of its inhabitants, hunting down and killing face-to-face, in retaliatory rage, five to twenty Vietnamese soldiers. He required psychiatric hospitalization immediately after the episode, as he did later on back in the United States, when he was thought to be suffering from "depression caused by post-Vietnam adjustment problems." He never got over his persistent "bad dreams," his guilt over having survived while his buddies died—or, as one psychiatrist put it, for "winning a high honor for the one time in his life when he lost complete control of himself," which made him wonder: "What would happen if I lost control of myself in Detroit and behaved like I did in Vietnam?" Three years after his heroic episode, he was killed, at the age of twenty-four, by the manager of a grocery store he was alleged to have attempted to hold up at gunpoint. All this was recorded in a *New York Times* obituary of May 26, 1971, as was his mother's concluding comment: "Sometimes I wonder if Skip [Sergeant Johnson] tired of this life and needed someone else to pull the trigger."

thing was wrong with this war was expressed in combat briefings (often by lieutenants or captains) as described to me by a number of former GIs:

I don't know why *I'm* here. *You* don't know why *you're* here. But since we're *both* here, we might as well try to do a good job and do our best to stay alive.

This was the very opposite of calling forth a heroic ideal or an immortalizing purpose. And while it is true that survival is the preoccupation of men in any war, this kind of briefing was not only a total disclaimer of any purpose beyond survival but a direct transmission of the absurdity and antimeaning pervading the Vietnam War. That transmission had a distinct psychological function. It inserted a modicum of out-front honesty into the situation's basic absurdity, so that the absurdity itself could be shared; it paved the way for the intense cooperation, brotherhood, and mutual love characteristic of and necessary to military combat. In the end, however, everybody felt the absence of larger purpose. Hence the deadpan professional observation by a Veterans Administration psychiatrist, in response to a query from his chief medical director concerning the special characteristics and problems of the "Vietnam Era Veteran": "Vietnam combat veterans tend to see their experience as an exercise in survival rather than a defense of national values."[7]

The distinction is important. Huizinga, in discussing the connection between play and war, speaks of the concept of the "ordeal," its relationship to "the idea of glory," and ultimately to the warrior's quest for "a decision of holy validity."[8] This theological vocabulary conveys well the immortalizing appeal battle holds for the warrior. But in Vietnam one underwent the "ordeal" or test without the possibility of that "idea of glory" or "decision of holy validity." There was all of the pain but none of the form.

What we find instead is best understood as an *atrocity-producing situation*. It is created by a special combination of elements that Jean-Paul Sartre has described as inevitably genocidal: a counterinsurgency war undertaken by an advanced industrial society against a revolutionary movement of an underdeveloped country, in which the revolutionary guerrillas are inseparable from the rest of the population. Those elements in turn contributed greatly to the draconian American military policies in Vietnam: the "free-fire zone" (where every civilian was a target), and the "search-and-destroy mission" (on which everyone and everything could be killed, or as the expression had it, "wasted"); the extensive use of plant defoliants that not only destroyed the overall ecology of Vietnam but, if encountered in sufficient concentration by pregnant women, human embryos as well; and the almost random saturation of a small country with an unprecedented level of technological destruction and firepower both from the air and on the ground. These external historical factors and military policies led, in turn, to a compelling internal sequence that constituted the psychological or experiential dimension of the atrocity-producing situation.

My Lai provides a grotesque illustration of that sequence, and makes clear that *the psychology of the survivor is central even to the killing process*. I was able to reconstruct events at My Lai on the basis of my interviews with the veteran who had been there, additional informal talks with several writers who have investigated various aspects of the atrocity, and descriptions of the event in various articles and books.[9] My assumption, based upon all this (and much other) evidence was that My Lai was exceptional only in its dimensions, and that these very dimensions reveal the essence of the atrocity-producing situation.

Many forms of desensitization and rage contributed to My Lai, some of them having to do with specifically American aberrations around race, class, and masculinity. But my assumption in speaking of an atrocity-producing situation was that, given the prevailing external conditions, men of very divergent backgrounds—indeed just about *anyone*—can enter into the "psychology of slaughter."[10] This assumption was born out by an examination of the step-by-step sequence by which the American men who eventually went to My Lai came to internalize and then act upon an irresistible image of slaughter.

During basic training, the men encountered (as did most recruits) drill sergeants and other noncommissioned officers who were veterans of Vietnam, and as such had a special aura of authority and demonic mystery. From these noncoms the recruit heard stories of Vietnam, of how tough and "dirty, rotten, and miserable" (as one remembered being told) it was there. He also heard descriptions of strange incidents in which it became clear that Vietnamese civilians were being indiscriminately killed—tales of Americans creeping up to village areas and tossing grenades into "hootches," of artillery strikes on inhabited areas, and of brutal treatment of Vietnamese picked up during patrols or combat sweeps. Sometimes pictures of badly mutilated Vietnamese corpses were shown to him to illustrate the tales.

Here and later on there is a striking contrast between the formal instruction (given rotely if at all) to kill only military adversaries, and the informal message (loud and clear) to kill just about everyone. That message, as the My Lai survivor put it, was that "It's okay to kill them," and in fact "That's what you're supposed to do"—or as a former marine received it: "You've gotta go to Vietnam, you've gotta kill the gooks."[11] The process resembles the Japanese use of *haragei* or "stomach talk"—perhaps more accurately translated as a "gut message"—in which what is really meant and acted upon is the opposite of what is actually said. Thus, Japanese statesmen, toward the end of World War II, publicly proclaimed that Japan must fight to the last man; the meaning intended—Japan has no recourse but to surrender—was considered too dangerous to state directly because of the threat of right-wing assassinations. Not surprisingly, there was considerable confusion about what the words were actually supposed to mean.[12] Similarly, American leaders found it politically inexpedient, and morally unacceptable (to themselves as well as to others) to state outright that all Vietnamese (or "gooks") were fair game; instead they turned the other cheek, underwent their own psychic numbing, while permitting—indeed making inevitable—the message of slaughter.* In both cases the stomach talk reflected profound moral contradictions—something close to what we shall later speak of as a counterfeit universe—as well as deep-seated ambivalence all around. But in contrast to the Japanese ambiguity, the American version was all too clear, the message unmistakable.

Thus the message of slaughter became inseparable from the death-and-rebirth process of basic training. The coercive desymbolization of basic training, its "systematic stripping process" in which the civilian self was "deliberately denuded" so that the recruit could "reject his preexisting identity . . . envelope himself instead in the institutional identity of the military organization . . . [and] accept his impotence in the face of military discipline and recognize the crushing recrimination it can inflict if he should seek to challenge it"—all this became a means by which he was not only "acculturated to the military system" but also acculturated, in an anticipatory sense, to the atrocity-producing situation awaiting him in Vietnam. The "masculine initiation rite" of basic training and the "manly status"[15] acquired in it became inseparable from what is best called the *machismo of slaughter*. That machismo was in turn directly associated with simple fear, with the message that *any* Vietnamese—man, woman, or infant—may be setting the booby trap that will kill you—the implication being that to survive you must "kill them all."

For many at My Lai the message was reinforced in concrete racial terms by the special environment of the "Jungle Training Center" at Schofield Barracks in Hawaii: facsimile Vietnamese village with booby-trapped huts and slant-eyed dummy targets. There Charlie Company of the Americal Division, initially in disarray, was taken over and revitalized by an able and on the whole well-liked commanding officer, whose somewhat over-zealous inclinations earned him the nickname "Mad Dog Medina." The by-now specific image of slaughter became more intense and immediate shortly after the company's arrival in Vietnam. They quickly became aware of random kill-

---

*Sometimes the informal message of slaughter can be conveyed by such crude symbolism as what the marines came to call the "rabbit lesson": On the last day before leaving for Vietnam, the staff NCO holds a rabbit as he lectures on escape, evasion, and survival in the jungle. The men become intrigued by the rabbit, fond of it, and then the NCO "cracks it in the neck, skins it, disembowels it . . . and then they throw the guts out into the audience." As one marine explained: "You can get anything out of that you want, but that's your last lesson you catch in the United States before you leave for Vietnam."[13] Prior to the exposure of My Lai, very little was likely to be said about those provisions of the U.S. Army Field Manual, "The Law of Land Warfare," which define as war crimes various forms of massacres and atrocities including the killing or harming of civilians and specify that "members of the Armed Forces are bound to obey only lawful orders."[14] And when these principles were taught, *that* unconvincing lesson was likely to be treated as "stomach talk" for the more compelling rabbit-lesson principle.

ing: "If you can shoot artillery and bombs in there every night," one of the men was quoted as saying, "how can the people in there be worth so much?"[16] Still more graphic was the sight of a troop carrier driving by with "about twenty human ears tied to the antenna."[17] The men were at first shocked ("It was kind of hard to believe. They actually had ears on the antenna"), but not long afterwards some of the men, having spotted a few Vietcong and called in artillery, came back with an ear of their own, to the approval of their commanding officer: "Medina was happy; it was his first kill."[18] Others began to mark their estimated kills with notches on their rifles. The imagery is that of the hunt. The "animals" one shoots serve merely to provide trophies, evidence of one's prowess.

But the men were hardly relaxed in their "sport"—the company spent its first ten weeks in Vietnam in a confusing, fatiguing, and frightening combination of construction work, patrols, and fruitless maneuvers. The men underwent a gradual but profound process of numbing, reflected in their increasing callousness and brutality toward Vietnamese. They justified their behavior by the unpredictability and "unfairness" of an environment in which friendly gestures toward a particular village were no guarantee against sniper fire: "We give the medical supplies and they come and kick our ass."[19] This image of justified slaughter was furthered by the resentful observation that South Vietnamese troops seemed to be "laying around doing nothing," causing the men to wonder, "Why should I fight for them?" Still stronger feelings could be expressed on a similar basis, as quoted to me during an individual interview: "I'm gonna go out and get me a gook—because those bastards are responsible for me being here."

And there was the perpetually enraging elusiveness of the enemy, as described by the My Lai survivor:

No matter how much effort you put into it, you can't find him. You can't lay your hands on him. And the fact that he also might be anywhere, you know . . . as though you were hunting a specific deer and you don't know which one it is and there's a deer herd all over you.

There is, in other words, confusion and reversal within this hunting image: the invisible enemy, being able to track down the GI, becomes the hunter, the GI the hunted.* The only possibility for overcoming this combination of helpless passivity, bitter impotence, and general terror lay in a real confrontation with the enemy—in getting him (as some of the men would put it) "to stand up and fight like a man." For the men of Company C that idea of a true battle—of a *genuine ordeal*—became something of a dream, no doubt both wishful and fearful.

*The "deer" in the image suggest a sense of one's enemies as relatively gentle creatures, as does a good deal of additional imagery in which genuinely human contact with the Vietcong and North Vietnamese is sought. But they can also be seen as tough, determined, and strong; and where there has been evidence of mutilations by them, as brutal.

The combat they actually did experience over the next month hardly lived up to that dream. Instead of a proud ordeal, they experienced only a series of hit-and-run blows and losses. There was the first death, always a profound event for men in combat, shattering the myth of group invulnerability and thrusting the men into the conflicts of the survivor. Each inwardly asks himself the terrible survivor question—"Why did *he* die, and not me?" Each struggles with the unconscious sense that his own life was purchased through his buddy's death, with the variety of ways in which he feels responsible for that death. One must make it up to the man killed, do something that gives significance to his death, in order to justify one's own survival and avoid the experience of overwhelming death guilt.[20] In combat that means getting back at the enemy, and in most wars there are prescribed forms for doing that— battlefield rituals in which one can demonstrate courage and initiative that take their toll on the enemy. In the absence of such forms, and for the most part of a visible enemy, the men were left with their acute survivor grief, with their sense of guilt and loss, which could in turn become quickly transformed into rage.

Hence, Company C's first death—that of a GI named Bill Weber—was "the turning point. Suddenly we realized a guy could get killed out there. So let's get our revenge before we go." Their lieutenant also changed: "He was no longer a GI [preoccupied with petty regulations]. He got to be a savage too."[21] After several additional ambushes in which men were wounded, the company experienced its greatest blow: a minefield disaster in which twenty percent of the men were incapacitated—four killed and twenty-eight severely wounded (another report had six killed and twelve severely wounded). Now survivor guilt became much greater: "There were men dying," as one of them later put it, "and you weren't one of them." More than guilt, there was the sense that the company as a unit—virtually the entire universe the men then inhabited—had been annihilated. Extreme images were needed to reconstruct self and world, and these, not surprisingly, took the form of absolute revenge. Fantasies previously held by individual men now were pooled, as the My Lai survivor recalls, into open discussions of "wiping the whole place out," or what he called "the Indian idea . . . the only good gook is a dead gook." The idea of the enemy, though increasingly hazy, was also broadly extended to include "anybody but them, anybody but an American soldier."*

Finally, there was Sergeant Cox—blown to pieces by an artillery shell he found in a booby trap he was attempting to dismantle. These hidden, hand-set, and grotesquely deadly arrangements, released by either direct touch, a

---

*The My Lai survivor claimed that there was strong evidence that the mines had been set, not by Vietcong, but by our Korean allies who had encamped in that area a short time before— which would place much of the responsibility with higher American headquarters, since they would presumably have been notified about the mines by the South Koreans. In any case, he noted that the men resisted this idea and preferred to place all the blame on the Vietcong (or "the gooks") so that their imagery of revenge could remain justified.

timing device, or (through wiring) by the hand of an outsider observer, contributed greatly to the combination of helplessness and terror the men felt. The name given to the devices suggests the sense in which they not only maim the victim but make him into a hoodwinked fool—they are "trap[s] for the booby."[22] The men had special feelings toward Cox, an older person with extensive war experience whom many of them leaned on for emotional support. His grotesque death exacerbated their sense of loss, their fear, and above all their rage. The next day a memorial service was held for Cox and for the others recently killed. The importance of the occasion was marked by the presence of a chaplain, but the main statement made was the combination eulogy-pep talk delivered by Captain Medina, the Company Commander.

Eulogies have the function of extending the significance of the life just ended; survivors can then justify remaining alive by taking on the mission of perpetuating that life, by carrying on the dead man's work. There are many versions of what Medina said that day, but all accounts agree that he spoke movingly about Cox and the other men who had been killed, brought his listeners close to tears, and provided them with a compelling survivor mission. It was something like:

We lost a lot of guys. Pinkville caused us a lot of hell. Now we're gonna get our revenge. Everything goes.[23]

Or, as the My Lai survivor recalls Medina saying, "Here's our chance to get back at them. . . . There are no innocent civilians in this area"—so that the men listening could conclude: "We were supposed to wipe out the whole area—waste it." Others remembered similar phrases such as "kill everything in the village" or "destroy everything with life"[24]—the message somewhere in-between exhortation and military orders, and perhaps received as both. There was also the strong impression (according to the My Lai survivor) that "he wanted a big body count . . . [because] this was a chance to go out and really show the brigade that we're something." Whatever Medina's actual words, his eulogy-pep talk provided the men with a concrete 'survivor mission' that gave significance to deaths being mourned. Now they had a psychological link between the deaths that had so overwhelmed them and the actions they could take in order to reconstitute themselves.

Medina apparently did not give a direct order to kill women and children. Rather, he combined "combat orders" from above,* his own impulses as a zealous officer, and an appeal to the shared emotional state of his company—which, within the standards prevailing in that environment, re-

---

*Later investigations of My Lai revealed that Medina had attended a higher-level briefing earlier that day, at which a similar "pep talk" had been given by Colonel Oran K. Henderson, who had just taken command of the brigade. Henderson was quoted as saying that he wanted to "get rid of [the Vietcong unit located in that area] once and for all," that he wanted the three companies to "get more aggressive." The Task Force Commander, Colonel Barker, also spoke and was reported to say that he "wanted the hootches burned, and he wanted the tunnels filled in, and then he wanted livestock and chickens run off, killed, or destroyed."[25]

sulted in a logic of slaughter. His talk was both command and release—as the My Lai survivor put it, "more or less permission . . . just sort of like, 'You can do it. . . . Whatever you do is up to you.'"

Medina's talk also enabled the men to form a rather strong psychic image anticipating their actions the next day, the day of My Lai.* The nature of that image undoubtedly varied, and in many cases contained elements of actual combat; but it mainly had to do with diffuse destruction and killing. Thus, one of the men recalled that, as he listened to Medina talking of burning huts, destroying livestock and food supplies, and poisoning wells, another man leaned toward his ear and said: "It's gonna be a slaughter, you watch."[26] The My Lai survivor described his own anticipatory image, which, significantly, was in the third person:

They could run into a bunch of ARVNs [South Vietnamese troops] and wipe them out—or Koreans and wipe them out . . . or they could run into a bunch of civilians. I thought one way or another somebody is going to get shot to pieces and it would just as soon be civilians. . . .

Following an artillery and gunship assault, the men landed from their helicopters at about 8:00 A.M. on the day of My Lai, fully armed for combat. The killings started almost immediately—some of them seemingly random and individual, but the larger number performed en masse, after "herding" together groups of men, women, and children, and then firing into them. Some Vietnamese were first manhandled; several of the young women were raped and then killed; homes were set fire, and livestock were shot. The killing was consistent with the men's anticipatory image of slaughter; it was exacerbated by the direct zeal of certain individuals—as for instance, by the now well-known orders of Lieutenant William L. Calley to "take care of" and "waste" large groups of captured Vietnamese. There was at no time any opposition, and no Vietcong were found. Most of the killing was done during the first two hours. By the time the company took its lunch break at about 11:00 A.M., between four hundred and five hundred residents of the village were dead. It later turned out that an additional hundred Vietnamese were killed that morning in the neighboring village by another company from the same task force involved in the same "combat operation."[27]

During all this killing the men behaved in many ways *as if* they were in a combat situation. The My Lai survivor noted that they kneeled and crouched while shooting—"like some kind of fire fight with somebody." For, as he went on to explain:

If you're actually thinking in terms of a massacre of murder, going in and shooting a bunch of defenseless people, why crouch? Why get down? Why do any of this? You

---

*This kind of anticipatory image is of enormous importance, as it has a great deal to do with the kind of behavior that follows. One can in fact say that all behavior occurs in response to some form of anticipatory image, which is in turn continuously modified on the basis of past and immediate experience. These issues are discussed at greater length in Lifton, *The Broken Connection: On Death and the Continuity of Life*, New York: Simon and Schuster, 1979.

must have something else on your mind. You must be thinking there's a possibility that you're going to get it yourself . . . that they pose some kind of a threat to you. . . .

He went even further in emphasizing the confused perceptions of the men (his continued use of the second person suggesting that he himself shared some of this confusion): "Because your judgment is all screwed up . . . they actually look like the enemy, or what you think is the enemy." What this, along with much additional evidence, suggests is that there existed in American soldiers at My Lai (and at other scenes of atrocity) the illusion, however brief, that, in gunning down old men, women, and babies, they had finally "engaged the enemy"—had finally got him to "stand up and fight."

One could say that the men sought to make this their "baptism of fire." The term is used for a soldier's first experience of actual combat conditions and is associated with the idea discussed earlier of an immortalizing ordeal. The combat conditions the men had already experienced—humiliating skirmishes and devastating encounters with mines and booby traps—lacked sufficient nobility or possibility for glory to qualify for this general category. So they sought their baptism, their beginning ordeal, at My Lai, and when that did not qualify either they acted as though it did. They were engaged in a double level of "play": military combat, in any case, is a male game and they were engaged in a particularly murderous *imitation* (as-if rendition) of the game of combat. Even the play element, in other words, was degraded and desymbolized.

I thus encountered conflicting descriptions about the kind of emotion Americans demonstrated at My Lai. Some recollections had them gunning down the Vietnamese with "no expression on . . . [their] faces . . . very businesslike,"[28] with "breaks" for cigarettes or refreshments. Yet others described the men as having become "wild" or "crazy" in their killing, raping, and destroying. The My Lai survivor described one GI engaging in a "mad chase" after a pig, which he eventually bayoneted; and others, in uncontrolled ways, tossing grenades or firing powerful weapons into the fragile "hootches" that made up the village. There is psychological truth in both descriptions. The businesslike demeanor of the men had to do with their advanced state of psychic numbing, a state enhanced by their (partial) sense of carrying out orders and of thereby being engaged in a "professional" military endeavor. The wildness and craziness had to do not only with the actual nature of what was going on (and the capacity of an observer to separate himself sufficiently from the situation, then or later, to contrast it with normal behavior) but also with the passions that lay beneath the numbing: the force of the "survivor mission," propelled as it was by death anxiety and death guilt. Thus, as they killed, the men were said to have shouted such things as "VC bastards, you dirty VC bastards," and "that's for Bill Weber," and "Cry, you dirty gook bastards, cry like you made us cry."[29] They were "bearing witness" to the deaths of their buddies; only later could many come to understand that it had been *false* witness. Underneath the combination of numbness and passion in each man was the central or controlling image of slaughter energizing the actions of virtually all of them.

To be sure the image was accompanied by doubt ("We only had a half-assed idea of what we were supposed to do"[30]) to the point of emptiness: "The people didn't know what they were dying for and the guys didn't know why they were shooting them."[31] Yet that very emptiness and absurdity served as a further impetus toward killing—toward pressing the logic of slaughter to the very end, until some kind of meaning could be squeezed from it. The illusion—the as-if situation—is pressed to the limit, until one has no choice but to see it as real.*

For example, one very confused young soldier remembered, in the midst of the My Lai holocaust, trying to make up his mind whether or not to kill a dazed little boy with one arm already shot off. He remembered thinking that the boy was about the same age as his own sister, and found himself wondering, "What if a foreign army was in my country and a soldier was looking at my sister just as I'm looking at this little boy. Would that foreign soldier have the guts to kill my sister?" He decided, "If he'd have the guts then I'd have the guts," and pulled the trigger.[33] So strong was the collective image (and now, program) of slaughter that intimations of wrongdoing or absurdity had to be subsumed by it, explained away within that image. By means of this bizarre criterion for guts or courage, the murder of a child is turned into a test or an ordeal. One met the test and stamped out inner doubt by carrying out the most extreme moral inversion and seeing the whole thing through to the end.

There was both compulsion and satisfaction in doing so. The My Lai veteran spoke of the killing as "scratching an itch . . . it's going to drive you nuts unless you do it." And he went on to explain:

You have a need to explode . . . and . . . like in Korea . . . and in World War II you could do it. When they used to have those battles I imagine a lot of guys were really tremendously relieved. . . . [At My Lai] they could just sit there and mow them down. And that's what I guess they wanted to do.

He admitted experiencing a similar impulse, which he consciously restrained:

---

*The process of rendering the as-if situation real, by means of accelerating slaughter, is described by another GI in relationship to a different atrocity:

. . . wandering and peeking around between hootches and inside hootches we realized we were just in a village . . . and they were going about their tasks, hardly noticing us until we came in strength. That is, fifteen or twenty of us showed up at once. And then all of a sudden they . . . got a little excited . . . pretty soon . . . a couple of the NCOs were shouting orders to "take those two and put them over here and this one and put him with those two." And pretty soon we had a crowd of people there, all yelling and screaming and kicking and wondering what's going on. . . . Pretty soon . . . a shot or two'd go off and somebody would yell: "You dirty Vietcong bastard!"—you know, something like this. . . . I fired into the crowd myself in the excitement. And I saw a few people go down. . . . It was horrifying to me at the moment. But in order to justify it I did it more, you know. It doesn't seem logical, I guess. But as you do something absurd sometimes you . . . add to it, or maybe do it repetitively just to make that appear to be . . . some part of your makeup. . . .[32]

It's a matter of controlling it, you know, saying, "Well . . . no, I can't do that. That's not right. I'd sure like to." . . . I think I can understand the men in the company because the things that were working on them were working on me too.

Another GI compared the situation to "the first time you masturbate. . . . You feel guilty because you think you shouldn't do it, yet somewhere you heard that it's perfectly natural and anyhow it's irresistible, so what the hell."[34]

Beyond this masturbatory imagery, there is sexual innuendo throughout the descriptions of My Lai—the sense of men who had been inactivated and rendered impotent suddenly asserting a form of violent omnipotence. The pattern is epitomized by the rape-murders which took place. In one of these, as described by Gershen, a GI finds a girl alone outside of a hut, forces her inside, tears her clothes off, and just before mounting her has the following thoughts, paraphrased by Gershen:

. . . you dirty bitch you killed Wilson and you killed Weber and Cox and Rotger and Bell, and you got me out here and look what you're making me do and look what my buddies are doing, and I hate this war and it's your fault that I'm here.[35]

Though she resisted him at first, according to the account, she gradually showed pleasure and sexual passion. But the GI, still in a state of rage and confusion, shot her and burned the hut, "Because [still in Gershen's paraphrase] he knew he hated these people and he didn't know why he was doing it." The rape scene undoubtedly lent itself to distortions in its re-creation, but the way in which the rape itself is subsumed to the false witness of the survivor mission of "revenge," and ultimately to the overall image of slaughter, is nonetheless significant.

Some experienced a more general sense of satisfaction. Paul Meadlo, who did considerable firing and killing, much of it in compliance with Calley's on-the-spot orders, said (during a television interview eighteen months later) that immediately after My Lai he "felt good." He explained that feeling more fully on another occasion:

I lost buddies. I—I lost—I lost a good, damn buddy, Bobby Wilson. And it was on my conscience. So after I done it I felt good. But later on that day, it kept getting to me.[36]

Meadlo also said (during the same television interview) that "It seemed like the natural thing to do at the time."* "Natural" here (as in the earlier reference to masturbation) means that slaughter was the norm in that situation; that it

---

*Later Meadlo's public position hardened, undoubtedly because of both legal and psychological pressures. During the Calley trial he pointedly used the term "Vietcong" as interchangeable with My Lai villagers, and when asked about having joined in shooting women and babies sitting on the ground, he answered: "I assumed at every minute that they would counterbalance [counterattack] . . . [by means of] some sort of chain or a little string they had to give a little pull and they blow us up, things like that."[37]

was psychologically necessary and felt psychologically right (however temporarily). In this sense the whole massacre was a "natural" consummation of the collective "survivor mission" and accompanying image of slaughter. Once begun, the slaughter was self-perpetuating; each expression of it confirmed and strengthened the overall image. Carrying the massacre through to the end was related not only to completion or consummation but also perhaps to an impulse, at whatever level of consciousness, not to leave survivors to tell the tale. (As it turned out, there were survivors, both Vietnamese and American, who did just that.)

The sense of their survivor mission having been accomplished gave the men, almost for the first time, a sense that their efforts—their very deaths—had significance: "Until now, we were dying uselessly,"[38] was the way one of them put it. Men who had been extremely tense and distraught since the minefield incident now (according to the My Lai survivor) "more or less loosened up" and "seemed more relaxed." More than that, the company "became more effective."* Moreover, right after My Lai the Vietcong "disappeared," company casualties dropped, and "It seemed . . . there wasn't any threat anymore." Though he knew that there were other reasons for these developments, such as better awareness of minefields and the NLF's hit-and-run tactics, the overall psychic effect was that My Lai "almost made some kind of sense." He compared the situation to "baking something," using the wrong formula and the wrong ingredients and yet having it "work." And since "Everything seemed to fit. . . . it made my arguments [against what was done at My Lai] sound a little bit hollow."

Buoyed by their new confidence, he explained, the men went on to find justification for what they did, claiming "They were all VC anyhow, and VC couldn't get along without their support"—even down to the killing of infants: "Well, they'll grow up [to help the VC]." Unlike higher military authorities, the men in no way sought to cover up what they had done—at least not to one another. On the contrary, they seemed pleased at their change in fortune: "Now instead of discussing the horrors of the minefield incident, My Lai was the new thing they had to talk about." They compared notes, often boastfully, in the manner of men looking back at a battle:

How many did you get? . . . It was really something terrific. . . . How many I got . . . the record and all this other stuff. One guy was very proud of the record. It was over one hundred. . . . There were probably a lot of exaggerations.

There were also extensive and admiring discussions about technical functioning of weapons—the damage done by grenades, forty-five-caliber automatic pistols, and the extent to which a seventy-nine artillery shell will blow someone to pieces. In all this they were recreating My Lai, treating it *as if* it were a

---

*He thought that replacements the company received could have been helpful as well. In any case this new "effectiveness" was, at best, short-lived—before long the units involved at My Lai were broken up, and the entire Americal Division was disbanded.

great battle and a noble victory, and themselves *as if* they were all-powerful warrior-heroes who had magnificently endured their ordeal.

This kind of post-slaughter rationalizing and boasting was partly in the service of suppressing doubts about whether My Lai qualified as that kind of immortalizing event, doubts that could lead to the kind of guilt Paul Meadlo referred to when he said, "Later on that day, it kept getting to me." The next day Meadlo accidentally triggered a mine that blew off his right foot. Since he was quoted at the time as saying "God punished me" and as angrily informing Lieutenant Calley that "God will punish you for what you made me do," it was quite possible that self-punitive components of his sense of guilt contributed to this accident. For residual guilt was undoubtedly strong in many of the men, and was to emerge in various forms later on.* More impressive, however, and much more disturbing, is the extent to which guilt could be at least temporarily refused or sloughed off by means of the advanced numbing and perverse meaning extracted from the many levels of "as if" pervading the environment. The most malignant actions can be performed with minimal guilt if there is a structure of meaning justifying them, even an illusory pseudo-formulation of the kind existing at My Lai. Only when achieving a certain independence from that environment and its pseudo-formulation can one begin to experience an appropriate sense of guilt. This way of avoiding guilt can render extremely dangerous any group of more or less ordinary people (that is, devoid of any diagnosable psychiatric illness) who happen to possess lethal weapons, while themselves possessed by lethal (and numbed) impulses toward false witness.

This state of numbed false witness was the norm at My Lai, as it was for Americans throughout Vietnam. One had to be a bit exceptional or, in that situation "abnormal," in order to avoid taking part in slaughter. The My Lai survivor, who did not fire at My Lai, was heard muttering during the killing, "It's wrong, it's wrong." But he had long been "maladjusted" to the combat situation—not in the sense of being unable or unwilling to fight, as he believed in his country and was a soldier of outstanding size, strength, and ability—but in his mounting disapproval of the way the men in his unit were treating the Vietnamese, and his increasing alienation from them on that basis. Well before My Lai he had reached the point where "I often got along better with the Vietnamese than with the guys in my outfit."

While it is difficult to know exactly why he was able to join the handful of men who stepped out of the norm and did not participate in the firing, three long-standing psychological patterns seemed significant. First, he had sensi-

---

*Gershen describes the men in Charlie Company whom he visited more than eighteen months after My Lai, as "frightened, conscience-stricken, terrified kids." One of them "still sees bodies in front of his eyes at night," another "feels terribly guilt-ridden," two more "have had nervous breakdowns," and at least four have difficulty finding or holding or concentrating at jobs. Nor did refraining from killing at My Lai prevent one from feeling guilty later on, as in the case of the man we have been referring to as the My Lai survivor.

tive access to guilt on the basis of particularly strong feelings of right and wrong imbued by family and by protracted Catholic religious training. Second, his lifelong inclination to be a loner, to engage in activities that kept him both physically and psychically separated from others, helped him to maintain a certain degree of autonomy from group influence and from the atrocity-producing situation itself. Third, he had an unusually strong sense of military pride and identification, a form of warrior ethos stressing honor; in Vietnam, and especially at My Lai, he felt both the code and himself to be violated.

After My Lai, he was further isolated from the others by his sense of disappointment in the few men he had been close to: "I'd seen people I thought I could depend on . . . that were going ahead and shooting, shooting people up like that." By joining in, in other words, his friends had failed to give further support or reality—had, in Buber's sense, failed to "confirm" him in his own autonomous stand. Moreover, such were the group pressures that the few others who apparently did not fire tended to hide that fact. As one man, who concentrated on killing animals in order to avoid shooting at people explained:

I didn't do it [kill people]. But nobody saw me not doing it. So nobody got on me.[39]

As the only one in his unit publicly identified with opposition to My Lai, he felt himself somewhat ostracized. This made him uneasy, and he was himself sufficiently sensitive to group pressures to speak cautiously about the event and hide much of his revulsion. Moreover, all this, and the continuing "as-if logic" and illusion surrounding the event, caused him to experience strong doubts about his own critical views. Eight months later, just before leaving Vietnam, he encountered Ronald Ridenhour, an acquaintance (from earlier days in the unit) who had not been at My Lai but had heard stories of the slaughter and was gathering information for his eventual exposure of the incident to the American public. The My Lai survivor spoke to Ridenhour at length, contributed much to that store of information, and at the same time experienced great personal relief. For the encounter convinced him that

I wasn't the only nut. . . . I wasn't really crazy. [Condemning what happened] was the right thing.

He was finally confirmed in his own previously isolated ethical imagery. Yet his words ("I wasn't the *only* nut") suggest that even then he was by no means fully liberated from the inverted morality—and inverted sanity (he still had a partial image of the rest of the men as the sane ones and Ridenhour and himself as the "nuts")—of the My Lai illusion.

A key to understanding the psychology of My Lai, and of America in Vietnam, is the body count. Nothing else so well epitomized the war's absurdity and evil. Recording the enemy's losses is a convention of war, but in the absence of any other goals or criteria for success, counting the enemy dead can become both malignant obsession and complusive falsification. For the combat GI in Vietnam killing Vietnamese was the entire mission, the number killed his and his unit's only standard of achievement, and the falsification of that count (on many levels) the only way to hold on to the Vietnam illusion of noble battle. Killing *someone*, moreover, became necessary for overcoming one's own death anxiety. We have seen how, at My Lai, killing Vietnamese enabled men to cease feeling themselves guilty survivors and impotent targets, and become instead omnipotent dispensers of death who have realized their mission. Only killing, then, can affirm power, skill, and worth.

In the end, Charlie Company was credited with only 14 of the 128 "kills," and the majority of these attributed to "artillery fire" as a way of giving the incident a greater aura of combat. The official report referred to "contact with the enemy force," and the colonel in command of the task force was quoted as saying that "the combat assault went like clockwork."[40] We may thus say that the body count serves the psychological function of making concrete the whole illusionary system; it is the locus of falsification.

One learns more about this phenomenon from other impressions of how the bodies were counted. The My Lai survivor told me that the prevailing standard was:

The ones that could walk they counted as bodies. The ones that couldn't walk they counted as, you know, sort of, they didn't count them. Because they couldn't have been Vietcong. They thought about this later.

He went on to say that he had heard talk of a body count of over 300 (undoubtedly the early count made by Medina) and was never clear about why it was reduced to 128. But the distinctions he describes, the informal attempts to impose a standard according to which one counts some bodies and not others, all this suggests the need to hold on to fragmentary aspects of actuality and logic in the service of the larger illusion.

Needless to say, these standards varied greatly. I heard descriptions of totals inflated in every conceivable way: by counting severed pieces of corpses as individual bodies; by counting a whole corpse several times on the basis of multiple claims for credit (by the man or unit doing the killing, the patrol encountering the body, the headquarters outfit hearing about the killing, etcetera); and by counting murdered civilians, animals, or nonexistent bodies according to the kinds of needs, ambition, and whim we have already encountered. Once a corpse has been identified (or imagined) it *becomes* that of a slain "enemy," and, therefore, evidence of warrior prowess—as the My Lai survivor makes clear:

If it's dead it's VC. Because it's dead. If it's dead it *had* to be VC. And of course a corpse couldn't defend itself.

He went on to place the body count into a frame of corrupt competitiveness—a company commander "obsessed with the body count" who "wanted a body count that would just beat all," that would "satisfy him . . . [and] satisfy higher headquarters . . . even if he knows this body count is a big dirty old lie." For, "Probably higher headquarters knows also. So they're fooling each other and theirselves as well." The whole thing, as he goes on to explain, resembles a cheater's golf game:

There was A Company over on the other side. They were counting bodies too. . . . He [the Company Commander] did sort of envy those people counting their bodies, keeping score. . . . Expressing sort of a disbelief that they had actually got that many. Which is like playing golf with somebody and carrying your own strokes and having some guy say, "I'm on [the green] in three." "You're on in *three?*" If it didn't matter to you how many *you* were on in, it wouldn't matter to you how many *he* was on in.

I am convinced that the ethically sensitive historians of the future will select the phenomenon of the body count as the perfect symbol of America's descent into evil. The body count manages to distill the essence of the American numbing, brutalization, and illusion into a grotesque technicalization: there is something to count, a statistic for accomplishment. I know of no greater corruption than this phenomenon: The amount of killing—any killing—becomes the total measure of achievement. Concerning that measure one lies, to others as well as to oneself, about why, who, what, and how many one kills.

In earlier work, I found that survivors of the Hiroshima holocaust experienced what I described as "a vast breakdown of faith in the larger human matrix supporting each individual life, and therefore a loss of faith (or trust) in the structure of existence." The same is true not only for large numbers of Vietnam veterans but, perhaps in more indirect and muted ways, for Americans in general. This shattered existential faith has to do with remaining bound by the image of holocaust, of grotesque and absurd death and equally absurd survival. Even Americans who did not see Vietnam felt something of a national descent into existential evil, a sense that the killing and dying done in their name could not be placed within a meaningful system of symbols, could not be convincingly formulated. The result was widespread if, again, vague feeling of lost integrity at times approaching moral-psychological disintegration.

What distinguishes Vietnam veterans from the rest of their countrymen is their awesome experience and knowledge of what others merely sense and resist knowing, their suffering on the basis of that knowledge and experience, and, in the case of antiwar veterans, their commitment to telling the tale. That commitment, especially for rap group participants, meant asking a question very much like that of Remarque's hero in *All Quiet on the Western Front*: "What would become of us if everything that happens out there were quite clear to us?" "Out there" means Vietnam, their own minds, and in the end, American society as well.

By a number of criteria, the group I have worked with represents a small minority of Vietnam veterans. For one thing, most saw active combat, as opposed to the majority of men stationed there in support assignments. For another, they emerged with an articulate antiwar position, in contrast to the majority who take no public stance on the war, and to another minority who emerged strongly supporting it. Concerning the first issue, my impression was that the intensity of residual conflicts were roughly parallel to one's degree of involvement in (or closeness to) combat, but that the sense of absurd evil radiated outward from the actual killing and dying, and that every American in Vietnam shared in some of the corruption of that environment. Hence Polner found that no Vietnam veteran was free of doubt about what he had been called upon to do.

Similarly, even those who later came to insist that we should have gone all-out to win the war—should have "nuked Hanoi" or "killed all the gooks"—have struggled to cope with their confusions and give some kind of form and significance to their survival. There is much evidence that antiwar and prowar veterans (the categories are misleading, and the latter hardly exists in a public sense) have been much closer psychologically than might be suspected—or to put the matter another way, have taken different paths in struggling to resolve the same psychological conflicts. Clearly the great majority of Vietnam veterans have struggled silently, and apolitically, with that specific constellation of survivor conflict associated with Vietnam's atrocity-producing situation. So that one antiwar veteran could comment:

I hear a lot of people say, "We know Vietnam veterans and they don't feel the way you do." My immediate reaction to that is, "Wait and see. If they are lucky they will. If they are lucky, they will open up."[41]

NOTES

1. Quotations are from report on Vietnam Era Veterans contained in Appendix to Chief Medical Director's letter of December 22, 1970, Veterans Administration, Department of Medicine and Surgery, Washington, D.C. See also *The Unique Problems of the Vietnam Era Veterans Workshop*, VA Hospital, New Orleans, La., October 8–9, 1970, ms; *The Vietnam Veteran: Challenge for Change—Administrative Seminars in Five Cities*, Washington: Veterans Administration, U.S. Government Printing Office, 1972; *The Vietnam Veteran in Contemporary Society: Collected Materials Pertaining to the Young Veterans*, VA Department of Medicine and Surgery, U.S. Government Printing Office, 1972; and Marc J. Musser and Charles A. Stenger, "A Medical and Social Perception of the Vietnam Veteran," *Bulletin of New York Academy of Medicine*, Vol. 48, July 1972, pp. 859–869.

2. Erik Erikson, *Identity: Youth and Crisis*, New York: Norton, 1968, p. 17.

3. Murray Polner, *No Victory Parades: The Return of the Vietnam Veteran*, New York: Holt, Rinehart and Winston, 1971.

4. "The Vietnam Veteran: Characteristics and Needs," Marcul R. Stuen, M.D. [VA Hospital, American Lake, Tacoma, Wash.], and Kristen B. Solberg [VA Hospital, Fort Meade, S.D.], mimeo, for observations made from 1968 through 1971.

5. Erich Maria Remarque, *All Quiet on the Western Front*, Fawcett Crest Books, Greenwich, 1958, p. 83.

6. Lifton, "America in Vietnam: The Counterfeit Friend," in *History and Human Survival*, New York: Random House, 1970, pp. 210–37.

7. Appendix 2, Veterans Administration Memorandum from Chief Medical Director, December 22, 1970, ILIO-70-95, p. A-11.

8. Johan Huizinga, *Homo Ludens: A Study of the Play Element in Culture*, Boston: Beacon Paperback, 1955, p. 91.

9. Seymour M. Hersh, *My Lai 4: A Report on the Massacre and Its Aftermath*, New York: Random House, 1970, and *Cover-Up: The Army's Secret Investigation of the Massacre at My Lai 4*, New York: Random House, 1972; Richard Hammer, *One Morning in the War: The Tragedy at Son My*, New York: Coward-McCann, 1970, and *The Court-Martial of Lt. Calley*, New York: Coward-McCann and Geoghegan, 1971; Martin Gershen, *Destroy or Die: The True Story of Mylai*, New Rochelle, N.Y.: Arlington House, 1971; *Lieutenant Calley: His Own Story, As Told to John Sack*, New York: Viking, 1971; and Arthur Everett, Kathryn Johnson, and Harry F. Rosenthal, *Calley*, New York: Dell, 1971.

10. W. Barry Gault ("Some Remarks on Slaughter," *American Journal of Psychiatry*, October 1971, Vol. 128, pp. 450–54) used this term in his thoughtful discussion of factors that led to atrocity in Vietnam. His ideas both blend with and extend my own earlier observations.

11. Vietnam Veterans Against the War, *The Winter Soldier Investigation: An Inquiry into American War Crimes*, Boston: Beacon Press, 1972, p. 5.

12. Robert Butow, *Japan's Decision to Surrender*, Stanford, 1954.

13. *Winter Soldier Investigation*, p. 6.

14. Richard A. Falk et al., *Crimes of War: A Legal, Political-Documentary, and Psychological Inquiry into the Responsibility of Leaders, Citizens, and Soldiers for Criminal Acts in Wars*, New York: Random House, 1971.

15. This and all previous quotations in this paragraph are from Peter Bourne, "From Boot Camp to My Lai," in *Crimes of War*, pp. 462–68.

16. Hersh, *My Lai 4*, p. 11.

17. Ibid., p. 23.

18. Gershen, p. 186.

19. Ibid., pp. 186–92 (includes quotations in following sentence).

20. See Lifton, *Death in Life*, discussion of "the survivor," pp. 479–539.

21. Last two quotations, Gershen, pp. 208–09.

22. Charles J. Levy, "ARVN as Faggots," *Transaction*, October 1971, pp. 18–27, 23.

23. Gershen, p. 288.

24. *My Lai 4*, pp. 40–41.

25. Hersh, "Cover-Up," *New Yorker*, January 22, 1971, p. 54.

26. Gershen, p. 290.

27. Documented in Hammer, *One Morning in the War*; and Hersh, *Cover-Up*.

28. Gershen, p. 28.

29. Ibid., pp. 37–38.

30. Ibid., p. 297.

31. *My Lai 4*, p. 187.

32. Interview by Jerry Samuels with former GI, transcript from Canadian Broadcasting Corporation program, "Ideas," July 1971, p. 16.

33. Gershen, p. 47.

34. Ibid., p. 43.

35. Ibid., p. 45.

36. Ibid., p. 24.

37. *The Court-Martial of Lt. Calley*, p. 161.

38. Gershen, p. 17.

39. Ibid., p. 31.

40. *Cover-Up, The New Yorker*, January 22, 1971, pp. 76, 79, and in Random House Book.

41. Statement by Arthur Egendorf, American Orthopsychiatric Association meeting, Washington, D.C., April 1971, transcript. pp. 19–20.

18

THE NARCISSISTIC PERSONALITY
OF OUR TIME

CHRISTOPHER LASCH

The last essay in this collection closes a circle in the sense that it returns us to the dread that entranced the Puritan villagers of seventeenth-century Salem: if self-indulgence is endemic to our (fallen) nature, at what point does it become an evil; and if change can befuddle and even anger us, when do our adaptive devices become symptomatic of sickness themselves? In many ways Christopher Lasch's *The Culture of Narcissism* (1979) does read like the sermons of Samuel Parrish, the Salem minister who warned his listeners that the devil's hand was visible in their everyday lives. Today's cult of intimacy, Lasch charges, does not champion personality so much as testify to its collapse. Poets and novelists, rather than glorifying the self, speak to its disintegration. "Our society," he writes in the chapter preceding the one excerpted below, "far from fostering public life at the expense of the private life, has made deep and lasting friendships, love affairs, and marriages increasingly difficult to achieve. As social life becomes more and more warlike and barbaric, personal relationships, which ostensibly provide relief from these conditions, take on the character of combat." "The quintessential doomsday book," Paul Zweig said in *Harper's* magazine (July 1979), referring to Lasch's study, "one hopes its very Germanic throughness will explode the genre."

People traditionally turn deaf ears to jeremiads, and critics of Lasch have noted—essays in this anthology underscore the point—that individualism is as American as apple pie, ambivalence about its costs inviting psychological treatment of issues as superficially different as the career of Jonathan Edwards, reform in the 1840s, and Populism. Moreover everyone agrees that a classic conflict in Western history has been the tension between the individual and society at large. If one finds narcissism in America today it may only mark a tip toward one end of an ancient set of scales, and we should be grateful for being comparatively free to strike a balance between individual will and communal needs. Thus on quick examination Lasch seems either to find what has always been noteworthy in American life or to excoriate the free expression that we rightly cherish. Other objections are more prosaic. Central to Lasch's argument is an increase in the number of clinical narcissists in the past twenty years or so, but statistics are not entirely trustworthy. In any case, our suddenly becoming aware of the narcissistic syndrome may both lead therapists to label as narcissistic patients who earlier would have been treated as something else and produce patients who describe themselves as suffering from the narcissism now in vogue.

Lasch's essay nonetheless repays close attention. For one thing it recapitulates several issues that this collection has touched upon and aimed to illuminate. Because empirical evidence on narcissism is weak and because clinical diagnoses are inherently subjective, Lasch reminds us that—although psychohistorical findings rarely grow out of "hard" data as do those of new politicial history—the most provocative questions often do not lend themselves to such measurement. Too, he addresses directly the relationship between self and society, in fact redirecting the usual view that society imprints personality; criticism of contemporary American culture, he says, must begin with individual pathology. Lasch goes on to demonstrate that attention to theoretical precision carries the discussion of narcissism far beyond mere references to self-love or individualism. Once more, the lesson is that theory and clinical experience give interesting perspectives and produce new historical questions. The essence of narcissism, according to Freud, is not self-love but disguised self-contempt; relying on the most recent clinical writings of Otto Kernberg, Lasch notes that narcissists, instead of exhibiting the sharply defined symptoms of earlier patients, complain of ill-defined dissatisfactions, and that instead of repressing the impulses that nineteenth-century culture forbade, narcissists "act them out." Narcissism, neither just another neurosis nor simple self-indulgence, offers a highly revealing comparative view of value shifts in recent American life.

Furthermore, since Lasch's essay raises serious questions about recent American history (and its course in the late twentieth century), it asks us to think about the responsibilities that students of history bear and the value of historical understanding or an appreciation for continuity in our lives. Historians write from the available evidence and adhere to rules of logic. They also speak to problems of interest to them and from the vantage point of their own society. Without simply moralizing, students of history therefore do well, and stand uniquely prepared, to consider the consequences of human acts in the past and the alternatives for the future—to be "moral critics," in John Higham's phrase. The essays of Lifton and Lasch (one a clinician, the other a historian) suggest that psychologically informed history can cast especially penetrating glances back from the historical subject to the society from which we take our look. Finally, if today narcissism is indeed the prevailing malady of men and women who seek therapeutic help, it is worth noting that the study of history supplies at least one hope—a sense of continuity to offset the impersonality and shallowness that pervade popular culture.

RECENT CRITICS of the new narcissism not only confuse cause and effect, attributing to a cult of privatism developments that derive from the disintegration of public life; they use the term narcissism so loosely that it retains little of its psychological content. Erich Fromm, in *The Heart of Man*, drains the idea of its clinical meaning and expands it to cover all forms of "vanity," "self-admiration," "self-satisfaction," and "self-glorification" in individuals and all forms of parochialism, ethnic or racial prejudice, and "fanaticism" in groups. In other words, Fromm uses the term as a synonym for the "asocial" individualism which, in his version of progressive and "humanistic" dogma, undermines cooperation, brotherly love, and the search for wider loyalties. Narcissism thus appears simply as the antithesis of that watery love for humanity (disinterested "love for the stranger") advocated by Fromm under the name of socialism.

Fromm's discussion of "individual and social narcissism," appropriately published in a series of books devoted to "Religious Perspectives," provides an excellent example of the inclination, in our therapeutic age, to dress up moralistic platitudes in psychiatric garb. ("We live in a historical period characterized by a sharp discrepancy between the intellectual development of man . . . and his mental-emotional development, which has left him still in a state of marked narcissism with all its pathological symptoms.") Richard Sennett reminds us that narcissism has more in common with self-hatred than with self-admiration; Fromm loses sight even of this well-known clinical fact in his eagerness to sermonize about the blessings of brotherly love.[1]

As always in Fromm's work, the trouble originates in his misguided and unnecessary attempt to rescue Freud's thought from its "mechanistic" nineteenth-century basis and to press it into the service of "humanistic realism." In practice, this means that theoretical rigor gives way to ethically uplifting slogans and sentiments. Fromm notes in passing that Freud's original concept of narcissism assumed that libido begins in the ego, as a "great reservoir" of undifferentiated self-love, whereas in 1922 he decided, on the contrary, that "we must recognize the id as the great reservoir of the libido."[2] Fromm slides over this issue, however, by remarking, "The theoretical question whether the libido starts originally in the ego or in the id is of no substantial importance for the meaning of the concept [of narcissism] itself." In fact, the structural theory of the mind, set forth by Freud in *Group Psychology* and in *The Ego and the Id*, required modifications of his earlier ideas that have a great deal of bearing on the theory of narcissism. Structural theory made Freud abandon the simple dichotomy between instinct and consciousness and recognize the unconscious elements of the ego and superego, the importance of nonsexual impulses (aggression or the "death instinct"), and the alliance between superego and id, superego and aggression. These discoveries in turn made possible an understanding of the role of object relations in the development of narcissism, thereby revealing narcissism as essentially a defense against aggressive impulses rather than self-love.

Theoretical precision about narcissism is important not only because the idea is so readily susceptible to moralistic inflation but because the practice of equating narcissism with everything selfish and disagreeable militates against historical specificity. Men have always been selfish, groups have always been

388 CHRISTOPHER LASCH

ethnocentric; nothing is gained by giving these qualities a psychiatric label. The emergence of character disorders as the most prominent form of psychiatric pathology, however, together with the change in personality structure this development reflects, derives from quite specific changes in our society and culture—from bureaucracy, the proliferation of images, therapeutic ideologies, the rationalization of the inner life, the cult of consumption, and in the last analysis from changes in family life and from changing patterns of socialization. All this disappears from sight if narcissism becomes simply "the metaphor of the human condition," as in another existential, humanistic interpretation, Shirley Sugerman's *Sin and Madness: Studies in Narcissism.* [3]

The refusal of recent critics of narcissism to discuss the etiology of narcissism or to pay much attention to the growing body of clinical writing on the subject probably represents a deliberate decision, stemming from the fear that emphasis on the clinical aspects of the narcissistic syndrome would detract from the concept's usefulness in social analysis. This decision, however, has proved to be a mistake. In ignoring the psychological dimension, these authors also miss the social. They fail to explore any of the character traits associated with pathological narcissism, which in less extreme form appear in such profusion in the everyday life of our age: dependence on the vicarious warmth provided by others combined with a fear of dependence, a sense of inner emptiness, boundless repressed rage, and unsatisfied oral cravings. Nor do they discuss what might be called the secondary characteristics of narcissism: pseudo self-insight, calculating seductiveness, nervous, self-deprecatory humor. Thus they deprive themselves of any basis on which to make connections between the narcissistic personality type and certain characteristic patterns of contemporary culture, such as the intense fear of old age and death, altered sense of time, fascination with celebrity, fear of competition, decline of the play spirit, deteriorating relations between men and women. For these critics, narcissism remains at its loosest a synonym for selfishness and at its most precise a metaphor, and nothing more, that describes the state of mind in which the world appears as a mirror of the self.

Psychology and Sociology

Psychoanalysis deals with individuals, not with groups. Efforts to generalize clinical findings to collective behavior always encounter the difficulty that groups have a life of their own. The collective mind, if there is such a thing, reflects the needs of the group as a whole, not the psychic needs of the individual, which in fact have to be subordinated to the demands of collective living. Indeed it is precisely the subjection of individuals to the group that psychoanalytic theory, through a study of its psychic repercussions, promises to clarify. By conducting an intensive analysis of individual cases that rests on clinical evidence rather than common-sense impressions, psychoanalysis tells us something about the inner workings of society itself, in the very act of turning its back on society and immersing itself in the individual unconscious.

Every society reproduces its culture—its norms, its underlying assumptions, its modes of organizing experience—in the individual, in the form of personality. As Durkheim said, personality is the individual socialized. The process of socialization, carried out by the family and secondarily by the school and other agencies of character formation, modifies human nature to conform to the prevailing social norms. Each society tries to solve the universal crises of childhood—the trauma of separation from the mother, the fear of abandonment, the pain of competing with others for the mother's love—in its own way, and the manner in which it deals with these psychic events produces a characteristic form of personality, a characteristic form of psychological deformation, by means of which the individual reconciles himself to instinctual deprivation and submits to the requirements of social existence. Freud's insistence on the continuity between psychic health and psychic sickness makes it possible to see neuroses and psychoses as in some sense the characteristic expression of a given culture. "Psychosis," Jules Henry has written, "is the final outcome of all that is wrong with a culture."[4]

Psychoanalysis best clarifies the connection between society and the individual, culture and personality, precisely when it confines itself to careful examination of individuals. It tells us most about society when it is least determined to do so. Freud's extrapolation of psychoanalytic principles into anthropology, history, and biography can be safely ignored by the student of society, but his clinical investigations constitute a storehouse of indispensable ideas, once it is understood that the unconscious mind represents the modification of nature by culture, the imposition of civilization on instinct.

Freud should not be reproached [wrote T. W. Adorno] for having neglected the concrete social dimension, but for being all too untroubled by the social origin of . . . the rigidity of the unconscious, which he registers with the undeviating objectivity of the natural scientist. . . . In making the leap from psychological images to historical reality, he forgets what he himself discovered—that all reality undergoes modification upon entering the unconscious—and is thus misled into positing such factual events as the murder of the father by the primal horde.*[5]

*"On . . . its home ground," Adorno added, "psychoanalysis carries specific conviction; the further it removes itself from that sphere, the more its theses are threatened alternately with shallowness or wild over-systematization. If someone makes a slip of the tongue and a sexually loaded word comes out, if someone suffers from agoraphobia or if a girl walks in her sleep, psychoanalysis not merely has its best chances of therapeutic success but also its proper province, the relatively autonomous, monadological individual as arena of the unconscious conflict between instinctual drive and prohibition. The further it departs from this area, the more tyrannically it has to proceed and the more it has to drag what belongs to the dimension of outer reality into the shades of psychic immanence. Its delusion in so doing is not dissimilar from that 'omnipotence of thought' which it itself criticized as infantile."

Those who wish to understand contemporary narcissism as a social and cultural phenomenon must turn first to the growing body of clinical writing on the subject, which makes no claim to social or cultural significance and deliberately repudiates the proposition that "changes in contemporary culture," as Otto Kernberg writes, "have effects on patterns of object relations."*[6] In the clinical literature, narcissism serves as more than a metaphoric term for self-absorption. As a psychic formation in which "love rejected turns back to the self as hatred," narcissism has come to be recognized as an important element in the so-called character disorders that have absorbed much of the clinical attention once given to hysteria and obsessional neuroses.[7] A new theory of narcissism has developed, grounded in Freud's well-known essay on the subject (which treats narcissism—libidinal investment of the self—as a necessary precondition of object love) but devoted not to primary narcissism but to secondary or pathological narcissim: the incorporation of grandiose object images as a defense against anxiety and guilt. Both types of narcissism blur the boundaries between the self and the world of objects, but there is an important difference between them. The newborn infant—the primary narcissist—does not yet perceive his mother as having an existence separate from his own, and he therefore mistakes dependence on the mother, who satisfies his needs as soon as they arise, with his own omnipotence. "It takes several weeks of postnatal development . . . before the infant perceives that the source of his need . . . is within and the source of gratification is outside the self."[8]

Secondary narcissism, on the other hand, "attempts to annul the pain of disappointed [object] love" and to nullify the child's rage against those who do not respond immediately to his needs; against those who are now seen to respond to others beside the child and who therefore appear to have abandoned him.[9] Pathological narcissism, "which cannot be considered simply a fixation at the level of normal primitive narcissism,"[10] arises only when the ego has developed to the point of distinguishing itself from surrounding objects. If the child for some reason experiences this separation trauma with special intensity, he may attempt to reestablish earlier relationships by creating in his fantasies an omnipotent mother or father who merges with images of his own self. "Through internalization the patient seeks to recreate a wished-for

---

*Those who argue, in opposition to the thesis of the present study, that there has been no underlying change in the structure of personality, cite this passage to support the contention that although "we do see certain symptom constellations and personality disorders more or less frequently than in Freud's day, . . . this shift in attention has occurred primarily because of a shift in our clinical emphasis due to tremendous advances in our understanding of personality structure."

In light of this controversy, it is important to note that Kernberg adds to his observation a qualification: "This is not to say that such changes in the patterns of intimacy [and of object relations in general] could not occur over a period of several generations, if and when changes in cultural patterns affect family structure to such an extent that the earliest development in childhood would be influenced."

love relationship which may once have existed and simultaneously to annul the anxiety and guilt aroused by aggressive drives directed against the frustrating and disappointing object."[11]

Narcissism in Recent Clinical Literature

The shifting emphasis in clinical studies from primary to secondary narcissism[12] reflects both the shift in psychoanalytic theory from study of the id to study of the ego and a change in the type of patients seeking psychiatric treatment. Indeed the shift from a psychology of instincts to ego psychology itself grew partly out of a recognition that the patients who began to present themselves for treatment in the 1940s and 1950s "very seldom resembled the classical neuroses Freud described so thoroughly." In the last twenty-five years, the borderline patient, who confronts the psychiatrist not with well-defined symptoms but with diffuse dissatisfactions, has become increasingly common. He does not suffer from debilitating fixations or phobias or from the conversion of repressed sexual energy into nervous ailments; instead he complains "of vague, diffuse dissatisfactions with life" and feels his "amorphous existence to be futile and purposeless." He describes "subtly experienced yet pervasive feelings of emptiness and depression," "violent oscillations of self-esteem," and "a general inability to get along." He gains "a sense of heightened self-esteem only by attaching himself to strong, admired figures whose acceptance he craves and by whom he needs to feel supported." Although he carries out his daily responsibilities and even achieves distinction, happiness eludes him, and life frequently strikes him as not worth living.

Psychoanalysis, a therapy that grew out of experience with severely repressed and morally rigid individuals who needed to come to terms with a rigorous inner "censor," today finds itself confronted more and more often with a "chaotic and impulse-ridden character." It must deal with patients who "act out" their conflicts instead of repressing or sublimating them. These patients, though often ingratiating, tend to cultivate a protective shallowness in emotional relations. They lack the capacity to mourn, because the intensity of their rage against lost love objects, in particular against their parents, prevents their reliving happy experiences or treasuring them in memory. Sexually promiscuous rather than repressed, they nevertheless find it difficult to "elaborate the sexual impulse" or to approach sex in the spirit of play. They avoid close involvements, which might release intense feelings of rage. Their personalities consist largely of defenses against this rage and against feelings of oral deprivation that originate in the pre-oedipal stage of psychic development.[13]

Often these patients suffer from hypochondria and complain of a sense of inner emptiness. At the same time they entertain fantasies of omnipotence and a strong belief in their right to exploit others and be gratified. Archaic, punitive, and sadistic elements predominate in the superegos of these patients, and they conform to social rules more out of fear of punishment than from a sense of guilt. They experience their own needs and appetites, suffused with rage, as deeply dangerous, and they throw up defenses that are as primitive as the desires they seek to stifle.

On the principle that pathology represents a heightened version of normality, the "pathological narcissism" found in character disorders of this type should tell us something about narcissism as a social phenomenon. Studies of personality disorders that occupy the border line[14] between neurosis and psychosis, though written for clinicans and making no claims to shed light on social or cultural issues, depict a type of personality that ought to be immediately recognizable, in a more subdued form, to observers of the contemporary cultural scene: facile at managing the impressions he gives to others, ravenous for admiration but contemptuous of those he manipulates into providing it; unappeasably hungry for emotional experiences with which to fill an inner void; terrified of aging and death.

The most convincing explanations of the psychic origins of this borderline syndrome draw on the theoretical tradition established by Melanie Klein. In her psychoanalytic investigations of children, Klein discovered that early feelings of overpowering rage, directed especially against the mother and secondarily against the internalized image of the mother as a ravenous monster, make it impossible for the child to synthesize "good" and "bad" parental images. In his fear of aggression from the bad parents—projections of his own rage—he idealizes the good parents who will come to the rescue.

Internalized images of others, buried in the unconscious mind at an early age, become self-images as well. If later experience fails to qualify or to introduce elements of reality into the child's archaic fantasies about his parents, he finds it difficult to distinguish between images of the self and of the objects outside the self. These images fuse to form a defense against the bad representations of the self and of objects, similarly fused in the form of a harsh, punishing superego. Melanie Klein analyzed a ten-year-old boy who unconsciously thought of his mother as a "vampire" or "horrid bird" and interalized this fear as hypochondria. He was afraid that the bad presences inside him would devour the good ones. The rigid separation of good and bad images of the self and of objects, on the one hand, and the fusion of self- and object images on the other, arose from the boy's inability to tolerate ambivalence or anxiety. Because his anger was so intense, he could not admit that he harbored aggressive feelings toward those he loved. "Fear and guilt relating to his destructive phantasies moulded his whole emotional life."[15]

A child who feels so gravely threatened by his own aggressive feelings (projected onto others and then internalized again as inner "monsters") attempts to compensate himself for his experiences of rage and envy with fantasies of wealth, beauty, and omnipotence. These fantasies, together with the internalized images of the good parents with which he attempts to defend himself, become the core of a "grandiose conception of the self." A kind of "blind optimism," according to Otto Kernberg, protects the narcissistic child from the dangers around and within him—particularly from dependence on others, who are perceived as without exception undependable. "Constant projection of 'all bad' self and object images perpetuates a world of danger-ous, threatening objects, against which the 'all good' self images are used defensively, and megalomanic ideal self images are built up." The splitting of images determined by aggressive feelings from images that derive from libid-inal impulses makes it impossible for the child to acknowledge his own aggression, to experience guilt or concern for objects invested simultaneously with aggression and libido, or to mourn for lost objects. Depression in narcis-sistic patients takes the form not of mourning with its admixture of guilt, described by Freud in "Mourning and Melancholia," but of impotent rage and "feelings of defeat by external forces."[16]

Because the intrapsychic world of these patients is so thinly populated—consisting only of the "grandiose self," in Kernberg's words, "the devalued, shadowy images of self and others, and potential persecutors"—they experi-ence intense feelings of emptiness and inauthenticity. Although the narcissist can function in the everyday world and often charms other people (not least with his "pseudo-insight into his personality"), his devaluation of others, together with his lack of curiosity about them, impoverishes his personal life and reinforces the "subjective experience of emptiness." Lacking any real intellectual engagement with the world—notwithstanding a frequently in-flated estimate of his own intellectual abilities—he has little capacity for sublimation. He therefore depends on others for constant infusions of ap-proval and admiration. He "must attach [himself] to someone, living an almost parasitic" existence. At the same time, his fear of emotional depen-dence, together with his manipulative, exploitive approach to personal rela-tions, makes these relations bland, superficial, and deeply unsatisfying. "The ideal relationship to me would be a two month relationship," said a border-line patient. "That way there'd be no commitment. At the end of the two months I'd just break it off."[17]

Chronically bored, restlessly in search of instantaneous intimacy—of emo-tional titillation without involvement and dependence—the narcissist is promiscuous and often pansexual as well, since the fusion of pregenital and Oedipal impulses in the service of aggression encourages polymorphous per-versity. The bad images he has internalized also make him chronically uneasy about his health, and hypochondria in turn gives him a special affinity for therapy and for therapeutic groups and movements.

As a psychiatric patient, the narcissist is a prime candidate for intermina-ble analysis. He seeks in analysis a religion or way of life and hopes to find in the therapeutic relationship external support for his fantasies of omnipotence and eternal youth. The strength of his defenses, however, makes him resistant to successful analysis. The shallowness of his emotional life often prevents him from developing a close connection to the analyst, even though he "often uses his intellectual insight to agree verbally with the analyst and recapitulates in his own words what has been analysed in previous sessions." He uses intellect in the service of evasion rather than self-discovery, resorting to some of the same strategies of obfuscation that appear in the confessional writing of recent decades. "The patient uses the analytic interpretations but deprives them quickly of life and meaning, so that only meaningless words are left. The words are then felt to be the patient's own possession, which he idealizes and which give him a sense of superiority." Although psychiatrists no longer consider narcissistic disorders inherently unanalyzable, few of them take an optimistic view of the prospects for success.

According to Kernberg, the great argument for making the attempt at all, in the face of the many difficulties presented by narcissistic patients, is the devastating effect of narcissism on the second half of their lives—the certainty of the terrible suffering that lies in store. In a society that dreads old age and death, aging holds a special terror for those who fear dependence and whose self-esteem requires the admiration usually reserved for youth, beauty, celebrity, or charm. The usual defenses against the ravages of age— identification with ethical or artistic values beyond one's immediate interests, intellectual curiosity, the consoling emotional warmth derived from happy relationships in the past—can do nothing for the narcissist. Unable to derive whatever comfort comes from identification with historical continuity, he finds it impossible, on the contrary, "to accept the fact that a younger generation now possesses many of the previously cherished gratifications of beauty, wealth, power and, particularly, creativity. To be able to enjoy life in a process involving a growing identification with other people's happiness and achievements is tragically beyond the capacity of narcissistic personalities."[18]

Social Influences on Narcissism

Every age develops its own peculiar forms of pathology, which express in exaggerated form its underlying character structure. In Freud's time, hysteria and obsessional neurosis carried to extremes the personality traits associated with the capitalist order at an earlier stage in its development— acquisitiveness, fanatical devotion to work, and a fierce repression of sexuality. In our time, the preschizophrenic, borderline, or personality disorders have attracted increasing attention, along with schizophrenia itself. This "change in the form of neuroses has been observed and described since World

War II by an ever-increasing number of psychiatrists." According to Peter L. Giovacchini, "Clinicians are constantly faced with the seemingly increasing number of patients who do not fit current diagnostic categories" and who suffer not from "definitive symptoms" but from "vague, ill-defined complaints." "When I refer to 'this type of patient,'" he writes, "practically everyone knows to whom I am referring." The growing prominence of "character disorders" seems to signify an underlying change in the organization of personality, from what has been called inner-direction to narcissism.

Allen Wheelis argued in 1958 that the change in "the patterns of neuroses" fell "within the personal experience of older psychoanalysts, " while younger ones "become aware of it from the discrepancy between the older descriptions of neuroses and the problems presented by the patients who come daily to their offices. The change is from symptom neuroses to character disorders." Heinz Lichtenstein, who questioned the additional assertion that it reflected a change in personality structure, nevertheless wrote in 1963 that the "change in neurotic patterns" already constituted a "well-known fact." In the seventies, such reports have become increasingly common. "It is no accident," Herbert Hendin notes, "that at the present time the dominant events in psychoanalysis are the rediscovery of narcissism and the new emphasis on the psychological significance of death." "What hysteria and the obsessive neuroses were to Freud and his early colleagues . . . at the beginning of this century," writes Michael Beldoch, "the narcissistic disorders are to the workaday analyst in these last few decades before the next millennium. Today's patients by and large do not suffer from hysterical paralyses of the legs or hand-washing compulsions; instead it is their very psychic selves that have gone numb or that they must scrub and rescrub in an exhausting and unending effort to come clean." These patients suffer from "pervasive feelings of emptiness and a deep disturbance of self-esteem." Burness E. Moore notes that narcissistic disorders have become more and more common. According to Sheldon Bach, "You used to see people coming in with hand-washing compulsions, phobias, and familiar neuroses. Now you see mostly narcissists." Gilbert J. Rose maintains that the psychoanalytic outlook, "inappropriately transplanted from analytic practice" to everyday life, has contributed to "global permissiveness" and the "over-domestication of instinct," which in turn contributes to the proliferation of "narcissistic identity disorders." According to Joel Kovel, the stimulation of infantile cravings by advertising, the usurpation of parental authority by the media and the school, and the rationalization of inner life accompanied by the false promise of personal fulfillment, have created a new type of "social individual." "The result is not the classical neuroses where an infantile impulse is suppressed by patriarchal authority, but a modern version in which impulse is stimulated, perverted and given neither an adequate object upon which to satisfy itself nor coherent forms of control. . . . The entire complex, played out in a setting of alienation rather than direct control, loses the classical form of symptom—and [misses] the classical therapeutic opportunity of simply restoring an impulse to consciousness."[19]

The reported increase in the number of narcissistic patients does not necessarily indicate that narcissistic disorders are more common than they used to be, in the population as a whole, or that they have become more common than the classical conversion neuroses. Perhaps they simply come more quickly to psychiatric attention. Ilza Veith contends that "with the increasing awareness of conversion reactions and the popularization of psychiatric literature, the 'old-fashioned' somatic expressions of hysteria have become suspect among the more sophisticated classes, and hence most physicians observe that obvious conversion symptoms are now rarely encountered and, if at all, only among the uneducated."[20] The attention given to character disorders in recent clinical literature probably makes psychiatrists more alert to their presence. But this possibility by no means diminishes the importance of psychiatric testimony about the prevalence of narcissism, especially when this testimony appears at the same time that journalists begin to speculate about the new narcissism and the unhealthy trend toward self-absorption. The narcissist comes to the attention of psychiatrists for some of the same reasons that he rises to positions of prominence not only in awareness movements and other cults but in business corporations, political organizations, and government bureaucracies. For all his inner suffering, the narcissist has many traits that make for success in bureaucratic institutions, which put a premium on the manipulation of interpersonal relations, discourage the formation of deep personal attachments, and at the same time provide the narcissist with the approval he needs in order to validate his self-esteem. Although he may resort to therapies that promise to give meaning to life and to overcome his sense of emptiness, in his professional career the narcissist often enjoys considerable success. The managment of personal impressions comes naturally to him, and his mastery of its intricacies serves him well in political and business organizations where performance now counts for less than "visibility," "momentum," and a winning record. As the "organization man" gives way to the bureaucratic "gamesman"—the "loyalty era" of American business to the age of the "executive success game"—the narcissist comes into his own.[21]

In a study of 250 managers from twelve major companies, Michael Maccoby describes the new corporate leader, not altogether unsympathetically, as a person who works with people rather than with materials and who seeks not to build an empire or accumulate wealth but to experience "the exhilaration of running his team and of gaining victories." He wants to "be known as a winner, and his deepest fear is to be labeled a loser." Instead of pitting himself against a material task or a problem demanding solution, he pits himself against others, out of a "need to be in control." As a recent textbook for managers puts it, success today means "not simply getting ahead" but "getting ahead of others." The new executive, boyish, playful, and "seductive," wants in Maccoby's words "to maintain an illusion of limitless options." He has little capacity for "personal intimacy and social commitment." He feels little loyalty even to the company for which he works. One executive says he experiences power "as not being pushed around by the company." In his upward climb, this man cultivates powerful customers and attempts to use them against his own company. "You need a very big customer," according to his calculations, "who is always in trouble and demands changes from the company. That way you automatically have power in the company, and with the customer too. I like to keep my options open." A professor of management endorses this strategy. "Overidentification" with the company, in his view, "produces a corporation with enormous power over the careers and destinies of its true believers." The bigger the company, the more important he thinks it is for executives "to manage their careers in terms of their own . . . free choices" and to "maintain the widest set of options possible."*[22]

According to Maccoby, the gamesman "is open to new ideas, but he lacks convictions." He will do business with any régime, even if he disapproves of its principles. More independent and resourceful than the company man, he tries to use the company for his own ends, fearing that otherwise he will be "totally emasculated by the corporation." He avoids intimacy as a trap, preferring the "exciting, sexy atmosphere" with which the modern executive surrounds himself at work, "where adoring, mini-skirted secretaries constantly flirt with him." In all his personal relations, the gamesman depends on the admiration or fear he inspires in others to certify his credentials as a "winner." As he gets older, he finds it more and more difficult to command the kind of attention on which he thrives. He reaches a plateau beyond which he does not advance in this job, perhaps because the very highest positions, as Maccoby notes, still go to "those able to renounce adolescent rebelliousness and become at least to some extent believers in the organization." The job begins to lose it savor. Having little interest in craftsmanship, the new-style executive takes no pleasure in his achievements once he begins to lose the adolescent charm on which they rest. Middle age hits him with the force of a disaster: "Once his youth, vigor, and even the thrill in winning are lost, he

---

*It is not only the gamesman who "fears feeling trapped." Seymour B. Sarason finds this feeling prevalent among professionals and students training for professional careers. He too suggests a connection between the fear of entrapment and the cultural value set on career mobility and its psychic equivalent, "personal growth." "'Stay loose,' 'keep your options open.' 'play it cool'—these cautions emerge from the feeling that society sets all kinds of booby traps that rob you of the freedom without which growth is impossible."

This fear of entrapment or stagnation is closely connected in turn with the fear of aging and death. The mobility mania and the cult of "growth" can themselves be seen, in part, as an expression of the fear of aging that has become so intense in American society. Mobility and growth assure the individual that he has not yet settled into the living death of old age.

becomes depressed and goalless, questioning the purpose of his life. No longer energized by the team struggle and unable to dedicate himself to something he believes in beyond himself, . . . he finds himself starkly alone." It is not surprising, given the prevalence of this career pattern, that popular psychology returns so often to the "midlife crisis" and to ways of combating it.

In Wilfrid Sheed's novel *Office Politics*, a wife asks, "There are real issues, aren't there, between Mr. Fine and Mr. Tyler?" Her husband answers that the issues are trivial; "the jockeying of ego is the real story." Eugene Emerson Jennings's study of management, which celebrates the demise of the organization man and the advent of the new "era of mobility," insists that corporate "mobility is more than mere job performance." What counts is "style . . . panache . . . the ability to say and do almost anything without antagonizing others." The upwardly mobile executive, according to Jennings, knows how to handle the people around him—the "shelf-sitter" who suffers from "arrested mobility" and envies success; the "fast learner"; the "mobile superior." The "mobility-bright executive" has learned to "read" the power relations in his office and "to see the less visible and less audible side of his superiors, chiefly their standing with their peers and superiors." He "can infer from a minimum of cues who are the centers of power, and he seeks to have high visibility and exposure with them. He will assiduously cultivate his standing and opportunities with them and seize every opportunity to learn from them. He will utilize his opportunities in the social world to size up the men who are centers of sponsorship in the corporate world."[24]

Constantly comparing the "executive success game" to an athletic contest or a game of chess, Jennings treats the substance of executive life as if it were just as arbitrary and irrelevant to success as the task of kicking a ball through a net or of moving pieces over a chessboard. He never mentions the social and economic repercussions of managerial decisions or the power that managers exercise over society as a whole. For the corporate manager on the make, power consists not of money and influence but of "momentum," a "winning image," a reputation as a winner. Power lies in the eye of the beholder and thus has no objective reference at all.* The manager's view of the world, as described by Jennings, Maccoby, and by the managers themselves, is that of the narcissist, who sees the world as a mirror of himself and has no interest in external events except as they throw back a reflection of his own image. The dense interpersonal environment of modern bureaucracy, in which work assumes an abstract quality almost wholly divorced from performance, by its very nature elicits and often rewards a narcissistic response.[25]

---

*Indeed it has no reference to anything outside the self. The new ideal of success has no content. "Performance means to arrive," says Jennings. Success equal success. Note the convergence between success in business and celebrity in politics or the world of entertainment, which also depends on "visibility" and "charisma" and can only be defined as itself. The only important attribute of celebrity is that it is celebrated; no one can say why.

Bureaucracy, however, is only one of a number of social influences that are bringing a narcissistic type of personality organization into greater and greater prominence. Another such influence is the mechanical reproduction of culture, the proliferation of visual and audial images in the "society of the spectacle." We live in a swirl of images and echoes that arrest experience and play it back in slow motion. Cameras and recording machines not only transcribe experience but alter its quality, giving to much of modern life the character of an enormous echo chamber, a hall of mirrors. Life presents itself as a succession of images or electronic signals, of impressions recorded and reproduced by means of photography, motion pictures, television, and sophisticated recording devices. Modern life is so thoroughly mediated by electronic images that we cannot help responding to others as if their actions—and our own—were being recorded and simultaneously transmitted to an unseen audience or stored up for close scrutiny at some later time. "Smile, you're on candid camera!" The intrusion into everyday life of this all-seeing eye no longer takes us by surprise or catches us with our defenses down. We need no reminder to smile. A smile is permanently graven on our features, and we already know from which of several angles it photographs to best advantage.

The proliferation of recorded images undermines our sense of reality. As Susan Sontag observes in her study of photography, "Reality has come to seem more and more like what we are shown by cameras." We distrust our perceptions until the camera verifies them. Photographic images provide us with the proof of our existence, without which we would find it difficult even to reconstruct a personal history. Bourgeois families in the eighteenth and nineteenth centuries, Sontag points out, posed for portraits in order to proclaim the family's status, whereas today the family album of photographs verifies the individual's existence: its documentary record of his development from infancy onward provides him with the only evidence of his life that he recognizes as altogether valid. Among the "many narcissistic uses" that Sontag attributes to the camera, "self-surveillance" ranks among the most important, not only because it provides the technical means of ceaseless self-scrutiny but because it renders the sense of selfhood dependent on the consumption of images of the self, at the same time calling into question the reality of the external world.[26]

By preserving images of the self at various stages of development, the camera helps to weaken the older idea of development as moral education and to promote a more passive idea according to which development consists of passing through the stages of life at the right time and in the right order. Current fascination with the life cycle embodies an awareness that success in politics or business depends on reaching certain goals on schedule; but it also reflects the ease with which development can be electronically recorded. This brings us to another cultural change that elicits a widespread narcissistic response and, in this case, gives it a philosophical sanction: the emergence of a therapeutic ideology that upholds a normative schedule of psychosocial development and thus gives further encouragement to anxious self-scrutiny. The ideal of normative development creates the fear that any deviation from the norm has a pathological source. Doctors have made a cult of the periodic checkup—an investigation carried out once again by means of cameras and other recording instruments—and have implanted in their clients the notion that health depends on eternal watchfulness and the early detection of symptoms, as verified by medical technology. The client no longer feels physically or psychologically secure until his X-rays confirm a "clean bill of health." Medicine and psychiatry—more generally, the therapeutic outlook and sensibility that pervade modern society—reinforce the pattern created by other cultural influences, in which the individual endlessly examines himself for signs of aging and ill health, for tell-tale symptoms of psychic stress, for blemishes and flaws that might diminish his attractiveness, or on the other hand for reassuring indications that his life is proceeding according to schedule. Modern medicine has conquered the plagues and epidemics that once made life so precarious, only to create new forms of insecurity.

In the same way, bureaucracy has made life predictable and even boring while reviving, in a new form, the war of all against all. Our overorganized society, in which large-scale organizations predominate but have lost the capacity to command allegiance, in some respects more nearly approximates a condition of universal anomosity than did the primitive capitalism on which Hobbes modeled his state of nature. Social conditions today encourage a survival mentality, expressed in its crudest form in disaster movies or in fantasies of space travel, which allow vicarious escape from a doomed planet. People no longer dream of overcoming difficulties but merely of surviving them. In business, according to Jennings, "The struggle is to survive emotionally"—to "preserve or enhance one's identity or ego."[27] The normative concept of developmental stages promotes a view of life as an obstacle course: the aim is simply to get through the course with a minimum of trouble and pain. The ability to manipulate what Gail Sheehy refers to, using a medical metaphor, as "life-support systems" now appears to represent the highest form of wisdom: the knowledge that gets us through, as she puts it, without panic. Those who master Sheehy's "no-panic approach to aging" and to the traumas of the life cycle will be able to say, in the words of one of her subjects, "I know I can survive . . . I don't panic any more." This is hardly an exalted form of satisfaction, however. "The current ideology," Sheehy writes, "seems a mix of personal survivalism, revivalism, and cynicism"; yet her enormously popular guide to the "predictable crises of adult life," with its superficially optimistic hymn to growth, development, and "self-actualization," does not challenge this ideology, merely restates it in more "humanistic" form. "Growth" has become a euphemism for survival.[28]

The World View of the Resigned

New social forms require new forms of personality, new modes of socialization, new ways of organizing experience. The concept of narcissism provides us not with a ready-made psychological determinism but with a way of understanding the psychological impact of recent social changes—assuming that we bear in mind not only its clinical orgins but the continuum between pathology and normality. It provides us, in other words, with a tolerably accurate portrait of the "liberated" personality of our time, with his charm, his pseudo-awareness of his own condition, his promiscuous pansexuality, his fascination with oral sex, his fear of the castrating mother (Mrs. Portnoy), his hypochondria, his protective shallowness, his avoidance of dependence, his inability to mourn, his dread of old age and death.

Narcissism appears realistically to represent the best way of coping with the tensions and anxieties of modern life, and the prevailing social conditions therefore tend to bring out narcissistic traits that are present, in varying degrees, in everyone. These conditions have also transformed the family, which in turn shapes the underlying structure of personality. A society that fears it has no future is not likely to give much attention to the needs of the next generation, and the ever-present sense of historical discontinuity—the blight of our society—falls with particularly devastating effect on the family. The modern parent's attempt to make children feel loved and wanted does not conceal an underlying coolness—the remoteness of those who have little to pass on to the next generation and who in any case give priority to their own right to self-fulfillment. The combination of emotional detachment with attempts to convince a child of his favored position in the family is a good prescription for a narcissistic personality structure.

Through the intermediary of the family, social patterns reproduce themselves in personality. Social arrangements live on in the individual, buried in the mind below the level of consciousness, even after they have become objectively undesirable and unnecessary—as many of our present arrangements are now widely acknowledged to have become. The perception of the world as a dangerous and forbidding place, though it originates in a realistic awareness of the insecurity of contemporary social life, receives reinforcement from the narcissistic projection of aggressive impulses outward. The belief that society has no future, while it rests on a certain realism about the dangers ahead, also incorporates a narcissistic inability to identify with posterity or to feel oneself part of a historical stream.

The weakening of social ties, which originates in the prevailing state of social warfare, at the same time reflects a narcissistic defense against dependence. A warlike society tends to produce men and women who are at heart antisocial. It should therefore not surprise us to find that although the narcissist conforms to social norms for fear of external retribution, he often thinks of himself as an outlaw and sees others in the same way, "as basically dishonest and unreliable, or only reliable because of external pressures." "The value systems of narcissistic personalities are generally corruptible," writes Kernberg, "in contrast to the rigid morality of the obsessive personality."[29]

The ethic of self-preservation and psychic survival is rooted, then, not merely in objective conditions of economic warfare, rising rates of crime, and social chaos but in the subjective experience of emptiness and isolation. It reflects the conviction—as much a projection of inner anxieties as a perception of the way things are—that envy and exploitation dominate even the most intimate relations. The cult of personal relations, which becomes increasingly intense as the hope of political solutions recedes, conceals a thoroughgoing disenchantment with personal relations, just as the cult of sensuality implies a repudiation of sensuality in all but its most primitive forms. The ideology of personal growth, superficially optimistic, radiates a profound despair and resignation. It is the faith of those without faith.

NOTES

1. Erich Fromm, *The Heart of Man: Its Genius for Good and Evil* (New York: Harper & Row, 1964, chapter 4; Richard Sennett, *The Fall of Public Man* (New York: Alfred A. Knopf, 1977), p. 324.

2. Sigmund Freud, *Group Psychology and the analysis of the Ego* (1921), in James Strachey, ed., *The Standard Edition of the Complete Psychological Works of Sigmund Freud*, 24 vols. (London: Hogarth Press, 1955–64), 18:130.

3. Shirley Sugerman, *Sin and Madness: Studies in Narcissism* (Philadelphia: Westminster Press, 1976), p. 12.

4. Jules Henry, *Culture against Man* (New York: Alfred A. Knopf, 1963), p. 322.

5. T. W. Adorno, "Sociology and Psychology," *New Left Review*, no. 47 (1968), pp. 80, 96.

6. Otto Kernberg, *Borderline Conditions and Pathological Narcissism* (New York: Jason Aronson, 1975), p. 223.

7. Warren R. Brodley, "Image, Object, and Narcissistic Relationships," *American Journal of Orthopsychiatry* 31 (1961):505.

8. Therese Benedek, "Parenthood as a Developmental Phase," *Journal of the American Psychoanalytic Association* 7 (1959):389–90.

9. Thomas Freeman, "The Concept of Narcissism in Schizophrenic States," *International Journal of Psychoanalysis* 44 (1963):295.

10. Kernberg, *Borderline Conditions and Pathological Narcissism*, p. 283.

11. Freeman, "Concept of Narcissism in Schizophrenic States," p. 295.

12. On the distinction between primary and secondary narcissism and the characteristics of the latter, see also H. G. Van der Waals, "Problems of Narcissism," *Bulletin of the Menninger Clinic* 29 (1965):293–310; Warren M. Brodey, "On the Dynamics of Narcissism," *Psychoanalytic Study of the Child* 20 (1965):165–93; James F. Bing and Rudolph O. Marburg, "Narcissism," *Journal of the American Psychoanalytic Association* 10 (1962):593–605; Lester Schwartz, "Techniques and Prognosis in Treatment of the Narcissistic Personality," *Journal of the American Psychoanalytic Association* 21 (1973):617–32; Edith Jacobson, *The Self and the Object World* (New

York: International Universities Press, 1964), ch. 1, especially pp. 17-19; James F. Bing, Francis McLaughlin, and Rudolph Marburg, "The Metapsychology of Narcissism," *Psychoanalytic Study of the Child* 14 (1959):9-28; Freud's "On Narcissism: An Introduction" (1914) appears in *Standard Edition*, 3:30-59.

13. For more on the characteristics of character disorders, see Peter L. Giovachinni, *Psychoanalysis of Character Disorders* (New York: Jason Aronson, 1975), pp. xv ("very seldom resembled the classical neuroses"), 1 ("vague, diffuse dissatisfactions"), 31 ("general inability to get along"); Heinz Kohut, *The Analysis of the Self* (New York: International Universities Press, 1971), p. 16 ("feelings of emptiness and depression"), 62 ("sense of heightened self-esteem"), 172 ("elaborate the sexual impulse"); Annie Reich, "Pathologic Forms of Self-Esteem Regulation," *Psychoanalytic Study of the Child* 15 (1960):224 ("violent oscillations").

14. See also, for an early description of borderline conditions, Robert P. Knight, "Borderline States" (1953) in Robert P. Knight and Cyrus R. Friedman, eds., *Psychoanalytic Psychiatry and Psychology: Clinical and Theoretical Papers* (New York: International Universities Press, 1954), pp. 97-109; and for the importance of magical thinking in these conditions, Freeman, "Concept of Narcissism in Schizophrenic States," pp. 293-303; Géza Róheim, *Magic and Schizophrenia* (New York: International Universities Press, 1955).

15. Melanie Klein, "The Oedipus Complex in the Light of Early Anxieties" (1945), in her *Contributions to Psychoanalysis* (New York: McGraw-Hill, 1964), pp. 339-67; Melanie Klein, "Notes on Some Schizoid Mechanisms" (1946) and Paula Heimann, "Certain Functions of Introjection and Projection in Early Infancy," in Melanie Klein et al., *Developments in Psychoanalysis* (London: Hogarth Press, 1952), pp. 122-68, 292-320; Paula Heimann, "A Contribution to the Reevaluation of the Oedipus Complex: The Early Stages," in Melanie Klein et al., *New Directions in Psychoanalysis* (New York: Basic Books, 1957), pp. 23-38.

16. Kernberg, *Borderline Conditions and Pathological Narcissism*, pp. 36, 38, 161, 213. On the psychogenesis of secondary narcissism, see also Kohut, *Analysis of the Self*; Giovacchini, *Psychoanalysis of Character Disorders*; Brodey, "Dynamics of Narcissism"; Thomas Freeman, "Narcissism and Defensive Processes in Schizophrenic States," *International Journal of Psychoanalysis* 43 (1962):415-25; Nathaniel Ross, "The 'As If' Concept," *Journal of the American Psychoanalytic Association* 15 (1967):59-83.

On mourning, see Freud's "Mourning and Melancholia" (1917), *Standard Edition*, 8:152-70; Martha Wolfenstein, "How Is Mourning Possible?" *Psychoanalytic Study of the Child* 21 (1966): 93-126; and on psychoanalysis as a way of life, Gilbert J. Rose, "Some Misuses of Analysis as a Way of Life: Analysis Interminable and Interminable 'Analysts'," *International Review of Psychoanalysis* 1 (1974):509-15.

17. Kernberg, *Borderline Conditions and Pathological Narcissism*, p. 282; Roy R. Grinker et al., *The Borderline Syndrome* (New York: Basic Books, 1968), p. 102; Herbert R. Rosenfeld on a narcissistic patient's use of words to defeat interpretation quoted in Otto Kernberg, "A Contribution to the Ego-Psychological Critique of the Kleinian School," *International Journal of Psychoanalysis* 50 (1969):317-33.

18. Kernberg, *Borderline Conditions and Pathological Narcissism*, pp. 310-11.

19. On changing patterns of pathology, see Giovacchini, *Psychoanalysis of Character Disorders*, pp. 316-17; Allen Wheelis, *The Quest for Identity* (New York: W. W. Norton & Co., 1958), pp. 40-41; Heinz Lichtenstein, "The Dilemma of Human Identity," *Journal of the American Psychoanalytic Association* 11 (1963):186-87; Herbert Hendin, *The Age of Sensation* (New York: W. W. Norton & Co., 1975), p. 13; Michael Beldoch, "The Therapeutic as Narcissist," *Salmagundi*, no. 20 (1972), pp. 136, 138; Burness E. Moore, "Toward a Clarification of the Concept of Narcissism," *Psychoanalytic Study of the Child* 30 (1975):265; Sheldon Bach, quoted in *Time*, 20 September 1976, p. 63; Rose, "Some Misuses of Analysis," p. 513; Joel Kovel, *A Complete Guide to Therapy* (New York: Pantheon Books, 1976), p. 252.

20. Ilza Veith, *Hysteria: The History of a Disease* (Chicago: University of Chicago Press, 1965), p. 273.

21. Rosabeth Moss Kanter, *Men and Women of the Corporation* (New York: Basic Books, 1977), *passim;* Eugene Emerson Jennings, *Routes to the Executive Suite* (New York: McGraw-Hill, 1971), *passim,* especially ch. 5 ("The Essence of Visiposure").

22. Michael Maccoby, *The Gamesman: The New Corporate Leaders* (New York: Simon & Schuster, 1976), pp. 100, 104, 106–8; Jennings, *Routes to the Executive Suite,* pp. 3, 307–8.

23. Maccoby, *The Gamesman,* pp. 110, 115, 122, 162; Seymour B. Sarason, *Work, Aging, and Social Change* (New York: Free Press, 1977), chapter 12.

24. Wilfrid Sheed, *Office Politics* (New York: Farrar, Straus & Giroux, 1966), p. 172.

25. Jennings, *Routes to the Executive Suite,* pp. 61, 64, 66, 69, 72, 181.

26. Susan Sontag, "Photography Unlimited," *New York Review of Books,* 23 June, 1977, pp. 26, 28, 31.

27. Jennings, *Routes to the Executive Suite,* p. 4.

28. Gail Sheehy, *Passages: Predictable Crises of Adult Life* (New York: Dutton, 1976), pp. 59, 199, 201, 345.

29. Kernberg, *Borderline Conditions and Pathological Narcissism,* p. 238.

SELECTED BIBLIOGRAPHY

I

Conceptual, Methodological, and Bibliographical Works

A dress parade of the theoretical articles, review essays, and other disquisitions on psychology-in-history would almost require a separate volume. Below are the published short pieces in English that probably will prove most helpful to the beginning student or inquiring reader. Not all of them, of course, focus only on American history; I have included surveys of recent work in that field as a guide for specialists. Note that the *Psychohistory Review* originally appeared as the *Group for the Use of Psychology in History Newsletter;* deMause's *Journal of Psychohistory,* to be relied on at one's own risk, was first entitled the *History of Childhood Quarterly.*

Alexander, Franz. "Psychology and the Interpretation of Historical Events." In *The Cultural Approach to History*, ed. Caroline Ware. New York: Columbia University Press, 1940. History and psychology are inseparably linked.

American Psychiatric Association, Task Force on Psychohistory. *The Psychiatrist as Psychohistorian.* Task Force Report 11. Washington, D.C.: American Psychiatric Association, 1976. Warnings, from within the clinic, especially against instant analyses of living public figures.

Barzun, Jacques. "History: The Muse and Her Doctors." *American Historical Review* 77 (February 1972):36–64. Psychohistory is nonsense.

Besancon, Alain. "Psychoanalysis: Auxiliary Science or Historical Method?" *Journal of Contemporary History* 3 (April 1968):149–62. How can the "historical" methods of psychoanalysis enhance historical inquiry, which reaches from individual "text" to the web of society and culture?

Brugger, Robert J. "Note on Psychological References." In *Beverley Tucker: Heart over Head in the Old South*. Baltimore: The John Hopkins University Press, 1978. An accounting of a quest.

Bushman, Richard L. "On the Uses of Psychology: Conflict and Conciliation in Benjamin Franklin." *History and Theory* 5, no. 3 (1966):225–40. Psychological patterns prompt psychological questions.

Byrnes, Joseph F. "Suggestions on Writing the History of Psychological Data." *History and Theory* 16, no. 3 (1977):297–305. A primary professional responsibility "is to be aware of the greatest possible number of really different and potentially relevant psychological theories to work with" (303).

Chodorow, Nancy. "Family Structure and Feminine Personality." In *Woman, Culture, and Society*, ed. Michelle Zimbalist Rosaldo and Louise Lamphere. Stanford: Stanford University Press, 1974. Is there a gender personality?

Coles, Robert. "Shrinking History." *New York Review of Books*, February 22 and March 8, 1973. Timely words on uneven books.

Coskey, N. H., et al. "Assessing Historical Figures: The Use of Observer-Based Personality Descriptions." *Historical Methods Newsletter* 10 (Spring 1977):66–76.

Cott, Nancy F. "Notes toward an Interpretation of Antebellum Childrearing." *Psychohistory Review* 6 (Spring 1978):4–20.

Crews, Frederick.. "American Prophet." *New York Review of Books*, October 16, 1975. A critique of Erikson's work.

Crosby, Faye. "Evaluating Psychohistorical Explanations." *Psychohistory Review* 7 (Spring 1979):6–16. Excellent on what psychological theory can and cannot do in history.

deMause, Lloyd. "The Evolution of Childhood: A Symposium." *History of Childhood Quarterly* 1 (Spring 1974):503–606. Does childhood determine personality?; why has the quality of child care improved in modern times.?

Demos, John. "Demography and Psychology in the Historical Study of Family Life: A Personal Report." In *Household and Family in Past Time*, ed. Peter Laslett and Richard Wall. Cambridge: Cambridge University Press, 1972. An encouraging word on a topic of burgeoning interest.

Donald, David Herbert. "Between Science and Art." *American Historical Review* 77 (April 1972):445–52.

Edel, Leon. "The Biographer and Psycho-Analysis." In *Biography as an Art*, ed. James L. Clifford. New York: Oxford University Press, 1962. A master of biography speaks on the craft.

Ellman, Richard. "That's Life." *New York Review of Books*, June 17, 1971. "How intimately can we know the self of another person?"

Erikson, Erik. "On the Nature of Psycho-Historical Evidence: In Search of Gandhi." *Daedalus* 97 (Summer 1968):695–730.

Fitzpatrick, John J. "Erik H. Erikson and Psychohistory." *Bulletin of the Menninger Clinic* 40 (July 1976):295–314. A useful reappraisal.

Garraty, John. "The Interrelations of Psychology and Biography." *Psychological Bulletin* 51 (November 1954):569–82. An early but still helpful discussion.

Gay, Peter. "Introduction: Dimensions of Cause." In *Art and Act: On Causes in History—Manet, Gropius, Mondrian*. New York: Harper & Row, 1976. Superb on the need to scratch away at motives.

George, Alexander L., and George, Juliette L. Research Note to *Woodrow Wilson and Colonel House: A Personality Study*. New York: John Day, 1956. Pioneering synopsis of "how it was done."

Gilmore, William J. "Critical Bibliography: Paths Recently Crossed: Alternatives to Psychoanalytic Psychohistory." *Psychohistory Review* 7 (Winter 1979):43–49; and 8 (Winter 1980):55–60.

———. "The Methodology of Psychohistory: An Annotated Bibliography." *Psychohistory Review* 5 (September 1976):4–33 (and later issues). Both guides most helpful.

Glad, Betty. "Contributions of Psychobiography." In *Handbook of Political Psychology*, ed. Jeanne N. Knutson. The Jossey-Bass Behavioral Science Series, ed. William E. Henry and Nevitt Sanford. San Francisco: Jossey-Bass, 1973. Review of works on political leadership.

Goerler, Raimond E. "Family, Psychology, and History." *Group for the Use of Psychology in History Newsletter* 4 (December 1975):31–38.

Graubard, Stephen R., ed. *Generations*. New York: W. W. Norton & Co., 1980.

Griffin, Clifford S. "Oedipus Hex." *Reviews in American History* 4 (September 1976):305–17. Reflections on the deMause approach to childhood and history.

Hiner, N. Ray. "The Child in American Historiography: Accomplishments and Prospects." *Psychohistory Review* 7 (Summer 1978):13–23.

Hoffer, Peter C. "Psychohistory and Empirical Group Affiliation: Extraction of Personality Traits from Historical Manuscripts." *Journal of Interdisciplinary History* 9 (Summer 1978):131–45.

———. "Is Psychohistory Really History?" *Psychohistory Review* 7 (Winter 1979):6–12. A call for empirical studies.

Illick, Joseph E. "More on the Child in American Historiography." *Psychohistory Review* 7 (Spring 1979):24–25. Contra Hiner, above: personality *has* changed through the centuries.

Keniston, Kenneth. "Psychological Development and Historical Change." *Journal of Interdisciplinary History* 2 (Autumn 1971):329–45. Historians should acquaint themselves with developmental concepts in order to study differences, in time and place, in the way societies provide the setting for psychological growth.

Lifton, Robert Jay. "On Psychohistory and History: Further Comment." *Comparative Studies in Society and History* 7 (January 1965):127–32. On the need for, and difficulties of, the new "historical psychology" and "psychological history."

———. "On Psychohistory." In *The State of American History*, ed. Herbert Bass. Chicago: University of Chicago Press, 1972.

———. "The Sense of Immortality: On Death and the Continuity of Life." *American Journal of Psychoanalysis* 33, no. 1 (1973):3–15.

McClelland, David C. "The Use of Measures of Human Motivation in the Study of Society." In *Motives in Fantasy, Action, and Society*, ed. J. W. Atkinson. Princeton, N.J.: Van Nostrand, 1958.

Mack, John E. "Psychoanalysis and Biography: The Narrowing Gap." *Journal of the Philadelphia Association of Psychoanalysis* 5 (1978):97–118.

Madden, Edward H. "Explanation in Psychoanalysis and History." *Philosophy of Science* 33 (September 1966):278–86. Neither history nor psychoanalysis are subject to scientific verifiability; that "weakness" may be a strength in leading therapist or historian to engagement and insight.

Manuel, Frank. "The Use and Abuse of Psychology in History." *Daedalus* 100 (Winter 1971):187–213. A classical discussion; must reading.

Mazlish, Bruce. "Group Psychology and Problems of Contemporary History." *Journal of Contemporary History* 3 (April 1968):163–77.

———. "Reflections on the State of Psychohistory." *Psychohistory Review* 5 (March 1977):3–11. Especially valuable.

———. "Psychoanalytic Theory and History: Groups and Events." *Annual of Psychoanalysis* 6 (1978):41–57.

Mischel, Theodore. "Concerning Rational Behavior and Psychoanalytic Explanation." *Mind: A Quarterly Review of Psychology and Philosophy* 74 (January 1965):71–78. Rebutting an earlier essay in the same journal, Mischel argues that there are indeed important parallels between psychoanalytic and "ordinary" explanations.

———. "Psychology and Explanation of Human Behavior." In *Readings in the Theory of Action*, ed. Norman S. Care and Charles Landsman. Bloomington: Indiana University Press, 1968.

Platt, Gerald M. "The Sociological Endeavor and Psychoanalytic Thought." *American Quarterly* 28, 3 (1976):343–59. Helpful on psychohistory beyond biography.

Pomper, Philip. "Problems of a Naturalistic Psychohistory." *History and Theory* 12, no. 4 (1973):367–88. "The systematic use of epidemiology for the psychohistoric description of entire cultures is a far more enticing prospect to a contemporary historian, weaned from an exclusive preoccupation with psychobiography and highly sweeping and speculative statements about entire ages" (378).

Rycroft, Charles. "Actions Louder than Words." *New York Review of Books*, May 27, 1976. A review of Roy Shafer, *A New Language for Psychoanalysis*. New Haven: Yale University Press, 1976: careful attention to language promotes clear thinking and prevents reification.

Saffady, William. "Manuscripts and Psychohistory." *American Archivist* 37 (October 1974):551–64. On preserving what can be read between lines.

Schoenwald, Richard L. "Using Psychology in History: A Review Essay." *Historical Methods Newsletter* 7 (December 1973):9–24. A thoughtful survey.

Small, Melvin. "Some Suggestions from the Behavioral Sciences for Historians Interested in the Study of Attitudes." *Societas: A Review of Social History* 3 (Winter 1973):1–19.

Spitzer, Alan B. "The Historical Problem of Generations." *American Historical Review* 78 (December 1973):1353–85.

Stannard, David E. *Shrinking History: On Freud and the Failure of Psychohistory*. New York: Oxford University Press, 1980. A lusty attack on psychoanalysis and the psychohistory derived from it.

Stone, Albert E. "Psychoanalysis and American Literary Culture." *American Quarterly* 28, no. 3 (1976):309–23.

Strout, Cushing. "Ego Psychology and the Historian." *History and Theory* 7, no. 3 (1968):281–97. One must develop an ear for "overtones" and "undertones."

———. "The Uses and Abuses of Psychology in American History." *American Quarterly* 28, no. 3 (1976):324–42. Excellent on the state of the field.

Walker, Lawrence B. "Psychological Dimensions of Historiography." *Psychohistory Review* 7 (Summer 1978):44–46.

Weinstein, Fred, and Platt, Gerald M. "The Coming Crisis in Psychohistory." *Journal of Modern History* 47 (June 1975):202–28. After biography and flawed generational studies, what?

Wellman, Judith M. "Culture and Character: Some Perspectives from Psychological Anthropolgy for Psychohistorians." *Group for the Use of Psychology in History Newsletter* 4 (December 1975):12–20.

Wyatt, Frederick, and Willcox, William B. "Sir Henry Clinton: A Psychological Exploration in History." *William and Mary Quarterly*, 3d ser. 16 (January 1959):3–26. Illuminating on the way historian and clinician can cooperate.

II

Representative Works in Psychologically Informed American History

The following titles make up a short list of suggested further reading. It largely confines itself to published works. It includes but a few references to American literary history—the reader may consult the Stone essay, above, for that material—and says nothing of the psychoanalytic criticism available on American authors—although Frederick Crews, *The Sins of the Fathers: Hawthorne's Psychological Themes* (New York: Oxford University Press, 1966) and Stephen Railton, *Fenimore Cooper; A Study of His Life and Imagination* (Princeton, N.J.: Princeton University Press, 1978) are two good examples of that genre. Nor does the list below make any attempt to include the many works touching on subjects like childhood, adolescence, religious experience, sex roles, the life cycle, aging, and death (all of them, one can argue, inherently psychological topics) unless an author deliberately makes use of psychological theory in his or her analysis. For treatments of those and other subjects, see Gilmore, "Paths Recently Crossed," in the first section. It should also be noted that this bibliography is concerned with studies of the American past, where understanding it in its own terms is a primary object, or of the near-present, where—Lasch's work on narcissism provides an example—an author seeks causation and looks at his topic through time. I therefore have omitted (but urge the reader to examine) the important writings of James D. Barber, Robert Coles, Glen Elder, Fred I. Greenstein, Kenneth Keniston, Harold Lasswell, David C. McClelland, Stanley A. Renshon, David Riesman, and William H. Whyte, Jr. Finally, the books and articles below are recommended in most cases, though not in every one, because they illustrate the use rather than abuse of psychology in history.

Anderson, James William. "In Search of Mary James." *Psychohistory Review* 8 (Summer–Fall 1979):63–70.

Bartlett, Irving. "New Light on Wendell Phillips: the Community of Reform, 1840–1880." *Perspectives in American History* 12 (1979).

Battis, Emery. *Saints and Sectaries: Anne Hutchinson and the Antinomian Controversy in the Massachusetts Bay Colony.* Chapel Hill: University of North Carolina Press, 1962. Psychological and somatic roots of a religious persuasion.

Beckman, Alan C. "Hidden Themes in the Frontier Thesis: An Application of Psychoanalysis to History." *Comparative Studies in Society and History* 8 (April 1966):361–82.

Brobeck, Stephen. "Images of the Family: Portrait Paintings as Indices of American Family Culture, Structure, and Behavior, 1730–1860." *Journal of Psychohistory* 5 (Summer 1977):81–106. Interesting use of material evidence.

Brodie, Fawn M. *Thaddeus Stevens: Scourge of the South.* New York: W. W. Norton & Co., 1959. An early study in anger and compensation.

———. *Thomas Jefferson: An Intimate History.* New York: W. W. Norton & Co., 1974.

Brugger, Robert J. *Beverley Tucker: Heart over Head in the Old South.* Baltimore: The Johns Hopkins University Press, 1978.

Bushman, Richard L. "Jonathan Edwards and the Puritan Consciousness." *Journal for the Scientific Study of Religion* 5 (Fall 1966):383–96.

———. "On the Use of Psychology: Conflict and Conciliation in Benjamin Franklin." *History and Theory* 5, no. 3 (1966):225–40.

Capps, Donald. "Orestes Brownson: The Psychology of Religious Affiliation." *Journal for the Scientific Study of Religion* 7, no. 2 (1968):197–209.

Capps, Donald; Capps, Walter H.; and Bradford, M. Gerald, eds. *Encounter With Erikson: Historical Interpretation and Religious Biography.* Missoula, Mont.: Scholars Press, 1977. Papers include Bushman on Edwards, Strout on the Great Awakening, and Michaelson on nineteenth-century conversions.

Cavallo, Dominick. "Social Reform and the Movement to Organize Childrens' Play During the Progressive Era." *History of Childhood Quarterly* 3 (Spring 1976):509–22.

———. "Adolescent Peer Group Mortality: Its Origins and Functions in the United States." *Psychohistory Review* 6 (Fall–Winter 1977–78):88–101.

Cover, Robert M. *Justice Accused: Antislavery and the Judicial Process.* New Haven: Yale University Press, 1975.

Davis, David Brion. *The Slave Power Conspiracy and the Paranoid Style.* Baton Rouge: Louisiana State University Press, 1969.

———. "Some Ideological Functions of Prejudice in Ante-Bellum America." *American Quarterly* 15 (Summer 1963):115–25.

———. "Some Themes of Counter-Subversion: An Analysis of Anti-Masonic, Anti-Catholic, and Anti-Mormon Literature." *Mississippi Valley Historical Review* 47 (September 1960):205–24.

Davis, Glenn. "The Early Years of Theodore Roosevelt: A Study of Character Formation." *History of Childhood Quarterly* 2 (Spring 1975):461–92. Clever use of childhood drawings.

———. "The Maturation of TR: The Rise of an Affective Leader." *History of Childhood Quarterly* 3 (Summer 1975):43–74.

Deck, Raymond H., Jr. "Notes on the Theology of Henry James, Sr." *Psychohistory Review* 8 (Summer–Fall 1979):60–62.

Demos, John. *A Little Commonwealth: Family Life in Plymouth Colony.* New York: Oxford University Press, 1970. Eriksonian archeology.

———. "Underlying Themes in the Witchcraft of Seventeenth-Century New England." *American Historical Review* 75 (June 1970):1311–26.

Demos, John, and Demos, Virginia. "Adolescence in Historical Perspective." *Journal of Marriage and the Family* 31 (November 1969):632–38.

Donald, David Herbert. *Charles Sumner and the Coming of the Civil War.* New York: Alfred A. Knopf, 1960.

———. *Charles Sumner and the Rights of Man.* New York: Alfred A. Knopf, 1970.

Dowling, Joseph A. "Psychoanalysis and History: Problems and Applications." *Psychoanalytic Review* 59 (Fall 1972):433–50. A study of the Populists' backward glance as serviceable regression.

Duberman, Martin. "The Abolitionists and Psychology." *Journal of Negro History* 47 (July 1962):183–91.

Edel, Leon. *The Life of Henry James: The Untried Years, 1843–1870; The Conquest of London, 1870–1881; The Middle Years, 1882–1895; The Treacherous Years, 1895–1901; The Master, 1901–1916.* Philadelphia: J. B. Lippincott, 1953, 1962, 1969, 1972. An American classic.

———. "Willa Cather and *The Professor's House.*" In *Psychoanalysis and American Fiction,* ed. Irving Malin. New York: Dutton, 1965.

———. "Revision of a Chapter from the Life of Henry James." *Psychohistory Review* 8 (Summer–Fall 1979):23–25.

Edelstein, Tilden G. *Strange Enthusiasm; A Life of Thomas Wentworth Higginson.* New Haven: Yale University Press, 1968.

Erikson, Erik H. "Reflections on the American Identity." In *Childhood and Society.* Rev. ed. New York: W. W. Norton & Co., 1963.

———. *Dimensions of a New Identity: The 1973 Jefferson Lectures in the Humanities.* New

York: W. W. Norton & Co., 1974. On Jefferson's characteristically American "protean" personality.

Feinstein, Howard M. "The Chronicles of Reuben: A Psychological Test of Authenticity." *American Quarterly* 18 (Winter 1966):637-54. Highly interesting effort to uncover Lincoln's relationship to this ribald story.

———. "William James and the Emotions." *Journal of the History of Ideas* 31 (January–March 1970):133-42.

———. "The Prepared Heart: A Comparative Study of Puritan Theology and Psychoanalysis." *American Quarterly* 22 (Summer 1970):166-76.

———. "Benjamin Rush: A Child of Light for the Children of Darkness." *Psychoanalytic Review* 58, no. 2 (1971):209-22.

———. "The Double in *The Autobiography* of Elder Henry James." *American Imago* 31 (Fall 1974):293-315.

———. "Words and Work: A Dialectical Analysis of Value Transmission between Three Generations of the Family of William James." In *New Directions in Psychohistory; The Adelphi Papers in Honor of Erik H. Erikson*, ed. Mel Albin. New York: Lexington Press, 1980. On the interplay between crises of identity and generativity among the Jameses.

Finkelstein, Barbara. "In Fear of Childhood: Relationships between Parents and Teachers in Popular Primary Schools in the Nineteenth Century." *History of Childhood Quarterly* 3 (Winter 1976):321-36.

Fitzpatrick, John J. "His Father's Son." *New West*, January 16, 1978. An interesting psychohistorical portrait of Jerry Brown.

———. "Senator Hiram W. Johnson: A Life History, 1866-1945." Ph.D dissertation, University of California, Berkeley, 1975.

George, Alexander L., and George, Juliette L. *Woodrow Wilson and Colonel House: A Personality Study*. New York: John Day, 1956.

———. "Dr. Weinstein's Interpretation of Woodrow Wilson: Some Preliminary Observations." *Psychohistory Review* 8 (Summer–Fall 1979):71-72. Rebuttal of the view that neurological injury—rather than a developmental pattern—accounts for Wilson's quirks as president.

Gilmore, William J. "Orestes Brownson and New England Religious Culture, 1802–1827." Ph.D. dissertation, University of Virginia, 1971.

Glad, Betty. *Charles Evans Hughes and the Illusion of Innocence: A Study in American Diplomacy*. Urbana: University of Illinois Press, 1966.

Gottfried, Alex. *Boss Cermak of Chicago: A Study of Political Leadership*. Seattle: University of Washington Press, 1962.

Greenspan, Henry Miller. "William James's Eyes: The Thought Behind the Man." *Psychohistory Review* 8 (Summer–Fall 1979):26-46.

Hamilton, James. W. "Some Reflections on Richard Nixon in the Light of his Resignation and Farewell Address." *Journal of Psychohistory* 4 (Spring 1977):491-512. Childhood traumas produced a compulsive personality and low self-esteem.

Harris, Irving. D. "The Psychologies of Presidents." *History of Childhood Quarterly* 3 (Winter 1976):337-50. A precarious attempt at generalization from rhetorical imagery and early family.

Hiner, N. Ray. "Adolescence in Eighteenth Century America." *History of Childhood Quarterly* 3 (Fall 1975):253-80. The experience was as psychologically significant as in the nineteenth or twentieth.

Hofling, Charles K. "General Custer and the Battle of the Little Big Horn." *Psychoanalytic Review* 54 (1967):303–28.

Holsti, Ole. "The 'Operational Code' Approach to the Study of Political Leaders: John Foster Dulles' Philosophical and Instrumental Beliefs." *Canadian Journal of Political Science* 3 (March 1970):123–57.

Isaac, Rhys. "Evangelical Revolt: The Nature of the Baptists' Challenge to the Traditional Order in Virginia, 1765 to 1775." *William and Mary Quarterly*, 3d ser. 31 (July 1974):345–68.

Jardim, Anne. *The First Henry Ford: A Study in Personality and Business Leadership.* Cambridge, Mass.: M.I.T. Press, 1970. Flawed but interesting.

Jordan, Winthrop. "Familial Politics: Thomas Paine and the Killing of the King, 1776." *Journal of American History* 60 (September 1973):294–308. Fascinating attempt to connect an individual's life experience, his political language, and the public appeal of his writing.

Kaplan, Justin. *Mr. Clemens and Mark Twain, A Biography.* New York: Simon and Schuster, 1966.

Kearns, Doris. *Lyndon Johnson and the American Dream.* New York: Harper & Row, 1976. Use with caution.

Kedro, Milan James. "Autobiography in the Progressive Era." *History of Childhood Quarterly* 2 (Winter 1975):391–407.

Keller, Phyllis. "George Sylvester Viereck: The Psychology of a German-American Militant." *Journal of Interdisciplinary History* 2 (Summer 1971):59–108. Interesting on political life and loyalty in the early and mid-twentieth century.

Kiell, Norman, ed. *Psychological Studies of Famous Americans: The Civil War Era.* New York: Twayne Publishers, 1964.

Klass, Dennis. "Psychohistory and Communal Patterns: John Humphrey Noyes and the Oneida Community." In *Biographical Process*, ed. Reynolds and Capps.

Lebeaux, Richard. *Young Man Thoreau.* Amherst: University of Massachusetts Press, 1977.

Lewis, Mary Agnes. "Slavery and Personality." In *The Debate over Slavery; Stanley Elkins and His Critics*, ed. Ann J. Lane, Urbana: University of Illinois Press, 1971.

Lynn, Kenneth S. *William Dean Howells: An American Life.* New York: Harcourt Brace Jovanovich, 1970.

———. *A Divided People.* Contributions in American Studies, Number 30. Westport, Conn.: Greenwood Press, 1977.

McGavran, Margaret. "Mary and Margaret [Fuller]: The Triumph of Woman." Ph.D. dissertation, Cornell University, 1973.

McGovern, James R. "David Graham Phillips and the Virility Impulse of Progressives." *New England Quarterly* 39 (September 1966):334–55.

Mazlish, Bruce. "Leadership in the American Revolution: The Psychological Dimension." *Library of Congress Symposia on the American Revolution. Leadership in the American Revolution: Papers Presented at 3d Symposium, May 9 and 10, 1974.* Washington: Library of Congress, 1974.

Michaelson, Robert. "The Beecher Family: Microcosm of a Chapter in the Evolution of Religious Sensibility in America." In *Biographical Process*, ed. Reynolds and Capps.

Musto, David. "The Youth of John Quincy Adams." *Proceedings of the American Philosophical Society*, 113 August 15, 1969, pp. 269–82.

Neuman, Robert. "Priests of the Body and Masturbatory Insanity in the Late Nineteenth Century." *Psychohistory Review* 6 (Spring 1978):21-32.

Patterson, James T. *Mr. Republican: A Biography of Robert A. Taft.* Boston: Houghton Mifflin, 1972.

Potts, Louis W. "Arthur Lee: A Life History in the American Revolution." *Journal of Psychohistory* 4 (Spring 1977):513-28.

Renshon, Stanley Allen. "Psychological Analysis and Presidential Personality: The Case of Richard Nixon." *History of Childhood Quarterly* 2 (Winter 1975):415-50.

Reynolds, Frank E., and Capps, Donald, eds. *The Biographical Process: Studies in the History and Psychology of Religion.* The Hague: Mouton, [1976].

Rogin, Michael Paul. *Fathers and Children: Andrew Jackson and the Subjugation of the American Indian.* New York: Alfred A.Knopf, 1975.

Ross, Dorothy. *G. Stanley Hall: The Psychologist as Prophet.* Chicago: University of Chicago Press, 1972.

———. "The 'New History' and the 'New Psychology': An Early Attempt at Psychohistory." In *The Hofstadter Aegis: A Memorial,* ed. Stanley Elkins and Eric McKitrick. New York: Alfred A. Knopf, 1974.

Shaw, Peter, G. *The Character of John Adams.* Chapel Hill: University of North Carolina Press, 1976.

———. "Their Kinsman, Thomas Hutchinson: Hawthorne, the Boston Patriots, and His Majesty's Royal Governor." *Early American Literature* 11 (Fall 1976):183-90.

Slater, Peter Gregg. *Children in the New England Mind: In Death and in Life.* Hampden, Conn.: Shoe String Press, 1977.

———. "'From the *Cradle* to the *Coffin*': Parental Bereavement and the Shadow of Infant Damnation in Puritan Society." *Psychohistory Review* 6 (Fall–Winter 1977-78):4-24.

Smith, Daniel Blake, "Autonomy and Affection: Parents and Children in Eighteenth-Century Chesapeake Families." *Psychohistory Review* 6 (Fall–Winter 1977-78):32-51.

———. "Mortality and Family in the Colonial Chesapeake." *Journal of Interdisciplinary History* 8 (Winter 1978):403-37.

Smith-Rosenberg, Carroll. "The Female World of Love and Ritual: Relations between Women in Nineteenth Century America." *Signs: Journal of Women in Culture and Society* 1 (Autumn 1975):1-29.

Stannard, David E. *The Puritan Way of Death—A Study of Religion, Culture, and Social Change.* New York: Oxford University Press, 1977.

Stowe, Steven M. "The 'Touchiness' of the Gentlemen Planter: The Sense of Esteem and Continuity in the Ante-Bellum South." *Psychohistory Review* 8 (Winter 1980):6-15. "Reputation and variety, knowledge and ignorance, work and self-indulgence, were pivots on which the self-image of the planters turned" (7).

Strickland, Charles. "A Transcendentalist Father: The Child-Rearing Practices of Bronson Alcott." *Perspectives in American History* 3 (1969).

Strout, Cushing. "William James and the Twice-Born Sick Soul." *Daedalus* 97 (Summer 1968):1062-82. Reprinted in *Philosophers and Kings: Studies in Leadership,* ed. Dankwart A. Rustow. New York: George Braziller, 1970. A standard example of thoughtful exegesis.

———. "The Pluralistic Identity of William James: A Psychohistorical Reading of: *The Varieties of Religious Experience*." *American Quarterly* 23 (May 1971):135-52.

————. *The New Heavens and New Earth: Political Religion in America.* New York: Harper & Row, 1974.

————. "Fathers and Sons: Notes on 'New Light' and 'New Left' Young People as a Historical Comparison." *Psychohistory Review* 6 (Fall–Winter 1977–78):25–31. Interesting comparative patterns.

————. "Henry James's Dream of the Louvre, 'The Jolly Corner,' and Psychological Interpretation." *Psychohistory Review* 8 (Summer–Fall 1979):47–52.

Strozier, Charles B. "The Search for Identity and Love in Young Lincoln." In *The Public and the Private Lincoln: Contemporary Perspectives*, ed. Cullom Davis, Charles B. Strozier, Rebecca Monroe Veach, and Geoffrey C. Ward. Carbondale: Southern Illinois Press, 1979.

Thomas, Robert David. *The Man Who Would Be Perfect: John Humphrey Noyes and the Utopian Impulse.* Philadelphia: University of Pennsylvania Press, 1977. Heavily psychoanalytic; highly interesting.

————. "John Humphrey Noyes and the Oneida Community: A 19th-Century American Father and His Family." *Psychohistory Review* 6 (Fall–Winter 1977–78):68–87.

Tomkins, Silvan. "The Psychology of Commitment: The Constructive Role of Violence and Suffering for the Individual and for His Society." In *Antislavery Vanguard: New Essays on the Abolitionists*, ed. Martin Duberman. Princeton, N.J.: Princeton University Press, 1965. Applied Allport.

Touster, Saul. "In Search of Holmes from Within." *Vanderbilt Law Review* 18 (March 1965):437–72. A sensitive reading of Oliver Wendell Homes, Jr., at war.

Weinstein, Edwin A. "Woodrow Wilson's Neurological Illness." *Journal of American History* 57 (September 1970):324–52. See George and George, "Dr. Weinstein's Interpretation," above.

Weinstein, Edwin A.; Anderson, James William; and Link, Arthur S. "Woodrow Wilson's Political Personality: A Reappraisal." *Political Science Quarterly* 93 (Winter 1978):585–98.

Wolin, Howard E. "Grandiosity and Violence in the Kennedy Family." *Psychohistory Review* 8 (Winter 1980):27–37.

Zeligs, Meyer A. *Friendship and Fratricide: An Analysis of Whittaker Chambers and Alger Hiss.* New York: Viking Press, 1967. A controversial depiction of Chambers as vindictive homosexual.

Zuckerman, Michael. "The Fabrication of Identity in Early America." *William and Mary Quarterly*, 3d ser. 34 (April 1977):182–214.

NOTES ON CONTRIBUTORS

STEVEN L. ALLEN, a former graduate student in mathematics at New York University, works as a banker in New York City.

PAUL BOYER is associate professor of American intellectual and social history at the University of Wisconsin, Madison.

ROBERT J. BRUGGER spent a year of his graduate study in history at Johns Hopkins University as a fellow in the department of psychology. Having taught ante-bellum American history at the University of Virginia for six years, he now is working on a comparative study of Northern and Southern intellectual discourse in nineteenth-century America.

EDWIN G. BURROWS is associate professor of history at Brooklyn College.

RICHARD BUSHMAN, author of *From Puritan to Yankee: Character and the Social Order in Connecticut, 1690–1765*, chairs the department of history at the University of Delaware.

KATHLEEN DALTON, formerly at American University, now teaches at Phillips Andover Academy, Massachusetts. She has a book on Theodore Roosevelt in preparation.

JOHN DEMOS, a member of the history faculty at Brandeis University, spent 1973–1974 as a fellow at the Center for Psychosocial Studies in Chicago and is finishing a book on witchcraft beliefs among colonial New Englanders.

STANLEY M. ELKINS has written many articles on nineteenth-century America and is professor of history at Smith College.

JOAN ERIKSON, a writer and student of the arts in child therapy, is a consultant to the department of psychiatry, Mt. Zion Hospital, San Francisco.

HOWARD M. FEINSTEIN, M.D. and Ph.D. in history, is adjunct associate professor of psychology at Cornell University, a practicing psychiatrist, and a former fellow of the Tavistock Clinic in London.

GEORGE FORGIE, associate professor at the University of Texas, Austin, won the 1973 Allan Nevins Prize for his study of Lincoln and the "House Divided."

PETER C. HOFFER, assistant professor at the University of Georgia, is working on a full-length study of political loyalties during the American Revolution.

N. E. H. HULL teaches political science at the University of Georgia.

WINTHROP D. JORDAN is professor of history at the University of California, Berkeley.

CHRISTOPHER LASCH, who has published widely on twentieth-century American intellectual and cultural history, teaches at the University of Rochester.

ROBERT JAY LIFTON, M.D., Foundation's Fund For Research Professor of Psychiatry at Yale University, is co-editor of *Explorations in Psychohistory: The Wellfleet Papers.*

BRUCE MAZLISH, professor of history at the Massachusetts Institute of Technology, is author of *James and John Stuart Mill: Father and Son in the Nineteenth Century.*

STEPHEN W. NISSENBAUM is associate professor of American social history at the University of Massachusetts, Amherst.

CARROLL SMITH-ROSENBERG teaches at the University of Pennsylvania and is completing a study of women in Victorian America.

CUSHING STROUT, Ernest I. White Professor of American Studies and Humane Letters at Cornell University, has published a great many studies in American cultural and literary history, including *The New Heavens and New Earth: Political Religion in America.*

MICHAEL L. WALLACE teaches nineteenth-century American history at the John Jay College of Criminal Justice, New York.

RONALD G. WALTERS, editor of *Primers for Prudery: Sexual Advice to Victorian America* and author of *American Reformers, 1815–1860*, is professor of history at Johns Hopkins University.

JAMES M. YOUNGDALE is a longtime student of Midwestern radicalism who worked almost twenty years as a farmer before embarking on a doctorate in American Studies at the University of Minnesota.

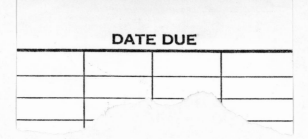
E
169.1
O9

Our selves/our past : psychological
approaches to American history /
edited by Robert J. Brugger. --
Baltimore : John Hopkins University
Press, c1981.
xiii, 416 p. ; 24 cm.

Bibliography: p.405-414.
ISBN 0-8018-2382-X (pbk.). -- ISBN
0-8018-2312-9

1. Psychohistory--Addresses, essays, lectures.
2. United States--Civilization--Psychological
aspects--Addresses, essays, lectures.   I.
Brugger, Robert J.